D1543066

SOUTHEAST ASIAN HISTORY
AND HISTORIOGRAPHY

Essays Presented to D. G. E. Hall

D. G. E. HALL (photograph by Blackstone-Shelburne)

SOUTHEAST ASIAN HISTORY
AND HISTORIOGRAPHY

Essays Presented to D. G. E. Hall

EMERITUS PROFESSOR OF THE HISTORY OF SOUTH EAST ASIA
IN THE UNIVERSITY OF LONDON,
SOMETIME PROFESSOR OF SOUTHEAST ASIAN HISTORY
AT CORNELL UNIVERSITY

EDITED BY

C. D. Cowan and O. W. Wolters

with a Foreword by John M. Echols

CORNELL UNIVERSITY PRESS
ITHACA AND LONDON

DS
503.4
.S 715

This book has been published with the aid of grants from the Hull Memorial Publication Fund of Cornell University and from the Southeast Asia Program.

First published 1976 by Cornell University Press.
Published in the United Kingdom by Cornell University Press Ltd.,
2-4 Brook Street, London W1Y 1AA

International Standard Book Number 0-8014-0841-5
Library of Congress Catalog Card Number 75-18726
Printed in the United States of America by Vail-Ballou Press, Inc.

Foreword

In 1976, Profeesor D. G. E. Hall will have completed more than fifty-six years of teaching and research in history, particularly the history of Southeast Asia. To commemorate this occasion, C. D. Cowan of the School of Oriental and African Studies in the University of London, and O. W. Wolters, David K. Wyatt, and I of the Southeast Asia Program at Cornell University invited faculty members of these two institutions where Professor Hall has taught most recently, a few of his former graduate students, and some others who had known him well to contribute papers that would fittingly honor him and his contributions to the study of Southeast Asian history.

Southeast Asia is a region on which serious historical research is still a relatively new activity, and Professor Hall has always insisted that historians are bound to gain from working within an interdisciplinary company of colleagues. In this way they are likely to cultivate new perspectives and, indeed, new working methods, thereby ensuring that Southeast Asian historical studies will play their role in enriching the process of historical inquiry in general. For this reason we invited the authors to present papers on a wide range of subjects, reflecting Professor Hall's diverse interests. The contributors have undertaken research in anthropology, art history, economics, linguistics, and literature, as well as in what is usually known as history, and the professional insights of those who are not officially historians in the sense of being members of a history department assist the historians in assimilating the yield of evidence that the historian is not always trained to understand.

Although I cannot claim to be a historian, my involvement in this undertaking stems from membership in Cornell's Southeast Asia Program, from my long friendship with the editors, and from the fact that in June 1954 I chanced to be in London. In the course of that visit I joined Professor Hall and some of his colleagues at the School of Oriental and African Studies in the Senior Common Room. This was the first of my many enjoyable meetings over the years, both in London and in Ithaca, with the doyen of Southeast Asian history.

George Hall, as he is affectionately known to his legion of friends all over the world, at eighty-four still maintains a strenuous regimen of research and writing that would daunt many a younger scholar. He is ever willing, nay eager, to assist colleagues and students alike. At his office he practices an "open door" policy, and untold numbers have benefited from his counsel and knowledge.

Those of us who have been directly involved in preparing this volume take pride in being able to offer evidence of the great respect, admiration, and friendship that so many persons have for George Hall. We, on our part, share this feeling and fondly salute him.

As anyone knows who has participated in similar transoceanic enterprises, books of this kind take time to assemble and produce, and in a few cases the contributors have not been able to take account of recent publications.

We are grateful to the Breezewood Foundation for assistance in preparing the manuscript for publication. Our appreciation also goes to the editors at Cornell University Press for their assistance. Thanks are due Mrs. Tazu Warner and Mrs. Hazel Kay for retyping a number of the essays.

JOHN M. ECHOLS

Ithaca, New York

Contents

Abbreviations

AA   *Artibus Asiae* (Ascona)
AHR   *American Historical Review* (New York)
ASB   Archaeological Survey of Burma
BEFEO   *Bulletin de l' Ecole Française d' Extrême-Orient* (Hanoi)
BKI   *Bijdragen tot de Taal-, Land- en Volkenkunde*
            [van Nederlandsch-Indië] (The Hague)
BM   British Museum
BSEI   *Bulletin de la Société des Etudes Indochinoises* (Saigon)
BSOAS   *Bulletin of the School of Oriental and African Studies* (London)
DNB   *Dictionary of National Biography*
FMJ   *Federated Museums Journal* (Kuala Lumpur)
JA   *Journal Asiatique* (Paris)
JAOS   *Journal of the American Oriental Society* (New Haven)
JAS   *Journal of Asian Studies* (Ann Arbor)
JBRS   *Journal of the Burma Research Society* (Rangoon)
JGIS   *Journal of the Greater India Society* (Calcutta)
JMBRAS   *Journal of the Malayan Branch Royal Asiatic Society* (Singapore)
JSEAH   *Journal of Southeast Asian History* (Singapore)
JSEAS   *Journal of Southeast Asian Studies* (Singapore)
JSS   *Journal of the Siam Society* (Bangkok)
JTG   *Journal of Tropical Geography* (Singapore)
Lg   *Language* (Baltimore)
LOr   Leiden University Library, Oriental Department
PA   *Pacific Affairs* (Vancouver)
PMS   *Papers on Malay Subjects* (Kuala Lumpur)
TBG   *Tijdschrift voor Indische Taal-, Land- en Volkenkunde* (Jakarta)
TP   *T'oung Pao* (Leiden)
VBG   *Verhandelingen van het Bataviaasch Genootschap van Kunsten en*
            Wetenschappen (Jakarta)

D. G. E. Hall: A Biographical Sketch

C. D. COWAN

School of Oriental and African Studies,
University of London

Daniel George Edward Hall was born an Englishman on 17 November 1891. The eldest son of a well-to-do Hertfordshire farmer, he received his early education at the Grammar School in Hitchin, the local market town, and his youth was spent in the pursuits of his age and class. Riding his father's hunters over the rolling farmland round about and making and enjoying music were the high points of his early life, and when he entered King's College in the University of London as an undergraduate in the autumn of 1913 there can have been little to indicate, even to the most prescient observer, the future historian of Southeast Asia. His own ambitions indeed pointed in quite a different direction. Nature had endowed him with a strong physique and a fine bass voice, which, developed by training, opened for him the possibility of a career as a professional musician, and in 1910, when he was eighteen, he was offered a scholarship at Trinity College of Music, in London. But the financial prospects were uncertain, and family and friends mostly against taking the gamble. So, not wholly convinced in his heart, he was persuaded instead to take a post on the teaching staff of Hitchin Grammar School while he worked externally for the intermediate examination of the University of London. Success in this won for him in due course direct entry to the second year of King's College history school at the age of twenty-one.

In the Department of History at King's in 1913, Sir J. K. Laughton, the naval historian and biographer of Nelson, was coming to the end of his tenure of the chair of Modern History. F. J. Hearnshaw held the chair of Medieval History and Hilda Johnstone the Readership, and the main core of the undergraduate curriculum, judging from the surviving examination papers, was traditional in character, beginning with Stubb's *Charters* and covering the well-worn paths of medieval and modern English and European history and Western political ideas. But there was also a group of younger teachers at King's with wider interests. A. P. Newton and Sidney Low held lectureships in American, Colonial, and Imperial history, and in

1916, in what was to be Hall's last year at the college, R. W. Seton-Watson joined them as Lecturer in East European history. Perhaps as a result of World War I, there seems to have been a strengthening of these interests, and between 1915 and 1917 a number of public-lecture courses on Imperial themes were offered at King's under the auspices of the Imperial Studies Committee.

Hall's own interests were in modern history, and he took first-class honours in the degree examinations of June 1915.[1] He had already been awarded the Gladstone Memorial Prize for his work as an undergraduate. Now, on the strength of the degree examinations, he was awarded an Inglis Studentship for postgraduate studies and, the degree of Ph.D. not yet having been introduced into the University of London, he embarked on an M.A. under the guidance of A. P. Newton, whose postgraduate seminar on colonial history at this time also included Lilian Penson, later Professor of Modern History and Vice-Chancellor of the University of London.

Hall's thesis on the mercantile aspect of English foreign policy during the reign of Charles II caused him to look for the first time at aspects of Anglo-Dutch overseas rivalry, to which he was to return in later years in his studies of the Dutch and English East India Companies in Southeast Asia. He does not at this stage, however, seem to have been particularly interested in the Asian scene, and the thesis, which is chiefly remarkable for the vigour and clarity of its prose, is a well-balanced survey of the Restoration colonial system and the commercial rivalries of the European maritime powers, based on the then available printed sources. It was presented in June 1917. But by the time its examiners had read and approved it, Hall himself had exchanged the pen for the sword, or rather for those more practical tools, the rifle, bayonet, and grenade. He spent the remainder of the war years as a member of the Inns of Court Regiment, being trained and training others in the basic skills of trench warfare. It was not until the beginning of 1919 that he was able to return to historical studies and, as senior history master at the Royal Grammar School, Worcester, to the teaching of history.

Looking back with the historian's advantage of hindsight one would guess that the years between 1916 and 1920 must have been something of a crossroads for George Hall, when new opportunities and interests opened before him, old ones seemed to present themselves once more, and decisions lay there to be taken. His time as a graduate student at King's College, when in addition to working on his thesis and serving as president of the Students' Union he had also acted as an Assistant Lecturer, had opened for him not only a field of study, but a way of life as a university teacher.

1. He did not formally graduate until 1916, when he had been registered for three years as an internal student.

But he had not altogether turned his back on the world of music. Singing engagements had provided an important source of income during his student career, and as opportunities offered in 1916 and 1917 he toured the Western Front with the Lena Ashworth concert parties. As he mixed again with professional musicians he was clearly tempted to look again at his earlier decision not to join their ranks. Then there was the matter of Miss Banks. Helen Eugenie Banks had been two years junior to Hall as an undergraduate at King's. Like him she was awarded the Gladstone Memorial Prize and graduated in history. Her influence, together with that of Hearnshaw, seems to have been an important factor in tilting the scales against a full-time career as a singer. By the beginning of 1919, when he took up the post in Worcester and she was teaching in Eastbourne, they had known each other for almost five years, and marriage was clearly on the cards. But there were problems. The job at Worcester, though not a university post, was a reasonable start for a young historian, especially with the large number of recently demobilized men seeking posts at that time. It was not, however, quite so good a prospect for a married man with a wife and possibly a family to support. And perhaps more important, it offered no solution to the question of how she, once married, was also to follow her chosen vocation as a teacher of history.

The solution proved to be delightfully simple, not unconnected with music, and reminiscent of a fairy story in the happiness of its ending. Hall's sister, a pupil of Myra Hess and a concert pianist of repute, was teaching music at Bedales, a progressive coeducational school at Petersfield, in Hampshire. Through her he learnt that a post in history was vacant there. "Would he care to come for interview?" At the interview he was told that there were in fact two history posts vacant. "Could he suggest someone for the second?" He could. On the strength of their appointment to the two posts at Bedales they married during the summer of 1919 and were in residence at the school by the beginning of the atumn term that year.

For the new husband and wife team this period was a great success, and they often recalled it with pleasure in after years. It was not, however, to last long. Before they had completed two years at Bedales, Hall, largely through the good offices of Hearnshaw, was offered and accepted the chair of history in the newly founded University of Rangoon.

The University of Rangoon came into existence in December 1920 incorporating two constituent colleges, University College (formerly Rangoon College) and Judson College (formerly the American Baptist College), both of which had previously prepared students for the external degrees of Calcutta University. The new university started its career at a time of stress, and in particularly unpropitious circumstances. Dyarchy, the first stage towards the achievement of the "responsible" government promised to India by Edwin Montagu in 1917 and embodied in the Government of India Act of 1919, was at first withheld from Burma. This evoked an outburst of Burmese national sentiment, and the quarrel between the Burmese nationalist leaders and the British government was in full swing at the time of the foundation of the university. It was complicated by a further quarrel over the constitution of the university itself. The government had rejected Burmese proposals for a federal-type university, with a system of external degrees to be taken by students in affiliated colleges at various places, including Mandalay, the centre of traditional Burmese culture. Instead they opted for a centralised residential university in Rangoon, a cosmopolitan commercial and administrative colonial city where Burmans were in a minority. For many students the journey to Rangoon was a long and expensive one, and once there they were exposed to an unfamiliar environment and a highly charged political atmosphere.[2]

The upshot was a widely observed boycott of government-sponsored colleges and schools and the establishment under nationalist auspices of a Council of National Education, with the task of building its own education system free of government or missionary control. The new University of Rangoon had not been in existence for many weeks when it lost some two-thirds of its students to the rival National College which the CNE opened in a group of Buddhist monasteries on the slopes below the Shwe Dagon Pagoda. This state of affairs did not last long, and when the university reopened in June 1921 after the long vacation, most of the students had returned. The link between the university and politics, and the tradition of political activism among the student body, however, was to continue.

Hall himself arrived in Rangoon in the middle of May 1921. He was alone, for Mrs. Hall had been left in England to await the birth of their first child. Before leaving England the new Professor of History in the University of Rangoon had spent a term studying Burmese at the School of Oriental Studies, then in Finsbury Circus, London. He had also looked at what little was then available in English on Burma's history, principally Phayre's *History of Burma*, published in 1883 and long out of print. But he was otherwise quite unprepared and unbriefed on the task ahead of him. Inevitably, therefore, some unpleasant surprises awaited him. The first was that no one in Rangoon knew anything of his appointment. The second was that the new university's history syllabus had already been laid down by a Department of Education committee headed by a Professor of History specially imported from an Indian university for the occasion. This syllabus

2. For the general political background see J. F. Cady, *A History of Modern Burma* (Ithaca, 1958). For the period 1921 to 1934 I am also much indebted to "Reminiscences of Rangoon University in the Nineteen-Twenties and Thirties", a paper read by Professor Hall to a seminar in the Southeast Asia Program at Cornell University on 15 October 1970.

involved a heavy concentration on classical Greece and Rome and on modern British and European history, while what Asian history was provided for was almost exclusively Indian. The committee had helpfully provided long lists of recommended reading, but no orders had been placed with any booksellers, and Messrs. Blackwell of Oxford were three weeks away by a "fast" surface mail which went via Calcutta, Bombay, Marseilles, and Dover, Nor had he any colleagues to turn to; only one other member of the History Department had been appointed, and he had not yet arrived. Only of one thing was there no shortage: there was no lack of students already registering for the session 1921–1922.

Hall's early years in Rangoon were therefore occupied with the long-term problems of fashioning and securing the acceptance of new courses more relevant to the needs and background of the Burmese students of the time, and of assembling a group of colleagues who could teach them, while coping almost on a day-to-day basis with the short-term problems of teaching the courses with which he had been presented on his arrival. Some of the expedients to which he was driven were a little startling. When Mrs. Hall arrived with their baby son, for instance, she was greeted before she had stepped ashore with the news that she was to lecture on Roman history at ten o'clock the next morning, and their first evening together was spent in studying the appropriate lecture notes. It was fortunate that the history degree at King's College, London, in 1915 had included that now unfashionable subject.

The revised history syllabus which was eventually accepted two years later substituted world history, including an outline study of the civilizations of the ancient Near and Middle East, India, and China, for the narrower concentration on the political history of Greece and Rome at the intermediate examination. In the final examinations courses were offered in modern Western history, Indian history, and the history of East Asia, the last including a special study of Burma. To teach Indian history Hall recruited W. S. Desai, a graduate of Bombay and Cambridge Universities who subsequently published a number of contributions to the early nineteenth-century history of Burma based on the India Office records, including a well-known monograph on the first British Residency at Ava.[3] For Burmese and East Asian history he was able, by a happy arrangement, to secure the services of G. H. Luce, for whose talent and scholarship he had conceived an admiration which was to continue for the remainder of their long association. Gordon Luce, whose early work had been in Classics and English literature, had originally gone to Burma as Professor of English in Rangoon College. But his interest had soon been captured by Burmese

3. W. S. Desai, *History of the British Residency in Burma, 1826–40* (Rangoon, 1939).

culture and by oriental studies generally. He devoted most of his leave to oriental studies, principally Chinese, at the School of Oriental Studies in London and at the Sorbonne, and by 1923 had already published with Pe Maung Tin (his brother-in-law) a translation of the Glass Palace Chronicle[4] and was at work on the inscriptions of Pagán. He needed little persuasion to accept an invitation to join the History Department, and a steady flow of contributions to the literature of the early history of Burma during the next fifty years established him as the outstanding authority in this field.[5]

Two other events must be mentioned to complete the academic background to Hall's work in Burma. One is the retirement of J. S. Furnivall (a founder of the Burma Research Society) from government service to devote himself to writing and to set up his Burma Book Club in one of the buildings of the university complex, where it became a centre for those interested in Burmese studies. The other is the publication in 1925 of G. E. Harvey's *History of Burma*, which for the first time provided a text of university quality around which the teaching of Burmese history to undergraduates could be built.

For all Professor Hall's eagerness to build up the Burmese content of the history syllabus and to encourage the development of research in the history of Burma, his own efforts were at first of necessity directed elsewhere. This was in part because of the many tasks associated with the growth of the university and its links with education in general, which added to the administrative burdens inevitably associated with his post. He was responsible, to mention but one achievement, for bringing together the teachers of history in schools for discussion groups within the university and for forming them into a branch of the Historical Association. Mainly however his inability to plunge at once into Burmese history was because it fell to him to teach most of the courses in modern Western history and political ideas; in the original university statutes, in fact, this had been laid down as part of the professor's duties. For Hall this involved not merely the teaching itself, but also the provision of textbooks suitable for the needs of his students. Before he had been in Rangoon five years he had produced three such books: *Imperialism in Modern History* (1923), *A Brief Survey of English Constitutional History* (1925), and (as coauthor) *The League of Nations: A Manual for . . . India, Burma and Ceylon* (1926). Only when this work was out of the way was he able to apply himself to his own research interests.

4. Pe Maung Tin and G. H. Luce, *The Glass Palace Chronicle of the Kings of Burma: A Translation of the Earlier Parts of the Hmannan Yazawin* (London, 1923; reprinted Rangoon, 1960).

5. Cf. Professor Luce's own contribution to this volume below (p. 31); see also Hall's review of Luce's great work, *Old Burma—Early Pagan* (3 vols., 1969–1970) in *Asia Major*, 17 (1971): 112–115, and "A Professorship of Far Eastern History," *JBRS*, 12 (1922): 169–170, justifying the creation of Luce's chair.

Hall's own research was at first concentrated upon problems of Anglo-Burmese relations and based in the main upon material which he collected from the India Office Library and Records during his periods of home leave. The first result of this work appeared as a paper in the *Journal of the Burma Research Society* for 1927 entitled "English Relations with Burma, 1587–1686."[6] Most of the material in this paper was incorporated in the more ambitious *Early English Intercourse with Burma, 1587–1743*, published in the following year,[7] an exhaustive account covering the subject from the reign of Elizabeth I to the destruction of the East India Company's factory at Syriam by the Mons. It was followed in 1931 by "The Tragedy of Negrais," published as a monograph number of the *Journal of the Burma Research Society*.[8] This was in effect a tailpiece to *Early English Intercourse*, telling the story of the East India Company's settlement on Negrais from its foundation in 1753 to its destruction by Alaungpaya in 1759. For some time before the publication of "The Tragedy of Negrais," however, Hall's interests had also been directed to nineteenth-century problems and to the period of the second Anglo-Burmese War. In 1925 the University of Rangoon had purchased eighty autograph letters written by Lord Dalhousie, when Governor General of India, to Captain Arthur Phayre, first British commissioner of Pegu and the Governor General's Agent in the negotiations with the Court of Ava at the end of the second Anglo-Burmese War. These Professor Hall collated with the texts in the Dalhousie Papers of a much larger number of letters written by the Governor General, by Phayre, and by Thomas Spears, British correspondent at the Court of King Mindon of Burma. He published the letters (some 262 in all), with lengthy elucidatory notes and a substantial introduction, as *The Dalhousie-Phayre Correspondence* in 1932.[9]

By that time, after more than ten years in Rangoon, George Hall could look back on a record of solid achievement. The university was by then housed in a new university estate, custom-built with its halls of residence, departmental accommodation, and Students' Union (a lively, not to say fiery, institution of great political as well as social importance), on the Prome Road, about five miles from the centre of the city. "One felt," as he later wrote, "a great sense of achievement, and the thrill of a new beginning."[10] He had served in 1923 and 1924 as a temporary member of the Legislative Council of Burma during the moves to amend the University Act to allow the development of affiliated colleges at Mandalay

6. "English Relations with Burma, 1587–1686," *JBRS*, 17 (1927).
7. *Early English Intercourse with Burma, 1587–1743* (London, 1928; reprinted London, 1968).
8. "The Tragedy of Negrais," *JBRS*, 21 (1931), reprinted with *Early English Intercourse* (London, 1968).
9. *The Dalhousie-Phayre Correspondence, 1852–1856* (London, 1932).
10. "Reminiscences of Rangoon University," p. 6.

and elsewhere, and as Warden of one of the university halls of residence had found his relationships with the students, politics and boycotts notwithstanding, as rewarding as his meetings with the teachers of history in schools had been earlier. The Department of History was flourishing, as was his own growing family, and his scholarly achievements had been recognized after the completion of *The Dalhousie-Phayre Correspondence* by the award of the degree of Doctor of Literature from the University of London. He was in fact already feeling the need to extend the scope of his studies; in his next visit to England he spent much time in the British Museum making the acquaintance of some of the Portuguese, Dutch, and French literature, and conceived the plan of writing a history of European relations with Southeast Asia as a whole, beginning with the arrival of the Portuguese early in the sixteenth century.

All seemed set fair when events developed which forced him to take his family back permanently to England. As he himself explained later,[11] "I had to give up my job in Burma because my wife and all five children developed trachoma . . . and I was warned never to go East again." The crisis in his affairs which followed was not only personal and professional, but potentially also financial. Where with his rather specialized background was he to find a post in the United Kingdom which would enable him to maintain and educate five children? There were one or two university posts possibly open, but salaries were low and the severest retrenchment seemed inevitable. For three years he stayed on alone in Rangoon, going home on leave every year to see his family and to work in the India Office Library. It was a trying time for him and for Mrs. Hall. The solution, when it came, was reminiscent of events in 1919, when Bedales had come to the rescue. Now in 1934 he was offered the headmastership of Caterham School, in Surrey, which carried with it a house and free education for his three sons, and he resigned the chair in Rangoon to return to schoolmastering.

Dr. Hall, as he was now known, retained the headship of Caterham from 1934 to 1949, steering it through the difficulties of World War II, and building it up from a small and somewhat struggling institution to a thriving public school with its own preparatory school attached. In their way these were achievements as outstanding and as valuable as those of his years in Rangoon. They were the more noteworthy in that they were accomplished without the cessation of his scholarly activities, and despite the loss of his left eye as the result of an infection which developed behind it during a severe attack of influenza in 1941.

In his historical work his efforts to widen his approach so as to take in the activities of other European nations in Asia, which we have already noted,

11. In a letter dated 23 January 1948 to Professor C. H. Philips, to whom I am indebted for allowing me to consult it.

bore fruit in the shape of two papers in the *Journal of the Burma Research Society* on Dutch trade in Burma and Arakan in the seventeenth century,[12] and the publication in 1945 of *Europe and Burma*,[13] which, after a summary of Burmese history down to 1635, surveys the course of European relations with Burma from the sixteenth century to the British annexation of Upper Burma in 1886. Also written while he was still at Caterham, but not published until 1950, was the small volume on Burma in the Hutchinson's University Library series which, covering the entire history of the country in its highly compressed but very readable pages, is a small masterpiece.[14] In addition Hall, while at Caterham, published as coauthor *A High School British History, 1714–1930* (1935), and in 1939 a revised and enlarged edition of *A Brief Survey of English Constitutional History*, which had originally been written in Rangoon.

In 1949, Hall's period as headmaster at Caterham came to an end when he was appointed to the newly established chair of the History of South East Asia in the University of London, tenable at the School of Oriental and African Studies. As we have seen, his first acquaintance with the School of Oriental Studies went back to 1921, when he had visited it as a student of Burmese. He had re-established contact with it after his return to England, and since 1939 had served on its panel of Additional (that is, occasional) Lecturers, being called upon whenever work in Burmese history was required. Since his first contact with the School it had extended its field of interest to Africa, added departments of history, law, linguistics, and anthropology to its establishment, and moved from Finsbury Circus to premises on the central university precinct in Bloomsbury. The Scarbrough Committee, reporting in 1946 on the development of Oriental, African, and Slavonic studies in the United Kingdom, had recommended the expansion of the School's activities, and additional financial resources were made available for this purpose.

As one of the very few established British scholars with experience in the Southeast Asian field Professor Hall was expected not only to build up work on that area in history, but also to preside over the development of the Department of the Languages and Cultures of South East Asia and the Islands, whose head he became. Once again, as in his early years in Rangoon, his own studies would often have to wait on the wider responsibilities of his post. But he was now in his fifty-seventh year, with only ten years ahead of him before the university's compulsory retirement age was reached. During the summer of 1949, as he and Mrs. Hall moved from

12. "Studies in Dutch Relations with Arakan," *JBRS*, 26 (1936); "The Daghregister of Batavia and Dutch Trade with Burma in the Seventeenth Century," *JBRS*, 29 (1939).
13. *Europe and Burma: A Study of European Relations with Burma to the Annexation of Thibaw's Kingdom, 1886* (London, 1945).
14. *Burma* (London, 1950; rev. ed., 1956).

Caterham to Hitchin and settled into their new home in the area in which his youth had been spent and where many of his family still lived, the newly appointed professor must in his thoughts have returned more than once to the question of his priorities in the next decade.

Of one thing there seems almost from the beginning to have been no doubt; the project of writing a history of Southeast Asia began to take shape in his mind. Earlier he had thought in terms of a history of European relations with the area. To attempt a history of Southeast Asia itself had seemed beyond his powers, the many language skills required to deal with the masses of unworked materials beyond the compass of a single scholar. Now, although there were still many parts of the subject on which little or nothing had been done, the amount of secondary material available from the work of other scholars was beginning to accumulate, and for an English scholar with a reading knowledge of Dutch and French the task began to seem within the bounds of possibility. Hall was already at work on the Southeast Asian section of *A Handbook of Oriental History*.[15] From 1950 onwards he set himself to collect material for a history of Southeast Asia, bit by bit, during the intervals of his working day, and to tussle with the intractable problems of the organization of the material as the earlier draft chapters began to take shape. An important stage in the working out of his ideas was probably the period he spent on study leave in Southeast Asia between July 1952 and April 1953, when he made lengthy visits to Indonesia, Thailand, Malaya, and Burma, delivering lectures, talking to scholars, politicians, and former students, and visiting important historical and archaeological sites. The resulting *History of South-East Asia*, which appeared in 1955,[16] was a formidable achievement. Modestly described by its author in his preface as "a bare outline . . . an introduction to South-East Asian history," it embraced within its forty-five chapters and extensive bibliography the results of virtually all the secondary literature on the subject and paid generous tribute to the authors on whose work it drew.

A History of South-East Asia was the centre-piece of Hall's years at the School of Oriental and African Studies, but there was much else besides. In Southeast Asian history he sponsored the early work of the three junior colleagues for whose appointments he was responsible, H. R. Tinker, C. D. Cowan, and O. W. Wolters, and introduced for the first time in any university a full degree-course in the subject. As head of the Department of the Languages and Cultures of South East Asia and the Islands he presided over the appointment of scholars in the fields of Thai, Mon, Cambodian, Vietnamese, and Pacific linguistic and literary studies,

15. "South-East Asia and the Archipelago," *in* C. H. Philips (ed.), *Handbook of Oriental History* (London, 1951).

16. *A History of South-East Asia* (London and New York, 1955; 2d ed., 1964; 3d ed., 1968).

strengthened the existing work in Burmese, Malay, and Indonesian, and introduced work in Southeast Asian art and archaeology. He was also able to bring into play once more his association with Gordon Luce, who at his invitation spent the years 1950 to 1953 at the School as a visiting professor, conducting seminars and directing research. Perhaps of equal importance to all this was his work with the graduate students he supervised, many of them from Southeast Asia, who subsequently took up teaching appointments in the expanding universities overseas. This contribution to his subject he reinforced as an external examiner in the Universities of Malaya (1953–1955), Ceylon (1954–1956), and Hong Kong (1955–1957). In addition to the publication of *A History of South-East Asia* and numerous articles, he also collected and edited for the press Michael Symes's journal and related documents connected with the latter's second embassy to Ava in 1802[17] and played the principal part in organizing the Southeast Asian section of a "Conference on Historical Writing on the Peoples of Asia," held at the School of Oriental and African Studies in 1956. The resulting volume of papers on Southeast Asian historiography which was published under his editorship in 1961[18] demonstrated in a remarkable fashion the great strides which had been made in the field since World War II.

That his retirement from the University of London in September 1959 proved to be merely the beginning of another phase in his career was mainly due to Hall's association with Cornell University, which dated from a chance meeting with Professor Lauriston Sharp in Bangkok in 1952. Cornell at this time was already the best-known centre of Southeast Asian studies in the United States. Its reputation was founded on the unique and rapidly growing Wason Collection of material on China and Southeast Asia, and on strength in the social sciences and in its Indonesian, Burmese, and Thai language programs. But its Southeast Asia program had as yet been unable to make a permanent appointment in history, and it was a logical step to propose that Hall might temporarily fill the gap as a visiting professor. When the suggestion was first made in 1955 and 1957 his commitments in London had made it impossible for him to accept, but in 1959 he was at last able to take it up, and he began teaching in Cornell in the fall semester of that year. The arrangement proved an outstandingly happy one. Cornell's beautiful campus at Ithaca, in the "finger lakes" region of upstate New York, became for him a second home, and from then on his time was divided between it and Hitchin, with occasional teaching forays to other universities in North America and Australia. The tragedy was that

17. Michael Symes, *Journal of His Second Embassy to the Court of Ava in 1802*, ed. D. G. E. Hall (London, 1955).
18. D. G. E. Hall (ed.), *Historians of South East Asia* (London, 1961).

Mrs. Hall was not to share all this with him. His first visit to Cornell was clouded by her illness, and they were forced to return prematurely to England in February 1960. She died in Hitchin after a long illness in 1962.

From October 1961 to the end of 1962 Hall was again teaching on a temporary basis at the School of Oriental and African Studies, but he returned to Cornell in 1963. His teaching there, though he taught under-graduate classes from time to time, was mainly concerned with the super-vision of graduate students and the conduct of seminars; a zealous teacher, with the knack of communicating his own enthusiasm to others, he valued above all the day-to-day contact with younger scholars and the opportunity to keep in touch with the development of research work on Southeast Asia. This stood him in good stead in his own work, particularly in the task of revising *A History of South-East Asia*, new and substantially enlarged editions of which appeared in 1964 and 1968. In addition to revisions of the original text to take account of the advances of scholarship since it had first been written, these new editions also incorporated treatment of topics such as the history of the Philippines and the economy of Southeast Asia before the sixteenth century, which had not been included in the first edition. His work in recent years has not, however, been confined to this task. He has played an active part in conferences of the Association of Asian Studies and the American Historical Association, and has published many papers of importance for the development of Southeast Asian historiography.[19] When he returned to England from Cornell at the beginning of 1973 he brought with him the completed typescript of another book—a full-scale biography of Henry Burney, British envoy to Thailand and the first Resident at the Court of Ava.[20]

It would be out of place here, and probably premature at this point in time, to attempt a critical evaluation of the work of D. G. E. Hall. But it is clear that more than any other man Professor Hall has been responsible for the emergence of Southeast Asia as a recognized field of study, in particular of historical study, in English-speaking universities. This, as it seems, has not been solely or even mainly because of the volume and quality of his published work, formidable though that is. What has told most has been his own conviction of the importance of his subject, and the way in which his personality and the nature of his relations with colleagues, students, and friends has communicated that conviction to them. Of the many universities in which he has worked—Rangoon, London, Cornell, British Columbia, Michigan, and Monash—he has left none of them without leaving behind in other minds the impression of his own.

19. See Publications of D. G. E. Hall, below.
20. Published as *Henry Burney: A Political Biography* (London, 1974).

D. G. E. Hall, as we remarked at the beginning of this essay, was born an Englishman, and in many respects he has remained throughout a long life deeply rooted in the values of the culture in which he was born, with a strong feeling for the countryside and the people of his native country. Yet perhaps the strongest features of his intellectual life have been his flexibility and modesty, and his capacity to adjust the framework of his ideas to changing events and the changing intellectual climate of the world around him. Although the work he did in Burma arose from a deep and genuine interest in that country and its people, it was almost exclusively devoted to European activities and Eurocentric themes, and reflected the thought-world of early twentieth-century England. But the author of *A History of South-East Asia* had moved away from that position to one where his interest was predominantly in indigenous Asian themes, and as the attentive reader of subsequent editions will have noted, this development of his ideas has continued. It is this capacity to continue to think, and to seek the ideas of others, which has made the acquaintance and friendship of D. G. E. Hall an honour and a pleasure for his colleagues and students.

Publications of D. G. E. Hall

Compiled by HELEN CORDELL

The Library, School of Oriental and
African Studies, University of London

1922   "A Professorship of Far Eastern History." *JBRS*, 12:169–170.

1923   *Imperialism in Modern History: Six Lectures.* Rangoon: Superintendent, Government Printing.

1925   *A Brief Survey of English Constitutional History.* London: Harrap. Rev. ed., 1939.

1926   "Prefatory Note to 'A Brief Account of the Kingdom of Pegu'; Translated from Portuguese by A. MacGregor." *JBRS*, 16:99–100.

1927   "English Relations with Burma, 1587–1686." *JBRS*, 17:1–79.
The League of Nations: A Manual for the Use of University Students and Teachers of Secondary Schools in India, Burma and Ceylon. By D. G. E. Hall and Jitendra-Mohana Sena. Calcutta: Macmillan.

1928   *Early English Intercourse with Burma, 1587–1743.* Rangoon University Publications, no. 1. London: Longmans Green.
"Materials for the Study of the Early Relations of the East India Company with Burma." Indian Historical Records Commission, *Proceedings*, 10:48–52.
"New Light upon British Relations with King Mindon." *JBRS*, 18:1–11.

1929   "The Dalhousie-Phayre Correspondence, 1852–1856." Indian Historical Records Commission, *Proceedings*, 11:131–136.

1931   "Note on Maung Maung's Paper 'The Beginnings of Christian Missionary Education in Burma, 1600–1824.'" *JBRS*, 21:13–14.
"The Tragedy of Negrais." *JBRS*, 21:59–133.

1932   *The Dalhousie-Phayre Correspondence, 1852–1856.* Edited with an introduction and notes by D. G. E. Hall. London: Oxford University Press.
"The English Settlement at Negrais, 1753–1759." Indian Historical Records Commission, *Proceedings*, 13:109–115.
"Felix Carey." *Journal of Religion*, 12:473–492.
"Phayre's Private Journal of His Mission to Ava in 1855." *JBRS*, 22:68–89.

1933 "The Journal of Felix Carey: A New Burma Document." *JBRS*, 23:123–125.

1935 *A High School British History, 1714–1930, for Burma, India and the East.* By A. M. Druitt and D. G. E. Hall. London: Oxford University Press. Rev. ed., 1946.

1936 "Studies in Dutch Relations with Arakan." *JBRS*, 26:1–31. Reprinted Burma Research Society, *Fiftieth Anniversary Publications*, no. 2, pp. 67–97. Rangoon: 1960.

1939 "Burma: The State of Historical Research." International Committee of Historical Sciences, *Bulletin*, 11:542–554.
"The Daghregister of Batavia and Dutch Trade with Burma in the Seventeenth Century." *JBRS*, 29:139–156. Reprinted Burma Research Society, *Fiftieth Anniversary Publications*, no. 2, pp. 99–116. Rangoon: 1960.

1942 "Burmese Religious Beliefs and Practices." *Religions*, 40:12–20.

1943 "English Relations with Burma, 1587–1886." *History*, n.s. 28:182–200.

1944 "Early Days of European Trade with Burma: With discussion." Royal Society of Arts, *Journal*, 92:173–181.

1945 *Europe and Burma: A study of European Relations with Burma to the Annexation of Thibaw's Kingdom, 1886.* London: Oxford University Press.

1950 *Burma.* London: Hutchinson's University Library. 2d ed., 1956. 3d ed., 1960.

1951 "South-East Asia and the Archipelago." *In* C. H. Philips (ed.), *Handbook of Oriental History.* London.

1954 "Some Present Tendencies in the Study of South-East Asia History." *Proceedings* of the 23rd International Congress of Orientalists. Cambridge.
"Thoughts on the Chinese Question in South-East Asia." *Asian Review*, 50:138–148.

1955 "From Mergui to Singapore, 1686–1819: A Neglected Chapter in the Naval History of the Indian Ocean." *History*, 40:255–272.
A History of South-East Asia. London: Macmillan; New York: St Martin's Press. 2d ed., 1964. 3d ed., 1968.
Michael Symes, *Journal of his Second Embassy to the Court of Ava in 1802.* Edited with an introduction and notes by D. G. E. Hall. London: George Allen and Unwin.

1956 "The European Impact on Southeast Asia." *In* P. W. Thayer (ed.), *Nationalism and Progress in Free Asia.* Baltimore, Md.: Johns Hopkins University Press.

1957 "Burney's Comments on the Court of Ava, 1832." *BSOAS*, 20:305–314.

1958 "Henry Burney, Diplomat and Orientalist." *JBRS*, 41:100–110.
1959 *East Asian History Today: A Lecture Delivered in the University of Hong Kong on May 20th, 1959.* Hong Kong: Hong Kong University Press.
"Vietnam's Political History: A Review Article." *PA*, 32:94–96.
1960 "Looking at Southeast Asian History." *JAS*, 19:243–253.
"On the Study of Southeast Asian History." *PA*, 33:268–281.
"R. B. Pemberton's Journey from Munipoor to Ava and from Thence across the Yooma Mountains to Arracan, 14 July–1 October 1830." *JBRS*, 43:1–96.
1961 "British writers of Burmese History from Dalrymple to Bayfield." *In* D. G. E. Hall (ed.), *Historians of South East Asia*. London.
Historians of South East Asia. Edited by D. G. E. Hall. Historical Writing on the Peoples of Asia, vol. 2. London: Oxford University Press.
1964 *Atlas of South-East Asia.* With an introduction by D. G. E. Hall. Amsterdam: Djambatan.
1965 "International Conflicts in South-East Asia: An historical survey." Oriental Society of Australia, *Journal*, 3:27–38.
"Problems of Indonesian Historiography." *PA*, 38:353–359.
1966 "Anglo-Burmese Conflicts in the 19th Century: A Reassessment of Their Causes." *Asia*, 6:35–52.
"Recent Tendencies in the Study of the Early History of South-East Asia." *PA*, 39:329–348.
1968 *Early English Intercourse with Burma, 1587–1743.* 2d ed., with "The Tragedy of Negrais" as a new appendix. London: Cass.
1971 Review of Gordon H. Luce, *Old Burma—Early Pagan. Asia Major*, 17:112–117.
1974 *Henry Burney: A Political Biography.* London: Oxford University Press.

SOUTHEAST ASIAN HISTORY
AND HISTORIOGRAPHY

Sources of Early Burma History

G. H. LUCE

Jersey, Channel Islands

In a diary published in 1926,[1] Aldous Huxley describes a voyage up and down the Irawady. He does not mention Pagán. His reading "was *The Glass Palace Chronicle of the Kings of Burma.*[2] This curious work was prepared in 1829 at the command of King Bagyidaw, who appointed a committee of the most famous scholars to compile a definitive and authoritative chronicle from the existing records. The result is probably the most learned edition of a fairy tale that has ever been published. . . . It is as though a committee of Scaligers and Bentleys had assembled to edit the tales of the nursery. . . ." He concludes: "In America, it would appear, there are still people who can discuss the first chapter of Genesis, the stories of Noah and Joshua, with all the earnest gravity of Burmese pandits discussing the Sun Prince and the eggs of the female Naga."

When Professor D. G. E. Hall, in the 1920's, rose to his feet in the Senate of the young Rangoon University, to propose the creation of a new Chair of Burma's history, he faced an audience partly imbued with the same derisive attitude to the whole subject. Has Burma any history worth studying?—inquired the Head of the Education Department. "Any Burmese undergraduate anxious to take up the study of history would be better advised to start on Thucydides' history of the Peloponnesian War."

Hall won his case, but by a narrow margin. The Sub-Department was born. It has since had a chequered career. It was almost ruined by the Japanese War, in which it lost all its library and nearly all its collection of estampages, readings, card indexes, translations and other records.— Forget it!—Here, if only to meet such criticisms as those instanced above, let me try to answer the question: What sources of real value are there, or were there, for studying Burma's early history?

Were there?—For there was once much evidence available which negligence or delays or just bad luck have lost for ever. Chief of these is the loss

1. *Jesting Pilate* (1957 edition, London: Chatto and Windus), pp. 168–171.
2. *The Glass Palace Chronicle of the Kings of Burma* transl. by Pe Maung Tin and G. H. Luce (London, 1923); see introduction, p. ix; text, pp. 33–39.

of so many languages—links in the long chains running east and west (Mon-Khmer) and north and south (Tibeto-Chinese), without which it is now hard, if not impossible, to trace origins before written history began. Genetic and anthropological evidence will help;[3] indeed may prove invaluable; but for recent pre-history the surest evidence, I venture to think, will come from language-study.

Once, we assume, Burma was inhabited by Negritoes, who still people the Andaman islands, parts of the north of the Malay Peninsula, and the Philippines. Valuable pioneer work was done on Andamanese by E. H. Man, R. C. Temple, M. V. Portman and others near the end of the last century, and on the "Andaman Islands" by Radcliffe Brown, and the "Pagan Races of the Malay Peninsula" by Skeat and Blagden[4] at the beginning of the present one. But few sure connections have been traced; and the Negrito languages of the Philippines are lost.

Consider next the Wet-Rice-cultivators. They started, it seems, from Tongking, and expanded west, between Central Yünnan, Cambodia and the Nicobars, as far as the Narbadda in Central India. Burma, north and south, was once an important stage on their spread westwards; and here they have left the noble legacy of Old Mon inscriptions (dating from the eleventh century onwards), now clearly revealed by the labours of Charles Otto Blagden[5] and Harold Shorto.[6] But many Mon-Annam dialects, even in the Shan States,[7] have still to be fully recorded. These are links in the chain, precious, irreplaceable, some almost extinct.

Arakan in the first millennium A.D. was a part of Eastern India, and its written language Sanskrit. Greek sources, chiefly Ptolemy,[8] provide glimpses of it in the second century. Professor E. H. Johnston's death in 1942 put a temporary stop to the study of Arakan's inscriptions. Those published,[9] notably the West face of the Shitthaung Pillar (now at

3. Note recent contributions by M. Mya-tu, *The Tarons in Burma* (Rangoon, 1966); A. E. Mourant and others, "The Blood-Groups and Haemoglobins of the Burmese," *Man*, 4, 1 (March 1969):118–122.

4. A. R. Radcliffe-Brown, *The Andaman Islanders* (Cambridge, 1932); W. W. Skeat and C. O. Blagden, *Pagan Races of the Malay Peninsula*, 2 vols. (London, 1906).

5. C. O. Blagden, *Epigraphica Birmanica*, vols. I, III, IV (Rangoon, 1919–1934).

6. H. L. Shorto, *A Dictionary of the Mon Inscriptions from the Sixth to the Sixteenth Centuries* (London, 1971). The northernmost point where Mon writing has hitherto (1971) been traced is at Shwezali village near Möng Mit in the Northern Shan States (eleventh-century writing by Aniruddha on the back of a votive tablet).

7. For example, Wa (Vü), Hkamŭk, Rumai, Yang Sek, Yang Wan Kun, Danaw, Darāng, En, Amök (Hsen Hsun), Loi of Möng Lwe, Āng-kú (Hka-La), Tai Loi, Sŏn: see *Upper Burma Gazetteer*, I, 1 (Rangoon, 1900), pp. 626–727; Rumai, Kyusao, Palê, etc.: see Leslie Milne, *A Dictionary of English-Palaung and Palaung-English* (Rangoon, 1931), pp. 355–383; Danaw, Riang, Panku, Tung Va: see G. B. Milner and Eugénie J. A. Henderson, *Indo-Pacific Linguistic Studies* (Amsterdam, 1965), I, 98–129.

8. Louis Renou, *La géographie de Ptolémée, L'Inde (VII, 1–4)* (Paris, 1925).

9. See E. H. Johnston, "Some Sanskrit Inscriptions of Arakan," *BSOAS*, 11, 2 (1944): 357–385.

Mrohaung), give roughly dateable dynasties of kings from the end of the second century to the eighth; and several are confirmed by a series of coins, Vaishnava at first, but mostly Shaivite. The change to Mahāyāna Buddhism, not noted by Hsüan-tsang or I-tsing in the seventh century, must have occurred soon after their visits to Samataṭa (say Chittagong). Johnston was hoping to edit the inscriptions on the North (tenth century) and earlier Shitthaung faces; but he did not live to do this. Stone sites, such as the old capital Vaiśālī eight miles north of Mrohaung,[10] and Mahāmuni a score of miles further north, likely to yield early inscriptions and other historical and artistic data, still await full-scale scientific excavation.

Most of Burma's languages are classed as Tibeto-Chinese; and the links between Old Burmese (twelfth century), Classical Tibetan (seventh-eighth century onwards), and Archaic Chinese (first millennium B.C.), are roughly assured, thanks to the work of Bernhard Karlgren, H. A. Jäschke, R.-A. Stein and others. Burmese itself broke away from Lolo in the ninth century. In 1916 Berthold Laufer[11] established the link between these languages and Tangut, spoken and written in the twelfth century on the borders of Ordos Desert, some fourteen hundred miles north of Pagán. There should be evidence of Burmese origins anywhere along that line.

Take only languages still spoken in Burma. Perhaps half of the vocabulary of KAREN is Tibeto-Burman or Mon-Khmer in origin.[12] Such words seem fully absorbed into the regular Karen eight tone-patterns. But there is still the other half which I cannot find in Tibeto-Burman or Mon. Provisionally I call it 'Pure Karen', very likely Pre-Tibeto-Burman. Still to be recorded fully are a number of Karen hill languages,[13] both in Burma and North Siam. Study of the four volumes of the *Karen Thesaurus* (Tavoy, 1847) and other works of the great early missionaries, Jonathan Wade, Francis Mason, etc., should help.

MRU[14] (mǎru[2] ts'a[1] = children of men) is now a language of North Arakan, infiltrated with K'umi, a western group of Kuki-Chin. But often its vocabulary is different; and when it is the same, the tones may differ. So the infiltration is superficial. I suspect that Mru was once a language

10. For recent finds at Wethali, see Report of the Director, Archaeological Survey, Burma, for the year ending 30 September 1964: pls. 31–32 and pp. 28–34; 1965 Report, pl. 18 and p. 37.

11. Berthold Laufer, "The Si-hia Language," *T'oung Pao*, March 1916, pp. 1–128.

12. In my article "Introduction to the Comparative Study of Karen Languages," *JBRS*, 42, 1 (June 1959): 10, I crudely described the Karen language as "Tibeto-Burman." I beg to withdraw this most inaccurate statement.

13. For example, Yintalè, Zayein, Mèpauk, Kawnsawng: see *Upper Burma Gazetteer* I, pt. 1 pp. 647–659; Wewaw, Monnepwa, Mopwa, Brek, Padaung, Yinbaw, Gheku, Zayein: see L. F. Taylor, *Census of India, 1921, Burma*, pt. 1, *Report*, Appendix B, pp. 288–289; also references in Robert Shafer's useful *Bibliography of Sino-Tibetan Languages* (Wiesbaden, 1957).

14. See Shafer's article, "The Linguistic Relationship of Mru," *JBRS*, 31, 2 (Aug. 1941): 58–79. My own conclusions are based on recordings of about 900 words.

of hunters, Pre-Tibeto-Burman, spoken on the west side of Central Burma.

SAK (Thet), called CHAK in East Pakistan,[15] is an old Tibeto-Burman language still spoken in a dozen villages north of Buthidaung in Arakan, and fourteen villages in the Chittagong Hill Tracts. Its speakers appear to know nothing of their relatives three hundred miles away to the north (Andro, Sengmai, etc.) who once peopled the Valley of Manipur;[16] nor of their relatives to the northeast, the KANTŪ (Kădu and Gănan) at the source of the Mu River, and the Mingin Range between Pinlèbu and Banmauk. These once lorded it over Upper Burma from their capital at Tagaung. The Chinese called them CHIEN-TU. They appear to have ranged, 600 miles west and east, over the lower ranges from the borders of Silchar in the plains of India to the Chien-ch'ang valley in the north of Yünnan.[17]

Another series of invasions from the north brought in the MEITHEI and the KUKI-CHIN. According to Grierson,[18] the Meithei "have been settled in the Manipur Valley for more than a thousand years," reducing to serfdom their predecessors, the 'Lui', i.e. the Sak tribes of Andro and Sengmai. But in various arts and crafts the 'Lui' have remained freer and superior to their Hinduized masters.

From the north-east, in the sixth to the ninth century, must have come the TIRCUL or PYU, with megalithic religious and funerary customs like those of the early inhabitants of the Plaine des Jarres, east of Luang Phrabang.[19] Not numerous, the Pyu were strongest in Upper Burma; but they occupied, for about a century, *Śrī Kṣetra* (Old Prome) and the Irawady plain down to the sea. In language apparently Tibeto-Burman, they appear already to have lost all final consonants, but distinguished in writing eight tones. Royal ashes were preserved in large stone urns, with names and dates beautifully engraved. They have left a number of Buddhist inscriptions in a strange archaic West Indian script, the oldest interlined with Brāhmī. Most are still unread or uninterpreted, except for about a hundred words identified by Blagden.[20] Their sculpture, North Indian in type, has a

15. See Lucien Bernot, *Les Cak* (Paris: Centre National de la Recherche Scientifique, 1967).
16. For vocabularies of Andro and Sengmai, see W. McCulloch, *Account of the Valley of Munnipore and of the Hill Tribes* (Calcutta, 1859), and for their various occupations see the index (s.v. *Loi, Lui*) of T. C. Hodson, *The Meitheis* (London, 1908).
17. For the *Saw* and *Kantū* of the Pagán period (the *Chien-tu* of the *Yüan-shih*), see *JBRS*, 42, 1 (June 1959):56–60. In the *JSS*, 46, 2 (Aug. 1958):183–184, n. 82, I tried (wrongly, as I now feel) to distinguish them from the *Chien-tu* (same characters) of the Chien-ch'ang valley in North Yünnan, mentioned in the same history, around the same dates.
18. *Linguistic Survey of India*, III, pt. 3, p. 2.
19. See Colani, *Mégalithes de Haut-Laos*, 2 vols. (Paris, 1925).
20. For read Pyu (Tircul) inscriptions, see C. O. Blagden, *JRAS*, 1911:365–388; *Epigraphia Indica*, 12, 16 (1913–14):127–132; *Epigraphia Birmanica*, I, pt. 1, pp. 59–68. Note their peculiar words: *tpū* "twenty"; *tdū* "water"; *phrụ* "day."

realism of its own. Their architecture employs the radiating arch and four-pendentive groining well in advance of their time.

I have considered elsewhere[21] the evidence (mostly linguistic) for the early history of the CHIN. All I would add here is what one can perhaps deduce from confused Perso-Arab and Chinese sources.[22] Early in the ninth century Burma was divided into three kingdoms, all threatened by Nan-chao: (i) the MI-NO (*mye-nak) or Chindwin kingdom of the Zo (Chins), perhaps around Mingin; (ii) the Central Burma capital of the P'IAO (TIRCUL) centred at *Hanlaṅ* (Halin) south of Shwebo, but including what is now the Northern Shan States; (iii) the Mon kingdom of MI-CH'ÊN, probably north-east of Pegu, near the old mouths of the Pegu River and Sittaung. The *Man-shu* dates the destruction of all three kingdoms in A.D. 832–835. Their fall was followed (or accompanied) by the descent of the MRANMĀ (Burmans) to the Central Burma plain, their occupation of the two irrigated rice lands of the Dry Zone, Kyauksè and Minbu, and the building of the walls of Pagán in A.D. 850.

The word 'Chindwin' means "the Hole or Well of the Chins." The word 'Chin' is the ancient Sino-Burmese word for "Comrade."[23] When the Mranmā seized Central Burma, they had to fight the Mon-Palaung-Wa, the Sak, and (very likely) the Karen. But the Chin were their "comrades," and have remained so ever since. After the fall of Pagán in 1286–1287, it was the Shans, not the Burmans, who drove the Chins west of the Chindwin, back into the Chin Hills. And this partly accounts for the great cultural and linguistic gap between the advanced Northern and Eastern Chins of Aijal, Tiddim, Falam, and Haka, and the Western and Southern Chins, still largely illiterate. Kuki-Chin languages extend at present all down the Arakan Yoma, from Lay-shi in the Somra Tract five hundred miles to Sandoway; and in breadth from the Chindwin border far into India (the Lushai Hills) and parts of East Pakistan. From her profound study of only five pages of Tiddim Chin, Eugénie Henderson[24] has opened a wide linguistic and grammatical vista, reaching (I venture to say) halfway to Europe.

Turn finally to written sources. Throughout the first millennium A.D., and indeed before it, our main, if only occasional source has been Chinese. From the date (90 B.C.) of the first of the twenty-four dynastic histories, the *Shih-chi* of Ssǔ-ma Ts'ien,[25] we have a reliable record of events, year

---

21. *JBRS*, 42, 1 (June 1959):23–28.

22. See V. Minorsky, *Hudud al-'Ālam* (982 A.D.) (London, 1937), pp. 242–243; *Man-shu* of Fan Ch'o (863 A.D.), trans. Cornell Southeast Asia Program Data Paper no. 44, pp. 90–91.

23. "Comrades," *Arch. Chin.* 彊彊 kian-kian (Karlgren, *Grammata Serica* 710 e) O. Burm. k'yaṅ:.

24. Eugénie J. A. Henderson, *Tiddim Chin* (London, 1965). For the Chin of East Pakistan, see Denise and Lucien Bernot, *Les Khyang des Collines de Chittagong* (Paris, 1958).

25. See Ed. Chavannes, *Les mémoires de Sse-ma Ts'ien traduits et annotés* (Paris, 1895–1898).

by year and often day by day, unrivalled in western histories. As a young man, Ssŭ-ma Ts'ien had visited K'un-ming, and clearly noted the difference (which gets blurred in later literature) between the MAN ("Southern Barbarians") of Eastern Yünnan, with their towns, agriculture and settled civilization (query Austroasiatic?), and the HSI-NAN-I ("South-western Barbarians") of Western Yünnan, with their plaited hair, absence of chiefs, and nomadic pastoral life. Already by 100 B.C., under Chinese pressure from the north, Tibeto-Chinese immigration into Southeast Asia had begun. The third and fourth dynastic histories (*Hou-han-shu* and *San-kuo-chih*) have many references to the Burma border. Indeed none of these histories can be disregarded.[26] The Old and New T'ang Histories have detailed sections on the P'iao (Pyu).[27] The *Yüan-shih* and *Ming-shih* have the fullest information. But there are many other equally essential texts, encyclopaedic, geographic, regional, provincial and district gazetteers, too numerous to mention. Shortly before the War reached Burma, I was asked to give a lecture in Rangoon on these Chinese sources; so I asked our University Library to count the number of Chinese volumes already acquired. It was over 20,000; and we were still badly short of district gazetteers along the Yünnan-Burma border. All had been neatly numbered, catalogued, and often indexed for Burma references by my beloved teacher, the late Bhikkhu Wan Hui. All these were looted by the Japanese, not a single volume recovered. Unless steps are taken to replace (so far as is now possible) this source material, the early history of Burma can never be adequately covered.

Burma's local histories are, in general, inward-looking; concerned with the present (based on a legendary past); centred on the plains rather than the hills (that is, only one third of Burma). As a new régime replaces an old, the latter (often the pioneer) gets pushed usually from centre to circumference, and may perish without sign. This is not to say that Burma histories are valueless. Indeed, from the founding of Ava (A.D. 1365) onwards, they tend to increase in accuracy. But before that date (as the experience of Rangoon University has shown), the collection and collation of source material were quite inadequate. By 1956 the University had published five portfolios including 609 large collotype plates of original inscriptions down to 1364.[28] This is the very stuff of history, nearly all engraved on stone, mostly in Burmese, but rarely cited in Burmese Chronicles. The inscrip-

26. See, e.g., *JBRS*, 14, 2 (Aug. 1924) (repr. at pp. 187–306 of *Burma Research Society Fiftieth Anniversary Publications*, no. 2).

27. *Ch'iu-t'ang-shu*, ch. 197; *Hsin-t'ang-shu*, ch. 222 C. Cf. "The Ancient Pyu," *JBRS.*, 27, 3 (Dec. 1937):239–253 (reprinted at pp. 307–321 of *B.R.S. Fiftieth Anniversary Publications*, no. 2)

28. *Inscriptions of Burma*, Portfolios I to V [down to 726 *s.*/1364 A.D. and the founding of Ava] Rangoon University, Oriental Studies Publications 2–6 (London, 1933–1956).

tions are factual, like those on Chou bronzes, but Buddhist, often deeply religious, mostly free from Indian flamboyance and exaggeration. One has only to read them, card-index dates, proper names, place names and other words of interest, to form a fair conspectus of a period or a reign. Problems, of course, arise: particularly in checking dates,[29] and deciding by palaeography and spelling whether an inscription is really original. But once this is settled, it can generally be accepted as a true statement of what happened on that date.

I have often wondered why Burmese scholars of the past, so justly famous in literature, poetry and the arts, neglected their own inscriptions. Ignorance of Pyu and Old Mon made Early Prome and Pagán history a closed book to them; as indeed it did to everyone until Blagden's genius found us the key. But from the accession (A.D. 1174) of *Cañsū* II (Narapatisithu) the language is normally Burmese; and though, phonetically, Burmese has changed greatly since that date, in spelling and writing it has changed little. Twelfth-century Burmese is far easier for a Burman to read than twelfth-century English for an Englishman. Being mostly religious, were the inscriptions deemed sacred, matter for piety rather than scholarship? I doubt it: for, in fact, the Chronicles did, not seldom, cite inscriptions—usually late ones, or 'Copies',[30] ones which I should tend to reject as not original.

In January 1833 Captain George Burney, brother of Colonel Henry Burney, the British Resident at Ava/Amarapura, accompanied two Burmese envoys on a visit to Bodhgayā in India. There they noticed a black marble inscription engraved in Old Burmese,[31] fixed upside down "against

29. For this vital checking of dates, see "Old Burma Calendar" in my *Old Burma—Early Pagan*, 3 vols. (Locust Valley, N.Y., 1969–1970), II, 327–337, especially "A Tribute to U Ka" on pp. 335–337. The six "elephant volumes" of inscriptions (1892–1913), listed on page 230 of the same volume, lose much of their historical value, not merely by "their modernized spelling, negligent copying, unreliable dates," but by confusing original and late inscriptions. C. Duroiselle's *List of Inscriptions Found in Burma* (Rangoon, 1921) distinguishes "Originals" from "Copies"; but he includes among the former many in pre-Kônbaung dynasty script which certainly do not belong to the early dates to which they refer. In the five Portfolios we have tried scrupulously to exclude all such inscriptions, and so to lay a secure foundation for future research. How far we have succeeded, it is for future scholars to judge.

30. For *hsin-hto* and *sat-hto* Copies, see Pe Maung Tin's Introduction (pp. x–xi) to *The Glass Palace Chronicle* translation.

31. Old Burmese Inscription at Bodhgayā. See (i) Colonel H. Burney, *Asiatic Researches*, 20, 1 (Calcutta, 1836):161–189, with facsimile readings by Ava scholars and translation by Burney(?); (ii) Rajendralala Mitra, *Buddha Gayâ* (Calcutta, 1878), p. 209 (reading by the Burmese scholar, Hla Oung); (iii) *J. Bengal Asiatic Society*, 3 (May 1834):214 (reading by Ratnapāla [and Prinsep?]); (iv) Alexander Cunningham, *Mahābodhi* (London, 1892), pp. 75–77 (translations by Ratnapāla and Hla Oung compared); *Book of Indian Eras* (1883), pp. 70–73 (the dates); (v) *A.S.B.*, 1911 Report, pp. 18–19 (translation by Taw Sein Ko). I add my own readings and translation at the end of this article.

the wall of the inner court of the convent of Sanyásis." Captain Burney was told that it had been "discovered near the large Buddhist temple [the Mahābodhi Vajrāsana] about forty years ago." Copies were sent to Colonel Burney, for reading by the Burmese scholars at Ava, who had just finished compiling the Glass Palace Chronicle (Hmannan Yazawin). Other copies were studied independently by the Burmese scholar U Hla Oung, the Singhalese Pali scholar Ratnapāla, and the Secretary of the Asiatic Society of Bengal James Prinsep. There was a fair degree of agreement on the general sense, but enough divergence to make it clear that the study of Pagán epigraphy was then still in its infancy, both in India and Burma. The stone has since vanished. My own reading and translation (given at the end of this article) are based on a photograph supplied by the Archaeological Survey of India, shown at Plate 299 of Portfolio III of the *Inscriptions of Burma*. Here are some notable discrepancies:—

	Burney (+ Ava scholars) (1836)	Hla Oung	Ratnapāla (+ Prinsep) (1834)	Taw Sein Ko (1911)	Luce
l.4	Penthagoo-gyee	Penthagoo-gyee	Naik Mahanta	Mahāthera Pinthagugyi	Pansakū krī
ll.6–7	Theeri Dhamma Pada Rāja Goona	Sri Dhamma Râjguna	Sri Dhamma Raja Guna	Siridhamma rājaguru	Siri Dhamma rājākuru
l.9	Waradathi	Wardathi	Varadasi	Varavāsi, a junior Thera	Vanavāsi Skhiṅ Thera
ll.9–10	Pyoo-ta-thein-men (chief of 100,000 Pyoos)	Lord of the 100,000 Pyoos	Prince Pyutasing	King Pyuta-thein Min	Putasin Maṅ
l.10	Pyoo-thakhen-nge	Lesser lord of the Pyoos	The younger Pyusakheng	–	[kamu] skhiṅ ṅai [i.e. the junior monk, Kassapa]
l.10	Great officer Ratha	Prime Minister Ratha	Minister Ratha	–	mlat krī the [i.e. the Venerable Thera Dhamma-rājākuru]
l.11	year 467	year 667	year 667	year 657	year 65[7]
l.12	year 468	year 668	year 668	year 660	year [6]60

There is little or no doubt about the dates. The failure of the Ava scholars to read correctly four out of the six figures not only threw them two centuries out in their reckoning, but seduced them into the absurd misreading of

Putasin [?Buddhasena] as "lord of the 100,000 Pyu." The Pyu, I fear, must have been well-nigh extinct at Pagán by the end of the thirteenth century; and it seems unlikely that they had moved in such numbers to the neighborhood of Bodhgayā. Ava mistakes, in turn, led Cunningham to misread the Burmese date on the large copper-gilt umbrella[32] which was found buried "immediately to the west of the temple." This consisted of a single line, damaged apparently at both ends. To judge by the hand copy on his Plate XXIX, I suggest the reading:

[sa]karac [6]55 khu || siridhammarājākuru . . . (kusil ||)

"655 *s.* [1293–1294 A.D.]. The good work(?) of Siri Dhammarājākuru."

It seems that the mission was sent to Bodhgayā by the Pagán king 'Hsinbyushin', i.e. the *Rhuy-nan-syaṅ* (Klawcwā) of Burma inscriptions, after his return to the capital and *abhiṣeka* in A.D. 1289.[33] What with the Mongol capture of Pagán, and Shan inroads in the north and east, the realm must have been a shambles. But a pious act at the source of the Religion might possibly avail to save it from despair and ruin. The meagrely equipped mission set up its copper-gilt umbrella; and this helped to win local support in India, but not to save the kingdom. Klawcwā was dethroned by the Shan brothers in A.D. 1297,[34] and murdered on 10 May 1299.[35] It was almost, but not quite, the death blow to Pagán.

The previous rebuilding of the Mahābodhi by *Satuiw Maṅ*, "our lord the king," was doubtless done by the mission sent by Kyanzittha (c. A.D.1095) to repair "the holy *Śrī Bajrās* . . . which had been irremediably destroyed by the Turks, which other kings had been unable to repair."[36] Plate XXXI of Cunningham's *Mahābodhi* and Plate 190 of Volume III of *Old Burma— Early Pagán* point to Pagán workmanship of the Kyanzittha period; also the three votive tablets with Old Mon writing found at Bodhgayā.

The main work on Burma's inscriptions is still to be done, or redone. The five published portfolios lead up to the still unpublished "grand inscriptional art of Sagaing, which flowered late, but lasted long after Sagaing had ceased to be a capital." I quote the conclusion of the Preface to Portfolios IV and V (1956).

32. Umbrella inscription. See A. Cunningham, *Mahābodhi*, pl. XXIX and pp. iii, 27, 56, 75.

33. *Inscriptions of Burma*, Portfolio III, pl. 282[1] (Stone at Dayinpāhto temple, Minnanthu). The date of the *abhiṣeka* is given as Monday the 12th waxing of *Mlwaytā* (= Wazo), Caitra year, 651 *s*. This year [1289 A.D.] was a leap year; but I cannot reconcile the weekday with U Ka's calendar.

34. *Nan-kla-maṅ*, "the Dethroned King," is mentioned in a Kyaukse Myinzaing inscription under date Thursday, the 13th waxing of Pyatho, Mārgaśīrṣa year, 659 *s*. [Thurs., 26 Dec. 1274 A.D.] See *Inscriptions of Burma* Portfolio III, pl. 286[1].

35. Third year of *ta-tê*, 4th month, 10th day [10 May 1299]. See *JSS*, 46, 2 (Aug. 1958): 158 and n. 250 on p. 202.

36. See *Epigraphia Birmanica*, I, pt. 2, pp. 163–164 (Inscr. VIII A[4-7]); *Old Burma—Early Pagán*, I, 62–63, 77; II, 104; III, pl. 190d. For votive tablets from Bodhgayā with Old Mon writing, see *ibid.*, I, 102; II, 22, 24; III, pls. 30a, 30b, 36c, 36d.

The century between the founding of Ava and the beginning of modern Burmese literature is little known even to scholars in Burma. Yet it produced the grandest of her carved inscriptions, whose calligraphy can bear comparison with any in the world. It produced a rich crop of early Burmese poems, which are scarcely to be seen in modern anthologies. The earliest dated one, Plate V 542, falls just before the founding of Ava, and very likely commemorated it. Linguistically, it doubled the resources of the language, and affords in lasting stone the basis of textual criticism, and the test of modern editions. There is still at Sagaing (Htupayôn Shed, Stone 25) a poem of Shin Sīlavaṁsa, clearly engraved on stone, which has never been printed. That Rangoon University, in spite of its grievous losses and anxieties, will see its way ere long to fill this last gap in the salvage of Burmese literary culture, is the fervent hope of [the editors].

In January 1955, when the Burma Historical Commission was founded, our prayer seemed likely to be granted. There was full cooperation (as always) with the Burma Archaeological Department; with Rangoon University; and with the Army Research Department. A start was made on editing, translating and annotating the inscriptions of Portfolio I. Two substantial Bulletins were published. In 1964, when I had to leave Burma (for a year without my library), we had edited the first twenty inscriptions; Plates 6 to 20 (including the earliest original Burmese inscription of a Burmese king) were in final proof for the third Bulletin. I do not know if it has yet been passed for publication. Since then, one of the three editors, Colonel Ba Shin, has died. The other two are over eighty, half-blind, and unable to communicate.

Old Burmese Inscription at the Vajrāsana Temple at Bodhgayā (*Inscriptions of Burma*, Portfolio III, Plate 299)

(1) ‖ ‖ purhā skhiṅ sāsanā 218 lwan liy pri so akhā nhuik | camputip klwan kuiw acuiw (mi) ra so si-

(2) ridhammasoka mañ so maṅkrī cetī yhat soṅ 4 thoṅ a(thai) nhuik

(3) chwa[ṁ] tau phun (ph)iy rā pāyā[sa]ī than kuw akhā liy mlaṅ pyak

(4) ruy [p]laṅ so skhiṅ paṅsakū krī ta yok thuiw priy ta khyak pya-

(5) k khay rakā satuiw maṅ plu e‍ᶦ thuiw pri ta khyak pyak khay tuṁ

(6) rakā chaṅ phlu skhiṅ tryā maṅ kri mimi kuiwcā chiryā siri dhamma-

(7) rājākuru kuiw ciy t[au]mu lat so akhā nhuik pā la-

(8) t so tape' sā siri kassapa sañ lu[p] aṁ [sa] uccā hi lyak

(9) ma lup ra tat rakā wanawāsi skhiṅ thera kuiw chwaṁ khaim ciy rakā pu-

(10) tasin maṅ hu e‍ᶦ lup ciy kamu skhiṅ ṅai kuiw mlat krī the kuiw

(11) akhwaṅ mū rakā sakarac 65[7] khu plasuiw l = chan 10 ryak 6 niy plu tu[ṁ]e‍ᶦ

(12) sakarac [6]60 tanchoṅmhun l = chan 8 ryak tanhaṅkanū ni [lha]ce so

(13) taṁkhwan kukā taṁkhwan myā tuiw kuiw le pucaw e^l saṅput th[o]ṅ
      chi mi
(14) th[o]ṅ tuiw akrin myā cwā lhya[ṅ] pucaw e^l sā sami hu mhat ruy
      suṅai 2
(15) yok rhuy pan ṅuy pan khwak pu[ch]uiw chway so patañsā le pu-
(16) caw e^l akhā khapsim lhyaṅ saṅpu[t] wat [m]a prat tañ cim so
(17) kroṅ mliy kywan nwā tuiw kuiw le way ruy lhu khay iṅā[m]u
(18) so koṅ mhu kā nippan paccañ athok apañ phlac khyāṅ sa-
(19) te ||| myattañ purhā skh(i)ṅ . . . lakthak lhyaṅ rahantā chu luiw sate

Translation

"After 218 [years] of the Lord Buddha's religion had elapsed,[37] one amongst the 84,000 *cetī* of the king called *Siri Dhammasoka*, ruler of the Island of *Camputip* [Jambudīpa]—the one at the site of the giving of alms of Milk-Rice (*pāyāsa*),[38] fell into ruin through age and stress of time. It was repaired by a Senior *Paṅsakū* monk [sc. wearing rags from a dust-heap, *pāṁsukūla*]. Thereafter, when it had again fallen into ruin, *Satuiw Maṅ* ("our lord the king") rebuilt it. Thereafter, when it had once more fallen into ruin, the king of the Law [*tryā maṅkri* = dharmarāja], Chaṅ-phlu-skhiṅ ("lord of the White Elephant") sent, as his proxy, his teacher [*chiryā* = ācārya] *Siri Dhammarājākuru*, who took with him his pupil (*tape' sā*) *Siri Kassapa*. With the funds they had for doing the work, they were unable to do it. So on the occasion of giving almsfood to the lord Thera *Vanavāsi*,[39] *Putasin Maṅ* ("Prince Putasin")[40] granted permission to the junior monk [sc. Kassapa] and the Venerable Thera [sc. Dhammarājāguru] to carry on the work(?).[41] On Friday the 10th waxing of the month of Pyatho in the year 657 *s.* [Friday, 16 Dec. A.D. 1295] they resumed the work. When (final) dedication was made on Sunday the 8th waxing of the month Tazaungmôn in the year 660 *s.* [Sunday, 12 Oct. A.D. 1298], there was offering of many flags and flag-streamers, many offerings, time after time, of rice-alms by the thousand, oil lamps by the thousand; also two children styled as "son" and "daughter"; the offering also of a *patañsā* [sc. kalpavṛkṣa tree][42]

---

37. 218 A.B. [326 B.C.] is the conventional date given for the *abhiṣeka* of Aśoka. See *Mahāvaṁsa* V[21].
     38. Sujātā's offering of Milk-Rice under the *nigrodha* banyan tree was on the morning of the day before Gotama attained Buddhahood. It was his only meal for the next forty-nine days.
     39. *Vanavāsi*. The word means "forest-dweller."
     40. *Putasin* (? Buddhasena) was, I suppose, the local Rāja of Bodhgayā at the time. The reading *Pu* is certain: *Pyu* is impossible.
     41. I take *lup ciy kamu* to be a colloquial expression, like "Go ahead! Do whatever is needed!"
     42. O. Mon *kapparuk*. O. Burm. *padesā, pateñsā*. Cf. *Inscriptions of Burma*, II, 117 b[3]. A tree of the North Island (Uttarakuru), which bears perpetual fruit for a whole *kalpa*.

hung with gold and silver flowers, with cups and garments. In order that rice-alms may be offered without a break for ever and ever, land, slaves and cattle were also bought and dedicated. As for this good deed done by me, I want it to be a means and support for the attainment of Nirvana. At the time when *Myattañ* [Maitreya] . . . as the Lord Buddha, I pray for the boon of Sainthood."

Postscriptum

Since this article was written, in 1971, yet another editor, the great Pali and Burmese scholar Pe Maung Tin, has died. The Burma Archaeological Department also has lost its venerable archaeologist, U Mya. Yet it still continues its invaluable work, excavating old sites, finding and editing old inscriptions. Its full Annual Reports (the last known to me is for the year ending September 1965) are in Burmese. And the Director of Archaeology, U Aung Thaw, has published (in 1972) a well-illustrated book in English, *Historical Sites in Burma*.

G. H. L. (1974)

Prolegomena to a Phonology of Old Burmese

ROBERT B. JONES

Cornell University

A reconstructed protolanguage is seldom, if ever, satisfactory in all respects. It will of course constitute a systematic statement of relationship between the various languages and dialects from which it is derived, but one would like to hope, even believe, that it also represents a "real" progenitor in some sense. For unwritten languages the reality of the prototype represented by a reconstruction must remain a matter of conjecture, though this in no way affects the validity of the reconstruction as a statement of relationship between the later representatives. For languages with early written attestations the question of reality is perhaps nearer resolution, but at the same time the complexities of arriving at any such resolution are considerable, requiring a phonological interpretation of the early evidence and comparison of that interpretation with the reconstructed phonology and with those of modern dialects as well. Needless to say, it is most unlikely that one would ever find perfect congruity at all levels, and any lack of congruence again requires evaluations of the differences. It is perhaps at this level that the greatest difficulties arise. Some may well be insurmountable, but many can be resolved. The Burmese language provides examples of both kinds of difficulties, perhaps fewer of the former than the latter, and we may be able to come somewhat closer to a resolution of the question of "reality" for Old Burmese and a reconstruction of Proto-Burmese.

Burmese writings date from the twelfth century, and some initial attempts at reconstructing a Proto-Burmese have been made, but a history of the Burmese language is still far from being realized. Nevertheless progress has been made toward this goal. Proto-Burmese initial consonants and consonant clusters can be reconstructed from the evidence of modern dialects, and these reconstructions generally correlate well with the evidence from Old Burmese. Vowels and finals, on the other hand, present greater problems; this aspect of Old Burmese phonology is addressed in the present study.

43

While a protovowel system can be unambiguously reconstructed from the modern dialects, questions arise concerning the status of this reconstruction in the light of certain internal evidence in the vowel systems of some dialects and the evidence of both Modern and Old Burmese spelling. With the publication of the earliest lengthy Old Burmese text, the ink writings from the walls of the Lokahteikpan temple in Pagán[1] dating probably from the early twelfth century, it has become possible to investigate these questions more fully and come to reasonably firm conclusions concerning the Old Burmese vowel system. Prior to this time the earliest Old Burmese text, the Rājakumār (generally known as the "Myazedi") inscription, was too short to be very useful for these purposes. The Lokahteikpan writings provide a lengthy text of some two hundred verses which are descriptive captions accompanying pictures painted on the walls of the temple representing scenes from the life of the Buddha and various Jataka tales. The vocabulary is rich and many words appear several times, making it possible to study spelling variation and arrive at some conclusions concerning the phonology they probably represent. These converge with and at the same time help to clarify some tentative conclusions derived from modern evidence.

Based on both the modern and the archaic evidence the principal conclusions are that some time prior to the twelfth century, a period which will be called the Pre-Old Burmese stage (P-OB), the phonology of Burmese included a three-vowel system, that this was still the basic system at the period of Old Burmese represented by the Lokahteikpan writings (L-OB) but that at this time two additional vowels were in process of developing, and that this process continued until an as yet unspecified time when it resulted in a seven-vowel system which is that of Modern Standard Burmese.[2] A seven-vowel system also can be reconstructed for Proto-Burmese (PB) on the basis of comparative evidence from the modern dialects. In this respect, then, the OB vowel system appears to stand in relationship to a PB vowel system much as Latin does to Proto-Romance.

The vowel system of Modern Standard Burmese (SB) includes plain vowels, and nasalized and stopped vowels and diphthongs as follows, with nasalization symbolized as /-n/.

1. Ba Shin, *Lokahteikpan, Early Burmese Culture in a Pagan Temple* (Rangoon, 1962).
2. Some linguists have preferred a five-vowel and four-diphthong analysis of Burmese (for example, W. S. Cornyn, *Outline of Burmese Grammar*, Language Supplement, vol. 20 [1944]). But since their /ei, ou/ are monophthongs as plain vocalic nuclei, and diphthongized only when nasalized or stopped, I have preferred to analyze these nuclei as unit vowel phonemes /e, o/ with the diphthongization conditioned, as this analysis conforms better with both the phonetic facts and the historical development. For similar reasons I have preferred a tonal analysis which consists of two pitch levels, either of which could occur on morphemes with a phonemic final glottal stop having two allophones, full stop with low pitch but constriction with high pitch.

/i	u	/in	un	/ìˀ	ùˀ
e	o	en	on	èˀ	òˀ
ε	a	ɔ/	–	an	–	ὲˀ	àˀ	–
		ain	aun/	àiˀ	àuˀ/

Modern spelling, though it has undergone several revisions in the course of time, is still archaic in retaining a full set of final nasal and stop consonants, which in modern dialects have merged into simple nasalization and glottal stop respectively. These modern spellings provide one part of the evidence for an older three-vowel system. In the following list[3] of spellings of vowels with final nasal consonants note that the aberrant spellings ⟨uiŋ⟩ and ⟨oŋ⟩[4] seem clearly to fill the otherwise empty slots for "iŋ" and "uŋ."

	⟨im⟩	⟨am⟩	⟨um⟩
	⟨in⟩	⟨an⟩	⟨un⟩
⟨uiŋ⟩ → (iŋ)		⟨aŋ⟩	(uŋ) ← ⟨oŋ⟩
		⟨añ⟩	

Modern spellings with final stop consonants are parallel, including modern ⟨as⟩ from OB ⟨ac⟩.

	⟨ip⟩	⟨ap⟩	⟨up⟩
	⟨it⟩	⟨at⟩	⟨ut⟩
⟨uik⟩ → (ik)		⟨ak⟩	(uk) ← ⟨ok⟩
		⟨as⟩	

Here too it seems clear that the sequences which once were "ik" and "uk" have been respelled, and similar phonetic conditions must have prevailed regarding the vowels /i/ and /u/ before both stop and nasal velar consonants.

Further evidence for a three-vowel system within the nasalized and stopped sets of vowels may be found in the dialect of Tavoy. There we find only three nasalized vowels, /in, an, un/, and it should be noted that

3. For the purposes of this paper it has not appeared necessary to distinguish between final ⟨m⟩ and ⟨ṁ⟩ (Sanskrit *anusvāra*). Their occurrence in words so far extracted from the Lokahteikpan texts would seem to indicate that the former occurs with the front vowel and the latter with the central and back vowels, but this impression is, of course, not a conclusion, nor is there yet clear evidence of any correlation with pitch, as is partially the case in SB spelling. There is some slight indication in the sketchy information available on Hpon of a possible vowel contrast that is relatable to these two finals, so the question remains open.

4. The orthographic representation ⟨o⟩ is not a transliteration, as are other such representations, but a convention. The orthographic form is a complex one composed of the preposed symbol ⟨e⟩ and the postposed symbol ⟨a⟩. This spelling in SB represents /ɔ/ in open syllables, /au-/ in closed syllables. This complex symbolization does not occur in Sanskrit but does occur in many alphabets of India and Southeast Asia derived from devanagari script.

in this dialect /un/ represents a very open (lax) vowel which may vary in tongue height from high to low. In other words the structural contrasts are front, central, and back, other features being secondary and non-distinctive. A similar but not entirely parallel situation exists in the stopped set of vowels. The same basic system is present, /ìʔ, àʔ, ùʔ/, but to it have been added /èʔ, òʔ, ɛ̀ʔ/, which are not related to the stopped vowels of SB but rather to the vowels /i, o, ɛ/ with the constricted tone, which have shifted to stopped tone in Tavoy with lowering of the high front vowel. Thus we find SB /íʔ, óʔ, ɛ́ʔ/ corresponding to Tavoy /èʔ, òʔ, ɛ̀ʔ/. This system was further expanded symmetrically to include /ɔ̀ʔ/, corresponding to orthographic ⟨ok⟩, SB /àuʔ/, and the two diphthongs /àiʔ, àuʔ/, the former corresponding to orthographic ⟨uik⟩, SB /àiʔ/, as expected, but the latter corresponding to orthographic ⟨up⟩, SB /òʔ/.

In the Myohaung dialect of Arakanese we find similar evidence. Here the nasalized and stopped vowel sets are perfectly paralleled—four vowels /e-, o-, ɛ-, ɔ-/ and two diphthongs /ai-, au-/ in each set. The vowels /e-, o-/ correspond to orthographic ⟨im/n, um/n, ip/t, up/t⟩ as expected. /ɛ-/ corresponds to orthographic ⟨ap/t/m/n⟩, and the new contrast /ɔ-/ corresponds to orthographic ⟨ak/ŋ⟩ which yields SB /ɛ́ʔ, in/. The two diphthongs correspond as expected to ⟨uik/ŋ, ok/ŋ⟩.

For the plain vowels all modern dialects so far investigated show a seven-vowel system, and it is these which cast doubt on the three-vowel hypothesis since there is neither internal dialect evidence nor orthographic evidence for fewer than seven plain vowels at the modern level. There is, however, such evidence in the Lokahteikpan spellings. Even though these texts include such variation in spelling that Ba Shin called it "haphazard and diverse," it is nevertheless possible, by comparing these spelling variations among themselves and with their SB phonemic and orthographic forms, to arrive at criteria for identifying the basic spelling system and hence variants from that system. (Some variants may simply be misspellings, but many no doubt result from the fact that the writer, or painter, was often required to crowd a text into a space too small to accommodate it with normal spacing.)

In the following discussion, L-OB spellings which seem clearly to be variants from the norm are included in parentheses. Also, to avoid possible confusion in transliterating Lokahteikpan spellings, both "short" and "long" symbols are indicated for the vowels ⟨i, a, u⟩ even though to do so is redundant. These Indic short/long vowel symbols have no length significance in Burmese but relate in open syllables to tone, that is, the "short" vowel symbols regularly produce SB constricted tone /ʅʔ/. Two finals which also relate directly to SB tones were sporadically used in L-OB. The occasional inclusion of a final /-h/, or sometimes /-ː/ (Sanskrit *visarga*), either on the line or as a subscript, often relates to SB high tone

/ɂ/. Similarly, and somewhat more frequently, the inclusion of a final or subscript /-ɂ/ (with or without an accompanying final nasal) corresponds to SB high pitch with constriction, the constricted tone. For Pre-Old Burmese it is then assumed that pitch features were probably not distinctive, but by the time of L-OB final consonants were losing their distinctive qualities, and concomitant changes were taking place in the development of new vowel and pitch distinctions which probably had not yet acquired contrastive status.

The following lists give the system of vowels and final consonants[5] posited for Pre-Old Burmese along with the SB phonemic correspondences, including pitch features where pertinent.

P-OB	SB	P-OB	SB	P-OB	SB
i	ì	a	à	u	ù
ih	í	ah	á	uh	ú
iɂ	íɂ	aɂ	áɂ	uɂ	úɂ
iy	e	ay	ɛ	uy	we
		aw	ɔ	uw	o
im	en	am	an	um	on
in	en	an	an	un	on
iŋ	ain	aŋ	in	uŋ	aun
ip	èɂ	ap	àɂ	up	òɂ
it	èɂ	at	àɂ	ut	òɂ
ik	àiɂ	ak	ɛ̀ɂ	uk	àuɂ
		ac	ìɂ		

Some of the allophonic variations implied by the above correlations had apparently become distinctive enough, if not contrastive, to be indicated in some cases in the spelling of the Lokahteikpan texts. Modern orthographic ⟨e⟩ had come into limited use. With final velars it occurs as a variant spelling of words otherwise spelled with ⟨ă⟩, often when preceded by an initial or medial palatal.

L-OB		MB
⟨myek ~ myăk⟩	eye	/myɛ̀ɂ/
⟨khyek⟩	to cook	/thyɛ̀ɂ/[6]
⟨-khyeŋ⟩	fetters	/-thyín/
⟨-kheŋ⟩	affairs	/-khín/

5. The palatal nasal as a final consonant has been omitted here since the preliminary search of the Lokahteikpan texts yielded no examples.

6. The palatal affricates of SB have also been analyzed as unit stops /ch, c/, but phonetically they are complex and clearly begin from alveolar position and so I have preferred the cluster analysis to reflect this. Historically, then, the palatalization of velar stops is seen in SB to have resulted in fronting of the velar to alveolar position.

Compare also the following alternation, the only example so far discovered.

⟨săkhaŋ ~ săkhĭŋ⟩   lord   /θakhìn/

From such examples we may infer that the fronting shift of the central vowel before final velars was in process but there was not yet a contrast.

The vowel ⟨e⟩ with other finals is quite rare. The spellings ⟨et⟩ and ⟨ec⟩ occur in a few words, for example ⟨hyet⟩ "eight," ⟨khet⟩ "to love," and ⟨sec ~ sac⟩ "tree." All these have developed as if from ⟨ac⟩, having SB /ì²/ in each of the words involved, and from these we may again infer that the final stops were losing their distinctive qualities as the new vowel contrast was developing. It may be further noted here that the modern spelling of "eight" would indicate an OB spelling "hr-" but the L-OB spelling is ⟨hy⟩, and since there is not yet evidence of the shift /r > y/ this no doubt represents a modern respelling.

Except in the many Buddhistic proper names of Indic origin the vowel ⟨e⟩ is very rare in open syllables, being confined to only four or five words. Nevertheless, at least two of these are of high frequency, and they do not occur in variant spellings.

L-OB		SB
⟨te⟩	(plural affix)	/tè ~ twè/
⟨le: ~ le⟩	also	/lɛ̀/

The differing reflexes of these words in SB prevent a firm conclusion that the new vowel was now in contrast with ⟨ĭy⟩, though it is possible that this was indeed the case. The few remaining words with the spelling ⟨e⟩ are difficult to identify conclusively with modern forms, including the very frequent verbal suffix ⟨ye²⟩. The modern Burmese spelling of "also" departs sharply from the L-OB spelling in utilizing the final palatal nasal which now ambiguously represents the vowels /i ~ e ~ ɛ/, though one can find many examples of a regularized modern spelling with ⟨ɛ⟩.

As noted above, pitch was perhaps not a distinctive element of Pre-Old Burmese but became so on the loss of certain of the final consonants, and this change may have been in process by the time of L-OB. If so there may have been some correlations between pitch and vowel allophones as well that could to some extent account for variation in vowel quality. At least by the time a seven-vowel system had developed a new symbol had been introduced into the writing system, ⟨ɛ́⟩ with inherent high pitch, as opposed to /ɛ̀/ with inherent low pitch from OB ⟨ăy⟩, SB ⟨ăy⟩. A similar situation exists also in back position wherein SB ⟨o⟩ has inherent high pitch, and a diacritic which does not occur in L-OB has been added to the symbol to indicate low pitch when called for. In addition there is some evidence in relation to L-OB ⟨i⟩. It was indicated above that the proposed P-OB /i/ corresponds to SB /i/. It should now be further noted that all L-OB words of this type so far catalogued have SB reflexes with high pitch except two, which have SB reflexes with /e/ and low pitch.

L-OB		MB
⟨cī⟩	cause to	/sè/
⟨sī⟩	to die	/θè/

Arakanese furnishes a modern example of allophonic vowel variation conditioned by pitch. All plain vowels in that dialect are noticeably tenser, even constricted, with high pitch. In addition, the low central vowel /a/ has a raised back allophone [ʌ] with high pitch and with all occurrences after medial /-w-/.

Turning now to the back vowel of the proposed P-OB stage we note that development in this position was largely parallel to the front vowel, except that /uy/ shifted from a falling to a rising diphthong with lowering of the resulting peak vowel, producing SB /we/. It was accordingly respelled, though in L-OB alternate spellings ⟨ŭy ~ ūy⟩ continue parallel to the front vowel alternates ⟨ĭy ~ īy⟩, and in neither case does the alternation between long and short vowel symbols appear to be of any significance. P-OB /uw/ had been respelled in L-OB as ⟨uiw⟩, and the sequence ⟨ui⟩ (the regular modern spelling of /o/) occurs only a few times and only as a variant spelling of words that appear otherwise with the final ⟨w⟩. Also by this time P-OB /uŋ/ and /uk/ had been respelled ⟨oŋ⟩ and ⟨ok⟩, and we see the beginnings of the shifts which resulted in the establishment of a new back vowel contrast parallel to the newly developing front vowel contrast.

L-OB		SB
⟨khŭy (~ khūy)⟩	dog	/khwé/, ⟨khwe:⟩
⟨mrŭy⟩	snake	/mwè/, ⟨mrwe⟩
⟨tū⟩	to dig	/tú/
⟨nuiwˀ (~ nui)⟩	breast	/nóˀ/
⟨ŋuiw⟩	to cry	/ŋò/
⟨cuiwˀ⟩	to suck	/sóˀ/
⟨chuiw (~ chiw)⟩	to talk	/shò/
⟨pŭn⟩	to hide	/pón/
⟨sŭṁ⟩	three	/θón/
⟨chŭp⟩	to squeeze	/shòˀ/
⟨phŭt⟩	to burn	/phòˀ/
⟨khyŭt⟩	to end	/thyòˀ/ respelled ⟨khyŭp⟩
⟨khloŋ⟩	stream	/thyáun/
⟨sok⟩	to drink	/θàuˀ/
⟨myok⟩	monkey	/myàuˀ/

There are also many words in which ⟨o⟩ appears to represent an alternate spelling of medial ⟨-w-⟩, seemingly reinforcing the notion of a new allophone in back position.

L-OB		SB
⟨kyon⟩	slave	/tyùn/, ⟨kywan⟩
⟨kloy ∼ klwāy⟩	buffalo	/tywɛ́/, ⟨kywɛ́⟩

Medial ⟨-w-⟩ was normally written with the subscript ⟨w⟩, as in SB, only when the following vowel was ⟨a⟩, but at least one example occurs of ⟨tweŋ⟩ "inside" as a variant of ⟨twaŋ⟩, SB /twìn/.

Further evidence of the lack of full contrast in the as yet developing allophones of the back vowels may be seen in the following odd spellings which combine both ⟨u⟩ and ⟨o⟩.

L-OB		MB
⟨chŭ ʾ ∼ chŭoʾ⟩	reward	/shúʾ/
⟨lūo⟩	person	/lù/

If we compare the word for "person" with the word for "to dig" listed above we may see some further support for the hypothesis that pitch differences and vowel allophones were correlated, but in this case no vocalic difference is reflected in SB.

The evidence presented in this preliminary study for an original three-vowel system in Burmese appears persuasive, though many details remain to be clarified, and an exhaustive study of the Lokahteikpan texts may help in this respect. For the present, the proposed three vowel system seems quite realistic.

Dalhousie and the Burmese War of 1852

SIR CYRIL PHILIPS

School of Oriental and African Studies,
University of London

Empire builders, particularly those who feel they have been called to perform a national mission, seem destined to be ambivalent. Certainly, the East India Company's proconsuls in India offer a rich variety of examples, ranging from the large number of those who habitually proclaimed their high responsibility in carrying "the white man's burden" while losing no opportunity of doing well for themselves and their families, to those, somewhat fewer in number, who consistently disavowed aggressive intent while marching inexorably along the road of conquest. In the latter context in his governor generalship of India between 1848 and 1856, Lord Dalhousie, a man of honour and deep sincerity, provides a fascinating and revealing example, and nowhere in his career is this more vividly to be seen and studied than in the negotiations leading to the outbreak of the Anglo-Burmese War of 1852.

On this particular episode most modern writers have followed Sir William Lee-Warner's exposition in his authoritative biography of Dalhousie. There are good grounds for this. His able account of the Anglo-Burmese struggle rests on a concise and comprehensive analysis of both the official papers of the Government of India and the private correspondence of Dalhousie himself; and, in the absence of a substantial corpus of materials on the Burmese side, this large body of evidence was bound in Lee-Warner's day to constitute, as it still does, the major part of the first-hand available evidence.[1]

Lee-Warner also revealed in his Preface that he had looked at "some personal records, of which the diary kept by Lord Dalhousie from boyhood up to the day of his leaving India is the most interesting," and went on somewhat defensively to add that "care has been taken to publish no extract from it which can be termed of merely personal interest and slight

---

1. W. Lee-Warner, *The Life of the Marquis of Dalhousie*, 2 vols. (London, 1910). Professor D. G. E. Hall, for example, has taken this line in his generally excellent introduction to *The Dalhousie-Phayre Correspondence 1852–1856* (London, 1932).

importance." In fact he quoted very little from the diary generally, and on the causes of the Anglo-Burmese War referred directly to the relevant evidence once only and that very briefly.[2]

This is a cause for surprise and regret because the diary probably reveals more about Dalhousie's attitudes and policies than any other single source. That Lee-Warner actually quoted so little is astonishing, for he had avowedly set out to correct "the distorted accounts of which Dalhousie's own personal dignity of character forbade any attempt to justify himself," and claimed it as his "duty not to pass by in silence the accounts which have been laid before the public by writers who have condemned the Governor General upon imperfect information, or from motives less defensible."

On the origins of the Burmese war, the most formidable contemporary criticism of Dalhousie's role had come from Richard Cobden in the form of a pamphlet published in 1853 with the title, *How Wars Are Got Up in India*.[3] This virtually went unanswered at the time, even though it raised questions of considerable public importance. In view of this, and also of what he had claimed in his preface, we are bound to ask why Lee-Warner, writing fifty years later, did not specifically answer or even mention it.

Cobden had frequently upbraided the House of Commons for what he described as its "appalling indifference" on the subject of the British conquest of India. On the Burmese war in particular he claimed that he had not met "anybody, in or out of Parliament" who had read the official, published papers on the subject. Conversing at the time with "a magnate of the East India Company in the lobby of the House of Commons," he took up his familiar theme of the profound ignorance and unconcern of the public in relation to all India questions. "I have not met," said Cobden, "with any one who has paid the smallest attention to the origin of this Burmese war, except my friend here—pointing to the Rev. Henry Richard—who indeed dug the matter to light from the blue book."[4]

Two sets of parliamentary papers had been printed in 1852–1853 on the subject, and Cobden set himself to arrange and analyze the evidence.[5] But it proved to be no easy task, for the Government's presentation of evidence was confused. Some of the material had obviously been carefully edited by Government before publication, so that often extracts rather than the full, relevant documents were printed, but so close and perceptive was Cobden's

---

2. Lee-Warner, I, 419.

3. R. Cobden, *Political Writings*, II (London, 1867), 23–107.

4. *Ibid.*, p. 25. Henry Richard (1812–1888) was a congregational pastor in the Old Kent Road, London, 1835–1850, and in 1848 secretary of the Peace Society. He was an advocate of international arbitration for the settlement of national disputes. See *DNB*.

5. *Papers Relating to Hostilities with Burmah*, presented to both Houses of Parliament, 4 June 1852; and *Further Papers*, 15 March 1853.

scrutiny that he was able to show that entire and probably important documents had been altogether omitted. He did not blame Dalhousie for this, but on the evidence indicted him of personal responsibility for the immediate cause of the war in that he had sent as his negotiator to Rangoon to treat with the Burmese not a civilian or knowledgeable officer of the East India Company but a commodore of the Royal Navy, complete with a naval squadron, over whom he quite failed to exercise effective control. Cobden also questioned the way in which Dalhousie had condoned a rising and oppressive scale of demands for compensation on Burma, and concluded by challenging the entire policy of conquest on financial, racial, and moral grounds.

Britain, he asserted, would not have acted in this manner towards a power capable of defending itself. Although then also at loggerheads with the United States, for example, her behaviour in this instance was markedly different. "Why is a different standard of justice applied in the case of Burma? Ask your own conscience, reader, if you be an Englishman, whether any better answer can be given than that America is powerful and Burma weak."[6]

Lee-Warner by comparison saw the conflict as inevitable and placed the responsibility squarely on the ignorance and arrogance of the Burmese rulers, whose behaviour he said was characterized by "a long sequence of insults and aggressions." It was difficult, he argued, to make contact with them and to understand their attitudes, which were divided and contradictory. He absolved Dalhousie from responsibility for the war, claiming that he used "moderate counsels and diplomatic overtures" and tried by all reasonable means to avoid what he described as "the mortification of war."[7]

But in offering this simple interpretation Lee-Warner had missed, or more likely deliberately brushed aside, important clues which would have yielded a fuller understanding of Dalhousie's attitude and role in the events leading up to the outbreak of war. The critical questions, for example, raised by Cobden related not so much to what Dalhousie and his Council were saying in Calcutta, nor to the policy of the London Government, but rather to the manner in which the British representatives "on the spot" in Rangoon were conducting themselves and fairly reflecting Dalhousie's policy.

Responsibility at Rangoon rested firmly on the shoulders of Commodore Lambert. Dalhousie's own confidential view of Lambert's conduct as negotiator was conveyed in a private letter to his oldest and dearest friend

6. *Cobden*, p. 69.
7. Lee-Warner, I, 412.

and correspondent in London, Sir George Coupar.[8] Writing some two years after the event, he said:

There is no doubt that Lambert was the *immediate* cause of the war by seizing the King's ship, in direct disobedience of his orders from me. I accepted the responsibility of his act, but disapproved and censured it. He replied officially that he had written home, and he was sure Palmerston would have approved! However, I gently told him that while acting for this Government he must obey its orders and we have never ceased to be good friends. Those despatches are suppressed in the Blue Book.

But, while I say this, I do not at all mean that but for his act the war would not have been. On the contrary, I believe everything would have been just as it has been. Lambert's service during the war has been admirable.

It is easy to be wise after the fact. If I had had the gift of prophecy I would not have employed Lambert to negotiate. But being only mortal, hearing of Lambert from everybody just what you say of him, recognising the benefit of having negotiator and commander in one, if possible, and having to act through an officer of high rank, not under my authority, I can't reproach myself with a fault in employing him though war did follow.

From other similar references it is clear that Dalhousie deeply regretted not having personally interviewed Lambert in Calcutta before deciding to despatch him to Rangoon. Normally he was careful and successful in his choice of subordinates, and this was one of the few mistakes of this kind which he made during his governor generalship.

The extent to which Lambert regarded himself as directly responsible to Dalhousie had obviously become a sore point. The relationship of commanders under the Crown to the senior member of the Company was a long-standing difficulty, producing endless bitter controversies between governors general and their military commanders in chief, and also with their serving commanders of the Royal Navy.[9] Writing to the same correspondent five years later when retired and convalescent on the island of Malta, in relative "calm of mind, all passion spent," Dalhousie reflected on the need for "unions of civil and military authority in India," citing as a case in point the arrogant attitude of the British Mediterranean naval commanders towards the governor of Malta.[10] "On every occasion," he said,

8. 22 July 1853 (J. G. A. Baird, *Private Letters of the Marquess of Dalhousie*, [Edinburgh and London, 1910], p. 260).

9. Almost every governor general and governor of the East India Company experienced difficulties of this kind, especially, of course, in time of war. But even in periods of peace the controversies could be severe. For instance, in Bentinck's time, army officers regularly refused to accept his personal invitations, and so serious was the breach between Bentinck and successive commanders in chief, that the London government finally appointed Bentinck himself as commander in chief.

10. 30 April 1858 (Baird, p. 423).

these Tritons—the Naval service—deliberately show their contempt. . . . Not one of them in my time in India (or, I believe, in anybody else's) would ever attend a Governor General's levée. And the Admiralty at home, childishly jealous of their own exclusive authority, encourage the Navy in assuming airs of independence in relation to every Government abroad. When Commodore Lambert at Rangoon deliberately disregarded all my instructions, and did the act which produced the war with Burmah, he replied to my letter expressing disapprobation of his acts, that he was sorry that the G.G. did not like what he had done, but that he had reported his act to the Lords of the Admiralty, and had no doubt of their approval!!!

Passing lightly over this aspect and this evidence, Lee-Warner simply noted that Lambert "took upon himself the responsibility of deviating from his instructions," quickly adding that "Lord Dalhousie . . . unreservedly commended the discretion of Commodore Lambert." Completely ignoring Cobden's evidence and criticism he attributed any unease about the handling of policy to John Lawrence, who according to Lee-Warner had written to Dalhousie's private secretary, Frank Courtenay, asking "Why did you send a Commodore to Burma if you wanted peace?"[11] It is true that Lee-Warner felt constrained to say that "The events which followed may seem at first sight to justify the doubt thus expressed," but he promptly disposed of the thought by adding, "But the manner in which the Governor of Rangoon received the Commodore's letter, even before he knew its contents, is sufficient to justify the measure."

It is evident that in this whole affair Lee-Warner was unwilling or unable to see fault in either Dalhousie or Lambert. He also ignored the fact that the London Government when preparing the Blue Books on the war deliberately suppressed the relevant exchanges between Dalhousie and Lambert.

Lee-Warner's omissions become even more glaring when we turn to the evidence provided in Dalhousie's diary. The entry for 13 January 1852 indicates that Dalhousie was at first willing to condone Lambert's action in declining to treat with the Burmese Governor of Rangoon and addressing himself direct to the King of Burma. "I think he was quite right in doing so. Sir F. Currie and Mr. Lowis think he ought to have abided by the letter of his instructions.[12] I think he was bound to secure the declared object of the Government by the means which seemed to him most effectual at the time; and I think that he exercised a sound discretion in departing from the strict letter of his orders."

A month later, judged by the entry of 15 February, Dalhousie was evidently beginning to see things in a different light.

11. Lee-Warner, I, 416–417.
12. Sir F. Currie and J. Lowis were members of the Supreme Council of the Government of India between 1847 and 1853. The Diary itself is in the author's possession.

This week has to all appearance solved the present question of war with Asia or peace. It is grievous to think that the stupid arrogance of these Barbarians should have declared for war. . . .

Whether the Court of Ava was sincere in its desire for peace, as evinced in its reply to the Government of India, or whether it was in truth practising from the first its usual evasive and tricky policy, can never now be known. My own belief is that it did desire a reconciliation.[13] It is further my impression that had the management of the negotiations with the King's officers sent to Rangoon fallen into other and better hands, the untoward incident which suddenly and necessarily broke off all communication between the parties would never have occurred.

But no care could have foreseen nor could any precaution have averted that difference. The rank of Commodore Lambert in command of Her Majesty's ships was such as to render it very difficult, if not impossible, to place the demands he was employed to enforce in any other hands than his own; and the impression his mild, gentle and temperate demeanour had created in Calcutta caused him to be represented to me as to all appearance trustworthy and likely to effect a peaceable accommodation.

His management of the interviews with the Governor of Rangoon, and especially his unauthorised seizure of the King's ship, were acts which the Government of India may with reason regret and disapprove of; but of which the Government of Ava has no right whatever to complain. We learn from private sources that the British residents at Rangoon and the American missionary, Mr. Kincaid, were urgent in their counsels for "vigorous measures" to the Commodore and produced their natural effect.

From these entries, along with the evidence in his private comments to Sir George Coupar, Dalhousie's regret and resentment at the actions of Lambert are clear. He had been committed to war at a time inconvenient and not of his own choosing. This is not the impression which the Blue Books and later Lee-Warner sought to convey.

But the immediately following entries for that day in the diary revealed the essential ambivalence in Dalhousie's own thinking and policy towards Burma:

Still, the conduct of the Governor [of Rangoon] towards the British officers was so unjustifiable; his rejection of the deputation on the ground of the inferiority of rank of Captain Fishbourne, when his predecessor and himself had sent their communications always by inferior officers, who had always, notwithstanding their inferiority of rank, been received by the Commodore in person, was so unreasonable, and the ignominy and contumely which he publicly heaped upon those officers were so outrageous that the Commodore was by *the law of nations* fully warranted in holding his demands to have been refused in the rejection of his officers carrying his letter, and justified in the act he had recourse to as the consequences of such refusal.

13. For confirmation of this guess, see G. E. Harvey's statements in *The Cambridge History of India* (Cambridge and New York, 1929), V, 561.

This Government has acted with extreme, perhaps impolitic forbearance. It may by adding nothing to its demands except its stipulation for the submission of a written apology by the Governor, have given encouragement to the arrogance of the Burmese. But on the other hand it has thus given valuable proof to the world that the Government of India has truly sought for peace. . . . And now that its most forbearing and moderate ultimatum has been rejected, it may proceed to fulfill its declaration that it would exact reparation by force of arms if redress were not fully and promptly conceded in reply.

Dalhousie in fact always seemed ready to fall back on the view that however inconvenient, expensive, difficult, or even objectionable a certain line of imperial policy might be, it must be accepted if there was the slightest risk that by pursuing any other course the prestige of the Indo-British empire would suffer. This was the touchstone and ultimate, personal justification of his policies. The immediate question at issue with the Burmese Government was trifling. He could himself see little British advantage from a war with Burma. Indeed, he warmly avowed that "conquest in Burma would be a calamity second only to the calamity of war." But no insult however trifling could be overlooked because, as he put it, "The Government of India could never, consistently with its own safety, permit itself to stand for a single day in an attitude of inferiority towards the Court of Ava."[14] When the Governor of Rangoon declined to see the British representatives, his reaction was the same: "We can't afford to be shown to the door anywhere in the East." Respect for the Empire, in short, had to be total; an attitude which, when put into practice, was bound to become a prescription for the British conquest of the whole of South Asia.

With this outlook and policy, Lee-Warner himself was fully in accord. As Secretary to the Political Department of the India Office in Curzon's day, he made this abundantly clear, and when in his closing years in office he set himself to describe the historical relationship of the British Government and the Indian states this became his framework of reference.[15] He did not feel called on to explain or defend his attitude, and showed no embarrassment in ignoring and presumably rejecting Cobden's attack on Dalhousie and on British policy in India.

There is no reason to question the sincerity with which both Dalhousie and Lee-Warner held these views, and so far as Dalhousie is concerned, the diary makes this clear beyond doubt, for what he says there is completely consistent with what he wrote in private letters and in official despatches and minutes.

But Cobden had undoubtedly put his finger on the essential ambivalence which was part and parcel of Dalhousie's way of thought—indeed, an

14. Baird, p. 188.
15. W. Lee-Warner, *The Native States of India* (London, 1910).

ambivalence which is to be found in many of the British empire builders in Asia both before and after Dalhousie, and in Lee-Warner himself. And the evidence of the diary fully bears out this interpretation which Cobden had perceptively drawn from his study of the official documents and the omissions in the Blue Books.

"Let us," concluded Dalhousie, "fulfill our destiny, which in Burma as elsewhere, will have compelled us forward in spite of our wishes."

To this Cobden finally retorted that however sincere it might be, little could be said for it as a policy. "The fact is, and the sooner we all know it, the better, nobody gives us credit for sincerity when we protest our reluctance to acquire more territory, whilst our actions are thus falsifying all our professions. Nor, speaking nationally, are we entitled to much credit. Let us hope that the national conscience . . . will be roused ere it be too late from its lethargy, and put an end to the deeds of violence and injustice which have marked every step of our progress in India."[16]

16. Cobden, p. 104.

Arthur Phayre in Mauritius, 1874–1878: Social Policy and Economic Reality[1]

HUGH TINKER

Institute of Commonwealth Studies,
University of London

When *The Dalhousie-Phayre Correspondence, 1852–1856* appeared in 1932, the "British Burmah" of Arthur Phayre's day was not so distant, either in time or in spirit, from the land in which D. G. E. Hall was working. Burma was still an outlying, frontier province of the British-Indian Empire. The administration, especially in the borderlands, was still at a pioneer stage. There were even people alive who could tell stories about Phayre and the king Mindon, from their own or their parents' memories. And yet, Hall wrote of Phayre: "we know little of him personally . . . the veil obscuring the man is only partially lifted, since both in his letters to Lord Dalhousie and in his private journal he contrives in a quite remarkable way to hide himself."[2] Subsequent attempts by the present writer to achieve greater knowledge of Phayre may have contributed something to understanding Phayre's works: *the man* remained a shadowy figure.[3]

Now, in the 1970's, the British Burma which Phayre and Hall helped to fashion, in their different times, has become a fragment of history. But there is another former British colony, in which Phayre sojourned, where little has changed in the years since he presided over its affairs: Mauritius. Moreover, in that island, Phayre was being observed by shrewd and closely involved commentators and reporters. Plunged into a conflict of interests and values, Phayre employed the qualities he had developed in Burma to

1. Most of the research for this paper was carried out in Mauritius, November–December 1971, as part of a project being completed under a grant from the Ford Foundation to the Institute of Race Relations. My grateful thanks are due to Harold Adolphe, head of the Archives Department, who did everything to ensure that I was able to make the best possible use of the wealth of materials in the Mauritius Archives.
2. Hall, Introduction to *The Dalhousie-Phayre Correspondence, 1852–1856* (London, 1932), p. xxxii.
3. See my paper "Arthur Phayre and Henry Yule: Two Soldier-Administrator Historians," in D. G. E. Hall (ed.), *Historians of South-East Asia* (London, 1961), and my Introduction to *A Narrative of the Mission to the Court of Ava in 1855, Compiled by Henry Yule, Together with the Journal of Arthur Phayre, Envoy to the Court of Ava . . .*, Oxford in Asia, Historical Reprints (Kuala Lumpur, 1968).

promote better government and a better society. As we shall see, his efforts were not enough to overcome the economic forces which have maintained an oppressive system almost unchanged since the days of slavery. But perhaps we will come to know as much about Phayre through his limitations and failures as in his achievements.

In the private diary which he kept throughout his life (with ever increasing irregularity) Phayre recorded: "On the 2nd September 1874 I was unexpectedly offered the appointment of Governor of Mauritius. The only person I consulted was Grant Allen, whom I met at the Club, 16 St. James Square. The next day I wrote to Lord Carnarvon and accepted."[4] Did he realize what a cockpit of controversy and acrimony he was committing himself to? In 1830, the population of Mauritius was approximately 100,000, of whom over 66,000 were African slaves, bound to the sugar estates. In that year, sugar production amounted to 32,750 tons. With the termination of legal slavery, the African Creoles quit the plantations, where they had been degraded, and the frantic planters, looking for alternative sources of labour, turned to China and India. The attempt to import Chinese failed; but India provided an almost limitless supply of cheap labour, which could, under the penal provisions of the indenture system, be bound to the estates in a condition of servitude almost as complete as that of slavery.[5] By 1871, the population consisted of 216,258 Indians and 100,811 Creoles, mainly of African descent.[6]

The sugar crop of 1862–1863 was a record: 165,000 tons. The planters in their opulent mansions (which the most wealthy liked to call "chateaux") were confident of a period of sustained expansion. Then a series of disasters struck Mauritius. In the floods and drought of 1865 the crop was reduced to 120,000 tons. The planters had put in their requisitions for Indian labour. The ships unloaded their human cargoes. The remedy chosen was to discharge the "Old" immigrants and take on the "New" immigrants at lower wages.

Those of the Old Immigrants who could rent *morcellements* of land took up market gardening. Others became squatters on marginal mountainside

4. Grant Allen (1848–1899), novelist, born in Canada, taught in Spanish Town, Jamaica, assisted Sir William Hunter in compiling *Imperial Gazetteer of India.* "The Club" is the East India United Services Club, of which Phayre was a member.
5. For a full-length study of the indenture system, see my book *A New System of Slavery: The Export of Indian Labour Overseas, 1830–1920* (London, 1974).
6. The term "Creole" is ambiguous. Originally it was applied to persons of European descent, born and domiciled in tropical colonies. By the mid-nineteenth century it was being used to distinguish the native-born from the immigrants (thus contemporary literature in Mauritius spoke of "Indian Creoles"). In these pages I try to distinguish the French Creoles (the white Mauritians) comprising about 3 per cent of the population, and African Creoles—the descendants of slaves, with some "Liberated Africans"—who make up just under 30 per cent of the population. Creole, the lingua franca of Mauritius (as of the Caribbean), is a polyglot form of French with African loanwords.

land. Many drifted into Port Louis in search of casual work. A few took to petty crime. From 1866, the island was scourged by epidemics. The state of medical knowledge was insufficient to identify the diseases positively, but it appears as though a virulent form of malaria gripped the lower-lying country. The population of Port Louis declined from 74,128 in 1861 to 63,015 in 1871.[7] For all these calamities the Indian immigrants were blamed: they had brought the disease, and spread it around; they had been idle and absent from work on the estates, and lowered sugar pro- duction; their natural way of life was that of crime and vagrancy. This attitude on the part of the ruling elite, the French Creole planters, prepared the way for a most vindictive piece of legislation: the Labour Ordinance of 1867. The Indians were already subject to penalties greater than in any other sugar colony. The most notorious was the "Double Cut." If a man missed a day's work he lost, not one, but two days' pay. If a man was absent more than fifteen days during a month, then he actually worked for nothing during the remaining days and entered the next month with a debit against his wages. Because of the lax system of estate medical treat- ment, the absentee might well be sick and unable to work, though not under treatment: he was subject to the Double Cut, and in addition for- feited the rations which formed part of his emoluments.

The 1867 Labour Law tightened up the provisions whereby the inden- tured immigrants (like the slaves before them) were required to carry a pass outside the boundaries of the estate. Enforcement was directed most of all against the Old Immigrants, those who had served their five years of indentured labour and were supposed to be free to choose their own occupa- tions. The Old Immigrants were required to carry a "portrait-ticket" of identity, to be shown to the police on demand. The ticket or licence cost the Old Immigrant £1 or Rs. 10 (the monthly wage of the indentured labourer was Rs. 5; the Old Immigrant would receive Rs. 7–8 a month for labour in the canefields). If an Old Immigrant wished to move from one district to another he had first to report to the police station in his old district, and then again in the new. When the ordinance was introduced into the legislature there was only one challenger: W. W. P. Kerr, the Colonial Treasurer. He expressed "his belief in the existence of a general feeling of hostility in the colony against the Indian—who was more or less robbed by everybody."[8] In the outcry against Kerr, the Governor, Sir Henry Barkly, joined in. For, as Barkly's successor—and Phayre's pre- decessor—observed: "The whole community of Mauritius was under the dominion of the planters; they had ruled in the Legislative Council . . .

7. Auguste Toussaint, *Port Louis: Deux siècles d'histoire* (Mauritius, 1936).
8. *Report of the Royal Commissioners Appointed to Inquire into the Treatment of Immigrants in Mauritius*, Cd. 1115 (London, 1875), p. 124.

their influence was felt by all persons from the highest to the lowest." Sir Arthur Gordon continued: "Where the employers of labour form, as they do in most of the cooly-employing colonies, the whole of the upper class of society, and influence every other class, it requires a very great deal of courage . . . to stand up against that influence."[9]

Enforcement of the Labour Ordinance was enthusiastically carried out by Lieutenant Colonel J. T. N. O'Brien, who became Inspector General of Police in Mauritius in 1867 after a military career in India and Ceylon, which appears to have left him with something like total contempt for Indians. He organized "Vagrant Hunts," in which any Indians caught on the highway or off the estates were rounded up. In 1868, there were 22,359 arrests and 8,958 convictions for vagrancy against Old Immigrants.

The situation was transformed by the arrival at the beginning of 1871 of a new governor, Sir Arthur Gordon. Son of the Earl of Aberdeen, Gordon (b. 1829) was one of those aristocratic, humanitarian reformers prevalent in the nineteenth century. He had previously been Governor of Trinidad (1866–1870) and was therefore familiar with a plantation economy and the importation of Indian indentured labour. In this new situation, the few opponents of oppression could effectively speak. Judge Gorrie of the Supreme Court resuscitated the exiguous legal rights of the Indians, and a recently arrived planter, Adolphe de Plevitz, organized a petition among the Old Immigrants to Governor Gordon to which 9,401 Indians subscribed. We cannot enter into the complex events which followed; it must be enough to record that two inquiries were initiated by Gordon: a locally appointed Police Inquiry Commission, which reported in 1872, and a Royal Commission (V. A. Williamson and W. E. Frere), who arrived from London in 1872. They spent eighteen months accumulating evidence in Mauritius and then returned to London to write their report, finally submitted in November 1874. Meanwhile, relations between Gordon and the planters had become bitterly hostile. In October 1874, Gordon abruptly left Mauritius.[10] A typical verdict upon his administration was pronounced by a leading local paper, the *Commercial Gazette*: "His administration . . . had been unpolitic and unstatesmanlike, inefficient, unwise and arbitrary, unfortunate in its immediate effects and disastrous in its collateral consequences."[11]

To govern this unhappy island, Major General Sir Arthur Purves Phayre, K.C.S.I., C.B., embarked on 25 September 1874, landing at Port Louis late in October. We must remember that he was now elderly. When

---

9. *Report of the Committee on Emigration from India to the Crown Colonies*, Cd. 5192 (London, 1910)—cited as *Sanderson Report*—evidence of Lord Stanmore, pt. II, pp. 348, 351.

10. Gordon's stormy governorship in Mauritius did not prejudice his further career. He was Governor of Fiji, 1875–1880, Governor of New Zealand, 1880–1883, and Governor of Ceylon, 1883–1890. He was created a baron in 1893 (Lord Stanmore).

11. *Commercial Gazette*, 5 January 1875.

Dalhousie and Phayre began their memorable correspondence, both were forty years old (that age which seems old to the young but young to the old). Phayre was now a grizzled veteran of sixty-two.[12] The town he entered must have reminded him forcibly of the Rangoon he had laid out more than twenty years before. Port Louis follows a rectangular, gridiron pattern of streets and blocks. Wharves, warehouses, and shipping would all be familiar. What was different was the French character of houses and shops, with mansard roofs, shutters, balconies, and elaborate scrolled ironwork. Yet the principal building in the Royal Road, which leads from Government House through the town, was then (as now) the Jumma Mosque; and the muezzin call rang out more loudly than the bell of St. Louis cathedral. Despite its European architectural styles this was an Afro-Asian city. Gujerati merchants and shopkeepers plied their trade, while labourers from Madras, Bihar, and the North-Western Provinces sweated, hauling carts piled high with sacks of sugar. In the centre of town, there was "a marked increase in the number of Chinese immigrants, who are by degrees absorbing all the petty trade of the colony," as Phayre later observed.[13] In addition there were "various dark races composing the almost cosmopolitan population of Mauritius, including West Indians, East and West Coast Africans, Malagasy, Malay, Arab."[14]

All this was familiar. Phayre would also immediately recognize the administrative structure as similar to that of British Burma. Although an island of only 710 square miles, Mauritius was divided into eight districts, outside Port Louis, and possessed a full legal and administrative superstructure of Supreme Court and Secretariat. What was totally unfamiliar to Phayre was the existence in Mauritius of a political superstructure. Public opinion—which meant, of course, the viewpoint of the French Creoles—was highly organized. The Chamber of Agriculture (established 1853) vigorously and effectively represented the sugar interest. At this time there were six daily newspapers in French and English, as well as several weekly and monthly journals.[15] Most difficult to adjust to was the Council of Government, the legislature. When Phayre arrived, the Council

12. The portrait of Phayre which hangs in the East India United Services Club (and which is reproduced in *The Dalhousie-Phayre Correspondence*) shows him as he was at this time. For a portrait of Phayre at the age of forty-three, when Yule described him as "a very young-looking man," see my edition of the *Mission to the Court of Ava*, pl. 3.

13. Despatch, Phayre to Lord Carnarvon, Secretary of State for the Colonies, 18 May 1877, enclosing the *Annual Report of the Protector of Immigrants*, 1876.

14. Quoted from an application by W. J. Caldwell, Chief Interpreter of the Supreme Court, to Phayre, October 1877, asking for his recommendation to the post of Protector of Immigrants, Natal.

15. The daily newspapers appearing in Mauritius at this period were *Le Cernéen*, *Le Pays*, *Le Progrès Colonial*, *La Sentinelle de Maurice*, *The Commercial Gazette* (to February 1878), and *The Mercantile Record* (established October 1877; amalgamated with *Commercial Gazette*, February 1878). See A. Toussaint and H. Adolphe (eds.), *Bibliography of Mauritius, 1502–1954* (Mauritius, 1956).

had eight officials and ten "inofficials" (in the French-English of Mauritius). The great majority of the nonofficial members were French Creoles, educated in France, possessing considerable skill and persistence in debate. The outstanding members were Célicourt Antelme, a successful lawyer, and Virgile Naz, another lawyer with some claim to be a man of science. Both owned extensive sugar estates. In intellectual brilliance they were more than a match for the somewhat second-rate civil servants, who constituted the official bloc. However, the latter included one man who was to play the leading part in Phayre's legislative battles: Barthelmy Gustav Colin, the Procureur and Advocate General. Colin (b. 1822) was a Mauritian, a French Creole; but unlike most of his class he had been sent to Britain for his education—to King's College, London, and to Edinburgh University—where he had absorbed the rational, liberal, utilitarian ideas of the day. Having been a Supreme Court Judge he had become Procureur General in 1870 on the death of his brother, the first Mauritian to have held the office.[16]

Phayre's arrival was anticipated with a good deal of foreboding by the Creole establishment. After its capture from the French, Mauritius was regarded as the Malta of the Indian Ocean, and after the first (civilian) governor, his five successors were military men. But from the 1850's, all the governors were civilians. Phayre, ranking as Major General, seemed to represent a return to military governance. Writing later, a newspaper editor recalled the fears of the time:

He had been selected, it was said, because he belonged to Her Majesty's Army and the strongest possible objection had been evinced by the community, during many years, to being ruled by a Military Governor. . . . His Excellency was supposed to have come armed with powers to force unjust and inequitable legislation upon the colony, regardless of appeal or protest; with authority to silence our legislature, if it fought against oppressive edicts . . . from the home government, and with royal instructions to insist to the bitter end upon a passive obedience to the decrees of the Colonial Office in all things, especially the new labor law. . . . Sir Arthur Phayre was looked upon as an instrument of correction, designedly chosen because he would accept such a degrading position.[17]

Phayre had indeed arrived with categorical instructions. He was required to overhaul the entire public services, following a *Report on the Civil Establishments of Mauritius* by Sir Penrose Julyan, a Colonial Office efficiency expert.[18] He was also awaiting (as was the whole colony) the arrival of the Royal Commission's report, and the instructions of the Secretary of State thereon. But it was not Phayre's way to push measures through

16. Jules Colin, (1828–1870), a barrister of the Middle Temple.
17. *Mercantile Record*, 31 December 1878.
18. The Julyan report was signed 1 June 1874; he visited Mauritius in June 1873.

roughshod: he was quite prepared to adopt a waiting game (as the mission to Ava in 1855 had demonstrated). His stay in Mauritius falls clearly into three separate phases. During the first phase, he was occupied with observation, analysis, inquiry, and the formation of personal relationships with those whom he must engage in political contest. The second phase was one of planning and drafting: working out answers to the problems raised by the Julyan report and by the Royal Commission's report, and in accordance with his own ideas of development. The final phase was to be that of implementation: by legislation, by administrative reform, and by efforts to change the social and economic structure—which meant, in effect, giving the Indians a recognized (even if lowly) place in the system.

Phayre was sworn in as Governor on 31 December 1874. His quiet, cautious, careful approach to his task at first somewhat baffled the ebullient Mauritians. Thus: " 'Deeds not words,' telle est la devise profondément utilitaire de la Grande Bretagne, et nous devons reconnâitre que jusqu'á ce jour Sir Arthur Phayre a semblé s'en inspirer, car il s'est montré sobre de paroles."[19] Soon, the same bilingual newspaper was commenting that "he has made a most favourable impression on the public. . . . His courtesy and accessibility have been noted with pleasure"; and a little later that his "evident intention to act with candour and decision and to employ only legitimate means for the carrying out of his policy, whatever it be, has, perhaps because of the contrast between his mode of proceeding and that of his predecessor, augmented the good feeling of the community towards him."[20]

Phayre's first move was almost imperceptible. The senior nonofficial member of the legislature died, and the Governor announced to the assembly "that he thought it but right to announce that it was not considered necessary to appoint a successor to the late M. Montocchio because as a matter of fact his decease had not created any vacancy at the Board [of government]." This limitation was accepted by politicians and press. A few weeks later, the press concluded:

His Excellency has decided to make himself thoroughly acquainted with the real condition of the colony before either disclosing the policy he intends to follow or suggesting the legislative and administrative reforms which are anxiously awaited. . . . He is credited with the possession of that prudence and discretion which should always distinguish the Governors of Colonies, the absence of which qualities rendered his predecessor unpopular.[21]

19. *Commercial Gazette*, 5 January 1875.

20. A monthly *Overland* edition of the *Commercial Gazette* was also published, reproducing the most important features of the daily paper, for readers in South Africa and Europe. These excerpts are from the *Overland Commercial Gazette*, 8 January and 5 March 1875.

21. *Ibid.*, 2 April 1875.

Meanwhile, the Secretary of State had forwarded the published report of the Royal Commission, and his own observations thereon.[22] The report, massively documented, condemned most aspects of immigration and labour conditions in Mauritius. It observed that "the recklessness of the police in making arrests was only to be equalled by that of the magistrates in condemning those arrested"; that "the title of Protector being given to the head of the Immigration Department is calculated to mislead immigrants as much as it has misled us"; that "no man, except one who is never sick and never absent . . . can tell what his month's wages will be," and a host of other similarly damning criticisms. Lord Carnarvon accepted the report, almost without reservation. He passed similar judgments: for example, "Assaults on immigrants are of common occurrence, and on some estates they have been subject to systematic and continued ill-treatment." Phayre was told to take whatever immediate administrative action was possible to ameliorate conditions and to revise legislation. Among many specific directions, the Secretary of State called for regular payment of wages, abolition of forced corvée on Sundays, magistrates to have no shares in sugar estates, the Protectorate to set up a regular system of inspection. He was asked to consider the prospects for compulsory education. He was instructed by Carnarvon that "vagrant hunts should be absolutely prohibited."

In his speech to the legislature, reviewing the report, Phayre emphasized the necessity for prompt remedial action. But he also took care to reassure his audience: "He believed that many of the grounds of complaint . . . had been since removed, and he felt sure that the Council, when other reforms were submitted to it for enactment, would willingly accede to them." Meanwhile, he assured them that nothing hasty would be done.[23] The planters' reply was far from conciliatory. The Chamber of Agriculture prepared its own report on the findings of the Royal Commission, which dismissed the "small importance of most of the suggestions and recommendations," condemned the "benignant exaggerations" and "absolute inexactitude" of the findings, and emphasized whatever errors or contradictions the Commissioners had made. The Chamber of Agriculture refused to agree that reforms were needed and resolutely defended existing practices, such as the Double Cut. All they would concede was that some government departments were guilty of error.[24]

22. Reproduced in *Correspondence Relating to the Royal Commission of Inquiry into the Condition of the Indian Immigrants in Mauritius*, Cd. 1188 (London, 1875).

23. *Overland Commercial Gazette*, 30 April 1875.

24. *Report of the Committee Appointed by the Chamber of Agriculture at its Meeting on 20 May 1875 to Examine the Report [of the Royal Commission] . . . and also the Despatch [of the Secretary of State]. Adopted by the Chamber at its Meeting of 9 July 1875* (116 pp.). Forwarded by Phayre to Carnarvon, 20 July 1875.

Although it was evident that there was to be a showdown over this question, Phayre's personal position remained secure. His levée for the Queen's Birthday "was the most numerously attended" for many years. Phayre's deeper qualities were now understood. Though he "makes no postprandial speeches, nor does he except on rare occasions address the legislature," nevertheless "Sir Arthur Phayre is not a Governor who takes everything as granted, or accepts statements as accurate because they are officially submitted. . . . [He] is not satisfied with mere formal statements but seeks to discover the causes of the circumstances . . . and the motives of the opinions."[25]

In this first year, Phayre made one important proposal to the Secretary of State. The appointments of District and Stipendiary Magistrates had been jointly held. Phayre argued that they should be separate. The Stipendiaries, responsible for supervising the Indian labourers and their conditions of work, must be outsiders, over whom the planters could not exercise influence. But the District Magistracy should be opened to provide careers for Mauritians (the French Creoles).[26]

Early in 1876 a report in *Le Cernéen* that Phayre was going as Governor of Bombay aroused regretful protests (as did later rumours of his promotion). But Phayre was now set to begin his real work of reform. He sent a series of despatches to London with detailed proposals for implementing the Julyan report: framed altogether according to his own judgment. He began by reducing his own salary from £6,000 to £5,000 per annum (this was not among Julyan's suggestions).[27] Lord Carnarvon wrote instructing Phayre to send the draft of the labour legislation, to implement the Royal Commission's report directly to London before laying a bill before the Mauritius legislature.[28] Previously, there had been a suggestion that the legislation would actually be produced by the Colonial Office, and now the Secretary of State reserved "full discretion" to add to the bill Phayre submitted.

Colin, the Procureur General, gave his draft bill to Phayre in mid-May. His report reveals a rare spirit. He insisted that all British subjects, including the Indians, "should enjoy equal freedom." He urged the importance of education for "that most interesting class, the Indian immigrant, the future Lords and Masters of the land in Mauritius." Any development must take place in government schools, not in church schools: "Of course clerical opposition will have to be met." He wanted compulsory education, "to induce their children to be stronger than themselves in the battle of

25. *Overland Commercial Gazette*, 24 June 1875.
26. Despatch, Phayre to Carnarvon, 26 May 1875.
27. Despatch, Phayre to Carnarvon, 28 January 1875; cf. Julyan report, p. 21.
28. Carnarvon to Phayre, 2 February 1876.

life." Put beside this imaginative statement, Phayre's covering despatch appears quite matter-of-fact. He indicated that education would be dealt with separately. He proposed an increase in female immigration to overcome the grave imbalance between the sexes, so that a "vast evil will gradually disappear."

The charges for portraits and tickets, having been reduced, would now be abolished. Passes, as such, would be abolished: this "will give great relief to the Indian population." Then, in great detail, the bill provided for inspection, for regular wage payments, for improved medical treatment, and many other reforms, though no proposal was made for the abolition of the Double Cut, which Phayre accepted, under stricter controls. A major innovation was a provision (Article 264) to enable the Protector of Immigrants to withhold labour from employers guilty of neglect: this "will give a strong hold over all employers."[29] The despatch went off; and the usually well-informed newspapers did not obtain a prior view.

Once again, Phayre demonstrated his determination to limit the non-official element in the legislature. When Naz returned from a European visit, M. Ducray, who had been appointed to fill his place, was required to vacate his seat.[30] Phayre began to lean hard upon his Inspector General of Police. Sir Penrose Julyan had been especially critical of the police, and in particular wrote of the "demoralisation" of the European constables, 65 per cent of whom were charged with drunkenness (presumably on duty) in one year.[31] In his minute on the police report for 1875, Phayre went into thirty-three pages of detail. He wanted the Europeans "kept to a minimum." He insisted that only Indian detectives could work successfully among Indians. He rejected O'Brien's request for smart Sikh recruits from India: local Indians with local knowledge were required. He was severe about the report on Port Louis: "Having endeavoured to arrive at a clear understanding of the state of crime . . . from the returns before me, I regret to say that I have not been able to satisfy myself that I have done so."[32]

Phayre's strictures were not welcomed by the press. The *Commercial Gazette* observed, "We regret to find that our views on the matter are altogether at variance with those entertained by His Excellency." Phayre also caused comment by inviting an Indian leader, Rajuruthnam, to the Queen's Birthday Party and going out of his way to talk to him: "His Excellency's conduct . . . has not been approved in all quarters, but the

29. Phayre to Carnarvon, 20 June 1876.
30. *Overland Commercial Gazette*, 25 May 1876.
31. Julyan report, p. 469.
32. Minute by Phayre, 18 April 1876, on the *Police Report for 1875*, submitted by Inspector General of Police.

most that is laid to his charge is an error of judgment. Apart from this paltry business, it may be said that His Excellency each day gains in the esteem of the community."[33]

Now that Carnarvon had accepted his proposal for separate Stipendiary and District Magistrates, Phayre asked to recruit his Stipendiaries in India, to ensure they were "totally unconnected in this colony" and also to acquire men "acquainted with two Indian languages." He asked for five officers from the uncovenanted service recruited in India, including three who knew Tamil. They must live in their districts (the prevailing custom was for the District Magistrates to reside in Port Louis or an adjacent suburb).[34] Urgency was given to the need by Colin's *Report on Crime* for 1875, which showed that one in seven of the Mauritius population was prosecuted during 1875, mostly for trivial offences (including kite-flying), while a fatally murderous attack by a French overseer on an Indian field worker did not end in his conviction for murder: "a flagrant miscarriage of justice."

Phayre now embarked upon the most personal venture of his governorship: an attempt to introduce vernacular education of a popular, "village" sort to the Indian children on the estates. Indian children between six and twelve years old numbered 28,103. Of these, only 1,584 were at school in 1874. To improve this situation, Phayre proposed, in a minute to the Education Committee of the legislature, dated 20 November 1876, that, without disturbing the existing system, a number of vernacular schools of a simple type should be started for estate children. Phayre explained that in India there were many regional languages, but for common communication a small number of wider languages were employed. It was "a waste of time," Phayre said, to teach the mass of children in English, a language they would not use. They ought to learn their own language, and not the Creole tongue. There would be "secular instruction only"; religious exercises would be excluded. No child must have to walk more than a mile to school. Phayre was opposed to compulsory education, which in the prevailing circumstances could become "a grievance and a source of terror." He proposed to begin with "a few schools in carefully selected localities"; a full programme would mean setting up 150 schools, a major undertaking. So at first they would proceed with a small scale experiment. The head of the Education Department, J. Comber Browne, made his observations: he was not enthusiastic. Compulsion would be necessary, there was "the utmost difficulty" in persuading Indians to send their

33. *Overland Commercial Gazette*, 22 June 1876.
34. Phayre to Carnarvon, 15 and 17 August 1876.

children to vernacular schools; they insisted upon the inclusion of English classes.[35]

The verdict of the conservative *Commercial Gazette* on Phayre's record in 1876 remained favourable: "While he is prudent he has the spirit of initiative . . . albeit he anxiously seeks to inaugurate reforms where necessary, he is opposed to fanciful changes."[36] At the start of the new year he was able to tell Carnarvon that all departments had been "revised and reported on" except the Supreme Court, the Education Department, the Immigration Office, and the Gaols. The expected magistrates arrived from India. All were police officers: one Eurasian, the rest European. They began their work as Stipendiaries, with none too friendly comments from the press. Phayre's plan for police reform went to London. He wanted to reduce the number of European constables, to introduce fixed quotas of Europeans, African Creoles, and Indians, and to give a "considerable increase" in pay to the Indian constables to attract better men. Phayre quoted from the *Police Inquiry Report* the opinion that the rank and file could not be held responsible for the repressive policy because the Inspector General "pressed constantly upon the force the duty of arresting vagrants and of keeping up the numbers arrested." Phayre commented: "I fully agree with the justice of these remarks. . . . There has also been a regrettable activity displayed since my arrival in Mauritius to arrest as many Indians as possible." He told the Secretary of State that he was giving instructions to reduce arrests and to change the view that stopping the Indians was stopping crime. On the contrary, it was "not only a grave abuse of power and useless vexation of innocent men but . . . a waste of the working powers of the police." Phayre rejected O'Brien's objections to his proposed reduction in the numbers of the force as "wanting in any sound basis," adding that whenever he passed a police post they "seem . . . to have plenty of leisure." To the argument that a reduced security force could permit an uprising, Phayre replied: "They are of various races, differing from each other . . . as much as Russians do from Portuguese." He added, "If the Indians were not a very long-suffering people, the way they have been treated . . . would long ago have caused serious general disturbances."[37]

His report on prisons, which followed, was in the same vein. There was "much crime of which the perpetrators remain undiscovered," while people were prosecuted for petty offences "which involve little or no moral corruption . . . and as regards Indians, I may almost say, no fault at all."

35. Minute by Phayre on vernacular education, 20 November 1876, to the Committee of Education of the Council of Government. Enclosed with despatch, Phayre to Carnarvon, 14 August 1877.
36. *Overland Commercial Gazette*, 5 January 1877 (review of 1876).
37. Phayre to Carnarvon, 11 May 1877.

Convictions under the labour laws were imposed for "nothing more criminal than an impatience under considerable provocation." The social evil that worried Phayre most was the effect of drink upon undernourished labourers, stupefied by cheap, potent rum. "I have seen since I came to Mauritius more instances of drunkenness among Indians than I witnessed during the whole period of my service in India."[38] Phayre had cause to worry about law enforcement, because J. B. Colin, his courageous legal adviser, was asking to retire on health grounds: "he had been dangerously ill several times during the past few months."[39]

At last, the Committee on Education of the Council of Government accepted Phayre's scheme for an experiment in vernacular education, voting Rs. 3,000 for the first year. Four schools were opened up in Grand Port district between June and November 1877. The need for such schools was illustrated by the case of Robert Vilbro, a Creole headmaster of Rose Belle School, who resented the Indians in his school, which he wanted to fill with the offspring of estate managers and overseers "who objected to their children sitting by the sides of their servants or labourers." Vilbro marked the Indian children absent, to get them taken off his books. Also, he must have read about the Indian Mutiny and the sepoys' objection to the greased cartridges, for he smeared his pupils' mouths with grease, so that the labourers refused to send their children "to have grease put into their mouths and to have their religious views tampered with." In the oblique manner of nineteenth-century bureaucracy, Vilbro was transferred to the Registrar General's Department.[40]

Phayre explained his scheme for estate schools to the Secretary of State. The scheme previously launched in 1857 for compulsory education had failed, because it was alien to the culture of the Indians. Now, "the most suitable medium . . . would be the vernacular languages of the children to be taught." A pilot scheme had started, with the cooperation of three planters in Grand Port district. The schools were like village schools in India, with "a mat for the children and a cushion for the teacher," who was paid Rs. 40 a month. After being opened one month, the schools were "immediately filled with as many Indian children as could be accommodated." The teaching was based on schoolbooks in use in Bengal and Madras.[41]

About the same time, Phayre prodded one of the main cultural institutions of Mauritius into greater activity. The Royal Society of Arts and

38. Phayre to Carnarvon, 15 May 1877, replying to Secretary of State's despatch of 4 April 1877 on prisons.
39. Phayre to Carnarvon, 27 March 1877.
40. Phayre to Carnarvon, 17 July 1877.
41. Phayre to Carnarvon, 14 August 1877.

Sciences (which numbered Charles Darwin and David Livingstone among its visitors) promoted important scientific work in fields such as zoology, geology, and botany, all of which interested Phayre, who became the Society's patron, presiding over its annual meetings. In March 1877 he wrote to the President, asking how Government might assist the Society, and "how the museum might be reorganised, enlarged, and rendered more useful." The Society replied that the museum needed to move to a more central position in Port Louis. Government help in supporting a qualified curator was requested. The letter ended by hoping that Mauritius would, some day, "be proud of its 'Phayre Museum.'"[42]

Meanwhile, Phayre was at last able to see some results from his pressure upon the Inspector General of Police. The arrests of Indians for vagrancy, which had numbered 5,166 in 1875, were reduced to 1,949 in 1876. Reporting this, O'Brien laconically spoke of "the greater latitude granted . . . to the Indian population" under the instructions of the Governor.[43] Another security matter under Phayre's notice at this time was the arrival of Abdullah, former Sultan of Perak, together with "chiefs and their families and attendants." They had been banished to the Seychelles (then administered from Mauritius) for complicity in the murder of the British Resident, James Birch. Phayre was worried lest the Malays (whom he regarded as expert seafarers) should escape by sea.[44]

Everything was now overshadowed by the arrival of Carnarvon's despatch returning the labour ordinance sent to London over a year previously. Colin's draft had been scrutinized by Counsel in London, but had been little altered. The few additions "sought to assimilate the treatment of Indians in Mauritius to that which they receive in British Guiana." Carnarvon carefully reviewed each aspect of their situation. He observed that if the Double Cut was to be retained, "the power of enforcing the penalty should be surrounded with due precautions against abuse." Of Clause 282, which permitted the withdrawal of labour from a bad estate, Carnarvon added "I trust . . . that the provisions of this clause . . . will in practice be seldom if ever called into requirement." He ordered that his despatch should be laid before the legislature.[45]

The revised ordinance was received in Mauritius on 27 July 1877. It was published, and given its first reading on 9 August. The debate was to continue, occupying the Council for two full days every week, almost until Christmas. Amendments were moved to the great majority of the articles,

42. *Transactions of the Royal Society of Arts and Sciences, Mauritius*, n.s. 11 (1883): 81–87, 122.
43. *Police Report for 1876*, and Phayre's minute thereon (9 July 1877).
44. Phayre to Carnarvon, 18 August 1877. For details of the involvement of Sultan Abdullah in the killing of Birch, see C. D. Cowan, *Nineteenth-Century Malaya: The Origins of British Political Control* (London, 1961), esp. pp. 234–236.
45. Carnarvon to Phayre, 22 June 1877.

and the most controversial were put to the vote. The debate was as protracted as over the most bitterly fought bills in the United Kingdom
House of Commons, and was infinitely more contentious and unpredict-
able than with the usual nineteenth-century colonial legislation.[46]

Colin introduced the second reading on 4 September, with Phayre
presiding over the debate, as he was to do throughout. However, information had been received from London by the most speedy means then
available (cable to Suez, and thence by steamer) that Colin's request to
retire had been met by the appointment of a former Mauritius judge,
J. Ellis, as his successor. Ellis arrived, and was sworn in as Procureur
General on 25 September. Because Colin had been responsible for the
measure, he was appointed an additional *inofficial* member of the legislature.
This move—which Phayre could fully justify—gave a majority over the
planting interest, which was to be vital in some tight situations that
followed. As Colin was to write when all was over,

it became quite clear from the first that the planting interest . . . would not be
satisfied unless all the sections intended to protect the labourer were toned down
to the planters' sense of equitable legislation, and even in Council some members
(except myself, all the unofficial members of Council are deeply connected with,
and deeply interested in sugar estates) could not, so far as I can judge, understand
that such laws are made not to punish the honest or the just but to deter the evil-
minded.[47]

The debate on Article 118, which concerned the duration of time before
which an absentee from an estate was declared a deserter, nearly resulted
in deadlock. Eight officials voted for its passage; eight nonofficials voted
against; Phayre had to cast his vote for the article, in contrast to his usual
habit of remaining above the battle. Matters reached a climax on
19 October, over Article 292, empowering the Governor to withdraw
labour. The press had waged a wordy campaign against this provision.
The *Commercial Gazette* demanded, "Is it absolutely necessary to confer upon
a Governor of Mauritius the right of ruining the most humane planter
of Mauritius? . . . We appeal to the inofficial members of the legislature
not to give their assent to so dangerous a doctrine. . . . We could understand a man *professing* extreme liberal politics advocating such doctrines.

46. For example, compare the Indian Emigration Bill, 1883, a measure of comparable
length and complexity to the Labour Ordinance. The Bill had been under discussion, and
had been drafted and redrafted, since 1881. It was introduced on the afternoon of 14 December.
Although an unofficial amendment was moved, was opposed by the Law Member, and was
eventually passed only by the casting vote of the Governor General (Lord Ripon), the whole
measure was taken at one sitting. See *Abstract of the Proceedings of the Council of the Government
of India, Assembled for the Purpose of Making Laws and Regulations* (1883).

47. Confidential Report by B. G. Colin, enclosed with despatch from E. Newton (Officer
Administering the Government, in Phayre's absence in the Seychelles) to Carnarvon,
31 January 1878.

We look forward however for real and practical liberality at the hands of the Conservative Party."[48] When the day arrived, Virgile Naz made a long and emotional speech: "The proprietors of the soil form an honoured and respected class. They represent the foundation of riches and stability in society. The proprietors of the two hundred sugar estates in Mauritius . . . are at the same time the cultivators of the soil and the manufacturers of the returns . . . indirectly, all the prosperity of the colony rests upon the production of their estates. Nobody denies that with very rare exceptions they treat their labourers with kindness, justice and generosity." Antelme followed in the same exalted strain. Then (as the report of the proceedings declared) there was "a long silence." Colin rose to reply. He asked rhetorically whether it was true that there were abuses requiring "the most rigorous applications of the law." With one voice the nonofficials roared "No," sweeping away the evidence of the Royal Commission and the conclusions of the Secretary of State. Phayre intervened to make one of his rare speeches. It was, he said, "exceptional legislation" to cover "exceptional circumstances." So many safeguards were included that there could be no abuse of power. He expressed his sympathy to those members of the Chamber of Agriculture who "always proved themselves just, humane and upright to their labourers": the law was aimed at "very few persons." His attempt at calming the critics did not succeed. The article passed, with H.E. and the officials voting in favour, and all the nonofficials voting against.[49]

All the arguments were stated again upon the third reading, though Phayre asserted his opinion "that the discussion of the ordinance had lasted long enough, and that there was no need of a further delay." At the end, the nonofficials claimed the right to place their dissent on the record. They specifically dissented from Article 191 and Article 282, and they urged the Governor and the Secretary of State to withdraw the latter article. Ten signatures followed, headed by Célicourt Antelme.

This was only the beginning of organized opposition. Before the year ended, a petition to the Queen had been signed by 1,812 persons. It recapitulated the objections and also protested against the overturning of the nonofficial majority: "The inofficial members have been reduced to a minority by not replacing members . . . and by the nomination, while the Ordinance was before the Council, of an additional quasi-official or extra member" (Colin). It was extravagantly claimed that Article 282 had the effect "of altering the whole foundation on which property rests in

48. *Commercial Gazette,* 11 September 1877.
49. *Overland Commercial Gazette,* 8 November 1877. At this period there was no official record of the legislative proceedings, but the newspaper reports appear to be almost verbatim.

Mauritius." It is impossible not to conclude that, to the French Creole petitioners, the Indian labourers were a kind of property, like their former slaves.

Phayre now departed for a visit to the Seychelles, leaving the Colonial Secretary, Edward Newton, to send the ordinance to London for final approval. Newton also enclosed the petition to the Queen; he commented that the great majority of the signatories were "directly or indirectly connected with sugar." He also enclosed a confidential report by Colin, who observed that the ordinance "will prove, if not frittered away by incessant meddling and tampering, a very great boon to the community" and "an act of justice" to the Indian. He maintained that, despite all the pressures, the measure was carried "with all its essential provisions sustained." In a burst of anger he wrote:

In fact, the planting interest is all-powerful, and we see it everywhere; that it should have power in an agricultural colony is surely just; but that its power should be exercised as if everything centred in it . . . that the incidence of taxation should be such that the necessaries of life, corn, rice and wine are heavily taxed, [while] the wealthiest hardly pay taxes at all when their wealth is derived from sugar estates, is a state of things . . . against which every disinterested observer must protest.

Colin argued that the revised Article 282 "leaves the act far less stringent than it was before [amendment], than it is in the Guiana act." Referring to the accusations of government "hostility" to the planters, Colin loyally supported Phayre: "There never was a Governor less hostile to the inhabitants of this colony than the present Governor; no one has shown himself more conciliatory, has held the reins with more impartiality between the conflicting races, conflicting religions, and conflicting classes."[50]

However, Colin need not have worried about his chief. As a Mauritian, *he* had attracted far more enmity, as one who was supposed to have betrayed his own community. Phayre enjoyed a strange immunity from personal criticism. When, at the end of 1877, the unexpected news arrived that Phayre had been promoted Lieutenant General, this was "hailed with great pleasure."[51] No fear of military domination now! Unlike his predecessor, and the next governor but one—Sir John Pope-Hennessy—Phayre's

---

50. Confidential Report by Colin, cited in n. 47.

51. *Overland Commercial Gazette*, 7 December 1877. It was strange that a man who had never commanded a formation larger than a company and had never taken part in a regular campaign should attain almost the highest rank in the army. Under the rules, when Ensign A. P. Phayre was seconded to the Talaing Corps in Tenasserim, he was entitled to regular military promotion. These rules were changed after the Indian Mutiny, when army officers transferring to the civil administration retained the rank they held at the time of transfer.

Olympian personality somehow removed him from controversy. Here is the *Mercantile Record* in its verdict upon the notorious Article 282:

The colonists [i.e., the planters] entirely recognise that Sir Arthur Phayre, from his long experience in India, and that gained during his residence among us, was forced to admit that an enactment such as Article 282 could not be applied. The calm and dignified attitude of His Excellency has naturally increased his popularity. . . . The nobility, firmness and frank loyalty of his character are everywhere recognised, and the generosity of his sentiments admitted.[52]

Compliments of this sort have to be weighed against the criticism of Gordon, which was still being expressed (the *Mercantile Record* observed that Phayre was "anything but afflicted with the mawkish sentimentality of his predecessor"). By invariably contrasting his understanding with the hostility of the Home Government the French Creoles may have been trying to divide their local ruler from their distant rulers, in the interest of their cause. This tactic certainly worked with Sir John Pope-Hennessy only five years later.[53] But when we recall the regard in which all his friends and associates held Phayre, we may concede that there was a genuine element in the praises of the press. In May 1878 it was announced that Phayre wished to retire soon; simultaneously he was advanced to G.C.M.G., and the customary applause was mingled with regret ("No Governor before him has more carefully studied, in every detail, measures affecting the well-being of the community").[54]

It might have seemed that Phayre's last year in office would be less beset by problems. After several bad seasons the sugar industry had entered an upward cycle, and the prosperity was reflected in public and private finances. New developments could be undertaken. Phayre's *bête noir*, the Inspector General of Police, had departed on leave to England on medical grounds (the medical report spoke of "derangement of the liver in the hot season") and now an inquiry had arrived as to whether, if O'Brien retired, he would be entitled to a pension. Thankfully, Phayre replied that he would. The scheme for vernacular education, which had aroused opposition initially, now seemed to attract support, if only because it had been shown to be so economical! The importance of preserving the forests of Mauritius was emphasized (the squatters had denuded much of the hill country) and in one of his rare references to Burma, Phayre spoke of his experiences there, and called for the appointment of a Forest Officer from the Indian service.[55] In reviewing the condition of the Indians, Phayre

52. *Mercantile Record*, 8 November 1877.
53. James Pope-Hennessy, *Verandah: Some Episodes in the Crown Colonies, 1867–1889* (London, 1964).
54. *Mercantile Record & Commercial Gazette* (now combined), 1 March 1878.
55. *Overseas Mercantile Record*, 18 July 1878.

still found much to distress him. Looking again at the problem of alcoholism Phayre rejected the solution of closing the rum shops on Sundays: "the keepers of the shops are almost invariably non-Christian Chinamen, the vast majority of the customers being non-Christian Indians."[56]

Far away, in London, conditions were developing to ensure that Phayre would experience an eventful end to his governorship. In January 1878 the disdainful Lord Carnarvon, with his strong convictions—among which was a determination to end the wrongs of coolie migration—resigned from Disraeli's government in disagreement over Russia and Turkey. He was replaced by Sir Michael Hicks-Beach, a more modern politician of a temporizing disposition. The allies of the Mauritius sugar interest now followed up the petition to the Queen by organizing a deputation to the Colonial Office, and they also concocted a joint letter to Hicks-Beach asking that the power to remove labour from any estate should be reserved to the Secretary of State (thus ensuring at least a further year's delay before the penalty could be enforced). The humanitarian interest was not idle. The Aborigines Protection Society also organized a memorial to the Secretary of State, with weighty contributions from elder statesmen. Sir George Young, who had headed the Royal Commission in British Guiana, urged that the safeguards worked out in the West Indies should be applied to Mauritius. Sir George Campbell, formerly Lieutenant Governor of Bengal and now a radical Liberal M.P., went further in demanding that the administration of the law be reformed. He regarded the whole system of indenture as "a sort of moderated and temporary slavery"; and the object should be to make the Indians "free labourers as soon as possible." He judged, from his own experience, that in Mauritius "there have been Protectors [of immigrants] and Governors under whom great abuses have taken place." Shrewdly, he regarded the row over Article 282 as "a struggle for a triumph between Planters and Protectionists [rather] than one of very great practical importance," and he ended by emphasizing that much depended upon the stand taken by the Governor of Mauritius: "Very great firmness, and very great capacity to resist unpopularity are required, and very strong support from the Colonial Office when he does his duty; the contrary when he does not."

In addition to listening to these partisans, Hicks-Beach called for the views of J. G. Daly, lately appointed Protector of Immigrants and just then on leave in England. Daly was regarded in Mauritius as a "Gordonite"; and the fine imposed upon a planter for neglect in his estate hospital had made him unpopular with the Creole establishment. Daly now submitted an immensely lengthy memorandum, examining the Ordinance in microscopic detail. It might have been better had he concentrated on essentials,

56. Phayre to Hicks-Beach, Secretary of State for the Colonies, 18 June 1878.

for he did pick up one flaw which had escaped notice: by substituting the term "employer" throughout the ordinance for the old term "master," a great many of those for whom the coolies worked were placed outside the orbit of the act.[57]

Hicks-Beach now made his decision: it was for a compromise solution, such as politicians under pressure choose to make. On Article 282 (now numbered 284), he stated, "I should not be justified in directing the omission of this provision from the Labour Code." But the article was revised in a wholly different form, which was said to "maintain the principle." Originally, the Governor had been empowered to withdraw labour where an employer was convicted three times under the Labour Code. Now, action could only be initiated where an employer was "more than four times convicted of offences" within two years. The Governor could now take a choice of different courses of action, more or less severe: the ultimate being the withdrawal of all indentured labour. However, before the Governor's order would take effect, it first required to be confirmed by the Secretary of State.

Having thus emasculated the offending article, Hicks-Beach and his advisers determined to do something to propitiate the humanitarians. Campbell had drawn attention to the additional threat against the labourer in Article 110, which added to the many offences for which he could be punished "threatening or insulting language or gesture" (a formula nearly as all-embracing as the British Army's offence of "dumb insolence"). The Secretary of State asked for this to be removed. He added that he hoped the amended act would afford "signal proof of the humanity and wisdom of the Council of Government."[58]

When the amendments were received in Mauritius, in August, the post of Procureur General had again changed hands. Ellis had gone on leave, and his replacement, H. Wrenfordsly, had only just arrived. Once again, the help of Colin was needed, although his health was under considerable strain. Phayre had taken the precaution of keeping a balance in favour of the administration in the legislature: this was again to be crucial in the passage of the act. Because a number of minor amendments were to be incorporated, an entirely new ordinance (No. 12 of 1878) replaced the previous legislation (No. 1 of 1878), which was repealed without ever coming into force. Introducing the new measure in the legislature on 6 August, Wrenfordsly paid tribute to the care with which Colin had

57. Hicks-Beach to Phayre, Despatch no. 147, 27 June 1878, with enclosures (1) from Messrs. C. J. A. Ullcoq, W. M. Anderson, and H. J. Jourdain; (2) J. G. Daly, "Observations upon Portions of Ordinance 1 of 1878"; and (3) letters to and from the Aborigines Protection Society, with memoranda.

58. Hicks-Beach to Phayre, Despatch no. 145 and Despatch no. 146, both 27 June 1878.

drafted the original act: the new ordinance was coming forward because "of the amount of pressure which had been exerted," the new Procureur General stated bluntly. Article 284 was reached on 24 September. There was an "animated and protracted debate": the Secretary of State's compromise had not abated the sugar interest's opposition in the slightest. When the vote was counted, all the nonofficial members available— numbering six—voted for a proposal moved by Naz and Pitot: "That Article 284 do not pass." Colin and eight officials voted against the motion. The ordinance finished all its stages on 28 October.

Before then, Colin was dead. From the vote on 24 September he was driven in his carriage up to his home in Curepipe, where he died on 15 October. The *Mercantile Record* published an obituary notice in which the venom of its antagonism to the Labour Law was only barely disguised: it asked sanctimoniously, "What care we now if, in the later days of his existence, he betrayed a spirit of contradiction, a vehemence in defending his opinions, a firmness degenerated into obstinacy?" *Le Cernéen* showed more magnanimity: it recalled that at his last appearance in the legislature he had upheld the dignity of the Creole lawyers of Mauritius: "Il défendit l'élément créole." When the Council met again on 22 October, Phayre spoke of Colin's "noble patriotism" in promoting the welfare of his countrymen, regretting that no higher official recognition of his services had been bestowed (Colin had been awarded the C.M.G. in 1877). The Colonial Secretary and the Procureur General also paid their tributes. From the nonofficial benches, the only word came from Antelme, who merely thanked the Governor "for the honour paid to the memory of the late Mr. Colin." In that moment the charm and courtesy of the Creole establishment fell away to reveal the pettiness and vindictiveness that lay beneath.[59]

At last Phayre was able to report to the Secretary of State his "very deep satisfaction that this important measure has become law." It would come into effect in January 1879. Seemingly, all was nearly over. The Governor composed yet another painstaking despatch in his own sprawling, scrawling handwriting—this one in response to a memorial from the Catholic Union asking for additional financial support for the Catholic church, whose privileges under the French capitulation of 1810 had been jealously upheld. Phayre indicated that among the population of Mauritius, 95,000 adhered to Catholicism, 13,000 were Protestants, and all the rest— 246,000 people—were Hindus, Muslims, or Chinese Buddhists. "If asked" (as Phayre noted dryly) the great majority would declare themselves

59. Obituaries, *Le Cernéen* and *Mercantile Record*, 16 October 1878. *Overland Mercantile Record*, 8 November 1878 for Phayre's valedictory tribute.

against further support for the Catholic church; but as the public funds were buoyant, the increase (Rs. 12,000) might be allowed. Still, he reiterated his opinion that "the support of missionary clergymen, with the avowed object of the conversion of non-Christian persons, does not now come within the legitimate duty of this government."[60] It was a kind of epitaph upon his own conception of the British purpose in this remote Indian Ocean colony. A specific statement of his idea of what he had come to do was delivered in a speech at a banquet in the Masonic Loge La Triple Esperance: "A country . . . must depend for her prosperity on the exertions of her children. A Government can do nothing more to contribute to that prosperity than to attend to the advice of the worthiest and best of the community, to follow that advice with singleness of purpose, and to abstain from all obstructive meddling. The best omen for success is in the patriotism, the energy, and the enterprise of the children of the soil." Can Phayre have forgotten the relentless opposition to reform which all those seated around him had displayed? He made it easy for Antelme to reply: "This Colony has never doubted Sir Arthur Phayre's solicitude for it . . . each time the Government had [produced] a proposal favorable to our interests, we have given him credit for the same, and each time laws have been made . . . prejudicial to our interests, we have exclaimed with one voice: this does not emanate from the Governor, but from the Colonial Office."[61]

The Labour Law still had one last unexpected surprise for Phayre to handle. On 30 December he wrote a confidential despatch to Hicks-Beach (the "confidential" category was then reserved for the most secret communications). He announced that Daly had approached him, fifteen minutes before the last meeting of the legislature, to ask for a final amendment to the ordinance. The Protector insisted that the use of the term "employer" in the ordinance would leave thousands of Indians outside its operation. Phayre referred the problem to the Procureur General, but on 27 December, *La Sentinelle de Maurice*—the only radical newspaper—produced an article, addressed to the Government, which embodied Daly's argument. Phayre saw his Protector "and pointed out to him the strong resemblance which appeared between the particular article and his report." Daly admitted talking to people outside official circles. Phayre concluded: "I expressed very strong disapprobation of the extreme views to which he

60. Phayre to Hicks-Beach, 4 December 1878. Phayre's extraordinarily tolerant attitude to religion and religious practice was a source of worry to his brother, General Sir Robert Phayre, and his wife, they being strong Evangelical Christians. Following Arthur's death, Lady Phayre wrote: "I fear about his salvation. There is nothing to show that he was a saved soul" (December 1885).
61. *Overseas Mercantile Record*, 18 July 1878.

had given expression in his report."[62] There was nothing else Phayre could do. Next day, the last of the year, he reported to the Secretary of State: "I this day leave the limits of this Government to return to England."[63]

The muddle was soon cleared up, Ordinance 1, of 1879, enacted by F. Napier Broome, Officer Administering the Government until the arrival of the next Governor, became law on 11 February and clarified Ordinance 12 of 1878.

The press was afforded one last opportunity to express its contempt for the labour law and all it represented. But in the issue of *The Mercantile Record* which was placed in Phayre's hand as he stepped on board ship there was no sour note. The editor, Cohen de Lissa, broke his custom of anonymity to sign his valediction: Phayre, he said, possessed "that power of continuous application, that ready and sound judgment, quick embracement of facts, firmness of decision, earnest sincerity of purpose, genial courtesy, immoveable decision and rigid impartiality which have, and always should distinguish, statesmen and experienced and enlightened governors."[64]

It was a fine way to depart. Yet, in truth, what had Phayre left behind in Mauritius? The Royal Society of Arts and Sciences moved into its new building in 1880, but they did not call it the Phayre Museum. As in most former British colonies, the names of ancient governors are liberally distributed over streets, schools, colleges, hospitals. But the visitor looks in vain to find the name of Arthur Phayre recorded anywhere. The standard short history of the island has almost nothing to say about him, except to recall that he took no leave during the period of his governorship (austerity almost unique in Mauritian annals).[65]

Even if his name is almost forgotten in Mauritius, can we say that he is commemorated in his achievements? Certainly, the labour law improved the lot of the Indian estate worker. We have the evidence of Arthur Gordon, Lord Stanmore, delivered thirty years later, that the ordinance had "worked an enormous amount of good."[66] Giving evidence before the same committee, J. F. Trotter, Protector of Immigrants in Mauritius from 1881 to the end of indentured emigration, declared that wages had remained constant during the same thirty years. He also stated that no planter had ever been punished under Article 284, even to the limited extent of being refused further indentured labour. The Double Cut

---

62. Phayre to Hicks-Beach (Confidential) 30 December 1878.
63. Phayre to Hicks-Beach, 31 December 1878.
64. *Mercantile Record*, 31 December 1878.
65. P. J. Barnwell and A. Toussaint, *A Short History of Mauritius* (London, 1949).
66. *Sanderson Report*, pt. II, p. 348.

remained, in a somewhat modified form, throughout the same period, though it was abolished at the beginning of 1909.[67] What of Phayre's careful division of the district magistracy, making officials from India responsible for the work of the Stipendiary Magistrates in safeguarding the Indian workers' rights? Edward Bateson, Stipendiary Magistrate, Mauritius, from 1901 to 1903, gave a grim picture of the pressures put upon magistrates by the planters. When asked: "You were really placed there for the convenience of the employer?" he replied: "I was a machine for sending people to prison."[68]

Phayre's efforts to clean up the police were of little more lasting effect. Colonel O'Brien, once described by Gordon as "a conceited, pompous, empty-headed ass," returned to the island after Phayre's departure and remained Inspector General till July 1881. Thereafter he was appointed Governor of Heligoland and Newfoundland, islands in colder climates, but service there earned him the K.C.M.G. When Mauritius experienced disturbances in January 1911, which the establishment called "riots," the Commission of Inquiry concluded, "The reorganisation of the police force appears imperative."[69]

Finally, what became of the attempt to introduce a system of education designed to give the Indians something of their own cultural heritage? This was Phayre's own individual interest, whereas everything else was influenced by the philosophies and policies of other men. One of Phayre's last actions in Mauritius was to record a minute upon the second report submitted by the Reverend William Wright, who was supervising the vernacular schools. Phayre observed (24 December 1878): "It appears to me that the experiment has, so far, been encouraging, and that more schools on the same plan might be established." The number was increased to five, and all seemed to flourish after Phayre's departure. But the Education Department disliked this development, which was outside their control, and in 1880 the opportunity arose to reassert control. A Special Committee was constituted to examine the progress of the schools. The three members included A. Lanauze, a Eurasian from Madras, and R. Dempster from Bengal, whom Phayre had brought over as Stipendiary Magistrates. The

67. *Ibid.*, pp. 363–366. Trotter is also on record concerning the usefulness of Phayre's law: "The immigrants in this colony have thrived and prospered under the Labour Ordinance 12 of 1878 as it now exists, and . . . the Indians in Mauritius are more hard-working and industrious than those of any other country" (Protector to Colonial Secretary, 21 October 1905, enclosed with Despatch from the Governor [Sir Cavendish Boyle] to the Secretary of State for the Colonies, 12 November 1905 [*India Office Records: Emigration Proceedings*, 1906]). See also Secretary of State to Governor of Mauritius, 19 April 1907, and Governor to Secretary of State, 6 September 1907, on abolition of the Double Cut (*Emigration Proceedings*, 1909).
68. *Sanderson Report*, pt. II, p. 374.
69. *Report of the Committee of Enquiry into the Riots in Mauritius in January 1911* (Mauritius, 1911), p. 24.

committee spent two days in visiting the schools and then submitted a remarkable report in which the evidence and the conclusions are directly contradictory. Thus: "We are bound to state that when we proceeded to visit these schools we were not prepared to find them so good and so well-organised. The children generally were young, but appeared happy and cheerful. . . . They would compare favourably with any schools of the same class in India." The "highest credit" was due to the schoolmasters; the experiment was "so far a success." The committee went on: "*We are unanimously of opinion that continuance of the experiment would be of no advantage.*" The reason given was that Indian languages were "of little advantage here": Creole, the French-African patois, was the lingua franca of Mauritius, and their own languages "will gradually be forgotten." The committee was of the "decided opinion" that "it will be better for the Indians themselves that English alone should be taught in Government Indian schools," and they recommended that Phayre's schools should be "gradually amalgamated or should be transformed with tact and discretion."[70]

Poor William Wright protested, and petitioned the Secretary of State against the decision of the Department and the Governor to adopt the Committee's plan. Of course the Secretary of State, Lord Kimberley, listened to the Governor and accepted his recommendations.[71] The Acting Colonial Secretary, H. N. D. Beyts (who had first been selected by Phayre as Acting Colonial Secretary to officiate after his departure) wrote to the Lieutenant Governor on 18 August 1881 proposing that the remaining vernacular schools be closed by the end of the year.

The subsequent cultural history of Mauritius cannot be assumed to stem from this decision alone; but it is certain that, today, Creole remains the link-language throughout the population, while any Indian aspiring to social position must become a brown Frenchman. So the history of the Indians in Mauritius has been written in the language of France.[72]

The verdict on Phayre's administration in Mauritius can only be that he tried, that he laboured conscientiously and long, and that he failed to change a system rooted in the economic and social ascendancy of an alien minority. Writing some years earlier, Sir Henry Taylor (1800–1886), a literary, and distinctly conservative, Colonial Office official, commented: "It will be generally found that the steady pressure of one invariable pecuniary interest throughout a series of years will overcome the resistance

70. *Report of the Special Committee on Indian Vernacular Schools*, by Henry Finniss, F. Dempster, and A. Lanauze, 15 October 1880.

71. Lord Kimberley, Secretary of State for the Colonies, to Sir George Bowen, Governor, 9 October 1880.

72. Aunauth Beejadhur, *Les Indiens à L'Ile Maurice* (Mauritius, 1935).

of governmental bodies, in cases in which they have nothing else to support them but a feeling in favour of dumb interests."[73] In the British nineteenth-century colonial empire, governors were invariably outsiders, appointed to rule for a restricted period of four or five years. They came and they went. Their only mandate was the tenuous support of the Colonial Office, distant in space and time. Where colonies contained a powerful domiciled European community, whether of planters or merchants, these dictated the pattern of policy and practice. The permanent officials might look to individual governors for preferment, adopting their convictions and prejudices for a time; but they had to live their lives out amid the domiciled nonofficial community unless they were prepared to seek another field of influence (as the reforming Judge Gorrie had done in moving on to Fiji). Almost always, the crusading officials were broken; as Colin was broken, in health though not in spirit. The survivors tended to be men like Mr. Beyts who managed to please or placate a long line of governors—the reactionary Barkly; Gordon, with his sense of mission; Phayre; his faceless successor, Bowen; and the quixotic Pope-Hennessy—but who consistently served his permanent masters, the planters of Mauritius.

Mauritius is the extreme case. In few other Western colonial possessions are economic power, social and cultural ascendancy, and political influence so neatly and discretely fused together within one dominant elite. Looking beyond the remote Mascarenes at a wider arc of colonial territories, in Southeast Asia, we find similar contrasts between the theories of colonial policy and the realities of colonial practice. An older generation of historians subscribed to a view of policy as something absolute, emanating from the metropole and enforced by "the Man on the Spot." Marxist historians see Western colonialism as the expression of monolithic economic forces. A case can be made for re-examining the British colonial record as an expression of a remote system of control that introduced and enforced measures whose consequences were frequently not understood, and which were altered and sometimes reversed with the casual change of governments and rulers. The longer-term trends were often not the consequences of policy decisions at all, as in the transformation of Mauritius from a community facing Africa into a society drawing upon India. Much the same is true of the buildup of an Indian minority in Burma, or of the growth of the Chinese in Malaya and Singapore. Sometimes, the unintended long-term trends take a very long time indeed to work themselves out. Colin's prophecy that the Indians would become "the future Lords and Masters of the land in Mauritius" has not yet been realized one hundred

73. I. M. Cumpston, *Indians Overseas in British Territories, 1834–1854* (London, 1953), p. 161.

years later, even though the island is formally independent under a democratic form of government. Similarly, the Chinese in Malaysia still await the day when they will attain a political role commensurate with their population strength. It is less through studies of policy and more by analysis of the process of interaction of policy among the peoples, native and immigrant, of colonial and once colonial territories that we shall be able to reassess the effects of colonialism. Phayre, the Governor, acknowledged the limitations of policy-making in his public statement that colonial governments must "abstain from all obstructive meddling" and in his final advice to the Secretary of State that proselytizing "does not come within the legitimate duty of this government." Phayre, the Governor, saw his duty as the careful and meticulous scrutiny of all governmental activity, and the questioning of all that might be irregular. Phayre, the historian, followed the same course. He was methodical, he was precise. He respected his sources and his subjects. He sought to prove no higher theory; neither to defend nor to attack. "Let justice be done to the Burmese soldier," he wrote near the end of his *History of Burma*. That was always his intention. D. G. E. Hall has followed a path not essentially different. Amidst changing historical fashions he has continued patiently to search for conclusions without presuming to know the answers in advance.

A Short History of a Burmese-English Dictionary, 1913–1963

HLA PE

School of Oriental and African Studies,
University of London

This contribution is from a nonhistorian. With some diffidence I venture to put on record this brief history of *A Burmese-English Dictionary* to pay tribute to Professor D. G. E. Hall, a teacher, mentor, and friend since 1932.

The *Dictionary* is the *magnum opus* now being compiled at the School of Oriental and African Studies. It is sixty years old and has had an eventful life. Its history reveals how a handful of devoted and determined scholars worked selflessly together to achieve their objectives: first to collect the necessary material and then to give it a definitive shape and form under the many difficult and adverse circumstances that one is bound to meet in this world. This history will be terminated, however, at the *Dictionary's* fiftieth year, the year that marks the end of the era of the three men who struggled quietly but pugnaciously from the inception of the project till death or old age intervened: J. A. Stewart, C. W. Dunn and H. F. Searle. They lived and worked in Burma and in England contemporaneously with Professor D. G. E. Hall, who, though not one of the *dramatis personae*, did play a part in the making of the *Dictionary*.

The history of the *Dictionary* falls into two phases: its conception in Burma roughly between 1913 and 1933, and its birth and growth in England between 1934 and 1963, with the School acting as its benevolent godfather.

Burma: 1913–1933

What seemed to be one of those isolated insignificant incidents started off a train of events that culminated in the conception of the *Dictionary*. In 1913 the late C. W. Dunn, a member of the Indian Civil Service in Burma, suggested that the existing 1893 edition of the Judson dictionary should be revised.[1] The suggestion was made at the Co-operative Conference in Mandalay, and was commended by them to the Burma Research Society, without success.

1. *A Burmese-English Dictionary* (hereafter abbreviated to *BED*), I (London, 1941), Preface, p. v.

Mr. Dunn, who was then Commissioner of Co-operatives in Burma, was a Cambridge classical scholar in his thirties. He made the proposal partly for personal reasons, and partly perhaps with altruistic motives. He had laid, unwittingly, the foundation of a project that was to impinge on the lives of many people and would have great repercussions in the scholarly world. He had been learning the Burmese language and studying the literature, and had found Judson's dictionary wanting in many respects.

The dictionary by A. Judson, an American Baptist missionary who came to Burma in 1813 to propagate the Gospel, was first published, apparently without his knowledge, in 1826 by the Serampore Press, Calcutta.[2] A better edition came out with the author's preface in 1849. It ushered in a new era in Burmese lexicography. For the first time words were arranged in alphabetical order and in semantic groups. Each word was followed by combinations (that is, stock phrases or idiomatic expressions, as in the *Concise Oxford English Dictionary*) in which it appears. The 1849 edition was the fruit of Judson's more than thirty years' acquaintance with the Burmese language. In 1893 it was revised and enlarged by R. C. Stevenson, of the Burma Commission, as a result of a suggestion he himself made in 1881 to G. D. Burgess, then Secretary to the Chief Commissioner of British Burma, Sir Charles Bernard, about the desirability of a new edition.[3] It was further revised and edited in 1921 by F. H. Eveleth, an American Baptist missionary who, however, dispensed with the valuable illustrative examples given in the previous edition.

Linguistic development is too fast for any dictionary. A dictionary is out of date the moment it is completed, since during the period of preparation it is outrun by the language itself. Dunn was aware of this fact as well as of the inadequacies of Judson's dictionary for modern needs. But he was not as fortunate as Stevenson: his proposal was turned down by the Burma Research Society. Dunn should have taken a leaf out of Stevenson's book and approached instead the then Secretary to the Lieutenant Governor (who had replaced the Chief Commissioner in 1897), or the Lieutenant Governor himself, Sir George W. Shaw and later Sir Harvey Adamson, for financial and moral support. Quicker results are usually achieved from dealing with a person in executive position than with a committee or, worse still, with a society. The inherent nature of the composition of these bodies is such that there is always a conflict of interests, in which those of the people with dominating personalities often prevail; then there is the financial angle; and finally, these bodies are impersonal in their dealings.

2. Elizabeth P. Quigly, *Some Observations on Libraries, Manuscripts and Books of Burma* (London, 1956), p. 29.

3. Rev. A. Judson, *Burmese-English Dictionary*, ed. R. S. Stevenson (Rangoon, 1893), Preface, pp. 1–2.

The Burma Research Society was founded in 1910, on the initiative of the late J. S. Furnivall, another Indian Civil Servant, and a forward-looking Burman, U May Oung. Its aims and objects are "for the investigation and encouragement of Arts, Sciences and Literature in relation to Burma and neighbouring countries." It was still in its infancy when it received Dunn's proposal in 1913. The future scholars who were to leave their mark in the field of learning, like J. A. Stewart, an Indian Civil Servant, and G. H. Luce, Professor of English, Rangoon College—both brilliant classical scholars—were still soaking up Burmese language, literature, and culture. The young D. G. E. Hall was then an undergraduate in England. There were, however, scholars such as Charles Duroiselle (former Professor of Pali in Rangoon College), a founder member of the Burma Research Society and, at that time, Superintendent of the Archaeological survey; Maung Tin (afterwards Pe Maung Tin), Professor of Pali; and U May Oung, another founder member and a brilliant barrister. But they were perhaps in the minority or outvoted or lacking in influence.

The Society appointed a subcommittee of four including Professor Maung Tin and U May Oung, when B. Carey and other members put forward Dunn's suggestion. The two Burmese members of the committee were asked to report back "on the likelihood of obtaining sufficient help from Burmese scholars to make the task feasible."[4] But on 3 February 1914 the Society stated in its report the grounds for refusing to take on the responsibility. "In view of the fact that it is understood that the ABM Press is bringing out a revision of Stevenson's Dictionary and in view also of the fact that such an undertaking would be a matter of great expense and difficulty the sub-committee is of the opinion that the proposal is for the present, at least, premature." At the general meeting the report was discussed, and accepted by the Society. However, the matter was left in the hands of the subcommittee.[5]

Dunn's suggestion lay dormant for more than ten years. In the meanwhile, many changes were taking place. Burma, which had been under a Chief Commissioner (1862–1896), then a Lieutenant Governor (1897–1922), was ruled after 1922 by a Governor, with a Council of four members with executive powers. Rangoon College, which had been affiliated with the University of Calcutta, had been raised to the status of a university in 1920. In that year too D. G. E. Hall joined the University of Rangoon as Professor of History. Professor Maung Tin, who had been sent to Oxford at the request of the Burma Research Society as a State Scholar in 1920,[6]

4. Proceedings in *JBRS*, 3 (1913):195.
5. *JBRS*, 4 (1914):81.
6. *JBRS*, 10 (1920):32.

returned in 1923 after completing his postgraduate studies to occupy the Chair of Oriental Studies. Mr. Stewart and Professor Luce had their horizons considerably widened as regards language, literature, and culture. They were joined in their pursuit of knowledge by many like-minded newcomers on the scene—among them was H. F. Searle, an Indian Civil Servant and an Oxford classical scholar. U May Oung, now no longer a young barrister but a High Court Judge and still hankering after research work, became President of the Burma Research Society in 1924. There also emerged a change in attitude especially among the members of the Executive Committee of the Society.

In 1924 a scheme for the preparation of a new dictionary was put before the Society by Dunn, Duroiselle, Searle, and Stewart—three Britons and one Frenchman. By then Eveleth's enlarged edition of Judson's dictionary had been out for three years. (The prospect of its publication was one of the reasons for the rejection of Dunn's proposal.) Nevertheless the scheme was put forward because the four scholars envisaged a definitive dictionary, "intended not only to bring Burmese lexicography up to date, but to do for Burmese what Liddell and Scott did for Greek, and Lewis and Short for Latin: to give a comprehensive survey of the history and function of every word."[7]

The Society received the scheme favourably; while seeking the financial support of the Government of Burma, it provided from its own resources the sum of Rs. 2,500 (approximately £167) for one year from the date of commencement of the work, and appointed the four scholars as a dictionary Subcommittee for one year. These resolutions were made at a meeting of the Executive Committee of the Society.[8]

The Committee also resolved, among many other things, (1) that an appeal to the public for funds for the dictionary be considered; (2) that the Society's effort to have a new Burmese-English dictionary prepared and published be publicized in the Burmese papers; and (3) that the new subcommittee be requested to consider the feasibility of so arranging the material for the new dictionary as to facilitate the production of an English-Burmese dictionary subsequently. The subcommittee carried out only the second resolution: no appeal was made to the public for funds, and the stage of arranging the material for a subsequent English-Burmese dictionary was never reached, for reasons that will become clear.

The subcommittee started work in 1925 with the available resources. The next year the Society received a letter from the Government, dated

7. John Okell, "A New Burmese-English Dictionary," *Britain-Burma Bulletin*, 1 (1959–1960):4.
8. *JBRS*, 14 (1924):75–76; 15 (1925):96; 16 (1926):77–78.

22 January 1926, sanctioning a grant of Rs. 2,500 per annum for four years towards the dictionary.[9]

First the subcommittee itself was enlarged to seven by coopting three Burmese members:[10] Professor Pe Maung Tin; U Tin (of Pagan), a former Burmese court official and scholar; and U Kyi O, a retired government servant with drive and energy and a friend of Stewart. Then a Dictionary Office was set up with a full-time clerk at a monthly salary of Rs. 60 (later increased to Rs. 100), in November 1925. Finally, collection of material began at the end of 1925 under the supervision of Searle, and later Stewart, as secretaries of the Dictionary Subcommittee. Books on various subjects, dating from the fifteenth to the twentieth century, were issued to a number of people who had undertaken to read for the *Dictionary*, and they were requested to send word-slips to the Dictionary Office monthly. Most of the contributors did this work as a labour of love, but a few had to be paid a small honorarium.

Collecting material was a complicated process. Pamphlets in English— and in Burmese for those not acquainted with English—dealing with points to be observed when contributing to the *Dictionary* were printed and distributed. Each contributor was given a text from which to collect words; the slips received were checked with the text supplied; omissions, faults of methods, and so on were regularly pointed out.[11] Stewart enjoyed doing his stint: he was in constant contact with Burmese scholars and was consolidating his knowledge of Burmese, and was also having some amusing moments.

For some time, Stewart told me, he had been regularly receiving slips from two men with the letters "B.Litt." and "B.P.K.," respectively, after each signature. He knew that there was only one man in Burma, Professor Pe Maung Tin, who had received the B.Litt. degree from Oxford, and he did not know what B.P.K. stood for. In the end he tackled these two men and managed to elicit answers from them. One said that he put the letters B.Litt. after his name because he liked the look as well as the sound of it, and the other replied that he had obtained the degree of Bachelor of Poultry Keeping from an American university.

To make the *Dictionary* as comprehensive as possible the subcommittee turned its attention to the colloquial language and asked several people to collect the words they heard, particularly in their own locality. The cooperation of the University of Rangoon was sought through the good offices of Professors Pe Maung Tin and G. H. Luce, who was now established as an authority on Old Burmese and Far Eastern history. Inscriptions,

9. *JBRS*, 16 (1926):73, 78.
10. *JBRS*, 17 (1927):89–90; 19 (1929):i–iii.
11. *JBRS*, 19 (1929):i–iii.

unpublished historical records, and other manuscripts had to be read and explored for more words.[12] Undergraduates who were reading for Burmese honours degrees were roped in. The university also appointed a research officer in June 1926 to collect words and phrases from the inscriptions.[13] Furthermore, U Tin (of Pagan) was given a clerk to record palace idioms and usages.[14] Members of the subcommittee did not wish to leave any stone unturned.

To gain as much publicity as possible, lectures on the *Dictionary* were given by Stewart and others; "Dictionary Jottings" were published in the *Journal of the Burma Research Society*; and articles were written in both English and Burmese newspapers by members of the subcommittee and by well-known scholars such as the Reverend R. Halliday, an authority on Mon studies.[15]

The five years from the beginning of 1926 to the end of 1930 were a period not only of great activity but also of expansion and planning to convert the material in hand into a finished product. The collection of words started on a modest scale with thirty-eight persons and twenty-two books.[16] It had jumped by the end of 1929 to sixty-two readers and three hundred books. By then too the total number of slips received had amounted to 340,218, of which 2,050 were from the spoken language. Words found in inscriptions were being kept independently of the Dictionary Subcommittee by the university.[17]

Long before such heartening progress became apparent, the subcommittee was formulating plans for the publication of the *Dictionary*. The subcommittee itself was again enlarged by coopting Furnivall and the Reverend A. C. Hanna. It then (1) appointed Duroiselle, one of the four promoters of the project, as provisional editor; (2) resolved that the editorial work should begin not later than 1929; (3) drew up an estimate for the probable cost of editing, printing, and publishing the *Dictionary*; and (4) considered making inquiries with presses in Burma, in England, and on the Continent.[18]

Towards the end of 1929 the subcommittee had already agreed on the size and layout of the *Dictionary*: it should be in quarto of 1,000 pages, each page having two columns. To get a clear notion of the format Stewart drafted four sample pages. The subcommittee assumed that the cost of printing and publication would be met out of sales by arrangement with

12. *Ibid.*
13. *Ibid.*, p. 76.
14. *Ibid.*, pp. i–ii.
15. *Ibid.*, pp. vi, 67–82.
16. *JBRS*, 16 (1926):78.
17. *JBRS*, 20 (1930):xvi–xvii.
18. *JBRS*, 19 (1929):xxiii–xxiv, xxxiv.

the publisher; and it estimated the total cost at about Rs. 10,000 (approx. £667). It also agreed to propose to the Research Society that the latter should provide the estimated cost of compilation from its own resources, possibly with the help of contributions from the University of Rangoon and other public bodies.[19] But the members of the subcommittee, who had had plain sailing so far, were in for a rough ride that eventually capsized their boat.

The world economic depression hit Burma rather hard in 1930. The Government was forced to cut its coat according to its cloth. In such a process of economization the tailor often does away with some of the pockets and flaps and even buttons. He often becomes a Philistine. Culture usually suffers. The *Dictionary* was one of the victims. There was no further contribution from the Government after the close of the financial year 1930–1931, and the subcommittee also learnt that there was no possibility of procuring the funds for editing and publishing the *Dictionary* on the terms so far proposed.[20] This was a cruel blow to the project, which had already amassed more than 420,976 slips from over 400 books sent in by 149 contributors by the end of 1931.[21]

In this pragmatic world sentimentality is out of place. Nevertheless it must be said that Stewart and his colleagues felt that all the good work that they had built up with loving care had been demolished in one day for want of rupees, annas, and pies. They were voluntary workers who had sacrificed their time and energies. Some of them made special journeys to Rangoon to serve on the subcommittee. They met, deliberated, and planned—yet what was not to be was not to be.

Scholars are generally hesitant to come forward with plans to raise money. Influential rulers and philanthropists could have come to their aid. Sir Spenser Harcourt Butler, Governor of Burma, 1923–1927, had managed to secure a donor each for the University of Rangoon's gymnasium, library, and students' union by conferring titles on three gentlemen of wealth: one Chinese, one Indian, and one Burmese. In spite of the depression there were still many very wealthy people in the Chinese, Indian, and Burmese communities in Burma, any one of whom would have given a sum of Rs. 10,000 without batting an eye if similarly attractive inducements had been offered. Sir Charles Innes, Governor 1927–1932, however, did not resort to such tactics to keep the project alive. He may have had his reasons. And to the wealthy Burmese Buddhists, who believed that they acquired more merit from erecting a religious edifice such as a monastery or pagoda than from setting up a secular building like a hospital or a

19. *Ibid.*, pp. i–vii.
20. *JBRS*, 22 (1932):ix, xv.
21. *Ibid.*, p. xv.

library, the idea of donating money to the dictionary funds would appeal still less.

The subcommittee became moribund. Arrangements were made to put the *Dictionary* material (kept with Stewart, the honorary secretary, at Magwe in Upper Burma) in sealed containers to be sent to the Library of the University of Rangoon for storage.[22] And the work of the *Dictionary* was transferred to the university in 1932. The *Dictionary* itself, however, did not become moribund. The university appointed Stewart and Dunn to be editors[23] on their retirement from government service, and they took the material to England in 1933.

England: 1934–1963

The two editors were to work on the *Dictionary* without any remuneration, and the cost of printing and publishing would be borne by the University of Rangoon. Stewart was appointed lecturer in Burmese at the School of Oriental Studies in London, and Dunn was a gentleman of means. In 1935 Stewart was awarded a Leverhulme Fellowship, which enabled Khin Maung Lat, a member of the Burma Civil Service, who had worked under him in Burma, to collaborate with the editors in England.[24] Stewart had settled down in Bishop's Stortford, Hertfordshire, probably to be near Professor (later Sir) Ralph Turner, a great scholar and famous lexicographer, then Director of the School. Mr. Dunn was living in a village called Meredith, Cambridgeshire, not far from his colleague. Khin Maung Lat stayed at Bishop's Stortford. Compilation began in earnest in 1936.

This was the beginning of the second phase of the *Dictionary*. Its history in the next thirty years is marked by vicissitudes and surprises—pleasant as well as unpleasant.

In 1939, I found myself helping Stewart, now Reader in Burmese, with his *Dictionary*. As a schoolboy I had read about it with passing interest in the Burmese and English newspapers. As an undergraduate I learnt more about it in the *Journal of the Burma Research Society* and still more from Professors Pe Maung Tin and G. H. Luce, under whom I was reading for an honours degree in Burmese. My interest began to wane, however, when the *Dictionary* material was taken to England. There was a temporary revival when I met Khin Maung Lat on the eve of his departure for England, through U Wun, a senior Burmese honours student, who later was instrumental in bringing Stewart and myself together. Yet I never dreamed that I would find myself in this daunting situation.

22. *Ibid.*, p. iii; 23 (1933):vi–vii.
23. *BED*, I, Preface, p. iii.
24. *Ibid.*

The Government of Burma awarded me in 1938 a State Scholarship to do a postgraduate course in education at the Institute of Education, University of London. I was to get a diploma in teaching and then proceed to the M.A. degree. U Wun, who went to Oxford as a State Scholar in 1936, came to tell me after my diploma examination that Stewart was very keen to meet me. We went to see him at Bishop's Stortford. After a few preliminaries, he talked me into switching from the M.A. thesis to a thesis for the Ph.D. in Burmese. I joined the School with alacrity as a postgraduate student in 1939, at the same time Khin Maung Lat left for Burma. So began my involvement in the *Dictionary* undertaking.

World War II came in September of that year. Part I of the *Dictionary* was still in proof form. I gave what help I could to Stewart and Dunn, while preparing my thesis under Stewart's supervision. Dunn made a weekly trip to Bishop's Stortford to discuss problems and pose some conundrums.

The first part of the *Dictionary* was published in 1941. This is in every sense of the word the first dictionary of the Burmese language. It is in large quarto, containing two columns per page, and each part contains eighty pages. The work looks formidable. It deals with words from both the literary and spoken languages, none of which had ever been explored systematically, and it covers the whole gamut of Burmese culture.

During the war, in a far from congenial atmosphere, Stewart, Dunn, and I tried to keep the *Dictionary* alive and nourish it, but its growth was inevitably retarded by the war. Stewart had to divide his time between writing a book on learning Burmese for the Linguaphone Company,[25] working as a government censor of civilian correspondence, and discharging his duties as an air raid warden. Dunn served on many committees and in his local Home Guard unit. I was a fire-watcher, besides preparing my thesis and broadcasting at first twice and later four times a week to Burma when the Japanese invaded it in 1942.

To have faith in oneself and in one's undertaking and persevere with it through thick and thin often brings reward. In 1944, at the end of the war in Europe, a scheme to give impetus to the *Dictionary* was produced by the then Government of Burma in exile at Simla, India. It was to start with a fund of £10,000 to recruit three assistants to help the two editors and to publish the *Dictionary*, if possible, at the rate of one part per year. The trustees of the University of Rangoon Endowment Fund agreed to continue to meet the cost of printing.[26] This was an echo of the proposals put forward by the Dictionary Subcommittee in 1929 to the Burma Research Society: to publish the whole *Dictionary* of 1,000 pages in three years. It has been

25. This was later published under the title *Manual of Colloquial Burmese* (London, 1954).
26. *BED*, II (London, 1950), Editorial Note.

often the case that a well-thought-out theory when put into practice fails to come up to one's expectations. Human fallibility and unforeseen circumstances are the main factors that upset the apple cart. Be that as it may, the scheme was a challenge that the two editors accepted.

Stewart (now Professor) had an office built out of his own funds in the garden of his house. Dunn made arrangements to buy a house in Bishop's Stortford. In the meanwhile they made enquiries to find suitable candidates for the three posts. They asked me to accept one post. I had finished my thesis, but I could not get a release (under wartime regulations) from the B.B.C. until April 1946, when I officially joined them. The Reverend U Thitthila, who had come to England just before the war to propagate Buddhism, took on the second post. The third post was never filled, but from July of that year U Htet Htoot, a postgraduate student at the School from 1935 to 1940, came to help us three days a week.[27] But hardly had our team settled down to work than the editors received from the University of Rangoon a letter that almost broke their hearts.

The war with Japan was over in 1945. The University of Rangoon, dismembered during the war years, was reconstituted, and its new policy-makers held a different attitude to the *Dictionary*. In December 1946 the editors were informed that the Council of the University of Rangoon had resolved that the preparation of the *Dictionary* could best be expedited if the work were transferred to Burma after the publication of the parts in hand.[28] The editors tried to negotiate with the council while digging in their heels. Their main point of argument was that horses should not be changed in midstream. I backed them up, though I am a Burman.

The advancement of knowledge transcends all other considerations. Mine, however, were based on ethical, academic, practical, and sentimental grounds. That (1) the editors should not be relieved of their duties except for incompetence; (2) the *Dictionary* was a two-way matter, and as such at least one of the editors must be an English scholar; (3) since there were signs that the politicians in Burma were going to fight for her independence from the British (which was eventually granted in 1948), it would be unwise to transfer the rare books and priceless word-slips to Burma, and (4) Professor Stewart, my mentor, teacher, and friend, must be given my support when he needed it most.

However, there was worse to come. U Thitthila left us in July 1947, quite understandably, to give all his time to the service of the Buddhists in the United Kingdom; U Htet Htoot stopped coming in February 1948; and Professor Stewart, who was taken ill in 1947, died in May 1948.[29]

27. *Ibid.*
28. *Ibid.*
29. *Ibid*

To complete this chain of misfortunes, which left only Dunn unaffected, the postwar Government of Burma, perhaps at the instigation of the university, gave me notice in June that my salary would be stopped in September. This last straw, however, did not break the camel's back.

Since before Professor Stewart's death, cablegrams from persons both known and unknown and from the university had been reaching me. All of them urged me to come home. It transpired that the Government's latest move was a policy of "divide and rule." The powers that be felt that without me, Dunn would have no alternative but to acquiesce in the university council's demand. But I decided to go on with the compilation of the *Dictionary*. To enable me to fulfill my objective I made a provisional arrangement with my landlady in Cambridge to work part time in her shop. I never had to take such a step: the School of Oriental and African Studies offered me the post of Lecturer in Burmese in July 1948. This in a way changed the course of the history of the *Dictionary*.

The momentous decision I made was guided by my loyalty to my colleagues and my intense desire to see in print the part we had started—an achievement that would give me the greatest pleasure. I did not wish to leave Dunn in the middle of our work, nor did I intend to break the promise I had made to the late Professor Stewart on his deathbed that I would never consider returning home until we had finished at least Part II. The day before Stewart's death, the Rector of the University of Rangoon, who was in England at the time, came to see us at Bishop's Stortford. He offered me the post of Reader in Burmese in Rangoon. Stewart, very ill though he was, angrily told him that that was not good enough for me, and that I could become a professor one day, if I worked at the School.

Had Stewart lived long enough he would have had the great satisfaction of performing the joint duties of the head of the newly created Department of the Languages and Cultures of South East Asia and the Islands at the School, and the editor of the *Dictionary*. Even after his retirement in 1949, he would still have been able to work on it and see the transfer of his beloved *Dictionary* to the School.

The history of the *Dictionary* during the decade of 1938 to 1948 was made up of a series of untoward events. The only redeeming feature was the publication of Part I. But the next decade fully compensated for those unhappy happenings.

In 1949, Professor Hall, who had returned to England in 1934 to accept the headmastership of Caterham School, Surrey, was appointed Professor of the History of South East Asia and acting head of the Department of Languages and Cultures of South East Asia and the Islands. In 1950, Searle, one of the four promoters of the dictionary scheme in 1924, accepted a temporary lectureship in Burmese and came to strengthen the depleted and dejected staff of two. In that year, too, the University of Rangoon had a change of heart: the dictionary undertaking was transferred to the School, and I was recognized as an editor.[30] The Dictionary Office was moved to the School from Bishop's Stortford in 1953.[31] For the first time, there was a happy reunion under one roof of three men—Professor Hall, Dunn, and Searle—all members of the Burma Research Society, who had lived and worked contemporaneously in Burma.

Part II of the *Dictionary* was published in 1950 under the editorship of Dunn and myself. It filled us with pride, considering the bad patches we had hit and my having to fulfil my duties as a lecturer with ten to twelve hours of teaching a week, besides several other commitments such as research work. Dunn, Searle, and I brought out Part III in 1955.

While Part IV was being compiled, I returned to Burma for a year in 1957. Dunn, Searle, and Anna Allott, who was appointed a lecturer in Burmese in 1954, carried on with the work, and in October 1958, soon after my return, Dunn decided to withdraw from the editorship. The proofs were still sent to him at Bishop's Stortford for his approval. Three years later Searle followed suit, and John Okell took over the lectureship vacated by him in 1961. Part IV came out in 1963 under the editorship of myself, Searle, and Mrs. Allott.[32] It marked the end of the active association of Dunn and Searle with the *Dictionary*.

During Professor Hall's ten years of headship of the Department, which he relinquished in 1959, he was partly involved in the fashioning of the *Dictionary*. He had had a hand in the appointment of three lecturers in Burmese, in the financing of the *Dictionary* project by the School's Publications Committee, and in getting Burmese scholars to come to the Dictionary Office on British Council scholarships between 1954 and 1957.[33]

Since its inception the *Dictionary* project has had moral, physical, and financial support from various quarters: the Burma Research Society, the Government of Burma, the University of Rangoon, the Leverhulme Trust Fund, Burmese as well as foreign scholars, the British Council, and the School of Oriental and African Studies. The nature and extent of this support has been described. But to complete the picture, something more will have to be added to what has already been said, especially on the last three items, namely, the scholars, the British Council, and the School.

Mention has been made of the help rendered by the many scholars in building up the dictionary material. Since then, many more have been giving their time and talents generously to the making of it by offering to

30. *BED*, III (London, 1955), Editorial Note.
31. *Ibid.*
32. *BED*, IV (London, 1963), Editorial Note.
33. See the Preface and Editorial Notes to each Part of *BED*.

read the proofs, which they return with valuable criticisms and suggestions, and also by giving us etymological notes.[34]

The British Council was good enough to give awards to three young Burmese scholars from the Burmese-Burmese Dictionary Office at the University of Rangoon, so that they could come to the School to participate in lexicographical work to the mutual benefit of themselves and the editors.[35]

The School has done more for the *Dictionary* than has any other educational institution in any part of the world. Besides bearing the costs of the publication of Parts III, IV, and V, all the editors, except C. W. Dunn, who had private means, have been at one time or another in the employment of the School.[36]

The editorial note to Part V, which was published in 1969 under the editorship of myself, Mrs. Allott, and J. Okell, recorded two sad events: the death of Searle in 1965 and of Dunn in 1966.[37] Thus ended the era of the three men who scorned the idea of "instant knowledge" that is hankered after nowadays by many.

J. A. Stewart, C. W. Dunn, and H. F. Searle belonged to the much maligned Victorian Age, as D. G. E. Hall does. During my many years of working with them I had nothing but respect and admiration for these men of outstanding qualities. Besides their high standard of scholarship, they were men of integrity and industry; of magnanimity and compassion; of selflessness and self-effacement; and of tenacity and singleness of purpose. But for such qualities there would have been no *Dictionary* story to tell for the eighty-fourth birthday of Professor D. G. E. Hall.

APPENDIX

The following are extracts from a letter dated 13 January 1917 from Dr. (later Sir) Denison Ross, Ph.D., C.I.E., the first Director of the School of Oriental Studies, London Institution, London, to the Honourable Sir Spenser Harcourt Butler, K.C.S.I., C.I.E., I.C.S., Lieutenant Governor of Burma.

34. See *ibid.*
35. See *ibid.*
36. Long before the transfer of the *Dictionary* to the School, the School had had its connection, first with the Government of Burma, and then with the Burma Research Society, the Sponsor of the *Dictionary* (see the Appendix below). The connection was strengthened after the war in 1958 when the Burmese Government instituted two scholarships for British students who had completed the Burmese Honours Course at the School. These scholarships have been in abeyance since 1962.
37. *BED*, IV, Editorial Note. On various aspects of the Dictionary see also: "The New Burmese-English Dictionary", the Presidential address, *JBRS*, 16 (1926):82–87; J. A. Stewart, "Lecture on the Dictionary," *JBRS*, 17 (1927):105–117, Okell, pp. 4–5; B. Lewis, "Perpetual Search for Knowledge", *The Times* (London), 16 January 1967; p. iii, on "The School of Oriental and African Studies, 1917–1967"; R. Bourne, "When a Scholar Needs Nine Lives at Least," *The Guardian* (London), 11 March 1968.

I expect the news of my appointment as Director of this School will have reached you in Burmah. . . .

Burmese is to be one of the features of our School, also Pali, and I wish to feel that the School has your sympathy and also the sympathy of your Province.

We receive a handsome Grant from the Treasury and £1,250 per annum from the India Office, but it has been the policy of those who are responsible for the institution of the School to depend in part on financial support from the general public, and therefore we are actively engaged in begging.

The City Companies are behaving very generously in spite of the many calls made on them in connection with the War, but we need a great deal more support before we can obtain the Staff necessary to bring this School up to the desired level of efficiency.

. . . large firms trading in and with the East are being appealed to, and it occurred to me that you might be disposed to try and arouse interest in this important national undertaking which must affect the whole of our future relations with the East, and obtain from the people of Burma some response to our appeal.

Pious Buddhists might even feel disposed to contribute books to our Library.

In any case, I thought it would be all for the advantage of the School if, in view of the fact that we provide instruction in Buddhism, Pali and Burmese, the leaders of light and learning in Burma were made aware of this incident."

The Committee of the Burma Research Society, on receiving a copy of this letter, resolved (1) that the Society will present to the School a complete set of the Society's Journal and will continue to send the Journal as issued; (2) that the Society will make known among its members that the School desires contributions in money or books, the Society itself being unable to send books as it has no library of its own at present; and (3) that as the Educational Syndicate is known to be undertaking to supply books, any further effort on the part of the Society to obtain them would cover the same ground and was therefore unnecessary.

JBRS, 7 (1917):197–198

Reflections on a Problem Sculpture from Jaiyā in Peninsular Siam

STANLEY J. O'CONNOR

Cornell University

When the historian of early Southeast Asia turns to the evidence of art, as he frequently must do in order to supplement meagre textual evidence, his focus is almost necessarily on those features that objects share with each other and that allow them to be aligned in space and time. These features are usually readily isolated form elements or motifs susceptible to being ordered in a typological fashion. Since art products in a traditional society tend to be public documents with conventionalized systems of symbolization and a shared grammar of formal relationships, often enduring with only minor change for considerable periods of time, style classes may be established that embrace great numbers of objects. Objects casually discovered and completely without either archaeological context or textual documentation linking artist, patron, and art work may often be interpolated into such systems of classification. In those cases where the object resists interpolation into one of the established and datable style classes, it is often possible to place it at least in a relative chronology by internal comparative analysis. It is obvious, however, that the object must be one of a group that is sufficiently numerous within a cultural area to allow meaningful comparisons. An example of the use of both methods of ordering of objects is the late Pierre Dupont's relative chronology for the images of the Buddha attributed to the culture of Dvāravatī, which he established by internal comparative analysis but which also depended on analogies drawn from the well-established styles of Amarāvatī, Gupta, and post-Gupta Buddhist art in India.[1]

Methods that focus attention on the classing of readily abstracted features of form or symbol are likely to prove inadequate to an investigation of such matters as aesthetic quality, expressive content, contextual questions involving artist or patron, or to a consideration of that singular object which stands in solitude as a prime. It may be useful to publish here such

---

1. Pierre Dupont, *L'archéologie mône de Dvāravatī* (Paris, 1959).

an object, which has been ignored by scholars because, I think, it is intractable to typological, stylistic, or iconographic analysis and quite lacking in readily discernible aesthetic quality. While the choice of this art object may seem eccentric in an essay written in honor of Professor Hall, I venture to think that he may find some interest in a problem posed by grudging and unlikely evidence and that he will know I offer this little essay with admiration and gratitude.

The sculpture that will engage our attention (Figures 1a and 1b) is in the collection of the National Museum in Bangkok. It bears the number ŚV-38, is 90 cm. in height, stands on a circular base, and has lost its head and both of its arms. Its provenance is the town of Jaiyā in southern Siam. There is a strong possibility that it is the image that J. Y. Claeys noted in 1931 among the debris of four Hindu sculptures at Wat Mai Colathon near Jaiyā, and about which he remarked, with some understatement, that it was not among the leading sculptures of the peninsular portion of Siam.[2]

The image is basically a column of stone with a minimum definition of parts or surface complexity. Viewed from the side (Figure 1b), the brusque transition between the volume of the robe and the pipe-stem cylinders of the legs, with their anklets and slablike feet adorned with curious garlands, is especially awkward. The enormous reserve of stone that has been left engaged to the image in the rear contributes to the clumsy, stunted quality of the piece. This massive reinforcement, exhibiting the sculptor's concern to ensure against the fracturing of stone where undercut,[3] contrasts strangely with the small raised cylinder of stone on the base which served as the socket for an attribute such as a club or trident that would have been free-standing and subject to easy fracture.

In view of the damaged condition of the image, it is difficult to reconstruct its iconography. A. B. Griswold has made a passing reference to the image, noting its corpulence, the simplicity of its costume, the pronounced projection of its heels, and its *yajñopavita* (sacred thread), and he speculated that the figure might be a representation of a sage or *ṛṣi* such as Agastya.[4]

2. J. Y. Claeys, "L'archéologie du Siam," *BEFEO*, 31 (1931):391.

3. This method of supporting monumental stone sculpture is exceptional in the art of peninsular Siam. It is also not found in the pre-Angkorian art of Cambodia, with the possible exception of some similarity to the reserve employed in the unusual Śiva image of Kompong Cham Kau illustrated in plate XX-B of Pierre Dupont, *La statuaire préangkorienne* (Ascona, 1955). Images supported by a reserve of stone in the rear are known in Champa in the style of Dong-duong, dating from the early part of the tenth century, and in the succeeding style of Mi-son A. 1, which continued throughout the tenth century. See Jean Boisselier, *La statuaire du Champa* (Paris, 1963), pp. 136, 163, and figs. 73, 74, and 88. Similar arrangements are found in Javanese art in images of Viṣṇu and Agastya from Chandi Banon. See A. J. Bernet Kempers, *Ancient Indonesian Art* (Cambridge, 1959), pls. 41 and 42.

4. A. B. Griswold, "The Jalong Bronze," *FMJ*, 7 (1962):66.

Figure 1a. Unidentified deity. Stone. Front view. Found at Jaiyā, Thailand.
Bangkok Museum.

Figure 1b. Unidentified deity. Stone. Side view. Found at Jaiyā, Thailand. Bangkok Museum.

This interpretation would explain the socket on the base, which would have supported the trident associated with such *guru* figures. While there are no stone figures of Agastya in the extant art of peninsular Siam or Dvāravatī, the deity appears in the genealogical myths of the *Chên-la* kingdoms of Cambodia in the eighth century, and there is strong evidence of reciprocal artistic exchanges around the Gulf of Siam at that time.[5]

Java offers abundant representations of Agastya, and, according to F. D. K. Bosch, the main characteristics of the Agastya image—the beard, the big belly, and the *jatāmakuta*—are always present.[6] The Jaiyā image, however, shows no trace of beard on the chest. It seems very likely that the sculptor would have treated the beard as a solid mass on the chest and as an expedient to reinforce the juncture at the neck, avoiding the undercutting required to present the beard as a free-standing element. Unfortunately, while I think that Agastya can be eliminated from consideration, I can suggest no more plausible alternative identification.

Discussion up to this point has ignored the broader "aesthetic field," the context in which the artist works and in which the object is experienced as possessing value.[7] One can inquire, for example, whether the artist would have made the image as we now see it, that is, without head or arms. The obvious answer is that it is unthinkable in terms of the artistic decorum that must surround objects that are public works. Such a breach of decorum would have been unacceptable to the patron. An elimination of the head or arms would also have been unthinkable in terms of the workshop practices, with their rules of iconometry and the prescriptions necessary to make a ritually efficacious object, which guided the artist.

Can we assume, then, that the piece represents the unfinished work of an inept artisan? The breakage is too extensive to be explained in this way. In fact, the damage to the image, especially the deep fracture on the diagonal line running from the belt to the reserve on the right side, and at the fracture line just above the feet and continuing through the massive reserve in the rear, suggests deliberate vandalism. It is certainly difficult to imagine that either the collapse of a sanctuary roof or even the prying up and overturning of the image with a lever would lead to the kind of breakage we now see.[8]

This quite inelegant object is likely to have been executed in response

5. Dupont, p. 72, and S. J. O'Connor, "Satingphra: An Expanded Chronology," *JMBRAS*, 39, 1 July 1966:137–144.

6. F. D. K. Bosch, "A Remarkable Ancient Javanese Sculpture," *AA*, 24, 3/4 (1961):237.

7. For a discussion of the concept of the "aesthetic field" see A. Berleant, *The Aesthetic Field: A Phenomenology of Aesthetic Experience* (Springfield, Ill., 1970), chap. 3.

8. My attention has been drawn to the problem of iconoclasm by Richard Cooler of Northern Illinois University, and I have profited from reading his unpublished paper, "A Note on Iconoclasm in 11th Century Cambodia."

to the demands of a patron in the Jaiyā area sometime before the Thai conquest of the area in the thirteenth century. This circumstance should occasion some surprise, because sculpture has a long and distinguished history in the Jaiyā region from at least the fifth century and continuing through the fifteenth and into the nineteenth centuries, when the local ateliers still had sufficient vigor to maintain a degree of artistic autonomy despite the almost total adoption elsewhere in Thailand of the conventions and style of the national school of Ayuthyā.[9]

It could be argued, of course, that the image under discussion was made in a provincial workshop, while the much more sophisticated works for which Jaiyā is justly famous were the products of more sophisticated ateliers. This seems, however, an improbable explanation; the isthmus is a very narrow portion of the earth where travel is relatively easy, and it is difficult to imagine artisans with no knowledge of the sophisticated works that were to be seen at Surāṣṭradhāni, Sî Chon, Vieng Sra, Nagara Śrī Dharmarāja, or Takuapā. It is even more difficult to envisage elite patrons so innocent of critical standards that they would consider our image as being on a level of quality with work that they would almost certainly have been familiar with in the sanctuaries around the Bay of Bandon.

This statue therefore remains an enigma not merely because of its singularity of type and iconography but precisely because of its aesthetic quality. Its preservation at Jaiyā for centuries and the rage it appears to have excited from vandals suggest that it is an object that may have been more fundamentally important in human affairs than many of the distinguished sculptures that have found their way into the galleries of the National Museum in Bangkok. It would also seem that the interesting questions to be asked of it are not susceptible to answer by methods that are rigorously typological. Its presence makes a pause or "opening" in the smooth screen of expectations and assumptions by which we view the art of a distant people, and in that "opening" we recover the intimation that this object, now so like a dead star, was once a provocation, an occasion

9. The art of the Jaiyā region includes objects in the styles of Dvāravatī, Śrīvijaya, Ceylon, and Cambodia (both pre-Angkorian and Angkorian). A range of objects from the region may be found in the following sources: G. Cœdès, *Les collections archéologiques du Musée National de Bangkok* (Paris, 1928); P. Dupont, "Viṣṇu mitrés de l'Indochine occidentale," *BEFEO*, 42, 2, (1942):233–254, and "Le Buddha de Grahi et l'école de C'aiya," *BEFEO*, 42, 1, (1942):105–106; Luang Boribal Buribhand and A. B. Griswold, "Sculpture of Peninsular Siam in the Ayuthyā Period," *JSS*, 38, 2, (1951):1–68; A. B. Griswold, "Imported Images and the Nature of Copying in the Art of Siam," *in* A. B. Griswold *et al.*, *Essays Offered to G. H. Luce* (Ascona, 1966), II, 37–73; Brah Guru Indapannacharya, *A Brief Account of the Antiquities Surrounding the Bay of Bandon* (Chaiya, Thailand, 1950); and S. J. O'Connor, *Hindu Gods of Peninsular Siam* (Ascona, 1972) and "An *Ekamulhaliṅga* from Peninsular Siam," *JSS*, 54, 1 (1966):43–49.

by which men came actively to understand their situation, and by which they embodied their image of the divine.

But it is just here, at the level of interpretation, that our present methods fail us most. Stylistics, iconographic studies, typological classification, and archival research may surround this work, provide a horizon for it, and even dissect it, but they falter and fall silent before the meaning it intends. What is revealed by this radical deformation of the image of the divine, this assertive triumph of manner over artistic convention? The answer requires some means of approach that is more trusting and more subtle than those we now employ. It is an answer that requires some surrender to the power of the work rather than the direct assault of a method, and it will probably be an answer that is equivocal and ambiguous. Paradoxically, the most direct path to the fullness of significance immanent in the brute presence of things may be indirect.

Chronicle Traditions in
Thai Historiography

DAVID K. WYATT

Cornell University

Among Professor Hall's many important contributions to the development of the study and teaching of Southeast Asian history is his work
in connection with the series of conferences on historical writing on the
peoples of Asia, the Southeast Asia section of which met in 1956. The
volume which he edited from the proceedings of that conference, *Historians
of South-East Asia*,[1] made a significant impression on the many students
then just beginning their studies in the field. Some of us may surely have
been somewhat intimidated by the volume's description and analysis of the
voluminous sources in the many vernacular languages of the region, only
a few of which any of us could hope to master in a lifetime. At the same
time, most of us then could gain some encouragement that our arduous
language training and study of standard European sources were leading us
along a course which could only be rewarding in the long run. We looked
forward to immersing ourselves in the mysteries of Javanese chronograms;
or Burmese *yazawin* and *ayebon* and *ayegyin*; or Malay *hikayat* and *sějarah*.
And we came even more to appreciate the enormous accomplishments of
European scholarship on the history of Southeast Asia, upon which Professor Hall's own *History* was so splendidly built (and continues to grow
so gracefully).

It is surely among the highest of compliments to Professor Hall's work
to note now that the *Historians* volume has in numerous respects been
superseded by more recent work, just as the successive editions of his
History have had to incorporate much substantial revision. Our field of
historical studies has moved very rapidly, and very far, in the past decade
or two. We have available now a great many new monographs in previously
unexplored fields and editions and translations of previously neglected
texts. Nonetheless, not all branches of our field have moved ahead at the
same pace. More has been done with modern history than with that of
earlier periods; and much more work has been done on the history of

1. London, 1961.

Malaya, Indonesia, and the Philippines than on the other countries of the region. Probably the most dramatic improvement has come with respect to the history of Thailand, which seems to have been in such a languid state in 1956 that it proved impossible to include chapters on Thailand in the *Historians* volume. Since that time, one can enumerate nearly thirty completed doctoral dissertations dealing with Thai history submitted to American, British, Australian, and Continental universities, as well as a considerable number now in progress. With an increasing pool of research being published on the basis of this and the authors' subsequent work, one can expect substantial revisions to our present understanding of modern Thai history in the near future.

Work on earlier Thai history, however, has yet to receive the attention it deserves. A great deal of excellent work has been accomplished concerning the early kingdom of Sukhothai, on the basis of its epigraphy, by A. B. Griswold and Prasert ṇa Nagara;[2] and their work on several occasions (including an article in this volume) has ventured into the history of the kingdom of Ayudhyā (A.D. 1350–1767).[3] Very little has yet been done, however, on Thai history prior to the fourteenth century, especially on the early kingdoms of northern Siam, or on the internal history of Ayudhyā itself. That this has been so stems largely from the nature of the sources themselves. These include a wide range of materials, including inscriptions, miscellaneous records, literary sources, local legends and oral traditions, and foreign accounts. The core of this material, however, is an extraordinarily rich chronicle tradition.

Two separate sets of problems are involved here. Those for the Ayudhyā period are in some ways more manageable. The royal or dynastic chronicles—well known to Western scholars since the seventeenth century—might be considered to consist of a single linear tradition, with two major variants on a single theme. Though somewhat sparse and specialized in the sorts of information they convey to the historian, they can be checked against other sources, and particularly foreign accounts, and certainly can yield a connected narrative of major events in the history of the kingdom. This basically is what was done by W. A. R. Wood in the 1920's with his *History of Siam*.[4] Much more care has yet to be taken, however, in collating various versions of the Ayudhyā chronicles with each other and with other documentary sources, as well as in exploiting more systematically the nuances of meaning and subtle turns of events which can be discovered from careful consideration of the nature of such chronicles

2. In a series of articles entitled "Epigraphic and Historical Studies," beginning in vol. 56 of *JSS*.

3. Another is "Devices and Expedients, Vǎt Ṗā Mok 1727 A.D.," *in* Tej Bunnag and Michael Smithies (eds.), *In Memoriam Phya Anuman Rajadhon* (Bangkok, 1970), pp. 147–220.

4. W. A. R. Wood, *A History of Siam from the Earliest Times to the Year A.D. 1781* (London, 1925; reprinted Bangkok, 1959).

as historical sources and of the unspoken values and intentions of their compilers.

In dealing with the pre-Ayudhyā history of Siam, quite another set of problems arises. Rather than a single chronicle tradition, there are dozens, deriving from various localities, written from disparate points of view, and raising severe problems of dating and chronology. They have tended to be dismissed as worthless or unreliable, or to have been ignored for extraneous reasons. Without them, however, no solutions are possible to many of the basic problems of Thai historiography.

It has for some time—apparently from the middle of the nineteenth century—been customary for Thai authors to distinguish between two basically different types of chronicles: between *tamnān* and *phongsāwadān*. Both are essentially annals, arranging events chronologically and concerned not at all with analysis or interpretation, save implicitly. Although *tamnān* seemingly began to be written earlier, certainly by the fifteenth century, both were being composed as late as the nineteenth century. They may be distinguished by the purposes for which each was written, the identity of their authors, and their relative scope in time and space.

Tamnān History

What might be termed the "earliest" chronicle traditions indigenous to Siam are the *tamnān* (stories, legends) associated with the localities and principalities of northern Siam and generally (but not exclusively) with the predecessors of the major Buddhist kingdoms of Sukhothai, Lānnā Thai (Chiangmai), and Ayudhyā. As a genre of historical literature, these "chronicles" usually are characterized first and foremost by their Buddhist associations. In this connection, many such *tamnān* are cast explicitly within Buddhist chronological and geographical frameworks. Many begin in the time of the Buddha, or earlier Buddhas, and some go so far as to prophesy to the end of the current Buddhist Era. They frequently cover earlier events in the history of Buddhism in India and Ceylon and trace the extension of the religion to the locality, region, or institution with which they are concerned. Many may be considered to have been written by Buddhist monks.

The subjects of such *tamnān* are usually Buddhist principalities, religious institutions or foundations, images, or relics and reliquaries. They could be considered as having been composed, in a sense, to legitimize their subjects by demonstrating the means by which they are linked to the Buddha, or showing how their subject has become and remains a repository of merit. They can thus be seen as having also a certain didactic value. While most such texts are quite localized in their subject, they are at the same time universal in quality: for those who wrote and read them, these were truly universal histories.

When written down, most *tamnān* almost certainly were incised in Siamese, Northern Thai (Tai Yuan), Lao, or Khmer script on carefully prepared palm leaves.[5] Few of these survive from much before the seventeenth century,[6] yet we know many were written earlier. It thus is necessary to assume that most actual manuscripts are later copies, as some explicitly state.

There is sufficient variation in existing texts to suggest a variety of means by which *tamnān* may have been compiled. Many contain local origin legends and myths, the best-known archetype of which is the Khun Borom story from Laos, which has all the Tai peoples issuing from a pumpkin or gourd.[7] Similar stories are to be found incorporated in such texts as the Nan chronicle.[8] It seems likely that much of the earlier narrative in many *tamnān* must derive from oral traditions.

Another component of many *tamnān* is the succession of rulers, often related in the form of a list embellished with brief tales of their exploits as well as their services to the religion. These have much in common with the indigenous historiography of such Tai peoples as the Ahom of Assam, the Shan of Burma and Yünnan, the Lao of northern Siam and Laos, and the various upland Tai peoples of Laos, northern Vietnam, and southern China.[9] These customarily feature a chronological system employing concurrent ten- and twelve-year cycles, in which the same combination of two named years occurs only once in each sixty-year cycle.[10] On the whole, this chronology demands treatment with the utmost respect: when tested against similarly-dated inscriptions it is not often found erroneous.

Their general characteristics notwithstanding, the qualities and nature of the various *tamnān* texts that are presently available vary widely. Out of a considerable quantity known to exist,[11] only a relatively small propor-

5. See Montgomery Schuyler, Jr., "Notes on the Making of Palm Leaf Manuscripts in Siam," *JAOS*, 29 (1908):281–283; and Christian Velder, "Die Palmblatt-Manuskript-Kultur Thailands," *Nachrichten der Gesellschaft für Natur- und Völkerkunde Ostasiens* 89/90 (1961): 110–114.

6. Cf. Charles F. Keyes, "New Evidence on Northern Thai Frontier History," *In Memoriam Phya Anuman Rajadhon*, p. 225.

7. René de Berval (ed.), *Kingdom of Laos* (Saigon, 1959), pp. 379–381; and C. Archaimbault, "Religious Structures in Laos," *JSS*, 52, 1 (April 1964):57–74.

8. "Rüang rātchawongpakǭn, phongsāwadān müang Nān," *Prachum phongsāwadān*, pt. 10 (Bangkok, 1919; reprinted Bangkok: Kāonā, 1964, IV, 333–542); partial English version published as *The Nan Chronicle*, trans. Prasoet Churatana, ed. D. K. Wyatt (Ithaca, 1966).

9. This subject is much too vast to be discussed here. The reader is referred to the following: (Ahom) N. N. Acharyya, *The History of Medieval Assam* (Gauhati, 1966), pp. 17–30; (Shan) J. G. Scott and J. P. Hardiman, *Gazetteer of Upper Burma and the Shan States*, I, 1 (Rangoon, 1900), esp. chap. 6; and (Lao) L. Finot, "Recherches sur la littérature laotienne," *BEFEO*, 17, 5 (1917), esp. pp. 149–154.

10. See Prince Phetsarath, "The Laotian Calendar," in de Berval, pp. 97–125.

11. See G. Cœdès, "Documents sur l'histoire politique et réligieuse du Laos occidental," *BEFEO*, 25, 1–2 (1925):172–174; and Pierre-Bernard Lafont, "Inventaire des manuscrits des pagodes du Laos," *BEFEO*, 52 (1965):429–546.

tion has been published; and only a handful have received the editorial care they demand. The most prominent among these may be divided into three groups: first, the *tamnān* of the distant past in extreme northern Siam; second, the "universal histories" in Pali and Thai, the product of the Buddhist efflorescence in Lānnā Thai in the fifteenth and sixteenth centuries; and third, the "monumental *tamnān*" of Buddhist images, relics, and institutions.

Tamnān of the Distant Past

This group of texts, of uncertain date, provenance, and authorship, deals with early states of extreme northern Siam in the period prior to the thirteenth-century foundation of such states as Lānnā Thai, Sukhothai, and Nān. All of them are the subjects of considerable puzzlement and controversy among those who have studied them, owing to their relatively weak links with subsequent Thai history. All were written originally in Tai Yuan.

The *Tamnān Müang Suwannakhōmkham*,[12] which deals with the legendary origins and history, over numerous millennia, of a state apparently in the extreme north-central region of the Indochinese Peninsula, in the Mekong Valley, is remarkable for several reasons. First, other texts (particularly the Singhanāwati chronicle) refer to Suwannakhōmkham as a historical antecedent of the kingdoms of Chiangsāēn, Chiangmai, and Phayao, in northern Siam. Second, its references to the *krọm* people usually are taken to refer to the Khmer of Angkorian Cambodia.[13] The apparent impossibility of either dating or localizing the subject of this text is a source of considerable frustration to those who would seek to ascertain the history of the Thai in the middle Angkorian period, prior to their rapid rise to power in Siam. This text invites serious study, especially within the context of vaguely similar Lao traditions associated with the region of That Phanom and Nakhọn Phanom in northeastern Thailand,[14] and the so-called "Annals of the North" (*Phongsāwadān nüa*),[15] both of which share with it several points of similarity and congruity.

---

12. In *Prachum phongsāwadān*, pt. 72 (Bangkok, 1939; reprinted Bangkok: Khurusaphā, 1969, XLV, 132–240). A French translation was published by Camille Notton, *Annales du Siam*, I: *Chroniques de Suvaṇṇa Khamdëng, Suvaṇṇa K̂ôm Khăm, Siṅhanavati* (Paris, 1926), pp. 82–135.

13. See also G. H. Luce, *Old Burma—Early Pagan* (Locust Valley, N.Y., 1969), I, 21–23.

14. See Phra Phanomčhedīyānurak, *Urangkhanithān (tamnān phrathāt phanom phitsadān)* (Bangkok, 1949); and Sila Viravong (ed.), *Urangkhathāt thētsanā* (printed on palm leaves, Bangkok, 1943).

15. C. Notton, *Annales du Siam*, IV: *Légendes sur le Siam et le Cambodge* (Bangkok, 1939). Many Thai editions exist, of which the most accessible is included in *Phrarātchaphongsāwadān Krung Sī Ayutthayā . . . lae phongsāwadān nüa*, 2 vols. (Bangkok, 1961), II, 316–406. Note Prince Damrong Rajanubhab's comments on it, "The Story of the Records of Siamese History," *JSS*, 11, 2 (1914/15); reprinted in *Selected Articles from the Siam Society Journal*, I (Bangkok, 1954), 81.

Two extremely important texts associated with the same area, and with a protohistorical period prior to the thirteenth-century founding of Chiangmai, are the *Tamnān Singhanāwatikumān* and the *Tamnān Müang Ngȫn Yāng Chiangsāen*. The former first became generally known with the publication of a French translation by Notton in 1926;[16] the second became available only with the publication of Thai editions of both in 1936.[17] Their relatively late availability had the consequence of keeping them from the serious scholarly attentions of Prince Damrong Rajanubhab and George Cœdès when they worked on some of the texts of earlier Siamese history in the first three decades of this century.

The Müang Ngȫn Yāng Chiangsāen chronicle might be an extremely late work, as the last date mentioned in it is equivalent to A.D. 1905. This appears, however, in what must be considered an appendix to the main text, the bulk of which is concerned primarily with the history of extreme northern Siam from its legendary beginnings down to Mangrāi's founding of Chiangmai in 1296. The remaining third of the text centers mainly on Phayao, on King Ngam Müang and his successors down to modern times. Although, like the Singhanāwati chronicle, it contains numerous Buddhist references, it seems best to classfy it with that text as part of a group of chronicles sharing a common geographical focus, a single genealogical line, and a characteristic chronological framework featuring three separate eras: *paṭhama-*, *dutiya-*, and *tatiyasakarāja* ("first," "second," and "third" eras). All these features similarly are shared with the early section of the Nan chronicle, also a later compilation, which must be based on similar texts.[18]

The Singhanawati chronicle also deals with the Chiangsāen region, but does so in a more explicitly Buddhist framework. Its early portions deal with pre-Buddhist and early Buddhist times, and in places can be seen to be based on Pali Buddhist texts. The author's concerns here are to link the upper Mekong region with universal (Buddhist) history and to account for local states and sacred shrines by relating their foundation to Buddhist prophecies and mythology. In the process, a sacred and semipolitical geography is described which extends from the Chiengsāen-Chiangrāi region northward into southern Yünnan. The latter portion of the text has certain points of contact with the Suwannakhōmkham chronicle mentioned above, as it begins with the seizure of the Chiangsāen state by a "Krǫm" prince living at Umongsela.[19] Subsequent passages dealing with a

16. Notton, *Annales du Siam*, I, 141–202.

17. *Prachum phongsāwadān*, pt. 61 (Bangkok, 1936; reprinted Bangkok: Khurusaphā, 1969), XXXIII, 197–287; XXXIV, 1–204.

18. Cited in n. 8, above.

19. Notton, *Annales du Siam*, I, 185; Chanthit Krasāesin, "Tamnān Chiangsāen," *Thalāeng ngān prawattisāt ēkkasān bōrānkhadī*, 4, 2 (May 1970):137, writes "*khǫm*." Compare this passage with the *Suwannakhōmkham*: Notton, p. 120; Thai edition (1969), p. 206.

Khǫm (Khmer) occupation of Yonakanagara, the northern Tai state in present-day Thailand, and with a later Burmese or Mon invasion, cry out for careful study.

The Singhanāwati chronicle is by far the most interesting—and potentially important—of this genre, primarily because it purports to be a full chronological record. Its very dates, however, seem to have given rise to the disdain commonly accorded it. Three dating systems are employed in the text, and each date also is rendered with its place in the sixty-year cycle. Beginning with Notton's French edition, many have taken the dates employed in the latter portion to be dates expressed in the Mahāśakarāja Era (M.S. + 78 = A.D.), owing to such equivalences being explicitly made there.[20] The chronicle thus appears to cover a period from 674 B.C. to A.D. 637 (by Notton's calculations) and it has been accordingly dismissed as fabulous. These calculations seem to be based on *mistaken* conversions made by some late copyist of the text.[21] References to an invasion from Burma and episodes dated in other chronicles in the eleventh century A.D., which in the Singhanāwati chronicle are expressed with dates in the fourth and fifth centuries of an unspecified era, encourage a belief that these dates should be taken as Lesser Era (Cūḷasakarāja + 638 = A.D.) dates. One recent editor of the text has done so, attempting also to unravel the chronology of the entire chronicle.[22]

Of the host of local *tamnān* covering later history, some written in comparatively recent times, one demands special mention here: the *tamnān* of Chiangmai. It clearly falls within this tradition, set within universal Buddhist history in its early portions yet concerned primarily with the history of a particular *müang* in historical times. The chronicle of Chiangmai long was known only in its French edition, translated by Notton and published first in 1932.[23] Only very recently has a Thai version, transcribed from Tai Yuan, become available.[24] A colophon to the Thai edition suggests it was composed in 1827, yet Notton's French version goes only to 1805, the remainder being filled out with sections of the modern *Phongsāwadān Yonok*. The two clearly treat the same text: they are identically divided into "books" (*phūk*); but Notton has only seven, while the recent version comprises eight. They form a connected narrative of the history of Chiangmai, after a brief introductory passage in Book I which moves from

20. See, for example, Notton, *ibid.*, p. 201.

21. Notton's version derives from a copy made in 1880 (*ibid.*, p. 202).

22. Mānit Wanliphōdom, "Tamnān Singhanāwatikumān, chabap sǫp khon," *Sinlapākǫn*, 6, 4 (May 1962), continued serially through 9, 4 (May 1965). Another edition, without attempts to unravel the chronology, has been completed by Chanthit Krasāesin, "Tamnān Chiangsāen (Tamnān Singhanāwati) . . . ," *Thalaēng ngān prawattisāt ēkkasān bōrānkhadī*, 3, 3 (Sept. 1969):131–151; 4, 1 (Jan. 1970):141–156; and 4, 2 (May 1970):133–148.

23. *Annales du Siam*, III: *Chronique de Xieng Mãi* (Paris, 1932). Notton's translation should not be accepted uncritically.

24. *Tamnān phün müang Chiangmai*, ed. Rǫng Sayāmanon (Bangkok, 1971).

the Buddha's predecessors to the reign of Aśoka. The early portions draw briefly on the standard Pali sources and on the *Suwannakhōmkham, Singhanāwati,* and *Cāmadevi* chronicles, and then devote the fullest attention to the period from the end of the thirteenth century to the end of the eighteenth, with particular emphasis upon King Mangrāi (1259–1317, Book II), King Tilokarāt (1442–1487, Books IV–V), and relations with the Burmese. As the chronicle of a major state which was incorporated into the kingdom of Siam only in the nineteenth century, the history of which is hardly given its due in the royal chronicles of Ayudhyā, the *tamnān* of Chiangmai must be considered a major source for the history of Thailand.

Such texts as these doubtless have been around for a very long time, in some form or another. Their three types of content—miraculous legend, lists of rulers, and Buddhist embellishments and additions—suggest a sequence in which individual texts might have taken shape over the centuries. They contain both a degree of precision with respect to rulers and the length of their reigns and a degree of historical plausibility which have been neglected. Concluding as they commonly do with events prior to known events of the thirteenth century, they suggest the extent to which Thai historiographers (and presumably others) regarded that period as constituting a break in the continuity of Thai history. Even more importantly, with the demise of the "Nan-chao myth"[25] they suggest an alternative field of enquiry for those concerned with what one Thai historian has called the "Beachhead states";[26] namely, early Thai states in the upper Mekong region in the several centuries prior to the thirteenth, having some connections with Angkorian Cambodia and Pagán Burma, as well as with other Tai states of northern Southeast Asia.

"Universal Histories"

The Buddhist historiography of northern Siam is extraordinarily rich and relatively well known, especially from the work of the late Professor Cœdès in the 1920's. His monumental "Documents sur l'histoire politique et réligieuse du Laos occidental" of 1925 brought to full scholarly attention two major Pali historical works produced at Chiangmai in the early sixteenth century. There are, however, several others. These include "universal histories" written in Pali, both then and later; one in Thai; and several "monumental" *tamnān* to be discussed below.

25. See Hiram Woodward, "Who are the Ancestors of the Thais: Report on the Seminar," *Sangkhomsāt parithat,* 2, 3 (Feb. 1965):88–91; F. W. Mote, "Problems of Thai Prehistory," *ibid.,* 2, 2 (Oct. 1964):100–109, and "Prehistory of the Thai People," *ibid.,* special no. 3 (June 1966):24–31.

26. Kachorn Sukhabanij, "The Thai Beachhead States in the 11th–12th Centuries," *Sinlapākǭn,* 1, 3 (Sept. 1957):74–81, and 1, 4 (Nov. 1957):40–54.

The best-known of the Pali "universal histories" are the two works partially published and translated by Cœdès. The first, the *Cāmadevīvaṃsa*, was written by Mahāthera Bodhiraṅsī around the beginning of the fifteenth century.[27] A work of considerable length, its fifteen chapters begin with the time of the Buddha, and presage later Tai Yuan history with a prophecy as to the future establishment of the kingdom of Hariphunjaya, present-day Lamphun. Much of the text (chapters 4–11) is devoted to the reign of Queen Cāmadevī, brought by *ṛṣi* from Lavo (Lopburi). Her successors, perhaps of the period A.D. 825–1050,[28] are much more quickly dealt with, and the chronicle ends with the rediscovery of relics of the Buddha, deposited in Hariphunjaya much earlier by his disciples, by King Ādityarāja, who is thought to have reigned there in the mid-twelfth century.[29] The purpose of this chronicle thus might be considered to be to explain the presence at a major shrine in Lamphun of Buddhist relics, and its function to be the linking of that region, in which the text's author lived almost four centuries later, with the person of the Buddha, earlier Buddhist states in the region, and "universal history"—that is, the origins and progress of Buddhism.

The *Jinakālamālī* was written in Chiangmai by Mahāthera Ratanapañña in A.D. 1516.[30] It is certainly the best example of its type, providing a synoptic history of Buddhism from the Buddha's resolution to become a Buddha through the history of Buddhism in India and Ceylon and the establishment of Buddhism in Siam, particularly the spread of Sinhalese Buddhism from the thirteenth century up to the author's own lifetime in Chiangmai. Although its coverage of secular affairs is peripheral to its primary concern with the history of Buddhism, its utility as an accurate source for Siamese history has frequently been demonstrated, and it must be numbered among the classics of Thai historiography.

One other work, exceptional in some ways, also deserves special mention here. This is the *Saṅgītiyavaṃsa*, composed in Pali by the Bangkok monk Somdet Phra Wannarat (also known as Phonnarat) in 1789.[31] Written in honor of King Rāma I immediately after his famous revision of the Pali

27. *Rüang Chammathēwiwong, phongsāwadān müang Hariphunchai* (Bangkok, 1921; reprinted with Thai translation only, 1930 and 1967); partial romanized Pali text and French translation, Cœdès, "Documents," pp. 141–171; and also Notton, *Annales du Siam*, II: *Chronique de La:p'un, Histoire de la Dynastie Chamt'evi* (Paris, 1930).

28. Kachorn, I, 4:50.

29. *Ibid.*, p. 51; and G. Cœdès, *The Indianized States of Southeast Asia* (Honolulu, 1968), pp. 194–195.

30. Partial Pali text and French translation in Cœdès, "Documents," pp. 36–140; full romanized text ed. A. P. Buddhadatta Mahathera (London, 1962); English translation by N. A. Jayawickrama, *The Sheaf of Garlands of the Epochs of the Conqueror* (London, 1968).

31. *Sangkhītiyawong, phongsāwadān rüang sangkhāyanā phrathammawinai* (Bangkok, 1923); Pali text and Thai translation in parallel columns.

canon, this is a history of the successive Buddhist councils at which the
Tripiṭaka was revised. Its first two chapters discuss the first seven councils
convened in India and Ceylon, and then the spread of Buddhism in South
Asia is treated. There is extensive discussion of the history (treated
dynastically) of northern Siam, Ayudhyā, and early Bangkok (chapters
6–8), and it contains an especially moving description of the fall of Ayudhyā
in 1767. Its classification as "universal history" is problematic, yet it does,
in classical fashion, treat of the chronological development of a world
structured by a common religious heritage in such a manner as to suggest
no other world exists. Similarly, its temporal framework, like that of the
other texts, is at least implicitly delimited in both finite and infinite Buddhist
time: that is, the current epoch extending five thousand years forward
from the Buddha's enlightenment is set within the abstract infinitude of
cosmic time in which there are earlier buddhas and buddhas-to-be.[32]

The Singhanāwati chronicle, already discussed, might seem a likely
candidate for inclusion in the category of Thai "universal histories." Its
place here, however, is debatable owing to the strong possibility that it
is a composite work, perhaps a local historical tradition blown up to fit a
broader Buddhist framework. A much clearer example of this genre, one
more certainly an original work, is the *Mūlasāsanā*.[33] This work, still
seriously neglected, is thought to have been compiled in Lānnā Thai just
prior to the *Cāmadevīvaṃsa* and *Jinakālamālī*,[34] and perhaps to have served
as a source for them. The main portion of the text was written by a monk,
Buddhañāṇa, in the mid-sixteenth century, later material being added by
another monk, Buddhabhukāma.[35] In structure their work is similar to the
two main Chiangmai texts, extending in time from the Buddha's resolve
to become a Buddha to the early sixteenth-century kings of Chiangmai.
It has in addition, however, a long discursive closing section dealing with
Buddha relics and the future course of the religion.

"Monumental" *Tamnān*

There is another class of *tamnān* which shares with the "universal histories" a common Buddhist framework but whose scope is very much more
restricted. These are the *tamnān* of Buddhist images, monuments, and institutions, particularly common in northern Siam but also known elsewhere.
One group of these chronicles is of particular interest as deriving from the

---

32. My discussion of this point owes much to the recent work of Charnvit Kasetsiri, Anan
Ganjanapan, and Koson Srisang.

33. *Tamnān mūnlasātsanā* (Bangkok, 1939).

34. Cf. Cœdès, *Indianized States*, pp. 136; 322, n. 30. The latest date mentioned in the
text is equivalent to A.D. 1510 (p. 260).

35. I am indebted to A. B. Griswold for advice on this point.

same environment, and even the same individuals, as some of the "universal histories."

The *Sihinganidāna* was written in Pali by Mahāthera Bodhiransī, who is also the author of the *Cāmadevīvaṃsa*, and it may be considered to date from around the beginning of the fifteenth century, A.D. 1402–1442.[36] It is the story of the Sihinga Buddha image, which by legend was cast in Ceylon; it was subsequently brought to Sukhothai via Nakḥọn Sīthammarāt in the reign of King Rāmkhamhāeng and then taken to Ayudhyā in 1378. In the warfare of the succeeding decades it was moved to Kamphāengphet (1382), Chiangrāi (1388), and, finally, Chiangmai (1407). Bodhiransī probably wrote in celebration of its arrival in Chiangmai. Because of the image's involvement in the wars of this period, the chronicle is a useful supplementary historical source.[37]

The most famous Buddha image in Siam is the so-called Emerald Buddha, now housed in the Temple of the Emerald Buddha within the walls of the Grand Palace. Its history, written by a young Chiangmai monk named Brahmarājapaññā, is of considerable interest. The date of his work is unknown: we know only that he based it upon an already-existing version in Thai, and that only his Pali version existed by the reign of Rāma I (1782–1809), founder of the present dynasty. Titled in Pali *Ratanabimbavaṃsa*, it has been frequently translated.[38] Because of the image's considerable "wanderings" in Siam, Cambodia, and Laos prior to its installation in Bangkok in 1782, the chronicle has much to say to the historian.

Tamnān of Buddhist religious monuments are numerous, and indeed continue to be written today. The best-known (and perhaps the earliest) of these have been collected in a single volume by Thailand's Fine Arts Department.[39] This collection includes only chronicles of reliquaries, *phrathāt*, most of which have been transcribed from palm-leaf manuscripts written in northern Thai script. The ten *tamnān* are (with probable dates of composition, when known, in parentheses) from Chiangsāen (1515?),

36. Dhanit Yupho, in the foreword to a new edition of the text, translated from Pali by Sāeng Monwithūn, *Nithān phraphutthasihing* (Bangkok, 1963). This edition gives the full Pali text, pp. 1–32.

37. An English translation by Camille Notton was published in Bangkok in 1933 under the title *P'ra Buddha Sihinga*.

38. The Pali text is available only in a volume edited by the Fine Arts Department, *Tamnān Phra Kāeo Mọrakot chabap sombūn* (Bangkok, 1961), pp. 312–384. This volume also includes a Pali version and explanation by King Mongkut, and several modern versions including the translation into Thai made for King Rāma I in 1788. The best modern translation in Thai is by Sāeng Monwithūn, *Ratanabimbavaṃsa, tamnān Phra Kāeo Mọrakot* (Bangkok, 1967). There exists an English translation by the indefatigable Camille Notton, *The Chronicle of the Emerald Buddha* (Bangkok, 1932).

39. *Prachum tamnān phrathāt, phāk thī 1 lae phāk thī 2* (Bangkok, 1970).

Lamphun (1606), Lampang (1830), the Chumphit Nakhǫn Reliquary (1543), Dǫi Pūphūthap in Phrāē province, the Chǫ Hāē Reliquary in Phrāē (1864), Thāt Phanom in the northeast (1838), Nakhǫn Sīthammarāt (c. 1553),[40] Dǫi Suthēp in Chiangmai (1825), and Nān (1704). In most cases, these are chronicles of the palladia of individual *müang*, and the fortunes of both are closely interrelated. Thus they have much to offer the historian whose interests lie in more secular directions. These texts almost always contain numerous dates, expressed in their fullest form. Because they often overlap with local histories and chronicles, they may profitably be employed in cross-checking other sources.[41] This genre of works remains relatively unexplored and deserves careful scholarly attention.[42]

Phongsāwadān History

The major differences between *tamnān* and *phongsāwadān* historical traditions are obvious only through a comparison of the most extreme examples of the two types: the comparison is blurred when one considers later examples of *tamnān* such as the Chiangmai chronicle, which contains elements of both types. Taking as extreme examples the *Mūlasāsanā* and *Jinakālamālī tamnān* and any of the versions of the *phongsāwadān* of Ayudhyā, their differences are clear. Instead of treating "universal," Buddhist history, the royal chronicles (*phrarātchaphongsāwadān*) of Ayudhyā deal with dynastic, or, more properly, kingly history: the deeds of the rulers of Ayudhyā. Their inherent continuity is secular, not religious, save insofar as the compilers were concerned with the enduring "merit" of Ayudhyā itself. Rather than being written by Buddhist monks, they were written by scribes or officials at the royal court. Although too few early examples survive to allow easy generalization, it would appear that they were composed primarily for the edification of the ruler and his successors, though it has also been suggested that a ruler might have considered the royal chronicles as part of his royal regalia.

It is not known for certain when the first chronicle of Ayudhyā was written, although it is quite certain that the basic sources for early texts must have been kept from an early time in the form of astrologers' notebooks

40. See D. K. Wyatt, *The Crystal Sands: Nagara Śrī Dharrmarāja in Early Thai History* (Ithaca, 1975).

41. For example, the chronological puzzles of the Nan chronicle can be solved by reference to the Chāē Hāēng Reliquary chronicle.

42. Only one chronicle of this type so far has appeared in translation: E. W. Hutchinson, "The Seven Spires: A Sanctuary of the Sacred Fig Tree at Chiengmai," *JSS*, 39, 1 (1951):51–68. A wider sampling of this literature is available in condensed form in Sanguan Chōtisukkharat, *Tamnān müang nüa*, 2 vols. (Chiangmai, 1955–1960).

of extraordinary events.[43] The earliest full version of Ayudhyā history presently known was compiled in 1640 by the Dutch merchant Jeremias van Vliet. Beginning with three variant legends concerning the origins of the founder of Ayudhyā, it then gives a reign-by-reign chronicle of notable events down to the date of composition. As no dates are given in this version, but only reign lengths, and because of the discursive style in which it was written, pending further study it may be considered to be based primarily upon oral, rather than written, records of Siamese history.[44]

The earliest, the best known, and the only full translation of Siamese royal *phongsāwadān* is the so-called Luang Prasert version of c. 1680, first published in Thai in 1907 and in English translation in 1909.[45] This chronicle is known to have been compiled in the reign of King Narai the Great (1657–1688) by a court astrologer, Phra Hōrāthibǫdī. Although it ceases with events in the year 1604, Prince Damrong Rajanubhab was of the opinion that a second volume of the text once existed to carry events into Narai's reign.[46]

The Luang Prasert version of the Ayudhyā *phongsāwadān* is quite skeletal, giving only the barest details of events, and it is particularly thin on the earliest periods. Its chief virtue has always been held to be its chronological accuracy, attested to by comparison with foreign sources. It bears such strong similarities in structure to the later "abridged chronicle," noted below, that it is tempting to consider it as such, perhaps a version intended to answer foreigners' questions concerning Siamese history.

Prince Damrong's useful article of 1915, translated from comments in his introductory section of the "Royal Autograph Edition" of the *phongsāwadān*, generally describes the various versions of the Ayudhyā chronicles.[47] It is necessary to cover the same subject again, however, owing to considerable advances in the study of the subject in the past half-century. As Dr. Busakorn Lailert recently has explained, there are nine extant versions of the Ayudhyā chronicles besides the Luang Prasert

43. Examples of these are available in printed form: "Čhotmāihēt hǒn" and "Čhotmāihēt hǒn khǒng čhamün Kongsin," *Prachum phongsāwadān*, pt. 8 (Bangkok, 1917; reprinted Bangkok: Kāonā, 1964, IV, 86–162); and *Čhotmāihēt hǒn chabap phra Pramuanthanarak* (Bangkok, 1921).

44. Following a lead from Seiichi Iwao, this text was first discovered and photographed by Kachorn Sukhabanij. It is published as *The Short History of the Kings of Siam*, trans. Leonard Andaya, ed. D. K. Wyatt (Bangkok, 1975).

45. *Phrarātchaphongsāwadān Krung Kao chabap luang Prasoetaksǫnnit* (Bangkok, 1907), included in *Prachum phongsāwadān*, pt. 1 (Bangkok, 1914; reprinted Bangkok: Kāonā, 1963, I, 113–138); and translated by O. Frankfurter, "Events in Ayuddhya from Chulasakaraj 686–966," *JSS*, 6, 3 (1909):1–21, reprinted in *Selected Articles from the Siam Society Journal*, I (Bangkok, 1954), 38–62.

46. Damrong, "Story of the Records," p. 84.

47. *Ibid.*

version, all of which postdate the fall of the kingdom to the Burmese in 1767.[48]

Of the earliest version, that of Cūḷasakarāja (cs.) 1136 (A.D. 1774), only one small fragment has survived.[49] This covers only the years cs. 926–931 (A.D. 1564–1569) and is too fragmentary to shed much light on the *phongsāwadān* as a whole. Of a slightly later version of cs. 1145 (A.D. 1783), we similarly have only small fragments, dealing with portions of the reigns of Mahā Čhakkraphat and Mahā Thammarāchā (A.D. 1549–1590). This version has never been published.

Only with the later versions of the reign of King Rāma I (1782–1809) does a fuller picture of *phongsāwadān* history begin to emerge. The earliest full version, the Phan Čhanthanumāt version of c.s. 1157 (A.D. 1795),[50] clearly indicates that its compiler worked from an earlier version written in the reign of King Bǫrommakōt (1733–1758) and revised in the reign of King Taksin (1767–1782).[51] In c.s. 1169 (A.D. 1807), Rāma I had a leading Buddhist monk, Somdet Phra Phonnarat, the author of the *Saṅgītiyavaṃsa*, undertake a thorough revision of the chronicles, basing his work primarily upon the cs. 1157 version but heeding the king's sensibilities on certain delicate episodes.[52] This version, of which the best manuscript is in the British Museum, must be considered the last great example of the *phongsāwadān*.[53] Two features of its composition are especially remarkable. First, it is unusual in having a short introductory section dealing with the legendary events leading up to the foundation of Ayudhyā in 1350. This material is reminiscent generally of the *tamnān* traditions concerning northern Siam, with which it has some points of connection, and of the compiler's previous work within that tradition as expressed both in his *Saṅgītiyavaṃsa* and in two fragments of a more lengthy work on the pre-Ayudhyā period, the *Culayuddhakāravaṃsa*.[54] It is worth remarking that this introduction was deleted from subsequent reworkings of his *phongsāwadān*. Secondly, it is somehow appropriate to note the specific initiative taken by King Rāma I in ordering the compilation of this chronicle, an act perfectly in character for a monarch also responsible for the total revision of the Pali canon, the

48. "Phrarātchaphongsāwadān Krung Sī Ayutthayā," *Sinlapākǫn*, 12, 2 (July 1968):89–93.

49. "Phrarātchaphongsāwadān khwām kao," *Prachum phongsāwadān*, pt. 4 (Bangkok, 1915; reprinted Bangkok: Kāonā, 1964, II, 113–132).

50. *Phrarātchaphongsāwadān Krung Sī Ayutthayā chabap phan Čhanthanumāt (Čhǭem) kap phra Čhakkraphatdiphong (Čhāt)* (Bangkok, 1964); two versions in one volume.

51. Busakorn, p. 90.

52. *Ibid.*, pp. 91–93.

53. The manuscript was discovered by Kachorn Sukhabanij and is published as *Phrarātchaphongsāwadān Krung Sayām čhāk tonchabap thī pen sombat khǭng British Museum Krung Lǫndǫn*, ed. Tri Amatyakul (Bangkok, 1964).

54. *Culayuddhakāravaṃsa, phūk 2 rüang phongsāwadān Thai* (Bangkok, 1920); and "Culayuddhakāravaṃsa khwām riang (tǫn ton)," *Prachum phongsāwadān*, pt. 66 (Bangkok, 1937; reprinted Bangkok: Khurusaphā, 1969, XL, 260–278).

recodification of Thai law, and the composition of the most complete version of the *Rāmāyana* known in Siam.

Until the publication of the "British Museum" manuscript of the chronicle, that version was known only through subsequent versions based upon it, of which the most prominent was the edition published in two volumes by the American missionary Dan Beach Bradley in the reign of King Mongkut. This edition was commonly attributed to Prince Paramānuchit Chinōrot, who had been a pupil of Somdet Phra Phonnarat. Inasmuch as, with the exception of the deleted pre-Ayudhyā portion, it is virtually identical to the "British Museum" manuscript in which authorship is explicitly attributed to Somdet Phra Phonnarat, that long-standing misapprehension has been removed.[55] It remains highly likely that it was Prince Paramānuchit who prepared Bradley's version for printing, just as it is almost certain that this same version is that which served as the basis of the version edited personally in 1855 by King Mongkut, the "Royal Autograph Edition."[56] From one, or a combination, of these texts, Prince Paramānuchit himself compiled two abridged versions, probably in Mongkut's reign, which are unique in having in some places a chronology all their own.[57]

Two recent dissertations have begun the important task of demonstrating that there is much more to be learned from the Ayudhyā *phongsāwadān* than Wood even hinted.[58] Certainly they are heavily concerned with king and court and more interested in warfare than in peace; in short, they are what King Chulalongkorn termed tales of "dynasties and battles" (*wong wong čhak čhak*). They reveal little of provincial affairs, of economic life, or even of religion. They have, nonetheless, a great deal—perhaps much more than has been suspected—to tell the modern reader about a historically important segment of Thai society, about its political values, its

55. The authorship question was first solved by Tri Amatyakul, "Phūtāēng nangsü phrarātchaphongsāwadān chabap phim 2 lem," *Sinlapākǫn*, 5, 6 (March 1962):43–50, and 6, 1 (May 1962):25–34. The Bradley "two-volume" edition has been published as *Phrarātchaphongsāwadān Krung Sī Ayutthayā chabap Somdet Phra Phonnarat, Wat Phra Chētuphon* (Bangkok, 1962).

56. The latest edition is the first to be encompassed within the covers of a single volume: *Phrarātchaphongsāwadān chabap phrarātchahatlēkhā* (Chonburi, 1968). Mongkut's version here has had additional editorial attention from Prince Damrong Rajanubhab, to whose energy we owe the fact that almost all the texts mentioned in this article are available in print.

57. These were first published in the Bradley edition of the mid-nineteenth century. The most accessible texts are those included in *Phrarātchaphongsāwadān Krung Sī Ayutthayā chabap luang Prasǭētaksǫnnit, chabap . . . kromphra Paramānuchitchinōrot lae phongsāwadān nüa . . .* , 2 vols. (Bangkok, 1961), II, 281–315. A translation of the longer of these, by the present author, is published as "The Abridged Royal Chronicle of Ayudhyā of Prince Paramānuchitchinōrot," *JSS*, 61, 1 (Jan. 1973):25–50.

58. Busakorn Lailert, "The Ban Phlu Luang Dynasty, 1688–1767: A Study of the Thai Monarchy during the Closing Years of the Ayuthya Period" (Ph.D. diss., University of London, 1972); and Charnvit Kasetsiri, "The Rise of Ayudhya: A History of Siam in the Fourteenth and Fifteenth Centuries" (Ph.D. diss., Cornell University, 1973).

modes of behavior, and its style of rule. Until this material has been thoroughly analyzed, we will still lack all but the most elementary skeleton of Ayudhyā history within which to place such other material as is beginning to come to light.

Neither *taṃnān* nor *phongsāwadān* has disappeared from Thai historiography. They continue to be issued and read, and there are still many—provincial monks, retired officials, journalists—whose writings contain elements of one or both traditions. When a historian is pressed to apply a more "modern" analytical approach to their materials, they might suggest that he supply his own interpretations. Those who in the decades to come carry forward the work Professor Hall has so long promoted might begin by making these basic sources of Siam's history better known and more accessible.

A Fifteenth-Century Siamese Historical Poem

A. B. GRISWOLD

Breezewood Foundation, Monkton, Maryland

and PRASERT ṆA NAGARA

Undersecretary of State for State Universities,
Office of the Prime Minister, Bangkok

I

The anonymous poem *Yuan Pâi* ('The Defeat of the *Yuan*') was probably composed around 1475 at Ayudhyā, or perhaps at Biṣṇuloka. (For the two main systems of transcription used in this chapter, see below, p. 162.) Though this poem is one of the earliest Siamese literary classics of any length to have survived in a fair state of preservation, it has been, as Prince Dhāni Nivat observes, "neglected longer than it should have been" (*JSS*, 59, 1 [1971]: 277).

It is not known how the text managed to survive the destruction of Ayudhyā in 1767 when so much Siamese literature was irretrievably lost. None of the extant manuscripts appear to be any older than the nineteenth century; but some of them exhibit much older forms of spelling, with no more than haphazard attempts at modernization; so it can be gussed that they were copied from older manuscripts, now lost, rather than set down from memory.

During the reign of King Rāma II (1806–1824) the poet Brañā Trañ (c. 1765–c. 1835) composed two stanzas to replace some material that had dropped out of the manuscripts following stanza 124, which shows that the poem was admired enough at that time to be studied with some diligence.

Yuan Pâi, or *YP* as we shall abbreviate the title, was first printed in the Vajirañāṇa Magazine in 1901. Prince Damrong Rājānubhāb, when preparing his edition of the Royal Autograph Recension of the Annals of Ayudhyā, which appeared in 1913, made some use of the historical portions of the poem in his analyses of the reigns of Paramarājā II and Paramatrailokanātha (*AA/RA*, pp. 407–409, 424–425, etc.; for the abbreviations used in this paper, see below, page 162). In 1922, *YP* was printed in book form by the National Library, with an introduction by Prince Damrong

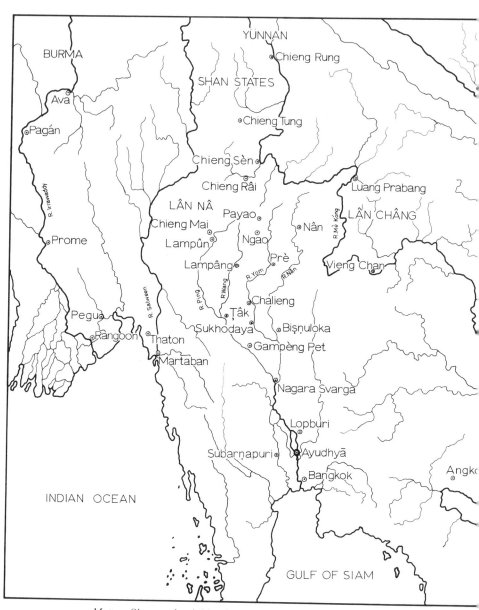

Map 1. Siam and neighboring regions in the fifteenth century.
(Maps were drawn by David K. Wyatt.)

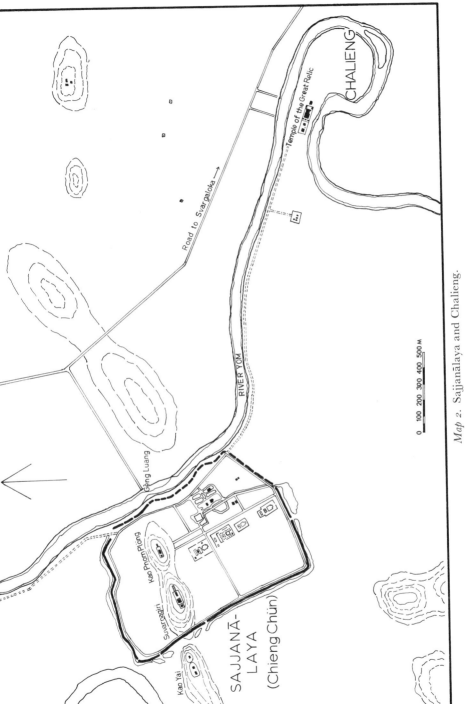

Map 2. Sajjanālaya and Chalieng.

Figure 2. The Temple of the Great Relic (Mahādhātu) at Chalieng, presumably built soon after 1475 by Paramatrailoka to celebrate his victory at Chieng Chün and to set the seal of his authority on the province recaptured from Tiloka.

in which he wrote: "The poem has not been appreciated at its full value because no one is able to interpret it properly, the verses of homage [stanzas 1–52] being so difficult to understand that they discourage anyone from going on to read the historical portion." This edition has been several times reprinted, most recently by the National Library in 1966 (see Bibliography, below).

In 1968, Mr. Chandijya Krasèsindhu published a study of *YP* in the Bulletin of the Faculty of Archaeology of the University of Fine Arts, Bangkok (vol. 1, no. 2). Prince Dhāni Nivat, in reviewing this issue of the Bulletin for the *JSS* (57, 2 [1969]:382f.), says that Mr. Chandijya's study "has been written with originality. . . . It touches on many aspects of interest [in the poem] such as its rhetoric, its valuable historical references (some of which however should have been pointed out as never having been brought to light in standard histories to date), its scholastic knowledge of the Indian classics, such as the Mahābhārata which has been forgotten [in Siam] until comparatively late times when it became known here through English translations."

More recently Mr. Chandijya, after studying eight different manuscripts—some belonging to the National Library and some in his own collection—has published a critical edition of *YP*, with variant readings, a paraphrase in modern Siamese, and numerous glosses and annotations (see "CK" in our Bibliography, below). Prince Dhāni Nivat, in his review of this work (*JSS*, 59, 1 [1971]:277f.) says: "The method of editing the poem adopted by Krasèsindhu is to take each stanza, commenting first on the text, going on to the history and topography of each scene, and offering where possible a solution of problems arising from the text. One of the main difficulties of interpreting the poem is its archaic language. . . . Topographical references are often quite difficult because many names have disappeared since the time of the epic." Elsewhere in the same review Prince Dhāni says of the poem: "Obviously written as a panegyric, it has the additional merit of being accurate in historical facts, as the editor points out by referring to other available histories of the period."

The late W. A. R. Wood refers very briefly to the poem in his *History of Siam* (p. 83). There is a short notice of it, together with a French rendering of several stanzas, in Mr. P. Schweisguth's *Etude sur la littérature siamoise* (pp. 50–51). These are the only two references to it we have been able to discover in Western writers, though a more thorough search might perhaps disclose two or three more.

As a source for history, *YP* is mainly useful for the light it throws on the long struggle between King Paramatrailokanātha of Ayudhyā (r. 1448–1488) and King Tilokarāja of *Lân Nâ Tai* (r. 1441–1487), two monarchs whose names we shall shorten to Paramatrailoka and Tiloka respectively.

The anonymous author writes as a devout panegyrist of Paramatrailoka, depicting his rival as a villain, a coward, and ultimately a madman. Prince Dhāni (*JSS*, 59, 1:278) agrees with Mr. Chandijya that the author was probably Paramatrailoka's son, who was later known as Rāmādhipati II (r. 1491–1529). The poem closes with Paramatrailoka's victory in the battle of *Chieng Chün* in 1474/5, and we think it was very likely composed soon afterward.

The correct identification of Chieng Chün is naturally vital for a proper understanding of the poem. Prince Damrong identified it with some place in *Lampâng* province, either *Müang Lòng* or *Müang Tön* (*AA/RA*, p. 423), which was accepted by Wood (p. 89, n. 2.) But in a fleeting cross-reference to *AA/LP*, Prince Damrong seems to have noticed that it might be *Chalieng* (*AA/RA*, p. 425). Prince Chand Rajanī has definitely identified it with Chalieng, which is certainly right; we had reached the same conclusion independently; and Mr. Chandijya (*CK*, pp. 229f.) agrees too. At stanzas 168–170 the ruler of Chieng Chün, who is preparing to defend the city against an expected attack by Paramatrailoka's troops, addresses his men as follows:

"This city and its defenses are not the work of human hands alone, and access to it is difficult in five respects. While the approaches by land are everywhere firmly held by our close-packed forces of infantry, elephantry, and cavalry, the *Meng* Swamp first forms an obstacle at one end [of the city]; there is the River *Yom* with its rapids to screen us on one of the long sides; and three mountains almost completely shield the glorious city. Along its edges there is a deep triple moat, filled with barbed spikes; and it has laterite walls to protect it, stronger than walls of iron, with stockades beyond."

The description exactly fits the old city of Chalieng (Sajjanālaya), whose extensive ruins can still be seen on the right bank of the Yom about thirty-five miles north of Sukhodaya (see Map 2). The plan of the city is an irregular quadrilateral, one side of which runs along the riverbank. At this point in the river there is a series of treacherous rapids, known as *Gèng Luang* ('the great rapids') which would make it almost impossible to attack the city from the water. Near the upper end of the city, three mountains, *Kao Yai*, Suvarṇagiri, and *Pnom Plöng*, lie close together in a straight line running at right angles to the river: the first is outside the city walls but close to them, while the other two are inside the walls. The walls themselves, built with huge blocks of laterite, are over fifteen feet high.[1] Except along the river side, where the erosion of the bank has washed away the greater part, they are mostly in a good state of preservation. The remains of a

---

1. The date these walls were built is uncertain. Griswold (*Towards a History of Sukhodaya Art*, p. 57) has suggested that it was in the sixteenth century, after artillery came into general use, but it now seems certain to have been earlier, though they may not have been built up to their present height until then.

deep moat are clearly visible just outside the walls and parallel to them. At the lower end of the city a portion of the moat is wider than the rest, as if a swamp (the "Meng Swamp"?) had been drained and the watercourse canalized. We do not know whether there are any visible traces of a second and third moat in the thick bamboo forest beyond the main moat, or of auxiliary embankments.

In the late thirteenth and the fourteenth century this was the second most important city of the kingdom of Sukhodaya. At that time it was known as Sajjanālaya. From a military point of view it formed the northern bastion of the kingdom; and when the Sukhodayan provinces were incorporated into the kingdom of Ayudhyā it retained its importance. A little over a mile downstream from the "great rapids" the river makes a hairpin turn, within which, almost completely surrounded by water, is the place that is now more particularly called Chalieng (see Map 2). Some of the inscriptions of Sukhodaya make a distinction between Sajjanālaya and Chalieng; but later the two names are used interchangeably. In the Annals of Ayudhyā, the whole complex is called *Salieng*, which is a doublet of Chalieng; in the Chieng Mai Chronicle it is called Chalieng, except in one entry where it is called Chieng Chün; in *YP* it is called Chieng Chün, except in one place where it is called Chalieng. Of course any of these names can mean the province as well as the city; but when the context shows they mean a city it is clearly the walled city formerly known as Sajjanālaya rather than the place in the river bend downstream from it.

For the political and military events of the period from 1431 to 1474—the same period that *YP* deals with in poetry—we have two excellent chronicular sources of information. One is the "Luang Prasert Recension" of the Annals of Ayudhyā (*AA/LP*), which has often been printed in Siamese and has been translated into English (see *AA/LP* in our Bibliography, below). The other is the Chieng Mai Chronicle (CMC), composed in *Tai Yuan*, the language of Chieng Mai; the text in Tai Yuan script, which survives in a fair number of manuscripts, has never been printed; but a good French translation by Camille Notton appeared long ago (CMC/N), and a transcription in modren Siamese characters has recently been published by the Historical Commission (see CMC/HC in the Bibliography, below). *AA/LP* is dry and laconic in style, with a chronology that is generally recognized as authoritative. CMC, on the other hand, provides a full and lively narrative, with a chronology which, if not faultless, is at least reasonably satisfactory. The two histories, besides supplementing each other admirably, have the merit of giving us two contrary points of view[2].

---

2. Unfortunately the *Jinakālamālī*, which is one of the best of our chronicles, will be of little use to us, because the portion of it covering the period from 1455 to 1476 has dropped out of the text. For the regnal years of some of the kings of Lân Nà, as well as the dates of certain events, there is a discrepancy of one year between Jinakālamālī and the CMC; and in those cases we have adopted Jinakālamālī's dates.

In Section II we shall tell the story of the conflict, using *AA/LP* and CMC as our chief sources. The dates in *AA/LP* are given in the era called Cūlasakarāja (cs.), plus the designation of the year in the twelve-year cycle; we transpose these dates into the Christian Era (with a possible error of one year) by adding 638; but our references to the entries are *sub annis*, in cs. with the cyclical designation omitted. The dates in the CMC are given in terms of the ten and twelve-year cycles, which can be easily converted into cs., and we then transpose them into the Christian Era as above. Our references to the CMC are by the page numbers in CMC/N and CMC/HC.

II

In 1438, it is reported, a miracle occurred in the city of Biṣṇuloka. When the newly appointed Viceroy, Prince Rāmeśvara of Ayudhyā, went to do homage to the statue named Buddha Jinarāja, tears of blood were seen to fall from it eyes (*AA/LP, sub anno* 800).

The kingdom of Sukhodaya, which had formerly been one of the strongest powers in Southeast Asia, was now, after a bitter struggle followed by a period of humiliating vassalage, being incorporated into the kingdom of Ayudhyā.[3] The last vassal king of Sukhodaya had spent the final years of his life at Biṣṇuloka; and it appears that the statue, which was the palladium of the city, was weeping at his death and the fate of the kingdom.

Rāmeśvara was the prince who latter became King of Ayudhyā under the name Paramatrailoka and, as such, the hero of *YP*. He was a son of Paramarāja II (r. 1414–1448). According to *YP* he was born while his father was engaged in the invasion of Cambodia, which as we know from *AA/LP* (*sub anno* 793) was in 1431. He was therefore only seven years old when he took office as Viceroy. His father may have intended the appointment as a gesture of friendliness to the former ruling princes; but at the same time he showed, by placing the boy in such an exposed position, that he would tolerate no insubordination on their part.

These princes were, in fact, in a state of chronic disaffection, which now and then broke out into open revolt. Though their prerogatives were much reduced, they still wielded great influence and seem to have retained the fierce loyalty of their subjects. They still ruled the tributary cities; and though the suzerain could remove them at will, he might well hesitate to do so. If he replaced one of them with some other member of the same family, the appointee might prove no more amenable than his predecessor; while if he chose an official from his own bureaucracy for the post the appointee would be unlikely to command the loyalty of his subjects.

3. For the history of Sukhodaya, see our *Ep. and Hist. Studies*, Nos. 1–5, 7–10; also Griswold, *Towards a History of Sukhodaya Art*.

In ruling a conquered kingdom such dilemmas must have arisen constantly. At first, usually, the conqueror would not depose a vanquished ruler, but require him to take an oath of allegiance and let him continue to reign. The oath was much more than a mere formality, for the person who took it called on his ancestral spirits and all sorts of divinities to witness it, begging them to inflict the most terrible punishments on him if he should prove false. This system might work very well as long as everyone believed in it; but if two or three conspicuous violators of the oath happened to meet with success, others might be tempted to imitate them. Another weakness in the system was that an oath of allegiance, in the very nature of things, was a personal bond between the two parties, and if one of them died there was nothing to bind his successor to the other. Often, therefore, a change of ruler must have been the signal for open revolt.

The kingdom of Lân Nâ was as eager to wrest the Sukhodayan provinces from Ayudhyā as Ayudhyā was to keep them, and was always ready to foment trouble.

As a result Lân Nâ and Ayudhyā in the fifteenth century often fought each other, with the former kingdom of Sukhodaya as their main battleground and the chief prize they were contesting. A look at Map 1, and especially the riverine system that provided the readiest means of communication, will help us to understand the nature of the contest. (For the toponymy, see below, p. 161.)

Lân Nâ, stretching from the Salween to the *Mè Kóng* and straddling two watersheds, was the home of the branch of the *Tai* called the Yuan. It was a land of mountain and forest interspersed with rice-rich valleys and plains. Besides northern Siam it controlled *Chieng Tung* in the Shan States and, at least intermittently, the *Sip-sòng Pan-nâ*, the home of the *Tai Lü* in Yün-nan. The most remote city it laid claim to was *Chieng Rung*, on the Mè Kóng in the Sip-sòng Pan-nâ. Farther down the Mè Kóng lay *Chieng Sèn*, which was one of Lân Nâ's chief cities, and on its western tributaries lay two others, *Chieng Rài* and *Payao*. *Chieng Mai*, the capital, was on the *Ping*; *Lampûn* was on one of its tributaries; and *Lampâng*, the southeastern bastion of the kingdom, was on the *Wang*.

The heartland of Sukhodaya was the home of another branch of the Tai, the Syâm. Here the plains and valleys were broader, the mountains lower and less numerous. The old capital, Sukhodaya, lay at its center, on the Yom. Like Mount Meru surrounded by its four lesser peaks, it was surrounded by four bastion cities: Chalieng at the north, Biṣṇuloka at the east, Nagara Svarga at the south, and *Gampèng Pet* at the west. Chalieng, on the Yom upstream from Sukhodaya, was less than 75 crow-flight miles from Lampâng but separated from it by a watershed. Biṣṇuloka ('the realm of Viṣṇu') was otherwise known as *Sòng Kwè* ('the confluence'), apparently because it was there that the *Kwè Nòi* ('lesser branch') flowed into the *Nân* in those days; Gampèng Pet ('walls of adamant') was on the Ping, 175 crow-flight miles downstream from Chieng Mai but only 50 from Lân Nâ's southern boundary. At the junction of the two main branches of this system, where the Ping and the Nân flow together to form the great stream of the *Jao Prayâ*, lay Nagara Svarga, dominating the riverine communications between the western and eastern halves of the Sukhodayan heartland and its access to the sea, 150 miles to the south.

The kingdom of Ayudhyā, or Ayodhyā as it was then called, was founded in 1351 by Rāmādhipati I, by consolidating two inheritances which together controlled nearly all of Siam south of Nagara Svarga. He was probably a Tai, related to the Syām of Sukhodaya, but this kingdom was deeply impregnated with Mòn and Khmer culture, and the Tai were apparently a minority among his subjects.

In 1370, less than a year after his death, the throne was seized by his brother-in-law, Paramarāja I, who undertook to conquer the kingdom of Sukhodaya. Though Ayudhyā's resources were far greater than Sukhodaya's, it took him several years to do so, from which we may measure his ability as a general and the stubbornness of the defense. The king of Sukhodaya continued the struggle until 1378 when, after losing three of his bastion cities, Nagara Svarga, Biṣṇuloka, and Gampèng Pet, he was taken prisoner and forced to become a vassal of Ayudhyā. Sukhodaya later regained its independence, but was again reduced to vassalage around 1410. In the 1420's the last king of Sukhodaya, presumably in compliance with his suzerain's wish, transferred his capital from Sukhodaya to Biṣṇuloka, which was easily accessible by river from Ayudhyā. Biṣṇuloka, which doubtless gained rapidly in population and wealth at the expense of the former capital of Sukhodaya, was the obvious choice for the seat of the viceroy.

Because of its historic past the heartland of Sukhodaya was the focus of Tai nationalism. In order to dominate it, Ayudhyā had either to crush the restless vassals or to win their loyalty; and the latter, it seems, was the course that Rāmeśvara's advisers laid out for him.

Soon after his arrival at Biṣṇuloka, a Sukhodayan prince named Yudhiṣṭhira, who was only a few years older than Rāmeśvara, came to do homage to him. Yudhiṣṭhira was a member of the former ruling family, very likely a son of the deceased king whom he would have succeeded if the kingdom had not been abolished. As he was by far the highest-ranking person at Biṣṇuloka after Rāmeśvara, the two soon became friends.

One day Yudhiṣṭhira said to Rāmeśvara, "When you become King, what rank will you give me?" To which Rāmeśvara replied, "The rank of Viceroy ruling half of my kingdom." (CMC/N, 112; CMC/HC, 65.)

The answer, which meant he would give him the same post he himself was then occupying, must have satisfied Yudhiṣṭhira, for not long afterward he showed his devotion in battle to his suzerain Paramarājā II.

From here on we shall continue the story as nearly chronologically as possible, translating or summarizing the entries in *AA/LP* and CMC, and adding our own comments when necessary. For ease of reference we shall break up the narrative into parts, which we shall designate by numerals preceded by the sign §.

§1. In 1441 the Mahārāja *Sâm Fâng Gèn* of Lân Nâ was deposed by his sixth son, who mounted the throne in his place, assuming the title Mahārāja Tilokarāja.[4] The father, because of his affection for him, abdicated without protest, but some of his followers plotted to restore him and asked Paramarājā II for help. The next year Paramarājā, taking advantage of the request, invaded Lân Nâ, accompanied by Prince Yudhiṣṭhira and the vassal rulers of Sukhodaya and Gampèng Pet. Their forces were routed. In the retreat Yudhiṣṭhira arranged for Paramarājā to escape first, while he himself took charge of the rear guard to protect him (CMC/N, 102–109; CMC/HC, 59ff; cf. *AA/LP, sub anno* 804). Yudhiṣṭhira was probably about sixteen years old at the time.[5]

§2. In 1443 Tiloka set out to attack Nân, while his mother, taking the field in command of another army, prepared to attack *Prè*. At that time both Nân and Prè, which had been tributary to Sukhodaya in the late thirteenth century, were independent principalities. Tiloka wished to gain control of them to use as bases in future operations against Ayudhyā in the Sukhodayan heartland. Tiloka's mother, with the help of a sorcerer, quickly frightened the Prince of Prè into submission, and then allowed him to continue ruling the place as a vassal of Chieng Mai. It was not until 1449 that Tiloka succeeded in taking Nân; the defeated ruler fled to Chalieng; and his brother or nephew was installed as Lord of Nân under Tiloka's suzerainty. After the new ruler's death in 1459, Nân was ruled by officials appointed from Chieng Mai. (CMC/N, 110–111; CMC/HC, 64; Jinakālamālī, Cœdès's translation, *BEFEO*, 25 [1925]: 109, which seems to give the right date for Tiloka's conquest of Nân. For further details about the campaigns against Prè and Nân, and about Nân's relations with Sukhodaya and Chalieng, see our *Ep. and Hist. Studies*, No. 3, esp. pp. 99–107.)

§3. In 1448 Paramarājā II died and was succeeded by Rāmesvara, who took the regnal name Paramatrailoka (*AA/LP, sub anno* 810). Instead

---

4. He is of course the villain in *YP*.

5. Sixteen was the age at which a prince would normally be considered old enough to engage in combat. He cannot have been much older than that; according to the CMC (CMC/N, 112; CMC/HC, 65), he and Rāmesvara were "still children" when they became friends, presumably around 1438.

of giving Yudhiṣṭhira the viceroyalty he had promised him, he only made him Lord of Sòng Kwè (Biṣṇuloka), an appanage which amounted to no more than a provincial governorship. Yudhiṣṭhira, bitterly disappointed, sent a secret emissary to Chieng Mai, asking Tiloka to help him throw off the yoke of Ayudhyā and offering in return to become his vassal provided he were given a suitable rank. When Tiloka replied that he would regard him as his own son, the matter was settled (CMC/N, 112). In other words, Tiloka intended to dislodge the whole of the former kingdom of Sukhodaya from Ayudhyā and make Yudhiṣṭhira its viceroy under his suzerainty.

§4. In 1451, when everything was ready, Tiloka led an army to the gates of Biṣṇuloka. Yudhiṣṭhira, who had up to now kept his intentions well hidden, threw open the gates of the city to welcome him, taking the Ayudhyan troops completely by surprise. Having thus secured the eastern bastion, Tiloka set out with Yudhiṣṭhira to win the rest of the Sukhodayan provinces CMC/N, 113; CMC/HC, 65; cf. *AA/LP, sub anno* 813.)

All seemed to be going well for them, until Tiloka received word that the King of *Lân Châng* (Laos) was preparing to attack Chieng Mai. By this time the Ayudhyan troops were beginning to recover from their surprise, so Tiloka and Yudhiṣṭhira found themselves in acute danger. Realizing they could not even hold Biṣṇuloka, much less their new conquests, they retired northward, taking 10,000 of Yudhiṣṭhira's followers with them, as well as a large number of elephants, horses and slaves, and much treasure. (CMC/N, 113; CMC/HC, 65; this entry gives no reason for their decision to withdraw; we have taken the news of the impending attack on Chieng Mai from *RBY*, p. 230, which is more or less confirmed by the preceding and succeeding entries in CMC/N, 112, 114f., and CMC/HC, 64, 66f.)

One day, when they were camped at a place called Nam Lüm (?), they were attacked by a numerous body of troops from Chalieng, who captured over a thousand of Yudhiṣṭhira's men and nearly routed Tiloka' troops. Tiloka's mounted crossbowmen, using poisoned arrows, counterattacked and put the Chalieng troops to flight (CMC/N, 113f.; CMC/HC, 65f.).

"Nam Lüm" ('the river Lüm') was obviously somewhere near Chalieng, though we are unable to identify it (the name may be corrupt).[6] The Lord of Chalieng at this time was very likely a member of the royal family of Sukhodaya who had been retained as ruler of the northern bastion by the suzerain power. He was probably, though not certainly, the same person who defected to Tiloka in 1460 (see §7). Whoever he was, he was obviously still loyal to Paramatrailoka in 1451.

Eventually Tiloka and Yudhiṣṭhira managed to reach Chieng Mai. Though the expedition could hardly be called a success, Tiloka rewarded

---

6. *RBY* (p. 229) identifies it as a river named *Nam Rüm* near Gampèng Pet, which is of course impossible. At the time *RBY* was composed, the location of Chalieng was still uncertain.

Yudhiṣṭhira by making him Lord of Payao and another province to the north of it (CMC/N, 114; CMC/HC, 66). For the next five years Tiloka and Paramatrailoka were too busy with other matters to fight each other.

§5. In 1456, according to *AA/LP* (*sub anno* 818), Paramatrailoka prepared an army to conquer *Li-sop-Tîn*; then, after reinforcing the army, he established headquarters at *Kón*. (The name Li-sop-Tîn, which is corrupt, apparently refers to the confluence of the *Lî* with another river, in the southern part of Lampûn province; Kón was on the Ping, about halfway between Gampèng Pet and Nagara Svarga.) According to the CMC (N, 115–117, HC, 66ff.) he was encouraged in his plans because one of his spies had told him that the bulk of Tiloka's forces were engaged far to the north, leaving the home country virtually undefended. He learned too late that his spy had been tricked, for when he invaded Lân Nâ, Tiloka's men lay in wait for him and beat him badly. What really happened is not clear, because *AA/LP*, after recording the plans for the invasion, says nothing about the invasion itself, while the CMC (N, 117–120; HC, 67ff.) describes an invasion in 1457 which contains at least one patent impossibility. According to this account, Paramatrailoka and his son Indarājā, accompanied by the vassal rulers of Gampèng Pet and Sukhodaya, set out to attack Prè and Lampâng; Tiloka lay in wait for them in a camp on the bank of the Rājadhānī river (the Yom), with large forces commanded by his son *Bun Rüang*, Yudhiṣṭhira, *Mün Dong*, and others. Yudhiṣṭhira fought three elephant duels in succession against Indarājā and the vassal Lords of Sukhodaya and Gampèng Pet. Later in the battle Indarājā was wounded in the face by an arrow.

If Paramatrailoka was born in 1431, his son Indarājā cannot have been old enough to fight in 1457. *AA/LP*, which does not mention this battle, reports another one, fought near Sukhodaya in 1463, in which Indarājā was wounded in the face by an arrow (see below, §9). As we can hardly believe that he was wounded in this manner in two different battles, we might guess that the CMC has put the battle too early and in the wrong locality; but apart from Indarājā's presence the account follows so naturally on *AA/LP*'s and CMC's entries for 1456 that we are reluctant to reject it altogether. A battle may really have been fought near Prè in 1457, but some of the details may be wrongly interpolated from the battle near Sukhodaya in 1463, which has dropped out of the CMC altogether.

Mün Dong, who makes his first appearance in the CMC in the account of the battle near Prè, was one of Tiloka's most capable and devoted commanders. He plays an important part in *YP*. His full appellation was Mün Dong *Nagara* (for the title "Mün," see our note to stanza 69 in Section IV, below), and he was the Lord of Lampâng (a place often called "Nagara" for short). Some writers have confused him with his predecessor as Lord of

Lampâng, *Mün Lók* Nagara, who was Tiloka's uncle. It is possible that Mün Dong was Mün Lók's grandson, which would make him Tiloka's cousin; but he may not have been related to him at all.

§6. In 1459, as well as we can make out from a corrupt passage in the CMC (N, 120; HC, 69), Tiloka advanced on Sòng Kwè (Bisṇuloka); Paramatrailoka shut himself up in the city, together with the vassal Lord of Gampèng Pet, and stayed there for a long time, while Tiloka besieged the place. Finally the Lord of Gampèng Pet slipped out of the city by night, and Paramatrailoka also escaped. He was followed by the Chieng Mai troops, who killed many of his men.

The next morning Mün Dong asked Tiloka's permission to pursue Paramatrailoka and capture him alive, but Tiloka refused, on the grounds that his enemy had already suffered enough. Then he took his troops back to Chieng Mai, where he rewarded Yudhiṣṭhira by bestowing the provinces of *Ngao* and Prè on him as appanages in addition to those he already held (CMC/N, 120; cf. CMC/HC, 70). By this time the vassal Prince of Prè (see §2) must have died or been removed, and Yudhiṣṭhira was being appointed to replace him, not only as a reward but doubtless also to prepare a secure base for the next year's campaign (§7). Ngao was between Prè and Yudhiṣṭhira's principal appanage, Payao (see §4).

§7. According to *AA/LP* (*sub annis* 822, 823), the Lord of Salieng (Chalieng) revolted and went over to Tiloka with all his followers in 1460; the next year he escorted Tiloka to attack Bisṇuloka, but as they did not succeed they deviated to Gampèng Pet; then Tiloka, being unable to take the city in a week, returned with his army to Chieng Mai.

In an entry dated 1458/9, but inserted after the entry for 1459, the CMC (N, 122–123; HC, 70–71) tells the same story a little differently, and with some additional details. Tiloka and Mün Dong were pursuing Paramatrailoka, who was in retreat. On the way Tiloka received the submission of the Lord of Chalieng, who was so terrified of him that he asked to be accepted as his vassal. After making unsuccessful attacks on Sòng Kwè and another place (Gampèng Pet?), Tiloka came back and confirmed the Lord of Chalieng as ruler of the province under his suzerainty. Then he returned to Chieng Mai with his troops, assigning Mün Dong the duty of supervising the Lord of Chalieng's administration of Chalieng.[7]

The bitterness with which the author of *YP* speaks of the Lord of Chalieng, for example at stanza 102, shows what a serious matter the loss of the principality was for Paramatrailoka.

---

7. The CMC seems to imply that Mün Dong was left at Chalieng in charge of a garrison (CMC/N, 123; CMC/HC, 71), but the account of subsequent events suggests that he was supposed to withdraw and keep in touch with affairs at Chalieng from a polite distance; so there may be a hidden lacuna in CMC. *RBY* (p. 236) says he was sent to *Ṭâk* to keep in touch with these affairs; but we think Ṭâk would be awkwardly placed for such a purpose; and his home town of Lampâng seems more likely.

In 1461, the CMC continues (CMC/N, 123–124; CMC/HC, 71), the Lord of Chalieng plotted to betray Tiloka. He invited Mün Dong to a cockfight at his palace, intending to kill him; but Mün Dong, seeing through the plot, surrounded the palace with his own men, seized him, and took him to Chieng Mai. Tiloka sent him to Müang Hâng (?), where he died. The province of Chalieng, which his removal left without a ruler, was bestowed on Mün Dong by Tiloka, in addition to Lampâng which he already ruled.

In *AA/RA*'s account of the Lord of Chalieng's defection (*AA/RA*, p. 108), there is a hidden lacuna, which caused the author of *RBY* to confuse the two vassal lords who deserted Ayudhyā in favor of Chieng Mai; this in turn has led other historians to do a posthumous injustice to Yudhiṣṭhira (cf. Prince Damrong's annotations in *AA/RA*, pp. 422, 440, etc.; Wood, *History of Siam*, pp. 87–89); and the impression is now somewhat general that the "Lord of Chalieng" and Yudhiṣṭhira were one and the same man. But a careful reading of *AA/LP* and the CMC shows there is really no room for confusion. Sòng Kwè (Biṣṇuloka) and Chalieng are two entirely different places, about seventy miles apart. Our principal source of information about Yudhiṣṭhira, the CMC, regularly calls him *Prayâ Sòng Kwè*, 'the Lord of Sòng Kwè', several times adding his personal name in a slightly garbled form. He was a brave man and an extremely proud one, a patriot by his own lights, deeply resentful of the humiliation heaped on the formerly brilliant kingdom of Sukhodaya by the Ayudhyan overlord. After being disappointed in his early hope that Paramatrailoka might grant the Sukhodayan provinces a greater measure of freedom, he had no reason whatever to be loyal to Ayudhyā. He went over to Tiloka in 1451, and lived at least until 1476, as we know from an inscribed statue which he cast in that year.[8] On the other hand, we have very little information about the anonymous person who is known to us only as "Prayâ Chalieng" (or Salieng). It is not clear whether he participated in the harassing action against Tiloka and Yudhiṣṭhira which was launched from Chalieng when they were retreating northward in 1451 (see §4). In any case he was frightened into joining Tiloka in 1460; he plotted to betray his new master a year or so later; he was exiled to Müang Hâng (?); and he died there, apparently soon after.

§8. Sukhodaya must have joined in the revolt against Paramatrailoka, because in 1462, as we learn from *AA/LP* (*sub anno* 824), the Kralāhoma attacked Sukhodaya and reduced the city to submission as of old. The Kralāhoma was one of Paramatrailoka's highest officers, his post being approximately equivalent to Minister of War.

§9. In 1463, as we gather from *AA/LP* (*sub anno* 825), Paramatrailoka transferred his capital to Biṣṇuloka in order to protect his northern frontier

8. For a further account of Yudhiṣṭhira, and the statue he cast in 1476, see Griswold, "Prince Yudhiṣṭhira," *AA*, 26, 3–4 (1963):215ff. and figs. 3–5.

more effectively, at the same time appointing his son (Indarāja?) to rule at Ayudhyā as regent with the title Paramarāja.[9] The same entry in *AA/LP* goes on to say that at that time the Mahārāja *Tâo Lûk* (Tiloka[10]) came with his army to take Sukhodaya, so Paramatrailoka and Indarāja went to defend the city; (Inda)rāja defeated the army of Prince Thiara (Yudhiṣṭhira); his army then encountered that of Mün (Dong) Nagara, and he fought an elephant duel with him; there was a great tumult, the Lâo soliders surrounded the royal elephant with four elephants of their own, and Indarāja was wounded in the face by an arrow; the Mahārāja's army then retreated (*AA/LP, sub anno* 825). Note that this passage appears to be corrupt, and it may have been wrongly placed in the entry for cs. 825; cf. above, §5.

§10. In 1464 Paramatrailoka built the Cuḷāmaṇī Monastery, about three miles south of Biṣṇuloka (*AA/LP, sub anno* 826). This monastery, the ruins of which are still visible, stood far enough away from the town to qualify as an establishment of Forest-Dwellers (Araññavāsī). According to the CMC (CMC/N, 124f.; CMC/HC, 72), Paramatrailoka, realizing he could not defeat Tiloka, decided to make friends with him, turn the throne over to Indarāja, and become a monk. Before being ordained, he sent envoys to Tiloka, asking for an alliance. Tiloka refused; but in accordance with custom, he sent him the "Eight Requisites" of monastic life (robes, almsbowl, etc.); and he also sent twelve monks of the sect of Forest-Dwellers to participate in his ordination. Paramatrailoka was ordained in 1465 at the Cuḷāmaṇī Monastery, as we know from a stone inscription, dating from 1681, which is still preserved there (the text is printed at the end of *AA/LP*). The inscription adds that the Kings of Lân Châng, Chieng Mai, and Haṁsāvatī sent him the Eight Requisites. Around March 1466 his son and the ministers of state requested him to leave the monkhood and resume his throne, so he complied and proceeded to Ayudhyā.

According to the CMC (CMC/N, 125–132; CMC/HC, 72–75) he did not devote himself entirely to piety while he was a monk. First he sent Tiloka a message asking for the province of Chalieng to furnish rice for almsfood; but Tiloka called an assembly of Chieng Mai monks, who said that such a request, coming from a king who was now a monk, was quite improper.

9. *AA/LP* says, *sub anno* 825: "H. M. Paramatrailoka went to reign at Biṣṇuloka appointing the King to reign at Ayudhyā under the name Samtec Paramarāja." Though the appointee was what we should call a regent, he technically became a king as soon as he assumed office at Ayudhyā. He was a son of Paramatrailoka, probably the same son who was called Indarāja before his appointment; both CMC/N (p. 124) and CMC/HC (p. 72) imply that he was Indarāja. In any case, he was the son who, after Paramatrailoka's death in 1488, reigned as Paramarāja III at Biṣṇuloka until his own death in 1491, after which the capital was transferred back to Ayudhyā.

10. *Lûk* is here a doublet of *Lok*, designating Tiloka, who was the sixth (*lok*) son of his father; O. Frankfurter (*JSS*, 6, 3 [1909]:6) mistakenly translates: "the Mahārāj sent his son . . . "

Then Paramatrailoka sent for a Burmese monk, who had a reputation as a magician, to make Tiloka powerless. From one of Paramatrailoka's spies, who knew Chieng Mai well, the magician learned that in the northeast quarter there was a huge banyan tree which was the *Sî Müang*, the 'luck [śrī] of the city'. He then went to Chieng Mai, where he gained Tiloka's confidence because his advice proved uniformly good and caused the country to prosper. At length Tiloka asked him if he knew some magic that would fulfill his wish to become a great conqueror. The magician said he could indeed make him ruler of all Jambūdvīpa (India and Southeast Asia) like King Aśoka, but he warned that it would be extremely sinful and make Tiloka incur very bad karma (which would bring him misfortune in future lives). Tiloka did not hesitate on that account, so the magician explained what had to be done. A palace was to be built, in the form of a lion, in the northeast quarter where the Sî Müang spirit resided. In order to do so the site was to be cleared of all trees, the adjacent parts of the city wall were to be razed, the moat filled in, and the place made perfectly level. Tiloka was to keep grilled rice and flowers over his bed when the palace was finished. If an enemy approached, all he had to do was to tap on whichever side of the house post the danger was coming from, and the enemy would be routed instantly. Everything was done as the magician ordered; the palace buildings were erected at the places he indicated; and the palace latrine was installed on the spot where the banyan had stood. In 1466 when the palace was finished the officials and vassals performed the ceremony of investiture on Tiloka to enable him to conquer all Jambūdvīpa.

§11. Instead of bringing success, the operation infuriated the Sî Müang spirit, and all sorts of misfortunes followed. Among other things, according to the CMC (CMC/N, 132; CMC/HC, 75), Tiloka's queen falsely accused his son Bun Rüang of plotting a rebellion; Tiloka relegated him to a provincial governorship; then the queen urged Tiloka to have him executed; and it was only afterward that Tiloka learned Bun Rüang was innocent. The CMC, without precisely saying so, implies that he was put to death. A separate passage (CMC/N, 135; CMC/HC, 78) says that Tiloka and the queen went to the Shan country in 1470, and adds: "Bun Rüang, the ruler of Chieng Râi, died in the Shan country during this trip."

It appears, however, that not everyone considered Bun Rüang innocent, because *AA/LP* (*sub anno* 830) says he seized the city of Chieng Mai from Tiloka in 1468. *AA/LP* does not mention Bun Rüang's death, but *YP* clearly says he was executed.

§12. Soon after resuming his throne Paramatrailoka sent an embassy to Chieng Mai, ostensibly to offer Tiloka presents, but really to find out how well the magician's schemes were working, and also to try some further means to bewitch Tiloka. Tiloka gave a dinner at the palace in honor of the envoys, during which the vice-ambassador was caught stealing a gold vase.

The envoys were thereupon expelled; and on their way home they were assassinated by Tiloka's men (CMC/N, 132–134; CMC/HC, 76f.).

§13. For the period following Paramatrailoka's retirement from the monkhood, both *AA/LP* and the CMC are rather reticent about the struggle between Ayudhyā and Lân Nâ. For the year cs. 835 (approximately from April 1473 to April 1474), *AA/LP* has a cryptic entry which, translated as literally as possible, seems to mean that Mün Dong stripped the gold leaf off an image of the Buddha and used it to coat the hilt of his sword: certainly an impious act, but one whose significance in the context of *AA/LP* is not clear.[11]

§14. According to a terse entry in *AA/LP* for cs. 836 (approximately April 1474 to April 1475), the King of Ayudhyā conquered Salieng (Chalieng). According to *AA/LP*'s entry for the following year, the Mahārāja asked to enter into friendship (sc. Tiloka asked the King of Ayudhyā for a truce).

The entry for cs. 836 in CMC/N (pp. 135–136) is too defective to be of any use. The entry for the same year in CMC/HC (p. 78), being based on a better manuscript, makes more coherent reading. It may be translated:

In the year *gâp sangâ*, sakarāja 836, Mün Dong, the ruler of Chieng Chün [Chalieng], died. Mün *Kwèn*, the ruler of *Chè Hom* [a district in Lampâng province], was sent to rule Chieng Chün in his place, and Mün *Gòng*, the ruler of Chieng Lü [Chieng Rung], was sent to rule Nagara [Lampâng]. In that year the King of Sukhodaya came with an army to attack Chieng Chün, killed Mün Kwèn the ruler of Chieng Chün, and recaptured Chieng Chün. At that time the ruler of Nagara [Mün Gòng, ruler of Lampâng], who went to supervise affairs at Chieng Chün, took flight and escaped.

After this entry—the sense of which we shall later try to extract by relating it to information from *YP*—the CMC passes on to other matters; no truce is mentioned; and we hear nothing more about Chieng Chün.

III

Yuan Pâi is written in a particular form of *Klóng* (gloṅ) known as Elephant's Feet (pāda kuñjara). Each stanza has four lines; and each line

11. Frankfurter (*ibid.*, p. 7) translates: "presented gold threads to cover the sword" and glosses the expression as "acknowledged the sovereignty"; but we cannot see anything about gold threads in the entry, and even if we could, we can see no reason why it should imply acknowledging anyone's sovereignty. Some scholars have recently suggested that the use of a sword with a gold hilt was a royal prerogative, so that if a vassal coated the hilt of his sword with gold he was setting himself up as an independent monarch. The explanation appears plausible; but as *YP*, an Ayudhyan source which is certainly as reliable as *AA/LP* in this matter, gives a circumstantial account of Mün Dong's extreme devotion to Tiloka, we may well doubt if Mün Dong was guilty. Perhaps the author of *AA/LP* was misled by a report circulated by Tiloka.

has five syllables plus an expletive of either two or four syllables. Certain syllables must have the *mai-ék* accent, certain others the *mai-tó*. The second syllable of the expletive rhymes with the third, fourth, or fifth syllable (usually the fifth) of the next line but one, continuing indefinitely from stanza to stanza.[12] Ornaments such as alliteration and internal rhymes are added at will.

As a work of literature *YP* is powerful and exciting. Though a good deal of it is incomprehensible, everyone admires it—which proves the author's remarkable skill. He is more impressionistic than explicit. In his description of the great battle, for example, there is a marvelous sense of tumult and confusion which leaves the reader as bewildered as the soldiers who got separated from their units. Of course there is no attempt to bring Paramatrailoka to life as an individual; as convention requires, he is godlike and rather abstract, as in some majestic bas-relief portraying scenes of worship and vast battles. Tiloka is more picturesque; while the Chieng Mai Chronicle depicts him as headstrong, ruthless, vengeful, and madly ambitious—but at the same time generous, energetic, and sometimes chivalrous—the poet allows him no redeeming qualities whatever. Several of Tiloka's officials, of whom we are given short but vivid glimpses, are crafty schemers like himself. The outstanding exception is Mün Nagara, a man of perfect honor who goes knowingly to his death rather than disobey his impossible master. The poet obviously admires him even though he belongs to the enemy, and gives a touching accout of him.

YP, being a poetical composition, naturally gives no dates, only a sequence of events. But by referring to *AA/LP*, to the CMC, and occasionally to other sources, we have been able to establish a reasonably satisfactory chronology for them. The process has given us a good deal of respect for the historicity of the poem. Of course the poet glosses over certain things in which Paramatrailoka would not show up to the best advantage; of course he transforms minor successes into brilliant victories; of course he fabricates speeches and conversations. But the events he recounts, so far as we can check them, actually occurred. We are therefore inclined to accept his testimony on three matters for which he is our sole source: (1) that Paramatrailoka was born during his father's campaign against Cambodia (stanzas 61, 62), which *AA/LP* places in 1431; (2) that a monk from Ceylon was present at Paramatrailoka's ordination at Biṣṇuloka) (stanza 76), which *AA/LP* places in 1465; (3) and that Mün Nagara did not die a natural death but was executed by Tiloka (stanza 124, 125), whereas the CMC, in recording his death in 1474, says nothing of its cause.

---

12. For short descriptions of this verse form, see R. B. Jones and R. C. Mendiones, *Introduction to Thai Literature* (Ithaca, 1970), p. 205, and Schweisguth, *Etude sur la littérature siamoise*, p. 23.

A careful study of *YP* would certainly add to our knowledge of several phases of Siamese life in the fifteenth century—above all, warfare, military organization, and tactics; but also Court protocol, statecraft, civil administration, and so on.

As our present purpose is not to study the poem for matters of this sort, or as literature, but to see what historical information we can extract from it, we have translated only those portions which seem to us to be pertinent, contenting ourselves with a short summary of the remainder. In order to make reference easier, we have numbered the stanzas (our numbering corresponds to CK's).

In one respect the design of the poem is rather odd: the period from 1451 to 1466 is covered twice. At stanza 61 the poet says he will begin by outlining the story in verse; but in fact the outline he gives from there to stanza 80 covers only the period from 1431 to 1466; so we wonder whether there was not originally some material following stanza 80, now lost, which carried the outline up to 1474. At stanza 83, after two stanzas of eulogy, he says he will relate the main subject of the poem in more detail, whereupon he goes back to 1451 and continues the narrative in more or less chronological sequence up to and including the events of 1474/5, with which the poem ends.

In our translation, or perhaps we should say paraphrase, we have aimed above all at clarity. To achieve it is no easy task: the vocabulary includes many words that are lacking in all dictionaries known to us, or used in senses that are lacking in them; the syntax is eccentric, sometimes to the point that we are uncertain which is the subject of a verb and which the object; and in places the text is so corrupt that we have either to guess at the meaning or give up altogether. Because of such difficulties, a great deal of our rendering is conjectural, but we call the reader's attention to our perplexity only when it seems most urgent. We have ruthlessly jettisoned a great number of honorifics, epithets, and literary flourishes. Whatever string of honorifics may be applied to Paramatrailoka, we render the lot as "His Majesty" or "the King" (with a capital *K*). The poet usually refers to Tiloka as "the Yuan king" or "the Lâo king," and this is the example we regularly follow (writing "king" with a small letter so as to distinguish him clearly from Paramatrailoka). Though the term "Lâo" properly designates the Lâo who have given their name to Laos, the author of *YP*, in common with other Ayudhyan writers, uses it as equivalent to "Yuan."

In the notes to Section IV, the numerals at the beginning of each refer to the stanza numbers we have given in brackets in the poem. The references preceded by § and a numeral are to the corresponding parts in Section II.

IV

THE DEFEAT OF THE YUAN

[1. Eulogy of Paramatrailoka]

[The first fifty-two stanzas contain the opening eulogy of Paramatrailoka. He is compared in turn to eleven great gods of Hinduism—Brahmā, Viṣṇu, Śiva, Indra, Yama, Marut (the wind god), Varuṇa (the rain god), Agni (the fire god), Upendra (Kṛṣṇa), the Sun, and the Moon—and declared to be a mixture of all of them (stanzas 1–11). His remarkable qualities are extolled in relation to the symbolism of numbers from one to ten (stanzas 12–31). He is then compared to various gods, whose powers and functions are discussed (stanzas 32–36). His knowledge of the śāstras, āgamas, etc., and his other accomplishments are compared to those of different gods; for example he is as steadfast in battle as Arjuna, as cunning as Kṛṣṇa, and as expert in archery as Rāma (stanzas 37–40). He is unsurpassed in his knowledge of military affairs, including strategy, surprise attacks, sieges of cities, tricks for attacking and tricks for escaping; he is unrivaled in the useful arts, in intelligence, in sweetness of voice in chanting, in knowledge of ancient customs, etc. (stanzas 41–52). In stanzas 53–60 the author apologizes for his own deficiencies as a poet and expresses his hopes for good fortune, etc.]

[2. The Poet's Synopsis of Events from 1431 to 1466]

[61] First we shall outline the story in verse.

We tell how His Majesty's father invaded Yaśodhara, [62] how His Majesty's mother gave him birth in an open field at Tāṃpal braḥ Udaya, and how the army advanced to capture the glorious city. [63] The city was sacked; everything was brought to the divine capital, Ayodhyā; and the King placed a son on the throne [of Cambodia].

[64] When the King died and went to heaven, the abode of the gods, his remains were honored by his grieving son [Paramatrailoka]. [65] The latter, who ruled his people justly, making Ayodhyā more blissful than heaven, erected a stupa for [the relics of] the deceased monarch, [66] and invited monks from all over the country to assemble [to dedicate it].

We tell how the Lâo came down to Jayanāda [Biṣṇuloka] because Yudhiṣṭhira deserted, [67] how His Majesty, upon being informed, went there with his heart set on capturing the Lâo king [Tiloka], and how the Lâo king was brought to grief after some of his men, learning the news [that they were in danger], saved their lives by running away. [68] His Majesty's brave men followed the enemy to attack and harass them, fought the bewildered Lâo whom they overtook at the River *Lip*, and vanquished them.

[69] [We tell] how the rebellious *Sèn*, almost choking to death [with fright?], went over to the enemy, delivering his province to them, and how the Lâo king intended to get his revenge by helping him in his revolt. [70] His Majesty, coming on a pleasure trip to the north without knowing that the man had rebelled, learned the news only when he arrived with his swift boats. [71] He entered Jayanāda [Biṣṇuloka] to resist the foe, showing the wisdom of Mahosadha, and started to harass the enemy, who were unable to hold out and retired of their own accord.

[72] His Majesty proceeded everywhere in the region without fear of any lord, presenting the monks with gifts, a hundred of each kind, and distributing the merit to others. [73] Then he returned, leaving his troops at their posts, and commanded an officer with the rank of *Kun Mün* to capture Sukhodaya, which he easily did. [74] Chieng Chün was in distress and its people trembled because His Majesty's power, being widely reported, struck fear into their hearts. [His men,] moving in swiftly, seized [a huge quantity of] rice so as to make the price expensive for the enemy.

[75] When his mother died and went to heaven, which is set with jeweled spires, he split off the southern [?] part of his city and presented it to the Lord Buddha.

[76] When His Majesty, bent on abstaining from sin and seeking merit, [decided to enter the monkhood,] his son went to Ceylon to invite a saintly monk [to come to Biṣṇuloka for the ordination]. [77] Ardent in promoting virtue and exposing evil, His Majesty, after renouncing the throne and the kingship, received his ordination as gracefully as the Omniscient Ones, which brought bliss to the kingdom, [78] and the news caused all mankind to strew flowers [in celebration]; but the arrogant foe swaggered while heaven and earth praised His Majesty.

[79] His Majesty's officers and his son, saluting him respectfully, invited and begged him to watch over them; so he retired from the monkhood and resumed the throne; and all the kingdoms and vassals paid him tribute. [80] He built a residence called the Buddhaiśvarya; and he erected a wall at Biṣṇuloka so that it would be easy for him to bear down and kill the enemy.

[We omit from our translation stanzas 81 and 82, which are eulogies of Paramatrailoka, serving to mark the end of Part 2.]

[3. Campaigns in the Sukhodayan Provinces, 1451–c. 1463]

[83] Now we shall relate in more detail the main subject of our poem. After His Majesty showed his power by coming to strike down the Lâo who greedily stole the place [Biṣṇuloka] when Yudhiṣṭhira, transferring

his allegiance to the enemy, [84] treacherously welcomed [the Lâo king] who, swaggering boldly, came to stay in the good city, and the unexpected news arrived that His Majesty, having raised an army, was hastening forward, [85] the Lâo king was terrified and turned as pale as death. If he stayed in the city he was afraid he could not defend it, so in his fear he moved his army out, fleeing from His Majesty in utter defeat, [86] swaying like an elephant beaten by a lion, reeling like a nāga beaten by a garuḍa, and rushing to escape like Vaipacitti, the King of Asuras, slipping away from Indra.

[87] His Majesty, skilled in warfare, followed, attacking the routed army, displaying his might like the god Viṣṇu, the whirr [of whose arrows] is enough to overturn Mount Meru. [88] His Majesty, moving his ele-phantry and his troops boldly forward, destroyed the Yuan army utterly after overtaking them at the River Lip. [89] Then he drew back his elephantry and cavalry to his own city [Biṣṇuloka], like the mighty Pāṇḍava at whose terrible reputation the Kaurava people grew sick with fear. [90] His Majesty remained there long enough to bestow rewards on his army of a hundred thousand brave men. Possessing great wisdom, by which he could distinguish absolutely between honest men and traitors, [91] he appointed the governor of his palace to replace Yudhiṣṭhira and rule the province [of Biṣṇuloka]. Then he moved his army back [92] to the glorious capital, Ayodhyā, resuming the throne and the overlordship of the kingdom.

Long afterward His Majesty, wishing to take a pleasure trip to the north, [93] prepared swift boats and set out expecting to enjoy himself, for the news of his vassal [the Lord of Chalieng] had been concealed from him. [94] Then upon his arrival he learned that the false-hearted villain had betrayed him. His Majesty, heroic and powerful, was not to be despised in the slightest degree. [95] When the envious ruler devised evil tricks against him, he frustrated them all, like Kṛṣṇa destroying the weapons of Duryodhana's warriors, so that he could not withstand him and retired of his own accord. [96] The Lâo troops, having come to grief, and shivering in a panic, ran away without looking back, for fear of being killed, while the Lâo king, hiding his fright, tried to look composed. Some of his men escaped with their lives, but with faces like the white of an egg. [97] His Majesty advanced his massed troops rapidly to attack and lay waste the famous might of the Lâo, moving boldly like Indra assaulting the foe, [98] and quickly deploying his troops everywhere. The enemy were so downcast and sick at heart that it was easy for His Majesty to bear down and kill them.

[99] Later on, His Majesty placed an officer who was skilled in warfare in command of an army to capture Sukhodaya, [which he did] with the snap of a finger. It was widely reported that the Lâo were secretly sad,

shaking their heads [in perplexity], [100] and the Lâo king, frightened and downhearted, dreaded His Majesty, since a ruler like himself dared not fight to take the city [of Biṣṇuloka], and even when he got it by stealth he could not hold it long.

[101] His Majesty, whose renown spread its rays farther than the rays of the sun, proceeded [to Biṣṇuloka] to display his authority.

[102] The Sèn, hard-pressed and half unconscious, was examined and all his tricks were counted. By the force of his evil plotting to forsake His Majesty he was ruined by his own crimes. He died, leaving the memory of unspeakable guilt behind him.

[103] At that time the Mahārāja [Tiloka] appointed Mün Nagara to restore Chieng Chün to its former status and to place his bravest men all around its borders. [104] Fearing His Majesty's army might attack, [Tiloka] reinforced the city, and then, after entrusting it to his officer [Mün Nagara], he withdrew his own troops and returned [to Chieng Mai].

[4. Tiloka's Madness, c. 1468; Execution of Mün Nagara, 1474]

[105] From that time on, the Lâo king [Tiloka], exhausted and sick at heart, acted like a madman. Everything he did seemed strange beyond words, his heart ached as if pierced by thorns, and he turned to brutalities of every kind. [106] For example, he was so afraid someone might usurp his throne that he had his beloved son Bun Rüang arrested and executed.

[107] Long ago the greedy Lâo king had arrogantly wronged his own father [Sâm Fâng Gèn], even though the father, trying to find some good in one who came from a good family, treated him indulgently.

[108] [Now,] seeing that Mün Nagara—the admirable officer who was loyal and devoted to him—was braver and more intelligent than himself, and respected by the rulers of all countries, [109] the Lâo king reflected in his heart that he detested him, fearing that he might revolt. Though [Mün Nagara] had done nothing wrong, [Tiloka] pretended to be angry, for he wished to kill his faithful and experienced officer. [110] He secretly sent word to the [rulers of] Nân and Prè to send him a lying message; and they, wishing to take advantage [of Mün Nagara] because of jealousy, collaborated together to fabricate this message, which had no truth in it: [111] "Your Majesty:—*Âi Dang* is scheming to desert your exalted Lordship and leave the country. There can be no doubt whatever that he is about to leave, so do not delay for a moment!"

[112] When the Lâo king understood their crafty trick, he immediately praised them for being on his side, and said: "Let us not divulge the matter at all. When the man comes we shall have him put to death to fulfill our wish." [113] Thereupon he sent for a very wily official and gave him instructions full of every sort of ruse, [adding]: "Go without fail to Chieng

Chün, find the gallant Mün, and have him come here at once!" [114] With that, the eager official, quickly discerning the plot, and fixing all the king's instructions precisely in his mind, hurried off to Chieng Chün in accordance with the king's command, selecting words that would be suitable in every way. [115] [When he arrived at Chieng Chün he addressed Mün Nagara in these words]: "*Dâm Prâ* and *Pân Pât* are striving to do evil; Nân and Prè have joined together to revolt against the king; and I have a secret command from him to find you, valiant Sir, and have you return with all speed." [116] In accordance with the perfidious king's instructions [he added]: "He regards you alone as his eldest son. Please go in time to protect him by killing the evildoers. [117] It is said that a king who is kept waiting for his troops is ill at ease." When Mün Nagara had heard him, everything was clear, because he saw through all aspects of the plot to deceive him. Then he spoke deliberately: [118] "Sir, do not waste time trying to cajole me with tricks and lies. In accordance with the urgent command you bring, I shall go. . . . [119] If any officer of the king is killed because of his devotion to his master, he will have been a man during his lifetime in this world, and in the next world he will be surrounded by as many heavenly nymphs as Indra. [120] When anyone the king has raised up and made rich is disloyal to him, then even if he were to live a hundred thousand years it would be as if he were dead, and when he dies he will go to hell. [121] It would not be right for me to think of staying here; I must hasten to the king and make obeisance to him. Even if he arrests me and then kills me, let it be so. Let the report be spread that I am totally loyal to my master."

[122] Thinking thus, he went quickly [to Chieng Mai]. After doing obeisance to the king, he spoke fearlessly: "As for those who hate me and conspire to accuse me of doing wrong, whoever they may be, I beg you, Sire, to reflect upon the matter."

[123] The Lâo king exploded with rage, and roared down [from his throne]: "Don't delay by asking questions about the case; everything is clear. If I so much as drop my hand, the ground you stand on will rock. [124] There is evil everywhere! If I were to point it all out, when would I come to the end? You are a parasitic vine growing all over the tree. I have caught you trying to thwart me many times. Now I can hold back no longer!"

[124a] He commanded *Sèn Fâ Rüa* to arrest Mün Nagara for secret disloyalty: "Sèn, you are to cut off his head, put it on a stake, and place it at the borderline between the north and the south." [124b] Sèn Fâ Rüa, after doing obeisance with his hands, carried out the command. He tied [Mün Nagara's] elbows [behind his back], hurried away in response to the king's wrath, cut off [Mün Nagara's] head, and put it on a stake

exactly as [the king had commanded]. All the rulers of provinces and towns were sick at heart at the frightful news.

[5. Chieng Chün Submits to Paramatrailoka but Is Lost Again]

[125] The ruler of Chieng Chün, Lady *Nâng Mün Non Müang*, was overwhelmed and convulsed with grief, and all the Chieng Mai people [in Chieng Chün] felt the pain of being abandoned, as if their hearts were torn out. [126] Nâng Müang consulted with the people, for she did not want [to persist in] allegiance to Chieng Mai, but proposed instead to go and seek the support of His Majesty, who was much more powerful; so she decided to speak frankly: [127] "There are many honest people whom [the Lâo king] has accused of doing wrong; he finds fault and casts aspersions; he is wicked, and while they repay him with good deeds, he in return accuses them of evil and suspects them of treachery or of running away in fear. [128] He even vexed and abused his own father [Sâm Fâng Gèn] who was devoted to him; then he even killed his own beloved son [Bun Rüang]. He not only [oppresses] his officers; he oppresses everyone, whether an officer or not. [129] Why should we remain loyal to this king who is so unreasonable and so malicious? I think we should turn over our province to His Majesty yonder [at Biṣṇuloka] and return to our former status as his subjects." [130] Then the ministers and officials of Chieng Chün, praising the fearless words she uttered, closed the city gates and built embankments in the hope that His Majesty would bring up his army.

[131] *Mün Lâo*, leaving his friends, hastened away with his family to His Majesty [at Biṣṇuloka]. When he arrived he presented [Nâng Müang's] letter, prepared beforehand to state the case with careful consideration: [132] "At this moment I, Nâng Müang, who am Your Majesty's slave, have shut the city gates and built broad embankments to make the city steadfast in the hope that Your Majesty will bring a large force of infantry, elephantry and cavalry here." [133] Then one of her devoted ladies-in-waiting, whom she had sent with golden utensils, presented them to His Majesty in witness to the message beseeching him to come quickly.

[134] His Majesty had not yet reached [Chieng Chün] when [the Lords of] Nân and Prè advanced to the stockade; but Nâng Müang refused to surrender, and in her devotion to His Majesty she held firm while waiting for him. [135] Defending the city, watching the road to descry His Majesty while she waited, she almost escaped defeat. But it was all in vain, because *Pan* Manorāja opened the gates to the enemy.

[136] The numerous population were stout-hearted; the nobles, mounted on elephants and horses, made a sortie; and measures were improvised for mass resistance. But Nân and Prè attacked fiercely, [137] and when they rushed forward with their elephantry on their flanks, the people

of Chalieng, unable to resist them, abandoned their own war elephants on the battlefield and fled to His Majesty. [138] Some of those who galloped away on horses reached [Biṣṇuloka] first; the fleeing foot soldiers who got lost on the way were slower; and the men who brought their families with them arrived in groups one after another.

[Stanzas 139–146, omitted from the translation, give a list of the refugee nobles.]

[147] Hastening to His Majesty, [the refugee nobles] did obeisance and invited him to move his troops forward. After listening to the whole story he exclaimed, "It is shameful for [the city] to have been taken like this!" [148] He went quickly in order to gratify the Yuan people [who had transferred their allegiance to him]. When his troops arrived at Chieng Chün they made a sudden massive attack, battered the stockade down, and moved in. [149] His Majesty considered, from every angle, how to act with a view to pleasing the troops who had transferred their allegiance from the Yuan king to himself, and making them happy. [150] He put Lâo princes in charge of the city and all its wealth, and presented Lâo nobles with the [captured] troops as slaves, together with their wives and children, elephants and horses.

[151] When the Lâo king learned that His Majesty had withdrawn his army he came to Chieng Chün and made arrangements to defend the city. Seeing that *Sè Hom* was brave and bold, he chose him [152] as governor to succeed Mün Dang and rule the people; he replaced many officials with others who were said to be certain to remain loyal to him; and he reinforced the troops to hold the province. [153] Having made these appointments he returned [to Chieng Mai], for he feared His Majesty too much to remain long [at Chieng Chün]. After reaching Chieng Mai he learned that His Majesty was indeed preparing to attack.

[6. Paramatrailoka Prepares to Attack Chieng Chün]

[154] His Majesty, though his vassals were eager to fight, undertook a stratagem before advancing. While he had no fear whatever, he pretended to be downcast, repaired the stockades [at various cities], and equipped his forts.

[Stanzas 155–163, which we have not translated, describe Paramatrailoka's preparations.]

[7. Preparations by the Yuan to Defend Chieng Chün]

[164] Sè Hom, the intrepid ruler of the city, rides all around it on an elephant, inspecting the gates and giving instructions to swordsmen, infantry, elephantry, and cavalry [stationed] in great number everywhere. [165] The sunshades flap and the canopies sway; the defenders cheer

exultingly in unison for victory; musical instruments, drums, and gongs are sounded together. [166] The officials follow in a mass; spearmen, swordsmen, and lancers form lines around [the ruler's] elephant; the noise of marching companies of elephants and horses resounds all over the city; shields and armor are seen everywhere. [167] Everywhere the gates are blocked with earth, pointed bamboo stakes, and sharp iron poles; sharpshooters are stationed at every opening [in the ramparts]; the troops of the city, reinforced by Chieng Mai men, stand as dense and firm as a protecting wall.

[168] [Sè Hom addresses his men as follows:] "This city and its defenses are not the work of human hands alone, and access to it is difficult in five respects. While the approaches by land are everywhere firmly held by our close-packed forces of infantry, elephantry, and cavalry, [169] the Meng Swamp first forms an obstacle at one end [of the city]; there is the River Yom with its rapids to screen us on one of the long sides; and three mountains almost completely shield the glorious city. Along its edges there is a deep triple moat, filled with barbed spikes; [170] and it has laterite walls to protect it, stronger than walls of iron, with stockades beyond." Then the ruler [Sè Hom], calling out loudly to the citizens of the left and right, addresses the entire throng: [171] "Let us not think of wavering in the slightest! There are plenty of us, and the city is strong. Our king can reach us by an uninterrupted route, and the rivers are not such as to hinder us from communicating with him. [172] This city is guarded by our ancestral [spirits]. Let us be confident and cheer for victory! It is not enough to say that [we could withstand] ten thousand or a hundred thousand [enemy soldiers]; even if there were a million we could still protect ourselves."

[8. Further Preparations by Paramatrailoka]

[At stanza 173 the scene shifts back to Biṣṇuloka, where Paramatrailoka continues his preparations to attack Chieng Chün. Troops are trained; weapons are gathered; elephants, horses, and war boats are assembled; reconnaissance parties are sent out to get information on routes and campsites (stanzas 174–181). The vassal rulers of Sukhodaya and Gampèng Pet, each with 8,000 men under his command, have orders to join forces and march together to Chieng Chün, while the war boats under Khun Indra are sent out with men to erect bridges, build causeways, repair roads, and wait for the King to arrive (stanzas 182–185). The King goes to *Tâ Chai* ('Victory Landing-place') to wait for the auspicious moment as foretold by astrology and omens (stanza 186). He inspects the war boats and their men (stanzas 187–188). Description of the boats and their occupants; names of the boats; their sailing regulations; their music and flags (stanzas 189–195). The main army is under direct command of the King, the rear is under the command of his son; description of the army, which totals 30,000 men; its armor, weapons, etc. (stanzas 196–208). Description of the elephantry with its 1,000 elephants; their names and dignities (stanzas 209–246). Description of the cavalry and names of the horses (stanzas 247–253). Banners, flags, music, etc., of the elephantry and cavalry (stanzas 254–257). The infantry; the rear under the King's son; the King's army and his vassals; banners, music, weapons, etc. (stanzas 258–263). The King deploys his immense host, like the elephant-borne god [Indra] deploying his forces all over the sky (stanza 264).]

[Quite a lot of material has obviously dropped out of our poem between stanzas 264 and 265, and six lines of *râi* eulogizing the King have been inserted in an unsuccessful effort to repair the lacuna. Originally, it may be guessed, there was a description of Paramatrailoka's advance toward Chieng Chün, his attack on the city, the beginning of the battle, and perhaps a good deal of other matter. In any case, stanza 265 opens with the battle in full swing.]

[9. The Great Battle of Chieng Chün]

[265] Yonder are the Lâo king's elephantry, their shields glittering with gold; but the virtues of the officers who command [our men] for His Majesty have no equal in all the universe. [266] Elephants are driven about swiftly, to meet in head-on collision, their tusks clashing together or goring [their adversaries]; some try to steal away and leave the main army; soldiers help one another to fall back and hide. [267] [The enemy] push forward into battle; the Lâo form a dense mass in front of the stockades; and their ruler quickly moves his army after them to help them cut our cavalry to pieces. [268] How can our brave men withstand them? The huge elephants attack and overturn one another; [the enemy] rush forward in great number to stop us; their elephantry and cavalry move in rapidly to help kill our men. [269] The tall [elephant named] *Song Bun* clashes in the midst of the battlefield with [the elephant] *Fòng Samut*, who falls down, and other elephants come to his rescue by joining their tusks together to shield him. [270] Song Bun recedes, then advances to gore his adversary, and the fleeing Lâo meets death by beheading. Wielding their hooks and weapons, our elephant-footguards add to the carnage. [271] The [body of the] headless Lâo hangs from his elephant's neck; and blood flows in great abundance.

Braḥ Deba Prahāra attacks mercilessly. Shields clash against shields, as [our men] kill [the enemy] with their swords. [272] Our troops advance in a body to tangle with the Lâo, and when they close in battle they transfix them with their swords in great number. The Lâo are terrified of His

Majesty. Trumpets are sounded, echoing everywhere. [273] The awesome din [of battle] strikes against the sky and shakes the earth: if the world were not firmly fixed it would soon lose its balance. Hlvaṅ Śrī Rājaputra's troops shake the earth as they approach. The enemy elephants advance boldly, but our men overwhelm them. [274] Their cavalry are braver than tigers, their spearmen bold in striking, and their soldiers numerous enough to cover the face of the earth. The uproar they make is enough to set the sky on fire.

[275] His Majesty, who is as active, graceful and brilliant as Rāmarāja and Ṛīdaiya, and as handsome as Nārāyaṇa [Viṣṇu], possesses the supernatural power of the four-armed god [Viṣṇu]. [276] His elephants are as quick as lions; the weapon he wields [in his right hand] is as sharp to sever heads as a cakra which never misses its mark; and he brandishes his shield with his other hand, while his brilliant canopy sways above him. [277] His swordsmen and spearmen, [seated on their elephants] in front of gilded back-rests, are eager to fight the enemy to the death before His Majesty's eyes; skilled [in the art of war], they take delight in deeds of valor as His Majesty moves them forward. [278] The "Golden Helmets" slash out [with their weapons] as they enter the fray, meeting the enemy as unconcernedly as a snap of the finger: ten of them can fight a thousand Lâo and cut off their heads to offer His Majesty. [279] Lines of swordsmen go into hand-to-hand battle against the Lâo, to fight them to the death, inflicting heavy losses. Peacocks' tails give the signal to advance.

Our swordsmen pounce upon the innumerable Yuan troops and force them to retreat. [280] The uproar, more intense than the fire that destroys the universe at the end of a kalpa, fills the whole earth. [When our] Brahmans wearing the sacred cord perform sacrifices, the ancestral spirits [of the Lâo] lose heart in great numbers and take flight. [281] The [enemy's] elephants run away into a dense forest of tamarind trees; and the bewildered Lâo, entangled among the corpses, are sick to death as they try to extricate one another in the immense confusion, looking like slashed banana trees. [282] When they see the royal canopy sheltering His Majesty's son, their spirits fly away into the forest, their faces turn pale, they shrink in alarm [like tortoises] withdrawing their heads into themselves.

The Yuan flee into the forest in utter disorder. [283] They have lost their bewitching ladies; they have lost a vast number of weapons of all kinds; they have lost an immense quantity of gold and treasure.

[284] See how our men follow the enemy everywhere to surround them! [See how] they pounce forward to attack the city and destroy it! [See how] they carry off a profusion of silver and gold on their shoulders, and take the glorious ladies of the city, the horses and elephants, to present to His Majesty! [285] The prisoners of war, with their hands tied, are pulled

along the road by horses; and when they are exhausted they are bartered [by our men] for liquor.

His Majesty's renown fills the earth and sky with fragrance!

[10. Conclusion]

[Stanzas 286–291 are a paean of victory of no historical interest. The first and third lines of each of these stanzas begin with the words "jaya jaya." We paraphrase stanza 291 as a sample:]

[291] Victory! victory! His Majesty has conquered far beyond Gampèng Pet, greatly enlarging his territory. Victory! victory! Let us extol his renown, his perseverance and his merits!

[Stanzas 292 and 293 are a kind of peroration:]

[292] His Majesty has enhanced his fame by defeating the Yuan king, and by his accumulated merits he has overcome the calamities of our age in every continent. A hundred kingdoms girdling the earth live in peace, [293] and a hundred kings hasten to come and do him honor, offering him golden lotuses as tribute. His accumulated merits shine like the sun. The Mòn and the Yuan have been defeated.

NOTES TO SECTION IV

61. "His Majesty's father" is Paramarājā II, who invaded Cambodia in 1431 (see **63**, below). Yaśodhara is Angkor Thom, the capital of Cambodia. The expression we have translated as "we tell how" is thlèṅ pāṅ (thlèṅ, 'recount'; pāṅ, 'incident'). It recurs constantly in the next eighteen stanzas, and as the repetition is much less effective in English than in Siamese we have generally omitted it.

62. Prince Damrong (*AA/RA*, 409) plausibly surmises that Paramarājā II, when he was planning to invade Cambodia, built a temporary residence on the plain of Braḥ Udaya where he was marshaling his forces; the Queen, who was far advanced in pregnancy, went to say good-bye to him, and gave birth to Paramatrailoka while she was staying there. Tāṃpal braḥ Udaya, 'the township of the royal birth', is evidently named *ex post facto*. Prince Damrong locates it on the plain called *Tung Han Ṭrâ*, east of Ayudhyā. The "glorious city" is Angkor Thom.

63. *AA/LP* (*sub anno* 793 = A.D. 1431) says: "King Paramarājā attacked and took Nagara Hlvaṅ [Angkor Thom], and appointed his son Braḥ Nagara Indra to rule over the land of Nagara Hlvaṅ. At that time he commanded Brahyā Kèv, Brahyā Daiy, and all the statues to be brought to Ayudhyā." Note that the spelling in *AA/LP* is modernized while that of our poem is, for the most part, old. Braḥ Nagara Indra was an elder half brother of Paramatrailoka. The statues in question were the palladia of the kingdom of Cambodia; see Jean Boisselier, "Notes sur l'art du bronze dans l'ancien Cambodge," *AA*, 29, 4 (1967):312–334.

64. Paramarājā II died in 1448; see §3. The terms we have rendered as "heaven" and "the gods" are more literally "the upper land" and "the beloved one(s)."

66. For the term "Lâo" in the sense of Yuan, see above, p. 142. In the fourteenth and fifteenth centuries, "Jayanāda" was an alternative name for Biṣṇuloka; see our note on Toponymy, below. For the incident alluded to in this stanza, see §4.

67. *Grung Lâo* (kruṅ lāv), 'the Lâo king'. In this poem *grung* regularly means 'king' rather than 'city'.

68. CK (p. 124) identifies "the *Nam Lip*" (the River Lip) with the Lî, and refers to Prince Damrong's location of Li-sop-Tîn in Lampûn province, which Paramatrailoka prepared to attack in 1456 (see §5). But as the battle in stanza 68 seems to have been fought in 1451 rather than five years later, and near Chalieng rather than in Lampûn province, we think it more likely that the "Nam Lip" is the same as the "Nam Lüm" in §4. One or both of these names must be corrupt. In any case, we think the battle referred to in stanza 68 is the one that was fought when the Chalieng troops assaulted the retreating forces of Tiloka and Yudhiṣṭhira in 1451 (see §4). *YP* features this battle as a victory for Paramatrailoka, whereas for the CMC it was a victory for Tiloka.

69. The first line of this stanza is obscure and perhaps corrupt; we have done the best we could with it. The "rebellious Sèn" is the Lord of Chalieng who defected to Tiloka in 1460; see §7. In both the Ayudhyan and the Chieng Mai tables of organization, civil and military officers were called by the number of persons theoretically under their command, for example (*Kun*) *Pan*, '(Lord of) a thousand'; (*Kun*) *Mün*, '(Lord of) ten thousand'; (*Kun*) *Sèn*, '(Lord of) a hundred thousand'. Most of the rulers of tributary states had the rank of Mün; but the Lord of Chalieng, perhaps in recognition of relationship to the former ruling dynasty of Sukhodaya, had the rank of Sèn.

71. Mahosadha is the hero of the Mahāummaggajātaka. The reference may be a discreet allusion to the siege of Biṣṇuloka (§6): the dates in this section of the CMC are rather confused.

72. "Everywhere in the region" did not include the provinces of Sukhodaya and Chalieng, which were still in the hands of Tiloka's men.

73. This stanza refers to the Kralāhoma's capture of Sukhodaya in 1462; see §8.

74. As the city of Chieng Chün (Chalieng) was still held by Tiloka's forces under Mün Dong Nagara (§7), "moving in swiftly" must mean sending raiding parties into outlying portions of the province.

75. We conjecture that *bon* (pan), 'upper', here means 'southern', by analogy with the expression *hua nòn* (hvva nòn), 'the head when sleeping', which in the Sukhodayan inscriptions means 'south' (because according to custom a man of rank was supposed to sleep on his right side, facing the east). As the next stanza deals with the King's ordination, we are inclined to think that the statement in stanza 75 refers to his allocation of land for the building of the Cuḷāmaṇī Monastery three miles south of Biṣṇuloka (see §10).

76, 77. Referring to Paramatrailoka's ordination in 1465; see §10. Although, as CK observes, none of our other sources mention the monk from Ceylon, the statement seems perfectly plausible (cf. Luang Boribal Buribhand, *JSS*, 43, 2 [1956]:138. Ever since the first half of the fourteenth century, if not before, Ceylon was regarded in Siam as the fountainhead of the Doctrine; and Sinhalese monks, especially "forest-dwellers," were held in high esteem.

79. The request at the beginning of this stanza is the usual formula that leads to a king's retirement from the monkhood. This was in 1466; see §10.

80. The "residence" (āvāsa, apparently used here in the general sense of a dwelling, rather than in the modern Siamese sense of a monastery or a residence for monks) was very likely a palace he built at Biṣṇuloka; Buddhaiśvarya means "dominion of the Buddha" (an Ayudhyan monarch was conventionally regarded as a Buddha). Or else the reference could be to some building he erected at the Buddhaiśvarya Monastery at Ayudhyā. The "wall" is the huge laterite and brick rampart, a good deal of which can still be seen, enclosing the city of Biṣṇuloka. Of course there was already a rampart enclosing the city; Paramatrailoka's work must have been either a reconstruction, an enlargement and improvement, or a replacement. The expression *yû châng* (^{1}ayū ^{1}jāṅ), in the last line of stanza 80, seems to have the same meaning as in stanza 51, 'conveniently' or 'easily'. The last line of stanza 80, *yû châng pra jao fî füang bòn* (^{1}ayū ^{1}jāṅ braḥ ^{2}cau ^{2}fî ^{1}föaṅ par), is identical to the last line of stanza 98 except that in the latter the words *fî füang* are replaced by *kâ kom* (^{2}khā ^{1}kham). We conjecture that *fî* has the same meaning as *kâ*, 'to kill', and that *füang* has the same meaning as *kom*, 'to bear down upon', 'to squeeze', oppress'.

83. Kalakāṇḍa (line 1) is for Skt. kalakāṇḍa, 'the main subject of a poem'. The author here returns to the events of 1451, which he has already dealt with "briefly" at stanzas 66 and 67; cf. §4.

85. See §4.

86. The garuḍas or solar birds are the inveterate enemies of the nāgas or serpent divinities. In Hindu mythology the Asuras are the titans who battle against Indra and the gods; from Sanskrit literature they passed into Buddhist Pali works, in which one of their kings is named Vepacitti (see G. P. Malalasekera, *Dictionary of Pali Proper Names* (London, 1960), II, 924ff.).

87. Viṣṇu is here called by his epithet, "the king who rides on a garuḍa."

88. Cf. **68**, above.

89. We have regularized the spelling of "Pāṇḍava" and "Kaurava," which in our poem are written "Pāndaba" and "Gauraba." The great war between the Pāṇḍavas and the Kauravas is the main subject of the Mahābhārata. In that poem Yudhiṣṭhira is one of the Pāṇḍavas, and it therefore seems odd for Paramatrailoka (the enemy of the Siamese Yudhiṣṭhira) to be compared to a Pāṇḍava.

92. For "long afterward" (sc. 1460), cf. stanza 69 and §7.

95. In the Mahābhārata, Duryodhana is the leader of the Kauravas in their war against Kṛṣṇa and the Pāṇḍavas; cf. **89**, above.

98. They were downcast because Tiloka failed to take Biṣṇuloka and Gampèng Pet in 1461; see §7.

99. See **73**, above.

100. A retrospective allusion to the events of 1451, when he "got it by stealth" (see §4).

102. The first line of this stanza is very obscure and may be corrupt; our rendering of it is conjectural. The Sèn is the Lord of Chalieng, who was caught trying to betray Tiloka and was punished for it; see §7.

103. Referring to Tiloka's appointment of Mün Dong Nagara as ruler of

Chalieng, c. 1461; see §7. The "former status" of the place means being ruled by someone loyal to Tiloka, as Tiloka had at first thought the Lord of Chalieng to be.

104, 105. Some material seems to have dropped out of *YP* between stanzas 104 and 105; at least the "detailed" account contains no reference to the transfer of the capital to Biṣṇuloka in 1463, Paramatrailoka's ordination in 1465, his resumption of the throne in 1466, or his building operations at Biṣṇuloka soon after (related in "outline" at stanzas 75–80).

105. The scene now shifts to Chieng Mai, and everything related from here to the end of the poem is new, in the sense that it has not been already related in the "outline" at stanzas 61–80.

106. The CMC intimates that Tiloka's irrational acts, including the execution of Bun Rüang, were the result of sorcery organized by Paramatrailoka; see §§10, 11.

107. See §1.

110. Nân had been subject to Tiloka since 1449, and Prè since 1443; see §2. It is not known whether Yudhiṣṭhira was still Lord of Prè, a post to which he had been appointed by Tiloka in 1459; see §6.

111. Despite the spelling, *Âi Dang* (written ²āy ¹taṅ) is of course Mün Dong Nagara (¹hmīn ²taṅ nagara). The term *âi*, used as a prefix before the name of a person who was the eldest son of his father, often became in effect part of the proper name. The expression we have translated as "your exalted Lordship" is *yua* (hñvva), a contracted form of *yû hua* (¹ayū hvva), 'dwelling above'.

115–116. This passage may be translated in two quite different ways. The one we have given, which seems to fit the context best, assumes that (Mün) Dâm Prâ and (Mün) Pân Pât are two of Tiloka's officials; the first may be *Mün Dâm Prâ Kot*, who acted as Tiloka's Minister of Works and died in 1482 (CMC/N, 92, 136, 142), or else *Mün Dâm Prâ Âi*, who is mentioned in CMC *sub annis* 1467, 1485, and 1486 (CMC/N, 134, 142, 143); we cannot identify the second. If this interpretation is right, the expression at stanza 116, "he regards you alone as his eldest son," would be intended to make Mün Dong believe Tiloka esteemed him above anyone else (in 1451 Tiloka had used a similar expression to Yudhiṣṭhira; see §4). On the other hand, according to the Sip-hā Rājavaṅśa (manuscript in the National Library, Bangkok), there was still another Mün Dâm Prâ, namely, Mün Dong's father, the former lord of Lampâng, who had first been known as *Mün Hân Ṭè Tòng*, then as Mün Hân Nagara, and finally received the title Mün Dâm Prâ late in life. If this is the person referred to, we must take *pân pât* (bān bāt) not as a proper name, but as a verb, *pân* (bān), 'to meet with', plus a noun, *pât* (bādh), 'distress', 'pain'; 'injury'. We should then translate: "Dâm Prâ is gravely ill [or gravely wounded?]; Nân and Prè have joined together to revolt against the king;" etc. In that case the sentence we have translated as "he [Tiloka] regards you alone as his eldest son" would be: "He [Dâm Prâ] thinks of no one except you, his eldest son." This is tempting: but we believe the wily official would be less likely to try to appeal to Mün Dong's concern for his father than to his single-minded devotion to the king.

118. We have omitted the last two lines of this stanza, which are corrupt and quite incomprehensible.

119. Sc., he has earned enough merit in past lives to have been reborn in this one as a human being, rather than in one of the inferior states of existence, and enough merit in the present life to be reborn in Indra's heaven, the Tāvatiṃsa.

124a, 124b. These two stanzas, composed in the reign of Rāma II (1806–1824) and inserted to repair a lacuna which occurs between stanzas 124 and 125 in all the known manuscripts of the poem, may be based on an oral tradition which preserved the original text with tolerable fidelity. In any case, they fit in very well with the context, and the stanzas that follow prove that the original text contained an account of Mün Nagara's execution. So far as we are aware, *YP* is the only old source that says Mün Nagara was executed; the CMC does not tell us how he met his death (see §14), and *AA/LP* does not mention his death at all.

125. Nâng Mün Non Müang, or Nâng Müang as she is called for short, was presumably Mün Nagara's wife, who had been acting as ruler of Chieng Chün since his departure for Chieng Mai.

128. See §§1, 11. The expression *bò röm* (¹pa ¹röm) occurs in Sukhodayan literature with the sense of 'even' or 'to such a degree'.

129. We conjecture that *nâ* (²nā) at line 2 of the stanza, which makes no sense in the context, is a mistake for *nâ* (hnā).

130. Sc., they closed the gates and built additional defenses to protect the city in case Tiloka should attack before Paramatrailoka could get there with his army and take over. The embankments were probably earthworks with stockades on top, built as auxiliary defenses outside the city walls; or else they may have been dams built across streams to divert water into the moat and raise the water level.

131. Mün Lâo, evidently an official who sided with Nâng Müang, was taking his family with him to give them as hostages to Paramatrailoka to guarantee Nâng Müang's sincerity.

134. Cf. **108**, above.

135. Pan Manorāja must be an official who secretly sided with Tiloka. For the rank of Pan, see **69**, above.

137. This is the only place in *YP* where the name Chalieng occurs.

151. The first two lines suggest that Paramatrailoka, having liberated the city as a point of honor, was not yet prepared to have his forces withstand a siege, so he withdrew them to gain time.

151, 152. See §14. Sè Hom is a doublet of Chè Hom (now *Jè Hom*, a district in Lampâng province). The person referred to in *YP* as "Sè Hom" is of course the same one the CMC calls "Mün Kwèn of Chè Hom."

152. For "Mün Dang" as a doublet of "Mün Dong," see **111**, above.

154. Sc., he disguised his preparations to attack as preparations to defend the territory he already held.

158. Among the preparations mentioned at stanza 158 are poisons to be put on arrowheads, poisons to be put in food, and *pün fai*, which could mean either arrows with flaming tips to be used as incendiaries or firearms such as matchlocks; cf. CK, p. 220. The Chinese are said to have possessed firearms since the tenth century or earlier; see Joseph Needham, *Science and Civilisation in Ancient China* (London, 1961), passim (we have not yet had access to the volume of this work that discusses firearms in detail); cf. Wood, *History of Siam* (p. 77, n. 1). Most scholars believe firearms were not in use in Siam until introduced by the Portuguese around the second decade of the sixteenth century; for a discussion, see H. Penth, "A Note on Pün," *JSS*, 59, 1 (1971):209f.

165. The sunshades are large leaf-shaped frames covered with cloth and set on top of long poles; the canopies are long-handled parasols of several tiers; both are carried in processions and serve as insignia of rank.

167. *Pün fai* (line 2) could mean either firearms or incendiary arrows (see **158**, above). In order to be noncommittal, we have translated the expression as "sharp-shooters." Note, however, that incendiary arrows were normally regarded as weapons for attacking a city, not defending it.

168. Peñcadūrgākāra (line 2) is for Skt. pañcadurgākāra (pañca, 'five'; durga, 'difficult of access'; ākāra, 'respects'. The "five respects" are enumerated at stanzas 169 and 170: (1) the Meng Swamp; (2) the River Yom; (3) three mountains; (4) a triple moat; (5) laterite walls.

169. *Küa* (line 1), literally the roof beam at one end of a house; *yè* (line 2), presumably equivalent to *bè*, literally purlin, a roof beam running along one of the long sides of a house. We therefore translate "at one end" and "on one of the long sides."

170. "Citizens of the left and right": it was the custom for the people of a city or province to be organized into two great divisions, the "left" and the "right," each under a high officer.

171. The last two lines of this stanza must refer to a land route between Chieng Chün on the Yom and Chieng Mai on the Ping, crossing only one river of any consequence, the Wang.

197. It is not clear which of Paramatrailoka's sons is in command of the rear, but he must be the same person who reappears at stanzas 259 and 282.

265–271. Our translation is conjectural, as the text is extremely obscure and probably corrupt. Cf. Mr. Schweisguth's partial translation of stanzas 266–282 (*Etude sur la littérature siamoise*, pp. 50, 51).

269. Mr. Schweisguth (*loc. cit.*) takes *song bun* as an epithet of Paramatrailoka ('plein de vertu') and translates *fòng samut* as 'de l'écume en abondance'; and there are numerous other differences between his interpretation of stanzas 266–282 and ours. In view of what we have said in the preceding note, he may well be right.

270. The "fleeing Lâo" who is beheaded in this stanza must be a man of very high rank, or else he would not have been singled out for special mention by the poet. Probably it is Sè Hom (see our Appendix, below).

271. Braḥ Deba Prahāra may be the name of an officer, though we cannot identify him. On the other hand the expression might mean "the King's warriors," i.e. the Ayudhyan forces.

273. Hlvaṅ Śrī Rājaputra must be a prince, but his identity is uncertain.

275. Presumably Rāmarāja is Rāma Gaṃhèṅ the Great of Sukhodaya (r. 1279?–1298) and Ṛīdaiya his grandson Ḷīdaiya (Mahādharmarājā I, r. 1347–c. 1370).

276. The cakra is the discus weapon of a cakravartin or a god (especially Viṣṇu).

280. For kalpa (eon) and the fire that destroys the universe at the end of it, see Benjamin Walker, *The Hindu World* (London, 1968), I, 6ff.

282. Very likely Mün Gòng was one of the Yuan who "flee into the forest in utter disorder." See our Appendix, below.

283. Our rendering of the last two lines of this stanza is an approximation only. Perhaps *pân* (bālya) means something like 'emblems' or 'tribute' (CK glosses the word as 'young girls', which seems out of place in the context); *panhao* (bălhau) must be *panhao* (barrhau), 'much', 'many'; *tòng tèng* (dòṅ dèṅ) usually means 'gold blocks'; *gantóng* (¹kanndoṅ) is perhaps for *gantóng* (karrdoṅ), a variant of *gratong* (kradaṅ), 'offering', 'float', or 'vessel' (CK reads *gantóng* (¹kăn ¹thoṅ), and glosses the term as 'howdahs' or 'bracelets'); *tuan ròi* (²thvan ²ròy) means 'a full hundred'; *mât malüang* (māś mlöaṅ) means 'shining gold.'

285. For the date of the battle and the events that led up to it, see our Appendix, below.

292. Palayakalpa (line 2), for Skt. pralayakalpa, a compound of pralaya, 'destruction' (in modern Siamese, 'calamity') with kalpa, an age or eon. According to the old belief, the age we live in has been preceded by an immensely long cycle of progressive deterioration leading toward the end of the world; cf. **280**, above. While no conceivable power can reverse the deterioration, the accumulated merits of individuals can mitigate it temporarily.

293. "Golden lotuses"; cf. the gold and silver trees that vassals offered their sovereign as tribute in more recent times. The Mòn people lived mainly in Lower Burma and central Siam at this time; but there was still a large population of Mòn descendants at Lampûn and other northern cities who were subjects of the Yuan king and presumably furnished contingents for his army.

APPENDIX

The struggle for Chieng Chün, as described in *YP*, falls into five phases:

Phase I: Soon after Mün Dong's execution, his widow Nâng Müang, the acting ruler of the city, sends a message of submission to Paramatrailoka, asking for his protection. (Stanzas 125–133.)

Phase II: Before Paramatrailoka can advance on Chieng Chün to protect it, the rulers of Nân and Prè, acting for Tiloka, arrive with their armies, and an official inside the city opens the gates to them. The troops who are loyal to Nâng Müang are defeated in battle and flee to Paramatrailoka at Biṣṇuloka. (Stanzas 134–138.)

Phase III: Soon afterward Paramatrailoka's forces make a quick assault and re-take Chieng Chün. Paramatrailoka puts the city in charge of Yuan nobles who have transferred their allegiance to him. Then he withdraws. (Stanzas 148–150.)

Phase IV: Tiloka goes to Chieng Chün and installs the Lord of Sè Hom as its ruler, at the same time replacing many officials with others. Then he returns to Chieng Mai. (Stanzas 151–153.)

Phase V: Paramatrailoka makes extensive preparations to attack the city (stanzas 154–163 and 173–264), while at the same time Sè Hom prepares to defend it (stanzas 164–172). A great battle is fought. Paramatrailoka wins it and takes the city (stanzas 265–285).

The victory in Phase V is certainly the one referred to in *AA/LP*, *sub anno* cs. 836, that is, between April 1474 and April 1475. True, this entry in *AA/LP*, if translated literally, says that Paramatrailoka "went to take Salieng," which might or might not mean that he succeeded in doing so; but as *AA/LP*'s entry for the following year clearly means that Tiloka asked for a truce (§14), we take it for granted that Paramatrailoka really did conquer Chalieng (Chieng Chün) in cs. 836. As the northern bastion of the Sukhodayan heartland, it was a place of immense importance; and it was Tiloka's last foothold of any consequence in the region.

Since there is no further reference to it in *AA/LP*, we assume that it remained firmly in Paramatrailoka's hands.

The entry for cs. 836 in *RBY*, however, seems to say that Tiloka reconquered it again before the close of that year, which is hard to reconcile with our data from other sources. As we cannot imagine the author of *YP* writing to celebrate Paramatrailoka's great victory if he knew it was soon followed by an equally great defeat, we should have to suppose the poem was written before Tiloka's reconquest of Chieng Chün. This, in turn, would require us to squeeze into a single year not only Mün Dong's death and the events of all the five phases of the struggle in *YP*, but also, after Phase V, the composition of *YP* and Tiloka's preparation and waging of still another battle.

Here is *RBY*'s entry for cs. 836, with the corresponding passages in CMC/N and CMC/HC placed in parallel. For CMC/N we give Notton's translation, with the spelling of names changed to conform to our system. For the other two we give our own translation. In all three this entry is immediately followed by the entry for 837, and no more is said about Chieng Chün.

		CMC/HC, p. 78 (already quoted above: §14)
RBY, p. 243	CMC/N, pp. 135–136	
In śakarāja 836, a year of the horse and sixth of the decade, Mün Dong, the ruler of Chieng Chün, died. Mün Kwèn, the ruler of *Jè Hom*, was sent to rule Chieng Chün in his place, and *Mün Gòng*, the ruler of *Chieng Rüak*, was sent to rule Nagara.	Mün Dong, gouverneur de Chieng Chün, mourut en l'année *gâp sangâ*, 836 de l'ère (A.D. 1474), et fut remplacé par Mün Kwèn de Chè Hom. Mün Gòng de *Chieng Lü* fut envoyé à Nagara.	In the year *gâp sangâ*, śakarāja 836, Mün Dong, the ruler of Chieng Chün, died. Mün Kwèn, the ruler of Chè Hom, was sent to rule Chieng Chün in his place, and Mün Gòng, the ruler of Chieng Lü, was sent to rule Nagara.
In that same year the King of Sukhodaya came up with an army to attack Chieng Chün, and killed Mün Kwèn the ruler of Chieng Chün. The king [Tiloka] led an army to attack the army of Sukhodaya; [the latter] retreated, and [Tiloka] retook Chieng Chün. He sent the ruler of Nagara to supervise affairs at Chieng Chün.	Cette année-là, le souverain de Sukhodaya arriva avec son armée pour s'emparer de Müang Chieng Chün . . . . ont tué . . . . Mün Kwèn reprit son gouvernement à Chieng Chün comme auparavant. Mün . . . . gouverneur de Nagara, alla provisoirement administrer Chieng Chün, se sauva en emmenant des partisans.	In that year the King of Sukhodaya came with an army to attack Chieng Chün, killed Mün Kwèn the ruler of Chieng Chün, and recaptured Chieng Chün. At that time the ruler of Nagara, who went to supervise affairs at Chieng Chün, took flight and escaped.

The similarities and differences between the three accounts show that they are based on different manuscripts of the same text. Up to a point they agree well enough. None of them mentions the events of Phases I to III, which probably occurred very rapidly. Tiloka's appointment of Mün Kwèn (Sè Hom) as ruler of Chieng Chün corresponds to Phase IV. At the same time, though *YP* does not mention it, Tiloka appointed Mün Gòng as ruler of Lampâng, evidently giving him general supervision over Mün Kwèn's administration of Chieng Chün; around 1460, Mün Dong, when ruling Lampâng, had been given general supervision over the Lord of Chalieng's administration in the same way (see above, §7). The conquest of Chieng Chün by "the King of Sukhodaya" refers to Paramatrailoka's great victory in Phase V. It is not clear why the capture of the city is credited to the vassal King of Sukhodaya rather than to Paramatrailoka; perhaps something has dropped out of the statement, which may have originally said that Paramatrailoka, supported by the King of Sukhodaya, took Chieng Chün.

The discrepancies that follow must stem from differences in the manuscripts used. Notton, working from a defective manuscript, scrupulously indicates the lacunae, but translates wrongly because the context is lost. The author of *RBY*, working from a manuscript with somewhat different lacunae, conjecturally repairs them without saying so, and makes some bad guesses. CMC/HC is based on a much better manuscript, which belongs to Professor Hans Penth of Chieng Mai, and its entry for cs. 836 is not only coherent in itself but also fits in well with the information derived from *YP*. We shall therefore do well to disregard the entries in CMC/N and *RBY* for that year when they are in conflict with CMC/HC.

The CMC/HC puts less into the year cs. 836 than *RBY*, but it still puts everything from Mün Dong's death to the end of Phase V in that year. We conclude that Mün Dong was executed early in cs. 836, say around April 1474; and that Paramatrailoka won his final victory at Chieng Chün toward the end of cs. 836, say in the first three months of 1475.

The last time *YP* mentions Sè Hom by name is at the beginning of Phase V, when he is inspecting the defenses and making speeches. As CMC/HC implies that Mün Kwèn (Sè Hom) was killed in the big battle, he may be the "fleeing Lâo" who meets death by beheading at stanza 270. Mün Gòng is doubtless one of the Yuan who "flee into the forest in utter disorder" at stanza 282.

TOPONYMY

Ayodhyā. The old name for Ayudhyā.

Biṣṇuloka. One of the names of the city that was the administrative capital of the Sukhodayan provinces in the 15th century. In the inscriptions of Sukhodaya and in the CMC, it is called *Sòng Kwè*. *AA/LP* calls it Biṣṇuloka. *YP* calls it Jayanāda; not to be confused with modern Jayanāda (*Chainât*), which is more than 100 miles to the south.

Chalieng and *Chieng Chün*. Alternative names used in the fifteenth century for the city and province formerly called Sajjanālaya. The walled city, which was of great strategic importance, fell into Tiloka's hands in 1460 and was not recovered by Ayudhyā until 1474/5. In the sixteenth century the city and province became known as Svargaloka. In the late eighteenth the population of the city was removed to the present site of Svargaloka, on the Yom about ten miles downstream, and the abandoned city became known as "Old Svargaloka." It is still sometimes called that; but scholars now generally prefer the name "Old Sajjanālaya" for the city and "Chalieng" for the site of the temple a mile downstream.

Chieng Chün. See *Chalieng.*

Jayanāda. See Biṣṇuloka.

Nagara (*Nakòn*). In Lân Nâ this name, when used without qualification, means Lampâng.

Sajjanālaya. See *Chalieng.*

Salieng. A doublet of *Chalieng.*

Sòng Kwè. See Biṣṇuloka.

Svargaloka. See *Chalieng.*

TRANSCRIPTION

We transcribe Sanskrit and Pali words by means of the "graphic" system which is commonly in use for those languages; for Siamese words that are obvious borrowings from Sanskrit or Pali we usually use the same system; and we also use it for all Siamese words when we wish to show the exact spelling. For the system, see *JSS* 56, 2 (1968):247. Words written in this system are printed in ordinary type.

Otherwise we usually transcribe Siamese words of Tai origin by means of a simplified phonemic system, in which consonants have their English values (with ṭ and p as in "string" and "spring") and vowels their Italian values (an acute accent over e or o indicates its Italian "closed" sound, a grave accent its "open" sound; the circumflex indicates a long vowel; ü and ö are as in German). See *JSS*, 56, 2 (1968):248–249. We sometimes use the same system for loanwords from Sanskrit, Pali, or Khmer which are thoroughly naturalized into Siamese. Words written in this system are printed in italics at their first appearance, and thereafter generally in ordinary type (but again in italics when it seems desirable to call attention to the system used).

The names of Siamese authors are mostly transcribed in the way they themselves use. Familiar names like "Bangkok" are written in the common manner, which does not necessarily correspond to any system.

BIBLIOGRAPHY AND ABBREVIATIONS

AA. Annals of Ayudhyā. See *AA/LP* and *AA/RA.*

AA/LP. The "Luang Prasert Recension" of the Annals of Ayudhyā (Braḥ Rājabaṅśāvatāra Kruṅ Kau, Chpăp Hlvaṅ Prasröṭh, in Prajum Baṅśāvatāra, Vol. 1, Bangkok, 1914; often reprinted since). English translation by O. Frankfurter in *JSS*, 6, 3 (1909); cf. W. A. R. Wood's comments at *JSS*, 19, 3 (1925/26):153 ff. Our references to the entries in *AA/LP* are *sub annis*, in Cūḷasakarāja, with the cyclical designation of the year omitted.

AA/RA. The "Royal Autograph Recension" of the Annals of Ayudhyā (Braḥ Rājabaṅśāvatāra, Chpăp Braḥ Rājahatthalekhā), annotated by Prince Damrong

Rājānubhāb (Bangkok, 1914; often reprinted since). We have used the Odeon's reprint (Bangkok, 1965), and our references are to the page numbers in that edition.

Bulletin of the Faculty of Archaeology of the University of Fine Arts: *Archaeology* (Porāṇagatī), Bangkok, 1967 to present.

Bulletin of the Historical Commission. See CMC/HC.

Chandijya Krasèsindhu. See CK.

Chieng Mai Chronicle. See CMC.

CK. Chandijya Krasèsindhu, *Yuan Pâi Klóng Dan* (Bangkok: Mitrasyām Press, 1970).

CMC. The Chieng Mai Chronicle. See CMC/HC and CMC/N.

CMC/HC. "*Ṭamnân Pün Müang Chieng Mai*," *Bulletin of the Historical Commission* (Thlèn-ñān Pravatiśāstra Ekasāra Porāṇagatī), vol. 3, nos. 2 and 3; vol. 4, no. 1 (Bangkok, 1969–1970). Unless otherwise stated, the page numbers in our references are those in vol. 4, no. 1.

CMC/N. C. Notton, *Annales du Siam*, III: *Chronique de Xieng Măi* (Paris, 1932).

cs. Cūḷasakarāja.

Ep. and Hist. Studies. See Griswold and Prasert ṇa Nagara.

Griswold, A. B. *Towards a History of Sukhodaya Art*, 2d ed. (Bangkok, 1968).

Griswold, A. B., and Prasert ṇa Nagara. *Epigraphic and Historical Studies*, nos. 1–5, 7–11, *JSS*, 56–60 (1968–1972).

HC. See CMC/HC.

"Luang Prasert Recension." See *AA/LP*.

N. See CMC/N.

Notton, C. See CMC/N.

RBY. Brayā Prajā Kicakaracakra, *Rüang Pongsâwadân Yónok* (Röaṅ Baṅśāvatāra Yonaka) (Bangkok, 1907).

"Royal Autograph Recension." See AA/RA.

Schweisguth, P. *Etude sur la littérature siamoise* (Paris, 1951).

Wood, W. A. R. *History of Siam* (Bangkok, 1933).

YP. Yuan Pâi. The edition we have used is that printed by the National Library (Bangkok, 1966) for distribution at the cremation of Lady Rājavarānurakṣa. We have also frequently consulted CK.

Yuan Pâi. See *YP*.

Toward a Bibliography of the Life and Times of Mongkut, King of Thailand, 1851–1868[1]

CONSTANCE M. WILSON

Northern Illinois University

The choices a nation makes depend on the nature and caliber of its leadership. Thailand was fortunate in the nineteenth and early twentieth century to be governed by a succession of able monarchs, members of the Chakkri dynasty founded in 1782. The Chakkri were exceptional leaders; they combined rare political skills with intellectual ability and a deep appreciation of cultural affairs. The dynasty produced a succession of political and cultural leaders beginning with Rama I, who restored the stability of the political and social order, sorely disrupted by the divisions which rent the kingdom after the Burmese attacks of 1767. Rama II oversaw the continued expansion of Thai influence in Laos, Cambodia, and the Malay States. Rama IV and Rama V guided the kingdom through sixty years of pressure from the West. Rama II and Rama VI were important cultural figures; the first found new ways to fuse Thai culture with an older literary tradition, while the second, a century later, adapted Western literary forms to the Thai.

In recent years scholars and popular historians, both Thai and Western, have been looking more closely at the life and reign of the fourth Chakkri monarch, Mongkut,[2] who ruled from 1851 to 1868. Mongkut is an unusually attractive subject to study; his reign has long been regarded as a pivotal one in Thai history. Born in 1804, Mongkut, a son of Rama II and his chief queen, spent his early years in training as a future monarch. His father died when he was twenty years old, and the Grand Council, responsible for the selection of a new king, decided that the throne should go to an older, more experienced person and named Mongkut's elder half brother, Chetsadabodin, Rama III. Mongkut retired to the Buddhist Sangha, where he stayed throughout his half brother's reign. In 1851,

1. This article is a revised version of the first chapter of Constance M. Wilson, "State and Society during the Reign of Mongkut, 1851–1868: Thailand on the Eve of Modernization" (Ph.D. diss., Cornell University, 1970), pp. 1–46.
2. Mongkut's full Thai title takes up an entire page. It is usually shortened to "Phrabat Somdet Phra Chom Klao Chao Yu Hua," and in some instances to "Phra Chom Klao."

164

after Rama III's death, the Grand Council brought Mongkut to the throne with great acclaim. At his request, his younger brother, Chuthamani, was given the special position of Second King. Under Mongkut's leadership the Thai, long outward-looking in foreign affairs, worked out an accommodation with the expanding Western powers in Southeast Asia. This accommodation, based on Thai acceptance of treaty relations with the West, provided the basis for the country's continued independence as well as for its economic development and future modernization. Careful observation of changing circumstances in Southeast Asia, numerous discussions of new ideas, and their careful testing against Thai tradition led, under Mongkut's successor, Chulalongkorn, to a far-reaching series of reforms in the last thirty years of the nineteenth century. As a result, Thailand entered the twentieth century as the most modern state in Southeast Asia, Chulalongkorn's reforms having preceded those of the British in Burma and Malaya, the Dutch in Indonesia, and the United States in the Philippines.

The renewed interest shown in Mongkut and in his reign in recent years justifies an attempt to survey the materials which are available for a study of his life and work, as well as to evaluate the work which has been completed.[3] It is hoped that this will contribute to the provision of an adequate bibliography for Mongkut's reign and that it will provide a base for continued work in this period of Thai history.

The materials available for a study of Mongkut and his time are best discussed by language and by period. The first section of this essay is concerned with Thai-language materials of a documentary nature. These fall into two categories: unpublished records from the reign kept in Thai archives, and published materials: books by members of the royal family and by high officials of the reign, and the reference works published by agencies of the Thai government. The second section discusses contemporary English- and French-language materials, including the records in the archives of Western governments. The final section deals with modern studies, in Thai and in English.

The most important materials for a study of Mongkut are the records from his reign kept in the National Archives, the National Library, and the Ministry of Foreign Affairs, Bangkok. The Ministry of Foreign Affairs continues to hold a number of records dealing with foreign policy during the fourth reign, although there has been some discussion of moving these records to the National Library. These records are closed to foreigners; however, on occasion, Thai nationals have been permitted to use them.

---

3. For reasons of space, scholarly articles about Mongkut are not discussed here. Several important ones have been published, most of them in *JSS*. Mention should be made of Seni Pramoj, "King Mongkut as a Legislator," *JSS*, 38, 1 (1950):32–66, and to David K. Wyatt, "Family Politics in Nineteenth Century Thailand," *JSEAH*, 9, 2 (Sept. 1968):208–228.

The records that are open to the foreign researcher, generally only with special permission, are kept in the National Archives and in the National Library. These documents are from Krom Kalahom (Ministry for the Southern Townships), Krom Mahatthai (Ministry for the Northern Townships), and the Court Secretaries Department. The records of Krom Kalahom, however, are not the original documents but a copy made for King Chulalongkorn's library. This copy is a series of imported, leather-bound, Western-style record books. There are two duplicate sets of records labeled as one; volume three is a copy of volume two, volume six a copy of volume five, and so on, with the exception of volume four, which is a copy of volume one. The last volume, number thirty-eight, contains copies of records from Krom Tha on the east-coast townships. The set is the only major group of records from the fourth reign kept in the National Archives.

The other records, those of Krom Mahatthai and the Court Secretaries Department, are kept in the Manuscript Division of the National Library. These records have been preserved in their original form and are known as the *nangsü khọi* (khọi books) or as *samut dam* (black books), references to the kind of paper on which they are written and to their color. The paper is the washed and dried pulp of the bark of the khọi tree. While it is some-times used in its natural tan state, in which it is almost as soft as a piece of cloth, it is usually coated with black lacquer or a substance containing charcoal to stiffen it. The normal writing material is white chalk; in very special cases gambodge or gold ink is used. If the paper is left in its natural state, the writing material is a piece of charcoal. The soft tan manuscripts, usually only two to three feet in length, are rolled or folded like a piece of cloth for storage. The longer stiffened black manuscripts, which can be more than twenty feet in length, are folded back and forth like the pleats in a fan to form a rectangular bundle that can be easily stored and read (by flipping the folds). These latter manuscripts withstand the tropical climate exceptionally well. They appear to be immune to dampness, their major enemies being insects and man.

The records in the National Library are classified under two headings: Chotmaihet (Records) and Mairapsang (Royal Orders). There are Chotmaihet and Mairapsang for each of the first five Chakkri reigns. The coverage of each reign varies with time, there being least coverage for the first reign and more complete coverage as the records approach the twentieth century. Few of these records refer to the process of decision-making at the Thai court or to any of the affairs of the royal family. The Mairapsang is basically a diary of events with occasional instructions for state and religious ceremonies. Records dealing with the inner workings of the Thai court do not exist for the first three reigns; they begin to appear among the records of the fourth reign, and show in number only in the fifth reign. Despite these absences, the available records are very valuable for what they reveal about Thai ceremonial life, the Thai economy, and, in greatest detail, the relationship between the capital and the outlying townships and satellite states. Most of these records are contemporary copies of correspondence from Bangkok to the townships and satellite states. In some instances there are also copies of letters sent to Bangkok, although these are relatively fewer. The extent and quality of these records show that Thai source materials do not neglect everyday aspects of administrative and economic life.

Published documents and records supplement the materials in the archives. One of the major responsibilities of the Thai monarchs was the preservation of Thai cultural life. All of the Chakkri kings were patrons of literature; a few of them were important literary figures in their own right. For example, Rama II made many contributions to the development of Thai poetry; his son, Mongkut, and grandson, Chulalongkorn, were accomplished authors in Thai prose. The written work of these three kings combined with the work of two other members of the royal family, Kromphra Paramanuchit Chinorot, the son of Rama I and patriarch of the Buddhist Sangha from 1849 to 1853, and Damrong Rajanubhab, a son of Mongkut, comprises a large portion of the Thai material available to the modern researcher.

Mongkut used the years he spent in the Buddhist Sangha for study and contemplation. He was deeply concerned with the reform of Thai Buddhism. As a result of his studies, he formed a new Buddhist sect, the Thammayut, and his religious interests are reflected in some of his writings. *Samanasan Phra Thera Thammayuttika Mi Pai Yang Langka Thawip* (Religious Letters from Thammayuttika Scholars Sent to Ceylon)[4] is a collection of letters to Ceylon dealing with various aspects of Thammayut doctrine. Thai translations accompany the Pali text of the letters. They are useful for what they reveal about the chief concerns of the Thammayut. Two volumes of Mongkut's sermons and essays on Buddhism were published in 1968 on the centenary of his death. Both bear the title *Mahamakut Ratchanusarani* (In Memory of Mongkut): one volume is the first in a projected collection in Thai; the other, the first of a series in Pali with Thai translations. Mongkut was very proud of his knowledge of Pali. He used Pali not only in the composition of his sermons, but also as a form of amusement. Mongkut's interest in his family and his delight in his children

---

4. Full bibliographical citations for works mentioned here will be found in the bibliography to Constance M. Wilson, "State and Society" (available from University Microfilms, Ann Arbor, Mich., no. 71-1084).

is illustrated in *Khatha Phraratchaniphon nai Phrabat Somdet Phra Chǫm Klao Chao Yu Hua Phraratchathan Phranam Phraratcha-orotthida* (Verses, Written by King Mongkut, Presenting Names to the Royal Children). The verses are in both Thai and Pali, with a Thai explanation of the Pali, and are dedicated to forty-three of his royal children. The verses express the father's wish for their happiness, comfort, good health, and long life.

Another of Mongkut's many interests was the study of Thai history. It was Mongkut who, when touring Sukhothai in 1833, discovered the inscription of Rama Khamhaeng and his stone throne. After the two valuable monuments had been brought to Bangkok for safekeeping, Mongkut and a group of Thai scholars were the first to attempt to interpret the meaning of the Rama Khamhaeng as well as other early inscriptions. The results of Mongkut's historical studies are revealed in the many essays he wrote on the derivation of Thai toponyms, the naming of Thai temples, and on the history of the relations between Thailand and other Asian kingdoms. Several of these essays have been published in four separate volumes, each of which bears the title *Chumnum Phrabǫromratchathibai* (Collected Royal Essays).

Multivolume sets of Mongkut's letters and proclamations have been compiled and edited for publication by his son, Damrong. Although about a half of the items in *Phraratchahatthalekha nai . . . Phra Chǫm Klao Chao Yu Hua* (The Royal letters of . . . Phra Chǫm Klao) are formal letters to the heads of foreign states, several deal with the royal family, thus giving some insight into Mongkut as a person. The *Prachum Prakat Ratchakan thi Si* (Collected Proclamations of the Fourth Reign) cover an incredibly wide range of topics. Mongkut was interested in virtually everything that could possibly affect the welfare of his kingdom or of the royal family. The proclamations include announcements of the new year, recommendations to the public to control thieves, discipline of the royal family, relations with foreigners, and the settlement of legal cases ranging from matters of inheritance to treason. The latest edition of these unusually valuable documents has been brought out by the Fine Arts Department in Bangkok. The Teacher's Institute Press (Khurusapha) has also published an edition of the collected proclamations.

Mongkut's intellectual endeavors were continued by two of his sons: his heir, Chulalongkorn, and Damrong Rajanubhab. Chulalongkorn as an author is best known for his famous diary and for his numerous published collections of letters. These humane documents, full of humor and wise advice, are much appreciated by all readers. Often a letter reveals some otherwise unknown facet of court life. Indeed, Chulalongkorn was very interested in Thai customs. One of the books he wrote, *Thamniam Ratchatrakun nai Krung Sayam* (Customs Concerning the Royal Family in

Siam)[5] describes the system of ranks used in the royal family with an account, based in part on personal observation, of the privileges associated with each position. Some of Chulalongkorn's remarks on the honors given to a *Chao Fa* prince refer to his own childhood.

Chulalongkorn's most valuable work for a study of the fourth reign is his detailed discussion of Thai state ceremonies, *Phraratchaphithi Sipsǫng Düan* (Royal Ceremonies of the Twelve Months), used as a major source by H. G. Quaritch Wales in his *Siamese State Ceremonies*. Most of Chulalongkorn's text is based on the *Kot Monthian Ban* (The Royal Palace Code) and his own observations at court. His use of the *Kot Monthian Ban* gives his text a highly Brahmanical cast which contrasts sharply with his comments drawn from personal experience. One wonders if the use of the *Kot Monthian Ban* misleads the reader, giving the impression that Thai state ceremonies were more Brahmanical in their structure than they actually were. Close reading of many passages in the book shows that Chulalongkorn's purpose in writing was to trace the development of Thai ceremonies from the Ayudhya period to his own reign. Like many Thai authors, he is not concerned with the exact dating of events. It is not always clear which period of Thai history is under discussion: the distant past of Ayudhya, the beginning of the Bangkok era, or his own reign. Many passages borrowed from the *Kot Monthian Ban* are included in explaining the origin and development of a ceremony in the past. The less formal, more humorous descriptions of current practice indicate that the Thai of the fifth reign did not take the Brahmanical elements seriously.

The greatest historian Thailand has yet produced was Prince Damrong Rajanubhab, one of the first Thai historians to break away from the strictly chronological narratives of the traditional Thai chronicle. He is one of the few Thai scholars who analyzed and commented on events. Damrong did not confine himself to the writing of history. In addition, he edited and published several volumes of documents of Thai history, including his father's letters and proclamations.

Among the collections of documents compiled and edited by Prince Damrong are the following basic works. The *Chotmaihet Luang 'Udom Sombat* (The Letters of Luang 'Udom Sombat) contains the letters sent to Bangkok by an official attached to the Thai troops sent south to crush a rebellion in the Malay States. These letters are unusually informative about conditions in the south during the third reign and Thai methods of local administration. The *Chotmaihet Rüang Thap Chiangtung* (Documents about the Troops in Chiangtung) is a carefully selected collection of letters

5. See Robert B. Jones, *Thai Titles and Ranks, Including a Translation of Traditions of Royal Lineage in Siam by King Chulalongkorn*, Cornell University Southeast Asia Program, Data Paper no. 81 (Ithaca, 1971).

and reports covering the two campaigns against Chiangtung (Keng Tung in modern Burma) in 1852 and 1853. The reasons for the Thai failure to capture the town are clearly discussed in the letters of Kromluang Wongsa, the commander of the expedition, to Mongkut.

Other of Damrong's books are useful sources for the study of Thai foreign relations. *Chotmaihet Rüang Thut 'American Khao Ma nai Ratchakan thi 3* (Records About the American Ambassador Who Came in the Third Reign), a collection of documents on the mission of Edmund Roberts in 1833, deals with the first treaty signed between Thailand and the United States. *Ruam Chotmaihet Rüang Thut Thai pai Prathet 'Angkrit, B.E. 2400: Siamese and English Records of the Siamese Embassy to England in 1857–1858* contains both Thai and English materials about the first Thai embassy to visit Europe since the seventeenth century. Most of the English records in the book are reprints of articles from the London press. By far the most valuable of these collections, however, is *Rüang Praditsathan Phra Song Sayamwong nai Langka Thawip* (The Establishment of Thai Buddhism in Ceylon). The title refers to the visits of Thai monks to Ceylon near the end of the Ayudhya period when the Singhalese Sangha asked the Thai to help them restore the purity of Buddhism in Ceylon. The extensive contacts between the two Theravada countries ceased during the Thai-Burmese wars of the eighteenth century. The Thai were anxious to renew relations in the second reign in an effort to determine the fate of Singhalese Buddhism under British rule. Much of the volume is composed of Damrong's text, a detailed history of Buddhism in Ceylon. The documents are Thai translations of the Pali letters sent to Ceylon. It is quite likely that Thai concern for Singhalese Buddhism was one reason for their interest in British activities in Southeast Asia. It is also possible that the support of the British government in Ceylon for the Buddhist religion inclined the Thai favorably toward contacts with Great Britain.

In addition, Prince Damrong compiled and edited a number of major reference works in Thai studies. *Chotmaihet Rüang Song Tang Phra Borom Wongsanuwong Krung Rattanakosin* (Documents on Appointments in the Royal Family) contains the appointment records of *krom* ranks granted to both male and female members of the royal family. Complete copies of these records cannot be found in the archives. *Rüang Tang Phraratchakhana Phuyai nai Krung Rattanakosin* (On Appointments of High Ecclesiastical Officials in the Bangkok Era) covers appointments made from the first to the sixth reign. Again, copies of these records cannot be found elsewhere. Another reference work is the *Thamniap Nam Phak 1* and *Phak 2* (A List of Names, Part 1 and Part 2). The first volume is a miscellaneous collection of lists of names including the names of chedi, royal palaces, gates in the wall along the Grand Palace and the Front Palace, forts, bridges, and streets in the capital city, royal barges, royal steamboats, royal elephants, and royal horses. The second part, printed separately, is a list of the titles and ranks of officials who served in the Front Palace (the palace of the Second King) during the fourth reign.

Damrong drew extensively on the Thai documents he edited as sources for his own historical studies and essays. Although he seldom footnotes his sources (rather he uses footnotes frequently to make additional comments on his text) any person familiar with Thai documentary material can often identify them. In addition to his knowledge of Thai documents, Damrong also relies on oral history. His books are full of anecdotes he must have heard from other members of the royal family or from high officials. In many cases, these amusing and often interesting episodes cannot be checked against other Thai sources, leaving the researcher in doubt about their authenticity. Any attempt to trace the source of these anecdotes is complicated further by the fact that Damrong's work is extensively quoted or paraphrased by other authors. On those occasions where Damrong's sources can be traced, he is shown to be a reliable and accurate historian. Damrong's account of the two Chiangtung expeditions in *Thai Rop Phama* (The Thai-Burmese Wars) obviously is based on the documents he previously had compiled and printed. He was fully aware of the reasons for the retreat and did not hesitate to discuss them. A modern historian could hardly improve on Damrong's account of the campaigns.

It is even more difficult to track down some of the source material Prince Damrong uses in his biographies; these appear to be based more on memory and on oral reports than on written records. The most useful of these biographies for a history of the fourth reign are the ones on Mongkut, *Rüang Phra Chǫm Klao*; the early life of King Chulalongkorn, *Phraratchaprawat Somdet Phra Chula Chǫm Klao Chao Yu Hua Müa Kǫn Sawoei Rat*; and the life of Mongkut's Kalahom, Chao Phraya Sisuriyawong, *Prawat Somdet Chao Phraya Bǫrom Maha Sisuriyawong Müa kǫn Pen Phu Samret Ratchakan Phaendin* (The History of . . . Sisuriyawong before He Became Regent). Much of the material in these biographies is very difficult to trace back to a documentary source. Yet, when cross references can be located, Damrong continues to stand out as a reliable commentator on events. For example, his portrait of Mǫm Kraison as an enemy of Mongkut is borne out by some of Mongkut's statements in his letters and proclamations. The National Library contains records of Mongkut's trip to receive the homage of the Mons in Thailand when he was a young boy and of the later controversy over the manner in which the Thammayut sect wore the yellow robe.

A more complex problem is Damrong's attribution of motives for the actions of the people he writes about. Thai documents often tell the reader what was done without explaining why it was done. The researcher, therefore, knows what actions were performed, but he has no information about the reasons behind them. Prince Damrong provides the explanations, which are always reasonable, but evidence to support them is difficult to locate. The modern historian accepts Damrong's reasons for the decision of the government to send troops to Chiangtung because he can compare Damrong's text with the original letters of the King. There is no similar evidence to support Damrong's statement that Mongkut personally rejected the Brahmanical elements in Thai ceremonies, maintaining them only because they had become the customary way of doing things. There is evidence in Chulalongkorn's account of Thai state ceremonies and in the description of Mongkut's coronation in the *Chronicle of the Fourth Reign* by Thiphakọrawawong that Mongkut, while he may not have changed the Brahmanical elements in Thai ceremonies, made many modifications to strengthen the Buddhist aspects of these ceremonies. Nevertheless, the author has not been able to find any statement by Mongkut which downgrades Brahmanism. When we examine Damrong's explanation for Sisuriyawong's desire to have the eldest son of the Second King appointed Crown Prince during Mongkut's lifetime, we can only note that the appointment was made immediately after Mongkut's death. In support of Damrong, we can say that in most cases, where his information can be checked, what he writes turns out to be correct.

Some people have noted that one of the problems of evaluating Damrong's work lies in what he left out rather than in what information he used. It was, after all, a modern biographer, Natthawut Sutthisongkhram, writing on the Front Place incident,[6] who found documented evidence of an underlying conflict between the Crown Prince and the young Rama V. This kind of problem is universal. The choice of what information to include and what to leave out is always a delicate one. Damrong was writing for a Thai audience, not a Western one. As a leading member of the royal family, he could not be expected to undermine its prestige by revealing some of its inner difficulties. The modern scholar still owes a great debt to Damrong; without him Thai history would be a far less developed field than it is.

A fourth Thai historian whose work must be considered in any study of the fourth reign is Chao Phraya Thiphakọrawong (Kham Bunnak). The royal family had no monopoly over the intellectual life of the Thai court. At all times, members of official familes—and even talented commoners— could participate in the literary and artistic activities at court. Talent,

---

6. For an account of the attempted *coup d'état* of 28 December 1874 and the subsequent negotiations between the Crown Prince and Chulalongkorn, see David K. Wyatt, "The Beginnings of Modern Education in Thailand, 1868–1910" (Ph.D. diss., Cornell University, 1966), pp. 77–80; *The Politics of Reform in Thailand: Education in the Reign of King Chulalongkorn* (New Haven, 1969), pp. 57–61; and Natthawut Sutthisongkhram, *Somdet Chao Phraya Bọrom Maha Sisuriyawong* (Bangkok, 1963), pp. 692–702, 766–769, 834–841, and 1880–1884.

wherever it appeared, was encouraged. Thiphakǫrawong was a member of the most important of the official familes, the Bunnaks. He was a second cousin to Mongkut, his father's mother having been a sister of Rama I's chief queen, the mother of Rama II. Thiphakǫrawong's father, Somdet Chao Phraya Bǫrom Maha Prayurawong (Dit Bunnak), had been both Kalahom (Minister for the Southern Townships) and Phra Khlang (Minister of the Treasury) under Rama III. Chao Phraya Sisuriyawong, Mongkut's Kalahom and the most powerful single official at court, was his half brother. When Mongkut died, Sisuriyawong assumed the post of regent for the minority of Chulalongkorn. During the fourth reign, Thiphakǫrawong was Phra Khlang (Minister of the Treasury) and head of Krom Tha (Department of Trade and the Eastern Townships). As a close relation of the Kalahom and a high official in the government, Thiphakǫrawong had a leading role in many of the events of the fourth reign.

Chao Phraya Thiphakǫrawong is best known for his work in the compilation of the official history of the first four reigns of the Chakkri dynasty. He undertook this task at the request of King Chulalongkorn in 1869. Thiphakǫrawong had already begun to collect the records he needed for a chronicle, but the king's approval was necessary if he was to obtain the cooperation of other officials at court. With the aid of Chao Fa Maha Mala, a member of the royal family who had held several positions including head of the Ministry of the Royal Palace, the Department of Religion, and the Royal Treasuries, Thiphakǫrawong was able to gain access to the records of the most important branches of the government, Krom Mahatthai, Krom Kalahom (virtually a Bunnak monopoly), Krom Tha, and the Court Secretaries Department. With these documents as his main sources, Thiphakǫrawong compiled historical chronicles covering the four Chakkri reigns from 1782 to 1868. When he completed his manuscripts, they were given to King Chulalongkorn for correction and approval. Other court officials were invited to comment on them. The chronicles were not distributed to the public until Prince Damrong became interested in them and edited them for publication. The chronicle of the first reign was probably published in 1902, but the third and fourth reign chronicles did not appear until 1934. The chronicle for the second reign was published last,[7] possibly so that it would not compete with Prince Damrong's own chronicle of the second reign, which was published in 1919.

Thiphakǫrawong's four chronicles closely follow the traditional pattern of Thai court chronicles. Events are discussed chronologically and separately. The discussions of extended events over time, such as military

7. It first appeared in 1961. This information comes from the Introduction to Chao Phraya Thiphakǫrawong, *Phraratchaphongsawadan Krung Rattanakosin Ratchakan thi 1* (Bangkok, 1960), pp. 1–10.

campaigns, are divided into sections and placed under the proper year. Thiphakǫrawong follows a strictly narrative style with no pauses for explanations or comments on his material. These chronicles are a major reference for the period, not only because they attempt to present a fairly coherent history, but also because they sometimes use documents which are no longer available, as, for example, in Thiphakǫrawong's description of Mongkut's coronation. The chronicle for the fourth reign also contains a list of all *krom* (departments) whose officials were appointed at that time. This list is not available anywhere else, although there are some individual appointment records in the Thai archives.

The chronicle for the fourth reign, whether by accident or intent, presents the Bunnak officials in a very favorable light. It is as much a chronicle of the Bunnaks in the government as it is a chronicle of the reign of the king. A fairly sizable portion of the text is given over to events in which the Bunnaks participated. Few references are made to the work of other officials. This is partly due to the fact that the Bunnaks held so many responsible positions, particularly in the consultations of the Great Council which was called at the end of each reign, and in foreign affairs and public works. However, other areas of activity such as religion and justice in which the Bunnaks showed little interest are not normally discussed in the chronicle.

Thiphakǫrawong's account of the Chakkri dynasty, especially in the mid-century, presents a portrait of Bunnak dominance that is impressive but should not, of course, be regarded as definitive. An examination of Mongkut's letters and proclamations soon shows that there were areas of Thai life into which the Bunnaks seldom penetrated. They were most dominant in those aspects of government which were most conspicuous; in less public areas of Thai life, their presence seems hardly to have been felt. There were limits to the power of the Bunnaks. In all of his references to them, Thiphakǫrawong was apparently very careful not to refer to any tension between the Bunnaks and the royal family, although other sources, including some of the books by Prince Damrong, show that tension did exist. Yet Thiphakǫrawong was willing, on occasion, to discuss unpleasant events in the royal family, such as the love affair of one of Mongkut's lesser wives, the death of the Second King supposedly by a love potion, and Mongkut's irritable temper as his fatal illness developed.

Prince Damrong's work in the editing and publication of Thai historical documents has been continued by a number of groups in Thailand. The Fine Arts Department (Krom Sinlapakon), the Royal Academy (Ratchabandit Sathan), and the Prime Minister's Office (Samnak Nayok Ratthamontri) have sponsored the editing of Thai documents for publication as cremation volumes or as works of merit. These books are distributed to the public after cremation ceremonies, after the opening of a public building, or in honor of a famous person. Some of the more valuable collections of documents edited by the Fine Arts Department include the *Chotmaihet Phararatchakit raiwan Ph.S. 2411* . . . (Royal Diary, 1868–1869 . . .), which is a collection of daily records on Mongkut's last illness, and the *Chotmaihet khǫng Phra Narongwichit (Chǫn Bunnak) rüang Ratchathut Thai pai Prathet Farangset nai Ratchakan thi 4* (The Account of Phra Narongwichit about the Thai Ambassadors who went to France in the Fourth Reign). The Fine Arts Department is responsible for the compilation of the *Chumnum Phra Bǫrom Ratchathibai* . . . (Collected Essays of Mongkut), both editions, and a short volume called *Phraratchaprawat Phrabat Somdet Phra Pin Klao Chao Yu Hua* (The Royal History of the Second King), a collection of essays by Mongkut, Damrong, and others. *Ruam rüang Muang Nakhǫn Ratchasima* (Collected Sources on Nakhon Ratchasima) is a selection of administrative records from the third reign printed with the addition of some essays by Prince Damrong on the establishment on the Monthon of Nakhon Ratchasima and the construction of the railway to the town. *Rüang Phra Pathom Chedi* (About Phra Pathom Chedi), is a collection of records from the "Chotmaihet Ratchakan thi 4" on the reconstruction of the monument in the fourth and fifth reigns. And *Rüang Thut Farang nai Samai Krung Rattanakosin* (About Foreign Embassies during the Bangkok Era) is a comprehensive compilation of Thai documents with commentary on Western ambassadors in Thailand during the first through fourth reigns.

The publications of the Royal Academy and the Prime Minister's Office are more limited in number. The Royal Academy is most famous for its dictionary, the standard Thai-Thai reference. Many of its definitions are more interesting than those provided in Thai-English dictionaries, reminding us that the attempt to find English equivalents of Thai words does not always succeed. The Royal Academy has also edited the *Chotmaihet müa Phrabat Somdet Phra Nang Klao Chao Yu Hua Sawankhot* (Documents on the Death of Rama III), an interesting set of records on the last days of the third reign, a few reprints of Mongkut's letters, and the *Rüang Chaloem Phra Yot Chao Nai* (About the Celebration of a Chao Nai), a second collection of appointments of members of the royal family to *krom* ranks. In 1962 the Prime Minister's Office issued *Thai Sathapana Kasat Khamen* (The Thai Establishment of Khmer Kings), a selection of letters between the Thai government and the king of Cambodia regarding Cambodia's relations with France during the fourth reign. The Fine Arts Department's *Ruam Rüang Kiao Kap Yuan lae Khamen nai Samai Rattanakosin* (About

Vietnam and Cambodia in the Bangkok Era) is compiled from Thipha-korawong's chronicles of the first four reigns and from Prince Damrong's book *Rüang Tamnan Phra Yuan* (About the History of Vietnamese Monks).

Still other sources of information are the local chronicles, several of which were compiled in the nineteenth century, among them chronicles of Chiangmai, Lamphun and Lampang, Nan, the northeast, Songkhla, and Phatthalung. The number of chronicles compiled in the 1890's, usually at the request of King Chulalongkorn, suggests that the Thai government was either anxious to preserve something of the past or that it was not especially knowledgeable about local administration or local history. Instead of turning to its own records, it may have been easier for the government to ask an interested person to compile a chronicle. In this respect it is noteworthy that no chronicles exist for the towns in the Chao Phraya Valley, apart from those dealing with the fortunes of Ayudhya when it was the capital. All of the local chronicles are concerned with the autonomous townships of the south, the northeast, and the Lao, Khmer, and Malay satellite states. These local chronicles are a valuable source of information about the local ruling elite. In many cases, these chronicles can be used as sources for local genealogies.

Another basic body of material is the genealogies of the royal family and the families of the leading officials. Several genealogies of the royal family have been published. The most complete edition is the two-volume set compiled by Thamrongsak 'Ayuwatthana, *Ratchasakun Chakkri Wong lae Ratchasakun Somdet Phra Chao Taksin Maharat* (The Genealogy of the Chakkri Royal Family and That of Taksin the Great). This work brings together the genealogies of Taksin, the nine Chakkri kings, the five Chakkri crown princes, and the eight queen mothers. For specific information about a member of the royal family, a useful reference is Saowanit's *Phranam Chao Fa . . .* (Names of Chao Fa Princes . . .), which presents brief biographies of the royal children in the order of their birth, a quicker means of reference than Thamrongsak's listing of royal children under their mother. The Fine Arts Department has published a similarly arranged collection of biographies of royal children under the title *Ratchasakun Wong* (The Royal Family).

Genealogies dealing with important official families are numerous. The most useful one is *'Athibai Ratchinikun Bang Chang* (Explanation of the Family of the Queen Mother Bang Chang) by Chao Phraya Phichaiyat and Phraya Phaibunsombat which covers the third, the fourth, and in some lines the fifth and sixth generations of the descendants of the Queen Mother. Among these were the families of Bang Chang, Chuto, and the Bunnaks. The four volumes of *Lamdap Sakun Kao bang Sakun* (Some Ancient Lineages) contain the genealogies of several official families, including the

Bunyaratthaphans and the Bunnaks. The fourth volume is a genealogy of Taksin's descendants through the eighth generation. Prince Damrong has compiled a genealogy of the Khotchaseni family, *Lamdap Sakun Khotchaseni*, and Tri Amatyakul has written one for the 'Amattayakun family, *Prawat Banphaburut lae Sakun Wong 'Amattayakun*. Other genealogies can be found in the biographical essays in cremation volumes.

The pivotal position of Mongkut's reign in Thai history was recognized at the time by Western visitors as well as by the Thai. In an Asia where foreign visitors were not always welcome, Thai hospitality attracted many Western travelers, and they sometimes kept journals of their experiences. Some were intended for publication in the popular press to meet the demands of a growing public for unusual adventures, while others were kept as part of an official record. Some of these accounts of Thailand are very useful to the scholar, although a few were exaggerated and intended to shock rather than to enlighten.

The reports of Western observers in nineteenth-century Thailand can be classified into three groups: the accounts of independent travelers, the journals of Protestant and Catholic missionaries, and the records maintained by foreign officials for the information of their home governments. Of these, the first category is the most mixed in quality. Trained observers, such as the naturalists J. G. Koenig, who visited Bangkok in 1779, and Henri Mouhot, who toured the Korat Plateau in 1858, 1859, and 1860, have left behind some very useful records. Independent adventurers, on the other hand, were usually more concerned with the making of their private fortunes than with the provision of reliable information. *Narrative of a Residence at the Capital of the Kingdom of Siam*, by Frederick Neale, is badly confused. In spite of the author's claim that he was employed to train Thai troops, he is unable to distinguish Mongkut (Chao Fa *Nai*, the elder prince) from his brother Chao Fa *Noi* (the younger prince). Often actions attributed by Neale to one brother were actually performed by the other. Some records that claim to be personal accounts are merely compilations of materials from other sources. George Bacon in *Siam, the Land of the White Elephant* borrows much of his material from *The Kingdom and People of Siam* by Sir John Bowring.

American and European missionaries had the advantages of a long residence in Thailand and close contact with the Thai people. Generally their journals and diaries are more valuable sources of information than those of the casual traveler. Of particular interest are the publications of the American missionaries Dr. Dan Beach Bradley and Samuel J. Smith, and the French bishop Jean Baptiste Pallegoix. Dr. Bradley was responsible for the publication of the *Bangkok Recorder*, a weekly newspaper that appeared from January 1865 to January 1867, and the *Bangkok Calendar*, published yearly from 1858 to 1873. Samuel Smith edited and published the quarterly *Siam Repository* between 1869 and 1874. The *Siam Weekly Advertiser*, also published by Samuel Smith, appeared from 1869 to 1884. Each of these serials contains information on the affairs of the foreign community in Bangkok, the growth of Thailand's foreign trade, and the continuing development of Thai international relations. The editors were always willing to print articles on local customs or reports of journeys into the interior and sought explanations of Thai ceremonies and the organization of the kingdom. On occasion, Mongkut himself would try his skill in the composition of brief English notices for publication.

The work of the American missionaries, both in publication and in the transmission of modern technology, should not be permitted to overshadow that of the French. Although French activities in Thailand were not as technically spectacular as those of the Americans who introduced modern engineering technology, they were of longer duration and possibly of more importance socially, for the small Christian communities in Thailand were Catholic in their faith and not Protestant. Bishop Jean Baptiste Pallegoix wrote the best general account of Thailand in the fourth reign. His *Description du Royaume Thai ou Siam* is more complete than any other single source. Nearly all of Sir John Bowring's information on the interior of the country is taken from Pallegoix. Bowring's visit to Thailand was brief and confined entirely to Bangkok and Paknam.

The French Catholic community also contributed to Thailand's growing knowledge of the West, for their presence gave the Thai a continuous living example of the variety of Western culture and religious practices. Owing to the presence of the French, the West did not appear to the Thai as monolithically Protestant and Anglo-Saxon: there were languages spoken other than the English of the Americans and British, religions other than Protestant Christianity, powerful nations other than Great Britain. This knowledge may have supported a pre-existing Thai sense of cultural relativism based on the variety in Asian cultures, which in turn may have helped to increase the cultural confidence of the Thai.

The most detailed descriptions of Thailand in the nineteenth century come from the pens of official visitors, servants of the East India Company, the government of India, and ambassadors to the Thai capital. Most of these men had had an excellent education and considerable experience in Asian affairs. They visited Thailand with the intent of compiling as much information as possible about the country. In many cases, their accounts are basic sources in Thai history. No student of Thailand can ignore John Crawfurd's *Journal of an Embassy from the Governor-General of India to the Courts of Siam and Cochin-China*; *The Burney Papers*, four volumes in five of documents on Thai-British relations from 1825–1846; and Sir John

Bowring's *The Kingdom and People of Siam*, which includes his journal of the negotiations culminating in the treaty of 1855. Less comprehensive but still useful standard sources are *The Complete Journal of Townsend Harris*, the American envoy in 1856, and the accounts of George Finlayson, chief surgeon to the Crawfurd mission; William Ruschenburger, who accompanied Edmund Roberts to Thailand in 1836 to exchange ratifications of the 1833 treaty; Captain McLeod and Dr. Richardson, who toured the northern Lao Kingdoms in the 1830's; Sir Robert Schomburgk, British consul in Bangkok; and Amédée Gréhan, Thai consul in Paris. Unfortunately these kinds of accounts stopped with the fourth reign. Later envoys, finding their duties less exotic, did not record their experiences for publication. General descriptive surveys of Thailand were left to the intrepid adventurers and laymen.

These official journals, while they duplicate the coverage provided by the missionaries, often go deeper into Thai affairs. Missionaries, even those who informally advised the court, seldom had direct contact with the workings of the Thai political system. The foreign envoys attempting to achieve their goals by negotiation did. The missionaries were private citizens for whom protocol was not a pressing matter; their meetings with Thai officials were usually private and therefore outside the formal system of etiquette. Foreign envoys, on the other hand, were very conscious of the proper protocol, and their activities were closely regulated by both Asian and Western customs. The private audiences held behind the scenes might be relaxed and confidential, but the formal public appearances never were. The missionaries' requests involved only one small group of people. Any special privileges granted them posed no threat to the social order. Foreign officials, however, sought concessions which would have the force of law and which would apply *en bloc* to a large and continually increasing number of foreign visitors and residents. The nature of the relationship between the foreign official and the Thai enabled him to comment on the intricacies of Thai politics in a way that few missionaries, if any, could match.

Much of this "inside" political information is not to be found in the published records. It is available, however, in the archives of those countries that maintained consular representatives in Bangkok: Great Britain, France, the United States, and Denmark. The British consulate was the only fully staffed and full-time mission operating in Bangkok during the fourth reign. The French government employed a full-time consul in Bangkok, but his frequent absences interfered with the continuity of record-keeping. The other consular representatives were part-time employees whose main interest was their own business activities. Consequently, the records of the British Foreign Office are more detailed and more informative than those of any other consulate. The British archives not only include the correspondence between the British consul and London; they also contain copies of the correspondence between the British consul and Thai officials, annual trade reports compiled by the consulate's staff from the ledgers of the customs house, special reports on the local economy, and a partial set of the internal records of the consulate, including some of the records of the consular court. The materials in the French and American archives are of a much more limited nature. The section of the French archives open to foreign scholars contains only the correspondence between the French consul and Paris. There are few records on the relationship of the French consul with Thai officials and nothing on the activities of the French consulate court; until other records become available, it will be impossible to trace the full story of the various controversies between the French consul and the Thai government. The correspondence between the French consul and Paris shows that the French consul was eager to expand French influence in Southeast Asia; however, the French Ministry of Foreign Affairs was reluctant to become involved in Asian affairs. The center of support for French adventure was the Ministry of the Marine.

The consulate of the United States was very poorly managed in this period. The American community in Bangkok was badly split by the competition of two groups for the control of the consulate: the missionaries and the merchants. The missionaries wanted a good stalwart Christian in the position of consul primarily to take steps to control the rougher merchants and sailors, whose behavior might give the American community a bad name. The merchants preferred a much more relaxed atmosphere. Both groups carried their complaints to Washington. The State Department, unwilling to invest the time, effort, and money needed to establish a proper consulate, kept removing and replacing its representatives, sometimes supporting the demands of the missionaries, at other times giving in to the merchants. The main concern of the American consul in these conditions was his defense against his fellow Americans rather than the compilation of information about Thai trade, politics, or government.

The Danish consul, D. K. Mason, was a British trader in Bangkok. When resident in the capital, he attended to his duties efficiently enough, but he did not take an active role in political affairs of the foreign community. While he refers to local events in his reports to Denmark, the same information in greater detail is available in the British archives.

The Western-language material on Thailand is very useful for the study of the development of Thai diplomatic and private relations with the West and its overseas representatives. No other body of material contains so much information on the origin of Thai studies in Western subjects and the kingdom's first steps toward modernization or the growth of its international diplomacy. These records are also important descriptive sources for some aspects of Thai economic and social life. They enable us, for example, to trace the growth of Bangkok from a relatively small Asian city inhabited primarily by the royal family, their officials and their retainers, Chinese traders, and Thai peasants, to a large, modern, international urban center serving numerous social groups and economic interests. From these sources, the reader can sense the impact of the introduction of brick buildings, paved streets, the telegraph, electricity, and, later, trains, automobiles, and streetcars.

Nevertheless, this material, useful as it is, has its limitations. Much of it is strongly biased—quite openly in the missionary records, more subtly in the official reports. The Westerners in Thailand were convinced of their superiority and their greater enlightenment. Their feelings were reinforced by the rapid advances Europe and the United States were making in technology and in the sciences. In the field of military activity the Europeans were supreme. The goals of the foreign community in Thailand were not the understanding of Thai culture or the advancement of Thai studies but the spread of Christianity, the introduction of Western customs and economic and political values, and the increase in the influence of their home governments in order to obtain more benefits for their own citizens. The standard they applied to Thailand was that of Europe, with the result that many successes and strengths of the Thai were ignored in their reports. They made loud demands for religious freedom when in fact the Thai had already provided it. The Buddhist religious tradition has always been one of great tolerance for divergent views. The missionaries tend to refer to religious freedom even though the real issue is something else, as, for example, the purchase of land for churches, missions, and graveyards. Except for a few isolated incidents at the end of Rama III's reign, the American missionaries and French priests enjoyed religious freedom in the 1830's and 1840's. Few governments at that time would have permitted their populations to come into such open contact with a group of foreign subjects preaching a foreign religion and versed in the strange knowledge of science. Western residents have also tended to exaggerate their own impact in Thai society by overlooking past precedents for actions undertaken by the Thai and attributing to themselves entirely too much credit for the steady progress the Thai made toward modernization.

Thai willingness to accept the presence of foreigners and to examine new ideas had long been evident in their contacts with the other peoples of Asia. Chinese, Indians, and Arabs had been permitted to establish residences, to carry on trade, and to practice their own religious beliefs. Some individuals had even been absorbed into the political structure, where they held high administrative positions. The anxious desire of the Chakkri dynasty to expand its foreign trade had already sent Thai vessels and Thai officials to Penang, Singapore, Canton, and Macao before British traders attempted to open the country. Trading contacts must have given the Thai a fairly keen appreciation of the changing power structure in Asia. Thai contacts with foreigners on a private level could easily have been motivated by a desire for further information about the changes which were taking place elsewhere in Asia. When the foreign observers refer to Thai receptivity (or in some instances to the lack of it), we should interpret this statement as evidence of Thai initiative in seeking the information they wanted. The Thai were eager to learn about mechanics, science, and medicine, whose benefits were immediately observable, but they ignored or rejected those things for which they felt no need. Modern conveniences like steamboats could readily be adopted because, as merchants, the Thai leaders quickly realized the competitive advantages of faster transportation. Is it not possible that the American missionaries were welcome because they could provide this type of knowledge? Royal responsibility for the construction of public works meant that an existing system of organization could be put to work constructing paved streets as well as digging canals. While many ideas and suggestions came from the foreign community in Bangkok, the responsibility for their implementation and the provision of the means to carry them out rested with the Thai.

Another important reason why Western-language materials on Thailand are of limited value as sources for study is that few Western residents took the time to learn Thai really well, and fewer took an interest in Thai history, literature, and art. Without a thorough knowledge of the language and without a serious interest in Thai culture, few Western observers were able to understand the basic ways in which the Thai social and political system operated. For example, no nineteenth-century observer noted the extent to which family connections were important in Thai politics. No foreign account correctly describes the structure of the Thai state or the workings of the Thai political system. Their assessment of the position of Mongkut's Kalahom, Sisuriyawong, whom they described as "Prime Minister," was acute, even though there was no such formal position in the Thai state, but their tirades on the absolutism and despotism of the monarchy were gross misinterpretations of the Thai system of government. While they did understand that the kind of slavery practiced in Thailand was different from that found in the United States, they did not understand the relationship between slavery and the Thai social system as a whole. While individuals were interested in some aspects of Thai law, Thai religion, or Thai administration, none of the early observers attempted a coherent study of these aspects of Thai life.

In spite of the amount of material available for a study of Mongkut's reign, it was not until recently that anyone began to examine these materials and to attempt modern studies of Mongkut and his era. The study of Southeast Asia, particularly in the United States, is a phenomenon of the period after World War II. Until quite recently only a few people were interested in Thai history: some foreign residents in Bangkok, some scholars from the Ecole Française de l'Extrême Orient, and some scholarly members of the royal family. In 1904 this small group of people formed the Siam Society. The society's journal was virtually the sole repository for articles and notes on Thai history and culture published before World War II. The journal continues to be an important source of material for Thai studies.

The first English-language study of Mongkut was a brief article by O. Frankfurter which appeared in the *Journal of the Siam Society* in 1904. With the exception of the work of George Cœdès and Robert Lingat, Thai studies never received the attention of the scholarly world in the way that Indian and Chinese did. Although Lingat was primarily interested in law and Cœdès in epigraphy, both took time from their regular work in the 1920's to introduce Mongkut to a wider audience. In 1927 and 1928 Cœdès published a three-part collection of Mongkut's English letters in the *Journal of the Siam Society* which retained all of the delightful peculiarities of the originals. Lingat, an admirer of the Thai historian Prince Damrong, wrote four articles during the same period as an introduction to some of Damrong's temple histories. The most interesting of these articles is his brief account of Mongkut's service in the Buddhist Sangha before he became king. His material is taken directly from Damrong's works.

While it was World War II and the creation of new, independent Asian nations that awakened the United States to the necessity of being well informed in Asian affairs, it was—of all places—Hollywood that made Thailand and Mongkut known to the average American and European. A semihistorical novel by Margaret Landon, *Anna and the King of Siam*, drawn from two poorly written books by Anna Leonowens, governess to Chulalongkorn in the 1860's, caught the attention of the American musical team of Rodgers and Hammerstein, who transformed it in 1951 into the musical *The King and I*. In 1956, after a long run on Broadway, the play became a Hollywood film with a worldwide audience. Yul Brynner's characterization of Mongkut had no basis whatever in reality but was accepted by the general public. The small, slight, and saintly king, who would stay up all night to preach to his wives, would have been horrified with his new image.

The reaction to the damage done to Thai-American relations was not long in coming. Concerned Thai and their American friends hastened to assure a relatively small audience that Anna's description of her experiences in Thailand was an unfortunate accident of the Victorian Era. A small flurry of articles and books designed to portray the real Mongkut soon appeared. The first person who stepped forth to restore Mongkut's image was the American art historian A. B. Griswold. He opened the counter-attack on Anna (although Hollywood was even more guilty), with a 1957 article in the *Journal of the Siam Society*, later expanded and published by the Asia Society under the title *King Mongkut of Siam.*

Meanwhile, Kukrit and Seni Pramoj, the editors of *Siam Rath*, Thailand's leading newspaper, prepared their own protest in the form of a volume of English translations from Mongkut's letters and proclamations. In this way they were able to illustrate his skill as a diplomat, the high quality of his leadership as head of state, and his genuine concern for the welfare of his wives, children, and subjects. This volume is appropriately called "The King of Siam Speaks." These documents, as translated by Kukrit and Seni Pramoj, were extensively quoted by Abbot Moffat in *Mongkut, The King of Siam.* All authors achieve their end very effectively. Anna's account is quite throughly crushed, directly by Griswold, indirectly by Moffat. In the process the reader is presented with a charming, although perhaps an overly idealized, portrait of one of Asia's great kings.

The effort to rescue Mongkut from Hollywood has been successful. The casual student of Thai history is no longer influenced by Anna, if, indeed, he ever really was. What is now necessary is an attempt to provide a more complete study of an unusually complex personality. However, we should not only look at Mongkut as an exceptional individual, but also as a person who was very much in touch with his people and his time. No man develops in isolation. Mongkut was a Thai and a member of the Chakkri family. He admired his father deeply and may have tried to pattern some aspects of his reign after his father's. Mongkut's achievements in religious studies could not have taken place without the support of his half brother, Rama III. His knowledge of the West could not have been obtained if it had not been for the religious tolerance of Thai Buddhism and the Thai state. The decision to enter into treaty relations with the West in 1851 was a joint decision by the King and the ruling oligarchy of Thailand. In the negotiations that took place with the European envoys, Mongkut was sometimes the leader, sometimes a follower. This interaction of the man with his society is missing from the current biographies of Mongkut.

During this same period, the late 1950's and early 1960's, several Thai-language biographies of Mongkut have also been published. One, *Lords of Life: The Paternal Monarchy of Bangkok, 1782–1932*, is available in both Thai and English editions. Although Prince Chula Chakrabongse wrote it as a series of popular biographies, his book is currently the best general survey of the Chakkri family. As a Thai, Chula is well aware of the important religious, cultural, and legal activities of the Thai kings. Although he handles the biography of each king as a self-contained entity, the reader can compare one Chakkri monarch with another, thereby developing a sense of the common values which motivated all Chakkri kings.

Five other Thai historians—Saen Thammayot, Kachorn Sukhabanij, 'Amrung Komonwatthana, 'Ophat Sewikun, and Prayut Sitthiphan— have also written biographies of Mongkut. Of their five books, *Rex Siamensium* by Saen Thammayot is the least interesting. The author uses a brief sketch of Mongkut's achievements as an occasion for introducing a variety of philosophical concepts on which he elaborates at great length. The history of the reign is lost in the flow of rhetoric. Kachorn and 'Amrung have assumed the roles of cultural middlemen seeking to inform their Thai audience about Western attitudes toward Mongkut. Kachorn, in his small volume *Phrakiatprawat Khǫng Phrabat Somdet Phra Chǫm Klao Chao Yu Hua* (Writings on the History of Mongkut), presents a summary of Crawfurd's, Burney's, Bradley's, and Pallegoix's comments on Thai foreign relations. Like most Thai commentators, he emphasizes Great Britain's changing relationship with China as a major factor in the creation of Thai foreign policy. 'Amrung has turned to Moffat's book for inspiration; several sections of his *Chao Fa Mongkut . . .* are based on Moffat. The rest of his material comes from the standard Western sources.

Both 'Ophat Sewikun and Prayut Sitthiphan have made intensive use of Thai sources. 'Ophat's *Phraratchabida Haeng kan Patirup* (The Royal Father of His Country) is a good general biography, one of the few Thai books to contain a bibliography of the sources used. The best available survey of the fourth reign is Prayut's *Phaendin Phra Chǫm Klao* (The Kingdom of Mongkut). All areas of Mongkut's responsibilities as king are covered— foreign affairs as well as his activities in support of religion, justice, public works, and taxation. Although Prayut does not use any archival material, his book provides an excellent summary of the published documents. He concludes his study with brief biographies of Mongkut's most important officials.

A recent useful collection of essays about Mongkut can be found in *His Majesty King Rama the Fourth, Mongkut*, published in honor of the centenary of his death. The volume opens with English translations of Pali verse composed by Mongkut for the monks to chant, followed by an English translation of Mongkut's essay "The Following of Buddhism." There are two English translations of works dealing with Mongkut's life: Prince Pavaresvariyalongkorn's biography and Seni and Kukrit Pramoj's translation of excerpts from Chao Phraya Mahindr's diary, "The Last Days of Mongkut." Still another, seldom discussed aspect of Mongkut's work is revealed in A. B. Griswold's essay "The Historian's Debt to King Mongkut."

Biographies of two other important figures closely associated with Mongkut likewise are available. Somthat Thewet has written a biography of Chao Fa Chuthamani, Mongkut's brother and Second King. It is a detailed compendium of references about him found in several sources, especially in Thiphakǫrawong's chronicles and the writings of Prince Damrong. Although less well known than Mongkut, Chuthamani was almost as versatile as his brother.

The life of the senior member of the noted Bunnak family in the fourth and fifth reigns is covered by Natthawut Sutthisongkhram in *Somdet Chao Phraya Bǫrom Maha Sisuriyawong.* Sisuriyawong was probably the most important official at the Thai court because he was responsible for most of the negotiations with foreign states. As the Thai court's main trouble-shooter he was involved in the settlement with Chiangmai after its attempt to establish a greater degree of local autonomy, with the negotiations with France over the fate of Cambodia, and with the issues raised by the consular courts in Bangkok. His official position was that of Kalahom, head of the ministry responsible for the administration of the southern townships. Mongkut's policies could never have been carried out without the support of Sisuriyawong.

Natthawut has also written several collections of brief biographies which include sections on other officials in Mongkut's court. *Sam Chao Phraya* (Three Chao Phraya) contains a fairly lengthy biography of Chao Phraya Thiphakǫrawong and refers to materials not found elsewhere, the most interesting being a selection reported to be a letter from Thiphakǫrawong to King Chulalongkorn on relations between the Bunnaks and the royal family during the fourth reign. The other two collections, *Yisip-chet Chao Phraya* and *Yisip-kao Chao Phraya* (Twenty-seven and Twenty-nine Chao Phraya) contain shorter biographies of officials from other leading families of the fourth reign. Another major biographical source is Prince Sommot 'Amǫraphan's *Rüang Tang Chao Phraya nai Krung Rattanakosin* (About Appointments of Chao Phraya in the Bangkok Era), which gives brief biographies of all of the major government officials in the nineteenth century.

The work of the American missionaries in Thailand is described in two books, one old, one new. George Bradley McFarland's *Historical Sketch of Protestant Missions in Siam, 1828–1928* is the standard reference. Relations between the Thai and Dr. Dan Beach Bradley, the leading missionary in the third and fourth reigns, are described in greater detail in a recent publication by Donald C. Lord, *Mǫ Bradley and Thailand.* This biography is based on Dr. Bradley's journal, now at Oberlin College Library, and on the records of the American Missionary Association and the American Board of Commissioners for Foreign Missions.

The most comprehensive general history of Thai-Cambodian relations is *Prawatsat Thai-Khom-Khamen* (History of the Thai-Khom-Khmer) by Thawit Suphaphon, whose bibliography shows that he has utilized a wide range of printed materials as sources. The text deals not only with the relations between the Thai and the Cambodians from the earliest period of contact to the French regime but also with Vietnamese relations with the two countries. Available documents are quoted at length, unfortunately without identifing footnotes. Many of the records for the fourth reign are taken from *Thai Sathapana Kasat Khamen* (Thai Establishment of Khmer Kings) referred to above. Thai-Vietnamese relations are discussed by Phra Khru Borihan 'Anampharot in *Prawat Phrasong 'Anam Nikai nai Ratcha-anachak Thai* . . . (The History of Monks of the Vietnamese Order in Thailand). The volume covers the period from 1782 to 1862, with emphasis on diplomatic exchanges and religious contacts between the two countries.

A very recent aspect of Thai studies has been the appearance of the first scholarly monographs on the history of Thailand. This development is an international one, taking place concurrently in Thailand, the United States, and Great Britain under the auspices of such institutions as Chulalongkorn University, Thammasat University, the University of California at Berkeley, Cornell University, and the School of Oriental and African Studies of the University of London.

The most important of these recent monographs is Neon Snidvongs' unpublished 1961 doctoral thesis for the University of London, "The Development of Siamese Relations with Britain and France in the Reign of Maha Mongkut, 1851–1868." This is an exceptional study, in large part because its trilingual author had full access to all known British, French, and Thai documents, including those held by the Thai Ministry of Foreign Affairs. This large body of source material enables her to trace diplomatic developments from the viewpoint of three capitals, with the emphasis naturally on Bangkok. Dr. Snidvongs places Mongkut's diplomatic activities in a much wider context than just the fourth reign, bringing forth evidence that there was a degree of continuity in Chakkri policy. The Thai are not passive reactors to Western moves; instead they are revealed as having a strong sense of the intricacies of international diplomacy, attempting first to follow a policy of neutrality, then seeking a rapprochement with France in 1840 to offset growing British influence in the Malacca straits, and, finally, when events were forcing their hands, accepting the offers of Great Britain. At all times the Thai kept the initiative. Even when the mission of Sir James Brooke in 1850 was in the process of failing, the Thai leaders were taking steps to prevent a similiar incident from occurring in the future. The Thai decision to look to Great Britain for diplomatic support was based on rational and well-considered premises.

A study of the internal history of Mongkut's reign, conceived in part as a companion study to that of Dr. Snidvongs, is Constance M. Wilson's "State and Society in the Reign of Mongkut, 1851–1868: Thailand on the Eve of Modernization," presented to Cornell University in 1970. The emphasis in this thesis is on internal affairs, especially administration, justice, religion, and economic practices. It utilizes source materials in English, French, and Thai from archives in Thailand, Great Britain, France, Denmark, and the United States.

A third doctoral thesis concerned with an aspect of Mongkut's work is "The Buddhist Monkhood in Nineteenth-Century Thailand" by Craig Reynolds, Cornell, 1973. A large section of this study deals with Mongkut's religious life, especially with his establishment of the Thammayut sect of Buddhism.

Two other recent monographs relevant to a study of the fourth reign are Akin Rabibhadana's 1968 master's thesis for Cornell University, published by the Southeast Asia Program as *The Organization of Thai Society in the Early Bangkok Period, 1782–1873*, and Nigel Brailey's doctoral thesis for the University of London, "The Origins of the Siamese Forward Movement in Western Laos, 1850–92," also presented in 1969. Akin, in his excellent study, regards the control of manpower as one of the major objectives of the Thai state. He examines the institutions—the *krom* (department) and its subunits, the *kong* (group) and the *mu* (small group)— used to maintain control over the labor of the *phrai* (commoners). Through a detailed examination of Thai laws, Akin identifies the social classes in Thai society and attempts to illustrate their shifting relationships. This very important material has been published as a Cornell Southeast Asia Program Data Paper.

Although Nigel Brailey knows Thai well and had access to the Thai archives, he chose to base his study of Thai policy toward the northern Thai kingdoms of Chiangmai, Lamphun, and Lamphan on English-language records. While the English-language record for this area and period is a more extensive one than that in the Thai language, it nevertheless presents some problems in interpretation. In order to improve their position at home, Western envoys and missionaries would claim that every change or reform which the Thai government made was the result of their benevolent influence. The British consuls, who were often judges in legal cases arising from the British teak trade in northern Thailand, were especially inclined to claim responsibility for any reforms undertaken by Thai officials. It is easy, in these circumstances, for scholars to overestimate the degree of influence the British had on Thai policy. Brailey at times misinterprets Thai policy, often describing Thai actions as "modern" when, in fact, they were based on previous precedents—in particular, earlier Thai policy toward the Malay States and Cambodia before foreign consuls were resident in Bangkok.

Other monographs useful for a study of some aspects of Mongkut's reign, although their central topic does not deal with it directly, are G. William Skinner's outstanding *Chinese Society in Thailand: An Analytical History*, Arsa Meksawan's *The Role of the Provincial Governor in Thailand*, Wira Wimoniti's *Historical Patterns of Tax Administration in Thailand*, and Walter Vella's *Siam under Rama III* and *The Impact of the West on Government in Thailand*.

Work on the fourth reign and related periods of Thai history continues. Many of the authors discussed above, particularly those who have worked with Professor Hall, are now engaged in training a whole new generation of scholars. Neon Snidvongs has founded a Thai Studies Group at Thammasat University in Bangkok. Busakorn Lailert, who has written on the dynasty which preceded the Chakkri, the Ban Phlu Luang dynasty of Ayudhya, is teaching at Chulalongkorn University. Kachorn Sukhabanij advises students at the College of Education at Prasarnmit. The number of Thai students working on materials in the National Archives and the National Library now exceeds the number of foreign scholars there. In the future the Thai will have even more to say about their history than they have in the immediate past.

In England, while the School of Oriental and African Studies remains the center for work on Thailand, the universities of Kent, Hull, and Bristol have become interested in the area. In the United States the universities of Hawaii, Michigan, Northern Illinois, and the University of California at Los Angeles have joined Cornell and Berkeley in preparing young scholars for work in Thai history. The work now in progress will add even more to our information about Mongkut and the society in which he lived.

Kinship, Genealogical Claims, and Societal Integration in Ancient Khmer Society: An Interpretation

A. THOMAS KIRSCH

Cornell University

In his essay on Mon historical sources H. L. Shorto observes: "It is possible that a preoccupation with the genealogical theme is one of the autochthonous elements in South East Asian culture."[1] It is true that indigenous genealogical material has held considerable fascination for Western students of Southeast Asian culture and history. In particular, certain royal genealogies recorded in ancient Khmer inscriptions have posed a number of interesting problems which have produced several alternative and sometimes conflicting interpretations. One problem with these Khmer genealogies has been the frequency with which genealogical links counted through women are emphasized, in some instances despite the known presence of male links. Several views have been offered to account for this situation.

The major protagonists in the dispute over the interpretation of Khmer royal genealogies are Eveline Porée-Maspero and George Cœdès. Porée-Maspero proposes that ancient Khmer society was grounded in a "mythico-social system" based on the existence of two intermarrying groups, the lunar race descended from the Nāgī Somā, and the solar race descended from the Mahārṣi Kambu.[2] She believes that the Khmer genealogies support her view that royal succession as well as succession in priestly families were based on a matrilineal principle. Rights to the throne were therefore the heritage of women of the lunar race. Though men became kings they did so because of their relationship to some woman who was descended from Somā and thereby belonged to the lunar race.

Though he agrees that matrilineal succession was the rule in priestly families and acknowledges the importance of matrilineal affiliation among royalty, Cœdès has expressed reservations about Porée-Maspero's interpretation.[3] Cœdès believes that Khmer royal genealogies are consistent

1. Shorto 1961:67.
2. Porée-Maspero 1962:155ff.; see also 1950:237–267.
3. Cœdès 1951; see also 1968:119, n.87.

with a rule of succession by primogeniture through the male line. According to him, Porée-Maspero has attempted to treat as "normal" a rule of succession that he believes to be "exceptional."[4]

Such a serious disagreement between two scholars so knowledgeable of the Khmer material suggests that, in fact, Khmer royal genealogies are highly ambiguous and hence open to a number of differing interpretations. In other words, the genealogies in question may not lend themselves to any straightforward interpretation which would unambiguously favour one side or the other in the dispute. That this may be the case seems to be confirmed when we observe that Kevin O'Sullivan has proposed yet another interpretation of ancient Khmer society based largely on these same royal genealogies.[5] Though O'Sullivan's interpretation is reminiscent of that of Porée-Maspero in hypothesizing an ideal "underlying matrilineality" in Khmer society, it differs in some essential respects from both hers and that of Cœdès. I shall quote O'Sullivan's summary of his view of the ancient Khmer situation: "We have established that the most sacred office [among the ancient Khmer] descended *as though* there were a classic matrilineal system, that although kings did not succeed each other in general in the female line, when they wrote out their genealogy they tried to pretend that they did, and that as far as we can tell the ordinary people at the time had a bilateral kinship organization."[6]

Having established these points, O'Sullivan attempts to explain the seeming inconsistencies in kinship practice. He contends that "matrilineal descent among the ancient Khmers was an ideal to which society 'ought' to adhere, and in fact did adhere in certain sacred and ritual situations, while the bilateral organization of kinship was in general effective and has since become almost totally effective."[7] O'Sullivan seems to suggest that Khmer society may be seen as increasingly matrilineal as one approaches "purely sacred" contexts. Thus, commoners live almost exclusively in the "profane" world and do not show this matrilineal element. The *purohita* (chief priest of the State *deva-rāja* cult) had a position which was almost "purely sacred," and his office therefore descended in the matrilineal line, from mother's brother to sister's son. The Khmer king had to bridge both the "sacred" and the "profane," and thus we find "mixed" genealogies, in which, for example, succession might actually pass in the patrilineal line but, in making genealogical claims, matrilineal descent might be stressed.

O'Sullivan's view of ancient Khmer society is especially interesting to the anthropologist concerned with the historical development of Southeast

4. Cœdès 1951:117.
5. O'Sullivan 1962.
6. *Ibid.*, p. 93.
7. *Ibid.*, p. 94.

Asian societies not only because it is based in Durkheimian social theory but also because it seeks to include Khmer commoners as well as the elite strata. By including commoners as well as royalty and priestly families, O'Sullivan provides a broader and more inclusive context in which to consider the role of kinship and the function of genealogical claims in ancient Khmer society.

Whether we wish to view ancient Khmer society in a broad or a narrow context, we are still faced with several differing interpretations concerning royal genealogies and succession to the throne. Each writer has offered a variety of evidence which supports his or her particular view and, in the case of Porée-Maspero and Cœdès at least, each has questioned the interpretation of the evidence put forward by the other. Is there any way to resolve the problems posed by these differences in interpretation? I believe that there is and that this resolution may be found by examining some of the general assumptions which lie at the base of the disagreement.

Despite their differing interpretations, all three writers appear to draw upon a common core of a priori assumptions when examining the Khmer genealogical material. One basic assumption they all hold in common is that some widely agreed norm of royal succession operated in ancient Khmer society. A second assumption is that this assumed norm of succession involved demonstrating, or at least claiming, purity of descent and that this was the primary aim of the genealogies. A third assumption is that such claims to purity of descent are being made exclusively in terms of some unilineal principle of reckoning descent,[8] either patrilineal in the case of Cœdès or matrilineal in the cases of Porée-Maspero and O'Sullivan. This set of a priori assumptions has set the stage on which the differing interpretations of Khmer genealogies have been acted out. Among other things, these assumptions have introduced into the discussion of ancient Khmer society assumed "pure" lines of legitimate succession and numerous "usurpers" of royal office who do not belong to the assumed pure line. Can it be that these assumptions are faulty and lie at the base of the disagreements in interpretation? May there be other assumptions which would provide a better vantage point from which to view the role of kinship in ancient Khmer society and also shed some light on the royal genealogies? I believe this is the case. I propose to question several of the assumptions which have commonly been applied to the Khmer material in order to set out another hypothesis and to offer still another interpretation of kinship and succession in ancient Khmer society.

While it seems highly likely that there were some generalized norms concerning legitimacy to rule in ancient Khmer society, it is by no means

8. See Cœdès 1951:129.

obvious that these norms had to do with demonstrating purity of descent or that they necessarily involved claims based on some unilineal principle. My alternative hypothesis is that, with the single well-defined exception of certain priestly offices, kinship reckoning in ancient Khmer society was generally bilateral, not unilineal. Therefore, if we examine royal Khmer genealogies as claims placed in the context of bilateral kinship reckoning, and couple this with other features of ancient Khmer society, many of the problems of interpretation may be easily resolved. However, as an anthropologist I wish to place my discussion in the same kind of broad context as that used by O'Sullivan. In particular, I wish to treat ancient Cambodia holistically, including commoners as well as royalty and priestly families.

The Case of the Khmer Commoners

Though the evidence concerning the kinship situation of Khmer commoners is extremely scanty, I agree with O'Sullivan that the available evidence suggests that they reckoned kinship relations bilaterally. One line of argument which may be more persuasive to the anthropologist than to the historian is that contemporary Cambodian peasants, the lineal descendants of the ancient Khmer masses, follow a bilateral kinship system. There is little evidence of any drastic change in the living conditions of Cambodian peasants which would account for a radical change in their system of kinship reckoning since the downfall of the Khmer empire. Hence, it seems likely that the ancient Khmer masses reckoned kinship in the same fashion as contemporary Cambodian peasants.

This argument is supported by the little direct evidence available to us concerning Khmer commoners. The evidence is based on historical summaries compiled in the seventh century and reproduced later by Ma Tuan-lin, and the observations of Chou Ta-kuan who visited the Khmer Empire in the thirteenth century.[9] Though referring to widely separated periods of time, this evidence suggests that Khmer commoners followed a practice of establishing neolocal residence at marriage, that marriage was to a considerable degree a matter of individual choice, that bride price was relatively unimportant, and that divorce was relatively easy. It also appears that at funerals the children of the deceased were ritually distinguished from other kinsmen. This evidence indicates the presence of a cluster of traits among Khmer commoners which are more consistent with a bilateral kinship system than a unilineal system. Ordinarily, in unilineal systems residence rules are also biased in the direction of either a matrilocal or a patrilocal pattern rather than a neolocal one. Unilineal kinship reckoning involves lineage groups, and marriages are commonly alliances

9. This evidence is summarized in O'Sullivan, 1962:92–93.

between lineage groups rather than matters of individual choice. In circumstances of lineage alliance, bride price is typically an extremely important factor in binding the alliance. For one thing, bride price serves as a surety for the maintenance of the alliance, hence making divorce difficult.[10] Further, in unilineal systems children are typically merged with other lineage members rather than distinguished as a distinct grouping. Although this evidence is by no means definitive, it supports the view that the ancient Khmer masses reckoned kinship bilaterally rather than unilineally.

The Case of Khmer Royalty

Although we have more data relating to Khmer royalty than to commoners, the royal genealogies have also provided the major arena of disputed interpretation. The main problem with the royal genealogies has been the frequency with which female links have been emphasized and, in some instances, the failure to cite male links even when they are known to have existed. For example, in his genealogy Indravarman II, who was reigning about 1243, seems to stake his claim to the throne by stressing his relationship through his mother, who was "of a family where kings succeeded each other." Similarly, Sūryavarman I (1002–1050) emphasizes his relationship to his mother, who was, according to the inscription, descended matrilineally from Indravarman I.[11] Cœdès notes that Sūryavarman claims a relationship through his wife to Yaśovarman I and interprets this as an instance of legitimizing power by means of marriage to the wife or daughter of a predecessor.[12]

Both Indravarman II and Sūryavarman I have been classed as "usurpers" of the royal power, but the stress on female links is found even in the genealogies of apparently "legitimate" claimants to the throne. For example, in his genealogy Yaśovarman I (889–910/12)[13] hardly refers to the fact that his father, Indravarman I, had been king. Instead, he emphasizes that through his mother, Indradevī, he is connected to the ancient kings of such pre-Angkorian centers of power as Vyādhapura. In Yaśovarman's genealogy Porée-Maspero finds support for her view of ancient Khmer society.[14] Cœdès, however, believes that Yaśovarman's "double ancestry," counted through both mother and father, served to "restore the pre-Angkorian legitimacy," which had been interrupted by a number of "usurpers."[15] In his reconstruction of Yaśovarman's genealogy

10. See Leach 1961.
11. Cœdès 1937:196.
12. Cœdès 1968:135.
13. For the length of Yaśovarman I's reign, see Jacques 1971:167–168.
14. 1950:584.
15. Cœdès 1968:111.

O'Sullivan notes that it does not exclusively consist of "pure" matrilineal claims; Yaśovarman's ancestry is traced out through two male as well as two female direct ascendants.[16] Hence, in O'Sullivan's terminology Yaśovarman's genealogy is "mixed" in the sense that it is not consistently either matrilineal or patrilineal but combines both types of linkage.

Yaśovarman's genealogy is particularly instructive with respect to the differing general interpretations of royal Khmer genealogies. The evidence that it provides has been sifted through the grid of assumptions held by each writer and interpreted to conform with these assumptions. The assumptions most relevant here are that the genealogy is an attempt to claim purity of descent and that these claims are being made within the context of some unilineal principle. If there were some unilineal principle operating, Yaśovarman's genealogy, stressing *both* male *and* female links, would be quite anomalous. But if Khmer royalty reckoned kinship bilaterally, as did Khmer commoners, counting kinsmen in this way is quite consistent. In a bilateral system, kinsmen, counted through either or both male and female links, are equally members of one's kindred. The genealogical claims of both Indravarman II and Sūryavarman I, emphasizing kinship links through their mothers, are also consistent with a bilateral system of kinship reckoning. However, even if Khmer royalty did reckon kinship bilaterally, this still does not completely account for the apparent emphasis on female links in royal genealogies. For example, Yaśovarman virtually ignores his claim to the throne through his father and goes to the trouble of tracing, through male and female links, his relationships to influential figures of the past. Perhaps the solution to this problem does not lie directly within the royal genealogies but in other aspects of ancient Khmer society and, in particular, its modes of integration.

It is widely agreed that a key problem for the persistence and stability of any society is to maintain a certain minimal level of internal integration.[17] Many primitive societies are able to maintain their integration primarily through their systems of kinship and marriage.[18] Ancient Khmer society was considerably more complex than those primitive societies which have been studied most frequently by anthropologists. The complexity of ancient Khmer society seems to have been based largely on the adoption and institutionalization of various cultural elements derived from India, a process which may have begun even as early as the first millennium B.C. This process of Indianization helped produce the political systems of ancient Cambodia, Champa, and others which were considerably beyond the level of complexity of a primitive society. The Angkorian empire might be

16. O'Sullivan 1962:91.
17. See Aberle *et al.* 1950.
18. See Leach 1954.

seen as the culmination of this process of Indianization of early Southeast Asia.

The mass of Khmer commoners appear to have lived in villages which were associated with particular temple complexes,[19] superintended by an elite bureaucracy composed of nobles and sacerdotal officials. The Angkorian king assumed the attributes of a *deva-rāja* and ruled over his empire from his capital city, which was also the center of the *deva-rāja* cult. The system of temples and the *deva-rāja* cult could be seen as key factors in integrating the Khmer masses, nobility, priesthood, and royalty into a single coherent social system.

Despite the centralization implicit in the *deva-rāja* system, it appears that in fact the king's effective control of outlying areas diminished as their distance from the capital increased. The hinterlands were composed of semiautonomous centers of power which potentially could pose threats to the central authority of the king. The elite therefore presented a special problem for the integration of ancient Khmer society which was met in part by the king's harem. High-ranking officials, priestly families, and semi-independent kings or princelings would marry their womenfolk to the *deva-rāja*. This procedure helped to ensure their loyalty and support to the king, while it also provided them with a bridge to the center of power. Though some of the king's wives may have had the status of "junior" wives, there were a number who, because of their own royal birth, were ranked as queens. Apparently it was not unusual for one of these queens to be singled out as a sort of "chief" queen, perhaps because of the king's favor or for reasons of political expediency. However, it seems likely that the chief queen could only have been a *prima inter pares* among the group of royal queens.

One of the important functions of the Khmer king was his identification with the fertility of the state, and his personal fecundity served as a symbol of his fertility. Hence, each of his queens can be presumed to have had a number of children. Contrary to the assumptions of Cœdès and Porée-Maspero, there does not seem to have been any simple rule of succession to the throne, though it seems likely that the children of junior wives of nonroyal status were ordinarily outside the usual circle of potential claimants. When the reigning king died, he left a number of widowed queens with kinship ties to outlying sources of power, each with her own brood of children. These children of queens could form a body of con-tenders for the kingship. Given the situation of polygamous royal marriage and a bilateral system of reckoning kinship, what would likely happen if two (or more) sons of queens sought to claim the throne? Clearly, if the rivals were actually children of the deceased king they would *share* the

19. See Cœdès 1963:96–97.

same patrilineal kinsmen. What would be unique about each of these claimants to royal power would be the powerful matrilineally related kinsmen they might call on to support their claim to kingship in opposition to the claims of their rivals. I therefore propose that, when we encounter Khmer royal genealogies which emphasize kinship connections through female links, these claims are not primarily aimed at demonstrating legitimacy by birth.[20] Rather, such genealogies are a list of the family lines of the claimants' political allies who have assisted them in gaining and holding royal power against their rivals. The rivals, however, would likely have been the claimants' own patrilineal kin. Yaśovarman's genealogy is particularly interesting, for it suggests that, having gone only one ascending generation in the matrilineal line, thereby stressing his uniqueness vis-à-vis any patrilineally related rivals, *any* line of relationship, patrilineal or matrilineal (that is, bilateral), may be stressed to gain the widest network of allies and supporters. Such claims are completely consistent with a bilateral system of kinship reckoning but unusual if kinship is reckoned unilineally. Such a situation is hardly inconceivable among the ancient Khmers when we observe that a similar state of affairs existed among a number of more contemporary Southeast Asian kingdoms up to recent times, where bilateral kinship and royal polygamy are also found.

That genealogical claims should be an important vehicle for asserting lines of political support is hardly surprising in the special circumstances of Khmer society. Societies such as that of the ancient Khmers are, compared with modern societies, relatively small. In particular, the elite group who wield power is quite restricted in size. As noted above, one of the ways in which such societies are integrated is through affinal alliances between influential family groups. In other words, a high degree of intermarriage prevails among the elite, so that most of those who hold power are likely to be interrelated in some fashion. This circumstance is also not unique to the ancient Khmers, for similar patterns can be found among recent and contemporary European royalty as well. What seems to be unique to the Khmer situation is the great stress on female links in genealogical claims. Anthropological experience in other societies provides a clue as to why this should be.

Edward Evans-Pritchard was among the first anthropologists to note that in societies in which polygamy is well established, even though these societies are highly patrilineal, kinship links through women (mothers) serve as important foci for political cleavages and lineage fission.[21] Uterine

20. Demonstrating legitimacy of birth might be a secondary factor in such genealogies in that it would indicate the claimant to royal power was the child of a woman of queenly rank rather than of a junior wife.
21. For example, see Evans-Pritchard 1940 and 1951.

siblings (children of the same mother) operate as a unit against their own patrilineal half siblings, who are children of the same father but a different mother. Uterine siblings are unique because they share the same matrilineal kin, as opposed to their nonuterine but patrilineally related half siblings. Anthropological research in other societies may provide yet another clue to the ancient Khmer case. Evans-Pritchard and Edmund Leach have observed that genealogical claims also serve to indicate "structural distance."[22] Leach has noted, for example, that very powerful Kachin chiefs have genealogies of greater depth than those of lesser chiefs. But these long genealogies do not only represent a lineage of great age; they also indicate a contemporary widespread geographic extension as well. We may therefore interpret Khmer genealogical claims which go back to very ancient times as indices of a contemporary widespread network of political support. However, such genealogical claims may also indicate that kings who had to resort to such wide-ranging support were also threatened by rivals for political power.

To summarize the situation of ancient Khmer royalty, I propose that the genealogical evidence is consistent with the view that Khmer royalty reckoned kinship bilaterally, as, it appears, did Khmer commoners. To account for the emphasis on female links in royal genealogies I hypothesize a state of affairs in which the custom of royal polygamy produced numerous rival candidates for succession to the kingship. The main contenders for the throne were likely to be half siblings, sons of the late king born of different mothers of queenly rank. These contenders then had patrilineal kinsmen in common but were distinguished by having different matrilineal kinsmen who might be called on to support their claim to royal power. Successful claimants to the throne were those who most effectively mobilized support from their powerful kinsmen counted through either or both male and female links. The royal genealogies set out the list of the family lines so mobilized. Such a view helps to resolve some of the problems that have resulted in the differing interpretations of Cœdès, Porée-Maspero, and O'Sullivan. There remains, however, the question of why, as is generally agreed, certain sacerdotal offices passed on unequivocally in a matrilineal line of succession.

Priestly Families and Sacerdotal Offices

Earlier I hypothesized that all segments of ancient Khmer society reckoned kinship relations bilaterally. But there is general agreement that in at least some priestly families succession to sacerdotal office was through a matrilineal line, from a mother's brother to a sister's son. This

22. See, for example, Evans-Pritchard 1940 and 1951, and Leach 1954.

was particularly the case for the office of *purohita*, the chief priest of the *deva-rāja* cult. Such a matrilineal succession appears to have been ascribed to the family of the Brahman Śivakaivalya, the first *purohita* of the *deva-rāja* cult under Jayavarman II (770–c. 834), the founder of the *deva-rāja* cult.[23] Why should this be?

Let me briefly review the case. I have argued that the scanty evidence on Khmer commoners suggests that they followed a bilateral form of kinship reckoning. I have also argued that the genealogical evidence from the Khmer kings is also consistent with bilateral kinship reckoning, if we take into account the role of royal polygamy and the king's harem as a mechanism for integrating the empire and the function of queens in differentiating rival claimants to the throne. Apparently the sole exception to the general pattern of reckoning kinship bilaterally in ancient Khmer society were priestly families linked with succession to particularly strategic sacerdotal offices such as that of the *purohita*. Might there be something about these priestly offices that would help us to understand this seemingly different pattern of matrilineal succession? As Cœdès has observed, celibacy is frequently a condition of holding a priestly office,[24] and if that office is ascribed to a particular family line, then matrilineal succession might be expected. Clearly, if the priest is celibate, he will have no sons to inherit his position.

There is some evidence to suggest that celibacy was a condition for such high priestly offices as that of *purohita*, though, it should be noted, Hubert de Mestier du Bourg doubts whether this was the case.[25] Lawrence Briggs observes that Sūryavarman I took his *purohita*, Sadāśiva, out of the religious state and married him to a sister of Sūryavarman's own queen: "On his marriage he relinquished the hereditary charge of the *purohita* of the *deva-rāja*."[26] This certainly suggests that there was some relationship between holding high sacerdotal office and being celibate. Under such circumstances, one possible way of ascribing such a priestly office to a particular family would be to make the succession matrilineal. However, because one (or a few) male members of a family had to be celibate to fulfill the requirements of some priestly office, it does not mean that *all* the males of that family had to be celibate. The succession, at least in theory, could go from a father's brother to a brother's son rather than matrilineally, as it did, from a mother's brother to a sister's son. Is there some factor to explain

23. See Briggs 1951:90. For the dates of Jayavarman II's reign, see Jacques 1972. Also see Chakravarti 1970–1971:29, n. 57 for a recent translation of the Sdok Kak Thom inscription which deals with the order of descent in the family of the *deva-rāja* priest.
24. Cœdès 1951:128, n. 1.
25. Bourg 1968.
26. Briggs 1951:150. See also Cœdès 1951.

why matrilineal succession was chosen in preference to other possible modes of arranging succession?

Whether my contention that all segments of ancient Khmer society reckoned kinship bilaterally is accepted or not, where an office (such as that of *purohita*) is ascribed to a matrilineal line of succession the fathers of the office holders are clearly of some interest. Or, put more precisely, who were the husbands of the *purohita*'s sisters, the women whose sons might succeed to priestly office? As Briggs observes, "Many of the hereditary sacerdotal families, which furnished ministers as well as priests to the kings until the time of Sūryavarman I at least, were descended from the wives of Jayavarman II."[27] Thus, at least some of the women of the *purohita*'s matrilineal family were married into the royal family, and, particularly, the wives and descendants of the wives of the very king who had not only established the *deva-rāja* cult but who had also ascribed the office of *purohita* to the matrilineal line.

Let me summarize the situation with respect to the matrilineal succession of important sacerdotal offices such as that of *purohita*. The *deva-rāja* cult was established by Jayavarman II. The rites of creating a new *deva-rāja* and the office of chief priest of the state cult were ascribed to a single family, that of Śivakaivalya. The office of chief priest (and possibly other high sacerdotal offices) apparently required celibacy. *Purohita*s were recruited from the children of the sisters of the celibates of this one family, and at least some of these women were married into the royal family. Thus, while the *purohita* had a measure of ritual power and control over the kings, the interests of the *purohita* and of the kings were deliberately merged through marriage of the *purohita*'s sisters with the king. Aside from this "co-option" or mutual accommodation between king and the family of the *purohita*, the king had a counterbalancing power over the *purohita*. The king could replace any incumbent chief priest, appointing a new *purohita*, and this new chief priest could be recruited from the king's own bilateral kindred, possibly including, in some cases, his own son.

Basing his comments on Briggs's reconstruction of the *purohita* Śivāchārya's genealogy, O'Sullivan observes that Śivāchārya succeeded to the office of chief priest "matrilineally" through his great uncle Ātmaśiva.[28] But it appears that Śivāchārya's family had rights to a number of lesser offices through the "patrilineal" line, and these went to Śivāchārya's son and grandson. This suggests that, in fact, even priestly families may have reckoned kinship bilaterally and that the sole exception to bilateral kinship reckoning involved matrilineal succession to a limited number of high sacerdotal offices. The case of Śivāchārya (as well as that of Sadāśiva) also

27. Briggs 1951:90, n. 6.
28. O'Sullivan 1962:89. See also Briggs 1951:143.

suggests that the condition of priestly celibacy may only have applied to the period of actual incumbency in the priestly office and not for an entire lifetime.

Conclusion

In an effort to clarify the role of kinship and genealogical claims in ancient Khmer society I have questioned some of the a priori assumptions which, in my opinion, have led to several conflicting interpretations offered by Cœdès, Porée-Maspero, and O'Sullivan. Basically, I have proposed that all segments of ancient Khmer society—the mass of commoners, the bureaucratic elite and royalty, and priestly families—reckoned kinship bilaterally rather than on the basis of some unilineal principle. I believe that this view helps to clarify certain otherwise anomalous features of royal Khmer genealogies as well as certain aspects of the matrilineal succession to high priestly office. Viewing royal genealogies within a framework of bilateral kinship, in conjunction with the institution of royal polygamy and with the role of the king's harem as an integrating mechanism in Khmer society, we can interpret royal genealogical claims not simply as attempts to establish legitimacy to rule by demonstrating purity of descent but as efforts to mobilize political support through emphasizing a ramifying network of kinship to a number of powerful families. These claims were put forward by using a bilateral rather than an exclusively unilineal principle. Royal genealogies are therefore not to be seen as exclusively directed toward linking a king with a noble past but rather as a practical recognition of a contemporary power struggle, in which he sought to win allies to aid him in gaining and maintaining paramount power. The rule of matrilineal succession to certain high priestly offices can be seen partially as a function of the condition of celibacy ascribed to priestly offices and partially as a means for maintaining a degree of royal power over the priests. The interests of the king and the family of the *purohita* were systematically merged through affinal alliances, similar to those the king maintained with other Khmer elite through his harem.

The English historian E. H. Carr has remarked: "the more sociological history becomes, and the more historical sociology becomes, the better for both."[29] This essay is offered in that spirit. As an anthropologist with a deep interest in historical problems I have tried to apply some ideas from my discipline to the ancient Khmer material. My alternative interpretation is offered solely as a hypothesis to be further explored. It will be the historian with his greater command of the detailed Khmer materials who will ultimately decide the utility of this hypothesis.

29. Carr 1964:84.

REFERENCES

Aberle, D., A. Cohen, A. K. Davis, M. Levy, and F. Sutton. 1950. "The Functional Prerequisites of Society." *Ethics*, 60:100–111.

Bourg, Hubert de Mestier du. 1968. "A propos du culte du dieu-roi (Devarāja) au Cambodge." *Cahiers d'Histoire Mondiale*, 9:499–517.

Briggs, Lawrence P. 1951. *The Ancient Khmer Empire*. Philadelphia, Transactions of the American Philosophical Society, vol. 41, pt. 1.

Carr, Edward H. 1964. *What Is History?* New York: Knopf.

Chakravarti, Adhir K. 1970–1971. "The Caste System in Ancient Cambodia." *Journal of Ancient Indian History*, 4:14–59.

Cœdès George. 1937. *Inscriptions du Cambodge*, Vol. 1. Paris: E. de Boccard.

———. 1951. "Les règles de la succession royale dans l'ancien Cambodge." *BSEI*, n.s. 26, 2:117–130.

———. 1963. *Angkor: An Introduction*. Hong Kong: Oxford University Press.

———. 1968. *The Indianized States of Southeast Asia*. Honolulu: East-West Center Press.

Evans-Pritchard, Edward E. 1940. *The Nuer*. London: Oxford University Press.

———. 1951. *Kinship and Marriage among the Nuer*. London: Oxford University Press.

Jacques, C. 1971. "Sur les donneés chronologiques de la stèle de Tuol Ta Pec." *BEFEO*, 58:163–176.

———. 1972. "Etudes d'épigrapie Cambodgienne, VIII: La carrière de Jayavarman II." *BEFEO*, 59:205–220.

Leach, Edmund R. 1954. *Political Systems of Highland Burma*. Cambridge: Harvard University Press.

———. 1961. "Aspects of Bridewealth and Marriage Stability among the Kachin and Lakher." In E. R. Leach, *Rethinking Anthropology*. London School of Economics Monographs on Social Anthropology, no. 22. London: Athlone Press. Pp. 114–123.

O'Sullivan, Kevin. 1962. "Concentric Conformity in Ancient Khmer Kinship Organization." *Academia Sinica*, 13:87–96.

Porée-Maspero, Eveline. 1950. "Nouvelle étude sur la Nāgī Somā." *JA*, 238:237–267.

———. 1962. *Étude sur les rites agraires des Cambodgiens*, vol. I, Paris. Mouton.

Shorto, H. L. 1961. "A Mon Genealogy of Kings: Observations on the Nidāna Ārambhakathā." In D. G. E. Hall (ed.), *Historians of South-East Asia*. London: Oxford University Press. Pp. 63–72.

Lê Văn Hưu's Treatment of
Lý Thần Tôn's Reign (1127–1137)

O. W. WOLTERS
Cornell University

In 1137, according to the *Đại Việt sử ký toàn thư*, three wives of the dying Lý Thần Tôn, fifth ruler of the Lý imperial family (1009–1225), persuaded him to change his mind in appointing his heir.[1] As a result, one of their sons, the future Lý Anh Tôn (1137–1175), aged two years, was nominated in preference to a concubine's son, Thần Tôn's original choice.

Lý Thần Tôn was the nephew of the fourth ruler, Lý Nhân Tôn (1072–1127), and he was also the first Lý ruler whose predecessor was not his father. He was only twenty-one years old when he died, and his reign is the shortest of all the Lý reigns with the exception of that of the ninth and final ruler, who ruled for less than a year. Thần Tôn's deathbed scene is not described in Lê Thành Khôi's invaluable survey of Vietnamese history, where even his reign is barely mentioned.[2] The reign is neglected because what happened in the period from 1127 to 1137 does not contribute to the themes in Lý history developed by this author, who concentrates on the expanding armature of the first long-lived Vietnamese dynasty and its devotion to Mahāyāna Buddhism. The significance of Lý history is seen in the rulers' victories against the Chinese, Chams, Khmers, and hillsmen and in their initiative in creating a more centralized monarchical system, supporting it by developing the country's agricultural resources and by creating a fledgling bureaucracy.

Thematic treatments of earlier Vietnamese history, of which Lê Thành Khôi's is deservedly the best known in a European language, owe much to

1. *Đại Việt sử ký toàn thư* (*TT*), bản kỷ 3, 41b–42a (Cornell University Olin Library microfilm of the Toyo Bunko copy of the Kŏng-yŏn-kim Library text, undated). Trần period citations are from this text. For the Lý period from 1137 to 1225 citations are from the Hikida Toshiaki text in Tokyo, believed to be of 1884 and in a printed edition in the Library of the School of Oriental and African Studies, London. The annals for the period from 1137 to 1225 are missing in the Olin Library text. For the date of 1137, see Hoàng Xuân Hãn, *Lý Thường Kiệt*, II (Hanoi, 1950), 424, to whose sources can be added Li Hsin-ch'üan, *Chien-yen i-lai chao-yeh tsa-chi*, Kuo-hsüeh chi-pen ts'ung-shu (1909, 1913), which states that Anh Tôn's mission reached Hangchou on 24 April 1138. The date is said to be based on the *hui-yao*.

2. Lê Thành Khôi, *Le Viet-nam: Histoire et civilisation* (Paris, 1955).

the circumstance that the dynastic records are arranged in chronological sequence. Long periods of time can therefore be surveyed with much more assurance than is possible with the earlier history of other parts of Southeast Asia. Surveys, in turn, encourage attempts to characterize conspicuous features of the past. Thematic surveys also enable topics that emerge in one period to be marshalled for discussion in the later periods. But characterizations, based on categories of happenings, bring with them the risk that the historian's own perspective sometimes determines what should be seen as significant in the record of the past.[3] Moreover, specific periods tend to lose their identity. Lý history is an important subject in its own right; it is the first long and relatively stable period in independent Vietnam after the withdrawal of the Chinese at the beginning of the tenth century. Because the Lý annals are presented as a year-by-year narrative, one becomes eager to know how different sections of the population responded to the situation evolving over more than two centuries. Their sense of what was significant in their lives is also part of the evidence. The historian may never recover it, but he can try.

Unfortunately, the establishing of Vietnamese perspectives more contemporary with the evidence is one of the difficult problems that face the historian of early Vietnam. The historian of other parts of early Southeast Asia handles materials which are almost entirely epigraphic and iconographic, and he has plenty of opportunities for studying how some people at a given moment in time were able to see themselves and their situations. Vietnamese inscriptions exist, but they have been much less frequently used as a basis for historical reconstruction. The historian of Lý Vietnam has relied chiefly on the annals, preserved in the Đại Việt sử ký toàn thư, which were compiled after the dynasty's fall and, even more discouraging, were subjected to editing by later historians.[4] Furthermore, these historians subscribed to the view that the past contained lessons for the present and the future, and they would not have flinched from allowing their sense of duty to influence them when they were compiling records. Thus, those who today interpret the general pattern of Lý history may sometimes be the

3. Louis Malleret notes this risk in "The Position of Historical Studies in the Countries of Former French Indo-China in 1956," in D. G. E. Hall (ed.), Historians of South-East Asia (London, 1961), p. 310.

4. This work incorporates Ngô Sĩ Liên's revision in the fifteenth century of the annals of the earlier centuries and also includes annals for the subsequent period. The standard edition of the TT was produced by Lê Hi in 1698. There is also the Việt sử lược (VSL), which is quoted below from the reprint of the copy in the Shou-shan ko ts'ung-shu, Ts'ung-shu chi-ch'êng collection, 3257. Its information, presented as a chronological record, can be compared with the TT's record. The VSL is believed to have been compiled in the second half of the fourteenth century. The text was preserved in China and not in Vietnam and may not have been subjected to editing.

victims of the discretion of earlier scholars, who also selected material that conformed to what they regarded as suitable categories of evidence.

One possibility, however, exists for studying a surviving perspective on Lý Vietnam, which, although not contemporaneous with Lý times, is no later than the thirteenth century. In 1272, Lê Văn Hứu presented to the Trần ruler Thánh Tôn a *Đại Việt sử ký* of thirty chapters, comprising Vietnamese history until the fall of the Lý. His work no longer exists, but, in the version of the Lý annals which survives in the *Đại Việt sử ký toàn thư* and precedes the annals of subsequent dynasties until the second half of the seventeenth century, thirteen comments on Lý history are attributed to Lê Văn Hứu. Of these comments, no fewer than five are concerned with Lý Thần Tôn's reign, while a further comment, although in the context of an event in 1028, also refers to that reign.[5] Lê Văn Hứu may have been considerably interested in the short and apparently undistinguished fifth reign.

But can one be confident that the narrative for the fifth reign, and even the comments attributed to Lê Văn Hứu, are exactly in the form that he originally wrote them? In 1479 another historian, Ngô Sĩ Liên, began to revise his work by supplying new facts, correcting his composition, and improving the language of the text in order, presumably, to make certain terms conform with fifteenth-century usage.[6] Ngô Sĩ Liên also reduced the length of his predecessor's work, though he used additional sources. Because of Ngô Sĩ Liên's intervention and because of the likelihood of even later editorial and copying changes, Lê Văn Hứu's criteria for selecting material may now be lost.

In 1934, Emile Gaspardone described the rules which Ngô Sĩ Liên invoked as the basis of his revision,[7] and, as early as 1904, Cadière and Pelliot were aware of his shadow.[8] Textual questions are bound to have had high priority for the few who have used the *Toàn thư*, and sometimes scholars have checked the text's accuracy and anachronisms by means of independent controls. Thus, Henri Maspero used the *Ling-wai tai-ta* as a check on Vietnamese sources for the political geography of Lý Vietnam.[9] Trần Hàm Tấn noted that, although the *Toàn thư* refers to the Temple of Literature in 1070 as the "Văn Miếu" 文廟, this name for Confucius' temple was not *en vogue* in China until the fifteenth century. He suggests

5. These comments are discussed in this essay.
6. See E. Gaspardone, "Bibliographie annamite," *BEFEO*, 34, 1 (1934) :54–58.
7. *Ibid.*
8. L. Cadière and P. Pelliot, "Première étude sur les sources annamites . . . ," *BEFEO*, 4, 3 (1904):617–671.
9. H. Maspero, "La géographie politique de l'empire d'Annam sous les Li . . . ," *BEFEO*, 16, 1 (1916):27–47.

that Ngô Sĩ Liên had updated Lê Văn Hưu's name for the temple.[10]

In spite of textual problems, however, efforts to identify Lê Văn Hưu's craftsmanship, though not necessarily every word he wrote, may not be fruitless.[11] Ngô Sĩ Liên reduced and revised Lê Văn Hưu's work, but he did not wish to supersede it. Indeed, in the surviving version of the Lý annals in the *Toàn thư*, he is represented as commenting on his predecessor's comments.[12] Anxious to teach the lessons of the past, he may have decided that some of the earlier annalist's lessons deserved to be retained.[13]

This essay will discuss one possibility for identifying part of Lê Văn Hưu's contribution to the surviving text of the Lý annals. The *Toàn thư*'s account of the fifth reign includes, as was remarked above, no fewer than five comments attributed to him. Perhaps his treatment of this reign was influenced by his interest in certain features of Lý history which were particularly prominent in the fifth reign. If so, the implication is that he not only commented on these features in Thần Tôn's reign but did so elsewhere when they were apparent. He may even have arranged his narrative of the different reigns in such a way that evidence was available to substantiate his views. A complementarity, recognizable today, between Lê Văn Hưu's comments and the organization of the narrative may be a means of identifying his work and of discovering a thirteenth-century perspective on Lý history.

For an investigation of his perspective we shall return to Thần Tôn's death-bed scene. The *Toàn thư*'s account is as follows:

The eldest imperial prince, Thiên Tộ, was appointed as imperial heir 皇太子. Thiên Lộc had originally been appointed by the emperor as his successor. When the ruler became bedridden, three wives, the Cảm Thánh, Nhật Phong, and Phụng Thánh *phu nhân* 夫人, wanted to alter the appointment. They sent someone to bribe the second privy councillor,[14] Từ Văn Thông, with the message: "If you are ordered to draft the ruler's last edict, do not then neglect the three wives." Văn Thông promised [to heed their wishes]. When the ruler became dangerously ill, he ordered his edict to be prepared. Văn Thông obeyed the ruler's order, but his concern was for the three wives. He held his pen but did not write. Suddenly

10. Trần Hàm Tấn, "Etude sur le Văn-Miếu de Hà-Nội," *BEFEO*, 45, 1 (1951):102. Professor Hoàng Xuân Hãn uses as an important control Li T'ao's *Hsü tzu-chih t'ung-chien ch'ang-pien*.

11. One word written by Lê Văn Hưu can certainly be identified. When the *TT* states that an envoy called "Nguyễn" went to China (he is called "Lý" in the Chinese sources), we know that Lê Văn Hưu is following the Trần convention of abandoning "Lý" in favour of "Nguyễn." Thus, the *TT* states that Nguyễn Quốc had returned from China in 1158 (*TT*, 4, 7b), whereas Li Hsin-ch'üan (p. 2868) states that Lý Quốc Dĩ was in China in 1156. Ngô Sĩ Liên did not check the Chinese sources on all points.

12. For example, *TT*, 3, 33b, in connexion with the fifth reign.

13. One warning of history, uttered by Lê Văn Hưu, is noted below.

14. For this translation of 參知政事 see E. A. Kracke, *Civil Service in Early Sung China* (Cambridge, Mass., 1953), p. 31.

the three wives, choking with tears, came and said: "We have heard that in ancient times when successors were appointed they were the sons of legal wives 嫡 and not of concubines 庶. Thiên Lộc is a concubine's son 嬖人之子. If you make him your successor, his mother will certainly usurp power and harmful sentiments of jealousy will arise. When this situation develops, how shall we and our children be able to avoid trouble?" The emperor accordingly issued this edict: "The imperial son Thiên Tộ is young,[15] but he is a legal wife's son.[16] Everyone knows that it is proper that he should succeed me in the imperial responsibility. The imperial heir 皇子 Thiên Lộc will [now] be appointed Minh-đạo vưởng."[17]

Lê Văn Hửu does not comment on this episode, but, in a comment on something that happened more than a century earlier, he anticipates it. In 1028 the founder of the dynasty died, and three brothers or half brothers contested the succession. Their efforts were foiled by those who respected the late ruler's last edict, and Lý Thái Tôn (1028–1054) became the second emperor. Lê Văn Hửu's comment is as follows:

The Lý family appointed all the sons of legal wives 嫡 as *vưởng* 王 and all the sons of concubines 庶 as imperial sons 皇子. But the post of imperial heir was not established. When the emperor was dying, [he] selected one of his sons to continue the imperial responsibility.

He discusses reasons for this custom. Perhaps the rulers wished to test their sons' qualities before making the final decision. The *Toàn thư*'s narrative certainly shows that the first two Lý rulers revealed their intentions during their reigns by giving one of their sons special educational and administrative experience, but, as the three wives in 1137 knew when they bribed the privy councillor, the imperial intention was officially binding only through the instrument of the ruler's final edict.[18] Lê Văn Hửu deplored this procedure, and, in a critical mood, he cites as a consequence what happened in 1137. He ends his comment thus: "Those who rule countries must take this as a warning ."[19]

The account of the appointment of Thần Tôn's heir is sufficiently detailed to suggest that the annalist took trouble over it as a convincing illustration of what was bound to be a critical time in Lý dynastic history.

15. According to the *VSL*'s chronology, he was born in 1136.
16. His mother was the Cảm Thánh *phu nhân*.
17. *TT*, 3, 41b–42a.
18. The *TT* states that "imperial heirs" were appointed in 1009, 1028, 1066, and 1118. On the other hand, the second and third rulers were also made *vưởng* when they were old enough to assume some responsibilities, and the symbol which rallied the new ruler's supporters in 1028 was his father's final edict. The third ruler was over forty years old in 1066 and had been childless. For him the case for appointing his first son, although a concubine's child, was overwhelming, and the narrative emphasizes the importance he attached to the birth of this son, the future Nhân Tôn. Thus the fifth ruler and his three legal wives had various precedents to guide them, but no precedent eliminated the authority of the final edict.
19. *TT*, 2, 13a–b.

He wanted his narrative to teach a lesson of history in support of his comment in the context of 1028. The *Việt sử lược*, while it refers to the princes' revolt in 1028, does not mention the scene at Thần Tôn's deathbed.

Two questions now arise. Is Lê Văn Hưu's interest in Lý dynastic practice reflected in other comments? And are there other instances of complementarity between comment and narrative?

His comment for 1028 is not an isolated criticism of the procedure for appointing heirs in earlier Vietnamese history. In connexion with Lê Ngọa Triều's murder in 1005 of his eldest brother, the second ruler of the ephemeral Lê dynasty (981–1009), he states:

Were not the misfortunes of the Lê family the results of the failure of Đại Hành [Lê Hoàn, the first Lê ruler] to establish early his successor and of Trung Tôn[20] to protect himself when he succeeded to the throne?[21]

Lê Văn Hưu provides further evidence of his interest in dynastic stability. On the occasion of Lê Hoàn's accession in 981, he compares the latter's achievements with those of the first Lý ruler. He concedes that Lê Hoàn's military achievements were greater,[22] but, in terms of influence exercised on posterity, the imperial *virtus* 德 of the first Lý ruler was greater.[23] Yet his respect for Lý Thái Tổ does not prevent him from criticizing another dynastic custom of the Lý family, who, like other dynasties before them, practised polygamy. His views on imperial polygamy are contained in his comment on the Đinh emperor's appointment of five empresses in 970.

From ancient times [that is, in the Chinese classics and history] only one empress was appointed to rule within [the female household 內治]. That was all. It was unheard of that there should be five. The Đinh ruler was lacking in ancient learning, and his subordinates at that time could not correct him. He therefore indulged himself and established five empresses. Later the Lê and Lý also often copied the Đinh practice. Đinh was the first to pave the way for disorders.[24]

He criticized the Lý because they practised polygamy and because their procedures for determining the succession were defective. The *Toàn thư*'s narrative gives so much detail, ignored by the *Việt sử lược*, about what happened when the emperors were dying that it reads as a verification of his criticisms. Here seems to be an instance of complementarity of comment and narrative in aid of teaching the lessons of history.

20. Trung Tôn was Lê Hoàn's immediate successor.
21. *TT*, 1, 26a.
22. Lê Hoàn repulsed a Chinese invasion in 981.
23. *TT*, 1, 14b.
24. *TT*, 1, 3a–b. The first ruler appointed three additional empresses in 1016 (*TT*, 2, 7b), and the second ruler had seven (*TT*, 2, 15b). According to the *VSL* (p. 33), the third ruler had eight.

Only the third ruler's accession in 1054 is uneventful. The succession in 1028 was contested.[25] The succession in 1072 was marred by the new emperor's mother, who murdered the late ruler's legal wife.[26] The succession of the fifth ruler in 1127 was, as we shall see, unsatisfactory because the new ruler was Nhân Tôn's adopted son but did not behave as such. The succession in 1137 took place after the scene at Thần Tôn's deathbed; the consequence, as we shall also see, was a palace revolution in 1150. In 1175 an empress was unsuccessful in persuading the dying sixth ruler to change his mind about his heir.[27] The seventh ruler died in 1211 after surviving a son's attempt to overthrow him.[28] The eighth ruler abdicated in 1224 in favour of a daughter, who married a young member of the Trần family, selected by senior Trần kinsmen to found a new dynasty.

Nevertheless, the Lý dynasty survived for more than two centuries. Do these family squabbles, emphasized in the *Toàn thư,* justify Lê Văn Hưu's harsh comments on dynastic customs?

His comments deal with matters that were far from trivial. During his lifetime the most serious question would have been whether the Mongols would continue to attack Vietnam, and he knew that the leadership provided by his own dynasty, the Trần, was indispensable in the face of this danger. He was bound, therefore, to have perceived the corresponding role of the early Lý rulers in the face of attack from China, Champa, and the hillsmen. Because he respected leadership, he could not fail to note that, of the eight rulers who followed the founder of the Lý dynasty, only the second and third were mature men at the time of their accession. This meant that an unstable situation in the imperial family could cause damage to the country as a whole, and he reviewed the dynastic record from this point of view.

The first minority began in 1072, which was not long before Wang An-shih's invasion, but the youthful Nhân Tôn was protected by two outstanding men, Lý Đạo Thành and Lý Thường Kiệt, whose loyalty to their dead leader, the third ruler, was probably absolute. But the subsequent young rulers were not so well served. Lê Văn Hưu, a Trần official, was qualified to diagnose the situation developing outside the imperial family as a result of the first Lý rulers' initiative. He knew that the eleventh-century emperors had not only been soldiers; they had also brought into being an enlarged royal service, with civilian as well as military components. Yet the records in the *Toàn thư* reveal that those in royal service, while depending on the dynasty for an administrative system in which they could

25. *TT*, 2, 10b–12b.
26. *TT*, 3, 6b–7a.
27. *TT*, 4, 10a.
28. This episode is summarized by Lê Thành Khôi, pp. 168–169.

prosper, had not evolved a code of conduct which reduced the need for imperial supervision. On the contrary, imperial control was more necessary than ever to prevent these servants from exploiting to their advantage the unstable family situation of the dynasty. The *Toàn thư*'s narrative, as we shall see, leaves one in no doubt that the royal service had acquired the capacity of influencing the dynasty at precisely the time in Lý history when imperial minorities in the wake of uneasy successions were beginning to cause stresses and strains in the dynastic institution and when Vietnam was also coming under attack from Chams and Khmers. This time began during the fifth reign, which is why it evokes more comments from Lê Văn Hừu than any other reign. The fifth reign is an opportunity for recovering a thirteenth-century perspective on Lý history.

We must first glance at the situation which had evolved by 1127. The dynasty was founded by a soldier from Bắc Ninh, north of Hanoi, who had served the Lê rulers and was the protégé of the monks. Lê Thành Khôi rightly stresses how the founder and his successor had to rely on a personal following.[29] Not many details are known of their partisans, but the evidence suggests a situation similar to that which A. Thomas Kirsch has discussed elsewhere in this volume. Important persons were bound by personal ties to the imperial family. The Đinh and Lê warlords of the tenth century had married their predecessors' wives, and Lý Thái Tổ gave his eldest daughter in marriage to Đào Cam Mộc, who had encouraged him to seize the throne in 1009.[30] Thái Tổ also appointed three additional empresses in 1016.[31] The identities of the second ruler's seven empresses are unknown, but it is noteworthy that in 1028 he gave titles of honour to three of his seven fathers-in-law.[32]

Among the valued allies of the first Lý ruler would have been those who possessed independent military power in the regions beyond the delta plains. The Lý family had come from the upper reaches of the delta. According to the *Sung hui-yao chi-kao*, Lý Nhân Nghĩa, who was sent as an envoy to China in 1011, was the "prefect" of Diễn, on the southern border.[33] He was loyal to the second ruler during the succession crisis of 1028.[34] Another "prefect" from a frontier area who was sent to China was Lương Nhậm Văn, from Trường, near the site of the former capital of Hoa Lư, who went to China in 1010;[35] he, too, was loyal when the

29. *Ibid.*, p. 145.
30. *TT*, 1, 34b.
31. *TT*, 2, 7b.
32. *TT*, 2, 15b.
33. *SHYCK*, Chung-hua shu-chü edition (Peking, 1957), 7728b. The *TT* states that the mission was sent in 1011 (*TT*, 2, 4b).
34. *TT*, 2, 11a.
35. *SHYCK*, 7728a. The *TT* also mentions this mission in 1010 (*TT*, 2, 2a). For Trường's location, see Maspero, p. 28, n. 4.

second ruler's brothers contested the succession in 1028.[36] The Chinese term "prefect" should not be taken literally. The first ruler lacked the authority to post his own officials to distant parts of the country. The "prefects" were merely local warlords.

The princely revolt of 1028 provides a further example of the way in which the Lý family was protected by regional support. As soon as the revolt had been suppressed, an annual oath of loyalty to the ruler was instituted at the temple of the Đông Cổ spirit at the capital.[37] This spirit of the Thanh-hóa mountain of Đông Cổ had, in 1020, offered its services to the future second ruler when, on behalf of his father, he was marching south against the Chams, and the grateful prince had built a shrine for its worship in the imperial city.[38] In 1028 the same spirit warned the new ruler that his brothers were about to attack him and gave him the opportunity of discussing the crisis with his supporters.[39] The spirit was now promoted to the rank of "prince."

The southern regions therefore supplied several and various means of support for the new imperial family. Lý Nhân Nghĩa came from Diễn, and Lương Nhậm Văn came from Trường. Moreover, in the fighting in 1028, the bravest general, Lê Phụng Hiểu, was born in Thanh-hóa, though not in the region of the Đông Cổ mountain. He had responded to the first ruler's call for soldiers.[40] In these circumstances, the annual oath of loyalty, with sanctions guaranteed by the spirit of the southern mountain, would have been appropriate and even prudent. The alliances, however, were not based on an acceptance of the abstract concept of dynasty but on personal sentiments. A tension between the second ruler's reluctance to fight his own brothers and his duty as his father's heir is reflected in his refusal to fight; he chose to mourn his father, leaving the fighting to his allies. The discussion in 1028 emphasizes his allies' sense of obligation to the dead ruler. They gave their support because the new ruler's father had deemed him worthy to succeed, and they reported the defeat of the rebels before the coffin and only then informed the new ruler. Again, the spirit's intervention in 1028 was because of his loyalty to the new ruler, first proferred in 1020. The spirit had observed the prince's refusal to shirk the difficulties of the campaign. Part of the inspiration behind the initial support given to the Lý family may have been the recognition of its ability to protect the southern regions of Vietnam from Cham attacks. Loyalty was

---

36. He was given a senior post by the new ruler (*TT*, 2, 16a).
37. *TT*, 2, 14b–15a.
38. The *TT* supplies the date of 1020, and the *Việt-điện u-linh tập* (*VDULT*), Nhà Sách Khai-trí edition (Saigon, 1960), pp. 196–197 mentions the spirit's assistance in the Cham campaign.
39. *TT*, 2, 15a.
40. *VDULT*, p. 207, and an interline note in *TT*, 2, 12b.

still only an acknowledgement of the heroic quality of an individual. Nevertheless, the consequence of these alliances was that the Lý imperial family survived its first major test, which involved no less fundamental a dynastic issue than the founder's choice of a successor.

The second Lý ruler continued to rely on regional support. For example, in 1031 the "prefects" of Phong and Ái, frontier districts, were sent to China as envoys.[41] The *Toàn thư*, while not disclosing these geographical details about the envoys, provides significant information about Lê Ốc Thuyên, the envoy of 1031 who was recognized by the Chinese as the "prefect" of Phong.[42] Phong is the district which controls the strategic river valleys between the upper delta and southern China. Lê Ốc Thuyên was the adopted son of one of Lê Ngọa Triều's empresses.[43] The new dynasty would have wanted to secure his obedience, and it is not surprising that in 1030 he is described as a *đại liêu ban*, a title of honour in the Lý court.[44] In 1036 the alliance was strengthened by a marriage between the second Lý ruler's daughter and Lê Thuận Tông, who appears in the *Toàn thư* as the "chief" of Phong.[45] The latter was probably a relative of Lê Ốc Thuyên, the "prefect" of Phong in 1031.

But the new dynasts wished to develop a system of government which depended on something more substantial than alliance with regional chiefs. They needed to emphasize the social distance between themselves and all other Vietnamese. A ready means of doing so lay at hand. Even the tenth-century Đinh and Lê warlords had sought to adopt some of the forms of a Chinese dynasty. They had assumed the imperial title, announced reign periods, and introduced trappings of rank in a ceremonial court. Lê Hoàn had minted coins and performed the ploughing rite.

The Lý family came from Bắc Ninh, in the neighbourhood of present-day Hanoi, where Chinese rule and influence had been most considerable and where a high rate of literacy provided the opportunity for studying Chinese secular literature as well as Chinese translations of Sanskrit Mahāyāna texts. Thus, as early as 1011, Thái Tổ's envoys to China successfully requested not only the Tripiṭaka but also imperial documents.[46] Further evidence of Thái Yổ's interest in Chinese models is his construction of a *Tập Hiền* office 集賢殿 in his new imperial city of Thăng

41. Li T'ao, *Hsü tzu-chih t'ung-chien ch'ang-pien* (Taipeh, 1961), pp. 110, 10. *TT*, 2, 20a, states that the mission was sent in 1030.

42. Li T'ao gives his surname as "Lý," but, in view of the evidence below, "Lý" is probably an error for "Lê."

43. *TT*, 1, 29a.

44. *TT*, 2, 20a.

45. *TT*, 2, 24b. On the title of "chief" (*châu mục*), see Maspero, p. 37.

46. *SHYCK*, 7728a. The *TT* ignores this request for secular literature and attributes the request for the Tripiṭaka to 1018.

Long at Hanoi.[47] In T'ang and Sung China this office possessed a library; its scholars were consulted on ritual and the preparation of official documents and examined policies in the light of ancient learning.[48] In 1029 the second ruler built a *Văn Minh* office 文明殿 where other literati would have been at his service.[49] The third ruler appointed an academician 學士 to this office at the time of his accession in 1054.[50] In 1046 the Chinese recognized a "librarian" 密書丞 and not a "prefect" among the Vietnamese envoys.[51]

Several Chinese institutions were particularly helpful for elevating and defining the social status of the *parvenu* Lý family. The first of these was the Ancestral Temple 宗廟, an institution which is not mentioned in the records of the tenth century. The concept of imperial *virtus* 德, symbolized by the Temple, is unlikely to have become quickly acceptable in Vietnamese society. Lê Văn Hừu criticizes the founder of the dynasty for postponing for ten years the erection of his Ancestral Temple.[52] Evidence of respect for the Temple becomes a little more frequent as the years passed,[53] though the only Lý ancestral tablet 神主 mentioned in the *Toàn thư* is that of the fourth ruler.[54]

The Ancestral Temple was the most prestigious symbol of the Lý family's imperial status, but additional and more efficacious means were necessary to establish its status. The family had to set itself as far apart as possible from other families in order to prevent it from being absorbed into a coalition of families, linked together by marriages and other modes of alliance. Otherwise, leadership would sooner or later be exercised by the person in every generation who could mobilize most support from these allied families, all of whom could regard themselves as being of comparable status. The successful adventurer's accession ceremony, corresponding elsewhere in Southeast Asia to a religious consecration, would then place him but not his own family at the head of the kingdom. In order to distinguish itself from other families, the imperial family had, as a matter of priority, to identify those whom it recognized as its members and to define their degree of access to the centre of the family, the emperor, by means of an unambiguous hierarchy of rank. Those inside the family would then know their relative subordination vis-à-vis their kinsmen, while everyone

47. *TT*, 2, 3a. The *Tập Hiền* office was still standing in 1281, according to the *TT*.
48. R. des Rotours, *Traité des fonctionnaires et traité de l'armée, tr. de la nouvelle histoire des T'ang* (Leiden, 1947–1948), I, 189, 194.
49. *TT*, 2, 19b.
50. *TT*, 2, 39b.
51. Li T'ao, 159, 15. The *TT* ignores this mission.
52. *TT*, 2, 3b. The building of the Temple is mentioned in *TT*, 2, 8b.
53. Victories were announced there in 1044, 1069, and 1119 (*TT*, 2, 35b; 3, 5a and 20b).
54. *TT*, 3, 34a.

else would be specifically excluded from the family and could approach the emperor only as his servants.

Two Chinese symbols of hierarchy were available: the imperial genealogy 玉牒 and the court 朝廷.

Unlike the Đinh and Lê families of the tenth century, the founder of the Lý dynasty possessed a genealogy, which was brought up to date 修 in 1026.[55] Unfortunately, little is known of its contents.[56] More is known of the succeeding dynasty's genealogy, which in 1267 had the hallmark of a genuine one; it provided for titles of descending rank for males and females into the fifth generation of descent from an emperor.[57] The *Toàn thư* refers to these titles in Lý times without explaining their genealogical significance; indeed, the titles are sometimes conferred on persons outside the imperial family. In Trần times, however, distant relatives of a reigning emperor were, by means of genealogical status, sloughed off and removed from close proximity to the head of the family. Diminishing rank from one generation to the next is not, of course, a specifically Vietnamese practice; the Thai royal family has observed the same rule.[58] But, when the rule is combined with the ruler's right to appoint his heir without consulting his nearest relatives, direct patrilineal succession can be achieved and palace revolutions avoided at the ends of reigns.

The Lý rulers certainly appointed heirs from among the next generation.[59] Lê Bá Ngọc, entrusted with the duty of executing Nhân Tôn's will on behalf of his nephew, expresses the hope that the dynasty's sons and grandsons will enjoy their right to the throne.[60] An instance also exists of the demotion of princes as a punishment; their reduced status, implied by their new and more junior titles, suggests that they were being removed from the centre of the imperial family.[61] None of this evidence proves conclusively that the Lý rulers used their genealogy for its essential purpose, which was to keep themselves apart from their numerous relatives. On the other hand, the absence of evidence in the *Toàn thư* of the activities of the descendants of earlier members of the imperial family indicates that

55. *TT*, 2, 10a.

56. Phan Huy Chú notes this omission in the evidence in his *Lịch triều hiến chường loại chí* (Saigon, 1957), ch. 13, 196.

57. *TT*, 5, *bảo phù*, 10.

58. Mary R. Haas, "The Declining Descent Rule for Rank in Thailand: A 'Correction,'" *American Anthropologist*, 53, 4 (1951):585–587.

59. The outstanding example is that of the childless Nhân Tôn, who in 1117 selected as his intended heir a son of one of his five brothers. The selection had, of course, to be legalized in his final edict (*TT*, 3, 18b).

60. *TT*, 3, 27a. The founder gave titles to his parents, showing the importance he attached to the principle of direct descent (*TT*, 1, 34a). Lê Văn Hữu criticizes these titles, comparing them with those conferred on his parents by the founder of the Sung dynasty.

61. *TT*, 4, 5a–b.

those who could claim descent from earlier emperors probably did not have a significant role in public life.

The introduction of a genealogy may have been one of the boldest measures undertaken by the Lý family. Their genealogy enabled the rulers to identify those whom they regarded as the most intimate members of the family. Because they could define relative seniority in terms of proximity to the ruler's own generation, they could limit the number of those with the most privileged position at court. In societies where genealogy was not used as an instrument to protect the ruler from his relatives, distant ancestors could be recollected when it was necessary to create bonds of alliance between a ruler and his distant living relatives. The ruler, by emphasizing his own descent from specified ancestors, was able to imply that he regarded all other descendants of these ancestors as belonging to the coalition of families which he led.[62] In Vietnamese genealogical practice, however, distant ancestors would have been recollected for exactly the opposite reason; the more distant they were, the more distant were their living descendants from the centre of power.

But the time was not yet ripe for the Lý rulers to carry their genealogical intentions to the logical conclusion. The two most important ranks in the imperial hierarchy were missing. Officially, there was no heir apparent; the succession was successful only because the Lý rulers, unlike their Đinh and Lê predecessors in the tenth century, were consistent in their choices of intended heir. Nevertheless, an heir's succession was achieved only when he paid homage to his father's coffin. Second, hierarchical distinctions were not observed among the legal wives. In theory, every legal wife could hope that her son would be appointed heir when the ruler issued his final edict. The consequence was that hierarchy was still imperfectly defined with respect to the reigning emperor's children and grandchildren until he was dying. Only his contemporaries and elders were clearly his subordinates.

The other hierarchical institution was the court, inherited from the Đinh and Lê and greatly elaborated by the Lý. The court was where the emperor presided over his family and where his relatives behaved according to the etiquette of their rank. To Lê Văn Hừu's surprise, the second ruler even insisted on being called "the Court."[63] The fourth ruler, aware that he was appointing a nephew to succeed him, made an impassioned appeal on his deathbed for loyalty to the new emperor. According to the *Toàn thư*, Nhân Tôn recalled: "When I was young I inherited the great treasure and ruled over the *vương* and *hầu*" (titled members of the imperial family).[64]

---

62. The author wishes to acknowledge his indebtedness to Professor Kirsch's analysis of the purpose of genealogy in Angkorian Cambodia, contained elsewhere in this volume.

63. *TT*, 2, 21a.

64. *TT*, 3, 25b.

In the first reign the court palace was called the Càn Nguyên palace.[65] Its name was changed to Thiên An in 1029.[66] The Thiên An palace was the scene of dynastic ceremonies and state occasions; administration was conducted in the Thiên Khánh palace.[67] At court the ruler performed the rite of feasting his subordinates, and the new ruler occupied the Thiên An palace as soon as he had succeeded, a ceremony that took place in front of the late ruler's coffin. At court Chinese rites and ceremonies, such as modes of addressing the emperor[68] and wearing formal clothing,[69] were increasingly stressed to enhance the ruler's prestige. On one occasion court style provided an opportunity to assert the ruling family's independent status vis-à-vis the Chinese court. In 1040 the second ruler ordered his warehouse staff to distribute Chinese brocade and satin among officials; the reason was that he had already taught the palace women to weave brocade and satin clothes. He was making the point that, because the court was Vietnamese, its own clothing should also be Vietnamese.[70]

Yet in Lý Vietnam the court was also the centre of activities which did not conform to a Chinese style of government. In the Thiên An palace the ideology of the Mahāyāna competed with that of the imperial *virtus*. Thus the *Nhân vương* 仁王 sūtra was recited there after Wang An-shih's invasion in 1077.[71] Vietnam was probably more confidently seen as being under the Buddha's protection than under that of the imperial ancestors. In 1073, Lý Đạo Thành inspected Nghệ An and erected a Buddha statue and a tablet in honour of the late emperor, worshipping both objects day and night.[72]

The Lý dynasty appropriated Chinese dynastic forms, but Vietnamese social practices and religious loyalties survived as a source of weakness of the dynasty. An irony of Lý history is that, when these dynastic weaknesses made themselves felt in the fifth reign for the first time since 1028, the year of the princes' rebellion, the royal government was, in other respects, stronger than ever. The eleventh-century rulers had known that "Chinese" forms were not enough to maintain their authority, and they exerted their influence in other ways. They raised a standing army, collected revenue from the villages, and sought to supervise the enforcement of their penal

---

65. *TT*, 2, 3a.

66. *TT*, 2, 19b.

67. *TT*, 2, 20a. The founder built an administrative palace in 1020 (*TT*, 2, 9a).

68. Lê Văn Hưu objected to the extravagantly long honorific names given to the rulers to emphasize their lofty status (*TT*, 2, 28a).

69. For example, in 1059 those who attended court were ordered to wear hats and boots (*TT*, 3, 2a).

70. *TT*, 2, 29b. Ngô Sĩ Liên was delighted.

71. *TT*, 3, 10a. This sūtra invokes the Buddha's protection on behalf of the country. It was also recited in 1126 and 1149 (*TT*, 3, 24a; 4, 4a).

72. *TT*, 3, 7b.

and civil laws.[73] For these purposes they were urgently in need of staff, and the first two rulers were sufficiently respected to be able to give their most promising sons a good education and early experience in the affairs of state.[74] Each son received his formal education in the "Eastern palace," and in the Long Đức palace he was trained in the chores of government.[75] A striking example of the employment of the favourite son was in 1040, when the second ruler's son was ordered to hear legal cases.[76] The advancement of trusted sons as intended heirs did not mean, however, that their status could be legalized before the issue of the ruler's final edict. Nevertheless, the father's prestige and administrative exigencies were such that the second and third rulers behaved as though they were the official heirs long before their fathers died.

But the burden of the dynasty's growing responsibilities made the early rulers realize that they required further staffing assistance. The *Toàn thư* mentions persons in the imperial entourage, whose posts correspond with the senior posts in the Chinese government. Their social origins and precise duties are not defined.[77] John K. Whitmore describes them as "counsellors" rather than officials.[78] Distinctions between military and civilian duties probably had little practical significance at this level in the administration, and, in fact, the counsellors are usually recorded as being on campaign. The wars of the eleventh century, fought by standing armies, would have brought to the fore new families of influence, as well as absorbing the energies of existing families with military aptitudes. The imperial army, and especially the palace guard, must have been an important avenue for promotion in the royal service. The counsellors in the eleventh century tended to be seasoned and loyal soldiers, to whom special duties were assigned as the need arose.

The *Toàn thư* indicates more clearly that the imperial administration needed teeth in the form of subordinate and literate servants who could keep treasury accounts, prepare documents, perform secretarial duties in the

73. On several occasions the *TT* records the early rulers' wish to be accessible to the people. In 1052 a great bell was erected in the imperial city for those who had been denied a hearing of their grievances (*TT*, 2, 37b). The second reign saw a great spurt of legal activity.

74. Lê Thành Khôi (p. 145) remarks that the first ruler had to rely on sons for governmental duties.

75. In 1012 the first ruler's son was given the title of *vương* and posted to the Long Đức palace to become informed about the people's affairs (*TT*, 2, 5a). In 1033 the second ruler's son left the Eastern palace on being appointed *vương* and was sent to the Long Đức palace (*TT*, 2, 21a–b).

76. *TT*, 2, 28b–29a. Ngô Sĩ Liên was amazed that a prince should undertake such duties.

77. The highest posts were *thái sư* 太師, *thái phó* 太傅, *thái bảo* 太保, and *thái úy* 太尉.

78. John K. Whitmore, "Vietnamese Adaptations of Chinese Government Structure in the Fifteenth Century," *in* Edgar Wickberg (comp.), *Historical Interaction of China and Vietnam: Institutional and Cultural Themes* (Lawrence, Kans., 1969), pp. 1–2. Phan Huy Chú (p. 54) remarks that the holders of these posts originally had no specific duties.

administrative palace, and implement the law code, promulgated in 1042. These persons were the junior members of the royal service. They are called *thư gia* 書家, for which an appropriate translation is perhaps "scribe." The method of recruiting them is ambiguously described. Law officers begin to appear in the narrative of the second reign as a result of Thái Tôn's emphasis on legal reform, and the first reference to the *thư gia* is in 1067, when ten of them became law officers.[79] According to the *Toàn thư*, in 1075 an edict was issued for the examination of those with "classical learning,"[80] but the statement in the *Việt sử lược* probably provides a more accurate description of what happened: at the beginning of the fourth reign monks with literary qualifications and "literate" monk-officials were selected to fill vacancies among the *thư gia*.[81] The appointment, but not by examination, of *thư gia* is also mentioned in 1088, and twenty law officers were appointed in 1122.[82] At the beginning of the fifth reign two senior ministers selected officials for service,[83] and probably at first informal means were used to admit the "scribes" into royal service. The *thư gia* must have come from families with the means of providing an education in the written Chinese language. The assumption need not be that they came from a class in society inferior to the class that produced the military officers.

References to *thư gia* become more numerous during the fourth reign (1072–1127). One reason may be that the third ruler, doubting whether he would live long enough to give his son, born in 1066 when he was already forty years old, the strenuous training which he himself had received from his own father, urged his faithful comrade, Lý Đạo Thành, to maintain during the minority his own policy of expanding the subordinate staff on behalf of the young ruler.[84]

The expansion of the subordinate staff in royal service had two consequences. In the first place, the supervisory posts at the top of the service became more important because those who held these posts were now controlling the actions of many subordinates. Secondly, the corps of *thư gia* was itself becoming an avenue for promotion. After the defeat of the Chams in 1069 and the withdrawal of the Chinese army in 1077, civilian opportunities for advancement would have been increasingly attractive.[85] The situation at the beginning of the fifth reign, which we shall now consider, reflects the changed nature of the royal service.

79. *TT*, 3, 4a.
80. *TT*, 3, 8a.
81. *VSL*, 38.
82. *TT*, 3, 20a (1088); *TT*, 3, 21a (1122).
83. *TT*, 3, 32a.
84. According to the *VSL*, 33, Lý Đạo Thành became *thái sư* in 1054 at the time of the third ruler's accession. Several of the events which Lê Thành Khôi categorizes as "development of instruction" (pp. 148–149) occurred during Nhân Tôn's minority.
85. In 1085 the scholar Lê Văn Thinh became *thái sư*.

Two senior officials were particularly important when the young Thần Tôn succeeded in 1127. They are Lê Bá Ngọc and Mâu Du Đô, and they are the special target of Lê Văn Hưu's disfavour. Lê Bá Ngọc is first mentioned in 1118, when he was dismissed from an executive post in the Board of Rites 禮部右侍郎 and demoted to the rank of *nội nhân thư gia* 內人書家.[86] In 1121 he regained some status by being appointed a *nội thưởng thị* 內常侍.[87] He was holding a military post when the dying Nhân Tôn urged him to help the new ruler.[88] Lê Bá Ngọc, who had been connected with the Board of Rites in 1118,[89] became *thái úy* 太尉 at the beginning of the fifth reign.[90] This is a high military post, and here is an indication that no clear division yet existed between military and civilian duties at the top of the royal service. Mâu Du Đô is first mentioned in 1120 as a *nội nhân thư gia* 內人書家.[91] At the beginning of the fifth reign he became *gián nghị đại phu* 諫議大夫, a post held by Lý Đạo Thành in 1073.[92] Further responsibilities, involving him in military as well as civilian duties, awaited him, and in 1144 he became *thái sư* 太師; he died in 1146.[93]

Lê Bá Ngọc and Mâu Du Đô are the two prominent figures in the fifth reign, and the developments with which they are associated show that the concept of "dynasty" was still imperfectly respected.

The Lý dynasty did not come to an end in 1127. Thần Tôn became emperor in spite of the fact that he was only eleven years old and Nhân Tôn's nephew. His real father, the Sùng Hiền hầu, Nhân Tôn's brother, did not take the opportunity of usurping, as his contemporary, Sūryavarman II of Angkor, had done by killing his uncle, the reigning Khmer ruler.[94] Yet the evidence indicates that a peaceful succession was not taken for granted. Special security precautions were enforced in the imperial city as soon as Nhân Tôn died, and troops were posted at the Thiên An palace.[95] Lê Bá Ngọc was careful to communicate the contents of Nhân Tôn's last edict to the princes and officials, and the village authorities were commanded not to allow outbreaks of violence.[96] The mourning ceremonies were elaborate, and the whole country was required to show respect for the dead emperor.[97]

86. *TT*, 3, 18b.
87. *TT*, 3, 21a.
88. *TT*, 3, 26a.
89. *TT*, 3, 18b.
90. *TT*, 3, 29a. He became *thái sư* at the end of 1128 (*TT*, 3, 32a). He died in 1134 (*TT*, 3, 39b).
91. *TT*, 3, 20b.
92. *TT*, 3, 29a. Many appointments were made at the beginning of the fifth reign, suggesting that a change of personnel took place.
93. *TT*, 4, 3a; 3b.
94. G. Cœdès, *The Indianized States of Southeast Asia* (Honolulu, 1968), pp. 154, 159.
95. *TT*, 3, 26b.
96. *TT*, 3, 27a.
97. The people were forbidden to ride horses or mount curtained chariots.

The honour paid to Nhân Tôn owed much, no doubt, to political calculation. Within the imperial city itself, less respect was paid. Within one month after Nhân Tôn's death, the new ruler's advisers allowed him to order the courtiers to discard their mourning clothes. Even worse, two females were welcomed into the palace. Lê Văn Hưu was indignant: "The court's servants rejoiced in the ruler's reduction of the mourning period, and no one remonstrated. It may be said that there were no men at court."[98]

Who were the females? One was the daughter of Lý Sơn, who appears as a guard commander in the long list of appointments at the beginning of the reign.[99] His daughter was appointed empress.[100] The other female was the daughter of Lê Xưởng, who was no less a person than Lê Bá Ngọc's nephew.[101] Both fathers-in-law were given titles in a manner reminiscent of the second Lý ruler's honours to three of his fathers-in-law in 1028.[102]

A few days later dynastic convention was again flaunted. The young ruler visited pagodas in the imperial city in order to thank the Buddha for a recent victory against more than 20,000 Khmer troops sent by Sūryavarman II to invade Nghệ An.[103] Lê Văn Hưu predictably criticizes the ruler on the grounds that the victory should have been announced at the Ancestral Temple.[104]

In the following year, 1129, a notable breach of dynastic convention took place. The young ruler was allowed to bestow high titles on his real parents, showing them an affection which should have been exclusively reserved for his adopted father, Nhân Tôn. The Sùng Hiền hầu was created "senior emperor" 太上皇, thereby reversing his correct hierarchical subordination to Nhân Tôn and Thần Tôn. Thần Tôn's mother was made an empress.[105] These honours incensed Lê Văn Hưu. As he puts it, "Did not the dynasty now have two roots 本?"[106] On this occasion he unambiguously blames those who were responsible for the enormity: "the ministers at Court such as Lê Bá Ngọc and Mâu Du Đô had no knowledge of propriety."[107] He knew what the sequel was going to be. The Sùng

98. *TT*, 3, 28a. Ngô Sĩ Liên, in a supplementary comment, supports Lê Văn Hưu's criticism.

99. *TT*, 3, 29a.

100. *TT*, 3, 30b.

101. *TT*, 3, 29b. In 1134 he is described as a *chi hậu thư gia* 祗候書家 (*TT*, 3, 39a).

102. *TT*, 3, 31a, states that these two women visited their family almost immediately afterwards. Here, surely, is a political marriage which could hardly have been consummated.

103. Khmer military pressure was continuous during this reign. In 1128 Sūryavarman II asked that envoys should be sent to Cambodia, presumably bringing tribute. The request was rejected (*TT*, 3, 32a).

104. *TT*, 3, 30b–31a.

105. *TT*, 3, 32b.

106. *TT*, 3, 32b–33a. Lê Văn Hưu considered that the ruler should have behaved as the Sung emperor Hsiao-tsung (1163–1190) did in similar circumstances.

107. *TT*, 3, 33a.

Hiền hậu died in 1130,[108] but the new empress lived until 1147.[109] Exploiting her undeserved status at court, she was able to introduce her brother, Đỗ Anh Vũ, into the palace, thereby causing considerable jealousy and unrest at court during the minority of the sixth ruler, Anh Tôn.

Early in 1129 something else happened which Lê Văn Hưu deplored. Lý Tử Khắc reported that a white deer had been discovered. The deer was captured, and Lý Tử Khắc was appointed a *khu mật sứ* and given a title.[110] Lê Văn Hưu points out that Lý Thử Khắc had no achievement to his credit and that his acceptance of the ruler's reward for so modest a service was equivalent to mocking his master 欺君.[111]

His fifth comment concerning this reign was aroused by an edict issued early in 1130, which forbad marriages of officials' daughters before the ruler had selected or rejected them as his concubines.[112] The annalist considered that Thần Tôn was appropriating a right which was not his.[113]

Court standards had evidently become slacker. The ruler had not treated Nhân Tôn, the Ancestral Temple, or even his subjects' daughters with proper respect. Relations between court and royal service were becoming personal on a scale that had not been known since the early years of the dynasty. Lê Văn Hưu's five criticisms all fall within the beginning of the fifth reign and are, by implication, aimed at the style of dynastic government encouraged by senior members of the royal service during the minority, who were now able to make the dynasty a facade behind which personal advancement could be gained.

The narrative reveals that, in the later years of the short reign, matters did not improve.

Gifts to the ruler are frequently recorded. The donors, with one exception, are not mentioned again, but some probably did well in royal service. One who prospered is Hứa Viêm, who gave a quantity of gold to Thần Tôn in 1137. He is mentioned again in 1141 in the capacity of *thái phó* 太傅.[114] Another and more interesting example is available of personal relations between the ruler and a member of the royal service. In 1133 an edict forbad court officials to leave the court without permission,[115] but in 1134 an exception was made in favour of Lý Công Tín.[116] This person first appears in 1128 under the name of Phi Công Tín, a *nội lệnh thư gia* 內令書家.[117] He was promoted in 1129, when the imperial surname of

108. *TT*, 3, 35b.
109. *TT*, 4, 4a.
110. *TT*, 3, 33b–34a.
111. *TT*, 3, 34a.
112. *TT*, 3, 35a.
113. *Ibid.*
114. *TT*, 4, 1a.
115. *TT*, 3, 38a.
116. *TT*, 3, 39a.
117. *TT*, 3, 21b.

"Lý" was conferred on him.[118] He received a title in 1136[119] and was still in royal service in 1163.[120] He began his career when the ruler was too young to influence the selection of junior personnel, and one wonders who were Lý Công Tín's patrons at court.

The forging of personal links between court and royal servants, reducing the distance between ruler and subject, seems to have been matched by the forging of similar links between prominent families outside the court.[121] We have observed that an edict in 1133 forbad court officials to leave the court without permission, and another edict of 1136 suggests that the ministers feared, among other things, that officials would take the opportunity of cultivating relations with powerful persons outside the court. The edict of 1136 laid down that all families, inside and outside the capital, had to guarantee that they would report court officials who reared their sons in the households of others "in order to depend on powerful families."[122] One can readily suppose that, in the absence of tight imperial control, patron and client relations were developing between officials and important families, on whose behalf the officials, sometimes themselves members of these families and other times coming from a less privileged background but ambitious, could perform services at court. Loyalty to the dynasty was bound to be endangered when outside interests could manipulate the dynasty's symbols and servants. In this light the venality of the privy councillor in 1137 is significant. The dying ruler's three wives were able to exploit the succession procedure, and those who stood to gain from the accession of the Cảm Thánh wife's infant son had probably encouraged them to suborn the privy councillor. Lê Văn Hưu expresses his opinion on one aspect of this situation at the time when the narrative deals with the princes' revolt in 1028 and he criticizes the unsatisfactory succession procedure, citing what happened in 1137. It was left to Ngô Sĩ Liên to deplore the other aspect of the deathbed scene, which were the close relations 交好 between corrupt servants of the dynasty and the inner palace 內庭.[123]

Only two of Lê Văn Hưu's comments on the period after 1137 survive.[124] Perhaps he thought that he had sufficiently emphasized the reasons for the

118. *TT*, 3, 34b.
119. *TT*, 3, 40a.
120. *TT*, 4, 8b.
121. One wonders what lies behind Lê Bá Ngọc's adoption of the surname "Trương" in 1128 (*TT*, 3, 32a).
122. *TT*, 3, 41a. The families were to be organized in groups of three in order to guarantee that each of them would disclose breaches in the provisions of the edict.
123. *TT*, 3, 42b.
124. They refer to the conspiracy of 1150, noted below, and to Anh Tôn's readiness to accept a Cham princess in 1154.

dynasty's decline and could now rely on his narrative to illustrate the consequences.[125]

The later reigns lie outside the scope of this essay, and only one episode will be mentioned briefly. Thần Tôn's last days had been clouded by collusion at court. His son's minority was disturbed in 1150 by a conspiracy among princes and officials, supported by Dương Tự Minh.[126] Dương Tự Minh was the *thủ lĩnh* of Phú Lương, in the foothills to the north of Hanoi.[127] The conspiracy was directed against Đỗ Anh Vũ, the brother of Thần Tôn's mother and the lover of the sixth ruler's mother, the empress Lê and former Cảm Thánh *phu nhân*.[128] The empress protected Anh Vũ, but tension at court persisted. Immediately after Đỗ Anh Vũ's restoration an edict was issued to prohibit court officials from mixing with princely families, from holding meetings, and from uttering criticisms.[129] When in 1158 an envoy, recently returned from China, successfully recommended the practice he had apparently observed in Sung China of placing a bronze casket in the imperial city for memorials, the casket was at once used to denounce Đỗ Anh Vũ.[130] The court had now become the scene of bitter factional feuds.

This essay has suggested that Lê Văn Hữu's comments, especially with regard to the fifth reign, and the detailed treatment of the relevant parts of the narrative in the surviving Lý annals seem deliberately to complement each other wherever matters of dynastic stability are involved. To this extent, then, we can recover a thirteenth-century and somewhat critical perspective on Lý history.

Independent support for the view that we are dealing with a genuine thirteenth-century perspective comes from what is known of the imperial Trần family, whose members were Lê Văn Hữu's contemporaries. They

---

125. In the introduction to the fourth reign, the fourth ruler is characterised as "the Lý dynasty's great ruler" 李朝之盛主 (*TT*, 3, 6b).

126. *TT*, 4, 4b–5b. Ngô Sĩ Liên assumes that the princes were of the imperial family (*TT*, 4, 5b).

127. For Phú Lương's location and Dương Tự Minh's post, see Maspero, pp. 34–35 and 37. Tự Minh may have been a local chief. He married an imperial princess in 1127 and again in 1144 (*TT*, 3, 25a; 4, 3a). Maspero (p. 34) notes that an imposter, claiming to be Nhân Tôn's son, was active in Phú Lương early in the sixth reign. Perhaps Dương Tự Minh was irritated when Đỗ Anh Vũ came to Phú Lương in 1147 to examine officials and hold a census (*TT*, 4, 4a).

128. *TT*, 4, 4b. Lê Văn Hữu notes in his comment that no crime could be greater than Anh Vũ's access to the forbidden palace and his relationship with the empress (*TT*, 4, 5b).

129. *TT*, 4, 6a.

130. *TT*, 4, 7b–8a. The text describes the envoy as 'Nguyễn Quốc', which is probably Văn Hữu's rendering of "Lý Quốc Dĩ" (see note 11).

Willingness to adopt useful practices from China had not ceased since the first reign (see pp. 212–213 above).

had no need to consult recorded lessons of the past, for, by means of marriage alliances, they had been able to infiltrate and control the Lý court. They were therefore uniquely well qualified to perceive and correct weaknesses in the dynastic institution which they inherited and rendered, they believed, foolproof a number of years before Lê Văn Hửu presented his history in 1272. Thus, the Trần family solved the succession problem by promoting the emperor to the rank of "senior emperor" 太上皇帝 as soon as his son was able to assume an active role in government under the title of "emperor" 帝.[131] Again, the early Trần emperors appointed only one empress.[132] Moreover, the second and third rulers married their cousins, also members of the Trần family, thereby relieving themselves of potentially embarrassing alliances with other families.[133] Finally, experienced members of the Trần family who were of the same generation as the senior emperor controlled the highest posts.[134] This is the situation with which Lê Văn Hửu, their servant, was familiar, and it helps to explain why he emphasized ways in which the customs of the fallen dynasty were less efficient than those of the new dynasty.

But a further observation can be made on Lê Văn Hửu's perspective. The Lý family's use of Chinese dynastic forms does not seem to surprise him. We, in the twentieth century, may wish to see the great achievement of the eleventh-century rulers as their attempt to fashion precedents of government, securing their family's uninterrupted rule for eight generations, which their successors could take into account as Vietnamese and not as Chinese precedents.[135] Not so Lê Văn Hửu.

Perhaps he, an imperial examinations graduate of 1247, took for granted the style of public life in his own day, when men with his literary attainments

131. The father of the Trần child, selected by his kinsmen as first emperor, was given the title of *thượng hoàng* 上皇 (*TT*, 5, *kiến trung* 2 [1226]). In 1258 this emperor became *thượng hoàng* and his son became emperor (*TT*, 5, *nguyên phong* 8). The senior emperor retained the right to depose the emperor; see the episode of 1299, narrated in the *TT*.

132. The first emperor, for reasons of state, married the ninth Lý ruler. In 1237 he was persuaded to discard her in favour of her pregnant sister. The discarded wife no longer held the title of empress; she was demoted to the rank of "imperial princess" (*TT*, 5, *thiên ứng chính bình* 6 [1237]). In 1258, immediately after his accession, the second emperor appointed one empress (*TT*, 5, *nguyên phong* 8).

133. The second emperor married his Trần uncle's daughter (*TT*, 5, *nguyên phong* 8 [1258]). The father-in-law/uncle received the title of *Yên Sinh vường* in 1237 when he surrendered his pregnant Lý wife to the first emperor (*TT*, 5, *thiên ứng chính bình* 6). In 1274 the third emperor married the daughter of the hero of the Mongol wars, Trần Quốc Tuấn, the *Hửng-đạo* prince. Quốc Tuấn was the son of the *Yên Sinh vường* (*TT*, *bảo phù* 2). By these marriages the Trần rulers not only avoided the danger of relatives by marriage from outside their family; they were also appeasing a branch of their own family which had been discontented since 1237.

134. Phan Huy Chú notes this practice (p. 54).

135. The records of the early Trần dynasty show that Lý precedents were examined in order to determine the institutions of the new court and that twenty-one items of the Lý penal laws and ceremonial rites were changed (*TT*, *kiến trung* 6 [1230]).

could prosper, though only as subordinates of the imperial family. Alternatively, he may have assumed that a millennium of Chinese rule would have familiarized Vietnamese with the opportunities which Chinese institutions offered ambitious men for strengthening their personal power. The early Lý rulers, in his eyes, could merely have been those who had seized these opportunities. Their initiative would therefore not have seemed particularly remarkable.

What is remarkable is not Lê Văn Hựu's tendency to withhold praise but his tendency to criticize. In order to understand the implications of this tendency, we must remember two things.

In the first place, in spite of his knowledge of ancient Chinese history, he was far from being the equivalent of a Sung scholar-administrator, working in an environment where officials were expected to take important initiatives at court. In the thirteenth century the Trần family was firmly in control of all the senior posts in the government.

We must also remember that the Ly family was not only the first Vietnamese dynasty about which Vietnamese in the thirteenth century were reasonably well informed. It was, in fact, their single dynasty of consequence before that time, and Lê Văn Hựu was unable to judge it in terms of Chinese models already assimilated before the first Lý ruler appeared in 1009. He could not even assume that the Chinese dynastic pattern of history would persist in Vietnam. When Vietnamese literati studied Chinese history, they would continually have been reminded that Vietnam was very different from China, and his own work reflects stubborn Vietnamese realities which affected dynastic history.

Lê Văn Hựu was not a Chinese-style official, and the Lý dynasty was an experiment. These are the reasons why his criticisms are significant. He is not a Chinese historian in the sense that he criticizes individual rulers' lapses from established imperial roles. Instead, the target of his criticism is the Lý dynastic structure itself, which was vitiated by an unsatisfactory succession procedure and by polygamy. The first Lý emperors, whose counterparts in Chinese dynasties would have been protected by their historians from undue criticism, are, according to Lê Văn Hựu, especially responsible for the system's defects. Thần Tôn's reign marks the beginning of dynastic decline not because of his own faults but because his dynasty is faultily organized at the time of its foundation; its faults merely become more pronounced in the fifth reign.

And so the implication of Lê Văn Hựu's attitude towards Ly history is that, for him, the two most recent centuries in the Vietnamese past had not, in spite of their innovations, provided a framework of successful precedents for strong government to determine the future shape of Vietnamese history. Instead, a variety of religious, political, and social possibilities remained. In spite, therefore, of the presence of a veneer of Chinese forms, he must have felt that history was still in the making, and we need not doubt that he knew that the future depended on Vietnamese performance rather than on the automatic efficacy of Chinese models.[136]

These reflections on the significance of Lê Văn Hưu's criticism lead to the hardly surprising conclusion that Lý Vietnam had acquired an armature of Chinese government forms without developing habits of mind which could see these forms as part of a sacrosanct system. The situation was still fluid, and expedients rather than precedents were important. The outlook of at least the governing elite would have been empirical rather than tradition-bound and therefore self-consciously Vietnamese.

An attempt to examine Lê Văn Hưu's treatment of the fifth Lý reign is offered as a tribute to Professor Hall, for whose guidance and friendship the author can never be sufficiently grateful.

136. Similarly, what at first seems to be the Lý rulers' un-Southeast-Asian attitude towards the past, represented by their genealogy, is probably no more than a new kind of example of Vietnamese response to contemporary exigencies. They used the unit of the generation as an instrument of government to guarantee the succession of power from father to son and probably also to keep the imperial family small and disciplined. They were not interested in differences between generations as the basis for social and moral obligations at every level of society, the setting for generational time in Confucian political and social philosophy. The author is grateful to James T. Siegel and C. A. Peterson for discussions of the significance of Lê Văn Hưu's criticisms of the Lý dynasty.

England and Vietnam in the
Fifteenth and Sixteenth Centuries:
An Essay in Historical Comparison

R. B. SMITH

School of Oriental and African Studies,
University of London

Professor Hall has, at different periods in his life, taught both the history of Europe (including England) and that of Southeast Asia. To present in his honour an essay in historical comparison therefore may not be entirely inappropriate. The paper that follows had its beginnings in a lecture given under the auspices of the British Council in Saigon, when I found myself embarking upon a comparison between the histories of England and of Vietnam. At first sight one is bound to be overwhelmed by the immense contrasts between the two countries, situated as they are at opposite ends of the Eurasian landmass, but as I proceeded I became increasingly aware of certain remarkable similarities between their histories: similarities that make the contrasts themselves much more interesting and worthy of investigation.

I

To begin with, there is a similarity of scale. In population Britain is somewhat larger, but not so much so that comparison is impossible. The present-day population of Vietnam (both North and South) stands at approximately the level which was reached by Great Britain and Ireland together during the 1890's, and by England, Wales, and Scotland about 1908. In surface area Vietnam turns out to be rather larger than the whole of the British Isles (including Eire).[1]

The two countries are alike too in the chronological extent of their history. Both emerged into recorded history (into Chinese and Roman history

1. Figures from United Nations, *Statistical Yearbook 1970* (New York, 1971):

	Area (km²)	Population (1969 est.)
Vietnam	332,000	39,000,000
Great Britain	230,000	54,000,000
U.K. and Eire	300,000	58,000,000

respectively) during the second and first centuries B.C., and both were firmly absorbed into neighbouring large empires during the first half of the first century A.D. In broad outline, at least, their histories can be written continuously since that time.

In terms of material culture, too, Britain and Vietnam were comparable at least down to the eighteenth century. Before that time, they were both agrarian societies in which the vast majority of the population lived in the countryside and in which trade and rural industries developed at the edges of the economy. Interestingly enough, by the seventeenth century both had flourishing textile industries in certain rural areas, and a small amount of mining, in addition to their agriculture. The fact that Britain belongs to the temperate zone and has always grown crops like wheat, barley, and oats, while Vietnam depends on wet-rice agriculture, does not affect this basic dependence on agriculture and the land over many centuries. True, after 1800 this similarity has disappeared, at least for the time being. Britain was by then beginning to experience its industrial revolution and the first stages of a complete social transformation. British colonial expansion had already reached North America, India, and Australasia, and during the next century it would produce an even vaster Empire, though most of it had become independent by the 1960's. Vietnam, on the other hand, was at the receiving end of Western imperialism, and during the nineteenth century its whole political and economic evolution was distorted by the French conquest. The country is still not finished with the consequences of colonial rule and of the struggle for national independence. A full-scale comparative study of the histories of Britain and Vietnam would need to take into account, perhaps even to try to explain, this great difference between them in the last two centuries. In the present paper, however, we shall confine our attention to a period before these differences became so marked.

In relation to the period before the nineteenth century, two other general similarities between English and Vietnamese history are worth noticing before we turn to the more detailed examination of a particular century. The first relates to their internal political development, and to the gradual inclusion of both countries, as they existed by 1800, within a single political framework which had not existed in, say, the tenth century. England itself was only effectively united during the tenth and eleventh centuries, and the process was not properly completed until the consolidation of unity by the Norman conquest. Wales was conquered in the thirteenth century by Edward I and finally absorbed into the English administrative system in 1536. Scotland, on the other hand, resisted the attacks of Edward I and his successors and remained a thorn in England's side until the two kingdoms were united by a peaceful dynastic succession in 1603. In the meantime, Ireland had been invaded by the Anglo-Norman kings in the twelfth century and was brought firmly under English control in the period between 1494 and 1540. But in the case of Ireland the process of conquest was never so complete that, despite further military campaigns in the sixteenth and seventeenth centuries and an act of union in 1801, it could not begin to be reversed in the twentieth century.

This gradual political expansion, from Athelstan to the Irish Union, can be paralleled to a remarkable extent in the history of Vietnam. The country which the Chinese lost about 900, and failed to reconquer in 937 and 980, was first unified as an independent kingdom by the Lý dynasty of the eleventh and twelfth centuries. But the Lý kingdom never extended beyond what is now North Vietnam, and its more southerly provinces were only conquered in 1069–1070. Central Vietnam was then, and for several centuries to come, occupied by the kingdom of Champa, while the whole Mekong delta was Khmer. The annexation of two Cham provinces by Đại-Việt in 1070 was followed by more than two centuries of border raids, without any significant territorial change. Then in 1306 the Vietnamese acquired two more provinces through a marriage treaty with the Cham king. There followed a long series of wars between the two kingdoms from 1371 to 1470, of which the eventual outcome was the Vietnamese conquest of all of Champa as far south as Bình-Định (including the former Cham captial of Vijaya). After another period of relative stability in the south, the Vietnamese resumed their expansion in the later seventeenth century, and by 1760 they had not only finally extinguished Champa but had also forced Cambodia to cede to them a large part of the Mekong delta. However, the Vietnamese kingdom itself became divided into two parts during the seventeenth century, and the present area of Vietnam was only finally united under a single ruler in 1802, the year after the union of Great Britain and Ireland. A further phase of expansion began in 1836–1840, when the Vietnamese tried to take over the remainder of Cambodia, but they had not succeeded in that aim by the time of the arrival of the French admirals in 1859.

The second of these general historical similarities concerns the external relationships of England and Vietnam: that is, their political and cultural relationships to Europe and China respectively. The Roman conquest of Britain, leading to nearly four centuries of government as a province of the Empire, has its parallel in the Han conquest of Chiao-chih, which made northern Vietnam a Chinese province from 111 B.C. to about A.D. 900. During these periods, England acquired a Roman culture without being completely Latinized, while Vietnam received a number of Chinese settlers and was deeply and permanently influenced by Chinese civilization. The Chinese failed to recover control of Vietnam despite invasions in 982,

1075–1077, and 1281–1288, and the Ming conquest of 1407 was reversed a mere twenty years later. Another Chinese invasion was repulsed in 1788–1789, and in 1884–1885 the Chinese were unable to prevent Vietnam from falling to the French. But, throughout the centuries from the fall of T'ang to the French conquest, Vietnam continued to look to China for cultural inspiration and often modelled its institutions on a Chinese pattern, while preserving its own language and insisting on its political independence (apart from tribute missions).

England might have had a similar experience in relation to Europe if the Roman empire had been reunified after the breakup of the fifth century. As it was, the cultural, spiritual, and, to some extent, political relationships between England and the Continent were reaffirmed by the conversion to Roman Christianity between 597 and 664, and then by the Norman conquest of 1066. In the latter year the victory of the Normans, coming immediately after the defeat of the Scandinavians, meant that England was embroiled in French-centred political conflicts down to the sixteenth century. Thereafter, with the final loss of its last French territory and the break with Rome which followed the Henrician Reformation, England went its own way and was strong enough to withstand attempts at invasion in 1588, 1805, and 1940. Like Vietnam, England preserved its own cultural and political identity, but within a cultural framework in which Latin played a role not unlike that of Chinese in Vietnam.

In this context, it seems not unreasonable to suggest a comparison between the two features which linked Vietnam to China between 982 and 1885 and England to Rome between 664 and 1534. In the former case it was a tribute system, in which all of China's close neighbours (including some not deeply influenced by Chinese culture) sent regular tribute missions, indicating their acceptance of the ultimate superiority of the Chinese Son of Heaven. Between England and Rome, the link grew out of the distinction between temporal and spiritual law; the Papacy was recognized as the supreme spiritual head of all Christendom, since the Pope had inherited the former imperial dignity of *Pontifex Maximus*. But the relationship between spiritual and temporal authority was often very far from harmonious, and the tensions which it generated came to a head in the sixteenth century: hence the Reformation of the 1530's.

To suggest that the tribute system played a role for Vietnam comparable to papal authority over the Church in England, however, is to identify a fundamental difference between their cultures. For the position of the Pope depended on a concept of divine law, emanating from an omnipotent God, which had little meaning for the Chinese and Vietnamese. Likewise, the tributary relationship depended on a cosmological notion of kingship which lay at the core of the Chinese political tradition. We shall return in due course to the implications of this important contrast, reflected in the Confucianization of Vietnam and the English Reformation.

II

The period between 1460 and 1560, which I propose to examine in more detail, was an important one for the political development of both England and Vietnam: a century during which their institutions and patterns of political conflict took on the shape which was to characterize the period from then until the nineteenth century. It was also the last period before the beginning of the British economic and colonial expansion which was to make their modern histories so very different: Drake's circumnavigation of the world, the foundation of the first American colonies, and the first visit of an Englishman to Southeast Asia all came in the decade from 1577 to 1587. The century before 1560 therefore seems to offer an excellent opportunity for comparative study, an opportunity to increase our understanding of both countries by measuring them against one another.

It is a curious coincidence—it can hardly be more—that in both England and Vietnam the years 1459–1461 saw a serious political conflict, which brought to the throne a new young king; more curiously still, Edward IV and Lê Thánh Tôn were both born in the year 1442. Since neither was yet twenty years old, it is hardly surprising that at the outset of both their reigns power should lie with court magnates of an older generation: in England with the Neville Earls of Salisbury and Warwick and in Vietnam with Nguyễn Xí and the alliance of military leaders and scholar-officials who had brought about the *xướng-nghĩa* coup of 1460.[2] But as the two kings grew older their power increased, and by 1471, despite the brief restoration of Henry VI in England, both were firmly in control of their respective courts and kingdoms. Their reigns marked important turning points in English and in Vietnamese history alike. Edward IV's policies began the trend towards the recovery of strength by the monarchy, which continued with only short interruptions between 1460 and 1560 and was thus a major theme of our period; Lê Thánh Tôn and his ministers were responsible for even more sweeping changes, which might well be summarized as the "Confucianization" of Vietnam, a phrase which will be explained in due course.

The stability which Edward IV brought to England was interrupted in 1483 when he died, leaving behind a child-king on the throne and an ambitious royal uncle. Two years of conflict followed, culminating in the

---

2. On the political history of the two countries in the fifteenth century, for Vietnam see John K. Whitmore, "The Development of Le Government in Fifteenth-Century Vietnam (Ph.D. diss., Cornell University, 1968); for England, E.F. Jacob, *The Fifteenth Century* (Oxford, 1961).

seizure of power by Henry Tudor. But under the new dynasty which he established, the monarchy became even stronger: a fact reflected in the peaceful succession of his son in 1509. As the sixteenth century wore on, this new strength of the Crown was to be of the greatest significance in the face of growing religious and potentially political strife, which in France and Germany produced long periods of civil war. In England, by contrast, the monarch not only survived but was able to prevent any breakdown in the territorial unity of the kingdom.

Henry VIII's decision to seize full spiritual independence from Rome in 1532 began a period of religious and political change and of institutional reform, which was comparable in many respects to the "Confucianization" of Lê Thánh Tôn after 1460; a later section of this paper will attempt a comparative analysis of the two movements of reform. Such changes could not have succeeded without a strong monarchy. Opposition was inevitable, but, when the Pilgrimage of Grace finally erupted in 1536, it was joined by only a small group of diehards who were quickly defeated. When a new phase of reform began in 1548–1549 the Crown, despite the fact that Edward VI was a minor and power was exercised by two successive regents during his reign, was strong enough to impose its will on the people once again. Even more remarkable, when the young king died and was succeeded by two sisters in turn in 1553 and 1558, the mere changes of monarch were enough to carry England back and forth between the extremes of Edwardian Reformation, Marian Reaction, and finally Elizabeth's "Middle Way." The change of 1558, however, may have averted a catastrophe: Mary's policies were sure to have provoked more opposition had she lived. As it was, by 1560 England had a strong monarchy and had been "reformed" without a civil war.

In Vietnam there was a reverse trend from stability to instability during the early decades of the sixteenth century.[3] Throughout the reign of Lê Thánh Tôn (1460–1497), there was no serious political conflict which could not be contained by the court or any important challenge to the Confucian scholar-officials. Trouble began with the premature death of his son, Hiến Tôn in 1505. How he died remains a mystery, but the consequence was that a young prince was placed on the throne by a court faction which had not previously been very powerful: the relatives and associates of a former concubine of Hiến Tôn, whose son now became king. In the absence of a rule of primogeniture such as existed in England, there was often no single candidate with a universally acknowledged claim to the succession, and this led quite often to succession conflicts between the candidates of

---

3. The account of the period 1505–1527 in Vietnam is based on Phan Huy Lê, *Lịch sử Chế độ Phong kiến Việt-Nam* (History of the Feudal Regime of Vietnam), II (Hanoi, 1962), 222–243.

different court factions. The faction which came to power in 1505, more-over, had its territorial roots in the region of Tongking immediately to the north of Hanoi. Its rise meant a decline in influence for the leading clans of the southerly province of Thanh-Hóa who had enjoyed royal favour and great influence ever since their support of Lê Lợi had led to the founda-tion of the Lê dynasty in 1427–1428. That these Thanh-Hóa clans would retaliate was all but inevitable. In 1509 (the year of Henry VIII's peaceful accession to the Crown of England) they supported a rebellion by a dissident prince, Lê Oanh, and led an army from Thanh-Hóa to Hanoi to place him on the throne. The Tongking clans who had held power since 1505 were thus driven out of the capital.

The new king, Lê Tướng Dực, reigned from 1510 to 1516, and the record of those years indicates a serious attempt at further reform and a new revival of Confucian scholarship. But these developments were brought to an end by the revolt of Trần Cào in 1516; there had been sporadic disturbances throughout the reign, but this new rising was of far more serious proportions. A native of Hải-Dương province in eastern Tongking, Trần Cào claimed descent from the Trần dynasty (1225–1400) and used his position as some kind of priest in a religious sect to become very in-fluential in his own region. In 1516 he made a bid for the throne, which briefly succeeded but failed in the end. More important than his own fate, however, was the fact that his revolt showed very clearly the extent to which the Lê dynasty depended for its survival on the power of the Thanh-Hóa clans. The leaders of the two most prominent clans, Trịnh Duy Sản and Nguyễn Hoằng Dụ, both had designs on the throne for themselves. During the course of 1516, the Trịnh leader killed Lê Tướng Dực and placed his own nominee on the throne, a usual preliminary move before attempting to establish a new dynasty, but he was prevented from getting his way by the intervention of the Nguyễn. Another prince was made king, becoming Lê Chiêu Tôn (1516–1522). But real power now lay with the clan generals, whose position was not unlike that of the noblemen of fifteenth-century England whom Sir John Fortescue dubbed "overmighty subjects." The years 1517–1519 saw virtual civil war between the various court factions. The conflict between the two main Thanh-Hóa clans (Trịnh and Nguyễn) eventually gave an opportunity for the re-emergence of the clans of Tong-king. The opportunity was seized by Mạc Đăng Dung, a native of the Tongking delta, descendent of a former scholarly family, but himself a military man. His intervention "saved" the Lê in 1519, and his opponents were forced to withdraw to Thanh-Hóa. He went from strength to strength at the court of Lê Chiêu Tôn, and he became so powerful that in 1522 the king fled from the capital in order to encourage a new rising by the Thanh-Hóa men. The Mạc not only survived this challenge but took control of

Thanh-Hóa itself in 1525, and in 1527 they seized the throne for them-selves.

Unlike Henry VII, with whom he might interestingly be compared, Mạc Đăng Dung was not able to restore the full might of the monarchy. His hold on Thanh-Hóa was still tenuous. In 1533, Nguyễn Kim, who had fled to Ai-Lao (Luang Phrabang), restored the Lê dynasty in exile in the person of Lê Trang Tôn (1533–1546); he then appealed to China for recognition. The Mạc averted a new Chinese occupation in 1540 by submitting to a Ming army and accepting the status of governors of Annam, a move which guaranteed them the disfavour of subsequent chroniclers.[4] Even so, the Chinese did not intervene to prevent the Lê supports, in effect the Nguyễn and the Trịnh, from returning to control Thanh-Hóa and Nghệ-An in 1542–1543. Thereafter, for the next fifty years, Vietnam was divided into two hostile states: a situation which was only brought to an end by the Lê "restoration" of 1592, after Trịnh forces had recaptured Hanoi. In the meantime, the death of Nguyễn Kim in 1545 had been followed by a growing conflict between the Trịnh and Nguyễn themselves. The Nguyễn avoided almost certain elimination by securing the governor-ship of Thuận-Hóa (the Huế area) in 1558. There they laid the foundations for what became virtually a separate kingdom in the seventeenth and eighteenth centuries.

Thus the history of Vietnam in the sixteenth century was even more disturbed by internal political conflict than that of England had been during the so-called Wars of the Roses. By 1558, the year of Elizabeth's accession, Vietnam had entered a period of political division which would end only in 1802.

III

In the broad sweep of world history, it is easy to lump together countries such as England and Vietnam had become by 1500 under the general heading "traditional societies." But when it comes to making detailed comparisons, comparability of scale and economic similarities must be set against cultural differences as great as any that were to be found in the world of 1500. It is not enough to attach labels to societies, be they universal epithets such as "traditional" or cultural identities such as "Christian" and "Confucian." It is necessary to compare in detail actual situations and social and political arrangements.

Both these countries were monarchies and both have been described, in very different contexts, as "despotisms." The Vietnamese monarchy be-

4. These events are very inadequately treated in most secondary works; see *Việt Sử Thông giám Cường mục* (trans. into *quốc-ngữ*, Hanoi, 1959), XIV, 23ff.

longed to the type which K. A. Wittfogel has dubbed "oriental despotism."[5] The power of the king was quite arbitrary, untrammelled by such limitations as the need to obtain parliamentary approval for taxation and other impositions on his subjects, or by the need to borrow money from rich merchants and financiers who enjoyed sufficient independence to charge him high rates of interest. Nor were there any restraints or precedents which obliged him to respect the rule of law; nor any Church to insist that in certain spheres the king had no jurisdiction at all. Yet we have seen that during the sixteenth century the Vietnamese monarchy became weaker while the Tudor monarchy went from strength to strength. And even though the Crown was forced to give way to Parliament in the seventeenth century, the government still remained strong by comparison with that of Vietnam. There is a paradox in this contrast which calls for some explanation.

One respect in which the English monarchy was strengthened by its principles was in the matter of legitimacy and succession. Primogeniture was the rule, and in England (as opposed to some other European countries) a first-born woman could succeed in the absence of direct male heirs. The importance of legitimacy is shown by the fact that, even in fifteenth century England, no "overmighty subject" ever actually seized the throne without having some pretence to a legal claim: all those who actually became king were ultimately offspring of the Plantagenet line. Great power might reside with a Warwick or a Norfolk, but he never stood any chance of becoming a monarch in his own right. His peers would never have accepted it. In the sixteenth century, likewise, the principle of legitimacy made it possible for the three children of Henry VIII to take England in successively different directions in matters of religious doctrine and the jurisdiction of Rome.

The Vietnamese monarchy placed no such emphasis on legitimacy. Quite apart from the fact that women could never occupy the throne (though one woman had considerable power as a mother-regent in the 1450's), there was no rule of primogeniture. In a country where kings had several wives and many concubines, the number of royal princes was far greater than in England; and on the death of a king no one of them had an automatic right to succeed to the throne. The heir was usually nominated by the king before his death. But this left open the possibility that his choice might be influenced by a powerful court faction, possibly the blood relations of one of his queens, so that the selected heir owed his very accession to a group among his own subjects. It is not surprising that from time to time some "overmighty subject" secured so great a control over the king and the

5. K. A. Wittfogel, *Oriental Despotism: A Comparative Study of Total Power* (New Haven, 1957).

court that he was able to overthrow the dynasty and establish himself on the throne. Where this final step was impossible, a family like the Trịnh was nevertheless able to become virtual rulers of Vietnam and to confine the king to his palace and to his religious roles. Thus changes of dynasty meant the passage of royal authority from one clan to another, without any blood connection between them—except that the usurper might marry the wives or daughters of his predecessor. Such a change was, moreover, justified by reference to the Confucian doctrine of the "decree of fate" (or the "mandate of heaven").

The concept of legitimacy in England was rooted in an even more fundamental element of its political culture: the notion of law. Originating partly in the Hebrew, partly in the Roman tradition, the belief in law was fundamental to political thinking and institutional practice throughout the Europe of the fifteenth and sixteenth centuries. It was especially strong in England, where it had long since become bound up with the idea of the community. What an Englishman meant by law was first and foremost the common law, more deeply rooted in English tradition than either the civil or the ecclesiastical law of Rome. The king himself was expected to rule according to this law, and since the thirteenth century successive monarchs had admitted as much by their frequent confirmations of the Magna Carta.

The Vietnamese, like the Chinese, had a different conception of law; or, rather, it may be true to say that they distinguished between three concepts which are all somewhat different from the English idea of law. *Pháp* (Chinese *fa*) was the decree of the king or emperor, and it could not therefore bind the throne in the same way as a Magna Carta; nor could *hình* (*hsing*), the list of penalties to be imposed on those guilty of various offences, for no offence that a king could commit was covered by them. On the other hand, *lẽ* (*li*) was a principle of justice and universal harmony which touched the behaviour of all men, but it was not embodied in any precise formulation of law.[6] The king or emperor might be measured according to *lẽ*, but there was no means for any of his subjects to force him to rule according to it. Only the impersonal "decree of heaven" could affect the position of a king. The importance of *lẽ* was not that it laid down specific rules or procedures which the king or his officials must obey but rather that it provided a means of measuring the ethical quality of men. Where the Christian view of monarchy held that a king should govern according to good laws, the Confucian view was that he should govern through the appointment of good officials.

This contrast between the two conceptions of government and law can be well illustrated by comparing the "Confucianization" of Vietnam under

6. For a discussion of Chinese concepts of law, from which these Vietnamese concepts are derived, see J. Needham, *Science and Civilisation in China*, II (Cambridge, 1956), sec. 18.

Lê Thánh Tôn with the "Reformation" of England under Henry VIII. John K. Whitmore, whose study of the period 1428–1471 represents one of the most significant Western contributions to historical writing on Vietnam in recent years, has shown how the reforms of Lê Thánh Tôn represented the victory of a class of scholar-officials or *quân-tử* (the Chinese *chün-tzu*) over the great counsellors (*đại-thần*, *ta-chen*) who had dominated the Lê court since the beginning of the dynasty.[7] The latter, mainly originating from Thanh-Hóa province, were military figures; whereas the *quân*, more frequently natives of Tongking, were scholars whose claim to authority stemmed from success in the Confucian examinations.

The method of selecting officials by testing their proficiency in the Confucian classics and in literary composition, at formal state examinations, was already established in Vietnam by the thirteenth century. But in the Trần period (1225–1400) the scholars occupied a relatively unimportant place in the government systems, and the *đại-thần* were very often Trần princes. The scholars become a little more prominent towards the end of the fourteenth century, when the exmination system was reformed to permit a small number of candidates to reach a higher grade; and during the Ming occupation (1407–1427) Confucian scholarship in general received a great boost, especially in Tongking. But the end of Ming administration and the triumph of Lê Lợi meant a setback for the scholars, who were only very gradually able to reassert their influence during the fifteenth century. Although significant examinations were held in 1442 and in 1448, it was only in 1460 that the *quân-tử* achieved the kind of prominence, under the patronage of Thánh Tôn, which enabled them to reshape the government and regulate affairs of state according to Confucian principles. Inevitably they took steps to make the examination system a regular part of national life, and the pattern of triennial examinations in the capital established in 1463 was maintained (with only a slight break in 1517–1518) until the end of the Mạc dynasty. Candidates who passed the examinations and obtained the highest grade (*tiến-sĩ*, or *chin-shih*) became members of the Hàn-Lâm academy, from which the highest official positions were now filled. In this way, Lê Thánh Tôn ensured that the country would be run by men whose qualifications were well established in Confucian terms, with a less dominant role being played by military mandarins. The latter, incidentally, were kept occupied by a policy of reforming the army from 1466 and then by the need to control the large area of territory annexed from Champa in 1471.

The rise to power of the scholar-officials was accompanied by an overhaul of the system of government more far-reaching than any attempted by earlier kings, and probably only comparable in later periods with the

7. Whitmore.

reforms of Minh Mạng (1820–1841). The general effect of the changes, whose details are much too complex to be covered by a short paper, was to bring into existence a more orderly pattern of government. In this situation a key role was played by the new "office of transmissions," which ensured communication between the throne and its numerous officials. Also important were the decrees for reforming provincial and local government and for regulating the communal lands, as well as the registration rolls, of the villages. The new system was enshrined in a number of officially inspired compilations of texts, notably the *Hoàng Triều Quan Chế* of 1471 and the *Thiên Nam Dư Hạ Tập* (a sort of administrative encyclopedia) of 1483. Another book of the period which reflects the new strength of the Confucian idea of government was the *Đại Việt Sử Ký Toàn Thư*, a revised and extended version of the national chronicle, which Thánh Tôn ordered to be written in 1479.

In the reforms made by Henry VIII of England with the able assistance of Thomas Cromwell, there was also an emphasis on the good ordering of the state; but it was an order based upon law. The Reformation was, in some measure, a reaction against the policies of Cardinal Wolsey, who had been in power from 1515 to 1529. Wolsey had tended to favour arbitrary rule, tempered by a sense of equity, and his administration had been highly personal in character. This was resented by his opponents, and the 1530's saw instead a new emphasis on legality and the formal enactment of statute law. Wolsey had feared Parliament. Cromwell, on the other hand, welcomed the idea of using Parliament to bring about what amounted to a revolution by legislation. G. R. Elton observes that the role of Parliament as a legislative assembly was virtually established by the Reformation Parliament of 1529–1536.[8] At the same time, Cromwell also brought about changes in the practice of administration which amounted to the creation for the first time in England of a formalized bureaucracy, as opposed to government by means of the royal household, changes which Professor Elton has called the "Tudor revolution in government."[9] These aspects of the Reformation were of the greatest significance, and they amounted to a reaffirmation of the importance of the common law. At a time when England was almost bound to undergo some kind of political and institutional change in response to both the new intellectual mood in Europe and new developments in its own society, Cromwell's reforms ensured that for the next two generations the changes would be in the direction of Parliamentary sovereignty.

The element of law also entered into the other major aspect of the Henrician Reformation, the assertion of the power of the Crown in spiritual

---

8. G. R. Elton, *The Tudor Constitution* (Cambridge, 1965), pp. 228ff.
9. G. R. Elton, *The Tudor Revolution in Government* (Cambridge, 1953).

matters and the ending of papal jurisdiction in England. This meant a decline in the status and independence of the clergy, a change reflected in the suppression of the monastic orders which quickly followed. In this respect, the changes of the 1530's had almost the reverse effect of the reforms of Lê Thánh Tôn. They brought to an end the spiritual ties between England and Rome which had been forged in the early medieval period, and they reduced the power of the clergy in the nation's affairs. England would never again have a cardinal for Chancellor. In Vietnam, on the other hand, the effect of "Confucianization" was to strengthen ties with China and to increase the influence of the group most inclined to look towards the Middle Kingdom for inspiration. The changes of the 1460's and 1470's brought Vietnam closer than ever to the Chinese model of government established under Ming T'ai-tsu. The tributary relationship to China continued and was strengthened by the events of 1540–1541, when Mạc Đăng Dung, and then his successor Mạc Phúc Hải, accepted the status of *đô-thống-sứ*, which made them virtually "governors of Annam."

The tributary relationship, however, had never been a form of jurisdiction, and it is important to insist on the difference between English and Vietnamese attitudes to religious law which underlies the contrast we are examining. The superiority of the Chinese emperor in the scheme of things might make it natural for a deposed Vietnamese dynasty to appeal for his intervention, as happened in 1405–1406 and in 1536–1537, but it did not give him any regular jurisdiction over the Vietnamese king or his subjects. In Christendom, such jurisdiction was a necessary consequence of belief in an omnipotent creator God and in an ultimate day of judgment for every human soul. That it was divided into the temporal and spiritual jurisdictions of king and bishops respectively is perhaps less fundamental than the fact that for every misdeed in his daily life any individual could be called to account before those charged with administering God's law. Absolutism such as this did not exist in traditional Vietnam, and it was quite alien to the Chinese religious tradition. For this reason it is necessary not to read into "Confucianization" the kind of religious changes that eventually followed upon the English Reformation.

Another contrast between the two countries relates to the question of religious tolerance. In 1462, a decree of Lê Thánh Tôn forbade the building of new Buddhist and other non-Confucian temples, and in the years 1468–1470 a series of decrees established new regulations for the maintenance of mourning rites and other Confucian ceremonies. Such concern for the Confucian proprieties stemmed naturally from the belief that the harmony of the kingdom and of the whole universe depends on propriety of conduct in the individual and on the correct performance of family rituals. On at least one occasion the King himself undertook a pious visit to the

ancestral tombs of his own clan in Thanh-Hóa province. But these decrees
did not involve a merciless persecution of Buddhist and other non-Confucian sects. Such sects lost royal patronage for a time, between 1460 and 1600,
and so disappear from the royal records. But there is nothing to suggest that
they ceased completely to exist or that Confucianization was accompanied
by large-scale execution of heretics such as occurred under the Marian
reaction. Confucianism was a religion that required a certain framework
of order. But it did not impose a rigorous catechism of belief on all members
of society and persecute those who refused to conform to it. In this respect,
the Vietnamese tradition was far less absolutist than the European.

IV

An aspect of the growing strength of the monarchy in England after 1460
which has received a good deal of attention from historians in recent years
was the question of the Crown's financial resources. Sir John Fortescue,
writing in the reign of Edward IV, lamented the fact that when a king had
smaller resources than his most powerful subjects the throne was bound to
be weak and the realm unstable.[10] He was thinking in particular of Crown
lands, which in the mid-fifteenth century were reduced to their smallest
extent before the losses of the late sixteenth and seventeenth centuries.
The period 1460–1540 saw a major recovery of land by the Crown,
beginning with the union of the Duchies of Lancaster and York in 1461
and culminating in the seizure of the monastic lands in the years 1536–1539.
By 1540 the Crown may well have owned as much as a fifth or a quarter of
the productive land of England, though the proportion was soon to be
reduced by the selling off of former monastic properties for ready cash.
The growth of the royal domain was accompanied by a new concern for
estate administration, and the process of reform which began under
Edward IV was completed by Cromwell's transformation of government
financial administration. Of course, the king was never able to live entirely
"of his own" even during this period. Edward IV borrowed from Florentine
merchants, and both the Yorkist and the Tudor kings depended for part of
their revenues on Parliamentary grants of taxation in various forms.
Henry VIII was reduced to debasing the coinage in an attempt to manipulate the whole monetary system in his own favour. But none of the monarchs
in the century before 1560 was faced with the kind of financial desperation
that compelled Charles I to summon a predictably recalcitrant Parliament
in 1640, an event which culminated in a civil war of a kind quite unlike
anything that occurred in either England or Vietnam during the period
currently under review. Thus the fact that English law protected the rights

10. Sir John Fortescue, *The Governance of England*, ed. C. Plummer (Oxford, 1885).

of the king's subjects, including their property, and gave certain merchant communities a special independence under royal charter did not prevent the monarchy from building up its own wealth and so dominating the realm.

Unfortunately this aspect of monarchy is not so easy to study in the case of Vietnam. Not only has less research been done; there is also a dearth of relevant source materials, for there are no surviving archives recording the day-to-day activities of Vietnamese administration before the nineteenth century. We are therefore dependent entirely on chronicles and on the records of formal edicts and decrees from the throne. These tell us a certain amount about the obligations of the king's subjects and about the rewarding of his officials but very little about the private lands of subjects and officials or even about the "treasury lands" of the government itself. It is impossible to say whether the proportions of land in various categories of ownership increased or decreased during our period. All that we can be sure of is that the confiscation of land from the Vietnamese traitors who had supported the Ming meant that Lê Lợi and his successors had a reserve of land which they could use to reward their supporters and officials and that they probably used it to make official grants, for life or a term, rather than to create hereditary fiefs. In the absence of any records of private estates, it is impossible to test the argument of the Vietnamese Marxist historians that the rise of the scholar-officials under the Lê monarchy of the fifteenth century reflected an important economic change, in which resources passed from an aristocracy to a sort of gentry landowning class from which the *quan* were drawn. We know that there were private estates of some kind, known as *trang-trại*, and a decree of 1397 reflects government concern lest they grow too large and draw away too many labourers from the village. But we know nothing of their extent or organization at this period.

One contrast between England and Vietnam, however, can be drawn with some confidence: that between the manor and the *xã*. In fifteenth and sixteenth-century England, there was an element of territorial lordship of a kind never found in Vietnam: the existence of large estates in which whole villages were owned in perpetuity by hereditary lords. Even though the feudal lordship of noblemen over their free tenants was declining at just this period, the landed estates actually owned by nobility and gentry alike consisted of numbers of manors each comprising all or part of a village. The manorial court, which managed an important part of village affairs, was as much a possession of the lord as was his land.[11] In Vietnam, lordship in this sense did not exist; nor was there ever a strictly feudal system in

11. The English manorial framework was of course undergoing important changes during this period, as highly formalized arrangements of the twelfth and thirteenth centuries were breaking down; cf. R. H. Tawney, *The Agrarian Problem in the Sixteenth Century* (London, 1912).

which great lords enjoyed rights over lesser ones within their territorial fiefs. Instead, we find a pattern of society in which the whole country consisted of semiautonomous communities known as the *xã* (Chinese *she*).[12] They were all subject to direct regulation by the throne, without any intervening lord—except insofar as a prince or a high official was sometimes granted the usufruct of their obligations to the throne. Each *xã* had its small group of officials, members of the community appointed to office by the king, who were responsible for the fulfilment of its obligations. It also had its guardian spirit, formally appointed by royal decree though usually a local ancestor or other spirit. In economic terms, each village was responsible for registering its own population and for the performance of whatever services the government might demand. The *xã* also had, in addition to the private lands of its inhabitants, a section of land set aside as *công-điền* (common land) and regulated by the state. This was public land which was distributed regularly among the members of the village, according to rank, every so many years; it could not be alienated, and it was regularly taxed by the king. How strictly the regulations were maintained was perhaps a measure of the strength of the monarchy and government, and it may therefore be significant that such evidence as we have suggests a greater measure of control over the *xã* under Lê Thánh Tôn than at any other period of Vietnamese history.

But here, too, the absence of archival records makes it impossible to go beyond the formal regulations affecting the *xã* and its obligations in order to see how its resources were used in practice. Was there, for example, a regular relationship over many generations between certain villages and certain offices? Were the affairs of supposedly semiautonomous village communities in effect dominated by local magnates, despite the formal differences between the Vietnamese and English land systems? These are some of the many questions which at present seem almost impossible to answer.

V

Power is never completely and automatically a consequence of wealth and control over land: it also depends on control over institutions and over people. The ability to wage war against one's rivals, or against the throne itself, must be related to the ability to raise an army away from the capital. The ability to influence or dominate affairs at court depends on an individual's ability to manipulate the institutions of government to his own advantage.

12. On the *xã*, see Lê Văn Hảo "Introduction à l'Ethnologie du Đình," *BSEI*, n.s. 37 (1962); Nguyen Huu Khang, *La Commune Annamite* (Paris, 1946), etc. The latter argues that in certain respects the *xã* was more rigorously controlled from the capital in the fifteenth century than in the nineteenth.

In England this aspect of the nature of power was changing quite fundamentally during the century between 1460 and 1560. The territorial lord-
ships which had been the most important form of lordship or patronage at
the height of the "feudal system" (in the twelfth and thirteenth centuries)
were by now declining in significance, though they were by no means
finished in 1460.[13] More important by the sixteenth century were three other
forms of patronage: the county community, the noble household (which
could include men who had no territorial associations with its lord), and
government appointments. At the local level the importance of the county
grew as that of private lordship declined, from the reign of Edward I onwards
but especially in the sixteenth century. It was an ancient English institution
which had never been totally eclipsed by Norman feudalism, and it was now
re-emerging into prominence as the focus of local justice and administration, and also of the militia. The power of the nobility tended to become
weaker territorially and to depend increasingly on the maintenance of a
large household and on the influence which a duke or an earl could exercise
at court. Patronage, in the sense of ability to secure for one's followers
appointment to an office in the expanding bureaucracy, was becoming
increasingly significant by the middle of the sixteenth century. But down
to 1560 the general effect of the changing nature of patronage was to
strengthen the position of the Crown, for it meant the end of the age when a
feudal nobility could use its power to raise private armies, at least in
England south of the Trent.

Vietnam did not have a "feudal system" at any time, in the sense of a
system of contractual tenure of large territorial fiefs from the throne and
a hereditary nobility owing military contingents in return for land. We do
not know a great deal about the internal structure of Vietnamese politics
and government in the Lý and Trần periods, but there is nothing to indicate
any arrangement of that kind. Royal grants of land may well have taken
place, but they seem to have been made on a temporary basis as part of the
rewards for office. That was certainly the case by the fifteenth century.
Lordship over territory, in the strictly feudal sense, was probably not an
element in Vietnamese patron-client relations.

What counted in Vietnamese political conflicts were offices in the
bureaucracy and membership in a clan. Had office alone been the most
important thing, with access to resources depending entirely on royal
appointment, Vietnam might well have been a much more stable polity,
as was the case in traditional Siam where kinship mattered much less.
But in Vietnam the clan framework was at least as important as lordship
in England. Kinship was the framework of the ancestral cult, which was the

13. On the question of territorial lordship in this period see R. B. Smith, *Land and Politics
in the England of Henry VIII: The West Riding of Yorkshire, 1530–46* (Oxford, 1970).

mainstay of Vietnamese religion and which was strengthened rather than weakened by the rise of Confucianism. A man was supposed to be in touch with all the descendants of his paternal ancestor of the fifth generation, and this was likely to be quite a large number of men. They were held together by a loyalty which might often conflict with their loyalty to the throne, and that loyalty was focussed upon a regional centre, because every family was obliged to maintain its ancestral tombs. This helps to explain why the Trịnh and the Nguyễn, and indeed the Lê clan itself, had special sources of strength in the province of Thanh-Hóa. They may well have had important private lands there; but above all they had kinsmen. It is unfortunate indeed that we have no records that might tell us something of the internal organization of a powerful clan in Vietnam at this period.

Compared with the English lordship, and also with the newer forms of patronage that were emerging, the Vietnamese clan was somewhat inflexible as a political grouping. Lordship was a bond that could be created, or broken, at will; even territorial lordship could incorporate new followers through new granting of lands or manors by a powerful lord. A rising lord could always attract new supporters, and they would immediately become equal members of his patron group. But kinship depends on birth, and while blood may be thicker than water it cannot be the basis of a highly flexible community which any new follower can enter at will. It was necessary to be born into the clan in order to be a full member of it; anyone who was not born into this clan, moreover, was very likely to have existing loyalties to another. For clan loyalties could have a divisive effect as often as being the basis of combined political effort.

The Vietnamese monarchy, "oriental despotism" or not, was in practice based on the occupation of the throne by one clan in a land which had many. Herein lies the most essential reason for the weakness of the monarchy, in this period as in all others. The Trần clan in the thirteenth century had sought to preserve the throne by a twofold policy: regular abdication of the king while still in the prime of life, so that he could rule as *thượng-hoàng* while his heir secured the throne; and marriage of leading princes entirely within the royal clan. But despite these precautions, which the Mạc seem to have revived after 1527, the Trần dynasty was unable to survive forever. By the mid-fourteenth century it no longer had a *thượng-hoàng* because a king had died on the throne before abdicating and a clan from Thanh-Hóa had been permitted to supply two royal wives, whose nephew was subsequently to overthrow the dynasty. The long history of Vietnamese political conflict under the monarchy suggests that there was no way of preventing outside clans from weakening and threatening the throne or from seizing it outright. The supposedly highly centralized bureaucratic system could not prevent it from happening, since clan patronage and official position were always too closely intertwined.

If nothing else, this brief essay in comparison has shown that the differences between England and Vietnam were essentially cultural and institutional rather than material. And it has tended to undermine the crude notion that oriental monarchies were always despotisms while the Western political tradition placed greater emphasis on the limitation of monarchy. Monarchical arbitrariness was a less sure foundation for the strength of governments than an institutional system based on law, however it might appear to limit the power of the monarch; while kinship was a less flexible, and therefore less stable, basis of politics than lordship and simple patronage.

The Anglo-Chinese College at Malacca, 1818–1843

BRIAN HARRISON

University of British Columbia

Britain's growing interest in China in the early nineteenth century is usually thought of in terms of trade and diplomacy—the East India Company's business in the tea and the "country" trade in opium at Canton, or such diplomatic approaches as the Amherst embassy to Peking in 1816–1817. But British interest in China was being manifested at the same time in other related if subsidiary modes, including a missionary one. The London Missionary Society, founded in 1795, planned to establish a foothold in China. It selected and trained Robert Morrison for the purpose and sent him to Canton in 1807. In the event, Morrison's work was severely limited by the restrictions placed on European activities in Canton at that time, and he was able to maintain his position of scholar-missionary there only by accepting appointment as secretary and translator to the East India Company's Canton factory. It seemed that an open and direct missionary approach to China would have to await much more favourable conditions. Morrison concluded that in the meantime an indirect approach should be made through the overseas Chinese in Southeast Asia. It was largely his enthusiasm for this idea that led to the founding of the Anglo-Chinese College at Malacca as a forward base and training centre for missionary operations among the Chinese people.

From the time of his arrival in Canton, Morrison repeatedly urged the London Society to set up a missionary base in Southeast Asia, suggesting at various times Penang, Malacca, and Java as possible centres. Penang (since 1786) and Malacca (from 1795) were both at this time under the East India Company's administration; Java, taken from the Dutch in 1811, was administered by the company until 1816. Penang was Morrison's first choice as a centre, "chiefly with regard to the Chinese who are there"; it could be "a stepping-stone to China, embracing at the same time the Malays." But by the end of 1812 he was thinking of Malacca as a more central base. "I wish that we had an institution at Malacca for the training of missionaries, European and native, and designed for all the countries beyond the

Ganges," he wrote. "There also let there be that powerful engine, the press."[1]

The arrival of William Milne as a second missionary for the London Society at Canton in July 1813 gave Morrison a chance to put his ideas into effect.[2] After spending some six months learning Chinese, Milne agreed to go on a missionary reconnaissance tour to Java, Penang, and Malacca, distributing copies of Morrison's recently completed Chinese translation of the New Testament and looking out for a suitable mission headquarters. Milne travelled in Java between March and August 1814, Sir Stamford Raffles, then Governor of Java, arranging for him to visit most of the main centres of Chinese settlement. From Java, Milne went to Malacca in early August and spent a week there. Then, as it was growing late in the sailing season, he decided to forego his intended visit to Penang and returned to China.[3]

Discussing the choice of a mission headquarters in Southeast Asia with Morrison on his return, Milne was inclined to favour Malacca rather than Java. While Malacca had a comparatively small number of Chinese residents, it was favourably situated for reaching the Chinese population of Southeast Asia in general; besides, it was both healthier than Batavia and "a quiet place," suitable for a centre in which "the Chinese, Malay and other Ultra-Ganges languages should be cultivated." Morrison agreed on the advantages of Malacca, where "preparations may be made for entering China with more effect, as soon as it shall please God to open a door for us." But the final decision seems to have been left for Milne to make in the light of circumstances (by the London Convention of August 1814, Britain had agreed to restore Dutch possessions in the Malaysian archipelago, including Java and Malacca, taken during the recent wars), and after Milne returned to Malacca in 1815, Morrison wrote: "Perhaps at Malacca or at Java an open door will be found. . . . It is yours, my brother, to seek for and found this important station. There we shall have our Chinese college."[4]

Reaching Malacca on 21 May 1815, Milne immediately set to work in organizing the various mission activities that were to lead eventually to the founding of the Anglo-Chinese College. In the field of education a small

1. Morrison 1839:I, 191, 273, 355. Robert Morrison (1782–1834), b. nr. Morpeth, Northumberland; works include *Dictionary of the Chinese Language*, 6 vols. (Macao, 1815–1823); translation (with William Milne) of *The Bible* in Chinese, 21 vols. (Malacca, 1823) (Ride 1957:43–44).

2. William Milne (1785–1822), b. Kennethmont, Aberdeenshire, trained at L.M.S. theological seminary at Gosport in Hampshire (to which Morrison had gone in 1804); ordained 16 July 1812; arrived at Macao to join Morrison 4 July 1815 (wall tablet in Christ Church, Malacca).

3. Milne 1820:114–119.

4. *Ibid.*, pp. 135–138; Morrison 1839:I, 377.

beginning was made in August 1815 with the opening of a free school for Hokkien-speaking Chinese pupils; and in the following year, a second school, for Cantonese pupils, was started. Milne himself knew no Hokkien, the dialect spoken by the majority of the Malacca Chinese; he could speak some Cantonese but had spent most of his time on the study of Mandarin.[5] A Malay school was opened in 1816 by C. H. Thomsen, another L.M.S. missionary (originally from Holstein in Lower Saxony) who had arrived at Malacca in September 1815 to join Milne especially in work among the Malays. Thomsen learned his Malay from the "munshi" Abdullah bin Abdul Kadir, a native of Malacca and later famous as the author of the autobiographical *Hikayat Abdullah*, which provides much valuable though not always reliable detail about the college and the men associated with it. An English school "for the children of Christians" had also been planned by Milne and a building allocated for the purpose by the authorities of the Dutch Reformed Church, but news of the likely early return of Malacca to Dutch rule soon damped what little local enthusiasm had existed for English-language training.[6]

Besides starting new schools Milne prepared the ground for the establishment of a publications centre. Morrison in Canton had often stressed the importance of the press as an instrument of missionary aims; he had sent a Cantonese printer, Leang Ah Fah, to accompany Milne to Malacca in 1815. Together they produced in August 1815 the first number of the *Chinese Magazine*, containing essays and papers "chiefly of a religious and moral kind" but designed "to combine the diffusion of general knowledge with that of Christianity" for free distribution "through all the Chinese settlements of the Eastern Archipelago" and in Siam and Cochinchina. Five hundred copies were printed monthly in small tract format during the first three years of publication; by 1819 production had risen to a thousand copies a month.[7] Printers, a printing press, and Arabic and English type founts were obtained from Bengal in November 1816, enabling Thomsen to publish some Malay tracts in the following year and in 1818 a Malay spelling book, "so far as we know the first work of the kind ever attempted in Malay."[8]

Thomsen was very much the Malay specialist, and Milne was left to carry the main burden of the mission's activities at this early stage. Even so he found time to continue the Chinese translation of the Old Testament in conjunction with Morrison and to complete his translation of *The Sacred*

5. Milne 1820:162.
6. *Ibid.*, pp. 174–175; Malacca Church Records, Kerk Boek, 19 Dec. 1815.
7. Milne 1820:138, 154–156.
8. *Ibid.*, p. 180; J. Noorduyn, "C. H. Thomsen, Editor of a Code of Bugis Maritime Laws," *BKI*, 113 (1957):238–251; *Indo-Chinese Gleaner*, 1, 2 (Aug. 1817):32; 4 (May 1818):131.

Edict of the K'ang-hsi emperor, which he dedicated to Stamford Raffles, in December 1815.[9]

But all such activities still lacked a focal point; the mission remained without a physical base. Milne therefore went to Penang in January 1816 to petition the government in person for a grant of land at Malacca as well as for formal authorization of a printing press. The governor in council decided that, pending the restoration of Malacca to the Dutch, the most that could be done was to allot a piece of waste ground to the mission under a conditional grant to be confirmed later by the Dutch government.[10] There was in fact no government-owned waste ground available nearer than one and a half miles from Malacca town, at St. John's Hill; but land obtained there was exchanged a few months later for a smaller though much more convenient property owned by a local merchant, Tamby Ahmud Said, on the sea front about a quarter of a mile west of the Malacca river, "at the western gate of the town."[11] Here the mission buildings and the Anglo-Chinese College were soon to be erected. A stone wall running across the sea front of the property was built in the summer of 1816. In January 1817 a row of buildings including a printing house, a paper store, and accommodation for employees of the mission was completed, with brick walls and tiled roof, along one side of the property. A second row of buildings was completed in June of that year on the same plan, about ninety feet in length, to accommodate additional printers and a large shipment of paper sent by Morrison from Canton for producing a new duodecimo edition of the New Testament in Chinese.[12]

Translation and publishing played an important part in attracting attention and support to the activities of the mission, and ultimately to the college. Most effective in this regard was the *Indo-Chinese Gleaner*, a quarterly journal in English, edited by Milne, which first appeared in May 1817. It contained accounts of mission activities, "general intelligence and miscellanea," designed to fill "the intellectual wastes which missionaries generally inhabit."[13] Though Milne himself admitted that it did not pay its way, Morrison considered it "an excellent publication" which had "gained considerable celebrity among the *literati* of Europe." It was the *Gleaner*, at any rate, that won valuable support from an English peer, Viscount Kingsborough, for the Anglo-Chinese College in 1824; he offered

9. *The Sacred Edict* (London, 1817; 2d ed., Shanghai, 1870); date of translator's preface: 16 Dec. 1815 at Malacca. Reviewed in *Chinese Repository*, 1, 8 (Dec. 1832):297–315. Milne 1820:144.
10. Straits Settlements Records, 54, Council Minutes of 25 Jan. 1816.
11. *Ibid.*, 55, Council Minutes of 8 June 1816; Milne 1820:173; Begbie 1834:368; Hill 1955:105 ("just outside the Tranquerah Gate").
12. Milne 1820:188; *Indo-Chinese Gleaner*, 1, 2 (Aug. 1817):32.
13. Milne 1820:192.

Morrison the gift of £1,500 and a collection of three hundred valuable books on condition that the college press should publish the *Notitia Linguae Sinicae* of the French Jesuit Father Prémare, "confessedly the most profoundly versed in the genius of the Chinese language of the Roman Catholic missionaries who visited China"—a condition that must have tested Morrison's scholarly detachment; but it was accepted, and the work eventually appeared in 1830.[14]

As the prime promoter of the idea of a college at Malacca, Morrison was most energetic in seeking support for the project. He formulated his proposals as early as October 1815 in the form of a rather high-pitched prospectus addressed from Canton "to the benevolent Christians of Great Britain and Ireland; proposals for establishing by voluntary subscription an English and Chinese College at Malacca in the East Indies." The immediate object of the college would be "to facilitate an amicable literary intercourse betwixt England and the nations in which the Chinese written language is employed"; the ultimate aim was to assist the process by which "the light of Science and of Revelation" might "peacefully and gradually shed their lustre on the eastern limits of Asia and the Islands of the rising sun." The teaching staff of the institution would include a European professor of English and Chinese and two assistant professors (one Chinese and one European) to start with, while provision would be made for six Asian and six European students. During 1817, Morrison also prepared an extensive report which served to publicize the work of the mission generally; this *Retrospect of the First Ten Years of the Protestant Mission to China*, further enlarged by Milne, was published by the Anglo-Chinese Press at Malacca in 1820.[15]

Plans for the college were carried a decisive stage further in the year 1818. The two partners in the enterprise met again in September 1817 at Canton, where Milne had gone for his health. Acting as a provisional committee of the Ultra-Ganges Mission, they drew up two sets of resolutions to regularize their activities, the second of which, signed on 2 January 1818, dealt specifically with the college. To get the project going, Morrison had decided to make a personal donation, anonymously at first, of 4,000 Spanish dollars towards the cost of building, with a promise of £100 a year for five years towards recurrent costs. A site was now allocated for building on the mission premises at Malacca. Milne was to superintend the construction, and meanwhile a "general plan" for the college was to be prepared for submission to the directors of the L.M.S. The *Indo-Chinese Gleaner* in its

14. Morrison 1839:I, 500; II, 288, 317, 439. Joseph Henri Marie de Prémare, S. J., missionary and sinologist, b. Cherbourg, July 1666, d. Macao, Sept. 1736; James Legge called his *Notitia* "an invaluable work."

15. Morrison 1839:I, 426, 475.

issue of February 1818 explained that the purpose of the college would be to cultivate "Chinese literature, general history, sacred criticism, Christian theology, etc.," as well as to teach English language and European literature to local students; and it went on to announce that although the building could hardly be completed within a year or so, "yet an application in behalf of any pious young man, whether born in India of European parents, or a native Chinese, or a European, well recommended, will meet with due attention."[16]

Milne returned from Canton to Malacca in February 1818. During his absence Walter Henry Medhurst, whose arrival in June 1817 had enabled Milne to take leave, was in charge of the mission, being especially responsible for printing and publication.[17] Another addition to the staff in 1817 was John Slater, a specialist in Chinese, and three new recruits who arrived in September 1818 were John Ince, Samuel Milton—both Chinese specialists—and Thomas Beighton on the Malay side. With their arrival Medhurst took general charge of the Chinese schools under the mission, now three in number, as well as the press.[18]

Although plans for the college were going ahead, there was still some uncertainty about their outcome pending the restoration of Malacca to Dutch rule. Major Farquhar, the British Resident at Malacca, wrote to the Dutch commissioners arriving for the transfer in September 1818 that the Protestant mission was "of first importance," and he hoped they would "favour and protect Rev. Mr. Milne of that institution" and confirm the conditional grant of land made by the Penang government. Milne himself also wrote to the commissioners, sketching the history of the mission and explaining the plan for a college.[19]

On 11 November 1818, after the transfer of government, the foundation stone of the college building was laid by Farquhar in the presence of the new Dutch governor and prominent residents.[20] The "general plan" for the college had been completed by October in readiness for the transfer and the foundation ceremony and for final submission to the directors of the Missionary Society in London. It reflected clearly the broad, humane outlook of the two men who had been behind the project from the beginning.

16. *Ibid.*, p. 502; *Indo-Chinese Gleaner*, 1, 3 (Feb. 1818):68–70.

17. Medhurst 1838:311. Walter Henry Medhurst (1796–1857), b. London, educated St. Paul's School and Hackney College, where he displayed "an unceasing activity of mind and a remarkable gift for languages"; served as a missionary in Malacca, Penang, Batavia and, from Dec. 1843, in Shanghai; compiled a Hokkien dictionary (Macao, 1832); author of *China, Its State and Prospects* (London, 1838).

18. Medhurst 1838:311–312; Milne 1820:211–213; *Indo-Chinese Gleaner*, 2, 7 (Jan. 1819):42.

19. Dutch Records, Buitenland 29 (Malakka): Farquhar to Commissioners Woltenbeck and Thyssen, 16 Sept. 1818; Milne to same, 18 Oct. 1818.

20. Milne 1820:350–364; *Indo-Chinese Gleaner*, 1, 6 (Oct. 1818):213.

The twin objects of the college were here described as "the reciprocal cultivation of Chinese and European literature, and the diffusion of Christianity"—in that order. The Chinese language and literature would be made accessible to Europeans, while the English language, with European literature and science, would be made accessible to the nations of "China, Cochinchina, the Chinese colonies in the Eastern Archipelago, Loochoo, Korea and Japan." The college would have an extensive Chinese library and a collection of European literature dealing with the languages, history, manners, and the like of the Asian countries mentioned. The staff would consist of European tutors of the Chinese language, capable also of teaching European learning, and native Chinese teachers. The Chinese language would be taught to European students for whatever purpose they chose to apply it to—"to religion, to literature, or to commerce." Asian students would be taught the English language, geography, history, arithmetic, and so on, together with moral philosophy, Christian theology, and Malay.

Admission to the college would be open to recommended persons from Europe or America, of any Christian communion, to persons from European universities with travelling fellowships, to Christian missionaries, and to persons belonging to commercial companies or attached to national consulates. Young men would be admitted from any of the Asian countries mentioned, and they would not be compelled either to profess the Christian religion or attend Christian worship. There would be accommodation in the college for a limited number of students—others might lodge in the town if they wished—and a fund would be set up for the maintenance of poor students.[21]

Underlying this whole document was a strong, though not exclusive, emphasis on the importance of the Chinese language and literature for the process of understanding—and gaining access to—China. Milne explained: "China, viewed as an object of literary and philosophical speculation, has scarcely been touched by Protestant countries . . . ; there is scarcely any foreign country of more importance for the British nation to investigate. The proximity of British territory to that of China, and the very important commercial relations which subsist between the two countries, certainly make it a point of high political consideration to understand fully Chinese laws, opinions, and manners; and that can only be done effectually by a knowledge of the language." At the same time, he added:

the other countries and languages of Ultra-Ganges India are also very important; their laws, manners, literature and religion . . . furnish ample subjects for investiga-

21. *Indo-Chinese Gleaner*, 1, 6 (Oct. 1818):217. The "general plan" is printed as a separate three-page prospectus after p. 217 of the microfilm copy (no. 2437) of *Indo-Chinese Gleaner* in the National Library, Singapore.

tion. The Malay language has indeed been long cultivated by the Dutch, and of late by the English; and several very interesting and useful books have been printed with a view to its illustration. But even here, there is still much to be done . . . ; the languages of the interior of Sumatra, of the Javanese, of the inhabitants of Borneo and the Celebes, of the Philippine Islands, of Japan, of Cambodia and Siam, are all (with the exception of some imperfect ideas of the Japanese given in Kaempfer's excellent *History of Japan*, and Thunberg's *Travels*) untouched by Protestant nations, or in a great measure so.[22]

However, Milne concluded frankly, while it was intended in the Anglo-Chinese College to unite the study of the languages and history of these countries with those of China so far as practicable, "our settlement at Malacca . . . was intended for China, and as a kind of substitute for a residence on the border of that country, which we would have preferred had it been attainable. Therefore objects connected with China will . . . hold a chief place in the seminary now proposed."[23]

The directors of the London Missionary Society accepted this "general plan" with some reservation; they must have found the spirit behind it rather too secular for their liking. Acknowledging the "liberal proposals" of the plan, they approved the general design for the college and confirmed the allocation of land for its building, but at the same time they observed that, as the institution appeared to be "intended to embrace other objects than such as are strictly missionary," they wished to see it given "a decidedly paramount direction towards missionary objects."[24]

Other developments in the mission's activities need only be touched on here in relation to the growth of the college, with which they were inevitably linked. In 1819 there were five schools under the direct care of the mission. C. H. Thomsen, Malay specialist with the mission, was placed in charge of a public school which opened early in 1819 under the patronage of the new Dutch governor. Thomsen at the same time was composing hymns and tracts in the Malay language.[25] Medhurst, always full of energy, "commenced preaching in the Fukien dialect four times a week in different parts of the town," opened a Chinese school in Penang (whither the mission's operations were extended during 1819), and published a *Geographical Catechism* in Chinese for use in schools, including maps and brief descriptions of the principal countries of the world.[26]

22. A footnote here cites as exceptions Marsden's *History of Sumatra*, Leyden's *Dissertation on the Languages and Literatures of the Indo-Chinese Nations*, the same author's *Comparative Vocabulary*, and Raffles's *History of Java* ("which we have had the pleasure to see since the first edition of this paper").
23. Milne 1820:356–359.
24. *Ibid.*, p. 350; Morrison 1839:I, 539–540. Confirmation of grant of land by L.M.S. dated 22 Feb. 1819.
25. *Indo-Chinese Gleaner*, 2, 9 (July 1819):168.
26. Milne 1820:220–221; Medhurst 1838:314.

Meanwhile the construction of the college building went ahead, though not without some delays, as in September 1819 when Milne noted: "We have been stopped in building the College a whole month from want of water in the river to float down the timber." But the work was finished by early August 1820, five years after the opening of the mission's first school.[27] Already in March, with the building well advanced and the first students being enrolled, Morrison in Canton felt that the time had come to draw up a code of laws and statutes for the institution as well as a deed of grant formalizing his donation of funds. Milne—who admitted, "I feel myself extremely ignorant of the proper method of College management"—drew up rules and regulations for the library and museum.[28]

The college building occupied the space on the mission premises between the two parallel ranges of buildings (containing printing offices, classrooms, and living quarters for local employees) already built at each end. It was an open and airy situation, commanding a fine view of the Malacca roads and the strait. When completed, the two-story building was described as "a plain substantial edifice," ninety feet long and thirty-four feet broad, with verandahs front and back extending the full length and supported by pillars. The front of the building, facing the sea, was shaded by a row of senna trees. The ground floor contained the library, museum, and classrooms; on the upper floor were living quarters for the missionary staff. The library in 1823 contained "about 3,380 volumes, of which 2,850 were in Chinese, the remainder in various languages Asian and European." The museum contained "Chinese drawings, maps and charts, Chinese anatomical plates, specimens of Chinese musical instruments, bronze figures, etc., specimens of the rocks in Palestine, birds of paradise, cups of Bacchus, and petrifactions." Around the building a botanical garden was originally planned; Morrison at one stage suggested that the Royal Horticultural Society send out a young botanist to collect the plants of the Eastern archipelago, learn Chinese, and translate scientific botanical works into that language; but the scheme seems to have fallen through.[29]

Curiously, the mission had no chapel until 1827. Two visiting officials from the London Society arrived to lay a foundation stone in January 1826, and the building, "plain but neat," was completed and opened for public worship the following year; by the early 1830's four services were being held every Sunday, in Chinese, Portuguese, Malay, and English.[30]

27. Morrison 1824:220–223.

28. Morrison 1839:II, 39–53.

29. *Ibid.*, p. 52; Morrison 1823:21; Milne 1820:350; *Indo-Chinese Gleaner*, 2, 14 (Oct. 1820):462; Broomhall 1924:107; Begbie 1834: facing p. 368 (view of Anglo-Chinese College, drawn by the author).

30. Tyerman and Bennet 1831:II, 274; Medhurst 1838:318; Begbie 1834:368.

As principal of the college, Milne began to admit students prior to the actual completion of the main building. The name of the first student on the college list was given as Yaou, admitted in October 1819 to study Mandarin. Eight students admitted in 1820 added strength to the international character of the institution; they were Loo, to study Mandarin; Rev. R. Fleming, who had arrived to join the Chinese side of the mission; James Bone, aged sixteen, of Malacca; Leang Ah Fah, the Cantonese printer who had been converted to Christianity in 1816, to study theology; and three Malacca youths—Chang Chun, Tsze Hea, and Ma King-tsuen—to learn Mandarin and English and to study the Chinese classics and Christian books in Chinese. Those students who were supported by college funds had to sign an undertaking "to study the language and literature of China according to the correct pronunciation of the Mandarin tongue," to study English language and literature, and to remain at the college for six years. But, as a prominent East India Company official reported after a visit to the college in 1828, "no profession of religious belief is required on entering the institution, nor are compulsory means in any way employed with a view to conversion."[31]

There was a modest but steady rise in student numbers in the early years: eleven in 1821, fifteen in 1823, twenty-six in 1824. The staff establishment during the first three years consisted of a president (Morrison, *in absentia*), a principal (Milne), a treasurer, a librarian, a professor of Chinese, and four masters in Chinese, Malay, Javanese, and Siamese. Milne wrote to Morrison in 1821: "I am quite happy at present, having Chinese, Siamese, Cochinchinese and Malay teachers all about me—Japanese alone is wanted." Two years later Morrison reported that, although not as much had been done in the department of Malayan and Ultra-Ganges literature as could have been wished, yet "a considerable number of Malay manuscripts have been collected; . . . for nearly these two years past a Siamese writer has been employed in collecting and transcribing manuscripts in that language; Cochinchina has also been kept in view, and a translation of a Christian catechism has been nearly completed by a native of that country who resided for some time in the College."[32]

With the position of the college reasonably assured by Morrison's deed of grant and the completion of the main building, financial support could be sought from outside sources. The L.M.S. itself voted £500 to the college in 1821. The East India Company granted an annual subsidy of 1,200 Spanish dollars. Largely due to the reputation Morrison had by now achieved as a scholar-missionary, as well as to his personal efforts and

31. Morrison 1839:II, 53–56, 61, 397; 1823:5–6, 20.
32. Morrison 1839:II, 124; 1823:7, 14–15; Medhurst 1838:316.

connections, individual donations were received from a wide variety of sources.[33]

In support of his fund-raising efforts Morrison produced two informative pamphlets: *To the Public* . . . (1823) and *To the British Public* . . . (1825). The first of these was completed during a visit to the college following Milne's death in June 1822. Milne, "that industrious and highly respectable character," as John Crawfurd described him a few months earlier, had burned himself out at the age of thirty-seven. With him died also the *Chinese Magazine* and the *Indo-Chinese Gleaner*. There seemed nobody quite capable of filling his place as principal. James Humphries, a young Scottish missionary who had entered the college as a student the previous year, took over for the time being. Morrison, feeling uncertain about the future of the college without Milne's leadership and drive, decided to go down to Malacca and assess the situation there himself.[34]

Passing through Singapore from Canton in late January 1823, Morrison had a meeting with Raffles, who at this time was enthusiastically promoting his own scheme for a college there. Out of their meeting emerged the proposal to combine and concentrate their efforts in a single institution to be located in Singapore. To Morrison this must have seemed at the time a providential answer to his doubts about the future of the Malacca College, and while at Malacca he added a postscript to his first pamphlet announcing the proposed move. He returned to Singapore in April and again in July for further discussions, and in the second fund-raising pamphlet written later for his visit to England in 1824 he publicly announced the proposal to remove the Malacca College to Singapore.[35]

However the proposal came to nothing in the end; for various reasons the plans for a Singapore college as conceived by Raffles did not materialize until much later. With the collapse of the original scheme, Morrison by November 1827 felt himself absolved from any obligation and concluded: "The removal of the Anglo-Chinese College is therefore now quite out of the question."[36]

Meanwhile, in face of this serious threat to its independent existence the college not only survived; it began to flourish as never before. Morrison was not a man to change horses in midstream. During his stay at Malacca for over five months in 1823 he devoted his time and energy to the college as if its separate identity had been unquestioned, not only taking a major

33. From, among others, William Farquhar, now Resident of Singapore and vice-president of the College; W. S. Cracroft of Penang; A. L. Johnstone of Singapore; T. Dent and C. Magniac of China; James Matheson and John Palmer of Calcutta; and Arthur Guiness of Dublin (Morrison 1823:8; 1825:18).

34. Morrison 1839:II, 174.

35. 1823:26 (postscript dated at Malacca, 15 March 1823); 1825:9.

36. Morrison 1839:II, 402; Wijeysingha 1963:6–54.

share in the administration but also acting as chaplain, teaching senior students, giving intensive tuition in Chinese to James Humphries and David Collie, a more recent arrival from Scotland, translating Joyce's *Scientific Dialogues* into Chinese for use in the college, and composing a memoir of the life of Milne. By the time of his departure for China in July 1823, Morrison's presence had given the college a new lease of life.[37]

Humphries and Collie, both "very promising Chinese scholars," were left in dual charge when Morrison went, but Collie gradually took over the main share of the work of principal. "Studious and retired," he completed a translation of the Four Books of Confucius in 1828, but died in the same year, after a short illness, before it was published.[38]

The student enrolment continued its slow but steady rise—from twenty-six in 1824 to thirty in 1827. In addition, there were about 200 boys in six Chinese schools maintained by the mission and supervised by members of the college staff. A useful addition to the staff in 1824 was Samuel Kidd, who joined as a Hokkien specialist. Morrison's visit to the United Kingdom in 1824–1826 helped to bring in new financial support that was badly needed. The transfer of Malacca from Dutch to British rule (agreed by the Treaty of London in March 1824 and effected a year later) helped to stabilize the college's long-term position in the community.[39]

Changes in the headship of the college became more frequent from now on. Kidd, who succeeded Collie as principal in 1828, returned to England in 1832, later becoming professor of Chinese at London University. An awkward situation developed for the college in Kidd's time with its involvement in a clash between the government of the Straits Settlements and J. H. Moor, editor of the *Malacca Observer* (as well as headmaster of the new Malacca Free School). The *Observer* was printed at the college press, and in its issue of 30 June 1829 it made what the government regarded as objectionable comment on its policy concerning the inland state of Naning. The governor, Robert Fullerton, noted ominously that both the Anglo-Chinese College and the Free School were being supported by government subsidies, and on a visit to Malacca in October he confronted Kidd, who however maintained that he had been "perfectly unaware of the mischief." The upshot of the affair was that the *Malacca Observer* closed down and Moor moved to Singapore; a further repercussion may perhaps be seen in Fullerton's recommendation to the governor general in India the following year that "the allowance to the Anglo-Chinese College at

37. Morrison 1839:II, 192–193.
38. *Ibid.*, pp. 219, 224.
39. Straits Settlements Records, 165, Malacca Diary, 4 Sept. 1826. Morrison 1825; Medhurst 1838:269. Samuel Kidd (1804–1843), b. Hull, trained at L.M.S. seminary at Gosport, served at Malacca 1824–1832, returned to England on account of ill health; professor of Chinese, London University, 1837–1843.

Malacca be discontinued, that institution being otherwise supported."
However, the company's Canton factory, doubtless with some prompting
from Morrison, came to the rescue and restored the subsidy.[40]

The college moved into the 1830's as a small but well established and
steadily growing institution. Humphries had left in 1829 but in the same
year Josiah Hughes arrived to strengthen the Malay side of the college's
work. Kidd was succeeded as principal in 1832 by Jacob Tomlin, a man
of immense energy and enterprise who had begun work among the Chinese
of Singapore in 1827, visited from Malacca the tin mines of Lukut and
Sungei Ujong in 1828, later in the same year travelled to Siam with Charles
Gutzlaff, the formidable German missionary of the China coast, then
visited eastern Java and Bali in company with W. H. Medhurst in 1829,
and returned to Siam in 1831.[41] Tomlin in 1833 felt that the college had
reached the point where it could dispense with the scheme of monthly
stipends for local students which had been in operation from the beginning.
His calculation seems to have been justified by the response: at the end
of the year there were fifteen stipendiary and seventeen nonstipendiary
students. Indeed there seems to have been a rapid increase in student
numbers after 1834, one that would have gratified the founder, Morrison,
who died in that year. Tomlin's successor, John Evans, took over as
principal in 1834; three years later the total student enrolment had risen
to seventy. A visitor to the college in 1837 pointedly remarked of Evans
that he was both "an experienced teacher and a skilful financier."[42]

The year 1837 was the most active and successful of any so far, and the
prospect for the college's future seemed brighter than ever. "The gloom
was passing away and the light springing up," wrote Samuel Dyer, who
had joined the college in 1835 from Penang and whose work on the casting
of movable metallic type for printing in Chinese greatly enhanced the
reputation of the college press at this time. But the light that Dyer saw
was not to last.[43]

What proved to be the final phase of the college's existence at Malacca
opened with the arrival of James Legge, later the famous sinologue, to take
over the office of principal in 1840. With the outbreak of the "Opium War"
a year later missionary interest and hope became increasingly concentrated
on events in south China and the prospect of entering the country itself.
On the conclusion of peace in August 1842, with the cession of Hong Kong
and the arrangements for treaty ports, the London Missionary Society

40. Morrison 1839:II, 445, 447; Newbold 1839:I, 184n.; Straits Settlements Records, 169,
Malacca Diary, 22 Oct. 1829; *ibid.*, ser. V, 4, 13 Nov. 1830.
41. Medhurst 1838:328, 356; Abeel 1834:200, 270.
42. Medhurst 1838:319–321; Horne 1895:307; Malcom 1839:II, 98.
43. Medhurst 1838:321, 327; Malcom 1839:II, 97.

decided to move its Southeast Asian bases forward to points in or near China. With Legge, Dyer, Medhurst, and three Chinese teachers, the college moved from Malacca to Hong Kong in 1843. There, failing to obtain land from the government for its own building, it ended by amalgamating—appropriately enough—with the Morrison Education Society.[44]

Malacca had served its purpose as a preparatory launching site for the mission to China, but in the process it had absorbed something of value from the presence of those who planned and prepared for the mission there. As a group, the men associated with the Anglo-Chinese College were outstanding for their energy and ability, for character and intellect. While seeking their own wider aims, they also worked for a time and after their own fashion for the good of the people around them.

China was undoubtedly the ultimate goal of all their endeavour, and in this aspect their aims may be seen as a reflection of the missionary image of that country in the early nineteenth century. "China, that object of wonder and of pity to Christendom, excited in their minds a deep interest," wrote Morrison, of Milne and himself; "China, one of the fairest portions of the globe, the most ancient, the most populous, the best skilled in the management of human nature, of any country under heaven." In their approach to this great goal they claimed to represent "the gospel of humanity and of literature," the belief that "literature and science are . . . the auxiliaries of true religion." Science and "revelation," they were convinced, would enter China hand in hand as soon as the door was opened.[45]

In the Southeast Asian aspect of their work the men of the Malacca College surely deserve a place—even if that of lesser luminaries in an era that produced Marsden, Raffles, and Crawfurd—as pioneers in the scientific study of the languages and cultures of the region.

The college which they served played a small but not insignificant part in the growth of the Western tradition of Chinese and Southeast Asian scholarship. Morrison claimed in 1831 that it was "the only place in the British dominions where Chinese is regularly taught . . . ; there is no school for Chinese in England." It was actively concerned with promoting the study, translation, and publication of works in Malay and other Southeast Asian languages as well as Chinese. It represented an early phase of experiment in the application of Western educational ideas and techniques

44. Ride 1960, for details of Legge's career (1815–1897); Lo Hsiang-lin 1963:17, 22–23; Endacott 1958:134.
45. Dutch Records, Buitenland 22, Duplicaat Missiven van Malakka, 1824; Milne to Thyssen, Governor of Malacca, 12 Jan. 1821.

to Southeast Asian conditions. True, its status as a college has been called in question,[46] but an institution in which a Chinese student "in little more than a year acquired such knowledge of English as to enable him to translate Keith's *Treatise on the Globes* into Chinese," or in which a Chinese Catholic Christian who understood Latin was supported while translating *Stockii Clavis Sacra*, would seem to have been something more than an ordinary school.[47] And if the college was small in size it was large in conception. For the principle on which it based itself was, as its founder declared, "that all the various tribes of men have equal rights, and every system . . . has a right to be heard; when this shall be the case, mighty truth shall prevail."[48]

REFERENCES

Unpublished Sources

Malacca Church Records (Kerk Boek, 1809–1822; Resolutie Boek, 1773–1825). Arkib Negara Malaysia.
Straits Settlements Records, series V. National Library, Singapore.
Straits Settlements Records, vols. 49, 54, 55. India Office Library, London.
Dutch Records (Buitenland, 22, 29: Duplicaat Missiven van Malakka). Arsip Nasional Republik Indonesia.

Published Works

Abeel, David. 1834. *Journal of a Residence in China and the Neighbouring Countries from 1829 to 1833.* New York.
Begbie, P. J. 1834. *The Malayan Peninsula.* Madras.
Broomhall, Marshall. 1924. *Robert Morrison, a Master Builder.* London.
Chinese Repository, The. Canton and Hong Kong, 1832–1851.
Cook, Rev. J. A. Bethune. 1907. *Sunny Singapore: An Account of the Place and Its People, with a Sketch of the Results of Missionary Work.* 2d ed. London.
Endacott, G. B. 1958. *A History of Hong Kong.* London.
Hardy, T. J. 1899. "Catalogue of Church Records, Malacca, 1642–1898." Singapore. Reprinted *JMBRAS*, 15, 1 (1937):1–24.
Hill, A. H. (trans. and ed.). 1955. "The Hikayat Abdullah." *JMBRAS*, 28, 3.
Horne, C. Silvester. 1895. *The Story of the L.M.S., 1795–1895.* London.
Lo Hsiang-lin. 1963. *Hong Kong and Western Cultures.* Honolulu.
Lovett, Richard. 1899. *History of the London Missionary Society.* 2 vols. London.
Malcom, Howard. 1839. *Travels in South-Eastern Asia.* 2d ed., 2 vols. in one. Boston.

46. Malcom 1839:II, 98: "an elementary school"; C. B. Buckley, *Anecdotal History of Old Times in Singapore* (1902), p. 123: "a small school." These and similar comments seem to have arisen from confusion between the work of the Anglo-Chinese College and that of the schools under the L.M.S. in Malacca.
47. Medhurst 1838:317; Morrison 1825:9. Christopher Stock, *Clavis Linguae Sanctae Veteris Testamenti* (Jena, 1717–1718; later editions with amended title, e.g. Leipzig, 1752).
48. Morrison 1839:II, 445; 1823:3.

Medhurst, Walter Henry. 1838. *China, Its State and Prospects*. London.

Milne, William. 1820. *A Retrospect of the First Ten Years of the Protestant Mission to China*. Malacca: Anglo-Chinese Press.

—— (ed.). 1818–1822. *The Indo-Chinese Gleaner*. 3 vols. Malacca.

Morrison, Robert. 1823. *To the Public, Concerning the Anglo-Chinese College*. Malacca.

——. 1824. *Memoirs of the Reverend William Milne, D.D., Late Missionary to China and Principal of the Anglo-Chinese College*. Malacca.

——. 1825. *To the British Public; Account of the Anglo-Chinese College*. London.

[——]. 1839. *Memoir of the Life and Labours of Robert Morrison, D.D., Compiled by His Widow* . . . 2 vols. London.

Newbold, T. J. 1839. *Political and Statistical Account of the British Settlements in the Straits of Malacca*. 2 vols. London.

Philip, Robert. 1840. *The Life and Opinions of Rev. William Milne, D.D., Missionary to China*. London.

Ride, Lindsay. 1957. *Robert Morrison, the Scholar and the Man*. Hong Kong.

——. 1960. *Biographical Note on James Legge* (reprinted from vol. I of a five-volume edition of *The Chinese Classics*). Hong Kong.

Townsend, William J. 1898. *Robert Morrison, the Pioneer of Chinese Missions*. London.

Tyerman, Rev. Daniel, and George Bennet. 1831. *Journal of Voyages and Travels*. 2 vols. London.

Wijeysingha, Eugene. 1963. *A History of Raffles Institution*. Singapore.

Wylie, Alexander. 1867. *Memorials of Protestant Missionaries to the Chinese*. Shanghai.

Malaya from the 1850's to the 1870's, and Its Historians, 1950–1970: From Strategy to Sociology

W. DAVID McINTYRE

University of Canterbury, New Zealand

"The old view is always right." With these words a somewhat cynical colleague of mine once gave vent to his scepticism about the self-conscious striving after revisionism which many historians feel is demanded of them. When we consider recent publications concerning Malaya during the third quarter of the nineteenth century, we may concede that in one important respect he had a point.

In 1948, Swettenham's *British Malaya*, completed in 1906, reached its fifth reprinting as the standard record of an imperialist success story. The author's "main idea" had been to set out the important facts which led to Britain's intervention in what became the Federated Malay States—facts which were "no discredit to the British nation."[1] The prosperity of the F.M.S. was due "(1) to Chinese, (2) to Europeans, and (3) to British officers in the service of the Malay government." Chinese energy and enterprise in the tin-mining industry had generated revenue for development. But the immigrant Chinese could not have operated without the British officers who created law and order, financial regularity, and administrative services. The Chinese also paved the way for European miners and planters, who brought new mining techniques, new crops, and the Indian labouring community. The Malays were, however, "the people of the country." The British had intervened "for their benefit, and . . . somehow managed to give them an independence, a happiness and a prosperity which they never knew before." Thus "all classes and nationalities" gained. But the credit was "due to a few British officers who strove ceaselessly for that object."[2] This version of events has been dubbed the "creation myth" of British Malaya.[3]

Swettenham's book had long been out of date, as Sir Richard Winstedt

---

1. F. A. Swettenham, *British Malaya: An Account of the Origins and Progress of British Influence in Malaya* (5th ed., London, 1948), p. xvi.
2. *Ibid.*, pp. 301 and 305.
3. W. R. Roff, *The Origins of Malay Nationalism* (New Haven, 1967), p. 99, and also in D. J. Steinberg (ed.), *In Search of Southeast Asia* (New York, 1971), p. 190.

did not hesitate to point out in the DNB.[4] Yet the first professional academics to write on Malayan history (both Americans) also wrote in the imperialist context. Lennox A. Mills's *British Malaya, 1824–67* (1925) was a history of the Straits Settlements in the pre-Crown colony phase and their relations with Thailand, the Peninsula, and Brunei. In contrast to Swettenham, Mills attempted to tell his story in a neutral way. But his conclusions (on the few occasions he ventured them) were similar to Swettenham's. "It is to the British Government alone, and most especially to the Government of the Straits Settlements, that the Malay States of the Peninsula owe the preservation of their independence." "British Malaya owes a debt of gratitude to the East India Company."[5]

It was left to Rupert Emerson in *Malaysia* (1937) to approach the subject as an "external and disinterested critic." A Harvard political scientist, he asserted that the "ultimate frame of reference must be a world of free peoples." Imperialism meant a denial of freedom. No dependency had ever been created "in the interest of the dependent society itself," nor had any colonial regime been created to hamper the legitimate activities of home investors.[6] He defined the primary function of colonial governments as "the creation of the conditions under which the western economy of the time could most profitably flourish."[7] Yet for all these seemingly doctrinaire assumptions (which infuriated Swettenham and others) Emerson was not intent on condemnation. He found that imperialist control had "not been an unmixed evil" for Malaya. "Capitalist industry has itself inadvertently done much to bring the Malay peoples into the modern world." He felt that "the incursion of European industrialism and 'modernism' into Malaysia was no more and no less peculiar and deplorable" than earlier Hindu and Islamic incursions. Emerson, indeed, "inclined strongly to the view" that imperialism had been "a necessary bridge from Malaysian medievalism to the modern world."[8] These words, written in 1937, may be compared with those of an up-to-date textbook published thirty-four years later which suggested that "direct Western rule in Southeast Asia may be seen as a short-lived frontier institution in a worldwide process of political change."[9]

4. "His education had not been such as to qualify him for research" (*DNB, 1941–1950* [London, 1959], p. 856).
5. L. A. Mills, *British Malaya, 1824–67*, new ed., Oxford in Asia Historical Reprints (Kuala Lumpur, 1966), pp. 173 and 286.
6. R. Emerson, *Malaysia: A Study of Direct and Indirect Rule*, new ed. (Kuala Lumpur, 1964), quotations from pp. 466–468.
7. *Ibid.*, p. 5. Cf. J. Gallagher and R. Robinson, "The Imperialism of Free Trade," *Economic History Review*, 6, 1 (1953):5, where they define imperialism as "a sufficient political function of this process of integrating new regions into the expanding economy."
8. Emerson, *Malaysia*, pp. 480 and 483.
9. Steinberg, *In Search of Southeast Asia*, p. 167. Cf. D. G. E. Hall, "Looking at Southeast Asian History," *JAS*, 19, 3 (1960):253.

Thus a student of the 1950's, whose introduction to nineteenth-century Malaya came from Swettenham, Mills, and Emerson (which was my experience in 1956) could hardly avoid entanglement in the scholarly debates about imperialism. It would take some time to realize that a balance of coverage which accorded most attention to the Straits Settlements and least to Trengganu, Kelantan, and Perlis was not necessarily the fairest picture of that awkward geographical expression "Malaya."

Nearly two decades later a student's endeavour to find a more truly "Malaysian" history is both easier and more hazardous. The debate about imperialism flows on, even though John Gallagher declared in 1961 that "the serious study of imperialism has ground to a standstill."[10] In the case of Malaya the most prolific area of publication in the 1960's concerned the motives, manifestations, and methods of British intervention from the 1860's to 1890's. Mills and Emerson were reissued. Tarling, Parkinson, Cowan, McIntyre, Chew, Thio, Sadka, Sinclair, Bastin, Reid, Turnbull, and Khoo[11] have all added to this particular "file on empire." Yet in introducing a new student to the modern history of Malaya we can now more readily avoid an imperialist framework since, as like as not, the context of studies will be a course on Asian or Southeast Asian history. If an earlier generation looked to Emerson as the scholarly landmark, today one would be tempted to select *The Origins of Malay Nationalism* by William Roff, whose opening chapter provides a good introduction to the mid-nineteenth-century period.

Roff seeks to redress a "marked neglect" by most recent historians "of the original possessors of the peninsular states, of the people about whose ears the elaborate superstructure of modern Malaya was built."[12] Harry Benda called this book "the first history of the *Malays* in modern times, strange as this may sound."[13] Roff singles out Gullick's anthropological monograph, *Indigenous Political Systems of Western Malaya*[14] for credit. A new perspective has also appeared from James de Vere Allen's work on Kedah, Kelantan, and Trengganu,[15] where the largest concentrations of Malay population lived. Some M.A. theses, published in the Oxford East Asia Historical Monographs series, try to bring out the economic and social

---

10. Gallagher, "Imperialism and Nationalism in Asia," *Studies in Asian History: Proceedings of the Asian History Conference, 1961* (Bombay, 1969), p. 393.

11. Specific titles are referred to below, nn. 26–29.

12. Roff, *Origins of Malay Nationalism*, p. xiv.

13. *Ibid.*, Foreword, p. viii.

14. J. M. Gullick, *Indigenous Political Systems of Western Malaya*, London School of Economics Monographs on Social Anthropology, 17 (London, 1958).

15. J. de V. Allen, "The Ancien Regime of Trengganu, 1909–1919," *JMBRAS*, 41, 1 (1968):23–53; "The Elephant and the Mousedeer—A New Version: Anglo-Kedah Relations, 1905–1915," *ibid.*, pp. 54–94, and "The Kelantan Rising of 1915," *JSEAH*, 9, 2 (1968):241–257.

development of the west coast states "from a local viewpoint."[16] Roff contributed to the nineteenth-century Malayan portion of the *Cambridge History of Islam*[17] and to Joel Steinberg's excellent new-style collaborative textbook *In Search of Southeast Asia* (1971), which deliberately strives to get away from a stress on "external stimuli, to the detriment of the study of indigenous institutions" and to explore adequately social change in the Southeast Asian environment.[18]

There is, however, one sense in which the new generation show less than justice to the "old view." Surely the most consistent trend in the pre-1950 historiography of nineteenth-century Malaya (apart from the memoirs or polemics of participants)[19] was the study of local history, usually Malay local history. In their state histories, dynastic, biographical, and local studies Wilkinson, Winstedt, Rentse, Lineham, Graham, Sheppard, Middlebrook, and Gullick (the scholar-administrators, who succeeded the proconsular publicists) provided the historiographical equivalent of the pro-Malay traditions of the M.C.S.[20] The range of Winstedt's contributions to a wide area of Malay studies is astonishing and includes the first modern history of Malaya in Malay, published in 1918.[21] In fact, when Victor Purcell issued *The Chinese in Malaya* in 1948 he complained that "historians of Malaya have almost without exception written as if the Malays were the central and self-sufficient theme and the Chinese were

16. Khoo Kay Kim, *The Western Malay States, 1850–1873: The Effects of Commercial Development on Malay Politics* (Kuala Lumpur, 1972); P. Loh, *The Malay States, 1877–1895: Political Change and Social Policy* (Kuala Lumpur, 1969).

17. W. R. Roff, "South-East Asian Islam in the Nineteenth Century," in *Cambridge History of Islam*, II, P. M. Holt, A. K. S. Lambton, and B. Lewis (eds.) (Cambridge, 1970), 155–181.

18. Steinberg, *In Search of Southeast Asia*, p. 3.

19. Especially O. Cavanagh, *Reminiscences of an Indian Official* (London, 1884); A. E. H. Anson, *About Myself and Others, 1745 to 1920* (London, 1920); W. H. M. Read, *Play and Politics—Recollections of Malaya by an Old Resident* (London, 1901); P. B. Maxwell, *Our Malay Conquests* (London, 1878); J. F. A. McNair, *Perak and the Malays, "Sarong" and "Kris"* (London, 1878); F. A. Swettenham, *Footprints in Malaya* (London, 1942).

20. R. J. Wilkinson, "Notes on Perak History," *PMS*, 4 (1908), and "A History of the Peninsula Malays," *PMS*, 7 (1932); with R. O. Winstedt, "A History of Perak," *JMBRAS*, 12, 1 (1934); R. O. Winstedt, "A History of Johore," *ibid.*, 10, 3 (1932); "A History of Selangor" and "Negri Sembilan," *ibid.*, 12, 3 (1934); "A History of Malaya," *ibid.*, 13, 1 (1935), and *The Malays: A Cultural History* (Singapore, 1947); A. Rentse, "History of Kelantan," *JMBRAS*, 12, 2 (1934):44–61; W. Linehan, "A History of Pahang," *ibid.*, 14, 2 (1935); W. A. Graham, *Kelantan, a State of the Malay Peninsula: A Handbook of Information* (Glasgow, 1908); M. C. Sheppard, "A Short History of Trengganu," *JMBRAS*, 22, 3 (1949):1–74; S. M. Middlebrook, "Yap Ah Loy," *ibid.*, 24, 2 (1961); J. M. Gullick, "Sungei Ujong," *ibid.*, 22, 2 (1949); "A Careless, Heathen Philosopher? [Abdul-Samad]," *ibid.*, 26, 1 (1953):86–103; "Captain Speedy of Larut," *ibid.*, 26, 3 (1953); "The War with Yam Tuan Antah," *ibid.*, 27, 1 (1954):1–23; and *Indigenous Political Systems*.

21. For a full bibliography see Bastin's Introduction to J. Bastin and R. Roolvink (eds.), *Malayan and Indonesian Studies, Essays presented to Sir Richard Winstedt on his Eighty-Fifth Birthday* (Oxford, 1964).

extraneous and incidental to it." To redress the balance he used terms reminiscent of Swettenham, asserting that without the Chinese, "Malaya would still be more or less as it was over most of its extent eighty years ago—a few clearings along the coasts and up the rivers, in the midst of jungle and swamp. . . . Modern Malaya is in the main the joint creation of British and Chinese enterprise."[22] Ironically, in the very same year, Winstedt's short *Malaya and Its History* appeared, and provides the great understatement of Malayan historiography in his remark that free trade and peace had attracted Chinese and Indians, "who have created a Malayan problem."[23]

In a sense the wheel has come full circle. Some of the most recent and important contributions, notably by Roff, Allen, Loh, Khoo, Sinclair, and Wake[24] are recognizing that the real groundwork of research in Malayan history must be in local history, just as Wilkinson and Winstedt did a half-century ago. Certainly the methodology and conceptual framework of the new local history is somewhat different from that of the administrator-scholars between the wars. Interest now tends to be demographic rather than dynastic, sociological rather than strategic, analytic rather than antiquarian. The context now preferred is that of the modernization of traditional societies, rather than the expansion of the West. Here again one cannot but acknowledge the extent of Rupert Emerson's pioneering. His work was conceived within a framework of comparative studies. He was impressed by the local variety he found in Malaya, being particularly puzzled by the anomaly of Johore: "closest" in relations to the British but most "independent" in constitutional theory. Indeed, Emerson produced an embryonic "development scale" for the Peninsula that has a distinctly modern ring to it. At one end he placed the F.M.S., representing the "superimposition of a modern political and economic structure on a simple agrarian people." At the other he put Kelantan and Trengganu, illustrating an experiment of raising a people by the development of its own forces from within. Of the two "independent" anomalies, which were adjacent to Singapore and Penang, he felt Johore inclined to the F.M.S. end of the scale and Kedah towards its neighbours Kelantan and Trengganu. If the modern town of Kuala Lumpur was "clearly no offspring of the Malays," Kota Bahru, a town with some modern trimmings, was "an obvious outgrowth of Malay society."[25]

22. V. Purcell, *The Chinese in Malaya* (London, 1948), p. vii.
23. Winstedt, *Malaya and Its History* (London, 1948), p. 107.
24. C. H. H. Wake, "Nineteenth Century Johore—Ruler and Realm in Transition" (Ph.D. diss., Australian National University, 1966), consulted on microfilm by courtesy of the author.
25. Emerson, *Malaysia*, p. 249. He was writing about the 1930's, but a similar "scale" of modernization for 1850–1880 would be instructive, and, one suspects, not dissimilar.

Thus Winstedt, with his emphasis on Malay language, culture, and institutions, and Emerson, with his political scientist's demand for a conceptually acceptable framework, were precursors of much recent research. One is, perhaps, left with the paradox that while the main theme of modern Malayan history has been a search for unity, the dominant historiographical trend has been the search for authentic local histories. For this reason a commentary on the main contributions to our subject in the 1950's and 1960's and on some current trends which seem promising, must be prefaced by a tricky question about the definition of our subject matter.

In writing about Malaya from the the 1850's to the 1870's,—should we write about geographical units, or about societies and their development, or about the antecedents of modern states, or should we select certain themes or problems? The last of these alternatives usually proves the easiest. Most published work of the past quarter-century falls into this category. By isolating a part of the subject, defining a theme, briefly linking it to a wider context, finding and exploiting some new sources, the researcher has every chance of making his own contribution to knowledge. Thus the role of the British in Malaya is the theme which has received greatest attention, largely because of the richness and accessibility of the sources. Within this wide theme, Tarling and Turnbull have both stressed the continuity of British interest from the days of Light and Raffles. Khoo stresses local propensities to intervene before 1873.[26] Parkinson, Cowan, McIntyre, and Chew give greater emphasis to the "decision to intervene" by the appointment of Residents, made in 1873, and place the decision in the wider context of British imperialism.[27] Thio, Sadka, and Loh have carefully delineated both the fluctuations in British interest after the incursions of 1874–1875 and the way in which the system of "government

26. N. Tarling, "British Policy in the Malay Peninsula and Archipelago, 1824–1871," *JMBRAS*, 30, 3 (1957) (reissued Kuala Lumpur, 1969); "The Relations between British Policies and the Extent of British Power in the Malay Archipelago, 1784–1871," *Australian Journal of Politics and History*, 4, 2 (1958):179–192; "Intervention and Non-Intervention in Malaya," *JAS*, 21, 4 (1962):523–527; "British Policy in Malayan Waters in the 19th Century," *in* K. G. Tregonning (ed.), *Papers on Malayan History* (Singapore, 1962), pp. 73–88; C. M. Turnbull, *Indian Presidency to Crown Colony: The Straits Settlements, 1826–67* (London, 1971) and "The Nineteenth Century," *in* Wang Gungwu (ed.), *Malaysia: A Survey* (London, 1964); Khoo Kay Kim, *The Western Malay States*.
27. C. N. Parkinson, *British Intervention in Malaya 1867–1877* (Singapore, 1960); C. D. Cowan, *Nineteenth-Century Malaya: The Origins of British Political Control* (London, 1961) and "Sir Frank Swettenham's Perak Journals, 1874–1876," *JMBRAS*, 24, 4 (1951); W. David McIntyre, *The Imperial Frontier in the Tropics, 1865–75* (London, 1967); "Britain's Intervention in Malaya: The Origin of Lord Kimberley's Instructions to Sir Andrew Clarke in 1873," *JSEAH*, 2, 3 (1961):47–69; and "Disraeli's Election Blunder: The Straits of Malacca Issue in the 1874 Election," *Renaissance and Modern Studies* 5 (1961):76–105; E. Chew, "The Reasons for British Intervention in Malaya: Review and Reconstruction," *JSEAH*, 6, 1 (1965):81–93.

by advice" was used to create a colonial-style bureaucracy and a policy of capitalist modernization, behind the facade of Malay rule.[28] Khoo, Bastin, and Sinclair have emphasized some of the commercial factors behind British intervention, especially as viewed from the Straits.[29] Wong Lin Ken has analyzed the Colony's trade in detail, Turnbull has traversed, in more analytical fashion the ground trod by Mills, and Reid has placed British policy in Malaya in the context of the surprisingly intricate diplomacy concerning Atjeh.[30] The improvement on Swettenham, Mills, and Emerson is impressive, but the approach remains severely topical. These works do not pretend to cover "Malaya" in general, although Cowan successfully places his detailed reconstruction of the origins of British political control in the context of the nineteenth century, and Thio defines her subject specifically as British expansion in the "Malay Peninsula."

If, instead of a topical approach, these authors had made the antecedents of the modern state their unit of study, they would, during the late 1940's to 1960's, have faced some tricky dilemmas. As "British Malaya" went through the vicissitudes of Malayan Union and Colony of Singapore, Federation of Malaya and State of Singapore, Federation of Malaysia (bringing in Sarawak and Sabah), then Malaysia (retaining East Malaysia) and Republic of Singapore, it must have provided an indexer's, cataloguer's, and archivist's nightmare. Clearly if the contemporary international scene had dictated the area of study, the relative weight to be accorded Singapore and the Peninsula would have been constantly under review. Penang, Province Wellesley, Malacca, Labuan, and northern Borneo would, no doubt, have become historiographical nuisance. It would be fair to say, then, that the topical approach, indeed the "imperial" approach, sustained historians through the era of "decolonization," with its peculiar "Malaysian" reverberations.

The trend now emerging, however, is a socioeconomic one. The subject

---

28. E. Thio, *British Policy in the Malay Peninsula, 1880–1910*, vol. I, *The Southern and Central States* (Singapore, 1969), and "Britain's Search for Security in North Malaya, 1886–97," *JSEAH*, 10, 2 (1969):279–303; E. Sadka, *The Protected Malay States, 1874–1895* (Kuala Lumpur, 1968) and "The Journal of Sir Hugh Low, Perak, 1877," *JMBRAS*, 27, 4 (1954); P. Loh, *The Malay States, 1877–1895: Political Change and Social Policy* (Kuala Lumpur, 1969).

29. Khoo Kay Kim, "The Origin of British Administration in Malaya," *JMBRAS*, 39, 1 (1966):52–90, and *The Western Malay States*; K. Sinclair, "The British Advance in Johore, 1885–1914," *JMBRAS*, 40, 1 (1967):93–110 and "Hobson and Lenin in Johore: Colonial Office Policy towards British Concessionaires and Investors, 1878–1907," *Modern Asian Studies*, 1, 4 (1967):335–352; J. Bastin, "Britain as an Imperial Power in South-East Asia in the Nineteenth Century," *in* J. S. Bromley and E. H. Kossmann (eds.), *Britain and the Netherlands in Europe and Asia*, conference papers (London, 1968).

30. Wong Lin Ken, "The Trade of Singapore 1819–69," *JMBRAS*, 33, 4 (1960); C. M. Turnbull, *Indian Presidency to Crown Colony*; A. Reid, *The Conquest of North Sumatra: Acheh, the Netherlands and Britain, 1868–1898* (Kuala Lumpur, 1969).

of study becomes the Malaysian communities, their economic and institutional preoccupations, and the sources of change working within them. The Chinese have received the greatest share of attention, partly because of their critical role in the nineteenth-century tin industry, but more, one suspects, because the secret societies puzzled, fascinated, and alarmed British and Malays alike for so long. Thus, apart from Purcell, who endeavoured to survey the origins, migration, and organization of the Chinese communities, Wong Lin Ken has provided a thorough economic analysis of the tin industry and Chinese mining, Comber and Blythe have taken up the regulation of the secret societies, and Khoo has indicated the complexity of the alliances that created the two "factions" who fought in Perak.[31] The Indian communities remained small until the expansion of rubber planting at the turn of the century, but the whole extent of Indian activities has been brought out by Arasaratnam and Sandhu,[32] particularly the point that a number of the Tamil migrants came, in fact, from Ceylon, and that there was a small but significant settlement by Indian professional and clerical workers, as compared with the Chinese and Indian mass of labourers. The small European and Eurasian mercantile community of the Straits and its financial entanglements with Malay rulers were touched on by Parkinson and Cowan and more thoroughly analyzed recently by Turnbull, and Khoo, who also looks at Chinese financiers who made loans to Malay rulers. Finally, attention has been drawn by Roff to the numerically small but (for the long term) intellectually significant Arab, Malayo-Muslim, and Indian Muslim communities in Singapore.[33] Beside these analyses of the immigrant communities, work on Malay society (or the aborigines) has been small compared with the great effort of Winstedt and others between the wars. Gullick's and Khoo's monographs deal with only Perak, Selangor, and Negri Sembilan; Wake considers Johore in

31. Wong Lin Ken, *The Malayan Tin Industry to 1914 with Special Reference to the States of Perak, Selangor, Negri Sembilan and Pahang* (Tucson, 1965) and "The Malayan Tin Industry: A Study of the Impact of Western Industrialization on Malaya," *in* Tregonning (ed.), *Papers on Malayan History*, pp. 10–39; L. F. Comber, *Chinese Secret Societies in Malaya: A Survey of the Triad Society from 1800–1900* (New York, 1959); W. L. Blythe, *The Impact of Chinese Secret Societies in Malaya: A Historical Study* (London, 1969); Khoo, *Western Malay States*, pp. 166–174. More detailed social analyses of the Singapore Chinese are available in Png Poh-Seng, "The Straits Chinese in Singapore: A Case of Local Identity and Socio-Cultural Accommodation," *JSEAH*, 10, 1 (1969):95–114; Yeng Ching-Hwang, "Ch'ing's Sale of Honours and the Chinese Leadership in Singapore and Malaya, 1877–1912," *JSEAS*, 1, 2 (1970):20–32.

32. S. Arasaratnam, *Indians in Malaysia and Singapore* (London, 1970); K. S. Sandhu, "Some Preliminary Observations of the Origins and Characteristics of Indian Immigration to Malaya 1786–1957," *in* Tregonning (ed.), *Papers on Malayan History*, pp. 40–72, and *Indians in Malaya: Some Aspects of Their Immigration and Settlement, 1786–1957* (Cambridge, 1969).

33. Roff, *Origins of Malay Nationalism*, chap. 2.

detail; Ahmat has looked at Kedah's political structure,[34] and Allen's revealing studies of Kedah, Kelantan, and Trengganu deal with a later period, as does most of Roff's work. So far no one has ventured a comprehensive sociologically inclined synthesis of the early phases of Malaya's multiracial society.

We are left with the geographical unit. Sandhu provides a definition at the start of his study of the Indians: "Malaya occupies the southern half of the long narrow peninsula that projects from the Southeast Asian landmass far southward into the Indonesian Archipelago. . . . Unless otherwise stated, the term 'Malaya,' or 'British Malaya' as it is called before independence, is used throughout the text to include both the Federation of the present-day States (West Malaysia) of Malaya and the State or Republic of Singapore. Although separated politically from each other, these two territories have nevertheless traditionally functioned together."[35] How, then, might we interpret the significant events in "Malaya," so defined, during the 1850's to 1870's?

By the middle of the nineteenth century the small riverine Muslim states of the Malay Peninsula were undergoing a series of demographic, economic, and political changes, which involved two phases of acceleration over the following three decades. These accelerations were marked by the "tin rush" of the 1850's and the beginnings of British administration in the 1870's. Certain technical and administrative innovations right at the end of the 1870's presaged the much faster accelerations which soon followed in the west-coast states.

The sources of change in Malaya were both indigenous and external. The usual starting point could be found among the Malay aristocracy. The shifting balance of influence and power between rulers, subordinate members of royal dynasties and the rest of the ruling elite, and, more dramatically, succession disputes on the death of a ruler were times of struggle which gave openings for the admission of external influences. These external stimuli varied in depth, intensity, and point of contact. But they depended, in the first instance, on existing "linkages," as between a Malay State and the outside world. First, there were dynastic links between the successor lineages of the Malacca and Johore empires. Second, the link provided by Islam extended to all the Peninsula states, to the Indonesian neighbours, and ultimately to Mecca, the Ottoman Khalifate,

34. Sharom Ahmat, "The Political Structure of the State of Kedah, 1879–1905," *JSEAS*, 1, 2 (1970):115–128. The same writer's "Transition and Change in a Malay State: A Study of the Economic and Political Development of Kedah, 1879–1923" (Ph.D. diss., University of London, 1969), is being prepared for publication.

35. Sandhu, *Indians in Malaya*, p. 1.

and involved the wider developments of the Muslim world. A pilgrimage to Mecca could enable a Malay to enhance his social status. Third, there were the links on the "periphery" of the state—with Thailand or Sumatra or Riau-Lingga or with the Straits Settlements. Finally, there were growing links with China, India, and Europe, which were increasing, at this time, by the spread of steamer lines, telegraphs, railways, and the opening of the Suez Canal.

The intensity with which these links promoted change in Malaya depended partly on the level of control achieved by the relevant Malay rulers and partly on the nature and location of contact. Some rulers, such as Abu Bakar of Johore, Baginda Omar of Trengganu, and Ahmad Tajudin of Kedah, increased their power. By selective adoption of new ways they delayed external domination. Modern methods of government (copied from the Straits Settlements) and more traditional methods of autocracy were both used to keep out alien rule. Another possibility, adopted by Sultan Abdul Samad of Selangor, was to affect a form of "neutrality," while his unpopular, "foreign" son-in-law Tengku Ziauddin from Kedah used all sorts of external aids (from Pahang, the Straits Settlements, Kedah, Sumatra, and elsewhere) to bring a new regime to Selangor which eventually meant exile for some of the local elite but allowed the Sultan to emerge from his stockades. In Perak, where occurred the most complicated of the mid-century succession disputes, one contender for power, Raja Muda Abdullah, used a Straits Settlements link with a Chinese merchant to such effect that he provided the "key to the door" for British administrative intervention. This left him, within a year, in the position of a ruler whose powers were steadily usurped by his backers, so he conspired to eliminate the first British Resident, which led to an invasion of his state and his own deposition. External influences were successfully "used" by some rulers; they were disastrous for others.

The intensity of the stimulus also depended on the nature of the contact. Thus the Islamic link was fundamental to traditional Malaya. In 1873, just as the rivals for power in Perak were turning to outsiders, the titular Sultan, Ismail, tried to unite the parties with the cry "We are all Mussulman."[36] In 1875, as a Gurkha expedition prepared to attack Yam Tuan Antah of Sri Menanti, the Malays could only hope that the Sultan of Turkey would come to their aid.[37] Yet Islam also became a major source of change (as Roff so skilfully shows) when British control over all matters except Malay religion and custom served to isolate Malayan Islam as the one major area of indigenous authority, from the mid-1870's. This led

36. Khoo, *Western Malay States*, p. 174.
37. Gullick, "The War with Yam Tuan Antah," *JMBRAS*, 27, 1 (1954):15.

gradually to religious conservatism, which in turn bred a radical response sustained by Islamic modernism emanating from the Middle East.[38]

The Chinese link tightened with the incursion of the miners, when the tin rush of the 1850's caused a major demographic shift on the west coast. In Perak the Chinese soon outnumbered the Malays in the Larut region; some estimates suggest that about 1870–1871 they outnumbered the Malay population of the state as a whole. Similarly, in Selangor, which had a very small and fluctuating Malay population estimated at between 5,000 and 10,000 in the 1870's, the Chinese around Kuala Lumpur fluctuated between 5,000 and 20,000, with a further concentration at Lukut. Across the border in Sungai Ujong were another 5,000 to 10,000 Chinese. By the first census in 1891 the Malays were a minority (181,451) in Perak, Selangor, and Negri Sembilan, compared to the immigrants (185,125), who were chiefly Chinese.[39]

The intrusion of these "colonies" of Chinese miners did not occur without the encouragement of the Malay aristocrats in whose districts the tin was found. The profits from tin mining promised them increased influence in their dynastic squabbles. When their traditional mining methods were inadequate for rapid expansion, the Malay chiefs borrowed money from Straits merchants and utilized the services of Chinese miners. But rapid expansion by these means had two effects on the traditional Malay system. Firstly, the Chinese immigrant communities with their new industrial requirements, especially relating to land use and control of water courses, hopelessly overtaxed Malay district administration, so in most cases the regulation of the miners was passed over to Chinese *Kapitans*. Only in Lukut (before the death of Raja Juma'at in 1864) and Johore (where the Chinese were mainly planters) were there Malay attempts at providing more "modern" government, borrowing European ideas about the administration of law and order and revenue. The second effect of the tin rush was that successful Chinese miners were not content to work for Malays. Straits merchants began to make loans directly to Chinese miners. The Malay monopoly was broken.[40] Thus, from the 1850's, the Malay aristocrats had to take a share of the profits of their region by levying taxes on the tin exports of the main rivers. This, in turn, sometimes became a source of dispute with the Chinese and also a major source of rivalry among Malay rajas.

38. Roff, *Origins of Malay Nationalism*, chap. 3.

39. Population estimates are reviewed by Gullick, *Indigenous Political Systems*, pp. 23–24. Early in the twentieth century Kelantan alone probably had a larger Malay population than the entire F.M.S. See also Allen, "Anglo-Kedah Relations," *JMBRAS*, 41, 1 (1968):55; for Selangor, J. C. Jackson, "Population Changes in Selangor State 1850–1891," *JTG*, 19 (1964):42–57.

40. Khoo, *Western Malay States*, pp. 51–52.

The link between the Malay states and the Straits Settlements became a direct source of change within the former when the alliances and disputes of the rival Malay aristocrats in Perak, Selangor, and Sungai Ujong and the rival groups of Chinese miners at Larut and on the upper Selangor, upper Klang, and Linggi rivers endangered the security of the British outposts. Although the precise point of contact between Malay State and Colony was through a seemingly slender thread made up of a small group of Straits investors (European and Chinese), a handful of British officials who occasionally called at Peninsula river mouths, and a few Malay aristocrats who visited the Straits, usually to borrow money or buy arms, it was a link which changed its potential in the 1860's.

For the first half-century after Raffles the Straits Settlements had been such a peripheral point of the British Indian Empire (especially after the ending of the China trade monopoly) that its ability to interfere in the Peninsula was restrained. Issues decided in Calcutta often did not come to the notice of the East India Company (or the India Office) for years, if at all.[41] The 1826 Treaty with Perak was not ratified. On the whole, events on the Peninsula did not stir the Straits Settlements unless the Colony's own trade or security were threatened.

Yet the Straits link was a point of contact which had virtually global implications. Just as Islam linked Malays with a great world religion, so the Straits Settlements linked them with a world power. In British commerce and strategy there lurked incalculable possibilities for the Malays. Those who understood these possibilities best were, no doubt, the handful of Straits merchants (not only British) who hoped to use British officialdom to "open up" the Malay States. They probably tried to convince Malay clients of the advantages for their wealth and power of British-sponsored "modernization" in their territories. It is highly unlikely that any of the Malay rulers (except Abu Bakar of Johore, who had just visited Britain)[42] realized that the potentialities of this link suddenly became nearer in 1867. With the transfer of the Straits Settlements from the control of the India Office, indirect supervision via an unwieldy Indian bureaucracy, uninterested in Malaya, gave way to more expeditious attention from an economy-conscious Colonial Office. New minds had to apply themselves to these incomprehensible, distant points of friction. Moreover the Colonial Office's global context of thought stretched to the tropical regions of the Atlantic and Pacific worlds, which appeared more analogous to Malaya than the northwest approaches to India which so obsessed Indian "foreign policy" makers in the 1860's and 1870's. Thus, if the Chinese link had already facilitated the colonization of parts of Malaya,

41. Turnbull, *Indian Presidency to Crown Colony*, p. 59.
42. Thio, *British Policy in the Malay Peninsula*, I, 95.

the Straits Settlements link was (unbeknown to the Malays) being sprung for action in a new form. This spring was released in 1873 by the decision to appoint Residents in the west-coast states, on the analogy of the political agents in the princely states of India.

There is little evidence that this is what the Malays wanted. Members of the Malay aristocracy were vying for power. In a period of rapid economic change they were prepared to try new ways of increasing their incomes. Monopolizing innovations was the traditional way of doing this. Thus the wealth of the upstart Temenggong Ibrahim of Johore had been based on his monopoly of the gutta-percha boom of the 1840's.[43] In subsequent years his son, Abu Bakar, kept a finger in multifarious economic and administrative developments. In Johore, European modes of government and even European personnel were employed to maintain the power of a new sort of "traditional" ruler. Abu Bakar let them work for him, but he gained advice "informally," not from a Resident.[44] The idea of the Residents was produced, not by the Malays, but by British officials.[45] And for both Tengku Ziauddin of Selangor and Abdullah of Perak, as for many of the Malay elite, the effects of their grasping at the British straw were unexpected and unwelcome.

In addition to Chinese "colonies" within the Malay States which soon began to increase and move into new regions such as Kinta, in Perak,[46] a new type of British-run administration developed. Traditional Malay usages were now changed in quite drastic ways. Revenue collection was centralized, with fixed allowances or pensions allocated to the chiefs. Traditional social relationships which the British regarded as "slavery" were prohibited. There followed attempts to change the system of land tenure and judicial processes. New crops were experimented with, the Chinese and Indian labour migration encouraged.[47] If the Chinese welcomed the end of warfare, a good number of the Malay elite decided to resist. In 1875 there was resistance in each of the states which accepted Residents. In Perak the Resident was killed, and the state was occupied by force.[48]

By the end of the 1870's a major new source of change had been introduced into the west-coast states. In economic terms, this meant develop-

43. Turnbull, *Indian Presidency to Crown Colony*, pp. 277–278.

44. Thio, *British Policy in the Malay Peninsula*, I, 97–99.

45. The links with India were Major McNair (chief engineer in the Straits Settlements), who sat on the Anson Committee of 1871, and George Campbell (from the Ceylon police), who acted as lieutenant governor of Penang in 1872 and specifically used the Indian analogy. See Cowan, *Nineteenth-Century Malaya*, p. 84, and McIntyre, *Imperial Frontier*, pp. 192–200.

46. Wong, *Malayan Tin Industry*, pp. 87–93.

47. See Sadka, *Protected Malay States*; Loh, *The Malay States*; and Chai Hon-Chan, *The Development of British Malaya, 1896–1909* (Kuala Lumpur, 1964), introd.

48. Discussed below, pp. 282–283.

ment by aliens. Tin mining prospered. By 1877 the introduction of the steam pump presaged the arrival of large-scale European mining enterprises alongside the Chinese. The expansion of tin mining led to changes in the land law, indicated by the General Land Code of 1879.[49] For the majority of Malay peasants engaged in rice cultivation, forest-produce gathering, and fishing, the new regime made little difference. To a few Malay aristocrats the new era brought great wealth. "Had I but foreseen!" declared former Sultan Abdullah of Perak at the end of the century after his return from exile in the Seychelles.[50]

In political terms, the protected states and the Straits Settlements underwent a process of modernization by government action, which began to impinge on the social life of the communities. The first efforts at regulating the migration of Chinese and Indians were made by the appointment of a Protector of Chinese in 1877[51] and of officials to supervise Indian migration in the same year.[52] In the states where Residents were accepted, state councils were formed in 1877, and the traditional Malay function of consultation between ruler and leading chiefs was gradually merged with modern advisory and legislative functions. In theory the ruler ruled on the advice of the Resident; in practice the Resident led a new administration and kept the ruler informed.[53] A vivid example of the type of change which flowed from Chinese mining success and British administrative control was the shifting of the seat of the state government of Selangor to Kuala Lumpur in 1881. At the same time, experiments in the Singapore botanical gardens with Brazilian rubber seed and Low's experimental plantings at Kuala Kangsar presaged the growth of Malaya's great twentieth-century staple, rubber, and also the introduction of its third largest ethnic community, the Indians. For some Malays, their world was changing rapidly in the

49. Wong, *Malayan Tin Industry*, chap. 3.

50. The Abdullah-Birch affair obviously fascinated Winstedt, who met the Malay who had recovered Birch's body in 1875 (Bastin in *Malayan and Indonesian Studies*, p. 3) and he endeavoured to catch its spirit in a number of later books. His concept of Birch as the "Victorian public school boy" or the "rationalist schoolmaster" pouring "new wine into old bottles" appears first in "A History of Perak," *JMBRAS*, 12, 1 (1934), chap. 9 and again in "A History of Malaya," *ibid.*, 13, 1 (1935):234–239, in *Malaya and Its History*, pp. 65–68, and in a chapter entitled "New Wine into Old Bottles" in *Start from Alif, Count from One: An Autobiographical Memoir* (Kuala Lumpur, 1969), probably written in the later 1930's (see p. xii). Parkinson takes up the Birch psychology lesson in *British Intervention in Malaya*, pp. 218–230, 236–238, using material from M. A. Mallal's "J. W. W. Birch: Causes of his Assassination" (M.A. thesis, University of Singapore, 1952), and suggests a suicidal element.

51. See R. N. Jackson, *Pickering, Protector of Chinese* (Kuala Lumpur, 1965) for the first incumbent.

52. The Madras government appointed a protector of emigrants, and the Straits government sent an agent to Nagapatnam (Arasaratnam, *Indians*, p. 13). Indian convict transportation to the Straits Settlements ended in 1873 with the transfer of the penal stations to the Andaman Islands (Sandhu, *Indians in Malaya*, p. 48).

53. See Sadka, *Protected Malay States*, and "The State Councils in Perak and Selangor, 1877–1895," *in* Tregonning (ed.), *Papers on Malayan History*, pp. 89–119.

1870's. In 1875 a district chief in Muar is said to have stopped a British surveyor with the words: "If we let the needle in the thread is sure to follow."[54]

Yet alien control was not the only option. Wan Ahmad of Pahang seized power in spite of Straits pressure.[55] Abu Bakar of Johore partially modernized his government, bowing to British example and cultivating good relations, but in order to retain control—perhaps even to enhance his own influence in the Peninsula.[56] The rulers of Kedah, Kelantan, and Trengganu (about whom much less is known for this period) seemed to have deliberately eliminated the major source of conflict which caused so much trouble to the south. By centralizing administration and reducing the number of intermediate titleholders, they reduced the area of competition for revenue and influence.[57] Perhaps they were fortunate that the impetus to turbulence provided by the buoyant tin trade of the west coast was not present. Yet Johore had a large Chinese population (probably a majority at the end of the 1870's), engaged in gambier- and pepper-growing, that did not upset Abu Bakar's rule.

During the course of the above survey various concepts have been freely used. "Power" and "influence," "intervention" and "administration," "tradition" and "modernization," "elite" and "resistance" are but a few of the labels which flow readily from an historian's pen. When we come to consider some of the present-day scholarly trends which affect our writing, we are faced with some tantalizing, possibly frustrating, possibilities. In short, virtually all our basic concepts are subject to review. Usually this is the work of political scientists, who demand precision in definition yet often argue, with some abandon, by analogy and comparison between quite diverse regions. Sometimes they exercise a salutary vigilance.

Take, for example, the concept of "power." In 1873 Lord Kimberley accepted that Britain was "paramount power" in the Malay Peninsula. Cowan suggests this "paramountcy" was established by the East India Company in the first half of the nineteenth century but "is difficult to define."[58] Swettenham tried to argue that the doctrine of "indirect rule" had been invented in the F.M.S. Johore was, says Cowan, "in many respects a British dependency"[59] even though in a famous law suit the court accepted a Colonial Office view that it was an "independent state."[60]

54. Quoted in Roff, *Origins of Malay Nationalism*, p. 92.
55. Linehan, "History of Pahang," *JMBRAS*, 14, 2 (1935), chap. 7.
56. Discussed below, pp. 282–284.
57. Sheppard, "Short History of Trengganu," *JMBRAS*, 22, 3 (1949):34–35; Allen, "Anglo-Kedah Relations," *JMBRAS*, 41, 1 (1968):57–58; Graham, *Kelantan*, pp. 47–48.
58. Cowan, *Nineteenth-Century Malaya*, p. 17.
59. *Ibid.*, p. 13.
60. Emerson, *Malaysia*, p. 202.

Clearly the legal and constitutional labels of colonial rule, which always ran into ambiguity when it came to "protectorate," "suzerainty," or "paramountcy," are not really very helpful in describing the nature of British power in the Malay States.

We need new labels, and D. A. Low found some useful ones for his work on Uganda. Adopting P. H. Partridge's suggestion that power may be exercised by varying nuances on a scale running from "influence" to "domination,"[61] Low found (in Uganda) a threefold progression of alien influence starting with *Impact*, when "influence" led to "sway," and developing through *Dominion*, when "ascendancy" was followed by "predominance," to *Control*, which involved first "mastery" and then "dictation."[62] Malaya, with its fascinating array of local variety, might be susceptible not only to a "chronological" typology like Low's, but to a pattern of "horizontal" labellings applied at different times. Particular interest now focusses on the growth of a modern bureaucracy and the creation of a partly indigenous class of bureaucrats. This has recently been called "a great cultural achievement," yet the very buoyancy of Malay State revenues (possibly, also, the fiction of royal rule) meant that Malaya became more "closely governed" by aliens than some areas under European sovereignty.[63]

If theoretical analysis of power and its exercise might help to illuminate long-term transitions, how could greater precision be applied to the discussion of "intervention" and the seemingly inevitable "resistance" that followed? One possibility could be the application of "decision-making theory," a framework of analysis devised by social scientists to "identify some of the crucial variables that determine national responses to concrete situations" on the assumption that "acts of state" represent deliberate choices by people who are "decision-makers."[64] However, such schemes have not identified any elements which historians would not normally look for, and an up-to-date exercise, for our purposes, needs to look at at least two different types of decision-maker: the Malay leaders who decided to seek "external" aid and the British officials who decided to "intervene." We need to ask, also: What were their alternatives? Did either side understand what it was doing? Did their respective objectives (insofar as they defined them) coincide?

61. P. H. Partridge, "Some Notes on the Concept of Power," *Political Studies*, 11, 2 (1964): 110.

62. D. A. Low, "Lion Rampant," *Journal of Commonwealth Political Studies*, 2, 3 (1964): 249–250.

63. See Steinberg, *In Search of Southeast Asia*, p. 197; Roff, *Origins of Malay Nationalism*, pp. 21–22; and Allen, "Malayan Civil Service, 1874–1941: Colonial Bureaucracy/Malayan Elite," *Comparative Studies in History and Society*, 12, 2 (1970):149–187, including a comment by a sociologist G. D. Ness.

64. R. C. Snyder, H. W. Bruck, and B. Sapin, *Foreign Policy Decision-Making: An Approach to the Study of International Politics* (New York, 1962), pp. 2, 65.

The situations which most commonly led to political change in the Malay states followed the death of a ruler. This occurred eleven times between 1850 and 1875. There were major dynastic disputes in Pahang, Selangor, Negri Sembilan, and Perak. Each had its peculiar characteristics, and while Wan Ahmad of Pahang managed to seize power in spite of the Straits Settlements attempt to intervene in 1863, ten years later some of the contenders in the west-coast states did facilitate British intervention.

Four ambitious Malays managed, indeed, to get into real difficulties. In 1872, Tengku Ziauddin and his allies in Selangor were reduced to controlling only the lower Klang region, while the rival Raja Mahdi's allies had gained the tin-rich interior and its northern and southern river outlets. In 1873 the two most active contenders for power in Perak, Nga Ibrahim of Larut and Raja Muda Abdullah, were both denied their revenue sources by a full-scale war between Chinese secret societies in Larut. In 1874 a newly appointed Dato Klana of Sungei Ujong tried to defeat his main rival officeholder and found himself in difficulties. All four schemed for outside help. Ziauddin successfully gained the alliance of Pahang. In Perak both Nga Ibrahim and Abdullah turned to the Penang government to end the Chinese miners' conflict and to gain recognition for their pretensions. In 1874 the Dato Klana of Sungai Ujong, having agreed to allow Straits supervision of the Linggi River and gained a promise of protection in return, went ahead with a rash attack on his rivals and got into a corner, from which he was rescued by British troops. Each of these rulers had their backs to the wall in their own disputes, the origins of which were quite different, even though common ingredients, such as rival Malay chiefs and rival Chinese societies, existed in each. There were also some more obscure Malay connexions which will be discussed below. But what the desperate, losing rajas failed to realize, as they grasped at their "external" straws, was that in the Straits Settlements and in London their problem was being viewed in quite a different way.

Reports on these local developments in Perak, Selangor, and Sungai Ujong reached desks in the Colonial Office in somewhat random order. But together they contributed to the decision to "do something," which issued in the general instruction to Sir Andrew Clarke, dated 20 August 1873, to consider the possibility of appointing Residents. Thus, in many ways, a series of unrelated incidents from three different states contributed to this one important preparatory stage of the decision to intervene.[65]

But other conscious acts of Malay rulers fed the British intervention in a

65. These stages are traced in my *Imperial Frontier in the Tropics*, pp. 199–206. For a slightly different interpretation see Chew, "The Reasons for British Intervention in Malaya: Review and Reconsideration," *JSEAH*, 6, 1 (1965):81–93, and for a major attempt at revision (emphasizing economic motives), see Khoo, "The Origin of British Administration in Malaya," *JMBRAS*, 39, 1 (1966):52–90.

more indirect way. In March 1873, Tengku Ziauddin granted his Singapore creditor, James G. Davidson, a monopoly concession for prospecting and mining in unoccupied land in Selangor. On the strength of this, plans for a Malayan Peninsula (East India) Tin Mining Company were drawn up; a letter from the London agent of its promoters to the Permanent Under-Secretary for Colonies alluded to the possibility that the Tengku might seek German intervention in Selangor, and this was probably the principal reason the Secretary of State, Lord Kimberley, was willing to approve intervention in July 1873. Although a company was formed and paid £100,000 for the concession in 1874, subscriptions were slow in coming and it went into liquidation after a year.[66] Another concession was granted by Raja Muda Abdullah of Perak, who by 1872 had already begun to claim the title of Sultan. Through an intermediary, he made contact with Tan Kim Cheng, one of the wealthiest Straits Chinese, whom he visited in Singapore in October 1873. In return for receiving Tan Kim Cheng's promise of support in his endeavour to be recognized as Sultan of Perak, Abdullah granted Tan the revenue farm of Larut for ten years.[67] Less than two weeks after this bargain Sir Andrew Clarke arrived at Singapore with Kimberley's instructions to consider the possibility of Residents. Within a few days Tan's business associate, W. H. Read, had told the Governor over dinner that he could supply a "key to the door," which turned out to be a letter from Abdullah requesting a Resident. Thus, insofar, as Malay contenders for power in Selangor and Perak "requested" a British Resident, those requests were engineered by Straits merchants who had just received large "concessions" for profit-making from desperate Malays, who no doubt felt that they had little to lose.

It would, therefore, probably be fair to say that the immediate background to intervention was marked by mutual incomprehension on the part of the major decision-makers. Certainly the objectives of Malays and British hardly coincided. The Malays wanted to beat their rivals, although not necessarily to eliminate them. They wanted certain claims to titles or territories recognized. They also wanted some way to stop the Chinese from squabbling, since this cut off the rulers' revenues. The British officials, in Whitehall, wanted to keep other European powers from a Peninsula which could dominate a major trade route, and to avoid the sort of disturbance to the trade and security of the Straits Settlements which the Malay wars caused. The critical "link" in this situation, which brought quite divergent interests together, was a handful of Straits merchants, who engineered Malay "requests" for intervention, having first gained concessions to exploit Malay resources.

66. For fullest account see Wong, *Malayan Tin Industry*, pp. 36–40.
67. For fullest account see Khoo, *Western Malay States*, pp. 214–217.

It is also ironical that few of the parties found the results very satisfactory. The Selangor tin concession and Larut revenue farm came to nothing. Abdullah gained recognition as Sultan of Perak and Tengku Ziauddin prevailed in Selangor, but within four years both had departed from the scene, Abdullah to exile and Ziauddin to retirement. If the Colonial Office sanctioned the new policies to gain security for the "turbulent frontier" of the Straits Settlements it soon had second thoughts when Malay resistance led to three armed expeditions in as many years, one of which disturbed the Disraeli Cabinet's Christmas.

In looking at the effects of "intervention" it is therefore appropriate to consider, finally, the concept of "resistance" in the light of recent scholarship. Few incidents have received such generous treatment as the "Perak war" of 1875–1876. Some attention has also been paid to the minor use of force in Sungai Ujong in 1874 and 1875–1876. Swettenham gave the orthodox view of the impact of military force: "The Malays had learned that the power of the British Government must be respected."[68]

Yet, on the face of it, British military efforts in Malaya were not particularly successful. "Gunboat diplomacy" was of limited value. The shelling of Kuala Trengganu in 1862 did not stop Wan Ahmad from gaining control of Pahang. The shelling of forts at Kuala Selangor in 1871 did not keep them out of the hands of Ziauddin's adversaries a year later. An attempted naval blockade of the Perak coast in 1872–1873 to cut off supplies from the warring Chinese in Larut only served to make things worse and forced the antagonists to plunder coastal shipping for food and arms. For much of 1873 fast-rowing boats with double-banked oars were able to elude the heavier cutters from the British warships.[69] It was Nga Ibrahim's Indian mercenaries who gained control of Larut, not the R.N. Even after the killing of the Resident in 1875, when British battalions lumbered in from India and Hong Kong they failed to capture some of the Perak fugitives, who were eventually apprehended through the help of the Sultan of Kedah and Maharajah of Johore. The limited resources of British power that were actually available in Malaya in the 1870's were only effective because parties in the Malay disputes were prepared to supplement them. Swettenham was convinced, however, that the moral effect had been salutary. Malays had told him, "in the silence of the night," that he and his fellow Residents were "thrown out as bait by the British Government." If the Malays swallowed the bait "they would find themselves on the British hook."[70] Resistance, it would seem, was not worth it.

However, the work of T. O. Ranger on "Primary resistance" movements

68. Swettenham, *Footprints in Malaya*, p. 67.
69. *Ibid.*, pp. 28–29, for a personal account.
70. *British Malaya*, p. 219.

and modern mass nationalism in eastern Africa[71] has opened up suggestive possibilities about resistance movements in traditional societies under stress. Eric Stokes has alluded to Ranger's thesis in relation to the Indian sepoy rebellion and Allen has tried to place the initial Malay resistances of 1875 in the context of the later Pahang rebellion (1891–1895) the Kelantan rising (1915), the Trengganu rising (1928), and the uproar over Malayan Union in 1945–1946. There are also interesting parallels in Maori resistance to Europeans in New Zealand from the 1840's to the 1920's.[72]

Obviously argument by analogy with such very different traditional societies is likely to be misleading. But even if his general scheme may not be applicable, some of Ranger's concepts are suggestive. First, he reminds us that while a colonial power would regard a minor punitive expedition as a passing, salutary incident (as Swettenham did), to the local populace it often set the environment of their later lives. The "trauma of defeat" sometimes shaped the attitudes of generations and bred a tradition of resentment or resistance. New taxes or differing disbursements often activated such feelings. Second, the very elements of traditional society that cooperated most closely with the Europeans bred New elites, which became a bridge between traditional rulers and modern political leaders. In both these respects it would be interesting to know the impact upon Perak Malays of the aftermath of Birch's murder, and also the extent to which modernizing rulers, notably Abu Bakar of Johore, might have aspired to a new-type leadership in Malaya.[73] For although the chronological type of "connexions" inherent in Ranger's African work seem somewhat tenuous as applied to Malaya, the "territorial connexions" between rival parties in the various states warrant investigation. The Malay wars of the 1860's and 1870's certainly connected with each other in many ways. Does any significant thread, "traditional" or "modern," provide a focus for these connexions?

In the Pahang war, 1857–1863, Wan Ahmad finally prevailed over his brothers with help from Trengganu and Kelantan, possibly Perak. He was opposed by the influence of the Temenggongs of Johore. Sporadic opposition to Wan Ahmad's rule attracted outside support from Raja Mahdi of Selangor. Thus Wan Ahmad was prepared to supply large forces to Tengku

71. T. O. Ranger, "Connexions between 'Primary Resistance' Movements and Modern Mass Nationalism in East and Central Africa," *Journal of African History*, 9, 3 (1968):437–453 and 9, 4:631–641.

72. E. Stokes, "Traditional Resistance Movements and Afro-Asian Nationalism: The Context of the 1857 Mutiny Rebellion in India," *Past and Present*, 48 (1970):100–118; Allen, "The Kelantan Rising of 1915," *JSEAH*, 9, 2 (1968):241–257; for an example of latter-day Maori resistance see P. O'Connor, "The Recruitment of Maori Soldiers, 1914–18," *Political Science*, 19, 2 (1967):48–83.

73. In which the British briefly encouraged him in the 1870's with regard to Negri Sembilan (Thio, *British Policy in the Malay Peninsula*, I, xxiv–xxx).

Ziauddin in 1872–1873, which helped bring the long Selangor war to an end. In this, Abu Bakar of Johore lent some support to Raja Mahdi. Outside support for Ziauddin was also forthcoming from Kedah and Perak. Sungai Ujong, on the southern border of Selangor, had its own particular disputes, notably between the two rival title holders who vied for control of the Linggi. Of these the Dato Klana tended to align himself with the Ziauddin of Selangor, while Raja Mahdi and his allies got help from the Dato Bandar. There were also connexions between Perak and Selangor. After losing in Selangor, Raja Mahdi's allies Syed Mashhor, Raja Mahmud, and Raja Asal moved on to new pastures in Perak. Moreover, as Abdullah sought support for his claims he looked to the Sultan of Kedah and his brother Tengku Ziauddin, who appeared somewhat mysteriously at a conference of Perak protagonists in Penang during August 1873.

Finally, after the Pangkor engagement and the appointment of the first Residents in 1874, some of the newly arrived British officials sensed a general feeling of resistance was brewing. Ismail, the deposed Sultan of Perak, is said to have addressed Wan Ahmad of Pahang and Abu Bakar of Johore on the possibility of united resistance.[74] In Perak the resentment of the Malay elite led to the killing of Birch and the British occupation. In Selangor the defeated parties were reforming late in 1875, so the Resident struck first and removed Raja Mahdi to Singapore.[75] In Negri Sembilan, Dato Klana Abdur Rahman, who took office in 1873 and accepted a Resident after the troubles of 1874, had designs on nearby Terachi. He also refused to recognize the election of Antah as *Yang di pertuan besar* of the Negri Sembilan. In fact, his pretensions caused Antah to attack Sungai Ujong at the end of 1875. This was just after Birch's death at Perak, and some Gurkhas were quickly diverted through Malacca to drive Antah off.[76]

Everything seemed to come to a head in the last months of 1875. Did anything connect these outbreaks? Three historians have suggested possibilities. Gullick feels there was no evidence to suggest "direct communication" between the leaders of the three resistance movements. "It just happened that the same factor of British intervention in 1874 had brought the Malays of the three States to the point of revolt at the same time a year later." But he finds it striking that all three groups of "rebels" had been in touch with Abu Bakar of Johore, who was the favoured Malay ruler in the eyes of the Straits government. "He would hardly have planned a revolt against his own patrons. But he was seeking to restore the ancient position of the Johore Sultanate as overlord of all Malay States." Gullick suggests that support for "the resistance party" suited his book. Abu Bakar

74. Linehan, "History of Pahang," *JMBRAS*, 14, 2 (1935):101.
75. Gullick, "A Careless, Heathen Philosopher?" *JMBRAS*, 26, 1 (1953):95–97.
76. Gullick, "The War with Yam Tuan Antah," *JMBRAS*, 27, 1 (1954):3–18.

"described the struggle in the Malay States as a Malay civil war in which the British had become identified with the wrong side; constitutional legality and popular support was with the rebels."[77] Unfortunately Gullick does not document this view. However, Wake's thorough examination of Abu Bakar's background and motives, using Johore sources, fills out the story. Abu Bakar, he says, did play a "double game," but his opposition to British intervention in the 1870's "amounted to no more than covert support for anti-British elements in the West Coast states."[78] His opposition to Ziauddin is also partly accounted for by the fact that Ahmad Tajudin of Kedah was married to the sister of Sultan Ali of Singapore. Abu Bakar would not want Selangor ruled by a prince "who might then support the ambitions of the old royal house of Johore."[79]

Khoo Kay Kim has also recognized that the interstate connexions have "never been fully brought out." Where Gullick and Wake see Abu Bakar as a focus, Khoo suggests that the Ziauddin-Mahdi war in Selangor provides "a useful unifying theme."[80] He notes how Kedah, Perak, Pahang, Johore, and parts of the Negri Sembilan were all drawn into the Selangor struggle. He makes two interesting suggestions: first, that Abdullah of Perak sought Tengku Ziauddin's support because the latter apparently had influence in the Straits Settlements; second, that Ahmad Tajudin of Kedah, a conservative Muslim, lent his support to his brother, Ziauddin, because of his disapproval of Abu Bakar's reforming ways, and inclined to Abdullah's side in Perak because the titular Sultan, Ismail (ousted at Pangkor), was not of royal descent.[81]

These views might suggest that the rulers of the two states "closest" to the Straits Settlements represented two opposing poles in Malaya. Ahmad Tajudin of Kedah stood by Islamic orthodoxy and dynastic legitimacy. Abu Bakar of Johore, himself from a parvenu line, inclined to religious and political expediency. We certainly need to know much more about Abu Bakar's supposed ambition to inherit the prestige of the Johore Sultanate. Was the model modernizer—the only ruler who ruled "in accordance with the practice of civilized nations"[82]—in reality the subtlest traditional resister? Or was he one of the intermediate "new leaders" who link traditional resistance with modern nationalism? Certainly both Kedah and Johore managed to utilize British influences to the end of preserving aspects of their own integrity. In recent times, too, leaders from these states have

77. *Ibid.*, pp. 4–5.
78. Wake, "Nineteenth Century Johore," pp. 305–306.
79. *Ibid.*, p. 309.
80. Khoo, *Western Malay States*, p. 176.
81. *Ibid.*, pp. 186 and 196.
82. Governor Ord's view, 10 February 1868, quoted in Cowan, *Nineteenth-Century Malaya*, p. 39.

been prominent in modern Malayan politics, notably Tengku Abdul Rahman from Kedah and Dato Onn from Johore.

Abu Bakar and his successor, Ibrahim, became so "modern" in their tastes that they dissipated much of their advantage. Ahmad Tajudin and his successors stood by Islamic orthodoxy, yet even Swettenham had to admit that, back in 1874, "Kedah was more advanced in its institutions, in observance of order, the well-being of its people, and the general development of the Country, than any other State in the Peninsula."[83] When the British tried to "take over" after 1909 they found a modernized bureaucracy and caused a civil-service strike.[84] Here perhaps was another case of the "modernity of tradition."[85]

These three examples of the way one might ponder such concepts as "power," "decision," and "resistance" indicate some of the ways in which uninhibited experimentation in the behavioural sciences might assist historians. If conceptual scheme-building or theorizing, on the basis of static fragments of the past, becomes the main preoccupation, it presages an arid scholasticism that is as bad, in its way, as earlier preoccupation with genealogies. But if comparative studies and the search for generalizations illuminate even small areas, none can cavil. There may even be room still for the study of "imperialism."

83. Swettenham, *British Malaya*, p. 331.
84. Allen, "Anglo-Kedah Relations," *JMBRAS*, 41, 1 (1968):56.
85. See L. I. and S. H. Rudolph, *The Modernity of Tradition: Political Development in India* (Chicago, 1967).

Some Notes on the Historiography of British Borneo

NICHOLAS TARLING

University of Auckland

The historiography of the British connexion with what was for a time "British Borneo" is not a rich one. The area, now covered by the two Malaysian states of Sabah and Sarawak and by the state of Brunei that still sustains a special relationship with Great Britain, has never in itself been a major source of political power or creative culture. Nor was it a major focus of British enterprise in the imperial phase that began in the late eighteenth century. Perhaps it is, at least at first sight, surprising that the historiography of the phase is not poorer than it is, rather than richer. In fact the history of the area through its not quite concluded period of connexion with Britain has been sufficiently interesting and challenging to produce substantial, if somewhat slanted, historical materials and historical writings. The area, though comparatively small and demographically immature, contains a diversity of peoples, languages, and cultures. Its connexion with Britain offers examples of experiment and expediency and eccentricity perhaps unique even in imperialist times. The contemporary legacy of this past and the contemporary problems of the Borneo states, if not of great international significance, are intrinsically fascinating. The nature and value of the material available for studying the history of the area have, of course, been affected by the historical events it has witnessed. The way historians have responded to the challenges the material offers has also been affected by historical factors. There is nothing unusual in this. Perhaps, indeed, because of the relatively slim volume of material and writing on "British Borneo," it illustrates especially clearly a factor common to all historiographies.

The earliest but by no means the least sophisticated writings on the area in this phase, in themselves sources for future historians, were closely connected with the activities surrounding the Sabah cessions of the 1760's and the first settlement on Balambangan in 1773. But the astute and thorough observations of Thomas Forrest, in *A Voyage to New Guinea and the Moluccas, from Balambangan*, recently beautifully reprinted by Oxford University

Press (Kuala Lumpur, 1969) with an excellent introduction by D. K. Bassett, are of more interest to historians of Sulu and Mindanao than to those of Brunei or northern Borneo. The other published writings of the period include those of Alexander Dalrymple, and printed in his *Oriental Repertory* (London, 1793, 1808) is John Jesse's "Account of Borneo Proper," or Brunei, where the Balambangan enterprise had a pepper-producing offshoot for a short time. But there is nothing equivalent in Dalrymple's political and promotional writings or in the *Repertory* to Forrest's sympathetic account of the other sultanates. Still more is this the case with the records the venture left behind in the archives of the East India Company in the Home Miscellaneous Series and Borneo Factory Records, which is particularly unfortunate in that this is a particularly obscure phase in the history of Brunei. Seemingly the relations of the sultanate with the northern territories, and even with those south of the capital, were greatly weakened during the eighteenth century. By the early nineteenth century its influence was substantially re-established south of Marudu. But the process is comparatively unknown.

It is true that at the beginning of the nineteenth century the British temporarily renewed their settlement on Balambangan and even momentarily established themselves in Marudu. These events produced no published work, and even the unpublished records perhaps are significant more for their indications of a change in British attitudes than for their contributions to the history of northern Borneo. Those attitudes are still plainer in Raffles who, no doubt influenced by the experiences of the "Balambangan gentlemen," advocated a forward policy in the area. As A. L. Reber has stressed in relation to the sultanate of Sulu ("The Sulu World in the Eighteenth and Early Nineteenth Centuries," M.A. thesis, Cornell University, 1966), the emphasis in Raffles's writings, based on no first-hand information of the area but rather, perhaps, on his knowledge of Johore, was on the reform and reconstitution of states that had allegedly declined. Fortunately his interest in the area produced the reports of John Hunt, a country trader whom he employed. These, covering Borneo and Sulu, were printed in *Malayan Miscellanies*, volume I (Bencoolen, 1820), and reprinted in J. H. Moor, *Notices of the Indian Archipelago and Adjacent Countries* (Singapore 1837), itself reprinted by Frank Cass in 1968. They are a basic source, even if Hunt's attitude is more unsympathetic than Forrest's. Yet even they are probably of more value in relation to Sulu than in Brunei.

The provision of material about and the writings on Brunei were, interestingly but perhaps unfortunately for the sultanate, ultimately to come from another peripheral direction. They arose from the extraordinary Brooke venture in Sarawak. This had a background in official British policy, which increasingly reflected dissatisfaction with that of the Dutch, to whom essentially the archipelago had been resigned under the treaty of 17 March 1824; but it was also the result of private ambition and enterprise. The tension between these two aspects of the venture remained throughout the history of what became the Raj of Sarawak and profoundly affected the history of British relations with the rest of northern Borneo also. A substantial body of material was published as part of the attempt to enlist official and public support for the initial plans of James Brooke in the 1840's: it included Brooke's original prospectus, focussing on Marudu; *A Letter from Borneo . . . addressed to James Gardner* (London, 1842), following his securing the government of Sarawak from Raja Muda Hassim; and the substantial extracts from his journals published in H. Keppel, *The Expedition to Borneo of H. M. S. Dido* (London, 1846), and in R. Mundy, *Narrative of Events in Borneo and Celebes* (London, 1848), which stress his interest in the reform of the Brunei sultanate with British support. With the second Keppel book, *A Visit to the Indian Archipelago in H.M.S. Maeander* (London, 1853), and *The Private Letters of Sir James Brooke*, edited by J. C. Templer (London, 1853) (only a small section of a vast family correspondence), the literature begins to reflect the controversy over Brooke's relations with the British Government following the clash with the Ibans in 1849. It includes, too, a number of pamphlets, producing more heat than light so far as Borneo is concerned, extensive debate in Hansard, and voluminous, if Palmerstonically edited, parliamentary papers. The Foreign Office built up archives on Borneo and Sulu, as did the Colonial Office following the acquisition of the island of Labuan in 1846. This phase thus greatly added to the materials available on northern Borneo. The emphasis was, however, very much on the making of British policy, so far as the archives and the polemical literature were concerned. Much of the other published material, on the other hand, either avoids political comment altogether or confines itself, so far as the indigenous political situation is concerned, to accounts that are perhaps less valuable than those of the earlier phase of British interest in the area. Strikingly, even observers like Hugh Low and Spenser St. John, both associated with the Brooke enterprise and later distinguished in the service of the British Government, seemingly believed that their readers were more likely to be interested in flora and fauna than in human society, though they were not unsympathetic to the Borneo peoples. True, Low was a botanist; but it is still a matter of regret that, following *Sarawak: Its Inhabitants and Productions* (London, 1848), he did not go on to record the events of his subsequent political career and his contacts with Brunei before moving, much later in life, to Perak. Spenser St. John's *Life in the Forests of the Far East* (London, 1862), shortly to be reprinted by Oxford University Press with an introduction by Tom Harrisson, is, though charming, ultimately in the same respect disappointing, too. No doubt government servants had to be cautious. But the result perhaps also reflected the decline in political interest in Borneo following Brooke's break with the British Government in 1855.

New factors thereafter helped, however, to create new historical writing and archive-building. One was the determination of the Brookes—Sir James, but still more his nephew and successor, Charles—to build a Sarawak state, independent of Brunei, independent also of Britain, but in close connexion with it. The character of the second Raja and his special feeling for the Ibans had been illustrated in his early work, *Ten Years in Sarawak* (London, 1866). Once he had become Raja in 1868, he was unwilling to launch into print openly. Nor did others find him an attractive subject: new biographies of Sir James were written by G. L. Jacob (*The Raja of Sarawak*, London, 1876) and by St. John (*The Life of Sir James Brooke*, Edinburgh and London, 1879). No similar account of the second Raja's reign was published: he did not do it himself; nor was he likely to encourage his subordinates to do so, though A. B. Ward prepared a manuscript subsequently published as *Rajah's Servant* (Cornell University, Southeast Asia Program, 1966). Nor are the archives of the Sarawak Raj substantial. Much has apparently been destroyed. But the archives, like the literature, in any case reflected the state's origins and character: it was autocratic, and it was amateurish. Autocracy meant that little was published unless the Raja published it: pioneering proceeded without the public glamour and clamour of the first Raja's reign. Amateurism, as well as autocracy, meant relatively lax secretarial methods in a state after all performing minimal functions and only in the process of establishment and growth. The most valuable part of the archives is characteristically the Raja's own letterbooks, which have mostly been preserved. But the maturing of the Raj and the Raja's role in it are also evidenced by the commencement of the *Sarawak Gazette* in 1870, another essential source; by the founding of the Sarawak Museum, which has also served as an archival repository; and by the publication of a semiofficial history (S. Baring-Gould and C. A. Bampfylde, *A History of Sarawak under its Two White Rajas*, London, 1909). The British Government's archives for the period are concerned in part with the problem of Labuan, a burden on the Colonial Office once open support for the Brooke venture had been dropped. They also cover relations with Sarawak and Brunei, complicated by the Raja's wish to retain independence with some British support and by his desire to extend at the expense of Brunei, even ultimately to incorporate it.

The resolution of these problems extended over a long period: it included the chartering of the British North Borneo Company in 1881, the establishment of British protectorates over Sarawak, North Borneo, and the remnant of Brunei by the 1888 agreements, and the installation of a British Resident in Brunei in 1905–1906. Strikingly little was published about these events: they were overshadowed by events elsewhere, in Southeast Asia, in India, in Africa; they were substantially diplomatic and thus confidential in character; and, apart from a reticent Raja, they were not dominated or directed by men of great personality, though the men involved in them were not without colour or character. The archives reflect some of the same features. The beginning of the Company meant the creation of new archives in North Borneo and in London and substantial correspondence between directors and governor: but a very thinly spread administration and very scanty resources demanded a desperate concentration on setting up some sort of rough-and-ready government in this fragment of empire. Possibly the most interesting sources are the diaries of the early Residents, particularly those of W. B. Pryer at Sandakan. The published work of his wife, *A Decade in Borneo* (London, 1893), supplements them, as do their notes for a second edition which they hoped to bring out, and which the present author hopes to incorporate in a reprint. In the routine correspondence of the administrators many gaps are unfilled: the material reflects the hand-to-mouth existence of the Company's government, though the *British North Borneo Herald*, like the *Sarawak Gazette*, published reports from outlying residencies that are sometimes of greater interest. In the twentieth-century phase, more discursive material appeared, including the work of Owen Rutter (*British North Borneo*, London, 1922). But it may be that, after about 1915, the archives themselves become less valuable: the files in London certainly seem to be less complete.

Something similar is evident in the case of the other territories, if for rather different reasons. Following the establishment of the Brunei Residency, C. P. Lucas and others at the Colonial Office had planned to strengthen the British hold on Sarawak. That proved more or less impossible while the old Raja lived. It also proved impossible after 1917 because his son and successor, Vyner, sought to retain Sarawak's independence, even when a personalized Raj was becoming, at least outside the Sarawak context, anachronistic. The fact that the Colonial Office's attempts to bring Sarawak under closer control were largely vain means that the Colonial Office archives are very scanty in this period; it may also explain why part of what does exist has been closed for one hundred years. On the other hand, Vyner himself, partly because of the difficulty of his position, kept silence. One of his few writings is an introduction to a book by his wife, Sylvia (*The Three White Rajas*, London, 1939). But her books themselves tell us little of Sarawak that is of value to the historian.

The establishment of the Residency in Brunei was preceded by an able but as yet unpublished report by Stewart McArthur, and it might have been hoped that the tradition of scholar–civil servants that developed in Malaya would develop in Brunei also. Yet this happened only in a partial degree. Low had set an example by publishing "Selesilah (Book of the Descent) of the Rajas of Brunei" in the *Journal of the Straits Branch Royal Asiatic Society*, volume 5 (June 1880), and W. H. Treacher published some notes on British Borneo in volumes 20 and 21 of the same journal (1889–1890). Later H. R. Hughes-Hallett wrote "A Sketch of the History of Brunei," *Journal of the Malayan Branch Royal Asiatic Society*, volume 18, number 2 (August 1940). But partly because Brunei was a short-term posting, Malaya remained the main focus of writing, as of administration, the chosen field for Wilkinson, Winstedt, Purcell. Private memoirs are also sparse: indeed, until oil became big business, the cutch company was the chief Western enterprise in Brunei; and it was as its employee that F. N. Butterworth gained that experience of which, as "Peter Blundell," he wrote in *The City of Many Waters* (London, 1923). The archives of the Residency appear no longer to exist. Much was no doubt referred to Singapore. But it seems that not much has been preserved. Very little was referred to London after the early years of the Residency, and so little is to be found there either. Other primary sources are scarce.

The Pacific war involved great destruction in British Borneo, and much of the archival material perished. The postwar phase saw the creation of colonial governments in Sarawak and North Borneo. The former involved considerable public controversy. The opening of the wartime archives in London has so far made but little more material available. The archives of the postwar period will, in any case, remain closed for some years. Formal colonial government and the intensification of administrative activity increased the published material available on Sarawak and North Borneo, while the political struggles in Brunei encouraged investigation of its past, and its growing wealth sustained a more elaborate form of government. The creation of Malaysia and the Philippines claim to Sabah attracted international interest to the area to a greater degree than any event since the time of James Brooke, and a considerable amount of material was published, though some of it was biased. But how much of the unpublished material of the period will ever see the light is to be doubted; and if it does not, the chance of correcting such bias will be diminished. The amateurishness of prewar governments and the destruction of the wartime period weaken our unpublished sources for that phase, when our published sources are also scanty. In relation to more recent times, there is perhaps some danger, though not only in the case of Borneo, that published sources will become a substitute for unpublished. The sheer volume of records may daunt archivists and government departments, and political reticence may respond to growing historiographical curiosity in a negative way by utilizing such considerations of expediency as the lack of storage space or reading facilities. The individual historian—or perhaps the historical profession as a whole in Southeast Asia and elsewhere—must strike a balance between the need for early access and the necessity to discourage destruction. But there are, of course, other approaches to the past than those provided by research in archives and in libraries, and historians have shown an increasing awareness of them. Possibly such approaches are especially important in the case of Borneo, in view of the value both of its archaeological sites and of its oral traditions, and the recently established *Borneo Research Bulletin*, edited first by G. N. Appell and now by Donald E. Brown, facilitates awareness of activities in a wide range of disciplines.

The writings on Borneo in the period of its connexion with Britain and the material created for its study have reflected primary events in its history. But in the past two decades in particular the nature of those writings and the utilization of that material have been professionalized to an unprecedented degree. That, in part, is the result of the general expansion of tertiary education and basic research in the historical as in other fields. It is also the result of a deeper interest in Southeast Asia as a whole, following the end of the colonial regimes and the involvement there of the United States and of Australia and New Zealand. The fact that this new interest in the area has produced a new historiography that seeks to conform to the highest standards demonstrates not only the strength of the best of European traditions but also the ability and devotion of practitioners and leaders in the field like D. G. E. Hall and his colleagues and students at the School of Oriental and African Studies and Cornell. In the case of "British Borneo," materials have come down from the past of varying range and usefulness. With the use of archives, where they are open, and of new techniques; with the expertise of scholars of diverse backgrounds, and the encouragement of men like the many-sided Tom Harrisson; with the opportunities provided in the *Sarawak Museum Journal*, the *Sabah Society Journal*, and Pengiran Shariffuddin's welcome newcomer, the *Brunei Museum Journal*, and by enterprising publishers like Macmillan and Oxford University Press East Asia: what has this new professionalism achieved?

The early phase of British involvement, that of Dalrymple and Forrest, had already, it is true, been partly examined before the war, both by Johannes Willi, in *The Early Relations of England with Borneo to 1805* (Langensalza, 1922), and by T. C. P. Edgell, in "English Trade and Policy in Borneo and the Adjacent Islands, 1667–1786" (M.A. thesis, University of London, 1935). The postwar study of this phase commenced with some sections in Vincent Harlow's first volume of *The Second British Empire* (London, 1952). Since then the Dalrymple venture has been re-examined from a number of points of view. H. de la Costa has written about the intriguing (in both senses) Sultan Alimuddin I of Sulu in the *Journal of the Malaysian Branch Royal Asiatic Society*, volume 38, number 1 (July 1965); E. A. Julian has studied anew all the British expeditions in the region in her "British Projects and Activities in the Philippines, 1759–1805" (Ph.D. thesis, University of London, 1963); and H. T. Fry has recently surveyed the whole career of Dalrymple, of which the "Felicia" adventure was only a part (*Alexander Dalrymple (1757–1808) and the Expansion of British Trade*, London, 1970). Possibly the nature of the material available will keep historians from writing more on Borneo itself in this phase.

The venture of James Brooke has been re-examined by several writers, in particular by G. W. Irwin, an Australian student of Purcell's who made the first attempt in Borneo historiography to combine English and Dutch archival material (*Nineteenth-Century Borneo: A Study in Diplomatic Rivalry*, The Hague, 1955). At issue still among historians are the origins and nature of British backing for the first Raja. C. D. Cowan, in his *Nineteenth-Century Malaya: The Origins of British Political Control* (London, 1961) stressed the importance of keeping open the route to China as a motive in British policy. In his thesis, *British Policy in the Malay Peninsula and Archipelago, 1824–1871* (reprinted Kuala Lumpur, 1969), the present author drew more attention to the background of dispute with the Dutch over the archipelago as a whole. In a more recent contribution, *Britain, the Brookes and Brunei* (Kuala Lumpur, 1971), he attempted a subtler interpretation: Peel and the Admiralty were at first more interested in Borneo than the Foreign Office; but, after an exchange with the Dutch, the Foreign Office became more enthusiastic, while the Admiralty's interest declined. This interpretation receives support from a thesis by J. E. Ingleson, who has enterprisingly made use of the papers of Lord Haddington, First Lord of the Admiralty ("Britain's Annexation of Labuan in 1846: The Role of James Brooke and Local Influences," *University Studies in History*, vol. 5, no. 4 [1970], University of Western Australia Press). The topic indicates the extraordinary complexity of motivation behind imperial involvement in the territory. That is important in the history of "British Borneo." It may be important in looking at other areas also, though the degree of complexity, of course, may vary.

The activities of the British took the form of or were represented as measures for the suppression of piracy. The controversy of the day largely centred upon them: Were the pirates really pirates? Should the Navy be involved? What were James Brooke's real objectives? In his *Piracy and Politics in the Malay World* (Melbourne and Singapore, 1963), the present author discussed some of these topics anew. No doubt he is justly reproached by Miss Reber, in regard to Sulu, for being influenced by the Rafflesian notions current in British policy-making and in the archives: to see piracy there as a symptom of "decline" is an exaggeration, though the spread of piratical Ilanun settlements into Sulu territory in the late eighteenth century and their patronage by influential Sulus still seem to require explanation. To some extent, the author is justly reproached by Robert Pringle also for failing to stress the subsequent role of the Ibans in the history of the Sarawak Raj. *Piracy and Politics in the Malay World* was at least justified by its re-examination of the problem and its provocation of others. Though there is still work to do in the Borneo field, the study of "piracy" is also perhaps a topic of wider interest in the history of imperialism: piracy is something that must be viewed in the context of a Western conceptualization, but it cannot be explained away by recognizing that fact.

Pringle's own book, *Rajahs and Rebels* (London, 1970), is possibly the most masterly of the historical works on Sarawak. His main subject is the Ibans and their relationship with the Raja, but in the course of the book he illuminates many other topics. The Ibans in the pre-Brooke period have been studied by an Iban, Benedict Sandin, till recently curator of the Sarawak Museum, through their own oral material (*The Sea Dayaks of Borneo before White Raja Rule*, London, 1967). Pringle takes up the story when they come into contact with the Raj, which others have studied from a Brookean or a British direction. The Ibans, under control by the early 1860's, were used by the Raj in spreading its authority and gave it a military sanction. They proved enterprising in other ways too: even in the Third Division Ibans actually employed Chinese or loaned money to them. Pringle also gives us an account of the administrative methods of the Raj, in particular of Charles Brooke, and an explanation of the present position of the Ibans in Malaysian Sarawak—indeed of the other communities also, whose loyalties shifted, as the Raj grew, from a local, but nonethnic focus, to a wider, but communal focus.

The actual expansion of the Raj, in which the Iban played a role, is not Dr. Pringle's major topic. It is substantially the subject of the present author's *Britain, the Brookes and Brunei*. This attempts to cover Britain's relations with Brunei from the first Balambangan settlement to the establishment of the Residency. But it is very much concerned, of course, with the Raj and its attempts to expand. Another work, partially on the same topic, appeared about the same time, L. R. Wright's *The Origins of British Borneo* (Hong Kong, 1970). This covers the period from about 1860 to about 1888. Perhaps the major difference between the two books on the interpretation of this phase relates to the extent of British involvement. Dr. Wright insists on a major change in British policy in 1860, a re-emphasis of British interest, a forward movement. My own conclusion is much more negative. So also over the refusal to approve Sarawak's expansion to the Baram: the emphasis should surely be placed on the wish to minimize the risk of deeper British involvement.

This is the context in which to see the change that the chartering of the Company surely represented. The stress was on minimum commitment. The actual administration the Company set up was minimum government, partly perhaps because of its concern to avoid criticism in Britain, partly because of its limited resources. The first major study of the Company, using its archives in London, was K. G. Tregonning's *Under Chartered Company Rule* (Singapore, 1958; revised as *A History of Modern Sabah*, Singapore, 1965). More recently, in a thesis awarded the Ph.D. degree at the Australian National University in 1971, "Native Administration by the British North Borneo Chartered Company, 1878–1915," I. D. Black has studied the Company's government up to the Rundum disturbances. He also puts the Mat Salleh revolt into a new context. Again the work raises a general question: Black suggests that "indirect" rule was adopted less for ideological than for financial reasons, except insofar as there was generalized respect for "native custom." It would be worth asking how far the shift towards more direct administration was forced on the Company by circumstances within the territory and how far it was the result of a wider change in imperial attitudes towards the close of the century. Indeed, late in the 1880's and in the 1890's, by contrast to the 1860's and 1870's, Britain—or the Colonial Office—sought to acquire the burdens of administration. Apparently certain Colonial Office officials had earlier contemplated that Sarawak might be encouraged to expand and then be taken over. But it was the Brunei Residency that gave shape to Britain's new readiness for responsibility.

On the period between the early twentieth century and the Pacific war, little has so far been published; little may ever be published. The archives in London offer some material on North Borneo. They offer little on the other territories, though the present author has, using them, published two rather tentative articles on Britain and Sarawak in the twentieth century. Unless substantial private archives are uncovered, this period seems likely to remain, rather curiously, the most obscure of all in the history of the relations of Britain and Borneo. Even the interviewing of administrators and administered seems to have been left too late. The major contributions of Emily Hahn (*James Brooke of Sarawak*, London, 1953) and of Sir Steven Runciman (*The White Rajahs*, Cambridge, 1960) do not relate to this period. Nor does the Ranee Sylvia's last book, *Queen of the Head-Hunters* (London, 1970), add anything of interest to the history of interwar Sarawak: it does little even to help us to comprehend Raja Vyner.

Was he really as weak as Pringle implies? Or was he rather faced with a problem more intractable than those his father faced, that of reconciling autocracy and modernity?

What historiography of the postwar period we can at present create depends largely on official documents and newspapers. Of these good use can be made, as is shown by M. H. Baker's *North Borneo: The First Ten Years, 1946–1956* (Singapore, 1962), and still more by James Ongkili's excellent *The Borneo Response to Malaysia* (Singapore, 1967), whose story is continued in *Modernization in East Malaysia, 1960–1970*, published by Oxford University Press East Asia in 1972. Interviewing is a further resource which must not be again neglected. The production of relatively instant history is important, not only in itself, but because it may provoke contributions from those who might otherwise remain silent. At the same time the archives at present accumulating must be far more substantial than ever they were for the prewar period. Impatience to get at these is natural. But in this respect a measure of discretion may serve historiography better than an overdose of valour.

Tribute to the God and Tribute to the King

F. H. VAN NAERSSEN*

In his *History of South-East Asia*, Professor Hall has written: "Among a host of petty rulers one would from time to time build up his power by forcing the 'rakryans' ruling the neighbouring localities to render him obedience and tribute. When from time to time such a ruler was able to extend his power over a wide area, he would proceed to demonstrate his greatness by building a 'chandi,' or monumental tomb, dedicated to the deity with whom he chose to be identified in life and united in death."[1]

Professor Hall throughout his *History* is always able to present the quintessence of a complex subject clearly and effectively. His statement above deals with the emergence of Hindu-Javanese kingship and the maintaining of it by the king's identification with a god, and I wish to offer the following essay on these two topics as a personal tribute to Professor Hall.

In an article written in 1937, I expressed the opinion that, before the reign of Çrī Mahārāja Rakai Kayuwangi, no centralized power, ruling over a large territory, yet existed in Java and that this situation is evident from, among other things, the heterogeneous nature of the inscriptions.[2]

Ten years later L. C. Damais wrote that he could not accept my opinion; his view of sovereignty was that, where there is no obvious royal title, we had for the time being to suppose that a charter was not issued by a king.[3] Thus, he believed that all who bore royal titles (*çrī mahārāja* or *ratu*) were kings, ruling in a chronological sequence over a wide area, and that there were no other contemporary independent rulers.

J. G. de Casparis agrees with Damais in so far as Çrī Kahulunnan is

* Before the volume went to press, the editors received the sad news of F. H. van Naerssen's death on 7 June 1974. They are grateful to P. J. Worsley for his assistance during the final stages of publishing this article.

1. D. G. E. Hall, *History of South-east Asia*, 2d ed. (London, 1964), p. 47.
2. F. H. van Naerssen, "Twee koperen oorkonden van Balitung in het Koloniaal Instituut te Amsterdam," *BKI*, 95 (1937):441–461; cf. 446–449.
3. L. C. Damais, "Epigrafische aantekeningen," *TBG*, 83 (1949):23–26.

concerned, believing that this was the title of the queen of the ruling king.[4] I had originally said of this person that "he was another independent ruler."[5] It is, of course, possible that Çrī Kahulunnan may have been the king's spouse and therefore able to grant land.

Nevertheless, I remain unconvinced that, in early Hindu Java, there was only one sovereign at a time. The historical sources at our disposal enable us to conclude that there were several independent rulers, some of them enjoying the title of *mahārāja* and others without that title. It does not necessarily follow, however, that the former were supreme rulers because they were known as *mahārājas*. To ascribe supreme authority to a ruler merely because the inscriptions mention him as a *mahārāja* and at the same time to deny authority to others who may possibly also have had sovereignty would be inconsistent with what is known of the social structure of the Hindu-Javanese period at this early stage of its history.

Not surprisingly, historians often attempt to identify a person attributed with a royal title in an epigraph with a king in a known dynastic list whenever the identification is chronologically feasible. But we have neglected to consider the native landed gentry as a political power in Old Javanese society. Because the gentry were not yet integrated into the Hindu culture and therefore lacked the support of a literate clergy, they have failed to leave records that clearly establish the credentials of their authority.[6]

In a lecture read to the Oriental Society of Australia in 1962, I discussed the genesis of the de facto ruler in early Javanese society.[7] My argument, briefly, was as follows: we can assume that the original smallest community was the *wanua*, a self-supporting and egalitarian unit organized in a communal and traditional system by a board of elders, presided over by the first among 'equals, styled the *rāma* or "father" of the *anak wanua*, the "children of the community," as the inhabitants were called. An authority of higher rank was the *raka*, the "older brother."

For the origin of the function of the *raka*, we can only surmise that he emerged from the ranks of the *wanua* heads (the *rāmas*, or "fathers") and functioned as an "older brother" (the original meaning of the word *raka*) among these *rāmas*. His role became necessary when the social and economic structure had developed to a level that required several communities to cooperate under one leader.

The *raka*-ship was undoubtedly a pre-Hindu institution. Perhaps its emergence can be ascribed to ecological factors. The introduction of the

4. J. G. de Casparis, *Inscripties uit de Çailendra-tijd: Prasasti Indonesia*, I (Bandung, 1950), 83.
5. Van Naerssen, p. 448, no. 15.
6. W. F. Stutterheim, "Een belangrijke oorkonde uit de Kedoe," *TBG*, 67 (1927):172–215.
7. F. H. van Naerssen, "Ancient Javanese recording of the past," *Arts, The Journal of the Sydney University Arts Association*, 5 (1968):30–46.

sawah, the irrigated rice field, would have required a complicated system of irrigation and therefore had to be based on the cooperation of several communities or *wanuas*, all dependent on the same river and its tributaries. Such an irrigation system obviously needed a head whose authority reached beyond a single *wanua*. The head of a *wanua* could have extended his power over a federation of *wanuas* and come to be considered the *raka* or "older brother" of the *rāmas* of the *wanuas*. It was essential that the *raka* had the right to dispose of the produce and labour to fulfil his function properly. Hence he became the sovereign of the federation. Possibly, with the appearance of the sovereign *raka*, a consumer class developed and shared rule with the *raka*, who now lived in a central *kraton*.

The social structure just before the Hindu-Javanese period therefore consisted of two main strata: the *wanuas*, each with its own *rāma*, and the *kratons* of the *rakas*. The former functioned as producers and the latter as consumers, but also as administrators and distributors of goods and services. There was an equilibrium between the power of the *wanuas* and that of the *kratons*; each depended on the other.

In this social structure of autochthonous Javanese origin a new social order emerged during the earliest Hindu-Javanese period. A *raka* might then be given a high-sounding title of foreign origin, which would give him a preponderant position measured first in status and then gradually also in power. This title was *"mahārāja."*[8]

What made the *mahārāja*'s position vulnerable was the fact that, because he himself was a *raka*, he had to compete with rival *rakas* who constituted a threat to his *kraton*. His unique position, his royal and even divine nature, needed legitimizing and, once legitimized, needed to be constantly confirmed and reinforced by aesthetic and religious display. Priests, literati, and artists were indispensable to a *kraton*; a magnificent display was needed in order to maintain its prestige and aura of divine majesty.[9]

Before proceeding with my argument, I should mention that I have gained support in my polykraton concept of the Hindu-Javanese period from Boechari, who, dealing with the changes in the administrative system during the Hindu-Javanese period, has written: "What remained unchanged during the whole period was that there never had been a centralised government. The kingdom was divided into a number of autonomous areas, governed by *rakais* or *rakryans*. . . . Those regional heads could act independently from the king."[10]

8. F. H. van Naerssen, "Some Aspects of the Hindu-Javanese Kraton," *Journal of the Oriental Society of Australia*, 2 (1963):14–19.

9. Probably for the first time by the *gurus* of the Çailendra dynasty. F. H. van Naerssen, "The Çailendra interregnum," in *India Antiqua: A Volume of Oriental Studies Presented . . . to Jean Philippe Vogel* (Leiden, 1947), pp. 249–253.

10. Boechari, "A Preliminary Note on the Study of the Old-Javanese Civil Administration," *Madjalah ilmu-ilmu sastra Indonesia*, I, 2 (1963):122–133.

A question, however, arises: how far could the *rakas* act independently, and was their independence acknowledged by the king? It seems to me that, although the centralizing process was under way during the course of the Hindu-Javanese period, every time there was a break in the continuity of a dynasty other rulers would seize the opportunity to gain their independence, and great efforts were made to subdue them. For instance, King Airlangga had to fight several "disloyal rulers" before he succeeded in rebuilding his predecessor's realm. Similarly, the history of early Majapahit is characterized by struggles with disaffected members of the landed gentry. And the downfall of this last Hindu-Javanese empire was in the first instance effected by its vassals in the coastal areas, who took advantage of the proselytizing zeal of recently-introduced Islam. Many other instances from historical sources indicate the potential readiness of the landed gentry to seize independence at the expense of the unstable sovereignty of the main Hindu-Javanese *kraton*.

My argument now leads me to the second part of the quotation from Professor Hall's book with which this essay began. The royal and divine nature of the king needed to be confirmed by a magnificent display. The question now is: how were the means acquired to erect the buildings and everything else that formed part of such a display?

We have seen that the ruler has the disposal of part of the produce and labour of the *wanua* people. The part due to him is called in the inscriptions *bwat haji*.[11] Another important institution was that of *anugraha* (literally, "favour," "grant"). Of course a ruler could renounce the *bwat haji* which he was entitled to take from the *wanuas* in favour of a monastery or community or even a person. He could also declare a community *swatantra*, or autonomous, and exempt from tribute.

Thus, by means of *anugraha* the ruler enabled sanctuaries to be built and supported existing ones. These and other examples can be seen in the inscriptions as objects of the ruler's *anugraha* or grant.

In investigating the origin and development of the *anugraha* institution, our initial focus will be the autochthonous and sacrosanct communities which we find mentioned in the Old Javanese epigraphs and literature as recollections from earlier periods but to a greater or less degree subject to the influence of Hindu culture. Among these old religious communities the Ḍihyang (Mountain of the Gods) was famous during the Hindu-Javanese period.

The Dieng plateau, as this area is named today, is situated about 6,500 feet above sea level. Its central part is formed by the floor of a dead

---

11. *Bwat haji* has the general meaning of "tribute due to the ruler." *Dṛwya haji* (literally, "properties of the ruler") probably means specifically the products due to the ruler as tribute.

volcano, through which a rivulet, the Kali Tulis, runs. This stream has its source a few miles north of the crater. Flowing southwards, it breaks through the southern rim of the crater and eventually becomes one of Java's biggest rivers, the Serayu. The water of this river is, one can imagine, "purified" at its source by flowing through the heart of the "Mountain of the Gods," where today the ruins of about a hundred buildings are found. One can also say, though more prosaically, that the river has been purified by the sulphur gases of the solvatara in the neighbourhood.

From prehistoric times, and long before Hindu culture infiltrated the island of Java, this isolated place in the upper regions of the mountains, chilly and covered by a blanket of mist during part of the day, must have been sacrosanct. Among other neolithic remains, a bronze kettle-drum has been found. The geophysical peculiarities of the region must always have impressed people. When Hinduism was introduced, the Çiwa religion gradually took over from nature worship.

The Dieng plateau during its heyday, from about the sixth to the tenth century, was the site of a Çiwaite temple town. Besides the numerous temples, there were dwelling places for the priests, their servants, and their slaves. From inscriptions we learn that this religious community was maintained by endowments and gifts from faithful rulers and pilgrims; some of the pilgrims even came from overseas.

In an inscription found on the Dieng,[12] we read that in A.D. 809 a *pamgat tiga* (? the "three *pamgats*") made a donation of several domestic utensils, including four rice-cooking pots and lamps. Moreover, free estates are enumerated as being situated at places known from other inscriptions. Probably the products of these lands, their *bwat haji*, were channelled to the Ḍihyang sanctuary by their respective *rakas*.

An interesting inscription, dated A.D. 827, gives us the name of a donor: Ḍang Pu Hawang Gĕlis and his wife.[13] He was a sea captain and trader from abroad. His gifts consisted of domestic utensils.

Another inscription, undated and not even mentioning a donor, is an inventory of the "properties of the God" (*dewadrawya*): twenty slaves, ten buffaloes, two beanfields, two bathing places, gold, mirrors, ivory combs, and so forth. The inscription ends with the words "Ika teja ḍanghyyang," which can be translated in all probability as "This is the wealth [literally, "glory"] of the deified ancestors."[14]

12. N. J. Krom, ed., "Oud-Javaansche Oorkonden Nagelaten Transcripties van wijlen Dr. J. L. A. Brandes" (hereafter OJO), *VBG*, 60 (1913), no. 11. According to R. Goris, "De inscriptie van Koeboreran Tjandi," *TBG*, 70 (1930):160, this inscription is dated A.D. 787.

13. L. C. Damais, "Études sino-indonésiennes," *BEFEO*, 50 (1960):25–29.

14. Cf. W. F. Stutterheim, "Oude gewichten in het Museum," *TBG*, 78 (1938):118–120. Stutterheim translated *ḍanghyang* as "voorouder(s)" or "ancestor(s)."

Names of famous religious foundations, or *dharmas*, survived several dynasties. Besides the Ḍihyang, there were, for example: Salingsingan, Wulusan, Tigangrat, Raja, Jambi, Airbulang, Airasih, and Mangulihi. These foundations are known in much later times and are even mentioned in a manuscript, the Ṛṣicāsana.[15]

The inscriptions tell us, for example, that in 869[16] and in 874[17] free estates were demarcated in favour of the *dharma* of Salingsingan; Tigangrat, Raja, and Jambi are mentioned together in an inscription of A.D. 877[18] and in other inscriptions;[19] Airasih is known from several inscriptions of east Java;[20] Mangulihi is mentioned in several inscriptions, together with other well-known *dharmas*.[21]

I have to limit myself to these few examples, which will give the reader an impression of the important place occupied by the religious foundation in the early Central Javanese period. The "divine household" of the God,[22] administered by the priests (*pitāmahās*), was made possible by the endowments and grants of its devotees, in the first instance the rulers (*rakas*). The *rakas* had converted the *bwat haji*, or tribute to the ruler, into tribute to the god, the *bwat hyang*, as it is sometimes appropriately named. In return they secured an elevation of their status.[23]

Different in origin were the *dharmas* of deified rulers. The first certain evidence of the *kraton* custom of identifying a once-living person with a god is found in an inscription in which a "Çrī Mahārāja sang lumah ing Pastika" (His Majesty the King who is buried in Pastika) is also named "sang Dewata Pastika" (the God of Pastika). Although this inscription is of A.D. 919,[24] we are acquainted with the "God of Pastika" from earlier epigraphs.[25] By the end of the ninth century not only Çrī Mahārāja Rakai

15. Cf. T. G. Th. Pigeaud, *Java in the 14th Century*, IV (The Hague, 1962), 373. Perhaps Pigeaud overlooked the epigraphical material when he discussed this passage of the Ṛṣiçāsana and gave an etymological explanation.

16. L. C. Damais, "Études d'épigraphie indonésienne, III," *BEFEO*, 46 (1952):36–37, no. 30.

17. *Ibid.*, no. 35.

18. *Ibid.*, no. 40. About Salingsingan in connection with another well-known free estate, Çri Manggala, see W. F. Stutterheim, "Beschreven lingga van Krapjak," *TBG*, 74 (1934):85–93.

19. Damais, "Études d'épigraphie indonésienne, III," pp. 42–43, no. 64.

20. OJO, 77, p. 186, 21. A *pamgĕt ing Airasih* is mentioned in an inscription of Kṛtanāgara's time. See F. H. van Naerssen, "Oudjavaansche oorkonden in Duitsche en Deensche verzamelingen" (Amsterdam, 1941), pp. 21 and 37–38. I plan to publish this stencilled thesis.

21. For example, Tigangrat in the inscriptions dealing with Pastika, discussed below.

22. For example, in the inscriptions dealing with Pastika; see below.

23. Cf. Gordon Childe, *What Happened in History*, 2d ed., rev. (Harmondsworth, England, 1964), p. 103.

24. Damais, "Études d'épigraphie indonésiennes, III," no. 98.

25. In 881 (30 July) "that was the date of the free-estate of the God of Pastika" (Damais, *ibid.*, no. 57). In 887 "the spouse of the God of Pastika demarcated a free-estate" (*ibid.*, no. 61).

Kayuwangi but apparently several other *rakas* joined in grants to the *dharma* of Pastika.[26]

The conception of the god-king may have existed from the beginning of the Hindu-Javanese period or even earlier. It seems to have developed, however, when the centralizing process of the Hindu-Javanese *kraton* got under way. The following evidence indicates this development.

In most of the *praçāstis* (land grants) there is a section in which witnesses of the solemn declaration of the founding of a free estate are invoked; the witnesses are the North, the South, the East, the West, the Zenith, the Nadir, the Sun and the Moon, as well as the gods Wiṣṇu, Brahma, Çiwa, Haricandana, and others. In an inscription of King Balitung of 907[27] this formula ends with an enumeration of the *rahyangta rumuhun* of the kingdom, the "previous gods," followed by the names of King Balitung's predecessors. In later inscriptions no individual names are mentioned, but the formula sometimes includes *dewata prasiddha*, "the accomplished gods" who protect the kingdom.

Finally, the apotheosis of the god-king becomes evident from the iconography of the Singhasari-Majapahit period. The *chandis*, or monumental tombs in which the kings of this period were portrayed in stone as gods, are well known. The veneration of the king as a god (Wiṣṇu, Çiwa, Çiwa-Buddha) distinguishes itself as a *kraton* institution. But the old *dharmas* of the autochthonous religion, which had been subject to some influence from Hinduism, were also supervised by the *kraton*.

The Nāgarakṛtāgama[28] makes a clear distinction between royal *dharmas* (*dharma haji*) and autonomous *dharmas* (*dharma swatantra* or *dharma lepas*). Documents such as the Pūrwādhigama are handbooks for the Çiwaite clergy, who, together with the Buddhist clergy, were represented in the *kraton* administration during the Singhasari-Majapahit period.[29]

Based upon the *bwat haji*, the tribute to the ruler which had its roots in pre-Hindu times, the *anugraha* institution became an intrinsic component of the social and economic structure of the Hindu-Javanese agrarian society. It was even an essential stimulus for the production and distribution of goods, and it was used by the rulers in this society in order to maintain the interdependent relationship between the Hinduized *kraton* and the autochthonous communities, the *wanuas*.

26. *Ibid.*, nos. 46 and 58.

27. Stutterheim, "Een belangrijke oorkonde uit de Kedoe," *TBG*, 67 (1927):172–215.

28. Pigeaud, I-V (The Hague, 1960–1963).

29. F. H. van Naerssen, "The Aṣṭadaçavyavahāra in Old Javanese," *JGIS*, 15 (1956):111–132; translated from the original Dutch article in *BKI*, 100 (1941):357–376. Cf. pp. 112–113, where I point out that this document is drawn up in the form of a *praçasti* from the time of Majapahit.

It seems to me that the possibility of creating such a social and economic link was the basic reason for the existence of the Hindu-Javanese agrarian *kraton*.[30]

30. For a maritime *kedatuan* such as Çrīwijaya, creating and maintaining a link with the surrounding autochthonous communities of the sea nomads of the Riouw-Lingga and Banka-Billiton areas, although different in nature, were also of prominent importance, as I pointed out in my chapter "The Economic and Administrative History of Indonesia" to appear in the *Handbuch der Orientalistik*.

Islam in Southeast Asia:
Problems of Perspective

A. H. JOHNS

The Australian National University

Professor Hall has made impressive contributions to history in his own right, and trained and inspired many generations of students. His lasting influence can be epitomized under two heads: his bold use of the term Southeast Asia as a historical category, exemplified in his *History of South-East Asia*,[1] still *the* standard work on the history of the region, and his exposure of the "Eurocentric" assumptions vitiating much Western writing about Asia. The former provided a focus that had previously been missing for a part of the world known only vaguely in Europe; to the newly established or independent states of the area, such as Indonesia and Burma, it provided a sense of regional community. The latter presented a challenge to historians concerned with the area, and the forgotten perspectives it offered were a powerful stimulus to a new generation of scholars. For Hall's *History of South-East Asia* was published at a time when the concept of area studies, understood "as a new integration of social sciences and cultural linguistic studies focused primarily upon the problems of specific parts of the modern world" was establishing itself, and served to underpin such studies as they concerned Southeast Asia, itself a major testing ground for the new concept.

Southeast Asia is indeed an area readily amenable to geographical classification, and anthropologists have not found it difficult to recognize within its boundaries many common cultural and ethnic characteristics which precede Indic, Chinese, and other cultural overlays.[2] Historians, however, attempting to use their discipline as a means better to understand the past of the region, even with the benefit of Hall's massive pioneering work, have found that the disparate and discontinuous nature of the sources available to them present serious problems of methodology to say the least. In many cases the solution has been to write on a specific area of Southeast Asia at a particular time which for the purposes of the investigator has the

---

1. D. G. E. Hall, *A History of South-East Asia* (London, 1955).
2. See Charles A. Fisher, "A View of Southeast Asia," *Southeast Asia*, 1, 1–2 (1971):11.

necessary spatial and temporal continuities to sustain a narrative, and then to call it Southeast Asian, relegating the focus of attention to the equivalent of "small print." This same disparateness and discontinuity in source material has likewise made the avoidance of Eurocentricity more easily said than done, particularly during the "European" period, since the scope of the unit to be treated and the type of sources then available coincided with the expectations of the European historian concerning area of study and sources. Materials for the internal history of the territories under European rule remained disparate, discontinuous, and intractable.[3]

Nevertheless "Eurocentric" served to pinpoint the dissatisfaction of Asians with narratives of their past written by foreigners, which focussed on the activities of the colonial powers, leaving the indigenous peoples either as rebels or shadows in the background. As a response, national histories of the new states appeared which, because they were nationalistic, could appear absolved of Eurocentrism.

Historians, however, are at the mercy not only of the attitudes and prejudices of the times in which they live, but even of its nomenclatures. The new nations have established themselves universally in a world of mass communications; they participate in the affairs of the United Nations, and they play the role in the modern world which is their right. In terms of the modern world their names stand on equal terms with those of the older nations, but to assume that these names stand for continuing traditions which have any historical reality is to misunderstand the processes of the past. Such expressions, then, as "a history of Indonesian Islam" have a limited use; even a sophistication such as "a history of Islam in what is now Indonesia" is in a very real sense begging the question. Does it mean a view of the past of Islam in the area that is now Indonesia seen through the eyes of the nationally self-conscious contemporary Indonesian, with all the limitations and distortions implicit in this standpoint? Does it mean a study of the beginnings of Islam in what is now Indonesia, the better to understand the various faces of Islam in Indonesia today? Or does it mean a study of the past of religion and society in Islamized Southeast Asia without reference to present-day political constructs and their frontiers? Unfortunately, the first of the these three alternatives has proved the most alluring, and Indonesian and foreign scholars alike have yielded to its seductions.

3. A clear statement of the difficulties of the historian in exorcising Eurocentrism is to be found in J. Bastin, *The Study of Modern Southeast Asian History* (Kuala Lumpur, 1959). An excellent example of the use of the era of European power as a frame of reference in which to organize typologies of indigenous response to foreign rule is J. Bastin and H. J. Benda, *A History of Modern Southeast Asia* (Englewood Cliffs, N.J., 1968). A valuable theoretical discussion is provided by J. R. W. Smail, "On the Possibility of an Autonomous History of Modern Southeast Asia," *JSEAH*, 2, 2 (1961):72–102.

It is with justice, then, that Soedjatmoko exclaims: "In what has hitherto been presented as Indonesian history . . . there is no coherent body, no single focal point of illumination, no particular frame of reference,"[4] and this is precisely the point. In the past of Southeast Asia there is no such entity, either in character or extent, as that designated by the modern term "Indonesia." There is thus no coherent body, no single point of illumination, no particular frame of reference in Indonesian history simply because before the beginning of the twentieth century when Dutch colonial rule reached its apogee there was nothing remotely comparable to "Indonesia."

If the concept of nation-states may not validly be used to provide a central core to which data from the past may be related, what are the alternatives? Southeast Asia is not coextensive with any great culture, whether Sinic, Indic, or Islamic, although each of these cultures has made an imprint on areas of the region; such a tradition in itself, then, cannot serve as a central core. Since the region consists mainly of peasant societies, literary documentation is sparse, although within limits archaeology can testify in lieu of written evidence. The failure of any Southeast Asian state to bring the whole isthmian tract under its rule[5] means that there is no single major kingdom or centre of authority upon which a narrative can be based. Essentially, then, we are left looking for a focus, a fundamental perspective.

The difficulties in finding such a historical perspective should not be underestimated. History writing presents special difficulties when the framework of documentation associated with urban settlements and centres of authority is absent. Just any urban settlement will not do. It must be one in which secular activities have a certain autonomy, and in which the preservation of written records has a key role in the maintenance and administration of the state and its dependencies. Almost by definition, these conditions did not hold in Southeast Asia (leaving Sinicized Indochina out of the discussion at this stage). The European scholar, as a result of his intellectual formation and experience of Western nation-states, is likely to perceive the past of the various Southeast Asian nations in the same way. Conditioned by the structure and source materials of European history to recognize certain types of spatial and temporal continuity, he expects to find them in Southeast Asia, and in consequence he even sees them where they do not exist and writes his history as if they did. The Western-trained Southeast Asian scholar, when he writes his national history, may see them

4. Soedjatmoko has expressed this view on various occasions. In Soedjatmoko (ed.), *An Introduction to Indonesian Historiography* (Ithaca, 1965), p. xii, he remarks, "There is no continuous historical narrative nor is there any central point of vision."

5. Paul Wheatley, *The Golden Khersonese* (Kuala Lumpur, 1961), p. 326.

too: on the one hand because his European training has conditioned him to expect them, on the other because his consciousness as a citizen of a modern nation-state leads him to feel that such continuities must be there.

Of course, as suggested earlier, certain generalizations are possible. From the geographer one can learn the configuration of mountain, river, forest, fertile plain, and swamp, the disposition of potential harbours and the role of the monsoons; from the anthropologist, types of social structure and ethnic relationships; and from the linguist, the spread and distribution of language families—all adding up to a picture of an interrelated network of peoples and language groups extending from continental Southeast Asia across the Pacific as far as Easter Island. For much of this area and many of these peoples, both the archaeologist and the modern historian may find material abounding. For the space of time between, however, there is a dearth. Yet at certain focal points in Southeast Asia from about the beginning of the Christian era it is possible to detect something new to the region, something erratic and short-lived but at times marvellously creative: the appearance of urban settlements, the generation of towns.[6] It must be stressed that it is this birth of urbanization that set in train the spread of Brahmanization across the Indian Ocean and the Bay of Bengal. Although this process never created Southeast Asian counterparts to the great urban civilizations of China and the Indian subcontinent, it effectively distinguished the region from the purely folk traditions of Oceania. The history of Southeast Asia, then, is largely the history of city-states, never far removed from their peasant base and richly permeated by the ethos and ethic of the peasant substrate, no matter how complex or Brahmanized became the ceremonial centre, the heart of the inland concentrations of population, or how important the role of international trade at coastal settlements. Thus the network of extended family relationships characteristic of peasant family structures continued to link town dwellers to the countryside and served to spread, dilute, and restructure elements of the urban culture in ever widening circles. What in the city was largely the possession of a community sharing the theology and organization of a world religion was, in the hinterland, absorbed into the village systems that in Islamic times were to be known as *adat*, and understood and practised, insofar as they were understood and practised, as elements of *adat*.

It may well be, then, that some of the problems of understanding the past of Southeast Asia can be elucidated through the use of a basic perspective of this kind. Because of the "exceptional focality with severe internal fragmentation" of the region, as Fisher puts it,[7] no starting point larger than the city-state is viable, and no unit larger than the city-state or the

6. Paul Wheatley, *The Pivot of the Four Quarters* (Edinburgh, 1971), pp. 248 ff.
7. *Loc cit.*

occasional federation of city-states appeared until the establishment of European power in the region. And the use of a broader framework becomes feasible only with the gradual extension of European power, which rendered possible the relating of an increasing area—the Dutch Colonial Empire, for example—to a single centre of authority, which provided its own documentation of this development. At the same time, it must be admitted that from these city-states one can learn not so much the personal history of rulers and ruled as the character of certain processes of the establishment of centres of trade or ceremonial complexes, of the extension and contraction of areas of influence, of the dissemination of religious ideas and cult practices.

Because these city-states were discrete, appearing in response to particular combinations of needs and circumstances that might cease to exist or might be better met elsewhere, they are discontinuous and often short-lived. With the decline of a state its population was gradually reabsorbed by the peasant system just as its monuments were covered up by the forest to decay undisturbed, and its literary heritage, if any, vanished.

This surely is the typology of the urban past of Southeast Asia, so that to be precise we should speak not so much of a history of Southeast Asia as of the histories of city-states in Southeast Asia, at least up to the modern period, nevertheless admitting that, although spatially and temporally discontinuous, they shared many cultural traits resulting from their generation in response to similar factors, similarities in environment, and the shared ethnic characteristics of their peoples.

Often their achievement was related to the intensity and length of contact with—for want of a better word—the outside world. It is clear from a study of the temple complexes of central Java, for example, that the Hindu-Buddhist iconography is eclectic, that waves of Indian influence are to be discerned, that periods and styles are combined, and that there is not to be discovered a steady line of growth and development.

Whereas details of relations between Javanese inland states and Indian centres of culture are simply unknown, it cannot be assumed that any relationship was constant in its intensity. And although it may be argued that the thirteenth and fourteenth centuries show a recrudescence of Javanese culture, breaking through its Indic overlay, it should be stressed that this can equally be seen as a reversion to more popular, peasant-type conceptualizations of Indian cultural elements. There are major changes in architectural style, although there appears no evidence of any technical advance on work done five hundred years earlier. In fact, it is not perhaps being unduly relativistic to point out the crudity of the stylizations of bas-reliefs of the Rama story on the East Javanese Panataran temple complex near Blitar and the shallowness of the engraving compared with those of the Prambanan complex. While the former is more Javanese, there is certainly evidence of cultural loss.

The size, importance, and area of authority of these city-states varied. Of some we know little but the name; of even the more outstanding such as Sriwijaya, even the fact of its existence was not rediscovered until the work of Cœdès in the 1920's. It is therefore all the more necessary not to exaggerate the importance of any particular city-state, which only held a degree of primacy in relation to others and rarely if ever exercised direct authority. On purely typological grounds, then, there is reason not to reject too hastily C. C. Berg's scaling down of the area of authority attributed to the "empire" of Majapahit. Perhaps in all discussions of this period the word "empire" is best avoided, suggesting as it does the bureaucratic structure and system of government of the British Empire in its heyday.

This framework, I suggest, remains valid for a discussion of Islamization of Southeast Asia. Islam is an urban religion, and Islamic civilization is essentially an urban (and largely middle-class) civilization. The point has been frequently made, by Montgomery Watt for example, who points out that no peasant religion could have tolerated the Islamic calender of twelve lunar months or 354 days for a single year.[8] The coming of Islam to Southeast Asia, then, is another chapter in the story of the generation of city-states noted in the spread of Brahmanization to Southeast Asia.

Much has been written on the origins of Islamization in Southeast Asia, usually beginning with Pasai and other port towns along the northeast coast of Sumatra. Little is known of their early history, no more than is known of the beginnings of Islamic port towns along the north coast of Java. This is not the place or the occasion to discuss possible qualitative differences between these Muslim port cities and their non-Muslim predecessors on the one hand, or between them and the inland sacral centres such as Majapahit on the other, although it may be argued that the Islamic ethos brought about an increased measure of autonomy in secular activities. Be this as it may, there is no denying the vigorous role of secular and mercantile activity in the Islamic city as known in the heartlands of Islam, whether in the ports or in inland staging centres on traffic arteries or intersections.

With the coming of Islam to the city-state world of Southeast Asia, then, is it prudent to say that Muslim city-state equals Islamic city? Unfortunately, social historians of Islam do not give much attention to developments in our region, and the excellent collection of papers on the Islamic city edited by A. H. Hourani and S. M. Stern makes no reference to Southeast Asia.[9]

8. W. Montgomery Watt, *Islamic Surveys*, IV (Edinburgh, 1965), 49.
9. A. H. Hourani and S. M. Stern (eds.), *The Islamic City* (Oxford, 1970).

In his introductory chapter,[10] Hourani constructs an ideal type of Islamic city, at the same time pointing out that it cannot be assumed that urban life in regions as diverse as Spain, Egypt, Syria, Central Asia, Iraq, Iran, and the Indian subcontinent—diverse in soil, climate, inheritance, and involvement in various commerical systems—should have taken the same form, and warning that the uneven distribution of research on the Islamic city in these widely differing regions creates the danger of imposing inappropriate models. The ideal type he proposes includes five components which might be common to many Islamic cities, although individually perhaps not exclusive to any one of them or necessarily characteristic of Islam.

These components are: a citadel or defence work; a royal city or quarter comprising the royal residence, administrative offices, and accommodation for the ruler's personal troops; a central urban complex with mosques, religious schools, and markets, with special places assigned for main groups of craftsmen or traders and the homes of the principal merchant and religious bourgeoisie; a "core" of residential quarters divided among resident foreign ethnic groups and religious minorities that enjoyed a degree of autonomy; and finally the outer quarters of "suburbs," where resided recent immigrants and temporary visitors to the city.[11]

There is nothing in this model irreconcilable with what we know, which is often little enough, of the Islamic port towns of Java and Sumatra already referred to or the later city-states of Malacca, Acheh, or Makassar. In each of them the presence of a fortress, royal compound, mosque and associated schools, commerical area, and the division of the residential parts of the city into quarters on the basis of ethnic groups—the kampong China, kampong Kling, kampong Java, and the like, each under its own captain—is sufficient to show that the concept of an "Islamic city" is a useful one and that, in any overall study of the Islamic city, such city-states deserve a place.

Such coastal city-states were centres for the diffusion of Islamic ideas to the peasant interior by means of kinship systems similar to those which had served to diffuse elements of Indic culture, adding a further colouring to the corpus of *adat* (a continually evolving code) already tinctured with Hindu-Buddhist beliefs. Though urban and peasant systems represent points on a continuum rather than mutually exclusive and alternative ways of life, the peasant end of the continuum is less likely to be intensely Islamic and more likely to reveal different levels of ideological tincture than the urban end.

The two most important Islamic city-states in the Malay world between

10. *Ibid.*, pp. 9–24.
11. *Ibid.*, pp. 21–23.

the fifteenth and seventeenth centuries are Malacca and Acheh, and these approximate closely in structure and function to Hourani's model. There is a large body of writing in Portuguese relating to Malacca, and an even larger body of material in various languages relating to Acheh. To each state likewise can be attributed a significant corpus of writing in Malay. The most comprehensive account of this corpus is given in Sir Richard Winstedt's *A History of Classical Malay Literature*.[12] Unfortunately, although the work contains a wealth of material not duplicated elsewhere, the assumptions and expectations which have determined its structure are analogous to those which bedevil Southeast Asian history generally: that Malay is an undifferentiated category, that it has a classical period, in which is to be defined a golden age, that it is susceptible of a linear historical treatment, and so on. A glance at the table of contents shows that a historical frame of reference cannot be maintained. Since there is little in much Malay writing to indicate a date of composition, Winstedt is forced to use cultural content and genre as guides to periodization, and on this basis he assigns works to a Hindu, Transitional or Muslim period, regarding the Malacca sultanate (1400–1511) as the central "core" to which all that is worthwhile in Malay letters can be related.[13]

A little reflection reveals what has gone wrong. The same types of temporal and spatial discontinuity are apparent in Malay letters as in the pasts of various Malay city-states, whether on the Malay Peninsula, Sumatra, or Borneo. Just as the peasant base of the urban centres absorbed successive cultural tinctures, and not in uniform proportions or in any particular distribution or consistency, so the varying proportions of Islamic or Hinduistic material in a manuscript which may date at the oldest from the eighteenth century may tell us something about the society in which the story was popular, but they can tell nothing about its position on a temporal continuum indicated by the terms Hindu-Transition-Islamic because of the continuing presence of elements of both these and earlier traditions in differing strata of society.

Accordingly, just as in our survey of the past of the region we found it necessary to avoid broad categories and to distinguish between city-states and the peasant background out of which they rose (and into which they were reabsorbed), so it is necessary to distinguish between works which can be ascribed to a court or bourgeoisie and those which belong to the folk tradition and at one stage or another were set down in written form; the latter require treatment and study rather different from that given to literature proper, although both may spring from the same cultural matrix. Such an amputation from the received body of Malay literature may appear

12. *JMBRAS*, 31, 3 (1958).
13. *Ibid.*, pp. 129–132, 141, 152, and passim.

radical, but it is necessary if we are to attempt to discover a clearer profile of Malay intellectual and literary life. The procedure in many cases is simple, but it reveals important perspectives that have often been over-looked. Every textbook tells us that Malay literature, at least until the time of Islam, is anonymous. But insofar as it is folk literature, of course it is anonymous, whether before Islam or after. And it is anonymous because it is folk literature, not because it is Malay. By the same token, if the first works in Malay to which we can ascribe an author are Islamic, this once again is not because they are Malay but because they are Islamic; they hail from an Islamic city-state in which the various components of the Muslim city exist in a particular constellation and the activities of the 'ulamā' play a significant role. And in Islamic learning, the foundations of every discipline are the authority on which any opinion or doctrine is based and its transmission.

A study of that body of writings which can be definitely associated with urban life in the Malay world reveals two foci of literary activity. In the first place there is the court. Under its aegis "chronicles" were compiled to legitimize the dynasty, record its family tree, and preserve its values and mores for the edification and example of later generations; and its library included stories of heroes, men of righteousness of before and after the call of the Prophet Muhammad, to be read as models of courage in times of crisis and around which hung an aura of sanctity, and *belles lettres* of various sorts.

Of a Malaccan court heritage, if heritage is not too grandiose a word, there is very little that remains directly, and not all that Winstedt thought derived from the Malaccan period is necessarily from Malacca. Even the Raffles manuscript of the *Sejarah Melayu*, the original text of which Winstedt believed dated from 1535, in fact is probably not earlier than 1612 and was compiled in Johore.[14] But if it presents a reliable picture of the cultural bric-a-brac extant a century earlier in a different place, then the Malacca court library could have included a version of the Alexander romance and epics of the heroes of Islamic tradition such as Muhammad Hanafiyyah and Amir Hamzah.[15]

In the second place there is the community of teachers of religion, the 'ulamā', to whose activities can be attributed the wide range of Muslim learning which became known in the Malay world. The exposition and administration of Islamic law, whether it concerns religious duties or the legal formulation of trade contracts, is a complicated but necessary chore in any Muslim society. Though we know little of the majority of these 'ulamā' as individuals, as a class we know they existed and had a function

14. R. Roolvink, "The Variant Versions of the Malay Annals," *BkI*, CXXIII, 3 (1967):311.
15. Winstedt, pp. 72–73.

and social disposition at least approximate to that of the '*ulamā*' in Hourani's model.

The great lacuna, of course, is in our knowledge of the bureaucratic processes of the state and details of business contracts and procedures. We lack a Malaccan or Achehnese equivalent of the Cairo Geniza, with its massive collection of trade contracts, marriage agreements, petitions to authorities, private letters, and even fragments of literary works, between the tenth and thirteenth centuries A.D.[16] Little of this kind of material survives except for a few blank forms for the manumission of slaves.

We are thus forced into a world of speculation. Yet there is one work which might be attributable to a Malaccan bourgeoisie, although later copies of it have been preserved only in court libraries. I refer to the *Hikayat Bayan Budiman* (Tale of the Wise Parrot), a fragment of which, now preserved at the Bodleian Library, may have found its way to Europe as early as 1598.[17]

It is perhaps the most remarkable work in old Malay secular literature. Although a rendering of a Persian work, there is nothing of "translationese" in the style: it is limpid and polished. The rhythmic character of its prose probably derives from the oral tradition, and the brief introduction setting out the parents and birth of the hero could reflect expectations conditioned by folklore, but it is none the less a work of considerable sophistication. A "miraculous" element such as the prescience of the parrot is used simply as a literary convention, not as a spectacle of wonder to hold interest. The setting is completely bourgeois: in the first demonstration of his wisdom, the parrot gives his master a business tip that enables him to buy up all the spikenard in Iran three days before a caravan arrives desirous of just this commodity, and thus to make a huge profit. The work shows a delicious irony in its asides at the morals of royalty and clergy, and its psychological insights are superb. One would expect it to be the property of a wealthy merchant family used to the finer things of life. One swallow, however, does not make a summer, and the vision of a wealthy Malaccan class of the third estate passing its leisure in the savouring of such works must be left as an alluring hypothesis.

That Acheh should be so often presented simply as a successor state to Malacca is another example of the distortions that occur when the past of Southeast Asia is viewed through the glasses of divisions created by the colonial powers. Malacca looms much larger in the past of twentieth-century Malaysia than Acheh in that of Indonesia, and thus it has a correspondingly greater role to play in the mythology of a modern nation. Yet in the seventeenth-century polity of city-states Acheh is not only much

---

16. S. D. Goitein, *Studies in Islamic History and Institutions* (Leiden, 1966), pp. 279–294.
17. Winstedt, pp. 95–98.

better known but on all available evidence it appears to have been the more important of the two, with a wider range of international relations and a far more clearly articulated religious intellectual life. It seems to have been a centre where a vigorous, intensely Muslim maritime kingdom, self-sustaining in trade as in religious life, could have developed. The number of religious works produced under its aegis, whether original or translations, is striking by Malay standards. Its role as gateway to the holy land for the *jawi*[18] pilgrims and students bound for Mecca, Medina, and centres of learning in Egypt and other parts of the Ottoman empire kept it in close contact with other Muslim port cities in the archipelago and made it a natural centre for an *'ulamā'*-bourgeoisie axis. Once again one can but hypothesize on the basis of Hourani's model, for only snippets of information are available. Of religious teachers, only four are relatively well known to us: Hamzah Pansūrī, (d. c. 1600), Shams al-Dīn (d. 1630), al-Rānīrī (d. 1657) and 'Abd al-Ra'ūf (d. 1690). Of al-Rānīrī it should be noted that he was a Gujerati scholar and prolific writer who won the favour of Sultan Iskandar Thani of Acheh in 1637 and led a witch hunt against the mystical doctrines of Hamzah Pansūrī and Shams al-Dīn.[19] Their works add up to a significant corpus of religious writing, which, although modest by Middle Eastern standards, gives some picture of the intellectual life of the city, its enthusiasms, shibboleths, and achievements, and provides a reference point for much transmission of learning to centres of Islam in other parts of the archipelago. While acknowledging this, one should be very cautious in assuming a linear development in Islam between one point and another. Rather, the same discrete character of the city-states of Southeast Asia is paralleled by autonomy and diversity in the distributions of emphases in their cultural and religious life. The point needs to be stressed since the expectations of Western historiography exert a kind of pressure to formulate generalizations based on larger units which appear to make sense yet somehow succeed only in obscuring the character of Islamization. Such a generalization, for example, is van Nieuwenhuijze's remark that Shams al-Dīn's mysticism in more than one respect "stands midway between the Indian and Javanese forms of Islamic mysticism."[20] It is simply not possible to plot a line of development between the forms of Indian and Javanese mysticism on which Shams al-Dīn can be allocated a place. The most that can be done is to compare his mysticism with that of a particular place in Java or the Indian subcontinent at a particular time. Neither India nor Java is a meaningful term in this context.

18. *Jawi* is the term used in Mecca for all pilgrims from the Malay world. It is both sufficiently specific and sufficiently general for our purposes.

19. Winstedt, pp. 113–122.

20. C. A. O. van Nieuwenhuijze, *Samsu'l-Dīn van Pasai* (Leiden, 1945), p. 239.

Islamic writing in Malay has not had a very good press. Winstedt complains bitterly about what he alleges to be the bad influence of the Arabic idiom on Malay and what he considers frequently unintelligible translations from Arabic in the tradition of *kitab* writing generally.[21] Hooykaas virtually excludes Muslim writing from his book *Over Maleis Literatuur* on the grounds that it is "more generally Islamic than Malay."[22]

In recent years Malay writing has been treated less patronizingly and with more insight.[23] The sad fact remains, however, that among Islamologists, Arabic religious writing of the seventeenth century does not have a good name, its authors being overlooked or regarded merely as transmitters of ideas better formulated and expressed elsewhere. This has two unfortunate consequences. The first is that the trained Islamologist is likely to regard Malay Muslim writing of the seventeenth century as at the lowest rank of a pecking order in a classification already well down on everyone's list. The second is that very little research has been done on the level of scholarship and writings of the Middle Eastern scholars under whom the *jawi* studied. The result is that the study of such Malay works has in great measure had to be the undertaken without that detailed study of the lines of transmission which can show a work in its proper perspective. The necessary infrastructure to make this possible is not yet available.

The seventeenth century, however, should be given its due. Perhaps its authors were not individually of the stature of the giants of Islam, but they were in close touch with the spirit and needs of their time. They belonged to the intelligentsia of their age, and they were guides to prince and pedlar alike. To them the Islamic world was one world, and they met one another on equal terms at Mecca, Medina, and other great centres of learning in the Middle East. Their writings are still human material, and within them can be discerned the pulse of human endeavour. And this is true even when Malay writing on Islamic matters has little to commend itself on the grounds of "originality."

We are thus returned to the role of a great tradition in attempting to assess and interpret the Muslim intellectual life of the Islamic city-states, taking as a fundamental point of departure that the holy cities of Mecca and Medina and University cities such as Cairo provide the norm, the core, the principle of order in all such activity, and supply that link with tradition that preserves the organic character of the Muslim world through a complex web of relationships between teacher and pupil, a network which in

21. Winstedt, p. 6.

22. C. Hooykaas, *Over Maleise Literatuur* (Leiden, 1947), p. vii.

23. Over the past decade or so G. W. J. Drewes and P. Voorhoeve have been adding steadily to texts at our disposal and to knowledge of personalities. Nor should one overlook the important contributions and reassessments provided by al-Attas S.M.N. in *The Mysticism of Hamzah Pansuri* (Kuala Lumpur, 1970).

the seventeenth century was reinforced and enriched by the great Sufi confraternities.

Thus, important as it is to see what can be made of the writings of *jawi* authors at particular port cities, accepting them as they are in terms of their own environment, it is equally if not more important to study the lives and works of their Middle Eastern teachers, in which are to be found the norms and lines of transmission we require.

A point of departure for a research project undertaken with an Egyptian colleague[24] is a brief Arabic treatise *al-Tuḥfa al-mursala ilā rūḥ al-nabī* (The Gift Addressed to the Spirit of the Prophet) written by an Indian author, Muḥammad b. Faḍl Allāh al-Burhanpuri (d. 1619) in 1590.[25] It became very popular in Acheh in the course of the seventeenth century, and the system of seven grades of being that it elaborated became established as *the* system throughout numbers of centres of Islamic teaching in Sumatra and Java. Knowledge and appreciation of the work spread in part *pari passu* with that of the Shaṭṭariyya confraternity; it was quoted extensively in Malay writings by Shams al-Din, al-Rānīrī, and 'Abd al-Ra'ūf, reiterated in fragments scattered among the Javanese *primbon* (religious notebooks), and a fairly full translation with some lacunae and interpolations has been made in Javanese verse.[26]

The work is brief and unpretentious, essentially a digest of the key theosophical formulations of the Unity of Being and its implications. But it was not only known in Southeast Asia. The author wrote a commentary on his own text *al-Ḥaqīqa al-muwāfiqa li'l-sharīca* (Reality Harmonized with the Law) of which several manuscripts are extant, including one eighteenth-century text from Bencoolen in south Sumatra with a codicil in Persian and marginal notes in Malay giving the meaning of Arabic words that Malay-speaking students of the text found difficult,[27] and one from Calcutta. In the Jakarta museum are two copies of another commentary with an interlineary Javanese translation.[28] Slightly more surprising for the scholar approaching the subject from the Southeast Asian perspective is that the major Syrian author 'Abd al-Ghani al-Nābulusī (1641–1730) found it worth his while to write a commentary on it entitled *Nukhabat al-masa'ala fi'l-tuḥfat al-mursala* (The Quintessence of the Matter in the Gift

24. Nagah Mahmoud al-Ghoneiymy, a graduate of Cairo University and al-Azhar University, at present engaged on what promises to be a standard work on al-Jīlī. The research project in question is a critical edition of the *Ithāf al-Dhakī* by Ibrāhīm b. Ḥasan al-Kurānī, 1616–1690. See Carl Brockelmann, *Geschichte der arabischen Literatur* (Leiden, 1943–49), II, 505, and SII, 520.

25. See A. H. Johns, *The Gift Addressed to the Spirit of the Prophet* (Canberra, 1965).

26. An edition of the Javanese text is included in *ibid.*

27. P. Voorhoeve, *Handlist of Arabic Manuscripts in the Library of the University of Leiden and Other Collections in the Netherlands* (Leiden, 1957), p. 381.

28. *Ibid.*

Addressed [to the Prophet]), of which Brockelmann lists various manuscripts still extant in libraries in Berlin, Cairo, and Alexandria.[29] A commercially printed edition is still available in Cairo.[30] Manuscript catalogues refer to yet others. But one such commentary has the scope and intellectual accomplishment of a major work. It is the *Ithāf al-Dhakī* (The Gift of the Discriminating) by a Kurdish author who spent most of his life at Medina, Ibrāhīm b. Ḥasan al-Kūrānī (1616–1690), a *khalīfa* of the Shaṭṭariyya order and teacher and close associate of the Achehnese teacher 'Abd al-Ra'ūf, referred to earlier. He was clearly a man of some stature, if only by seventeenth-century standards, and Brockelmann attributes at least forty works to him. More important, it was written after repeated requests made to him over the years by several *jawi* for a commentary upon it in order to enable their countrymen better to understand the principles of mysticism. Brockelmann lists two manuscripts of this work, one in the India Office, of which Snouck Hurgronje had a copy made for the Leiden University Library, and one in Berlin which has been lost.[31] Thus until 1965 the India Office text was in effect a unicum, complete, but abounding in errors and uncertain readings. During an extended stay in Cairo in that year I met my Egyptian colleague, who happened to be interested in the extension of Islam in South and Southeast Asia. In the course of his manuscript studies he discovered in Cairo alone three previously unknown copies of the work, all far superior to the Indian Office manuscript and of which the best is located in the library of al-Azhar University. Although relatively young, its value is enhanced—it is almost perfect—by a codicil stating the name of the copyist, and a line of transmission of copies and copyists back to a copy sighted by Ibrāhīm himself.[32]

Although professedly a commentary on the *Tuḥfa*, only a small proportion of the seventy folios of which the work consists are in fact commentary. The remainder is a scholarly apologia for the doctrine of the Unity of Being and an exposition of the significance of the Law in the life of the mystic. In the *Ithāf* it seems that Ibrāhīm has brought all his learning together in a supreme effort to plead the cause of the Unity of Being, showing himself a master of Qur'anic exegesis, of tradition, of grammar, of scholastic theology, of mysticism, and of philosophy. The last section of the work in fact discusses lengthy citations from ibn Sinā's *al-Shifā* and *al-Ishārāt wa'l-Tanbīhāt*. His purpose is to demonstrate that, throughout Islamic history, all the Islamic disciplines may be used to demonstrate that the Unity of Being is a metaphysical concept that violates none of the principles of revelation. His

29. Brockelmann, II, pp. 454–458.
30. Ed. 'Alī Abū al-Nūr al-Jarabi (Cairo, 1344/1926).
31. See n. 24.
32. Library of al-Azhar University, Cairo, Taṣawwuf no. 288.

most telling argument for the justification of legal obligation in answer
to those who claim that enlightenment brings exemption from the provisions
of the Law is the following: that Muhammad's enlightenment came when
he was called to prophethood in Mount Hira with the first visitation of the
angel Gabriel. The provisions of the Law, such as the daily prayers, the
fast of Ramaḍan, and the various other ritual and legal obligations were
revealed after the Prophet's enlightenment. How, therefore, could any
lesser mortal in later times claim that enlightenment meant liberation
from the law?

Throughout the text Ibrāhīm shows himself a scholar and a gentleman.
A sober but solid piety glows through the work, which is never disfigured by
any polemic or abuse, although the author is a master of dialectic. An
unexpected by-product of our study as it has proceeded so far is the discovery of a hitherto unknown work of al-Jāmī which it quotes, a text of
which Mr. Nagah has located in a volume of manuscripts at the Egyptian
National Library in Cairo.[33]

The question arises: Granted that this book was written for the *jawi*, did
it ever reach "the land below the wind"? The answer, unfortunately, is
that to date no copy has yet been discovered in any Southeast Asian
library. Accordingly, its status as a document relevant for the study of
Islam in Southeast Asia might be regarded as doubtful.

The point is well taken. But the manuscript holdings of the Egyptian
National Library are equal to the situation, for among them my Egyptian
colleague has discovered a biographical dictionary entitled *Fawā'id al-
irtiḥāl wa natā'ij al-safar fī akhbār al-qarn al-ḥādiya cashar* (The Benefits of
Travel and Results of Journeying in Reports of the Eleventh Century
[A.H.]) by Muṣṭafā al-Ḥamawī (d. 1711), a disciple of Ibrāhīm,[34] which
gives a detailed account of Ibrāhīm's dealings with the *jawi* in Medina
and the fame the *Tuḥfa* enjoyed among them. He relates that Ibrāhīm
told him what the *jawi* has told him (Ibrāhīm) of the *Tuḥfa*, that "in their
country its fame had spread far and wide, and it was read in Qur'anic
schools, and youths studied it as they studied other minor treatises on the
principles of the Islamic sciences . . . and it had reached this status only
by virtue of its dedication to the Prophet and the [pure] intention of its
author." Another passage of the dictionary explains the reason for its
dedication to the spirit of the Prophet: "it is a custom of scholars in Iraq,
India, Egypt, Syria, and the Hijaz, when one of them has compiled a book
into which he has put his best efforts, to dedicate it to the ruler of his

---

33. It is a brief commentary on his own work *al-Durrat al-Fākhirat* (see Brockelmann, II,
207; SII, 285–289) to be found in the Taymūr Library, Cairo, Taṣawwuf no. 134.

34. Dār al-Kutub, Cairo. Tārīkh 1093, folio 166–167. I am most grateful to Mr. Nagah for
typing out and sending to me from Cairo at short notice some relevant passages.

country . . . but the Imām [Muḥammad b. Faḍl Allah] knew of no one in the world greater or higher in rank than the Prophet of God, so he made this treatise of his as a gift dedicated to the spirit of the Prophet . . . because his holy spirit is the first of created things."

In yet another passage[35] al-Ḥamawī (the biographer) mentions that he read with Ibrāhīm part of his commentary on the *Tuḥfa*, and that the first time he met him was at the end of Rajab A.H. 1086 (A.D. 1675). Not only, then, do we have evidence of the *jawi* studying the *Ithāf* under its author, but we also have one of the earliest references in Arabic sources to *jawi* students at Medina so far discovered.

We have barely skimmed the surface of this bibliographical dictionary, which contains a wealth of information concerning Indian as well as *jawi* students and teachers of Islam. It came to light simply in the course of a search for background material concerning Ibrāhīm in connection with the critical edition we are preparing of the *Ithāf*. From Malay sources deriving from Acheh it appears that *jawi* were making the pilgrimage to Mecca well before the dawn of the seventeenth century. One must live in hope therefore that further search in the libraries of Egypt, Turkey, and the Yemen will supply documentation of the presence of *jawi* scholars and pilgrims at Mecca during earlier centuries.

Let it be stressed, however, that the object of such a search is not merely to find names of people and places—although in studies relating to Southeast Asia during this period the tiniest crumb of information is to be treasured like gold—but to discover a core of intellectual activity to which can be related the often fragmentary evidence of the process of Islamization and Islamic life in city-states in Southeast Asia and which can supply the sorely missed chains of transmission in the Muslim learning developed there.

And in this resides the importance of Ibrāhīm and his *Ithāf*. He is an example of one of the most outstanding minds of his age, devoting himself to the special needs of the *jawi* and their intellectual formation. His wisdom and learning must have had some influence on those from Acheh, among whom al-Rānīrī's witch hunts against mystics such as Hamzah, whose doctrines he alleged were heretical, were still a vivid memory; and in fact the impress of his personality is exemplified in that of his most famous *jawi* pupil, 'Abd al-Ra'ūf, who was renowned for his gentleness and piety.

The quality and range of the *Ithāf* gives a far better picture of the standards of Muslim education in the seventeenth century than the greater part of the corpus of Southeast Asian manuscripts which fortuitously has survived wars, persecution, a tropical climate, and colonialism. Clearly, then, although Muslim learning in Southeast Asia needs to be studied in terms

---

35. Dār al-Kutub, 1093, folio 34 v.

of its adjustment to local conditions, its nature and significance cannot be grasped outside the "great tradition" of Islamic disciplines which gave it birth.

The development of Dutch commercial power in the archipelago based on Batavia from 1620 onwards, the Dutch capture of Malacca in 1641 and of Makassar in 1667, and their growing power to enforce monopolies at the expense of local traders sounded the death knell of such centres of international maritime trade as Acheh and prevented the emergence of new ones. With what effects on the social structure of the towns can only be surmised: perhaps a withering away of the local bourgeoisie and "involution" among the *'ulamā'* who thereby lost in large measure the economic base which had made it possible for them to live and travel as citizens of the Muslim world.

Perhaps the main conclusion to be drawn from this essay is that a study of Islam in Southeast Asia requires a longevity and vitality equal to that of Professor Hall. It illustrates that the aspirant historian of Islamization in the Malay world cannot dispense with a double training: as a historian and as an Islamologist. Otherwise he has little chance of exploiting to the full the scattered fragments of information available to him and finding some truth worth the telling of the pilgrimage of man in Southeast Asia.

Awareness of the Past in the Hikajat Potjoet Moehamat[1]

JAMES SIEGEL

Cornell University

In writing of the Achehnese work *Hikajat Potjoet Moehamat*, Snouck Hurgronje said it was "a gem of Atjehnese, nay of Oriental literature."[2] This is one of two occasions known to me on which Snouck praised the Achehnese. To impress so knowledgeable and so antagonistic a critic the work must indeed be of value. I would like to deal here with the use it makes of the events of the past. For although the narrative portrays an actual struggle for the throne, it does not display the "confused, contradictory multiplicity of events, the psychological and factual cross-purposes, which true history reveals."[3] Moreover, the smoothness of explanation, the absence of notions of motivation, interest, and conflicting purpose make it seem like myth. Nonetheless, I shall try to show how the work differs from myth in its use of language. For both the construction of the story and the prosodic features of the work call attention to the difference between what is said and the nonsemantic features of language.

It will be helpful to set the historical context of the events recited in the epic. Acheh was important in the Malay world as a source of trade goods, particularly pepper, and was known as a center of Islam. It was a powerful state by the end of the sixteenth and in the early part of the seventeenth century. By the eighteenth century this power had declined considerably. Acheh differed from most of the kingdoms on the Malay peninsula in having an extensive, populated interior ruled by the chieftains who acknowledged the sovereignty of the Achehnese sultan but were largely free of any control by him.

1. I wish to thank Oliver Wolters and Sandra Siegel for their help in clarifying the issues in this paper.

2. C. Snouck Hurgronje, *The Achehnese* (Leiden, 1906), II, 99.

3. Erich Auerbach, *Mimesis* (Garden City, N.Y., 1953), p. 17. Snouck himself commented on "the occasional masterly touches in which the [authors] sketch, briefly but accurately, genuine pictures of Achehnese life" (Snouck, p. 80). Snouck's comparison was with the Indian stories recited in Acheh which were sheer fantasy. Also, he refers to particular scenes, rather than to the shape of the entire course of events, in characterizing the epic.

One must distinguish the culture of the sultan's court from that of the interior. The language of the court until late in the nineteenth century was Malay, and its literary productions were more like those of other Malay states than those of the interior. Its connection with the interior, apart from that with the chieftains who surrounded the court itself, was tenuous. The interior world must be pictured as isolated with little accurate knowledge of the world outside Acheh's boundaries. Its language was Achehnese, few people being able to speak Malay and thus having no direct connection with larger Malay culture. This picture may be overdrawn, but the intellectual universe of most Achehnese in the interior did not include much more than the names of kingdoms outside Acheh's borders.[4]

It is this interior world and not that of the court in which the *Hikajat Potjoet Moehamat* had its source.[5] The epic relates the conflict of two contenders for the throne.[6] The contest occurred probably about the first quarter of the eighteenth century, and the account was written about the middle of that century.[7] The point I will try to make is that, although the narrative tells about the restoration of unity of the kingdom, it is not a story about opposing forces of order and disorder. Rather, the accomplishment of the story is to direct attention to the nonsemantic aspects of language.

The story itself is a tale of the resolution of conflict. It begins quite abruptly; the youngest brother of the heir to the throne is deliberating with some chieftains, presumably about the state of conflict for the throne, though we are not told. However, in the midst of the consultations, the youngest brother, Potjoet Moehamat, wishes to see a "concealed meaning" in a dream and leaves the gathering to go to sleep. He dreams that he has climbed a mountain and that there he sees a tree "its top bowed, its roots twisted" (l. 8). Awake, he goes directly to his older brother and tells him that he sees Acheh gone to ruin, the palace become jungle, and its grounds become swamp. In the palace sits their brother, while in a place called Gampong Djawa sits Djeumaloj Alam, the usurper. Potjoet Moehamat finds this situation so shameful that he threatens to leave the country altogether, and he speaks a line that is still famous in Acheh: "What others have never had, we have: one land, but two kings" (l. 32).

4. For an overview of Achehnese history and culture see the entry "Atjeh" by Th. W. Juynboll, P. Voorhoeve, and A. J. Piekaar, *Encyclopedia of Islam*, rev. ed. (Leiden, 1960). The outstanding ethnography by Snouck Hurgronje contains a synopsis of the *Hikajat Potjoet Moehamat*, as well as essential information and analysis of Achehnese society and culture.

5. The author is said to come from the west coast.

6. The source used here is mainly the Romanized text to be found in the University Library at Leiden, Codex Ord. 8669d, and citations are to lines in this text. The Romanization was made by H. J. Damsté, supplemented by a text I collected in Acheh in 1968, a text which shows no significant deviations from Codex Ord. 8669d. The English translation is my own.

7. Snouck, p. 88.

His brother tries to dissuade him from doing anything about it, but Potjoet Moehamat shows himself to be fierce and powerful and defies his brother. In a series of incidents Potjoet Moehamat repudiates all relationships, including those to his brothers, if they conflict with the reunification of Acheh.

When it has been established that Potjoet Moehamat acts for the sultanate he makes a journey to the populated area of the east coast. There he presents himself in a way strikingly different from the picture we have of him originally. He says, at one place: "I am a small man, in the care of you who are here,/ like a flower in the midst of its blossoming, its fragrance nearly gone, about to fade./ My wish is for you to carry this flower to the grave" (ll. 441–443). He repeats similar sentiments in other villages, once saying that:

> I am a small man and have never before been in war.
> Let alone lead a war, I have never even seen one.
> If you have knowledge, tuan, tell me your wisdom now. [ll. 459–461]

This presentation of himself as helpless, fragile, and in need of protection is part of his appeal to villagers to join the war. Another part of this appeal is the statement which he repeats in every place he visits: "If there is love and pity, tuan, come help war on Gampong Djawa,"[8] the seat of the usurper. This appeal is successful, and the people pledge to follow him into battle.

His recruitment of soldiers is not, however, the only result of his trip. Everywhere he goes he also restores whatever has gone awry. In one place the irrigation system is blocked and he has it cleaned. In another place the laws are improperly administered and he instructs the people in their rightful application; elsewhere he restores a palace that was used as the stopping place for kings (ll. 462–565).

This restoration of order is incongruent with his presentation of himself as weak and passive. Indeed, he restores order locally, but the people invariably pledge that they will leave their villages, now set aright, and their families and follow him into battle. Furthermore, they do so not out of conviction that he represents the rightful sultan but because of their feelings for him. Here is the way he appears to them:

> His form was beautiful, his body lean; if one looked up at him everything
>   whirled about;
> His form was extraordinarily beautiful; his eyelashes arched acutely.
> His eyebrows were like the day-old moon; he was very beautiful and well
>   formed. [ll. 289–291]

---

8. The statement appears first in line 310 as "if there is love and pity, tuan, we wish to make war on Gampong Djawa."

His influence over the people does not stem from their concern that order should be restored. He creates instead an effect or sensation that they cannot express. In contrast with the sharp definitions of law or the unambiguous workings of irrigation systems and the restoration of palaces, there is a softness and descent into diffuseness in the way he is received:

> His words all were harmonious, like doves descending through the air.
> His commands and prohibitions were all soft-spoken so that the leaders all were frightened of him.
> He forbade nothing in the wrong manner, but all that he prohibited he did with calmness;
> The hearts of all the people softened; to hear his delicious voice pleased.
> [ll. 299–302]

Potjoet Moehamat, in addition to putting things right and asking for "love and pity," tells people about the chaos in Acheh. They seem to respond to chaos, to the disunity marked by one land but two kings. He tells them: "What the ears hear is discordant, what the eyes perceive makes one ashamed" (l. 587). And, listening to these words, they pledge to help him, "a feeling of pity rising [in them] as they listened to his voice" (l. 596). What is peculiar is the nature of their response; it is not terror but a feeling of peace. The response to Potjoet Moehamat's statement that all is in disorder is a feeling of tranquillity. "Because his voice was supple and sweet, their souls felt wholly at peace,/ His voice sounded continuously flattering, friendly and pleasant to the feelings" (ll. 598–599).

Potjoet Moehamat speaks of chaos, yet he creates order; and the response to his words about chaos is a feeling of peace. These contrasts distinguish order from the tangible qualities of the words used to talk about order. Potjoet Moehamat puts things together and restores, but it becomes evident that the restoration of order is not the focus of the story.

Though Potjoet Moehamat says that "what the ears hear is discordant," people respond not to his words, not to the organized meaning of speech, but to the sounds; his "continuously flattering [voice], friendly and pleasant to the feelings" (l. 598) overrides the message it carries. Similarly, Potjoet Moehamat's beauty has little to do with his actual appearance. In several places he is called "a very small man" (ll. 441, 459, 586, 599, and elsewhere), an unflattering description in Acheh. His beauty comes not from what he looks like but from his luminosity: his eyebrows are "like the day-old moon" (ll. 291, 1215); his light, not his shape, is important here. He "shone so extraordinarily" (l. 292) that no one could look at him. His radiance and the impressions of his features, as though detached from his body, obscure his actual figure. What prevents his audience from responding to his message of chaos with fear is the feeling created by perception of qualities which stand in contrast to organized meanings.

I cannot here go into detail about the other events of the *hikayat*. I want, however, to note one more incident that again shows the contrast between social and meaningful order on the one hand and sound and luminosity on the other. On his trip, Potjoet Moehamat learns that he cannot hope to win unless he has a great warrior named Bentara Keumangan on his side. But Bentara Keumangan is a close ally of the usurper, who has befriended him on many occasions. When Bentara is wounded in battle, Djeumaloj Alam, the usurper, has cared for him, and the usurper's wife has nursed him until he is healed. The extent of Bentara's obligation is such that he considers Djeumaloj Alam as his father and refuses to turn against him for any consideration.

Obligation and reciprocity are, in ways that I cannot detail here, shown to be the concepts that govern all social relations, familial as well as political. The whole of Acheh is pictured as a web of obligations. When these obligations are not in existence, Acheh itself ends. The epic makes it clear that Bentara Keumangan owes nothing to Potjoet Moehamat but owes an enormous amount to Djeumaloj Alam. Despite the costly presents that Potjoet Moehamat gives him and despite his appeal for the reunification of Acheh, Bentara Keumangan long refuses to change sides. His statement of his obligation and loyalty gives us a compressed and personalized view of the situation of all of the people whom Potjoet Moehamat has recruited. They are established in their homes and villages, places that are in fact improved by the prince, yet they leave all that behind in spite of their ties to their families simply because of their blindness to all organized meaning. Bentara Keumangan is unmoved by a rational appeal. The significance of Bentara's refusal rests on the fact that he is the only one who is able to look at Potjoet Moehamat and not be blinded. When he finally capitulates it is because he is caught in a moment of unawareness, a state described by the same term as that used for daydreaming.[9] He sinks into the same state that is described above:

> He saw the shining expression of [the prince's] face; each word tasted like *sròëkaya*[10] . . .
> He heard his voice, supple and sweet, and his soul was wholly at peace.
> [ll. 1216, 1218]

The state of blinded unawareness contrasts with a later moment of restored vision when Bentara confronts Djeumaloj Alam in battle. Djeumaloj Alam reminds Bentara of his obligations and then shoots down a tree branch. The shadow of the branch descends over Bentara, and he is

---

9. In the version I collected in Acheh, Bentara Keumangan faints when he first meets Potjoet Moehamat.

10. *Sròëkaya* is a delicacy made of eggs, sugar, spices, and coconut cream.

startled and dies. The narrator adds that Bentara was "jolted in the heart by Djeumaloj Alam; the warrior was his oldest son" (l. 2190).

With his change of allegiance, Bentara had become the commanding general of Potjoet Moehamat's forces. The remainder of the epic tells of their march to Gampong Djawa and the battle that ensues when they arrive there.

A large section of the *hikayat*, however, tells of the enormous devastation that these forces cause *before* they ever reach the enemy. Fields are leveled, shops looted, and whole villages razed. "They had not yet fought; even so, the land was already defeated; one saw that half the world had been devastated" (l. 1678). The forces raised through sound and luminosity and the consequent forgetting of obligations create chaos.

The battle itself is described in some detail. In the end Djeumaloj Alam is defeated and forced to flee into the wilderness. Djeumaloj Alam is a *sayyid*, a descendant of the prophet whom even Potjoet Moehamat agrees must be honored. He is in no way an evil man. At the end of the *hikayat*, the followers of Protjoet Moehamat are stopped from ransacking the palace because of the honor due a Muslim. God himself is angry that a *sayyid* has been defeated and sends an eclipse of the sun and the moon and a seven-day earthquake to show His displeasure. In the last few lines, peace returns to Acheh, and Potjoet Moehamat marries and repays his warriors for their help; it is added that God grants all that Potjoet Moehamat desires.

The *hikayat* does not betray any special preference for either of the sides. It is, at one level, about the rupture of Acheh, one land with two kings; the existence of this rupture is more important than the rightfulness of either claimant to the throne. There are, in fact, no arguments about the legitimacy of either side. Certainly Djeumaloj Alam is not shown as a creator of disorder fighting against the forces that maintain wholeness. If anything, he is more clearly identified with order than are the destructive forces of Potjoet Moehamat. At the close, however, Potjoet Moehamat and his side are established in a united kingdom.

What we have, then, is movement from an Acheh "in disorder, swerving back and forth in turmoil like a prau in the midst of waves" (l. 521), to its reunification. Yet the forces established when wholeness is restored are raised not by the vision of social order but by a blindness to it which is transformed into a devastating force before battle is even begun. We see here no synthesizing force but one which breaks down both mental and social order. That Potjoet Moehamat's side is in power at the end and that the rupture has been healed is not the focus of the *hikayat*. The process of restoration of order is not described; the *hikayat* directs attention to the breaking down of wholeness.

This reduction of event to imagery is seen again and perhaps most clearly in the prosodic features of the *hikayat*. All Achehnese *hikayats* have a certain metrical order, rhyme scheme, and shape to the line as well as a fixed style of chant and recitation. All these features, rather than serving to clarify and condense the meaning of the narrative line, stand in contrast to it.

The line of the *hikayat* is always divided into halves and sometimes into quarters, and the divisions are marked metrically. Here is an example (one slash marks the end of a metrical foot; two slashes indicate both a foot and a rhymed syllable):

> Hantòm/ di gòb/ na di/ geutanjöë// sabòh/ nanggròë// doea/ radja//[11]
> Never/ by others/ exists by/ us// one/ country// two/ kings//

"What others have never had, we have; one land, but two kings." The literal translation does not make sense, partly because no literal translation from Achehnese to English can do so. But, even in spoken Achehnese, one cannot say the words as they appear above because the words which indicate connection between the parts of the line have been left out. In this example one would have to make the line into two sentences. The word *njang*, meaning "that which is" or "that which has", would have to be added to the beginning of the line in order to indicate the relation between the two parts of the first half of the line. Alternatively, one could add *tapi* ("but") before *na* to gain the same end. In the second half of the line, one would add *njankeu* ("that is") before *sabòh* and *tapi* ("but") before *dua*, which would make the line into an Atjehnese sentence of two clauses. In the *hikayat*, however, these words, indicating conjunction and relationship, are omitted.

The consequence of recording events in a metrical line that omits the conjunctions between events is to break up whole images into smaller and discontinuous particles. One sees this in the descriptions of Potjoet Moehamat as well as everywhere else:

> His form was extraordinarily beautiful; his eyelashes arched acutely.
> His eyebrows were like the day-old moon; he was very beautiful and well formed.
> His body glistened extraordinarily; no one could look him in the eye.
>   . . . . .
> His words all were harmonious, like doves descending through the air. [ll. 290–292, 299]

The choppy, abrupt sound of the lines in English is not so pronounced in the Achehnese lines, but it is evident that we have no impression of what Potjoet Moehamat looks like. This is partly because we are not given very much detail. The reason we are not given much detail, I believe, is

---

11. This appears first at line 32.

that to do so would sound like a description on a police poster. The details would be laid next to one another, but there would be no way of fitting them together except by the shortest and least convincing generalization, such as "his form was extraordinarily beautiful." The *hikayat* does not allow of anything except detail joined to detail on the one hand or short and very broad generalizations on the other. The breaking up of the line into halves and the linkage through the fact of being set on the line means that parts are separated from one another and then linked solely by being adjacent to one another. Physical descriptions thus convey the quality of sensations, since the whole image never comes into focus.

    Achehnese prosody is very simple. As Snouck Hurgronje remarks, Achehnese meter depends on accent rather than quantity.[12] Each line contains four pairs of feet with the accent on the last syllable of each foot. The final syllables of the middle two pairs of feet rhyme with each other, as do the final syllables in each line. Here is our example again (one slash is an accent; two is both an accent and a rhyme):

    Hantòm/ di gòb/ na di/ geutanjòë// sabòh/ nanggròë// doea/ radja//

The rhymes occur in the syllables ending the fourth and sixth feet and the syllables ending the lines. The final syllable is usually the same throughout the *hikayat*, though occasionally the final rhyme is changed. In this case, the change is announced in the text and the final syllable then continues unvaried to the end. The rhymes in the middle of the line vary between lines and show no regularity.

    This scheme allows very little flexibility, and it is maintained unchanged from beginning to end. Its most important feature is that, instead of being adapted to the events described, it stands in opposition to those events. The meter does, of course, mark off the phrases which stand opposed to each other. But even here the system is not perfectly coincident with the meaning, because there are more feet than there are phrases and because the phrases are not always marked off by the same feet.

    In any system of prosody there is a distinction between the form and the meaning. Ordinarily, however, the poet attempts to make the two coincide so that the entire expression seems to be a "natural" and right coincidence of form and meaning. In the *hikayat*, however, the opposite seems to be true. We can see this more clearly when we look at the rhyme scheme. The important thing here is that the rhymes occur between the feet that are least likely to be linked in meaning. As we have seen, the divisions are between the two halves of the line and within each of the halves. The rhymes, however, occur between the fourth and sixth feet and at the ends of the lines, and these divisions are neither the natural units of meaning nor

12. Snouck, p. 74.

the units which are most likely to be contrasted. Rhyme so divorced from meaning makes it seem as though certain words respond to patterns of their own and so heightens an impression of discreteness.

Achehnese *hikayats* are composed to be chanted. There are two chant styles, the melody of each of which covers only a few lines. Each of these melodies is recited in either "quick" or "slow" tempo. There are generally two reciters; sometimes they chant in unison, at other times one will recite alone and the other will either remain silent or repeat the last syllable or two of each line. The monotony of the fixed metrical system is somewhat alleviated by changes in tempo and modes of recitation. The significant feature of the style of recitation is that it, too, is discoordinate with the meaning of the line. The chant melody, for instance, sometime ends in the middle of the line, while the action portrayed continues until the line ends. Similarly, the quick tempo will often be used in places where the action is slow, and conversely. Melody and tempo, like rhyme, are discoordinate with meaning and make clusters of words seem to respond to something other than events. The free-floating effect of melody, tempo, and rhyme, all without link to meaning, exaggerates the discreteness of imagery created by the bifurcated line.

Here is an example of how prosody and meaning work against each other. Unfortunately, it is not from the *Hikajat Potjoet Moehamat*, as I do not have a tape recording (necessary for the musical analysis), but from another, similar epic:

(1) [Kalheuëh] Toedjōh oeròë, toedjōh *malam*, /// *peudjam* daratan Saphan-Sapha
[After] Seven days seven *nights*, out of sight land Wholly *disappeared*
(2) Djipōt angèn *sapoe-sapoe*, meu'oe-'oe djiploeëng Behtra
Carried wind *mist sound of ocean*, ran Three-Masted Ship
(3) Ië dioelèë ban boengòng *meuloe* [seudang] ië *diikoe* ban kipah Tjina
Water ahead all *jasmine* blossoms, [while] water *astern* like fan Chinese
(4) Òh saré troïh lam *arōngan*, /// Pòteu jōh *njan* teumakōt Raja
After having arrived in *open sea*, Prince *then* feel terror Very[13]

(1) /After/ seven days and seven nights /// the land entirely disappeared.
(2) The wind carried a mist /as/ the three-masted ship ran on through the crash of waves.
(3) The water ahead was like jasmine blossoms, /while/ the water astern was like a Chinese fan.
(4) Having reached the open sea, /// the prince then was filled with immense terror.

13. Those lines are from a version of the *Hikajat Malém Dagang* I collected in Acheh in 1968. Somewhat similar lines, containing some identical phrases, appear in the edition edited by H. K. J. Cowan, between lines 872 and 876. *De "Hikajat Malém Dagang"* (The Hague, 1937). The musical analysis was made by Joseph Haletky of the Cornell University Music Department.

The bracketed words are those which would be spoken in normal speech but are left out of the *hikayat*. They are, again, words that indicate relationship. Lines 2 and 3 would have two sentences each, rather than the single sentence given in the text. The tempo of the recitation is fast, whereas there is actually a feeling of slowed motion in the passage, particularly in line 3.

The internal rhymes of each line are italicized, while the rhyme at the end of the line is capitalized. We should note that in line 3, "jasmine," which is said to be "ahead," is linked by rhyme with "astern," while in line 4 "open sea," rather than being linked with "terror," is rhymed with the relatively meaningless word "then," a word so unimportant that I would have left it out of the translation altogether, just as it would have been most likely omitted from spoken Achehnese. Also "mist" is incongruously connected with the onomatopoeia for "sound of the ocean."

The melodic phrase, whose beginning and end are marked by three slashes, contains two complete lines (sentences) about the water and ship, but it joins to that half of two other sentences, breaking these in the middle. In line 1, the words "the land entirely disappeared" are separated from the first half of the sentence and linked to the phrases about ship and water, an attachment that is syntactically senseless. Similarly the first half of the last sentence, which indicates cause, is detached from the second half, which indicates effect. Again, the result is to make words seem to respond to something other than their referents. Even to put it in this way is inadequate, as it is not one quality that is involved but four: tempo, rhythm, rhyme, and melody all work not only apart from meaning but largely independently of each other.

The audience is very much aware of the contrast between event and portrayal. I was warned that I would not comprehend *hikayats* till I understood that people listened for the sounds of the recitation as well as the story. A well-recited *hikayat* is said to be *mangat*, a word whose basic meaning is "good-tasting." This contrast between order, meaning, and sound focuses the listeners' attention.

The effect of relating events in Achehnese prosodic form is to reduce ordered perceptions and meanings to something near chaos. This is not, however, the chaos of the infinite variety of history but of language stripped of meaning and reduced to sound features, tempo, and discrete image.

It is important to see, however, that the reduction toward chaos is not a completed reduction. Rather it stops short of making a distinction between language and referent. The interest of the listeners of *hikayats* remains always with the contrast between what is portrayed and the effect of the way it is portrayed. The efforts of the audience do not go into completing the conjunctions omitted from the text, or toward recognizing the linguistic features. The narrative itself carries forward a stream of images, linguistic and visual, which the Achehnese try to abstract from their context. The result is that the same text is heard alternately in two different and exclusive ways. Achehnese prosody makes this possible, but the construction of the story itself directs attention to the two modes of registration. The writing of history in traditional Acheh, at least so far as this text is concerned, seems to have been governed more by a fascination with rhetoric than by myth or political interest.

Javanese Sources in the Writing
of Modern Javanese History

M. C. RICKLEFS

School of Oriental and African Studies,
University of London

In writing the history of the Javanese people after the sixteenth century, historians have been somewhat reluctant to accord a major role to the use of Modern Javanese source materials. The reasons for this are many, perhaps the most important being the availability of a large volume of European-language sources (predominantly Portuguese and Dutch) which has naturally attracted the attention of European scholars, among whom most of the historians of Modern Java have been found. The greatest problem raised by Javanese sources for the period after c. 1500 may be that they are simply inconvenient for these scholars. Indonesian writers have worked with greatest effect in the history of Old Java, and it is regrettable that they have, with a very few distinguished exceptions, left the writing of the history of Modern Java to Westerners. Since the beginning of the twentieth century, however, and particularly since the 1930's, considerable progress has been made in establishing the value of Modern Javanese sources.

It was very early recognized that the Javanese possessed historical literature of their own and that this might hold some interest for the outside observer. In 1779–1781, Josua van Iperen published the first European-language translation of a Javanese *babad* (chronicle). The original text had been acquired by the Dutch East India Company translator J. Gordijn in 1750 from his teacher of Javanese in Surakarta. Van Iperen introduced the translation with a brief note about the respect which the Javanese paid to such books, but he did not expand upon its historical value. The text was a version of the *Babad Tanah Jawi*, which will be discussed below, and the translation extended to the beginnings of the kingdom of Majapahit.[1] Van Iperen published only the first portion of the text, stopping well before the point at which most *Babad Tanah Jawi* versions begin to move from the realm of myth into that of history.

---

1. Josua van Iperen, "Begin van eene Javaansche histoire, genaamd, Sadjara Radja Djawa," *VBG*, 1 (1779):134–172; 2 (1780):262–288; 3 (1781):117–133.

The founders of Javanese studies are usually recognized to have been the Britons Sir Thomas Stamford Raffles and John Crawfurd, both of whom were prominent in the British interim administration of Java (1811–1816). Both considered the question of the value of Javanese *babad* sources. Raffles treated such accounts for the period after c. 1500 as reasonably accurate "records of the transactions of the times."[2] His description of Modern Javanese history was largely based on such records. Crawfurd, who was a man of strong opinions firmly expressed, took a somewhat different view: "No one, aware of the weakness of the human mind, and of the universal prevalence of superstition and credulity, in so rude a state of society as that which exists in Java, will reasonably expect to find the Javanese possessed of any remote records deserving the name of history. If the accounts of their ancient story be less monstrously extravagant and impudent than those of the Hindus, they are fully more childish and incongruous."[3]

For the *babad* accounts of Modern Javanese history after c. 1500, Crawfurd allowed more gentle condemnation: "Some common sense and moderation may be discovered, brightening slowly as we descend, and, for the last two centuries [c. 1620–1820], improving into records of *some* consistency and moderation."[4]

Crawfurd's criticisms were not without foundation, and many of them would be accepted today if expressed more moderately, as will be seen below. In the nineteenth century his view that Javanese *babads* were largely childish nonsense was widely accepted. Such historical studies of Java as were written shared two general characteristics: they were based upon European sources and they concerned primarily the activities of Europeans.

Those who did approach Javanese sources found them to be of little historical value. In the second volume of his standard work *Java* (1878), P. J. Veth attempted a history of Java. In discussing the sixteenth century, he encountered the problem which other writers have also found insurmountable, the multiplicity of historical traditions: "But as difficult and precarious as it is to reconcile the Javanese *babads* with [the Portuguese writer] Mendez Pinto, so dangerous also is the attempt . . . to bring harmony between the *babads* of Java and those of Madura."[5]

Javanese texts were not ignored generally in the nineteenth century, they were merely distrusted by historians. Meanwhile the study of Javanese language and literature began to achieve respectable scholarly standards

2. Thomas Stamford Raffles, *The History of Java*, 2 vols., 2d ed. (London, 1830), II, 67–68.
3. John Crawfurd, *History of the Indian Archipelago*, 3 vols. (Edinburgh, 1820), II, 293–294.
4. *Ibid.*, p. 294.
5. P. J. Veth, *Java, geographisch, ethnologisch, historisch*, 3 vols. (Haarlem, 1875–1882), II, 253.

and several texts were published. Some of these were of a historical or
semihistorical type, but it was generally agreed that they were so inaccurate as to be of no use to the historian. They were of interest primarily
as literature and were used especially as tools for language instruction.
Cohen Stuart dismissed the historical relevance of the *Sĕrat Baron Sakendher*
in 1850[6] and Meinsma observed in 1877 that the *Babad Tanah Jawi* grew
more accurate as its narrative approached the time of its composition but
that at all times "fantasy and belief in miracles" was present.[7] But in this
distrust of the historical veracity of narrative Javanese sources lay the
roots of a more sophisticated use of such sources for historical purposes.
Babads as literature began to be worthy of consideration quite apart from
their value as political history in the Western style. From this attitude
would grow an appreciation of Javanese texts as a cultural phenomenon
to be understood within the perspectives of Javanese rather than Western
culture. And this would lead to a more realistic appreciation of the value
of Javanese sources in the writing of history.

Around the end of the nineteenth century three events again attracted
the attention of Western scholars to Javanese sources for history. The first
was the publication of the Modern Javanese *Babad Tanah Jawi* (1874),[8]
the second the discovery and publication of the Middle Javanese (Javano-
Balinese) *Pararaton* (1897),[9] and the third the discovery and publication of
the Old Javanese *Nāgarakĕrtāgama* (1904).[10] Each of these had parts which
seemed to be "history" in the Western sense, and they were used by scholars
such as N. J. Krom to reconstruct political history.[11] But no scholar whose
primary training was in history rather than in literature gave serious
attention to these documents, and the effect was merely to move the
consideration of Javanese sources in writing history back to the stage of
inquiry of Raffles's and Crawfurd's time: were they or were they not
reliable political history?

    6. A. B. Cohen Stuart (ed. and trans.), *Geschiedenis van Baron Sakéndhèr, een Javaansch verhaal*
(Batavia, 1850), pp. vii–viii.
    7. J. J. Meinsma, *Babad Tanah Djawi, in proza*, vol. II: *Aanteekeningen* (The Hague, 1877),
pp. 7–8.
    8. J. J. Meinsma (ed.), *Sĕrat Babad Tanah Jawi, wiwit sangking Nabi Adam dumugi ing taun
1647* (The Hague, 1874).
    9. J. L. A. Brandes (ed.), "Pararaton (Ken Arok) of het boek der koningen van Tumapel
en van Majapahit," *VBG*, 49 (1897); 2d ed. (ed. N. J. Krom), *VBG*, 62 (1920).
    10. J. L. A. Brandes (ed.), "Nāgarakrĕtāgama, Lofdicht van Prapantja op Koning
Radjasanagara, Hajam Wuruk, van Madjapahit, naar het eenige daarvan bekende handschrift, aangetroffen in de puri Tjakranagara op Lombok," *VBG*, 54 (1904). Newly edited
and translated into English in Th. G. Th. Pigeaud, *Java in the 14th Century: A Study in Cultural
History*, 5 vols. (The Hague, 1960–1963).
    11. See N. J. Krom, *Hindoe-Javaansche geschiedenis*, 2d ed. (The Hague, 1931), pp. 14–26.
Krom was very skeptical about the historical value of the *babads*, but was less so about the
Nāgarakĕrtāgama and *Pararaton*.

The foundations for a more sophisticated view of Javanese historical sources was meanwhile being laid by three distinguished scholars, A. C. Vreede, J. L. A. Brandes, and Hoesein Djajadiningrat. Vreede's catalogue of the Leiden University Javanese manuscript collection (1892) took the first steps toward establishing the relationship among various *babads*,[12] and in 1900 Brandes attempted to clarify the origins and interrelationships among various *Babad Tanah Jawi* texts.[13] In 1913, Djajadiningrat's thesis on the *Sajarah Banten*[14] considered a large number of versions of Javanese history and the general characteristics of Javanese historical writing, without at all stages applying the single test of reliability or unreliability by Western chronological standards.

In the 1930's the attempt to define the role of Javanese texts within Javanese society progressed a step farther when a complicated and still-lively debate was initiated by C. C. Berg.[15] A large corpus of literature has grown from this debate, which cannot be adequately reviewed here. Two factors limit the relevance of this controversy to the practical problems faced by the historian of Java. First, that part of the debate which has concerned Modern Javanese materials has so far focused almost exclusively on narrative Javanese sources, in particular upon the Meinsma version of the *Babad Tanah Jawi*. Narrative sources comprise only one part of the body of literature available to the historian, as will be seen below. Furthermore, the *Babad Tanah Jawi* is not necessarily the most important of the narrative sources, and the Meinsma version is the least useful of the *Babad Tanah Jawi* versions. Second, while the literary debate has reached ever greater degrees of sophistication, its application to historiographical questions has rarely progressed beyond the Crawfurd-Raffles stage of assessing reliability as political chronology. Professor Berg's theories suggest an important new understanding of the function of certain Javanese texts within Javanese society and they must be considered carefully, but they are historiographically unsound insofar as they seem to argue that if texts are not reliable political history from beginning to end they are not the historian's province. It is more profitable to ask what it is that these sources are reliable for. If they are not always accurate political history, what are they and how may the historian use them? The debate which has grown

---

12. A. C. Vreede, *Catalogus van de Javaansche en Madoereesche handschriften der Leidse Universiteits-Bibliotheek* (Leiden, 1892), pp. 70ff.

13. J. L. A. Brandes, "Register op de proza-omzetting van de Babad Tanah Djawi (uitgave van 1874)," *VBG*, 51 (1900), pt. 4. Several other Brandes publications are also important in the development of *babad* studies.

14. Hoesein Djajadiningrat, *Critische beschouwing van de Sajarah Banten: bijdrage ter kenschetsing van de Javaansche geschiedschrijving* (Haarlem, 1913).

15. "Javaansche geschiedschrijving," *in* F. W. Stapel (ed.), *Geschiedenis van Nederlandsch Indië*, 5 vols. (Amsterdam, 1938–1940), II, 5–148.

from Professor Berg's theories is of great assistance in giving historians some of the tools to answer this question about particular texts.

Around the turn of the present century, concrete steps were being taken to integrate Javanese source materials into the writing of Javanese history. The key to this integration was less a consideration of the cultural background of these texts than the development of a historiographical technique which could join Dutch and Javanese narrative sources. This was less easy than it may seem. The two sources were written from different points of view and often concerned different events, different parts of the country, and different participants. The authors of *babads* often knew best what the Dutch knew least: the internal affairs of the courts. Thus the two types of documentation sometimes appeared simply to have nothing to do with each other. In 1894, P. J. F. Louw included a consideration of Javanese sources in his study of the Java War (1825–1830).[16] But the pioneer in marrying Javanese and Dutch sources into a consistent historical narrative was C. Poensen, whose two articles on the period from 1755 to 1813 (1901, 1905) attempted to join Dutch and Javanese material.[17] There were several things wrong with these articles; most notably, his Dutch sources were restricted to published ones and his Javanese source was biased.[18] But for the first time someone had written history by joining these two types of evidence. That the articles seem in retrospect to be somewhat clumsy makes them no less pioneers.

In 1935 the possibility of a successful historiography based upon Dutch and Javanese sources became much greater. In that year a thesis was published by H. J. de Graaf,[19] who was at that time one of the rarest figures in the study of Javanese history, a trained historian. He depended primarily upon Dutch-language sources, including Javanese letters and reports preserved in Dutch translation, but he also consulted the Meinsma *Babad Tanah Jawi*. This was perhaps not the best source for his purpose, but the important step of considering seriously a Javanese text had for the first time been taken by a professional historian. Since 1935, Dr. de Graaf has published many articles and monographs which have greatly increased the understanding of Javanese history after c. 1500, and as he has done so the range of Javanese sources he has employed and the success

16. P. J. F. Louw and E. S. de Klerck, *De Java-Oorlog, 1825–30*, 6 vols. (The Hague, 1894–1909); see I, 85–115.

17. C. Poensen, "Mangkubumi, Ngayogyakarta's eerste Sultan (naar aanleiding van een Javaansch handschrift," *BKI*, 52 (1901):223–361; idem, "Amăngku Buwănă II (Sĕpuh), Ngajogyakarta's tweede Sultan (naar aanleiding van een Javaansch handschrift)," *BKI*, 58 (1905):73–346.

18. See M. C. Ricklefs, "On the Authorship of Leiden Cod. Or. 2191, Babad Mangkubumi," *BKI*, 127 (1971):265.

19. H. J. de Graaf, *De Moord op Kapitein François Tack, 8 Febr. 1686* (Amsterdam, 1935).

of integrating them into an historical narrative have increased. B. J. O. Schrieke also used this technique for the purposes of more sociological analysis of Java's past institutions.[20]

The methodological significance of Dr. de Graaf's work has been somewhat obscured by the tendency he shares with many historians to practice his craft without adequately discussing its techniques.[21] Thus, at the simplest level, the reader is commonly left ignorant of the reasons why Dr. de Graaf has selected particular Javanese sources from among the thousands of volumes available to him. Indeed, the most pressing methodological task facing historians of Java now would seem to be the establishment of standards for selecting Javanese texts and the definition of criteria for their use. Here one must consider not only the technical problem of marrying Javanese and Dutch sources but also the theoretical problem of defining the function and relevance of Javanese sources within Javanese society, insofar as these affect the uses to which historians may put these texts.

To establish standards for selection and use of Modern Javanese texts in historical research, one must first classify these texts in terms of their use to the historian. There would seem to be two major classes, the narrative and the nonnarrative, each of which can be subdivided into several subtypes. Each major genre will be considered here in turn as a preliminary contribution to a more defined historiography of Modern Javanese sources. The distinctions proposed are not intended to be rigidly applied but are merely offered as tools to facilitate the consideration of sources for particular studies. The discussion here necessarily emphasizes sources for court history, with which the present writer is most familiar.

Narrative sources are those which are usually meant when one speaks of Javanese "histories." *Babads* are all narrative in that they relate the development over time of an episode or episodes. But narrative sources must for historical purposes be subdivided into those which are, for want of a better term, "mythical" (not describing actual occurrences) and those

20. For examples of this technique, see B. J. O. Schrieke, *Indonesian Sociological Studies*, 2 vols. (The Hague, 1955–1957). More recently Schrieke's approach has been adopted and extended by Soemarsaid Moertono's *State and Statecraft in Old Java: A Study of the Later Mataram Period, 16th to 19th Century* (Ithaca, 1968).

21. An important exception to this reluctance is Dr. de Graaf's essay "Later Javanese Sources and Historiography," *in* Soedjatmoko *et al.* (eds.), *An Introduction to Indonesian Historiography* (Ithaca, 1965), pp. 119–136. The present writer does not, however, accept all of the views expressed in that article. In particular, it seems misleading to refer to "the *Babad Tanah Djawi*, the so-called Javanese State Chronicles" (p. 119) as if this were a single text of which the various manuscripts merely represent variant readings. Similarly, it seems to this writer a misleading depiction of the multiplicity of *babad* texts and of their complicated interrelationships to say, "After the completion of the great *Babad Tanah Djawi*, the Javanese continued to write the history of their people. Several works were completed which should be considered as supplements and sequels to the Babad" (p. 131).

which are "historical" (describing actual events, however inaccurately). Clearly the boundary between these two is fluid and the distinction cannot be rigidly applied. Nor would Javanese authors necessarily have recognized such a distinction. Some literati were surely aware that, for instance, the *Sĕrat Baron Sakendher* did not describe the "true" genealogy of Jan Pieterszoon Coen. But they may have felt that the *Sĕrat Baron Sakendher* myth about the Dutch was a "real" description of the reasons for their distinguished role as the rulers of Batavia. Myth may have been merely an alternative way of describing a real situation.

Historical narrative texts, without mythical introductory sections, exist in abundance and are likely to attract the greatest historical attention. These describe the history of an actual kingdom or person. Among this class would be included such texts as *Babad Giyanti* (published by Balai Pustaka, 1937–1939; describing the period 1746–1760), *Babad Mangkubumi* (Leiden cod. Or. 2191; describing the reign of Sultan Hamĕngkubuwana I, from 1755 to 1792), *Babad Dipanagara* (published by Albert Rusche, 1914–1917; describing the adventures of the hero of the Java War, by himself), *Babad Pakunĕgaran* (BM add. MSS 12283, 12318; describing Prince Mangkunĕgara I, 1757–1796), *Babad Pakĕpung* (Sana Budaja MS 123; on the encirclement of Surakarta in 1790), *Babad Balambangan* (Leiden cod. Or. 2185; telling the history of Balambangan), *Babad Bĕdhah Ngayogyakarta* (Netherlands Bible Society 36 and other MSS; describing the British deposition of Hamĕngkubuwana II, 1812), and so on. These texts by and large describe events from the seventeenth century and after, most narratives of earlier periods being rather more myth than history. They are predominantly of eighteenth- and nineteenth-century origin. To these texts the historian can most appropriately apply the test of reliability as political history, by comparing them with European sources. Each text, indeed each section of a single text, must stand this test on its own, as must historical source material from anywhere else in the world. The results of such a test may vary enormously. Jasadipura I's *Babad Giyanti* seems on the whole to be reliable as literal history; *Babad Pakĕpung* is not.[22] One important test of relevance is the date when a particular text was written down. The Javanese did sometimes copy a book, word for word and line for line, but often it seems they rewrote. When a new version was written down, new stories, new details, new interpretations were often added wherever they seemed relevant or interesting. Thus the further in time a text is from the period it describes, in general the less likely it is to be of great historical veracity. Many of these texts are dated, but many are not. For the latter such technical matters as the paper they

22. See the discussion of these two texts in M. C. Ricklefs, *Jogjakarta under Sultan Mangkubumi, 1749–1792: A History of the Division of Java* (London, 1974).

are written on must be considered, as well as internal hints about date and authorship. In the building of specific historical studies these narrative historical sources will probably be most valuable. It is unfortunate that the considerable debate on Modern Javanese historiography has been written largely without reference to this genre. This is probably because few of these texts have been published, and those which have are in Javanese script and are of considerable length and difficulty. More convenient texts have naturally attracted first notice.

The narrative mythical texts are of great historical value but are not themselves works of history. Through them the historian can approach the ideas and perceptions of a particular time and place. Some of these texts are political allegory, as the *Babad Dipanagaran Surya Ngalam* (Leiden cod. Or. 6488) seems to be. Some are pseudo-history in which real characters are given pseudonyms and act out fictitious history, as did the Crown Prince of Yogyakarta (later Sultan Hamĕngkubuwana II) in the *Sĕrat Surya Raja* (Yogyakarta *kraton pusaka* copy). Some provide fictitious historical backgrounds to actual current situations, such as the *Sĕrat Baron Sakendher* (published by Cohen Stuart, 1850). Some are simply mythical prehistory, such as Ranggawarsita's *Paramayoga* and *Pustaka Raja Purwa* (published by Kolff-Buning, 1939–1941). Some written *wayang* texts are also allegorical, although many are not. These texts make it possible to reconstruct the myths of a particular time and place. In a more general sense, each type has the value of providing insights into the author's *Gedankenwelt*, which is particularly essential for the non-Javanese scholar. One learns not what particular persons did or did not do, but rather what types of things were ideally done. The reader learns of what heroes and villains were ideally made, how courts ideally functioned, how history ideally moved. The standards by which events were judged in a specific setting become more accessible, and the non-Javanese scholar in particular is left more confident of his ability both to describe events and to interpret them in the light of the standards of the time.

In using mythical narrative texts, a scholar must be certain of their date and origin. This is true of any historical source, of course, but it is so crucial for these texts that one which cannot be satisfactorily identified should ideally be ignored by the historian. Texts changed over time, and one can only assert that the ideas in a particular text were held by a particular author or social circle at a particular time. Each historian must decide how precise such identification must be for his own purposes. But one cannot, for instance, propose to describe with any reliability the *Weltanschauung* of Pakubuwana I (1703–1719) by reading a text from the reign of Pakubuwana X (1893–1939). There may be broad areas of myth which did not change over time, but these cannot be defined until texts have been examined historically and both similarities and differences seen in a chronological dimension. But these mythical narrative texts have one very major historical shortcoming. Like most Modern Javanese literature, they are largely later than c. 1775 in date. For earlier periods one may be forced by documentary circumstance to employ noncontemporaneous materials, but one should not be misled into believing that this is other than a necessary but basically unsatisfactory technique. For the eighteenth, nineteenth, and early twentieth centuries, however, this genre offers possibilities for reconstructing the intellectual history of Java during a period of great change and uncertainty.

The historical and mythical narrative texts merge in the case of the *Babad Tanah Jawi*, a title which covers a multitude of manuscript and published texts. It is perhaps unfortunate for historians that the debate on Javanese historiography has until now concentrated upon the Meinsma version of the *Babad Tanah Jawi*, the least useful among these texts, which are themselves no more typical of Javanese writing than is any other genre discussed here. The Meinsma *Babad Tanah Jawi*, published in 1874 and again in transliteration and Dutch translation in 1941, has severe short-comings as a source which have already been discussed elsewhere.[23] It is a short, edited prose summary of a major text. Its typicality has perhaps been exaggerated by the fact that whenever some other version of the *Babad Tanah Jawi* has been consulted, it has been most frequently the major Surakarta *Babad*, formerly known to Dutch scholars as the "groote babad" (Leiden cod. Or. 1786; published in part by Balai Pustaka, 1939–1941). Since this is apparently the text upon which the Meinsma summary was based, it is hardly surprising that their contents seem similar.

The *Babad Tanah Jawi* has sometimes been described as "canonical" or as the "official" imperial chronicle,[24] but both of these terms are somewhat misleading. They imply that the text was fixed at some point and thereafter copied precisely down through the centuries, except when it was altered by decree, for which view in this writer's opinion there is no evidence. Texts changed. The Javanese regarded *babads* as things of considerable spiritual power,[25] but that did not mean that the words must not be altered. There was, it seems, a shared fund of stories mythical (Watu Gunung, Banjaran Sari, Aji Saka, Baron Sakendher) and historical (Dĕmak, Pajang, Mataram, Kartasura) from which the selections for a *Babad Tanah Jawi* version were

23. M. C. Ricklefs, "A Consideration of Three Versions of the Babad Tanah Djawi, with Excerpts on the Fall of Madjapahit," *BSOAS*, 35 (1972):285–315.

24. For example, by E. M. Uhlenbeck, *A Critical Survey of Studies on the Languages of Java and Madura* (The Hague, 1964), p. 128.

25. See van Iperen, "Begin van eene Javaansche histoire," *VBG*, 1 (1779):134; de Graaf, "Later Javanese Sources," p. 131. See also P. J. Zoetmulder on Old Javanese works as "Sprach-Caṇḍi," in Waldemar Stöhr and Piet Zoetmulder, *Die Religionen Indonesiens* (Stuttgart, 1965), p. 273.

made. This selection was not always the same, and the details of the stories and their interrelationships might differ considerably. These differences probably reflected both the predilections of particular authors and the interests of their patrons. As with other texts, one must consider the date and origin of each text before deciding the relevance of its various sections. The point at which one draws the boundary between myth and history within any of these texts is to a large extent indicative of where one stands on the general question of the historical value of narrative sources. No one would argue that the opening genealogies are literal history, but some would argue that the final events, taking place in the eighteenth or nineteenth centuries, are still to be regarded as myth.

Perhaps some clarification of the historiographical value of these documents would result from abandoning the automatic use of the title *Babad Tanah Jawi*, the origin of which is unclear to the present writer. One sometimes suspects that it may have originated as a generic term with one of the early Dutch scholars of Javanese literature, such as C. F. Winter, Sr. Original Javanese texts of this genre seem usually to have some other name, such as *Babad Mataram*, *Babad Kraton*, *Sajarah ing Nata kina-kina*, and the like. Perhaps the use of such individual titles would remove the somewhat unhelpful impression of substantial uniformity among versions of "the" *Babad Tanah Jawi*.

Nonnarrative sources are very important to the historian, but to date only *sĕngkala* (chronogram) lists have been much employed. These are more or less extensive prose lists giving a brief description of major events followed by chronograms for these events and, often, an explanation of the value of the chronograms. These tend to be similar in structure to *Babad Tanah Jawi* texts, beginning with early mythical history (for example, from the year 1) and usually extending down to the time when the list was composed. The relationship between the two genres is unclear. Were *sĕngkala* lists used as the chronological skeletons upon which *babads* were constructed, or were they extracted from *babad* texts? In either case they would be important tools for the study of the chronological schemes found in *babads*. Or was there perhaps no direct relationship between *sĕngkala* lists and *babads*? Attention to such lists in the context of further study of Javanese literature in general may provide some answers to these questions. This writer suspects that no single answer will be sufficient to explain all *sĕngkala* lists. In like manner, no single judgment on their historical value will suffice. Some are useful as literal history, some are not but provide important insights into the mythical (or semimythical) chronological patterns which were important in Javanese thinking.

There are also collections of letters and official correspondence within Javanese circles and between Javanese and Europeans. These are found not only in various library manuscript holdings but in some Dutch archival collections as well, such as the Arsip Nasional Republik Indonesia, Jakarta. There are also copies of treaties among Javanese rulers and between them and Europeans, legal codifications, census figures, and lists of landholdings. These records are most likely to be of interest to students of legal, administrative, or economic history. Their exploitation has hardly begun, but they undoubtedly have great potential value. Because they cannot be called literature they have been largely ignored by literary scholarship, but the historian may nevertheless find them of great interest.

There remain several literary genres whose value for historical research is yet unclear. Nothing is without value to the alert historian, but faced with the enormous volume of documentation in Javanese and with ignorance of even the most important developments over long periods of Javanese history, he may place these items so low on the scale of priorities as to ignore them in practice. There is a large corpus of religious and ethical literature which one feels should be invaluable but which in fact is sufficiently mystical, ethereal, and timeless that it is difficult to use for historical reconstructions. The sixteenth century, for instance, is devoid of contemporaneous Javanese documentation with the exception of two religious texts.[26] These should, therefore, be eagerly seized upon by historians, but in fact they clarify none of the important historical problems of that century except to confirm the fact that Islam was known in a mystical form.

There are also the "romances," many of which derive from foreign legends but which in most cases have become indigenous literary works. These include such texts as *Sĕrat Yusup*, *Raja Pirangon*, the *Menak* stories, *Raden Ardi Kusuma*, *Dewa Ruci*, *Damar Wulan*, and so on. There are also Modern Javanese versions of the epics *Bhāratayuddha* and *Rāmāyana*. These are similar to the narrative mythical works in that they offer an approach to the ideas of a particular time and place. But they seem to be less frequently dated and hence more difficult to use. And they may perhaps be tied more closely to preceding versions than original mythical tales and therefore more difficult to define chronologically. Some of these texts are probably allegorical, but unless one has the good fortune to discover some evidence concerning the "code" of the allegory, so that it can be related to real circumstances, this fact is of little historical use. Some are probably built upon memories of actual historical events, but they cannot be used with much success to reconstruct these events. In most cases, the historical occurrence is so successfully obscured by romantic elaborations as to be irretrievable. And, finally, there are works on such matters as physiognomy, divination, and the like, which seem to be of very marginal value, indeed, unless the historian has a specific interest in such affairs.

26. G. W. J. Drewes (ed. and trans.), *Een Javaansche primbon uit de zestiende eeuw* (Leiden, 1954); *idem* (ed. and trans.), *The Admonitions of Seh Bari* (The Hague, 1969).

Some final comments should be made on technical matters which are of importance in selecting and assessing historical sources. These are still very much in need of investigation. Modern Javanese scripts may someday be of importance in assessing the date and origin of manuscripts, but paleographic standards are still in their infancy. Th. G. Th. Pigeaud has made an important contribution in this area by publishing facsimilies of several manuscript styles in volume III of his *Literature of Java*,[27] but much more remains to be done. At the present time, the writing material employed is a more tangible means of assessing the date of texts. Javanese paper (*dluwang*) seems to have fallen out of use almost entirely by the early nineteenth century. Heavy European paper of Dutch manufacture was used by the late eighteenth century and into the early nineteenth whenever it was obtainable. It is comparable to the paper used by the East India Company and the Dutch government for their own records in the same period. During the British administration (1811–1816) English paper was used, often bearing the date of manufacture in the watermark. Later in the nineteenth century and in the twentieth, paper was available with printed decorative borders on each page, with blank centers for the text. And in the twentieth century manuscripts were also written on lined notebook paper. Thus the type of paper used should provide at least a rough indication of the date of composition of even an undated manuscript. Palm-leaf (*lontar*) manuscripts are probably no older in date than those written on paper. *Lontar* was a cheaper writing material than paper and has survived in use in Bali into contemporary times. Modern Javanese texts on *lontar* are likely to be from rural areas and particularly from East Java. Some texts, most notably the *Sĕrat Yusup*, seem traditionally to have been written on *lontar* even after other writing materials were available.

Historians will normally seek texts least likely to have been edited specifically for foreign consumption. Such manuscripts may be somewhat rare outside of Indonesia. Only in the British sacks of Yogyakarta and Palembang (both in 1812) was a significant volume of texts acquired by conquest. The Dutch normally acquired Javanese manuscripts by purchasing them legally or by commissioning their copying. When a text was purchased it had probably not been written originally for foreign consumption, and there is no particular cause to worry about editing. But commissioned copies may have been edited. In this writer's experience, there seem to be two reasonably clear sorts of evidence of such copying specifically for European consumption. In some cases the paper on which the story was written was folded vertically in half to create a dividing line, and the text was then written only on one (usually the left) half of each page. This was apparently done in order that a translation or running notes on the text could be written

27. Th. G. Th. Pigeaud, *Literature of Java*, 3 vols. (The Hague and Leiden, 1967–1970).

on the other half of each page. The second such evidence is the use of prose rather than verse in narrative works. Modern Javanese books were not normally read in silence in the Western style but were intoned aloud to fixed chants in several standard poetical meters. The only exceptions seem to have been nonnarrative works such as *primbons*, legal codes, or *sĕngkala* lists. Thus, a *babad* in prose would be an anomaly: a Javanese book which could not be read as Javanese books were normally read, since prose cannot be chanted metrically. It was Europeans who preferred prose, which was very much more clear in meaning than verse. Hence, this writer strongly suspects that a recent narrative source in prose is self-evidently one composed specifically for a Westerner. The significance of editing as a historiographical problem is not yet clear, but it should be borne in mind when sources which may have been edited are being used.

The historian using Javanese sources stands now at an interesting stage in the development of his discipline. The propriety of using such sources can no longer be doubted, and the possibility of a successful integration of them with other forms of evidence has been demonstrated. The theoretical debate on the role of Javanese books within Javanese society goes on, and like all truly fundamental issues it is likely never to be resolved to everyone's satisfaction. It has already helped to raise the appreciation of the problems and possibilities of Javanese sources to a more sophisticated level, and will no doubt continue to do so. With this background, historians can now proceed to open up the vast range of historical sources in Javanese, of which so little has yet been investigated. In so doing, they will begin to create a greater understanding of the history of the largest and one of the most important cultural groups in the history of Southeast Asia.

Malay Borrowings in Tagalog[1]

JOHN U. WOLFF

Cornell University

Linguistic forms borrowed from one language by another are a source of information about the nature of the contacts between the peoples speaking the two languages: the origin of the speakers of the donor language, the amount and degree of bilingualism that existed, the purposes for which the donor language was used, and the status of the two languages vis-à-vis one another. Just as, for example, the English borrowings from medieval French alone are enough to tell us the character and nature of the contact and the purposes for which French was used in English society, so can borrowings among Southeast Asian languages provide clues as to the nature of the contact between different speech communities. For the English and French contact we have a large body of documents which independently bear out what we may deduce from the linguistic evidence alone. In Southeast Asia, however, where documentation is sparse, linguistic evidence may often be the best source of information. Here we shall look at Malay and Tagalog and see what we may deduce about the nature of Malay-Tagalog contacts. Tagalog is the only Philippine language outside of the Mindanao-Sulu area which shows appreciable Malay influence,[2] and a study of the Malay borrowings, as we shall see, is highly revealing.

The documentary evidence for Malay in the Philippines is slender. Antonio Pigafetta, the chronicler of Magellan's voyage around the world, which was the first European expedition to visit the Philippines, reports that the members of the expedition communicated with the Filipinos

1. My thanks are due to the following people whom I consulted about forms in languages I am not familiar with: Mathew Charles for Old Javanese, Nicholas Bodman for Chinese, James Gair and Fr. Michael Manickham for Tamil, and Alfred Ivry for Arabic. The decisions were my own, and I am solely responsible for any errors.

2. An exception is the language of Capul (Abak) Island in the San Bernardino Straits which shows heavy Malay and Arabic borrowing. However, it is closely related to the Samal languages of the Sulu Archipelago (languages found also in widely scattered coastal areas and islands of Borneo, Celebes, Mindanao, and in the Moluccas). Local tradition in Capul has it that Capul was settled from somewhere in the south, and the Samal-like character of the language bears this tradition out. (No doubt there is documentation on the settlement of Capul Island in existence.)

through an interpreter (until he escaped), a Sumatran-born slave brought
from Spain. There is no question that Malay was the language used. In
describing the negotiations with the king of Cebu, Pigafetta even quotes
a sentence in Malay that he alleges was uttered.[3] Further, the Cebuano-
language word list, which Pigafetta took down on Limasawa Island, in a
few cases gives Malay words or Malay synonyms for a Cebuano word.[4]
It may be possible to find evidence for Malay in the Philippines from other
sources, but it is clear that our best evidence is going to be the forms
themselves.

Our first task is to isolate borrowings: Malay and Tagalog are both
Austronesian languages—that is, they are related, deriving from the same
protolanguage. Therefore, it is necessary to distinguish forms which are
cognate by virtue of inheritance from those which are cognate by virtue
of having entered one (or both) of the languages after they became different languages. Also, if we are to study these forms for clues to the nature
of the contact between Malay and Tagalog, we must show that the
borrowings are indeed from Malay and not from a third donor language.

We may quickly dispose of the possibility that the Malay forms in
Tagalog came in through a third language. Most of the Tagalog forms of
Malay provenience are not found in other Philippine languages north of
Mindanao, and Tagalog was not in contact with Mindanao languages
until this generation, so the possibility that the Malay forms came into
Tagalog through another Philippine language may be ruled out. Also we
may rule out the possibility that the borrowings came into Tagalog from
Javanese, even though a good portion of the borrowings from Malay into
Tagalog also have Javanese cognates; for the Tagalog form always follows
the Malay shape when the Malay and Javanese forms have different
shapes: for example, we say that Tagalog *batas* 'law' is borrowed from
Malay *batas* 'boundary' and not Javanese *watĕs* 'boundary', because of
its shape.[5]

3. "Thereupon the Moro merchant said to the king [of Cebu] *Cata raia chita*." (Pigafetta
1903:I, 135). This is still normal Malay and means, "Our king has spoken."
4. They are: 'rice' *bughax baras* (Cebuano *bugas*, Malay *bĕras*); 'large' *bassal* (not a Cebuano
word, Malay *bĕsar*); 'drink' *minuncubil* (Malay *minum*; *cubil* unidentified); 'eat' *macan* (Malay
makan); 'fish' *jcam yssida* (Malay *ikan*, Cebuano *ʔisdaʔ*); 'all the same' *siamasiama* (Malay
samasama). There are some other Malay forms in the list which probably were loan words in
Cebuano. One can account for the existence of these Malay forms: natives often use a third
language of wider communication when they attempt to speak to outsiders who do not know
their language, whether or not the outsider speaks it. When I was eliciting forms in the
Mountain Province of Luzon, natives often gave Ilocano forms instead of their own or in
addition to their own. This appearance of Malay words in Pigafetta's list is clear evidence that
Malay was a language of wider communication in this part of the Philippines at that time.
5. There are four Tagalog forms of Sanskrit provenance for which I have found no cognates
in Javanese or Malay, but since only a portion of the Javanese and Malay forms which existed
are attested in our dictionaries, there is no reason to suppose that these forms did not also occur

In the case of Tagalog-Malay cognates which originated in a third language, it is necessary to separate those which came into Tagalog via Malay and those which were borrowed independently in both Malay and Tagalog. For forms originating in the modern European languages it is usually clear enough that they were borrowed independently. The things that the forms refer to, their sound patterns, and the history of the forms in the European languages from which they come, all preclude the possibility that they could have come into Tagalog from Malay or vice versa. Thus, we need not consider pairs like Malay *kĕreta* Tagalog *katīta* 'cart'; Malay *kĕmeja* Tagalog *kamísa* 'shirt', and the like: the Malay forms were borrowed from Portuguese and the Tagalog from Spanish, quite independently of one another. For forms of Chinese provenience we assume that they were borrowed independently unless there is evidence of parallel development in shape or meaning, developments of a sort which could not easily have taken place independently. Thus, the pair Tagalog *kawa* and Malay *kawah* 'cauldron' seem to be borrowings from Mandarin *kuɜ* [kwɔ] 'large pot'. It is not likely that Tagalog developed an *a* in the first syllable independently from Malay, and so we consider the Tagalog form to be a Malay borrowing. Forms of Indic and Arabic origin that are cognate in Malay and Tagalog were clearly introduced into Tagalog via Malay. In the case of Arabic forms, there is no evidence for direct contact or contact via any other language except Malay. There are no forms of Arabic origin in Tagalog which are not also attested in Malay. Further, the forms in Tagalog invariably follow any peculiar Malay treatment of the shape and meaning of Arabic loans: e.g., Tagalog *salabat* Malay *sĕrbat* 'ginger tea' show a common semantic development from the Arabic original *sharbat* 'drink'. The forms of Indic origin have also clearly been channeled through Malay. There are very few Philippine forms of Indic provenience which do not have a Malay or at least a Javanese cognate. Some of these Indic borrowings also undergo developments of meaning and shape in Malay that are invariably followed by the Tagalog forms. For example, Malay *puasa* and Cebuano *puʔása* 'fast' show a similar deviation in shape from the Sanskrit *upavása* 'fast'. Similarly, Tagalog *bása* 'read' and Malay *baca* 'read' show a parallel semantic development from Sanskrit *vac* 'speak'. There can be no doubt that Cebuano *puʔása* and Tagalog *bása* both come from Malay *puasa* and *baca*, respectively, and not independently from Sanskrit. Similar arguments can be made for

---

in Javanese and Malay. Also, the presence of a form in our Javanese sources but not in Malay is without significance. The documentation of Malay dialects is very poor. We may presume that these Javanese forms were in use in whatever dialect of Malay influenced Tagalog. There is no evidence for direct influence of Javanese on Tagalog. All the evidence indicates that the Javanese influence on Tagalog came via Malay.

many of the other forms of Indic provenience. That the donating language
is indeed Malay rather than Javanese or some other language in Indonesia
can be shown in those cases where Tagalog forms of Indic origin show the
Malay rather than the Javanese or some other shape. For example, we
say that Tagalog *halaga* 'price, value' is from Malay *harga* 'price' which
itself comes from Sanskrit *argha* 'price' because it shows the development
of initial *h* just as the Malay form does. The Javanese cognate *rĕga* 'price'
does not show this development of initial *h* and therefore cannot be the
source of the Tagalog form.

We now turn to the problem of distinguishing borrowings from inherited
forms. If we know the etymology of a form, we can, of course, eliminate
it from our list of possible inherited forms.[6] Also forms of anomalous shape
(of a phonological structure not normal for the protolanguage) can be
strongly suspected of being cognate by virtue of borrowing.[7] Further, even
if the Tagalog and Malay forms both derive from a form which can be
reconstructed in the proto-language and there are cognates in other
Austronesian languages, the Tagalog may be considered a borrowing
from Malay if the Tagalog and its Malay cognate show a sharp and parallel
semantic shift as opposed to the cognates in the other Austronesian languages. Thus Tagalog *salátan* 'southwest wind' is a borrowing from Malay
sĕlatan 'south' because the Tagalog and the Malay show a common semantic development as opposed to cognates in other languages which
have meanings comparable to Malay *sĕlat* 'strait'. However, if we do not
know the etymology, and if none of the other factors that indicate a borrowing is present, we identify borrowings on the basis of sound correspondences. Forms which are cognate by virtue of inheritance exhibit
regular correspondences, as shown in Chart 1. Forms which appear to be
cognate but fail to exhibit these regular correspondences must have come
into one (or both) of the languages by borrowing, if the forms are cognate
at all (with the exception of a few cases of analogical reshaping—see
footnote 8); and we have already concluded that such forms must have
been Malay forms that came into Tagalog if they are not known to be from

6. For example, there would be no way of recognizing that Malay *sabun* and Tagalog *sabon*
are not related by inheritance if we had no knowledge of the Arabic etymon. Of course, once we
know the etymology of a word and the approximate time of borrowing there is no reason to
treat the word as an inherited form.

7. For example, we have considered Tagalog *palayok* 'earthen cooking pot' to be a borrowing
from Malay *pĕriok* 'cooking pot' because the form in the protolanguage which could give rise
to this correspondence would be anomalous in shape, *$p(e, a)reyuk$*. Also, the correspondence
Tagalog *l* Malay *r* is probably an indication of borrowing (see n. 8). Third, the cognates of
pĕriok and *palayok* in other languages show irregular correspondences: e.g., Iloko *pariok* 'iron
pan'. And finally, the forms Tagalog *hiyaʾ* 'shame' Kinaray-a *heyaʾ* 'shame' show that it is
unlikely that Proto-Austronesian *ey* could have become Tagalog *ay*.

Chinese or from one of the modern European languages. The task is complicated by the fact that both Malay and Tagalog exhibit the same reflex for a number of protophonemes—that is, in the case of a number of sets of sound correspondences Malay and Tagalog have exactly the same reflex. Thus, if the form under consideration does not contain phonemes that enter into a correspondence which has different reflexes in Malay and Tagalog, there is no way of determining on the basis of its shape whether it is inherited or cognate by virtue of borrowing, and we must treat it as an inheritance.

Chart 1 shows the sound correspondences for Malay, Tagalog, and Javanese. Cognate forms which show correspondences other than these are considered borrowings.[8]

8. This table follows Dempwolff (1934, 1937, and 1938) as revised by Dyen (1947b, 1951, and 1953). The symbolization is that proposed by Dyen 1947a. We are dealing with probabilities, of course. To determine which set of sound correspondences reflects a sound of the protolanguage and which set is due to secondary developments requires weighing all the available data from related languages. This analysis differs from Dempwolff's and Dyen's on two points. The correspondence Malay *j* Tagalog *r* which Dyen takes to reflect the reconstructed phoneme *z we take here to indicate borrowing. *z is reflected as Tagalog *l*, as in Malay *tajam* 'sharp' Tagalog *talim* 'sharp' (from *$tazem$). There is only a handful of forms which show Tagalog *r* where Malay has *j*, and their meaning is very much of the same character as that of other forms described here as borrowings; and often they have other hallmarks of being borrowed. E.g., Tagalog *tári* ? 'gaff' is known to be a borrowing from Malay *taji* because of the final glottal. This confirms our conclusion previously that the *r-j* correspondence is indicative of borrowing. *Tári* ? is one of seven examples of terms related to cocks which are borrowings.

Similarly, we consider the handful of forms which show the correspondence Malay *c* Tagalog *s* as borrowings. Dempwolff considered these to reflect a protophoneme *c. Again, the forms which show this correspondence are invariably of the semantic categories of our borrowed words. Further, they appear only in Indonesia and the Philippines, not in Oceania and Formosa, and the vast majority have known etymologies or other phonological signs of being borrowings.

I am now convinced that the correspondence Malay *r* Tagalog *l*, which Dempwolff believed to reflect a protophoneme *r, is actually due to borrowing. Again, there are no good examples of forms showing this correspondence outside of the Philippines and Indonesia, and almost all of them are of a sort likely to be borrowings (Wolff 1974). If the correspondence Malay *r* Tagalog *l* can be shown to reflect borrowings, as I believe it does, we may enlarge our list of Tagalog borrowings from Malay by some 10 per cent with forms which have no known etymology outside of Austronesian and which show no correspondences other than *l-r* which mark a borrowing. These forms fit readily into the categories we have established for our borrowings and provide no new substantial information as to the nature of Tagalog-Malay contacts.

Further, borrowing is not the only explanation for irregular correspondences: the probability for an analogical change must also be weighed. Thus, Dyen ascribes the correspondence Malay final vowel–Tagalog vowel followed by a final glottal stop to an analogical development (Dyen 1953: Para. 91), whereas I take this correspondence as an indication of borrowing. There is a large number of such examples. A few of them may indeed be inherited, and the Tagalog glottal stop may in those cases be explainable by an analogical development; but the majority of the cases must be borrowings (and they usually have other signs of being borrowings as well).

Chart 1.   Malay, Tagalog, and Javanese reflexes of Proto-Austronesian phonemes

Malay			*Tagalog*	*Javanese*	*Protolanguage*
Penult	*Final open*	*Final closed*			
a	a	a*	a	a	a
i, e	i	e*	i, e	i, e	i
u, o	u	o*	u, o	u, o	u
ě	-	a	i*	ě	e
	b- -b- -p		b	b or w	b
	d- -d- -t		d- -r- -d	d	d†
	d- -d- -r		d- -l- -d	d or r	D
	g- -g-		g	g	g†
	-d- -t		-l- -d	r	j
	r		g	ø	R
	h- -ø- or -h- -h		ʔ	h- -ø- or -h- -h	ʔ
	h- -ø- or -h- -ø		h- -h- -ø	ø (but h in OJav)	h
	i		ay	i	ey
	ay		ay	e	ay
	i		uy	i	uy
	k- -k- -ʔ (orth. -k)		k	k- -k- -ʔ (orth. -k)	k
	l		l	l	l
	r		l	r	r†
	m		m	m	m
	n		n	n	n
	ng (ŋ)		ng (ŋ)	ng (ŋ)	ng (ŋ)
	ny		n	n‡	ny
	p		p	p	p
	t		t	t	t
	s		s	s	s
	j		d- -l-	j	z†
	j		d- -l-	d	Z
	ø or w		w	w	w
	aw		aw	o	aw

* The vowels of the antepenult all fall together in *ě* in Malay and are often reflected as *a* in Tagalog. Proto-Austronesian **e* in Tagalog becomes *i* except in syllables preceding *u*, in which enviroment it becomes *u*. The *i, e* and *u, o* contrasts are recent developments in Malay, Tagalog, and Javanese; and in any given form it is of no moment for our purpose whether *i* or *e* occurs, or whether *u* or *o* occurs.

† I question Dempwolff's reconstructions of the phonemes **d, *c, *g, *r,* and **z* in the Protolanguage (see footnote 8).

‡ The Javanese reflex of the Proto-Austronesian *ny* is /n/, not /ny/ as Dempwolff thought.

Chart 2 summarizes correspondences which we take to be prima facie evidence for borrowing. There is not necessarily any regularity of sound correspondences in borrowed forms: the same Malay sound may at one time be borrowed in one way and at another time in another way.[9]

9. In fact, we have doublets, Malay borrowings appearing in two shapes, which have persisted to the current time: *hári ʔ, hadyi* 'king' from Old Javanese (presumably via Malay) *hadyi* 'king'. That this should be the case is not surprising: languages frequently show variant pronunciations of borrowed forms—closer or further from the pronunciation in the original

Chart 2. Correspondences
indicating borrowing

Javanese	Malay	Tagalog
ĕ	a	a
ĕ	ĕ	a
-d or -r	-t	-t
ḍ	-d-	-r-
d	j	r
d or j	j	dy
-h	-h	-ø
-ø	-ø	-ʔ
-k or -ʔ	-ʔ	-ʔ
c	c	s

It is possible to make some educated guesses as to the period in which these borrowings came into Tagalog. There are two clues: one is the etymology of some of the borrowed forms; and the other is the shape of some of them. As for the etymology, there are at least two forms of demonstrably Portuguese origin: Tagalog *banyágaʔ* 'foreigner' from Malay *bĕniaga* 'trade' (from Indo-Portuguese *veniaga* 'merchant, merchandise') and Tagalog *linggo* 'Sunday, week' Malay *minggu* 'Sunday, week' (Portuguese *Domingo* 'Sunday')[10] These forms must have been borrowed in the decades prior to the Spanish conquest of Manila in 1570 (or shortly thereafter). The terms of Arabic origin also make it possible to date these Malay borrowings. Their character makes it almost certain that they were introduced into Tagalog together with Islam, and thus we may be certain that they do not antedate the fourteenth century.

A second piece of weak evidence points to a particular period of borrowing. The Tagalog forms which are borrowed from Malay and are of Sanskrit provenience reflect archaisms of pronunciation in certain cases that are not attested even in the oldest Malay documents. Thus, an argument can be made that these Tagalog forms which preserved archaisms must have been borrowed before the sixteenth century, the period of the earliest extensive Malay documents extant.[11] Accordingly, we may assert

---

language. For example, in English the word 'garage' (from French) is pronounced /gəraž/, /gərádž/, /gǽrədž/, and perhaps other ways as well.

10. Portuguese *veniaga* is itself of Indic provenience, being a borrowing of an Indic form which derives eventually from Sanskrit *vaṇija* 'trade'. Malay *minggu* 'week, Sunday' is from Portuguese *Domingo* 'Sunday'. Tagalog *linggo* 'week, Sunday' shows the same semantic development as the Malay. Further, the change of an initial nasal to *l* in a syllable preceding another nasal is attested for other borrowed forms in Tagalog (e.g., *langkaʔ* Malay *nangka* 'jackfruit'). Thus, the best explanation is that *linggo* is a borrowing from Malay.

11. Sanskrit forms in Tagalog often show an archaic pronunciation in retaining postconsonantal *h* where no attested Malay has it: Tagalog *mukhaʔ* 'face' Malay *muka* 'face' Sanskrit *mukha* 'face'; Tagalog *kathaʔ* 'story' Malay *kata* 'story' Sanskrit *katha* 'speech'; Tagalog *sithaʔ* 'cuttings of variegated pieces of cloth' Malay *cita* 'cotton print' (said to be from modern Indic [Gonda 1973:113]).

that the period of strong Malay influence on Tagalog began at least a century prior to the Spanish conquest. (It could, of course, have begun much earlier.)[12]

As regards the part of the Philippines which was under Malay influence, only the language of the Manila area was strongly influenced by Malay. Of the Malay borrowings in Tagalog, only a small portion are found in other languages (outside of Mindanao-Sulu), and these are invariably terms of trade or specific cultural phenomena (words like *bása* 'read' from Malay *baca* 'read'). To be sure, we have evidence from Pigafetta that Malay was a language of wider communication in the Visayas, but the Malay influence on the languages of this area is not of the same character or depth as that in Tagalog.

As to the exact locality from which the Malay borrowings into Tagalog come, there are a few clues which point to Borneo. The substitution of *a* for what is a mid-central vowel *ě* in most Malay dialects suggests that the Malay dialect was one which shows *a* for earlier *ě*.[13] This feature characterizes the Malay dialects of Borneo today and probably was already present in the early sixteenth century.[14] Moreover, many, but not all, Malay dialects underwent a loss of *h* initially and between unlike vowels, and that change most likely antedates the period of Arabic borrowings (for Arabic borrowings invariably retain *h* in these positions). Since Tagalog forms borrowed from Malay show retention of *h* with a handful of exceptions (e.g., Tagalog *ʔasta* Malay *hasta* or *asta* 'cubit'), the donor dialect must have been an *h*-preserving dialect. Other clues are dialectal forms, forms not general in Malay, but confined to certain regions. One

12. Pigafetta (1906:II, 37), writing fifty years before the conquest of Manila, reports that a son of the king of Luzon was the captain-general of the king of Brunei. Thus, we have documentation that Brunei-Manila relations go back this far. Spanish sources describing Legazpi's conquest of Manila emphasize the shallow penetration of Islam, but they need not be considered reliable on this point. Malay influence on Tagalog is deep and lasted over a period of time, and no doubt Islam had been present in the Manila area for a longer period of time than the Spaniards wanted to believe.

13. Tagalog had (and still has) no mid-central vowel, *ě*. An earlier mid-central vowel merged with *i*, a change which was probably already complete by the sixteenth century (as shown by the earliest Tagalog citations). Modern Tagalog substitutes *i* for a mid-central vowel (e.g., *tíbil* 'table' from English [teyběl]), and certainly mid-central vowels would have been handled the same way at a period much closer in time to the merger of older *ě* and *i*.

14. Pigafetta's word list of Malay shows the same substitution of *a* for *ě*. His Cebuano word list indicates a mid-central vowel, which Pigafetta transcribes sometimes *e* and sometimes *u*. Presumably he would have transcribed a Malay mid-central vowel *ě* in the same way if he had heard one. Because he transcribes Malay forms with *a* where standard Malay has *ě*, we may deduce that he got his list in a dialect which shows this substitution of *a* for *ě*. Pigafetta's Malay word list is clearly in a type of Brunei Malay. It has at least six forms which nowadays are confined to the Brunei dialect, and the circumstances of the voyage make it likely that he took down his list at around the time the expedition reached Brunei. Therefore, it is most likely that this substitution of *a* for *ě* was a feature of the Brunei Malay of the time.

form, Tagalog *binibíni* 'lady', is from a Malay form attested only for Brunei: *binibini* 'woman'. There are also many forms of Javanese provenience that even today are used mainly in dialects of Malay influenced by Javanese, e.g., Tagalog *bísaʾ* Malay *bisa* 'able'. The combination—*h*-preserving, *a* for *ĕ*, and Javanese-influenced vocabulary—indicates Borneo; but the exact location and final proof can only come when we have better information on Malay dialect geography than at present.[15]

Much can be said about the nature of the Malay-Tagalog contact. There are more than 300 Tagalog forms which can be shown conclusively to be of Malay origin (and probably an equal number I have failed to spot), plus a large number which surely are borrowings but do not exhibit any phonological or semantic features that would make them identifiable as borrowings. And probably an even greater number of Malay borrowings has gone out of use in the past four hundred years. Their very number as well as their character indicates that there must have been a considerable population in the Tagalog speech community which could speak Malay. Some of these Malay borrowings are words of an ordinary, everyday character: forms referring to personal characteristics, names and titles of relations, words for parts of the body, and others of the type that refer to things for which there must have been good native terms. Such basic vocabulary can only have come in if members of the Tagalog speech community could speak Malay. For a good portion of these forms we can well imagine the situation that could have led to their adoption into Tagalog. Some of them are clearly forms which ascribed status and came into Tagalog for that reason. Examples of this type are *binibíni* 'lady behaving in a manner proper to females' (Noceda's [1860] definition) from Brunei Malay *binibini* 'woman' as opposed to the native *babáʾe* 'woman'. (Cf. German *Dame* 'lady' from French as opposed to the native *Weib* 'woman'.) Tagalog *astaʾ* 'action' is a borrowing (presumably via Malay) of Javanese *asta* 'do (said of persons of high rank)'. We may presume that *asta* was used as a status form in the Malay that influenced Tagalog and most likely was originally a status form in Tagalog. Many of the polite forms still used in Tagalog are of this sort: Tagalog *poʾ* 'sir' Malay *empu* 'master'; Tagalog *tábi?* 'excuse me' Malay *tabik* 'with your permission'. The presence of these forms in Tagalog indicates clearly that Malay was not learned only as a language of commerce but that it had a certain amount of prestige, probably very much like the function of English

15. It may be impossible to pinpoint the location exactly. One would suspect Brunei Malay as the type which influenced Tagalog, but current Brunei Malay does not preserve the *h* in all cases (as contrasted with the Malay of Banjarmasin, for example, which preserves *h* almost invariably). On the other hand, the forms which now show no *h* in the Brunei dialect may have come in within the last few centuries.

in the Philippines today or French in old Russia. Forms of much the same character are being borrowed from English into the Philippine languages at the present time.

The borrowing of Malay forms which refer to personal characteristics bears out the view that Malay was used in the Manila region as a prestige language. The use of Malay forms to refer to personal characteristics (good or bad) is analogous to the behavior of present-day Filipinos, who often use forms from English or other Philippine languages as a sort of euphemism: making a negative judgment in terms of an allusion to another language in order to blunt the impact, make the statement witty, and keep the speaker in a good light. An example of such a Malay borrowing into Tagalog is *lapastángan* 'free-handed, daring to do things one has no right by his station to do' (Malay *lĕpas* 'free' and *tangan* 'hand'). Or something unpleasant is referred to with a borrowed form to take away the sting, e.g., Tagalog *sála* 'error' Malay *salah* 'error'. A good characteristic is referred to by a Malay form to enhance it or give it some special nuance: Tagalog *masúsi ʔ* 'meticulously clean'; Malay *suci* 'pure' (from Sanskrit *suĉi* 'pure'). The parallel between these types of borrowings and current borrowings into Philippine languages from English or other prestige languages is instructive. Cebuano, for example, has borrowed a huge vocabulary of deprecatory words from English and Tagalog. These forms give a nuance of wit or allusion, and with them one makes a joke at the same time that he says something nasty. As a consequence, one can make his point without putting himself in a bad light. For example, one may describe a person who is snobbish or puts on airs as *bústing* 'boasting' or *biri ʔanádir* 'haughty' (from English 'very another') or *ʔú ʔi* 'putting on' (from the abbreviation o.a. for 'overacting'). Using these English-derived forms one makes a joke while criticizing and thereby avoids public condemnation as a gossip. Or in current Cebuano one can avoid the harsh realities connoted by a native form through the substitution of the English-borrowed form: for example, a person who has been fired is said to be *gigirawut* (from English 'get out') or *nagrisayin* (from English 'resign'), terms which describe situations that do not seem quite so bad as to suffer the same action denoted by the native form *gipapaháwa ʔ*. Or positive characteristics have a special nuance when they are described as 'having (such-and-such) a characteristic like the Tagalogs', if the borrowing is from Tagalog (or Spaniards, if the borrowing is from Spanish; or Americans, if the borrowing is from English): Cebuano *bunítu* 'good-looking like a Spaniard', Cebuano *marúnung* 'smart and clever like the Manila people', and so on. From the modern Cebuano examples we can see how these kinds of Malay forms could have found their way into Tagalog, and further we see that Malay had very much the same sort of social status as English currently has in the Philippines.

There is a handful of forms of high frequency and of the most intimate part of the vocabulary whose existence is difficult to explain: these forms are *bísa* ⁾ 'can', *káya* 'can', *lálo* ⁾ 'more', *mula* ⁾ 'beginning', *maskin* 'even', *harap* 'facing', *samantála* ⁾ 'meanwhile', *sakásakáli* ⁾ 'occasionally'. At least one example of a loan translation occurs in the intimate vocabulary (and perhaps a number of others I have failed to spot). The Malay word meaning 'new', *baru*, has been extended to be used as a conjunction meaning 'before (doing)': *aku makan baru pergi* 'I ate before I left.' This sentence can be translated word for word into Tagalog *kumáin* ⁾*ako bágo lumákad* 'I ate before I left', where *bágo*, the Tagalog word for 'new', has been extended to mean 'before' just like the Malay *baru*. I do not know of this extension of the meaning of the word for 'new' anywhere else in the Philippines; it is clearly a loan translation of the Malay *baru*.[16]

For this type of borrowing of basic vocabulary, there are no parallels in borrowings from current English. Tagalog does have similar types of borrowings from Spanish, however, and these borrowings may perhaps shed some light on how Malay forms of this kind could find their way into Tagalog. The Spanish forms of a similar nature are forms like *puyde* 'can', *pero* 'but', adjective- and noun-forming affixes, and so on. The Spanish borrowings can be explained by the existence in the Philippines of a group that spoke Spanish (or creolized Spanish) better than Tagalog and thus spoke a Hispanized Tagalog. Although this segment of the community was always small, it was highly admired, and speech forms associated with it were widely imitated. Nineteenth-century novels provide illustrations of this behavior and serve as documentation for our deductions based on the linguistic evidence. (See also Schuchardt 1883.) The existence in Tagalog of these intimate forms of Malay origin seems to be analogous to the intimate borrowings from Spanish and points (but not conclusively, to be sure) to the existence of a segment of the community which was basically Malay-speaking and whose Tagalog was imitated. There are, however, no borrowings from Malay comparable to the many forms from

16. There is even a minor example of the borrowing of a syntactic construction. The king of Manila is referred to as the *raja mura*/*ladyá múra*/ (Malay *raja muda* 'young king'), and the king of Tondo is referred to as *raja matanda*/*ladyá matanda* ⁾/ 'old king', where *matanda* ⁾ 'old' is a form of purely Tagalog origin. (The citation comes from Morga's *Sucesos* as reproduced in Blair and Robertson 1906:XV, 48.) Normally, a phrase consisting of a title followed by another word does not occur in Tagalog, though it is normal Malay. In Tagalog there is a marker *ng* which must be inserted between the title and the word which follows it. The words which make up the phrase *ladyá matanda* ⁾ are Tagalog, but the way they are put together is Malay.

Spanish which indicate a master-servant relationship, so one cannot go too far in drawing parallels with the mestizo elite of the Philippines.[17]

The Malay spoken in the Manila area developed its own character just as Spanish and English in the Philippines have done.[18] Numerous forms, clearly of Malay origin, are used in combinations and meanings not attested for modern Malay such as *dalamhâti* ʔ 'extreme sorrow' (from Malay *dalam* 'within' and *hati* 'liver [as the seat of the emotions]'), other forms containing *hâti* ʔ, *lapastángan* 'daring, too free-handed' (from Malay *lĕpas* 'free' and *tangan* 'hand'), and the like. Also there are Malay-Tagalog combinations, like *bahaghári* ʔ 'rainbow' (Tagalog *bahag* 'G-string' and Malay *hari* 'day'). Many of the Malay borrowings have drifted considerably from the original Malay meaning, and these semantic shifts in many cases may well have characterized the Malay spoken in Manila.

Many of the borrowed forms suggest the spheres in which Malay was used. Some refer to intellectual activities (*siyásat* 'investigate', *hukum* 'judge'), some to geographical and nautical items (*lá* ʔ*ot* 'sea', *dalátan* 'land as opposed to sea', *salátan* 'southwest'), some to measurements, commercial activities, amusements. A good portion of the Malay borrowings into Tagalog refer to elements of civilization which were introduced to the Tagalog speakers: articles and devices (utensils, items of dress and ornament, foods and drinks, items of house construction, weapons, and so on), social institutions, medicine, religion. For a handful of terms there is no explanation. We have omitted from this study terms referring to flora and fauna which are not domesticated or which are not of some religious or commercial significance because the terms for flora and fauna common to Malay and Tagalog are widespread throughout the Philippines and Indonesia, and their spread into Tagalog has been under a different sort of impetus than the other terms described here; they offer no evidence as to the nature of the contact between the Malay and the Tagalog speech communities.[19]

17. Most of the Philippine languages influenced by Spanish are full of Spanish-derived commands, terms of reference and address to a master or mistress, and the like: e.g., Cebuano *anda* 'get going', *alibanta* 'heave', *nyur* 'term of address to a master' *ámu* 'boss', *mutsátsu* 'servant', and the like. These Spanish-derived forms all give an impression of a world in which the supervisors were Spanish-speaking and the servants speakers of a Philippine language (and, of course, we have plentiful documentation that this situation did indeed obtain). We have nothing from Malay into Tagalog of a similar character.

18. The Cebuano borrowings from English *biri* ʔ*anádir* 'haughty' (from 'very' and 'another') or *girawut* 'fire from a job (from 'get out') show how sharp the semantic shift may be in borrowed forms.

19. An example is the name of the fish called in Malay *haruan tasik* 'the snakehead of the sea'. This name recurs in scores of languages throughout Indonesia and the Philippines. It also occurs in Cebuano as *halu* ʔ*an tásik*, and the fishes thus referred to are approximately the same ones covered by the name *haruan tasik* in Malay. We know that the Cebuano form must be a borrowing because there is a form *tásik* in Cebuano, but its meaning has drifted

We now give a list of the forms on which our conclusions are based. An asterisk before the abbreviation Tag indicates that a cognate of the form occurs also in Cebuano. Since Cebuano is located farther away from Tagalog than most of the other languages outside of the Mindanao-Sulu area, we can get some idea of the extent to which Malay borrowings have spread beyond Manila and the character of the forms which did spread. In a few cases we quote forms from other Philippine languages when no Tagalog cognate is attested. The presumption is that these forms came from Tagalog into the other languages and subsequently disappeared in Tagalog.[20]

1. Forms referring to character traits and personal feelings: Tag *ʔalibughaʔ* 'irresponsible, squanderer' OJav *paribhoga* 'enjoyment' Skt *paribhoga* 'enjoyment'; *Tag *ʔasa* 'hope' Ml *asa* 'hope' Skt *āsā* 'hope'; *Tag *balísa* 'restless, fidgety' Ml *bĕlisah* 'restless, fidgety'; *Tag *bangis* 'cruel, fierce' Ml *bĕngis* 'cruel, indifferent to the suffering of others'; Tag *bani* (accentuation unknown) 'persuade with deceptive arguments' OJav *bani* (meaning unknown) Skt *vāṇī* 'eloquent speech'; *Tag *budhiʔ* 'will, intention, conscience' Ml *budi* 'quality of mind and heart' Skt *buddhi* 'intelligence, reason'; Tag *bunyiʔ* 'distinction, fame, glory' Ml *bunyi* 'sound'; Tag *dáyaʔ* 'deceit' Ml *daya* 'artifice, dodge'; Tag *dukhaʔ* 'poor, unfortunate' Ml *duka* 'grief' Skt *duḥkha* 'uneasiness, pain, sorrow'; Tag *duluhaka* (accentuation unknown) 'twist someone's words' Ml *durhaka* 'treason, insubordination' Skt *dorhaka* (Gonda 1973:115) 'injury, laying violent hands upon'; Tag *dunguʔ* 'stupid' Ml *dungu* 'obstinately stupid, dull-witted'; Tag *dustaʔ* 'treated with outrage, ignominiously' Ml *dusta* 'lying, falsehood' Skt *duṣṭa* 'false, inimical, offensive'; Tag *dalas* 'speed, frequency' Ml *dĕras* 'rapidity'; Tag *dálitaʔ* 'misery, suffering, poverty' Ml *dĕrita* 'endure' Skt *dhṛta* 'borne'; Tag *dúsa* 'suffering, punishment' Ml *dosa* 'sin' Skt *dosha* 'fault, transgression';

considerably from the original meaning of 'sea'. Moreover, the structure of the phrase is not normal for Cebuano; there should be a marker between the two nouns. Thus the form *haluʔan tásik* must have come into Cebuano by borrowing. For the same species of fishes there are at least five other names in Cebuano. This example shows how readily susceptible terms for flora and fauna are to replacement by newly borrowed forms. Terms of this sort travel faster and farther than other items in a language and do not provide information on the nature of contacts between speech communities.

20. We use the following abbreviations: Ar, Arabic; Jav, Javanese; OJav, Old Javanese; Ml, Malay; PAN, Proto-Austronesian; Skt, Sanskrit; Tag, Tagalog. For Tagalog we give Panganiban's (1973) gloss if the form is found there; if not, we give Serrano Laktaw's (1914), and if the form is only in Noceda (1860), we follow Noceda's gloss. Also in cases where the definition given by Serrano Laktaw or Noceda is more directly comparable to the meaning of the Malay form than Panganiban's, we follow Serrano Laktaw or Noceda. For Malay we quote Wilkinson's gloss (1932), and in the few cases where a form is not found in Wilkinson, we follow Iskandar (1970). Since the Malay glosses are in many cases based on the current meaning, we should not be surprised to find forms where the Tagalog borrowing is considerably more conservative in retaining earlier meanings than the Malay form we quote.

Tag *gahása* ˀ 'rash, precipitate' Jav *sahasa* 'violent' Skt *sāhasa* 'rash, precipitate'; Tag *hámak* 'vile, low' Ml *hamak* 'surly, disobliging' Ar *ḥamāqa* 'foolishness'. Tagalog forms ending in *-háti* ˀ referring to a state of mind or character from Ml *hati* 'liver' (a word added to adjectives to refer to a person's state of mind): Tag *dalamháti* ˀ 'extreme sorrow' Ml *dalam* 'within'; Tag *luwalháti* ˀ 'generosity' Ml *luar* 'outside of'; Tag *pighati* ˀ 'anguish', Tag *salagháti* ˀ 'resentment', Tag *salakháti* ˀ 'suspicious'; Tag *hímat* 'overcarefulness' Ml *hemat* 'solicitude, care' Ar *himmat* 'be worried'; Tag *hína* ˀ 'weakness' Ml *hina* 'mean, humble' Skt *hīna* 'inferior, vile'; Tag *kási* 'dear person' Ml *kasih* 'love'; Tag *labhasa* ˀ 'destructive, vile' Jav *rĕbasa* 'using force, overpowering' Skt *rabhasa* 'impetuous'; Tag *lapastángan* 'doing what is improper' Ml *lĕpas* 'gone beyond' *tangan* 'hand'; Tag *luksa* ˀ 'in mourning' OJav *rūksa* 'unkempt, as when going into mourning' Skt *rūksah* 'dry, rough, hard, harsh'; Tag *lubha* ? 'excessive, very much' Ml *loba* 'greed' Skt *lobha* 'greed'; Tag *palamára* 'careless, doing little with what one has' (no Jav or Ml) Skt *pramāda* 'negligence, carelessness'; Tag *sadya* ˀ 'intentional' Ml *saja* 'intentional'; Tag *sála* 'error' Ml *salah* 'error'; Tag *sapala* ˀ 'modest, humble' OJav *sapari-cāra* 'attendants, servants' Skt *saparyā* 'homage'; Tag *sigla* ˀ 'lively, animated' Ml *sĕgĕra* 'speedily, forthwith' Skt *śīghra* 'quick'; Tag *sinta* 'love' Ml *cinta* 'love' Skt *chintā* 'care, devotion'; Tag *súsi* ˀ 'cleanliness, orderliness' Ml *suci* 'pure, clean' Skt *śuci* 'unsullied'; Tag *taksil* 'disloyal, traitorous' Ml *taksir* 'neglect' Ar *taqṣīr* 'neglect'.

2. Forms of high frequency in speech.

2a. Those which have no apparent explanation: conjunctions, prepositions, pronouns, and the like: *Tag *maskin* 'even though' Ml *mĕski* 'even though'; Tag *mula* ˀ 'beginning' Ml *mula* 'begin' Skt *mūla* 'origin'; *Tag *samantála* 'while' Ml *sĕmĕntara* 'while' Skt *samanantara* 'immediately following'; Tag *sakásakáli* ˀ 'occasionally' Ml *sĕkalisĕkali* 'sometimes'; Tag *harap* 'facing' Ml *hadap* 'face something'; Tag *saríli* 'self'[21] Ml *sĕndiri* 'self'; *Tag *táma* ˀ 'enough, fitting in amount' Ml *tamat* 'done' Ar *tamma* 'be complete'.

2b. Forms meaning 'be alike, similar, complete', or their opposite: Tag *garil* 'defective in pronunciation' Ml *ganjil* 'odd, uneven in number'; Tag *ganap* 'complete' Ml *gĕnap* 'complete'; Tag *kambal* 'twins' Ml *kĕmbar* 'a pair of things that are alike' (as, for example, twins); *Tag *langkap* 'incorporated, joined with' Ml *lĕngkap* 'complete'; Tag *lálo* ˀ 'more' Ml *lalu* 'put through, done, past'; Tag *pára* 'like' Ml *pada* 'sufficiency' Jav *paḍa* 'like'; Tag *magka-písan* 'staying together' Jav *pisan* 'once'; Tag *salisi* 'askew, in

---

21. Tag *saríli* must be a borrowing because Ml *sĕndiri* is cognate with Ml *diri* 'stand' from PAN **Diri*. **DiRi* would be reflected in Tag as *d/ligi*. The form Tag *halígi* 'post' is cognate with Ml *diri* and *sĕndiri*.

opposite directions' Ml *sělisih* 'varying, not coinciding'; Tag *sáma* 'go together with' Ml *sama* 'together' Skt *sama* 'same, like'; Tag *sirha* ⁊ 'correct a fault' Jav *sida* 'really happen, go through' Skt *siddha* 'accomplished, perfect'; Tag *suwáto* 'in harmony' Ml *suatu* 'one'; Tag *tapat* 'directly in front' Ml *těpat* 'exactly, precisely'; Tag *túlad* 'like, similar' Ml *těladan, tauladan* 'model'.

3. Forms referring to a group or crowd; Tag *pangkat* 'section, group, portion' Ml *pangkat* 'tier, shape, rank' (a re-formation of the root *angkat* 'lift'); Tag *salamúha* ⁊ 'hobnob, mingle with' Ml *sěmua* 'all together' Skt *samūha* 'assemblage'; Tag *samaya* ⁊ 'accomplice' (no Jav or Ml) Skt *samaya* 'compact, agreement'.

4. Terms referring to sensations: Tag *díri* 'feeling of loathing for what is foul or filthy' Ml *jiji* or *jijek* 'feeling of disgust'; *Tag *lása* Ml *rasa* Skt *rasa* 'taste, sensation'; *Tag *pála* ⁊ 'grace, blessing' Ml *pahala* 'reward, grant' Skt *phala* 'fruit, benefit'; Tag *púri* 'honor' Ml *puji* 'praise' Skt *pūjya* 'honor, worship'; Tag *sarap* Ml *sědap* 'delicious'; Tag *pagta-tamása* 'enjoyment of abundance' Ml *těrmasha* 'spectacle, show' (said to be from Persian).

5. Forms referring to ability: Tag *bahagya* ⁊ 'it is just barely good, powerful, etc., enough to . . . ' Ml *bahagia* 'good fortune' Skt *bhāgya* 'luck, good fortune'; Tag *bihása* 'skilled, experienced accustomed' Ml *biasa* 'habitual' Skt *abhyāsa* 'habit, custom'; Tag *maka-bísa?* 'can' *bísa* ⁊ 'effect' Ml *bisa* 'can' Skt *visha* 'poison, active ingredient'; Tag *gunagunahin* 'enjoy something while one has the chance' Ml *guna* 'magical potency, use' Skt *guna* 'quality'; Tag *kawása* ⁊ 'endurance, tolerance' Ml *kuasa* 'power over'; *Tag *káya* 'ability, can do, wealthy' Ml *kaya* 'having power, wealth'; Tag *paham* 'sage, erudite' Ml *paham* 'understand' Ar *faham* 'understand'; Tag *lakas* 'strength' Ml *lěkas* 'fast'; Tag *pantas* 'nimble, acquitting oneself well' Ml *pantas* 'neat, nimble, graceful'.

6. Forms of politeness or which give status; euphemisms: Tag ⁊*asta* ⁊ 'posture, attitude of the body, action' Jav *asta* 'have, hold, do' (honorific form) Skt *hasta* 'hand, holding in hand'; Hiligaynon *buli* ⁊ 'buttocks' Ml *buri* 'buttocks'; Tag *binibíni* 'lady behaving properly and modestly' Malay *binibini* 'woman'; Tag *dalíri* ⁊ 'finger, toe' Ml *jeriji* 'finger'; Tag *gara* ⁊ 'stateliness, pomposity' Ml *gahara* 'of royal birth on both sides'; Tag *gawa* 'do' Ml *pěnggawa* 'functionary'; Tag *kálunya* ⁊ 'concubine' Ml *kurnia, karunia* 'bounty, favor' Skt *kārunya* 'pity'; Tag *mukha* ⁊ 'face' Skt *mukha* 'face'; Tag *param* 'disappear' Ml *padam* 'extinguish' Jav *paděm* 'honorific form referring to someone dead'; Tag *sira* ⁊ 'defective' Ml *cěděra* 'defect, flaw' Skt *chida* 'fault, defect'; Tag *sila* (accentuation unknown) 'leave something up to someone' Ml *sila* 'please, you are invited to . . . ' Skt *sīla* 'custom, practice, good disposition'; Tag *sila* ⁊ 'sit on floor with legs

crossed in front of one' Ml *bĕr-sila* 'sit squattering on floor'; *Tag *tábi*ʾ 'respectful request to be excused or pass in front of someone' Tag *pa-sintábi*ʾ 'ask to be excused' Ml *tabek* 'with your permission' Skt *kshantavya* 'expression asking pardon'; *Tag *salámat* 'thank you' Ml *sĕlamat* 'word of greeting' Ar *salāmat* 'safe and sound'; Tag *ʾupasála*ʾ 'flatterer, perfidious' Ml *upacara* 'ceremony, honor' Skt *upacāra* 'polite or obliging behavior'; Tag *ʾúsap* 'converse' Ml *ucap* 'speaking'.

6a. Titles, term of address and relationship, names: Tag *bunso*ʾ youngest son or brother' Ml *bungsu* 'youngest born'; *Tag *bansa, bansa*ʾ 'nation' Ml *bangsa* 'race' Skt *vaṃśa* 'lineage, race'; Tag *kaka*ʾ 'title for elder sibling or first cousin' Tag *káka* 'title for aunt or uncle' Ml *kakak* 'title for elder brother or sister'; *Tag *dáto*ʾ 'chieftain' Ml *datu, datuk* 'chief'; *Tag *hari*ʾ, *hadyi* 'king' OJav *haji* 'prince'; Tag *ladya*ʾ 'title of nobility' Ml *raja* 'king' Skt *rāja* 'king'; Tag *Laksamana* 'person's name' Ml *Laksamana* 'name of Rama's half-brother' (from Skt); *Tag *maharlika*ʾ 'noble' Ml *mĕrdĕheka* 'freedom' Skt *maharddhika* 'very prosperous, powerful' Tag *po*ʾ 'respectful term of address' Ml *empu* 'master'.

7. Forms referring to intellectual activities: Tag *ʾalipusta*ʾ 'determine something for oneself' OJav *paripṛṣṭa* 'examined' Skt *pariprishṭum* 'exam-ined'; Tag *ʾalusitha*ʾ 'verification, proof' OJav *ālocita* 'proven' Skt *ālocita* 'considered'; *Tag *ʾálam* 'known'[22] Ml *pĕng-alam-an* 'experience' Ar *'allām* 'known'; Tag *ʾalamat* 'legend, tradition' Ml *alamat* 'sign, portent of the future' Ar *'alāmāt* 'marks, signs'; Tag *ʾáral* 'instruction, advice' Tag *pag*ʾ*áral* 'study' Ml *ajar* 'instructed' *bĕlajar* 'study'; Tag *ʾásal* 'custom, habit' Ml *asal* 'source' Ar *aṣl* 'basis'; Tag *ʾakála*ʾ 'idea' Ml *akal* 'idea' Ar *'aqala* 'have intelligence'; *Tag *bása* Ml *baca* 'read' Skt *vac* 'speak, recite'; Aklanon *bisála* 'word' Ml *bicara* 'speak' Skt *vicāra* 'discussion'; Tag *dalubhása*ʾ 'expert' Ml *jurubahasa* 'translator'; *Tag *díwa*ʾ 'sense, conscious-ness, spirit' Ml *jiwa* 'life, soul' Skt *jīva* 'principle of life'; Tag *guro*ʾ Ml *guru* 'teacher' Skt *guru* 'preceptor'; Tag *haráya*ʾ 'imagination' OJav *hṛdaya* Skt *hṛdaya* 'mind'; Tag *hikáyat* 'sweet talk' Ml *hikayat* 'narrative, story' Ar *hikāyāt* 'stories'; Tag *ʾíngat* 'care, devotion' Ml *ingat* 'give attention' Jav *ingĕt* 'remember'; Tag *kalatas* 'letter' Ml *kĕrtas* 'paper' Ar *qirṭā* 'paper'; Tag *katha*ʾ 'literary composition' Ml *kata* 'speech' Skt *kathā* 'conversation, speech'; *Tag *kawáni* 'clerk' Ml *kĕrani* 'clerk'; Tag *kawi*ʾ (accentuation unknown) 'gibberish' Ml *kawi* 'poetic speech' Skt *kavi* 'sage, poet'; Tag *mantála*ʾ 'sacred text, charm' Ml *mantĕra* 'magical formula, incantation' Skt *mantra* 'sacred text'; Tag *palibhása*ʾ 'sarcastic, ironical' Ml *pĕribahasa* 'proverb'; Tag *paliksa* 'proof, essay' Ml *pĕriksa* 'examined' Skt *parīksa*

---

22. The Samar-Leyte cognate of this word is *ma*ʾ*áram*. Since SL has an *l* as well as an *r* phoneme, one would not expect an *r* in this form if it is cognate with the Malay and Arabic forms. Perhaps there is no connection between Tag *ʾalam* and Ml *pĕngalaman*.

'inspect'; *Tag *panday* Ml *pandai* 'smith' Skt *pāṇḍya* 'wise, learned'; Tag *salita*ʾ 'tell' Ml *cĕrita* 'story, tell' Skt *carita* 'deeds, adventures'; Tag *sampalatáya* 'believe' Ml *perchaya* 'believe' Skt *sampratyaya* 'faith, belief'; Tag *sapakat* 'plot, intrigue' Ml *sĕpakat* 'agreement' Ar *muwāfaqat* 'agreement'; *Tag *saksi* Ml *saksi* Skt *sākshi* 'witness'; Tag *siyásat* Ml *siyasat* 'investigate' Ar *siyāsāt* 'management'; Tag *surhi* 'ascertain' Tag *súri*ʾ 'analyze' Ml *sudi* 'purity, correctness' Skt *śuddhi* 'purity, justification, verification'; Cebuano *sudiya*ʾ 'criticize, point out a person's mistakes to him' OJav *codya* 'provoking criticism' Skt *codya* (Gonda 1973:143) ''be incited, criticized'; *Tag *pagka-taho*ʾ 'realization, comprehension' Ml *tahu* 'know'; Tag *tanto*ʾ 'realized' Ml *tĕntu* 'sure'.

8. Forms referring to supernatural beings or to religious, magical, or medical matters: Tag ʾagímat 'amulet' Ml *azimat, ajimat* 'amulet' Ar '*azīma* 'incantation, spell'; Tag *bakam* 'cupping glass' Ml *bĕr-bĕkam* 'cup'; Tag *baláta* 'vow' Ml *bĕrata* 'idol' Skt *vrata* 'solemn vow, holy practice'; Cebuano *bárang* 'kind of special insects used in witchcraft or the witchcraft using these insects'; Ml *bajang* 'kind of supernatural animal at the service of its owner'; *Tag *bathála*ʾ 'god' Ml *bĕtara* 'title of divinity' Skt *bhaṭṭara* 'noble lord'; *Tag *diwáta*ʾ 'nymph goddess' Ml *diwata* 'god' Skt *devatā* 'godhead, divinity'; *Tag *kapri* 'kind of supernatural being in the form of a large black man'[23] Ml *kapri* 'negro' Ar *kāfir* 'unbeliever'; Tag *kabal* 'something used to render oneself invulnerable' Ml *kĕbal* 'invulnerable'; *Tag *ngadyi*ʾ 'pray' Ml *mengaji* 'study, recite the Koran'; Tag *linga* (?*lingga*ʾ) 'kind of idol' OJav *lingga* 'image' Skt *liṅga* 'Shiva's emblem'; Tag *likha*ʾ 'statue' OJav *reka* 'image of a god' Skt *rekhā, lekhā* 'streak, line, drawing'; Tag *mantála*ʾ 'sacred text, charm' Ml *mantĕra* 'magical formula, incantation' Skt *mantra* 'sacred text'; Tag *nága* 'figure put on the prow of a boat' Ml *naga* 'kind of snake' Ml *naganaga* 'image carved on the prow of a boat' Skt *nāga* 'serpent demon'; Cebuano *pu*ʾ*ása* 'fast' Ml *puasa* 'fast' Skt *upavāsa* 'fast'; *Tag *pati*ʾ*ának* 'supernatural being that kills newborn babies' Ml *pontianak* (from *patianak) 'supernatural being that kills children'; *Tag *pintakási* 'intercessor, patron' Ml *pinta* 'ask for' *kasih* 'love'; Tag *pag-samba* 'worship, adoration' Ml *sĕmbah* 'obeisance'; *Tag *tanda*ʾ 'sign, mark' Ml *tanda* 'sign, token'; *Tag *batas* 'law, decree' Ml *batas* 'boundary' Jav *watĕs* 'boundary'; *Tag *hukom* 'pass judgement' Ml *hukum* 'decree, law' Ar *ḥukum* 'pass judgment'.

9. Forms referring to business, finance, and measurements: Tag ʾasta 'cubit' Ml *hasta, asta* 'cubit' Skt *hasta* 'measure, the length of the forearm'; Tag ʾemas 'grain of gold' (Noceda 1860:one-sixteenth of a gold *tahil*);

23. There is a form *cafre* 'kaffir, savage' in Spanish which originates from the same Arabic word. However, the Tagalog, because of its meaning, must be borrowed from Malay, not from Spanish.

Ml *ĕmas* 'gold'; *Tag *banyága* 'foreigner' Ml *bĕniaga* 'trade' Portuguese *veniaga* 'trade, peddler'; Tag *biyáya* 'favor, gift' Ml *biaya* 'disbursement, working expense' Skt *vyaya* 'disbursement, outlay'; Tag *dáli* 'inch' Ml *jari* 'finger'; Tag *dangkal* 'unit of measure from tip of thumb to tip of middle finger outstretched' Ml *jĕngkal* 'span of hand'; Tag *halaga* Ml *harga* Skt *argha* 'price'; *Tag *kaban* 'trunk, measure of 75 liters' Ml *kĕban* 'four-cornered matwork bag'; Tag *kati* 'ten million' Ml *kĕti* 'one-hundred thousand' Skt *koṭi* 'ten million'; Tag *laba* 'growth, increase' Ml *laba* 'gain, good return' Skt *lābha* 'gain'; *Tag *labi-* as in *labing isa sa ra'an* '101' (literally, one more than a hundred) Ml *lĕbih* 'more'; *Tag *laksa* Ml *laksa* 'ten thousand' Skt *laksha* 'one hundred thousand'; Tag *láko* 'peddle' Ml *laku* 'go'; *Tag *lapas* 'be free of debt, square' Ml *lĕpas* 'freed, unbounded'; Tag *múra* 'cheap' Ml *murah* 'cheap'; Tag *nílay* 'reflection, meditation' Ml *nilay* 'appraisal' Tamil *nilai* 'state, condition'; Cebuano *ka-saráng-an* 'average' Ml *sĕdang* 'average'; *Tag *tákal* 'measurement by volume' Ml *takar* 'measurement' Jav *takĕr* 'measurement'; Tag *tsúpa* 'a dry measure' Ml *cupak* 'a measure of weight'; Tag *talaro* Ml *tĕraju* 'balancing scales' (from Persian); *Tag *túnay* 'true, real' Ml *tunai* 'cash' (from Tamil); Tag *'úpa* 'rent, payment for work done' Ml *upah* 'payment for services rendered'; Tag *'úri* 'quality of something' (e.g., of jewelry, number of carats; purity) Ml *uji* 'measure, test something to see what sort of quality it is'; Tag *yúta* 'one-hundred thousand' Ml *juta* 'a million' Skt *ayuta* 'a myriad' Skt *niyuta* 'a million'.

  10. Forms referring to weather, geography, seafaring, seasons: Tag *bahaghári* 'rainbow' Ml *hari* 'day'; Tag *balakla'ot* Ml *bárat laut* 'northwest wind'; Tag *dalampasígan* 'seashore near the mouth of a river or inlet' Ml *dalam* 'at, in'; Tag *dalát-an* 'highland for cultivation' Ml *darat* 'land as opposed to sea' (cf. Jav *rat* 'world'); Tag *hulo* 'origin, head of stream' *hulu* 'upper part of stream'; Tag *kanan* 'right side' Ml *kanan* 'right side' (cf. Malagasy *havanana*, PAN **kawanan*); Tag *láho* 'eclipse' Ml *rahu* 'snake that causes eclipses' Skt *rāhu* 'demon that causes eclipses'; Tag *lá'ot* 'high seas' Ml *laut* 'sea'; (cf. Wolff 1974); Tag *linggo* Ml *minggu* 'Sunday, week' Portuguese *Domingo* 'Sunday'; Tag *magha* 'cloud' Ml *mega* 'cloud formation' Skt *megha* 'cloud'; Tag *masa* (accentuation unknown) 'season' Ml *masa* 'season, epoch' Skt *māsa* 'month'; Tag *páraluman* Ml *pĕdoman* 'compass'; *Tag *paraw* 'large sailboat' Ml *pĕrahu* (pronounced *pĕrau*) 'undecked ship of Malabar coast' Tamil *paṭavu* 'kind of boat'; Cebuano *pásil* 'rocky area along coast' Ml *pasir* 'sandy beach' (cf. Tag *pásig* 'sandy bank'); *Tag *sabang* 'intersection, crossing' Ml *cabang* 'branching bifurcation'; *Tag *salátan* 'southwest wind' Ml *sĕlatan* 'south', Tag *talága* 'small pond' Ml *tĕlaga* 'pond' Skt *taḍaga* 'pond'; Tag *tálang* 'dawn, red sky' Ml *tĕrang* 'clear, bright'; *tangháli* 'noon' Ml *tengah hari* 'noon'.

11. Forms referring to foods, drink: *Tag *ʔálak* 'liquor' Ml *arak* Ar *áraq* 'kind of liquor'; *Tag *ʔatsára* 'pickles' Ml *acar* 'pickles' from Indic, e.g. Hindi *achār*; *Tag *kari* 'precooked viands in native cafeterias' Ml *kari* 'food cooked with sauce'; Tag *múra*ʔ 'unripe, young' Ml *muda* 'young'; *Tag *patis* 'sauce made by boiling down fish, shrimp, meat' Ml *pětis* 'fish sauce'; *Tag *púto* 'steamed rice (cassava, etc.) cake' Ml *putu* 'steamed rice cake' Tamil *puṭṭu* 'steamed rice cake'; Tag *sapa* 'quid of chewed betel' Ml *sěpah* 'quid of betel'; Tag *santan* Ml *santan* (cf. Jav *santěn* 'juice extracted from coconut meat'); *Tag *salabat* Ml *sěrbat* 'ginger tea' Ar *sharbat* 'drink'; *Tag *súka*ʔ Ml *cuka* 'vinegar' Prakrit *cukkā* 'sorrel'.

12. Forms referring to goods and devices.

12a. Terms for wearing apparel and jewelry: Tag *báro*ʔ 'shirt, dress' Ml *baju* 'clothes'; *Tag *galang* 'golden bracelet or other ornament Ml *gělang* 'bracelet'; Tag *gáring* Ml *gading* Jav *gaḍing* 'ivory'; Tag *kása*ʔ 'bracelet of colored stones' Ml *kaca* 'glass' Skt *kāca* 'glass'; Tag *mánik* 'beads of mother of pearl' Ml *manik* 'beads' (of Indian origin); *Tag *mutya*ʔ 'pearl' Ml *mutia* 'pearl' Skt *mutya* 'pearl'; Tag *pákay* 'wearing apparel' Ml *pakai* 'wear'; Tag *palamata* 'bracelet made of glass, fancy jewelry' Ml *pěrmata* 'gem, jewel'; Tag *palara*ʔ 'tinsel, tinfoil' Ml *pěrada* 'tinsel, gold foil' Skt *pārada* 'quicksilver'; Tag *paruka*ʔ 'footgear' Ml *paduka* 'term of address to noble' Skt *pādukā* 'footgear'; Tag *sitha*ʔ 'cuttings of variegated pieces of cloth' Ml *cita* 'cotton print' (from modern Indic: e.g., Hindi *chiṃt* 'chintz', Gonda 1973:113); Tag *salawal* Ml *sěluar* or *sarawal* Ar *sarwal* Persian *shalwar* 'trousers'; Tag *sutla*ʔ Ml *sutra* 'silk' Skt *sútra* 'thread'; *Tag *singsing* Ml *cincin* 'ring'; Tag *tadyuk* 'tuft of feathers, plume' Ml *tajok* 'short, upward projection'; Tag *túrong* 'nipa hat' Ml *tudung* 'sun hat' Jav *tuḍung* 'kind of woven hat'.

12b. Terms for weapons, hunting and fishing devices: *Tag *balaraw* Ml *běladaw* 'curved dagger';[24] Tag *baril* Ml *bědil* 'gun'; Tag *dálat* 'snare' Ml *jěrat* 'noose, lasso for small animals'; Tag *dála* Ml *jala* 'casting net' Skt *jāla* 'net'; *Tag *bilanggo*ʔ 'prisoner, captive' Ml *bělěnggu* 'handcuffs, shackles; Tamil *vilanku* 'fetters'; *Tag *lantáka*ʔ 'culverin' Ml *rěntaka* 'type of swivel gun'; *Tag *kális* Ml *kěris* 'kris'; *Tag *paltik* 'homemade gun' Ml *pělantik* 'spring spear, spring gun'; Tag *sulígi*ʔ 'dart' Ml *sěligi* or *suligi* 'javelin, dart'; Tag *sandáta* Ml *sěnjata* 'weapon' probably from Skt *sajjatā* 'being equipped'; Tag *sula*ʔ 'impale' Ml *sula* 'sharp stake for impaling' Skt *śūla* 'stake for impaling criminals'; *Tag *sundang* Ml *sundang* 'kind of

---

24. Tag *balaraw* is recognizable as a borrowing on the basis of the *r*; see n. 8.) However, I do not know an etymology. In other languages in which cognates occur the shape indicates borrowing, e.g., Mongondow *baladow* Gorontalo *baladu*. Further, it is a trisyllabic root; therefore the chances are infinitesimally small that these forms are not related by borrowing from Ml, even though a Ml cognate is not attested.

sword' Jav *suḍang* 'gore' *sunḍang* 'horn'; *Tag *tanikala* ' 'chain' Ml *talikala* 'binding for the stomach of a woman in labor' Skt *śṛṅkhalā, śṛṅkhala* 'chain, fetter'; Tag *tárak* 'knife, dagger' Ml *tajak* 'grass cutter'.

12c. Other terms referring to warfare: Tag *ʔalága* ' 'care, vigilance' Tag *daga* ' (accentuation unknown) 'be awake' Ml *jaga* 'be vigilant' Prakrit *jaggai* 'be vigilant'; *Tag *bangga* ' 'collision, battle' Jav *bangga* 'recalcitrant, opposed' Skt *bhanga* 'breaking, overthrow, refutation'); Tag *halubílo* 'noisy crowd of confused mixture' Ml *haru biru* 'commotion, uproar';[25] Tag *káwal* 'soldier' Ml *kawal* 'watchman' Tamil *kāval* 'guard'; *Tag *kúta* ' 'fortress' Skt *kuṭa* 'house'; Tag *puksa* ' 'exterminated' Jav *muksa* 'disappear, sink away' Skt *mokṣa* 'emancipation'.

12d. Terms for devices for storing, serving, or preparing foods: Tag *balanga* ' Ml *bĕlanga* 'wide-mouthed earthen cooking jar' Tag *gúsi* ' 'large china vase' Ml *guci* 'water vessel'; Tag *kalan* 'stove for cooking' Ml *kĕran* 'chafing dish'; Tag *kawa* 'large cauldron' Ml *kawah* 'vat, cauldron' Mandarin *kuă* *Tag *kawáli* ' 'rounded frying pan' Ml *kuali* 'wide-mouthed cooking pot'; Tag *kumbo* ' 'decanter, cruet' Ml *kumbu* 'fish basket of wicker work shaped like a water vessel'; Tag *paso* ' 'earthen vessel, flower pot' Ml *pasu* 'deep bowl, flower pot'; *Tag *pinggan* 'plate' Ml *pinggan* 'plate' Tamil *pīngkan* 'chinaware'; Cebuano *panay* 'shallow earthenware basin' Jav *pane* 'basin, bowl' Tamil *pāṇai* 'big jar'; *Tag *sandok* 'ladle, scoop' Ml *sĕndok* 'spoon, ladle'; Tag *súro* ' Ml *sudu* Jav *suru* 'spoon'; Cebuano *tagyaw* or *tadiyaw* Ml *tajaw* 'large, narrow-mouthed earthenware pot'; *Tag *tungko* ' 'cooking place of three stones or edges to hold a pot' Ml *tungku* 'hearthstones for supporting pot over a fire'.

12e. Terms for musical devices: *Tag *bangsi* ' 'bamboo flute' Ml *bangsi* 'kind of flageolet' Skt *vaṃśi* 'kind of flute'; Tag *bidya* 'chord stop, fret' (no Jav or Ml cognate found) Skt *vedhya* 'kind of musical instrument'; *Tag *kudyapi* ' 'lyre, harp' Ml *kĕcapi* 'kind of four-stringed lute' Skt *kaccapī* (Gonda 1973: 125) 'kind of lute'.

12f. Forms referring to constructions or devices for construction: Tag *gusáli* ' 'large building' OJav *gosali* 'smithy' Skt *gośāla* 'cow stall'; Tag *lagári* ' 'saw' Ml *gĕrgaji* 'saw' Skt *krakaca* 'saw'; Cebuano *katsaw* 'rafter' Ml *kasaw* 'rafter'; Tag *katam* 'plane' Ml *kĕtam* 'grip firmly'; Tag *káwad* Cebuano *káwat* 'wire' Ml *kawat* 'wire'; Tag *kunsi* 'lock' Ml *kunci* 'key'; Cebuano *lansang* 'nail' Ml *rancang* 'stake'; Tag *pako* ' 'nail' Ml *paku* 'nail'; Tag *pasak* 'dowel' Ml *pasak* 'fastening or tightening with a twist, peg, or wedge' Jav *pasĕk* 'pressed tight'; Tag *pinto* ' 'door' Ml *pintu* 'door'; *Tag *sulambi*,

---

25. Tag *halubílo* is considered to be a borrowing of Ml *harubiru* because the formation *harubiru* is of a type not present in Tag and further Tag *hálo* ' 'mixed' is itself a borrowing of *haru* 'confused, disorderly'.

sulambi ⁾ 'eaves, overhang' Ml *s̆erambi* 'veranda'; Cebuano *táruk* 'implant
a post' Ml *tajok* 'shoot upward, projection'.

12g. Forms referring to other devices: *Tag *batubaláni* ⁾ 'magnet' Ml
batu b̆erani 'magnet'; Tag *bisa* (accentuation unknown) 'poison' Ml *bisa*
'poison' Skt *visha* 'poison'; Tag *lason* 'poison' Ml *racun* 'poison'; Tag *dupa* ⁾
'incense' Ml *dupa* 'incense' Skt *dhūpa* 'incense'; Tag *galagala* 'caulking
material' Ml *galagala* 'mixture of dammar and pitch for caulking boats'
Skt *gala* 'resin (esp. from Shorea spp.); Tag *gantala* 'spinning wheel' Ml
jĕnt̆era 'spinning wheel' (Gonda 1973:146) probably also Ml *ğentala*
'wheeled vehicle that moves by magic' Skt *yantra* 'engine, machine'; Tag
kulambo ⁾ Ml *kelambu* 'mosquito net'; Tag *malílang* 'sulphur, gunpowder'
Ngadju Dyak *marirang* 'sulphur';[26] *Tag *sabon* 'soap' Ml *sabun* 'soap' Ar
sābūn 'soap'; *Tag *salamin* 'mirror' Ml *c̆ermin* 'mirror'; Tag *sakla* ⁾ 'metal
ring around the handle of a knife' Ml *cak̆era* 'wheel, circle, discus' Skt
cakra 'wheel'; *Tag *timba* ⁾ 'bucket' Ml *timba* 'bucket'; *Tag *tumbága*
'copper' Ml *t̆embaga* 'copper'; Cebuano *pitáka* 'bag' (no Ml or Jav cognate
found) Skt *piṭaka* 'basket, box, bag'.

12h. Terms referring to games or cocks: Tag *híraw* 'white cock with
green admixture' Ml *hijau* 'green'; Cebuano *lumba* ⁾ 'race' Ml *lomba* 'race,
competition'; *Tag *sípa* ⁾ 'game of kicking rattan ball' Ml *sepak* 'kick';
*Tag *tári* ⁾ 'gaff' Ml *taji* 'gaff'.

13. Terms referring to domestic or supernatural plants and animals or
those which produce products of commercial importance: *Tag *bíbi*
'domesticated duck' Ml *bebek* 'duck'; Tag *dambuhála* ⁾ 'whale, sea or air
monster' Ml *jambuara* 'a monster fish'; Tag *gadya* Ml *gajah* 'elephant' Skt
gaja 'elephant'; *Tag *kalabaw* Ml *k̆erbau* 'water buffalo'; Cebuano *katyubung*
Ml *k̆ecubung* (*Datura metel*) 'a poison-yielding plant'; Tag *kasubha* ⁾ 'safflower'
Ml *k̆esumba* 'trees yielding yellow to red dyes'; Tag *lakha* ⁾ substance used
as base for preparation of tints and stains' Ml *kayu laka* 'henna' Prakrit
ḷakkhā; Tag *níla* ⁾ 'indigo plant'[27] Ml *nila* 'indigo' Skt *nīla* 'dyed with indigo';
Cebuano *sangki* 'cloves' Ml *c̆engkih* 'cloves' Chinese *ting gê* 'cloves'.

14. Unclassified terms: Tag ⁾*antála* 'get in one's way' Ml *antara* 'between'
Skt *antara* 'being in the interval'; Tag *pang-anyáya* ⁾ 'damage, hurt' Ml
aniyaya 'injustice' Skt *anyāya* 'injustice, impropriety'; Tag *bahagi* 'part' Ml
bahagi 'mete out' Skt *bhāgin* 'partaking of'; *Tag *bágay* 'thing' Ml *bagay*
'kind, variety' Tamil *vakay* 'kind, sort'; Tag ⁾*ambon* 'drizzle' Ml *ĕmbun*

---

26. The Ml word for 'sulphur' listed in our dictionaries is *b̆elerang*. However, there is a
Ngaju Dyak form *marirang*, which by its shape we know must be a borrowing (most likely
from Malay), so we may deduce that there is or was a form *marirang* 'sulphur' in Borneo Malay,
presumably the source of the Tagalog form *malílang*.

27. The name Manila (Tag *Mayníla* ⁾) comes from this form: *may* 'there are' and *níla* ⁾
'indigo'—i.e., 'place where there are indigo plants'.

'dew'; *Tag *bakas* 'vestige' Ml *bĕkas* 'traces'; Tag *bálam* 'late, retarded' Ml *bĕlam* 'dusk, late in day'; *Tag *balita* ⁾ Ml *bĕrita* 'news' Skt *vṛtta* 'event'; Tag *tayibasi* 'filings' Ml *tahibĕsi* 'rust' Tag *bátak* 'pull toward oneself' Ml *batak* 'plundered' (cf. Jav *batĕk* 'dragged'); Tag *dáti* 'custom' *ka-rati-han* (accent unknown) 'natural, way something is' Ml *jati* 'genuine, really' Skt *jāti* 'character, genuine state'; Tag *damá* 'touch, have in hand' Ml *jamah* 'physical possession'; Tag *darak* 'bran' Ml *dĕrak* 'rice dust'; Tag *dulo* 'end, extremity' Ml *dulu, dahulu* 'beginning'; Tag *ganti* 'reciprocal act' Ml *ganti* 'replace' Jav *gĕnti* 'replace'; *Tag *hálo* ⁾ 'mixture' Ml *haru* 'confusing, disorderly'; Tag *lambot* 'softness' Ml *lĕmbut* 'soft, pliable'; *Tag *landas* 'beaten path' Ml *landasan terbang* 'landing strip for airplanes, (cf. Jav *landĕsan* 'chopping block'); *Tag *latak* 'residue' Ml *latak* 'lees, dregs' (cf. Jav *latĕk, latĕk* 'lees, dregs'); Tag *lungga* ⁾ 'burrow, hole' Ml *rongga* 'cavity, hollow'; Tag *mánuṣya* 'human spoor' Ml *manusia* 'mankind' Skt *manushya* 'human'; Tag *mandala* ⁾ 'stack of rice on stalks prior to threshing' Tag *madla* ⁾ 'all, everyone' (no Ml or Jav cognates found) Skt *maṇḍala* 'collection, circle'; Tag *paksa* ⁾ 'purposely' Ml *paksa* 'force to do something'; Tag *pandi* ⁾ Ml *panji* 'banner'; Tag *pansol* 'spring of water from high source' Ml *pancur* 'spray, gush'; Cebuano *sambiri* 'embroidered edge' Ml *sĕmbir* 'fringe, edge of plate'; Tag *sadya* 'prepare' Ml *sĕdia* 'prepared' Skt *sajja* 'ready'; Tag *simpan* 'something kept' Ml *simpan* (cf. Jav *simpĕn*) 'keep'; Tag *suri* ⁾ 'fold, plait' Ml *suji* 'embroidery' OJav *suji* 'quill for sewing'; Cebuano *tanáman* 'flower garden' Ml *tanaman* 'plants' Jav *tanĕm* 'plant'; Tag *túlong* 'help'; Ml *tolong* Chinese *tō lóng* 'patronize, help a man on'; Tag *tulut* 'permission' Ml *turut* 'going along with, following line previously indicated' (cf. Cebuano *túgut* 'give permission, pay out a line').

REFERENCES

Aspillera, Paraluman S. (comp.). 1964. *A Common Vocabulary for Malay-Philipino-Bahasa Indonesia*. Manila: St. Anthony Book Service.

Bausani, A. 1960. "The First Italian-Malay Vocabulary by Antonio Pigafetta." *East and West*, n.s., 11:229–248.

Blair, E. H., and Robertson, J. A. (eds.). 1903–1909. *The Philippine Islands, 1493–1803*. 55 vols. Cleveland: A. H. Clark.

Blust, R. 1970. *Proto-Austronesian Addenda*. Honolulu: University of Hawaii. Department of Linguistics Working Papers 3.1.

Dempwolff, O. 1934, 1937, 1938. *Vergleichende Lautlehre des Austronesischen Wortschatzes*. Berlin: Zeitschrift für Eingeborenen Sprachen, vols. 15, 17, and 19.

Dyen, Isidore. 1947a. "The Malayo-Polynesian Word for 'Two.'" *Lg*, 23:50–55.

———. 1947b. "The Tagalog Reflexes of Malayo-Polynesian *D." *Lg*, 23:227–238.

———. 1951. "Proto-Malayo-Polynesian *Z." *Lg*, 27:534–540.

———. 1953. *The Proto-Malayo-Polynesian Laryngeals*. Baltimore: Linguistic Society of America. William Dwight Whitney Linguistic Series, 9.

Francisco, Juan R. 1964. *Indian Influences in the Philippines*. Quezon City: University of the Philippines.

Gonda, J. 1973. *Sanskrit in Indonesia*. 2d ed. New Delhi: International Academy of Indian Culture.

Iskandar, *Teuku*. 1970. *Kamus Dewan*. Kuala Lumpur: Dewan Bahasa dan Pustaka.

Juynboll, H. H. 1923. *Oudjavaansch-Nederlandsche Woordenlijst*. Leiden: E. J. Brill.

Lopez, Cecilio. 1939. *A Comparison of Tagalog and Malay Lexicographies*. Manila. Publications of the Institute of National Language, Bulletin No. 2.

Noceda, Juan J. de. 1860. *Vocabulario de la lengua Tagala*. Manila: Ramirez y Giraudier.

Panganiban, J. V. 1973. *Diksyunaryo Tesauro Pilipino-Inglis*. Quezon City: Manlapaz.

Pigafetta, Antonio. 1903. "Magellan's Voyage around the World." E. H. Blair and J. A. Robertson (eds.), *The Philippine Islands, 1493–1803*, vols. I and II. Cleveland: A. H. Clark.

Pigeaud, Th. G. Th. 1938. *Javaans-Nederlands Handwoordenboek*. Groningen/Batavia: J. B. Wolters.

Ronkel, Ph. S. van. 1902. "Het Tamil-element in het Maleisch." *TBG*, 45:97–117.

——. 1903a. "De oorsprong van het Maleische woord *bagai*." *TBG*, 46:241–242.

——. 1903b. "Tamilwoorden in Maleisch gewaad." *TBG*, 46:532–557.

Santa Maria, Luigi. 1967. *I Prestiti Portoghesi nel Malese-Indonesiano*. Napoli: Istituto Orientale di Napoli.

Schlegel, G. 1890. "Chinese Loanwords in the Malay Language." *T'oung Pao*, 1:391–408.

Schuchardt, Hugo. 1883. "Kreolische Studien IV: Ueber das Malaiospanische der Philippinen." *Sitzungsberichte der Kaiserlichen Akademie der Wissenschaften zu Wien (Philosophisch-historische Klasse)*, 105:111–150.

Serrano Laktaw, Pedro. 1914. *Diccionario hispano-tagalog*, Manila: La Opinión. Pt. 2: *Diccionario tagálog-hispano*.

Wehr, Hans. 1961. *A Dictionary of Modern Written Arabic*, ed. J. M. Cowan. Wiesbaden: Otto Harrassowitz.

Wilkinson, R. J. 1932. *A Malay-English Dictionary* (Romanized). Mytilene, Greece: Print. by Salavopoulos and Kinderlis.

Wolff, John U. 1972. *A Dictionary of Cebuano Visayan*. Ithaca, N.Y.: Southeast Asia Program, Cornell University. Linguistic Series VI, Data Paper No. 87.

——. 1974. "Proto-Austronesian *r and *d." *In* George Grace (ed.), *Proceedings of the First International Conference on Comparative Austronesian Linguistics*. Honolulu.

Southeast Asia: The "Colonial Drain" Revisited

FRANK H. GOLAY

Cornell University

A prominent feature of colonialism in Southeast Asia was the persistent and substantial export surplus which characterized the foreign trade of Thailand and the colonies of the area. That this major aspect of nineteenth- and early twentieth- century development came to be called the "colonial drain" can surprise no one.[1] This paper uses readily accessible trade and balance-of-payments statistics to examine the "colonial drain" of Southeast Asia and its subsequent transformation following World War II.

Colonial bureaucracies, like their counterparts in the more developed world, assiduously recorded imports and exports, and reliable statistics on the trade of Indonesia, the Philippines, and Thailand during much of the nineteenth century are easily accessible.[2] Comparable data covering the last quarter of the century for Burma, Indochina, and Malaya/Singapore undoubtedly exist in public archives, but they have not been given general distribution. The availability of trade statistics improves rapidly for the twentieth century, and beginning in 1920 official trade data converted to current United States dollars exist for the six major political entities in the area.[3]

1. For a late colonial-period analysis of issues raised by the "colonial drain" see J. H. Boeke, *The Structure of Netherlands Indian Economy* (New York, 1942), pp. 181–193.

2. Analysis of colonial-period Southeast Asia must include Thailand (Siam), which was never a colony. Thailand's economic development prior to World War II conformed in important features to that taking place in the colonies of the area, and Thailand is included in the analysis herein. It becomes exceedingly awkward, in referring to the "colonial world of Southeast Asia," to constantly acknowledge Thailand as the exception to this convenient generalization, and the writer apologizes at this time to those who are going to be offended by his failure to do so.

3. The political changes since World War II complicate attempts to analyze economic changes from the late colonial period through the mid-1960's. For example, colonial-period data for French Indochina cannot be disaggregated for areas corresponding to the successor states of the former French colony. Similarly, colonial-period data for Malaya and Singapore separately were not available to the writer. References to the trade of Indochina following World War II refer to the trade of South Vietnam, Cambodia, and Laos exclusive of mutual trade between these countries. Similarly, references to trade and payments of Malaya/

Reliable statistics for the late colonial period on the disposition of the surplus of foreign exchange earned by Southeast Asian colonies and Thailand through foreign trade are limited to only a few colonies and to only a few years in the 1920's and 1930's. The concept of the balance of payments has penetrated the consciousness of the layman and preoccupies political leaders and economists today, but, for most of the world, the concept has been fleshed out with data only since World War II. Although balance-of-payments estimates improve steadily, those available for Southeast Asia vary widely in quality and comparability, and many data used in this paper are reliable only as orders of magnitude—which is all that is demanded of them for the comparisons made herein.

I

The persistent export surplus in the trade of the Southeast Asian colonies and Thailand over the century following 1840 is not surprising since these states were net importers of shipping; insurance; financial, bureaucratic, and administrative services; payments for the services of foreign investment; and minor amounts of educational, travel, and tourism services.[4] What is surprising and anomalous is the size and rapid growth of the export surplus over the period of capitalist expansion following 1850. This development is particularly incongruous in view of the inflow of missionary remittances, expenditures of the colonial powers on their defense establishments in the colonies, and the inflow of private foreign capital to create modern plantation, mining, forestry, commercial, and financial enterprises and to fund the social investment projects of colonial governments.

During the last seven decades of the nineteenth century the value of imports into the Netherlands Indies averaged only seven-tenths of the value of exports, and in no year was an import surplus recorded. Over this same period the Philippines experienced a persistent export surplus which averaged one-fifth of the value of imports. Data for Thailand covering the last four decades of the century reveal an export surplus which, on the average, was more than a third again as large as the value of Thailand's imports. The annual trade balances summarized above include 162 observations, and in only twelve instances, all involving the Philippines, were import surpluses recorded.

Singapore include the external transactions of these two states exclusive of mutual exchanges. In the case of nontrade payments for the period following the formation of Malaysia, the tabulations for Malaya/Singapore include payments of the Bornean components of Malaysia.

4. All references to the balance of trade, exports, imports, and other categories of foreign transactions and to changes in various categories over time are in terms of recorded or estimated values of aggregate transactions in the indicated categories.

Although trade statistics for the other colonies in Southeast Asia comparable to those summarized in Table 1 were not available to the author,

Table 1. Southeast Asia: Dimensions of the "colonial drain" in the nineteenth century (annual average in millions of national currency; imports as a percentage of exports)

	Indonesia			Philippines			Thailand		
Period	Imports	Exports	Imports/Exports	Imports	Exports	Imports/Exports	Imports	Exports	Imports/Exports
1831–1840	26	40	65%	1.0	1.1*	91%	na	na	
1841–1850	34	62	55%	2.9	3.2	91%	na	na	
1851–1860	58	92	63%	5.7	7.6	75%	na	na	
1861–1870	69	118	58%	10.5†	12.3†	85%	6.8‡	8.3‡	82%
1871–1880	123	178	69%	17.1§	18.6§	92%	9.4	13.1	72%
1881–1890	149	190	78%	20.7	25.7	81%	14.2	20.8	68%
1891–1900	178	219	81%	25.1‖	32.2‖	80%	32.8	43.5	75%

Sources: For Indonesia, data copied from worksheets of the Centraal Kantoor voor de Statistiek, Mededeeling No. 160, by J. A. M. Caldwell, who kindly made them available to the author; for the Philippines, Census of the Philippines, 1903, IV, 564–565; for Thailand, James C. Ingram, Economic Change in Thailand since 1850 (Stanford, Calif., 1955), pp. 240–241.
* Includes data for 1831 and 1837–1840.
† 1861–1867 and 1870. Entries for 1865–1867 converted to pesos.
‡ 1864–1867 and 1870.
§ Less 1871.
‖ 1891–1895.

less comprehensive data support the impression that the rest of Southeast Asia experienced the same trade pattern. Trade statistics for Burma for every fifth year beginning with 1875 reveal that for the ten years tabulated, ending with 1920, no import surplus was recorded. Moreover, the ratio of the export surplus to the value of exports steadily increased until for the five years tabulated, beginning with 1900 and ending with 1920, this ratio fluctuated narrowly around the average value of 38 per cent.[5] In the case of French Indochina, trade transactions for the four years 1899–1903 resulted in a large import surplus, but a decade later, in 1909–1913, this had been converted to an export surplus amounting to almost one-fifth of the value of exports.[6] The colony which in the latter part of the nineteenth century departed from the pattern described above was Malaya/Singapore. Although the trade returns of the Federated Malay States displayed a large export surplus, this pattern was reversed by the import surplus of the Straits

5. U Aye Hlaing, A Study of the Economic Development of Burma (Rangoon, 1964), Table 11, p. 45. Another reference which tabulates the trade of Burma for four pairs of years, 1868–1869, 1872–1873, 1903–1904 and 1913–1914, also reveals a substantial and increasing export surplus; over these eight years, the ratio of the value of imports to the value of exports averaged 54 per cent (J. S. Furnivall, Colonial Policy and Practice [New York, 1956], pp. 551–553).
6. Charles Robequain, The Economic Development of French Indochina (London, 1944), p. 306.

Settlements, which more than counterbalanced the trade balance of their hinterlands.[7]

As we move into the twentieth century the "colonial drain" becomes even more pronounced as France and the United States, latecomers in the race for empire in the area, organized their colonies to produce large export surpluses. In the case of the Philippines the ratio of imports to exports declined in every decade following 1900 until, for the decade of the 1930's, imports amounted to less than three-quarters of the value of exports. This pattern was repeated for Indochina, where the ratio of imports to exports declined in three out of the first four decades of this century. Tin and rubber exports of Malaya, stimulated by strong international demand and supported by an inflow of foreign capital, quickly came to dominate the trade of Malaya/Singapore; for the combined colonies an export surplus first appeared in the 1920's, and by the decade of the 1930's it reached almost one-sixth of the value of exports.

For the first two decades of the century the trade of Indochina, Indonesia, the Philippines, and Thailand can be aggregated. During the decade 1911–1920 this trade resulted in an export surplus equivalent to 199 million U.S. dollars, which amounted to more than one-third of the value of exports of these states.[8] For the remaining two colonial decades through 1940 data are available permitting the trade of all of Southeast Asia to be aggregated. When this is done it becomes clear that by 1920 colonial development in the area was distinctive for the large and relatively stable proportions of export earnings which were not available to the colonies to pay for imports. This was true for the decade of the 1920's, a period of relative peace and economic stability when the average annual export surplus totaled $408 million, just as it characterized the 1930s, when economic depression originating in the United States was diffused to the rest of the world by trade and other economic exchanges. Although the average annual export surplus of Southeast Asia declined moderately to $364 million in the latter decade, it was virtually equivalent to one-third of the value of exports.

Understanding of the "colonial drain" is to be found in the processes of capitalist development which flourished in the colonial world. There, the savings of a rentier class of foreign investors and the capital and enterprise of aliens resident in Southeast Asia who participated actively in colonial economic development—predominantly Western, Chinese, and Indian— were combined with indigenous labor and readily exploitable natural

7. Frank Swettenham, *British Malaya*, rev. ed. (London, 1948), pp. 300 and 331. This reference includes data on trade of the Straits Settlements for fourteen years between 1868 and 1904 and for the Federated Malay States every five years from 1880 to 1905.

8. Unless otherwise indicated, all subsequent references to the dollar value of the trade and payments of Southeast Asia are in millions of current United States dollars.

resources to produce tropical foodstuffs and industrial raw materials in strong demand outside the area.[9] Relatively modest initial injections of alien/foreign-owned capital and alien entrepreneurship initiated a process of economic growth which became self-sustaining and increasingly independent of further geographic inflows of capital and entrepreneurial resources from the outside world. The contributions of capital and the skills of the alien capitalists/entrepreneurs to colonial development were essentially the same as those of their counterparts participating in the economic growth proceeding in the industrial world, but the consequences were markedly different. For the balance of payments, the result was a heavy export surplus as the ownership and control of modern economic activities became the private preserves of the alien/foreign participants in colonial development.

Economic growth was sustained, in large part, by alien businessmen who performed the essential capitalist function of "plowing back" a high proportion of the earnings of their enterprises in the colonies. This process served to enlarge the wages fund, thereby enabling more indigenous labor to be introduced into modern production, which raised the productivity of alien/foreign-owned capital and enterprise. At the same time, a portion of the earnings "plowed back" into the sector of modern enterprises enlarged the capital equipment with which labor worked, thereby raising the productivity of the latter. This process was reinforced by qualitative changes in indigenous labor as it assimilated to industrial employment in mines, plantations, and commercial and manufacturing enterprises. The capacity of these Southeast Asians to capture improvements in their productivity was severely limited, however, by urban migration, population growth, and the slow growth of employment opportunities outside peasant agriculture, processes which served to maintain the profitability of further expansion in the enterprises of the alien businessmen.[10]

The interstices between the large-scale modern enterprises of Western businessmen were filled by the smaller enterprises of Asian aliens—Chinese, Indians, and Arabs—who enlarged their firms by reinvesting earnings and

9. Hereinafter, nonindigenous participants in colonial development not resident in the area will be characterized as "foreign." If resident in the area, such participants will be called "alien." When reference is made to both categories of nonindigenous participants, "alien/foreign" will be used. In the same fashion, capital invested in Southeast Asia by investors residing outside the area will be called "foreign-owned." Capital invested in the area by alien capitalists/entrepreneurs residing in Southeast Asia and actively participating in colonial economic growth processes will be called "alien-owned." The combined capital of these two categories of investors will be categorized as "alien/foreign-owned."

10. The writer's debt to W. A. Lewis for the latter's insights into economic growth under conditions of enclave dualism, such as prevailed in colonial-period Southeast Asia, will be obvious to readers of Lewis's seminal essay, "Economic Development with Unlimited Supplies of Labor," *The Manchester School*, 22 (May 1954):139–191.

who, as moneylenders, retailers, and wholesaling agents for large Western trading firms, distributed imports and assembled for export the cash crops produced by Southeast Asia peasants. The appearance of cash crops, which more fully utilized the labor time of the peasants, markedly improved their productivity, but the capitalist organization of trade in such crops ensured that a disproportionate share of the improvement in peasant productivity would go to alien participants in commerce.

Insofar as geographic flows of commodities, services, and capital between Southeast Asia and the outside world are concerned, colonial economic growth produced steady expansion in the claim upon output accruing to the rentier class of foreign investors and to the resident alien capitalists/entrepreneurs. Over time, an increasing proportion of this claim upon the output of the area was transferred to the outside world as interest, profits and dividends, contributions to private pension reserves, and the family remittances of alien businessmen and their alien employees. To transfer the steadily growing share of output which accrued to the owners of alien/foreign-owned capital, and which they chose to spend outside Southeast Asia, required a steadily expanding export surplus.

The size of the "colonial drain" of Southeast Asia and its autonomous growth also reflected two aspects of colonialism which were not inherent in the processes of capitalist development underway in Southeast Asia. Most important was the role of portfolio investment and the rentier mentality of the foreign investor using this instrument as an outlet for his savings. The capital markets in London, Amsterdam, Paris, and New York were well organized to mobilize and transfer to the colonies the savings of small investors, which were used to fund social capital projects that supported and encouraged the private capitalist expansion.[11] The foreign investors who purchased bonds issued by colonial governments, in contrast to the alien capitalists/entrepreneurs participating in the development of the colonies, were interested in such instruments because they were motivated to consume the interest income to which they were entitled and, moreover, to consume this income in the West where they resided. As a result, a relatively large proportion of that part of the export surplus generated to service

11. Helmut G. Callis estimated that alien/foreign-owned investment in Southeast Asia totaled $3,754 million in 1930, including, *inter alia*, $2,887 million of entrepreneurial and $687 million of portfolio investment. Alien/foreign-owned entrepreneurial and portfolio investment in Indonesia in 1930, estimated to be $1,600 million and $397 million respectively, accounted for well over half of estimated alien/foreign-owned investment in the area. Professor Callis estimated that, by the late 1930's, alien/foreign-owned investment had increased to $3,836 million, of which $1,121 million was portfolio investment. Estimated alien/foreign-owned investment in Indonesia included $1,411 million entrepreneurial and $853 million portfolio. See Helmut G. Callis, *Foreign Capital in Southeast Asia* (New York, 1942).

alien/foreign-owned capital in Southeast Asia was used to transfer "interest" payments due to investors living elsewhere.[12]

Still another feature of colonialism not attributable to capitalist development was the stranglehold of aliens—Western and Asian—on administrative and professional employment provided by colonial bureaucracies. The colonial defense establishments were staffed disproportionately by aliens because of the anxieties of the Western rulers inherent in the colonial relationship. Similarly, the higher-level administrative and professional posts in the colonial bureaucracies were pre-empted by nationals of the colonial powers. Although these aliens were living in Southeast Asia, their pension reserves were invested abroad, they were frequently on home leave, their children were sent abroad for schooling, and, upon retirement at an early age and entitled to liberal pensions, they returned "home" to live.

For many students of colonial development confirmation of the exploitative nature of colonialism is found in the "colonial drain." Capitalist economic expansion without substantial indigenous participation in modern economic activities ensured that the value of Southeast Asian resources embodied in export commodities quickly came to exceed the value of outside resources embodied in commodities which Southeast Asia obtained through international specialization and trade. This state of affairs is at the heart of the moral issue raised by the "colonial drain": the capacity of the wealthier, developed world to exercise a constantly growing claim on the export earnings of the colonies without a compensating geographic movement of resources from the metropolitan powers to their colonies.

Similarly, it is little wonder that prior to World War II a succession of "heretical" economists—in the classical, neoclassical, and socialist traditions—were contributing insights that promised understanding of colonial development as a special case of capitalist growth. This intellectual ferment, which focused on the "theory of economic imperialism", failed to seriously distract orthodox economists, whose confidence in the validity and ethical impeccability of the marginal-productivity theory of income distribution remained unshaken. By the first decade of the century the controversy over economic imperialism, in which the contributions of socialist theoreticians were particularly fruitful, was increasingly focused on the evolving role

12. Boeke reports that the Netherlands Indies foreign debt increased fifteenfold between 1913 and 1934. By the latter year, the interest burden on the debt of guilders 65 million was equal to more than three-fifths of the estimated geographic outflow of "interest and dividends" (Boeke, p. 186). For the estimated outflow of interest and dividends in 1934, see League of Nations, Economic Intelligence Service, *Balance of Payments, 1938* (Geneva, 1939), pp. 55–57. In 1938, Indochina's expenditures for servicing the public debt "almost entirely held in France" accounted for one-fifth of expenditures of the central government of the colony (Robequain, pp. 150–158). For information on the cost of servicing the external debt of Burma during the late 1930's, see J. R. Andrus, *Burmese Economic Life* (Stanford, Calif., 1948), pp. 321–322.

of capital exports in economic relations between the industrial nucleus and the less developed periphery. Understanding of the process of capital accumulation in colonial development was clouded, however, by preoccupation with the rise of investment banking and concern for the increasing size of enterprises active in overseas development and the monopoly abuses threatened by their growth. Ultimately, the mainstream of socialist speculation over "economic imperialism" was diverted into a blind alley from which it has not emerged when Lenin—a better revolutionist than economist—pronounced economic imperialism "the monopoly stage of capitalism."

Before leaving the colonial period it is necessary to survey the fragmentary quantitative information available to assess the uses made of the foreign exchange earned by the export surplus of Southeast Asia. Here, in contrast with the trade data, we find only limited and relatively unreliable statistics on nontrade payments. For Indonesia, crude balance-of-payments statements exist for the years 1932–1938, with limited additional estimates for 1925–1931.[13] For Indochina, balance-of-payments statements are available for 1934–1937,[14] with additional estimates of the inflow of foreign investment going back to 1924. For the Philippines, crude but comprehensive statements exist for the period 1925–1940.[15] For Thailand and the other colonies of the area, only fragmentary data exist.

In the case of Indonesia, whose export surplus during the 1920's accounted for over half of the aggregate export surplus of Southeast Asia, the net outflow of "interest and dividends" for the six years 1925–1930 was estimated to have averaged $157 million annually.[16] For the Philippines, the net outflow of "interest and dividends" was estimated to have averaged $8 million annually over this period.

The same picture emerges from the available estimates for the 1930's. In the case of Indonesia, the net flow of "interest and dividends" was reduced markedly from levels estimated for the previous decade, but the average outflow for 1932 through 1938 was recorded as $71 million. For Indochina, the average annual outflow over the four years ending with 1937

13. League of Nations, *loc. cit.*
14. *Ibid.*, pp. 91–93.
15. For 1925–1931, see U.S. Tariff Commission, *United States-Philippine Trade*, Report No. 118, Second Series (Washington, D.C., 1937), pp. 37–38. For 1932–1940, see Technical Committee to the President of the Philippines, Report TC-1, *American-Philippine Trade Relations* (Washington, D.C., 1944), p. 227.
16. Estimates of "interest and dividends" paid to foreign investors in the Netherlands Indies are net of reinvested earnings accruing to owners of alien/foreign capital. Although documentation of the scattered estimates for other colonies is incomplete, it appears that retained earnings generally were not included in pre–World War II estimates. This practice resulted in estimates of the geographic flow out of the colony of the earnings of foreign-owned capital but substantially understated the total income accruing to alien/foreign-owned capital because a major part of such income was being reinvested or invested directly in the colonies in existing enterprises and in new enterprises.

was estimated to be $35 million; and for the Philippines, for the nine years ending with 1940, the average annual outflow was $15 million. These estimates aggregate to an outflow from the three colonies of $121 million and, together with the estimates available for the earlier decade, suggest that if comparable data existed for Thailand and the missing colonies the net outflow of "interest and dividend" payments probably averaged somewhat more than half of the average annual export surplus earned by Southeast Asia during the 1920's and the 1930's.

A second major use of foreign exchange earned from exports was to make private remittances. Here the coverage of balance-of-payments estimates is fragmentary but suggestive of the magnitude of this outflow. Estimates exist for the Philippines for the period from 1932 through 1940, for Indonesia for 1932 through 1938, and for Indochina for 1934 through 1937. The average annual estimated net outflows of private remittances from these three colonies during the middle 1930's total $26 million. In view of the fact that the proportions of Asian aliens in the populations of these colonies were low relative to those for Burma, Thailand, and Malaya/Singapore, private remittances from the whole of Southeast Asia during the interwar period may have averaged as much as $80 million annually.[17]

A remaining major category of expenditures that utilized the surplus of foreign exchange earned by Southeast Asia from trade includes government transfers abroad to pay the pensions of retired Western civil servants and personnel who had served in the military establishments in the colonies and, in the case of Indonesia, the large budgetary subvention transferred from the colony to the Netherlands government. Such estimates are limited to two colonies, Indonesia and Indochina. For the former, net pensions paid abroad averaged $18 million annually during the period from 1932 through 1938, and, in addition, the colony was contributing $24 million annually to the budget of the Netherlands government. In the case of Indochina, the net outflow in connection with pensions and the "pay of officials on leave" averaged one million dollars annually over the four years from 1934–1937. Although comparable estimates do not exist for Thailand or other colonies in the area, the occasional qualitative judgments expressed by economists

17. For estimates of the outflow of Chinese remittances from Thailand during periods in the 1920's and 1930's, see G. W. Skinner, *Chinese Society in Thailand* (Ithaca, 1957), pp. 224–227. In the case of Burma, J. R. Andrus concludes, "The phenomenal 'favorable' balance of merchandise trade of Burma [during the late 1930's] was accounted for by the fact that most of the million Indian immigrants were single males who sent surplus funds to the extent of approximately Rp. 30 million annually to their families in India by money order alone. Indians also sent money to India in other ways and when they returned to India, they took savings with them" (Andrus, p. 182). See also G. E. Harvey, *British Rule in Burma* (London, 1946), p. 71. Harvey's estimate of telegraphic transfers of remittances by Indians is twice that of Andrus.

and other scholars suggest that such out-payments were considerable in the case of Burma and Malaya/Singapore.[18]

It is obvious that attempts to locate, refine, and aggregate estimates of the pre–World War II payments of colonial Southeast Asia other than those arising in trade transactions are doomed to rapidly diminishing returns. It seems reasonably clear from the data summarized above, however, that the net geographic outflow of "interest and dividends" over the two decades from 1921 to 1940 utilized at least one-half of the area's foreign exchange earnings from trade; the net outflow of "private remittances" may have utilized a further one-fifth of such earnings, with bureaucratic pensions plus the heavy budgetary transfers from the Netherlands Indies approaching another fifth. In other words, the aggregate net geographic outflow of payments in these categories, on the average and for the area as a whole, probably accounted for 85 to 90 per cent of the "colonial drain" of Southeast Asia during the 1920's and 1930's.[19]

II

The remainder of this essay is concerned with the impact of independence and sovereignty on the "colonial drain" and seeks to assess the importance of changes in various categories of payments which dramatically transformed the trade balance of the area to a substantial import surplus. To initiate this analysis, the average annual trade balances for the major political entities of Southeast Asia over the course of three decades, 1921–1930, 1931–1940, and 1954–1963, are compared.

The decade 1921–1930 is a satisfactory base for this comparison because it was a period of relative peace and economic growth with minor fluctuations in real economic activity. By the end of 1920, the sharp recession following the war, for the most part, had completed its course, and trade expansion in the pre–World War I pattern was ready to resume. The last year in the decade, 1930, was somewhat abnormal because world trade was contracting under the impact of the depression, but this process was in its early stages.

The period 1931–1940 is introduced into the comparison because it is a time of great interest to economists, historians, and the peoples in the less developed world generally. The severe worldwide depression made it most

18. Andrus comments: "Pensions to civil servants (the retiring age was 55) amounted to a considerable sum and much of that sum was transferred abroad, as European civil servants also ordinarily retired in the United Kingdom" (Andrus, p. 182). These same comments also applied to the civil servants of prewar Malaya/Singapore.

19. A minor portion of cumulative export surplus of the area was accounted for by the slow growth of monetary reserves under the foreign-exchange reserve systems that extended the international gold standard to the colonial world.

unusual, and for this reason it would not be a satisfactory base period for analysis of the transformation of the "colonial drain." On the other hand, introducing this decade into the comparative analysis strongly corroborates the conclusions that emerge from analysis of changes from the previous decade.

The postindependence decade selected for comparison, 1954–1963, was chosen for three reasons. First, when it began, sufficient time had elapsed for the effects of the Korean War "boom" in raw-material prices on the trade of Southeast Asia to have been worked off, and a relatively normal pattern of trade expansion in real terms was underway. Second, a major new institution, economic aid for economic development, had undergone a few years of testing and experimentation and had settled into a relatively stable

Table 2. Southeast Asia: Dimensions of the "colonial drain" in the twentieth century (annual average value in millions of U.S. dollars; imports as a percentage of exports)

	1901–1910			*1911–1920*		
Area	*Imports*	*Exports*	$\frac{Imports}{Exports}$	*Imports*	*Exports*	$\frac{Imports}{Exports}$
Indochina	40	36	111%	45	59	76%
Indonesia	87	129	67%	202	382	53%
Philippines*	36	32	113%	83	82	101%
Thailand	21	30	70%	35	41	85%
Southeast Asia	184	227	81%	365	564	65%

	1921–1930			*1931–1940*		
Area	*Imports*	*Exports*	$\frac{Imports}{Exports}$	*Imports*	*Exports*	$\frac{Imports}{Exports}$
Burma	126	227	56%	76	173	44%
Indochina	92	112	83%	53	75	71%
Indonesia	326	559	58%	211	374	61%
Malaya/Singapore	430	462	93%	282	334	85%
Philippines	129	136	95%	102	140	73%
Thailand	73	90	81%	46	65	71%
Southeast Asia	1,176	1,584	74%	771	1,135	68%

Source of trade statistics: Except for Burma, U.S. Department of Commerce, *Foreign Commerce Yearbook* and predecessor publication, *Foreign Commerce* (both annual publications). Data for Burma from J. R. Andrus, *Burmese Economic Life* (Stanford, Calif., 1948), p. 183.

* Philippine import values which are recorded f.o.b. have been increased by 12% to convert them to c.i.f. basis. The import values recorded for the rest of Southeast Asia include insurance and freight charges. Similarly, the recorded values of Philippine exports have been increased by the value of Philippine gold production as Philippine exports of gold, which by the late 1930's accounted for one-quarter of foreign exchange earnings from commodity exports, were excluded from the recorded trade returns.

pattern. Third, the decade selected terminates before any major buildup in
the United States military expenditures occasioned by the war in Vietnam
had taken place. American military expenditures, which were relatively
modest and stable over the decade, were dominated by support of the
American military establishment in the Philippines.[20]

The impact of independence and sovereignty on the trade balances of the
major states of Southeast Asia and for the area as a whole is summarized in
Tables 2 and 3. During the 1920's every colony plus Thailand experienced

Table 3.   Southeast Asia: The postcolonial balance of trade, 1954–
1963 (annual average value in millions of U.S. dollars; imports as a
percentage of exports)

Area	Imports	Exports	Export surplus	Imports/Exports
Burma	223	234	12	95%
Indochina	356	127	−229	281%
Indonesia	641	790	149	81%
Malaya/Singapore	1,483	1,352	−131	110%
Philippines*	627	511	−116	123%
Thailand	429	377	−52	114%
Southeast Asia	3,759	3,391	−467	111%

Note: Rows and columns do not add exactly because amounts have
been rounded.

Sources of trade statistics: United Nations/International Monetary
Fund/International Bank for Reconstruction and Development,
Direction of International Trade, Statistical Papers, Series T, and IMF,
IBRD, *Direction of Trade* (supplement to *International Financial Statis-
tics*) *Annual, 1958–62* and *1962–66.*

* Trade data for Philippines obtained from United Nations, *Yearbook of International Trade Statistics, 1968*, Statistical Papers, Series G
(New York, 1970). Philippine imports adjusted to c.i.f. basis and
reported exports have been increased by value of gold production.

an export surplus. Moreover, only five annual trade balances—three for
Malaya/Singapore and two for the Philippines—of the sixty covered by the
decade were import surpluses. For the 1930's the same picture emerges,
and, again, only five annual trade balances were import surpluses.

The aggregate average annual export surplus for the area during the
1920's was $408 million, or more than $4 billion over the decade. In the
succeeding decade the aggregate export surplus declined by 11 per cent, to

20. Over the decade 1954–1963, U.S. defense expenditures in Southeast Asia averaged
$70 million annually, of which seven-tenths were outlays in the Philippines. See U.S. Depart-
ment of Commerce, Office of Business Economics, *Balance of Payments Statistical Supplement*,
rev. ed. (Washington, D.C., 1963), and *Survey of Current Business*, December 1969, p. 44.
By 1967, U.S. military expenditures in Southeast Asia had jumped to more than $1 billion
annually.

$364 million, but because the total value of exports declined even more rapidly, the export surplus as a ratio of the value of exports increased from one-quarter to slightly less than one-third.

When we turn to the postindependence decade, 1954–1963, we find that a major change has taken place. Four of the states experienced substantial import surpluses over the period, and, for the area as a whole, the "colonial drain" has been replaced by an import surplus of $467 million annually.

Although Burma and Indonesia—colonies whose export surpluses over the 1920's and 1930's were substantially larger, relative to export earnings, than those of the other states in the area—experienced export surpluses for the decade 1954–1963, these states made major contributions to the elimination of Southeast Asia's "colonial drain." Burma experienced an average annual export surplus of $12 million during 1954–1963, an amount equal to only one-eighth the dollar value of Burma's unrequited export surplus during the interwar decades.

In the case of Indonesia, the absolute value of the export surplus during 1954–1963 was less than two-thirds that experienced during the decade of the 1920's, and the ratio of Indonesia's unrequited exports to total exports declined from 42 to 19 per cent. Moreover, inflation over the periods compared wiped out much—probably half to three-quarters—of the real burden of an export surplus of a given dollar amount.

Measuring the "turnaround" in the aggregate balance of trade of Southeast Asia over the periods compared is a relatively simple matter, and the change can be expressed in terms of trade values prevailing in either of the periods used in the comparison. Since we are interested in analyzing the changes resulting from sovereignty and independence, and inasmuch as reliable data on the nontrade payments of Southeast Asia are concentrated in the postindependence period, analysis is facilitated by expressing the "turnaround" in terms of the value of trade during 1954–1963. If expenditures by Southeast Asia on imports had increased in proportion to the increase in Southeast Asia's export earnings between 1921–1930 and 1954–1963, the value of imports in the latter period would have amounted to 74 per cent of exports, or $2,510 million. Imports in the decade after independence, in fact, were valued at $3,759 million. Therefore, over the periods compared, changes occurred which enabled the states of Southeast Asia to consume $1,249 million more of imports annually during 1954–1963 than they would have been able to consume if these changes had not occurred.[21]

21. Behind this calculation lies the assumption that Southeast Asia's enlarged capacity to import has not resulted from improvement in the terms of trade; that prices received for Southeast Asian exports have not increased significantly relative to prices paid for imports into the area. The widely held conviction that the terms of trade for primary products are doomed to decline secularly assures that the above assumption will not be controversial, but the existence of such a conviction proves nothing.

Elimination of the "colonial drain" carries obvious implications for international income distribution, levels of welfare, and interregional movements of capital. In the 1920's and 1930's up to one-third of the exports of Southeast Asia did not result in imports, and a significant part of the real product and income of the area was being transferred to the outside world without a compensating geographic flow of resources into the area. Since World War II this transfer of income has been reversed, and whether assessed on grounds of need, equity, or the inefficiency evident in international differences in factor productivities, this is the desirable direction for internationally mobile capital to flow.

Why has this important change taken place? The obvious answer is that a new institution—economic aid—has materialized to mobilize and transfer a part of the savings of wealthier societies to those that are less well off. Such transfers enable the recipient countries to have more imports without compensating exports.

Aggregation of central government receipts of unrequited transfer payments (grant aid) in Southeast Asia (see Table 4), reveals that the annual inflow of government-to-government transfer payments over the decade 1954–1963 averaged $372 million. This geographic inflow of grant aid was supplemented, moreover, by capital transferred as government-to-government lending (loan aid), which averaged $110 million annually.[22]

Grant and loan aid combined of some $480 million annually accounted for about two-fifths of the average annual turnaround in the aggregate balance of payments of Southeast Asia between the decade of the 1920's and the decade after independence. There remains, therefore, the problem of accounting by other changes for the principal part of the postindependence expansion of imports into Southeast Asia.

The next obvious place to turn is private foreign investment. Here, the coverage of the estimates is less complete, and the meaning of the available estimates is confused by their frequent revision. For the period from 1954 to 1963, receipts of alien/foreign-owned private capital in Southeast Asia averaged $126 million annually. This magnitude cannot be considered a net contribution to the turnaround in the balance of trade, however, since private foreign investment, in contrast to grant and loan aid, is not a new institution; it was flourishing in the colonial world from 1850 onward. Whether or not the inflow and accumulation of alien/foreign-owned private capital contributed to the turnaround in the balance of trade of Southeast

22. For confirmation of the reliability of estimates obtained by aggregating the postindependence balances of payments of Southeast Asian states, see Organization for Economic Cooperation and Development (OECD), *Resources for the Developing World* (Paris, 1970), pp. 304 and 312, for aid transfers to Southeast Asia reported by the Soviet Bloc, and OECD, *The Flow of Financial Resources to Less Developed Countries, 1956–63* (Paris, 1964), Table V.3, and *1964–65* (Paris, 1966), Table VIII.2, for aid transfers to the area reported by non-Communist developed countries.

Table 4. Southeast Asia: Major balance-of-payments categories, 1954–1963 (annual average in millions of U.S. dollars; inflow = +)

	Central government		Monetary capital accounts	Private foreign investment	Investment income	Private transfer payments			Errors and omissions
	Transfer payments	Loans				Inflow	Outflow	Net	
Burma	18.1	4.6	−1.9	−2.0	−1.7	1.6	−5.0	−3.5	3.5
Cambodia*	29.7	—	−2.7	−2.2	−.3	.2	−.1	.1	1.8
Indonesia†	38.6	68.9	29.4	4.2	−85.1	8.6	.3	8.3	−11.1
Laos‡	36.2	−.3	3.5	neg	1.0	na	na	na	na
Malaya/Singapore§	5.9	9.1	−42.5	58.9	−52.0	na	−73.8	−73.8	42.4
Philippines	32.3	10.7	11.5	31.6	−48.9	57.2	−2.3	54.9	−36.8
Thailand	29.0	2.3	−24.3	27.5	−5.7	4.3	−4.9	−.6	16.8
South Vietnam‖	182.4	14.9	−10.8	1.9	−4.6	11.9	−.6	11.3	.6
Southeast Asia	372.2	110.2	−37.8	119.9	−197.3	83.8	−87.0	−3.2	17.2

Source: International Monetary Fund, *Balance of Payments Yearbook*, vol. 11, (1957–58) and subsequent issues. Estimates in U.S. dollars for all entries except private transfer payments were obtained from Summary Statements of this publication. Estimates of private transfer payments were obtained from Country Statements. Unless otherwise indicated, entries for 1954 were obtained from *Balance of Payments Yearbook*, vol. 11; for 1955, vol. 12; for 1956, vol. 14; and for 1957–1963, vol. 17.

* Averages for six years, 1958–1963.
† Estimates for 1957 and 1958, vol. 14; for 1959–1963, vol. 19.
‡ Averages for four years, 1958–1961; estimates from vol. 14.
§ Averages for eight years, 1956–1963; estimates for 1956–1959, vol. 12; for 1960–1963, vol. 16.
‖ Averages for eight years, 1956–1963; estimates for 1956–1958, vol. 16; for 1959–1963. vol. 19.

Asia can be assessed only by comparing postindependence net receipts with net receipts of alien/foreign-owned private capital in the decade of the 1920's. Unfortunately, for purposes of this comparison, the sketchy balance-of-payments statements for the Southeast Asian colonies in the interwar period appear generally to report capital receipts net of reinvested earnings, whereas the postindependence estimates, with some exceptions, include reinvested earnings.[23] Although the two colonies for which estimates are available for periods in the 1920's—the Philippines and Indonesia—report a net annual outflow of private capital of $18 million over the five years from 1925 to 1929, the large and growing export surpluses of these colonies confirm that alien/foreign-owned capital was accumulating steadily.[24] The expanding claims of the owners of such capital to domestic output, a part of which they chose to consume and invest abroad, was accounting for the growing export surplus at the same time that alien/foreign-owned capital was accumulating in the area.

Widespread political instability, inflationary pressures, government intervention in economic processes, and the relentless pressures of economic nationalism, including extensive expropriation of alien/foreign-owned enterprises, have inhibited foreign investment in postindependence Southeast Asia. Because of the investment climate prevailing in the area, the possibility that the inflow of private foreign capital including retained earnings during 1954–1963 was greater in dollar amount than the comparable inflow during the 1920's, in this writer's opinion, is quite remote.[25]

Next it is necessary to consider the possibility that the enlarged capacity to import is explained by the drawing down of foreign exchange reserves. The available estimates for the period from 1954 to 1963, which are relatively complete, show a net outflow of "monetary sector capital" of $38 million annually.

23. The irrelevance of comparing post–World War II estimates of capital movements into Southeast Asia, which include capital accumulation financed substantially by retained earnings and by the savings of aliens domiciled in the area, with crude estimates of the geographic inflow of capital in the 1920's is illustrated by recent Philippine balance-of-payments estimates. During the six years from 1954 to 1960 the Philippine estimates of receipts of private (nonmonetary) capital, including retained earnings, averaged $72 million annually. In 1961 the Philippines began reporting capital movements net of undistributed earnings, and over the five years ending with 1965 the official estimates report an average annual outflow of capital of $51 million annually. Who can fault an underdeveloped country for choosing to define capital flows in terms of geographic movements and excluding capital accumulation created out of resources existing within the country?

24. For sources of data, see nn. 12 and 15 above.

25. For extended treatment of the climate for alien/foreign-owned capital in Southeast Asia since independence, see Frank H. Golay, Ralph Anspach, M. Ruth Pfanner, and Eliezer B. Ayal, *Underdevelopment and Economic Nationalism in Southeast Asia* (Ithaca, 1969), passim.

To what extent is the improved import capability in Southeast Asia the result of military aid and big-power military expenditures in the area? Military expenditures by big powers which maintained defense forces in the area between 1954 and 1963 were dominated by those of the United States, which, as reported above, averaged $70 million annually.[26] Again, it should be emphasized that such expenditures are not unique to the postcolonial period. For example, between 1934 and 1937 government expenditures by the United States and France in Southeast Asia averaged $39 million annually, and the United Kingdom undoubtedly was making substantial expenditures in her colonies.[27]

To summarize the argument to this point: the balance-of-payments estimates available for the countries of Southeast Asia for the 1920's and 1930's and the postindependence decade 1954–1963 provide reasonably reliable evidence supporting the conclusion that about one-half of the improvement in the capacity of Southeast Asia to import between the 1920's and the decade after independence was accounted for by grant and loan aid, private capital inflows, the drawing down of foreign exchange reserves built up during the Korean War "boom," and big-power military expenditures in the area. The major changes that explain the remaining half of the improvement in the import capacity are readily identified, although they cannot be quantified with confidence.

The change in private remittances (private transfer payments) is confirmed by extensive balance-of-payments estimates. In the decade after independence the inflow of such payments into Southeast Asia of $84 million annually almost matched the estimated outflow of $87 million. Inasmuch as the net outflow of such payments in the 1920's may have been in the range of $75 to $90 million annually, independence has produced a sharp change in this flow. Vigilant economic nationalism, a general exodus of Western populations from former colonies, government regulation and monopolization of foreign exchange, strict control over immigration, repatriation of the Indian minority in Burma, improved balance in the sexual distribution of alien minorities, particularly in Malaya/Singapore, and the lapse of time and political changes which have weakened the personal and economic ties of Asian aliens to their homeland, all help to explain the decline in the outflow of private remittances. At the same time, remittances from Southeast Asian emigrants, particularly Filipinos in Hawaii and Guam, and expanded transfers of religious and international service agencies have augmented the inflow of private transfer payments.

26. See n. 20. The United Kingdom and Australia maintained military forces in the area, but data on expenditures in support of these forces were not available to the writer.

27. For sources, see nn. 14 and 15 above. Estimates for Indochina are classified "military expenditures"; for the Philippines, "United States government expenditures."

Achievement of independence was invariably accompanied by repudiation, or transfer to the colonial powers, of such obligations as pensions due Western civil servants and budgetary subventions such as that transferred by the Netherlands Indies to the colonial power. We can assume that the absence of these items in the postindependence balance-of-payments statements of the countries of Southeast Asia reflects the fact that no significant outflows now take place in these categories. In fact, a net inflow of such payments since independence has been substantial. In the case of the Philippines, for example, pension obligations to Filipinos inducted into the United States armed forces in the closing months of World War II have resulted in U.S. Veterans Administration payments which averaged in excess of $60 million annually during 1954–1963.

Finally, it is necessary to assess the change in the flow of investment income from Southeast Asia. Unfortunately, the data to quantify this change do not exist because the estimates of the outflow of such payments in the 1920's (a) were generally net of reinvested earnings which added to the equity of the alien/foreign owners of enterprises and (b) appear in general not to include investment income paid to resident aliens in Southeast Asia. Payments of "dividends and interest" servicing alien/foreign-owned capital in the area averaged $197 million annually during 1954–1963. Although such payments may have been little changed in dollar amount as compared to the net geographic outflow of payments servicing foreign-owned capital which can be inferred from the fragmentary estimates for the 1920's, the comparison is irrelevant. Conversion of the postindependence estimates to the same basis as those available for the 1920's, or the reverse, could only show a substantial decline in the net outflow of post-independence payments.

For example, a substantial part—perhaps as much as half—of the geographic outflow of such payments in the 1920's represented interest transferred to foreign owners of portfolio securities.[28] In a number of cases, achievement of independence was followed by repudiation of the external debt incurred by the colonial government. In other cases, responsibility for servicing the debt was transferred to the former colonial power by agreement. In every case, the debt service obligation of the successor state was drastically scaled down.

Since the 1920's, the proportion of foreign-exchange earnings required to transfer profits, interest, and dividends to foreign owners of capital invested in the area has declined substantially. This change has reflected the growing virulence of economic nationalism and the determination of Southeast Asian societies to transform the colonial-type economies they

28. See nn. 11 and 12 above.

inherited with independence into national economies in which the ownership and control of economic activities are in the hands of nationals. In
Indonesia and Burma this transfer was ultimately accomplished by overt
expropriation, reinforced in Burma by the repatriation of the Indian
minority which traditionally had played a major role in internal commerce
and moneylending. In the Philippines, Indochina, and Malaya, the transfer
of power was followed by the contraction in the relative importance of
alien/foreign ownership and participation, a process maintained by the
structure of policy measures erected to increase indigenous participation in
economic activities. Thailand also has not lagged behind her neighbors in
seeking to expand indigenous ownership and control of modern economic
activities.

III

The substantial improvement in the capacity of Southeast Asia to import
following the liquidation of colonialism in the area is explained by two
types of changes: first, those changes which reflect the initiative of the
developed world, the most important of which has been the emergence of
economic aid in the form of grants and loans to transfer savings from richer
to less wealthy countries. To a minor extent, economic aid has been
supplemented by various types of big-power expenditures, particularly
those of the United States in the Philippines, and by the drawing down of
the foreign exchange reserves of Southeast Asian countries. Examination
of the available data confirms the relatively minor role that the geographic
inflow of private foreign investment has played in directly enlarging the
import capacity of Southeast Asia over the periods compared. The data
support the conclusion that the dollar value of the inflow of alien/foreign-
owned foreign investment into Southeast Asia, if placed on a comparable
basis for the periods compared, has undergone little change, and probably
has declined.

The second category of changes are those that have resulted from the
actions of Southeast Asian societies themselves. The assertion of an economic sovereignty to match their hard-won political independence has been
reflected in each state in a structure of policies designed to expand the
ownership of productive assets outside traditional agriculture by nationals
and to ensure their pre-emption of rewarding economic functions. The
means adopted by Southeast Asian societies to achieve these goals have
been diverse, but the end result has been the same; the claims to the
foreign exchange earned by exports of alien/foreign participants in Southeast Asian economies—as owners of capital, entrepreneurs, pensioners, and
receivers of remittances—have steadily contracted in the face of the deter-

mination of Southeast Asian societies to organize economic progress which is national and not merely geographic.

It is necessary to close with two caveats. The basic argument of this paper constitutes a process of elimination which leaves roughly half of the improved capability of Southeast Asia to import following the collapse of colonialism in the area to be explained by changes in economic magnitudes which cannot be supported adequately by the available data. The argument is complex, and the findings can only be assessed as tenuous. Admittedly, the firmess of the conviction evident in the writer's qualitative judgments reflects his study of economic nationalism in Southeast Asia rather than the quantitative evidence introduced herein.

The economic implications of the reversal of the "colonial drain" of Southeast Asia into a substantial import surplus are cluttered with ambiguities. From the viewpoint of the distribution of a given volume of total world output, an import surplus represents an inflow of commodities and resources available to sustain a higher level of welfare in Southeast Asia. Economists are also agreed that an import surplus of goods and services is the measure of the inflow of net foreign investment in the sense that savings (foregone consumption) from the outside world are made available to the country experiencing such a surplus. The question of whether or not the recipient society is capable of converting such savings into additional capital equipment is another—and more crucial—issue.

More important to the societies of Southeast Asia, however, is the threat to their independence and sovereignty embodied in an import surplus. It results in a relationship of dependence and circumscribes, or threatens to circumscribe, autonomy and freedom of political action. There is probably no statesman or political leader in the underdeveloped world today— or in the developed world, for that matter—who does not understand the contribution which a buoyant export surplus makes to genuine sovereignty. After all, that is what nationalism is all about.

Southeast Asian History
and the Social Sciences

JOHN D. LEGGE

Monash University

The appearance of the first edition of D. G. E. Hall's *History of South-East Asia* in 1955 coincided roughly with a change in the character of Western writings about the region. Prewar Western scholarship had been of two main types: the study of the early history of Southeast Asia based partly on archaeology, partly on epigraphical sources, and partly on the analysis of the limited number of literary sources available; and the study of the colonial histories of those parts of Southeast Asia which had passed under the rule of one or another of the European powers. The former enquiry was devoted in considerable measure to determining a chronology of sometimes doubtfully known events and to discerning the outlines of institutions and material culture. It reached something of a climax with the publication by George Cœdès in 1944 of *Les Etats hindouisés d'Indochine et d'Indonésie*. The latter enquiry was perhaps more firmly grounded in the archival sources of the metropolitan powers—Portugal, the Netherlands, Britain, and France. In consequence, it produced what would now be regarded as incurably Eurocentric history, but nevertheless it yielded such standard contributions as J. S. Furnivall's *Netherlands India* (1939) and Rupert Emerson's *Malaysia* (1937).

World War II made a sharp break in the historiography as well as the history of Southeast Asia. The emergence after the war of the new nations of Burma, Indonesia, and the Philippines, the plans for the more rapid political development of Malaya, and the expansion of nationalist struggle in Indo-China focussed attention upon the restored autonomy of the various parts of the region and thus gave a fresh perspective to the study of its past. As the new nations of Southeast Asia sought a basis in history for their sense of national identity, so Western historians, too, were disposed to see the colonial period in Southeast Asia as an interlude in a much longer and essentially autonomous history. They were ready also to see common patterns in the region as a whole where their predecessors had concentrated most of their attention upon its separate parts which had come under the sway of this or that European power, writing the histories of Burma or Netherlands India or French Indo-China or the Philippines rather than the history of Southeast Asia. Separate national histories, it is true, continue to occupy most of the field, but the perception of Southeast Asia has nevertheless managed to establish itself.

Hall's *History* came aptly as the changing emphases were revealing themselves. It was at once a reflection of the change and a stimulus to it; it represented a kind of stocktaking of the state of knowledge of the region as a whole, on the basis of which the more detailed study of its parts could continue. It also insisted on the autonomy of Southeast Asian history, complaining of "the insidious tendency to overstress the part played by the imported cultures and to underrate the importance of the indigenous ones of the area."[1] In these words it appealed to historians to approach Southeast Asia as a field of study in its own right and not merely as a "cultural appendage," a mere branch of Indology or Sinology.

But the change in the character of Southeast Asian historiography was not merely a matter of perspective; there was also present a methodological change. The postwar study of the new republics of Southeast Asia was conducted in large measure not only by historians but by political scientists, sociologists, and economists who brought new techniques of comparative enquiry to their examination of emergent nations, of new elites, of the role of armies, of the problems of securing self-sustaining economic growth, and it was not surprising that historians should draw heavily upon their findings and sometimes even borrow their techniques. This of course was a development not confined to historians of Southeast Asia—the expansion of the social sciences had its impact in other fields of history also—but it was perhaps true that the Western study of Southeast Asian history was particularly open to the attraction of social-science theory, in part because the study of alien cultures might be better ordered by an awareness of basic structure, in part because the uncertainty of the chronology of early Southeast Asian history could in some measure be counterbalanced by an understanding of the general shape of early Southeast Asian societies. Hence a concern with what Harry Benda called "the structure of Southeast Asian history."[2] Hence, too, an interest in a variety of conceptual aids to enquiry. To Benda it seemed that the very fact that the study of Southeast Asian history was comparatively underdeveloped gave it the opportunity to borrow the techniques of other disciplines and advance in a more ordered and systematic way in consequence. He drew an analogy with the advantages of a late start in industrialization which enabled the latecomer to

1. D. G. E. Hall, *A History of South-East Asia* (London, 1955), p. 4.
2. H. J. Benda, "The Structure of Southeast Asian History," *JSEAH*, 3, 1 (March 1962):106–138.

avoid the mistakes of others and to draw on greater scientific knowledge and use far more modern tools. To John Smail it seemed that a history concerned with sociological realities would make possible a truer understanding of the continuing autonomy of Southeast Asian history.[3]

Hall's *History* was less reflective of these methodological shifts than it was of the shift in perspective. With his firm sense of the facts of the past he was not easily seduced by theoretical speculation. His purpose was to get the story down in coherent and straightforward fashion and to bring together the findings of the latest research. He was not much drawn to debate methodological questions. On the contrary, he took his own methodological premises for granted and left it to others to undertake a self-conscious consideration of the types of patterns that the historian might legitimately discern or the kinds of contributions that other social sciences might make to the understanding of the past. He could borrow when the insights of others seemed useful to him, but he did so in an unself-conscious way, without any desire to elaborate at a theoretical level a view of history's relationship to the social sciences.

During a period in which comparative analysis became the order of the day and the imperialism of the social sciences seemed to be invading history's traditional domain and perhaps undermining the very claim of history to be a separate and autonomous discipline, Hall's pragmatism and his concern with the accuracy of narrative might have seemed old-fashioned. But it may be wondered whether the social-science boom has in fact managed to deliver its promised goods or whether, on the contrary, history is not now in a position to reassert its own rights and to move to recover some of its too easily ceded territory.

A consideration of history's relations with neighbouring disciplines and of its dependence on them as against the independence of its own rules and methods of enquiry needs to be seen against the background of a more general debate, generated at about the same time, about the nature of the historian's enquiry. It is a debate that has engaged other than Southeast Asian historians, but the evolution of the discussion may seem to have implications for the way in which Southeast Asian historians see their task.

The debate has engaged the attention of philosophers rather than of practising historians, and perhaps for good reason, for the questions round which it has centred have been, for the most part, questions of logic rather than matters of practice. What is the nature of historical explanation? Is it logically of the same kind as explanation in the natural sciences? or

---

3. J. R. W. Smail, "On the Possibility of an Autonomous History of Modern Southeast Asia," *JSEAH*, 2, 2 (July 1961):72–102.

as explanation in the social sciences? Is it, like them, dependent on observed regularities of human behaviour which may be formulated as laws, so that an explanation of an event would involve the assigning of that event to its place in a class of events about which general knowledge already exists? Does the "covering law model" of explanation, as it has been called, fit the historian's practice? Or is historical explanation essentially of a different kind from scientific explanation? Does the uniqueness of historical events prevent generalization, or does the historian's concern with reason and motive mean that his explanation must involve entering into the minds of others and understanding their thoughts—a matter of *verstehen* rather than the counting of regularities. Many have argued so, believing with R. G. Collingwood that "for history, the object to be discovered is not the mere event, but the thought expressed in it. To discover that thought is already to understand it."[4] But the fashion has been, for the most part, the other way.

What influence were issues of this kind likely to have on the actual practice of historians, affecting the nature of their approach to their evidence, the kind of conclusions they might draw from it, or the way in which they might present their findings? For a time there did seem to be a direct connection between theoretical argument and practical application; and certainly the protagonists in the debate seemed to believe that critical issues of method and practice were at stake in the theoretical discussion. Those who argued that historical explanation is the same in logical form as scientific explanation seemed also to be suggesting that, if historians could only be persuaded of this view, it would affect what they did. It would allow them, and even encourage them, to concern themselves with general patterns rather than merely with particular events, and it would thus provide a logical basis for a breakthrough towards a new and more scientific history. Tremendous prestige attached to the notion that history is a science, a notion which involved not merely the traditional criteria of historical rigour—a critical approach to sources, care in the handling of evidence, an awareness of one's assumptions and of the possibility of bias, a determination not to go further than the evidence allowed in reaching conclusions—but went beyond these to the idea that the historian's job is to discover laws of human behaviour.

There was a considerable sense of euphoria among those who thought in this way. R. M. Crawford, for example, argued that events or conditions offered as historical explanations could only explain if they were seen as examples of general laws. Though historians might be concerned, on the whole, with the actual determining relationships of particular events to

4. R. G. Collingwood, *The Idea of History* (Oxford, 1964), p. 214.

each other, nevertheless, "we cannot speak of *actual determining relationships* unless we assume that the particular relationships are instances of regular relationships, that is, of regularities that could be formulated as laws."[5] From this he went on to hope that attempts to formulate laws would lay bare the implicit assumptions of historians, make their analyses more precise, enable a more exact testing of their generalizations, and blur the dividing line between historians and sociologists. If historical explanations implied the existence of general knowledge, then the discovery of these laws could be a legitimate object of historical enquiry.

The opponents of this view, on the other hand, looked with suspicion on the euphoria, and indeed on the whole idea that history could be made more scientific. Their objections were of several kinds. They held that arid generalization would rob history of the richness of texture that was its distinguishing feature and would replace its sense of "the contingent and the unforeseen"[6] by a false and indeed arrogant sense of confidence about the nature of the historical pattern. Or it was said that the specific nature of the events with which the historian is concerned rules out the idea of generalization. In the last resort the historian's explanation, said Herbert Butterfield, "is not a piece of general reasoning at all. He explains the French Revolution by discovering exactly what it was that occurred; and if at any point we need further elucidation all that he can do is to take us into greater detail, and make us see in still more definite concreteness what really did take place."[7] The covering law theorist would respond that Butterfield had misunderstood the point—that even where an explanation is given in all its definite concreteness, some kind of law will be implied—but it was important nonetheless that the working historian's concern was likely to be with the particular events and not with the law. His sense of specific events was likely to be so close that, even if it could be allowed that any historical explanation might be thrown into lawlike form, this would be an artificial process, and many of the resulting "laws" would be so precisely defined, so heavily burdened with specific detail, that they would hardly be laws at all, or would be laws with only a single case.[8] Further, where explanations were given in terms of motives and reasons it would not be correct to speak of covering laws at all. The understanding

5. R. M. Crawford, "History as a Science," *Historical Studies, Australia and New Zealand*, 3, 11 (November 1947):164. Crawford took as his point of departure the seminal article by C. G. Hempel, "The Function of General Laws in History," *Journal of Philosophy*, 39 (1942), but he was concerned, as Hempel probably was not, to draw practical lessons for historians from Hempel's analysis.

6. H. A. L. Fisher, *History of Europe* (London, 1936), p. v.

7. Herbert Butterfield, *The Whig Interpretation of History* (London, 1931), p. 72.

8. This point is made by W. H. Dray, *Laws and Explanation in History* (Oxford, 1960), p. 39.

of a situation was, in those circumstances, a direct and immediate matter: there could be no point in formulating, in lawlike form, the regular relationship between alleged mental events, such as motives and intentions, on the one hand, and subsequent actions on the other. To do so might make motives appear like causes, but this would be a quite unnecessary step. If the historian understood aright the purposes and ideas of his historical agents he would understand the actions in which they were involved. And having understood these actions, a knowledge of comparable cases would be superfluous. To quote Collingwood again, "If, by historical thinking, we already understand how and why Napoleon established his ascendancy in revolutionary France, nothing is added to our understanding of that process by the statement (however true) that similar things have happened elsewhere."[9]

To arguments of this kind the advocates of scientific history countered by insisting that there was no need for alarm. They pointed out that even historians who explained in terms of motives, reasons, or intentions also used covering laws by implication whether they were aware of it or not, and insisted that it was as well that they should bring their implicit assumptions out into the open. Collingwood's assertion that nothing could be added to knowledge of a problem by knowledge of other cases was in any case grossly overstated. While it might be true that his model described accurately enough much of what historians did and caught the flavour of their concern with choice, motive, and reason, and while it was also true there was no point in casting a motivational explanation into a lawlike form, not all legitimate enquiries are of that kind. Many acceptable explanations, on the contrary, do not depend on an understanding of individual thoughts and wills, but on a knowledge of the regularities of collective behaviour. It is always important, for example, to know in general something about the situations in which rebellions are likely to occur, or to succeed or fail, and to know about those in which authoritarian leadership may be likely to emerge, and so on. Such understanding would be based in part on a direct and detailed knowledge of how people thought and reacted, but in part it would not. In part it would depend upon noticing regular patterns of behaviour of men in the mass. Further, even where motive or reason or choice is centrally important, it would still be possible to enquire into the circumstances which led individuals to be moved, to reason, or to choose in particular cases. Even if all history is the history of thought, as Collingwood said, there is room for an enquiry into the causes of thoughts. The findings of such an enquiry might well be

9. Collingwood, p. 223.

unexpected. They might illuminate hidden motives and add new dimensions to reasons that were incompletely understood even by the historical actors themselves, who would probably have regarded their own choices as rational. Finally, and more fundamentally perhaps, was the claim that even where a grasp of reason or motive might seem to provide all the explanation necessary, the ability of the historian even to discern the play of motive and reason must depend in the last analysis on his general grasp of the way the world is, on his observation of regularities. In fact, the whole process of explanation is usually a subtle interplay of conscious generalization, unconscious grasp of general principle, imagination, and appreciation of motives and ideas.[10] If these arguments could be allowed it seemed that the way would still be open for historians to concern themselves with the general rather than the particular, with the discovery of the general patterns of human behaviour and not merely with the elucidation of particular situations.

These are the barest outlines of an involved, subtle, and continuing argument. It is not intended here to attempt a resolution of the debate, but rather to point to a later change in its tempo, to a lessening of the belief that "scientific" history is in some way dependent upon a particular view of the nature of historical explanation. It was ironical that the great expectations of those who had insisted that historians explained by reference to general laws should have been undermined by a defender of the covering law model of explanation. When Patrick Gardiner in 1952 attempted to lay the dust by surveying the debate as a whole, removing misconceptions about what the covering law theorists were saying, and thereby allaying, he hoped, the apprehensions of their opponents, he did so in such a way as to make some of his readers wonder what all the fuss had been about. Gardiner came down on the side of the view that indeed, for the most part, explanatory statements in history depend on the existence of lawlike statements, explicit or implicit, and that therefore in logical

10. On this point Hugh Stretton, a later critic of the claims that historical explanation depended on observation of regularities, is perhaps unfair (*The Political Sciences* [London, 1969], chap. 7). He argues that a genuine understanding of a single phenomenon (to take one of his examples, the connection between dancing and status systems in New Guinea society, as perceived by the anthropologist Murray Groves) depends not on repeated observation but on an inner grasp of the rationality of the phenomenon. The anthropologist's perception of the relationship does not result from the observation of regular association. "It is in Poreporenan minds, *once*, that Groves first understands the connection between the dance and the status of the host. . . . Repeated observations may still be appropriate. But their purpose will be to get a better look next time, or to see if different observers discern the same things, more often than merely to see whether the same actions recur regularly in the same circumstances" (*ibid.*, p. 203). This account does less than justice to the fact that the single perception depends in the last analysis on knowledge of regularity. The anthropologist brings to his "once only" observation a whole body of functional theory and an experience of many cases.

form historical explanation does resemble explanation in the natural sciences.[11] But it was clear from his argument that this was a logical rather than a methodological point. Many of the so-called laws were trivial in character, needing no explicit formulation and constituting no new discovery of how man behaves in general. To say that the historian explained under cover of laws was not to say that he was a scientist in the sense of seeking general knowledge rather than knowledge of particular events. Such a conclusion, on the contrary, had nothing to say, one way or the other, on whether history ought to be more like physics or whether it ought to be concerned merely with the reconstruction of a narrative. The "history as a science" debate, in brief, contained two quite separate issues: the covering law issue was quite distinct from the issue of whether historians should seek general knowledge. The former issue was concerned only with the logical analysis of explanatory statements—statements which might be of a most concrete kind, to use Butterfield's term, or of a most general kind.

Gardiner's contribution did not end the debate. It evoked a direct reply in the form of W. H. Dray's *Laws and Explanation in History* (Oxford, 1960), which pointed to ways in which the covering law model did not seem to correspond closely enough to much of what historians did and argued that, even when it did, the term "law" was hardly appropriate. But Gardiner, by pointing out how slender were the methodological consequences of the covering law analysis, had already taken much of the passion from the discussion. If history was not about to lay bare the laws governing man's progress through time it didn't matter much, for practical purposes, whether an explanatory statement implied a covering law or a direct understanding of mind and motive.[12]

The other aspect of the question, however, remained a real one, even if the philosophical debate had passed it by. How far should the historian try to make himself more like a sociologist or political scientist or anthropologist? If he did try to draw on the advancing techniques of the social sciences, what, if anything, would he see as distinctively his own technique? For the Southeast Asian historian in particular, because of his concern with culture change, emerging nationhood, integration of minorities,

11. Patrick Gardiner, *The Nature of Historical Explanation* (Oxford, 1952). Gardiner did allow rational or motivational explanations also but argued that these were not causal in character. To use them as arguments against the idea of explanation by reference to law was in his view the product of confusion arising from different uses of the world "explain" (p. 136).

12. Cf., also, A. C. Danto, *Analytical Philosophy of History* (Cambridge, 1965). In the course of developing his own view that narrative is a form of explanation Danto surveyed the earlier debate in a manner which reflected how little concerned it had been with practical questions of method, though he noticed that, for some of the participants, there had indeed been present a desire to reform the practice of historians.

economic development, and many other things that also concern the social scientist, the boundaries of history have tended to blur.

There is no doubt that the character of much of the work of practising historians of Southeast Asia has been affected in important ways by the stimulus of neighbouring disciplines. Harry Benda's influential article "The Structure of Southeast Asian History" was both a call to historians to make themselves more receptive to new techniques and a sign that the process was already well advanced. For Benda a sociological approach was useful in helping historians to perceive the shape of societies for whose detailed history evidence was simply lacking.[13] The available evidence would not allow them to reconstruct the details, but it was sufficient to enable them to see at least the sort of society that had existed—the early Southeast Asian infrastructure and the patterns of the classical era which had followed the intrusion of external cultural influences. But the utility of a structural approach did not stop there. Even for later Southeast Asian history, for which more extensive source material was available, a concern with social structure could inform the way in which the story was apprehended. Benda's own example was the way in which a sociological approach might suggest a revised scheme of periodization. After the thirteenth century the rise of Theravāda Buddhism on the mainland and of Islam in the peninsula and islands, and the ability of both religions to forge a link between Great and Little Traditions—which Hinduism and Mahāyāna Buddhism had failed to do—gave the fourteenth and fifteenth centuries the character of a more marked watershed than modern scholarship has often allowed. Similarly the post–van Leur fashion of emphasizing continuity is apt to miss the significance of structural change under European impact, even before the intensified "Westernization" of the late nineteenth century gave diverse Southeast Asia a new "intrinsic unity."

Some of this argument may merely have been a rehearsing of well-used categories which had long been part of the historian's stock-in-trade—the basic types of political and social structures, the contrasting religious systems of the region and their relationship to contrasting political orders— but it represented nonetheless a shift in the historians' conception of what is required in a historical interpretation. That this was so may be more apparent if one turns from Benda's clarion call to the actual practice of historians of Southeast Asia. Van Leur's seminal essay "On Early Asian Trade," written in 1934 and given wider circulation in its English translation in 1955,[14] owed its influence essentially to its self-conscious concern

13. "The Structure of Southeast Asian History," p. 109.
14. In his *Indonesian Trade and Society* (The Hague and Bandung, 1955).

with its conceptual apparatus. Its redefinition of capitalism[15] and its concept of a peddling trade around the coasts of Asia were the tools by which van Leur launched his challenge to the traditional periodization of Southeast Asian history. His thesis formed a point of departure for more detailed studies, of which M. A. P. Meilink-Roelofsz's examination of sixteenth-century trade was perhaps the most notable.[16] Kristoff Glamann's *Dutch-Asiatic Trade*[17] represented a different sort of attempt—this time by an economic historian—to apply the tools of another discipline to the study of the Indies' past.

For the study of more recent history the influence of the social sciences is equally evident. Clifford Geertz's concept of agricultural involution has pointed the way to a new appreciation of the nature of Dutch economic policy in the Indies in the nineteenth century, and his perception of primordial loyalties and his use of the notion of *alirans* (streams, currents, cultural solidarity groups) have combined to affect the way any student may look at the history of the Republic of Indonesia or at the emergence of nationalist feeling during the colonial era.[18] So do Herbert Feith's contrasting political cultures—Javanese-aristocratic and Islamic-entrepreneurial.[19] And the latter's polarized skill groups—solidarity-makers and administrators—formed a stimulating framework for his consideration of the political life of the Republic.[20] And many other tools of systematic analysis could be listed: the notion of shifting status systems,[21] the special definition given to the notion of an intelligentsia,[22] Fred Riggs's distinction between "diffused," "prismatic," and "diffracted" societies,[23] the idea of individual and collective identity crisis,[24] the definition of patrimonial-bureaucratic states and the variety of conceptual schemes that have been called into service in the debate about the extent to which traditional patterns persist in modernizing societies. How far such modes of analysis have become part of the standard equipment of the working historian may be seen in the most recent general history of the region. The six

15. *Ibid.*, chap. 1.

16. M. A. P. Meilink-Roelofsz, *Asian Trade and European Influence in the Indonesian Archipelago between 1550 and about 1630* (The Hague, 1962).

17. Kristoff Glamann, *Dutch-Asiatic Trade, 1620–1740* (Copenhagen, 1958).

18. Clifford Geertz, *The Religion of Java* (Glencoe, Ill., 1960); *Agricultural Involution* (Berkeley, 1963); *The Social History of an Indonesian Town* (Cambridge, Mass., 1965).

19. H. Feith, *The Decline of Constitutional Democracy in Indonesia* (Ithaca, 1962), pp. 31–32.

20. *Ibid.* pp. 133ff.

21. Leslie Palmier, *Social Status and Power in Java* (London, 1960).

22. J. H. Kautsky (ed.), *Political Change in Underdeveloped Countries: Nationalism and Communism* (New York, 1963).

23. Fred W. Riggs, *Administration and Developing Countries: The Theory of Prismatic Society* (Boston, 1964).

24. Lucien Pye, *Politics, Personality and Nation Building: Burma's Search for Identity* (New Haven, 1962).

authors of *In Search of Southeast Asia* move easily through the consideration of such matters as the creation of new bureaucratic frameworks of power as new modernizing elites emerged to challenge the position of traditional leaders, the reordering and incorporation of traditional political centres into a series of new states with new bases of legitimacy, and the effects of urbanization.[25]

It might seem, then, as though the social sciences were indeed fulfilling their promise to illuminate the study of the past as well as the nature of the present. In W. F. Wertheim's view, "the sociological approach has forever added a new dimension to historiography."[26]

But is the impact of new techniques so great, after all, as to represent a methodological revolution in the study of Southeast Asian history itself? Do they, as Benda seemed to suggest, promise the attainment of more solid answers? Has history, in drawing on the conceptual tools of sociological or political sciences, become more like these disciplines, more a generalizing study and less an independent enquiry with its own rules and its own autonomy? Or does the historian's awareness of his disciplinary neighbours represent a much less important shift of emphasis, a change of perspective, a readiness—perhaps a somewhat self-conscious readiness—to follow new insights for specific historical purposes without introducing any important theoretical or methodological implications? To call again on Wertheim's authority, historians have in some degree been sociologists all the time. "They will, in the fashion of Monsieur Jourdain," he said, "write sociology even without knowing it."[27] It is probably fair to judge that the enthusiastic expectations of those who believed the study of Southeast Asian history to be on the verge of a methodological revolution have been largely disappointed.

More specifically, two points need to be made, one methodological and one a matter of definition. If historians of Southeast Asia seem to have become more self-conscious in their borrowings from the social sciences, they have not changed fundamentally the nature of their enquiry nor become necessarily more "scientific." Their methods of understanding the past remain varied; they will use conceptual analysis at one time and an examination of reasons and intentions at another according to the nature of their subject matter and the questions they ask of it. But even if they have become more aware of the utility of the former, they have not thereby committed themselves to a behaviouralist position. The question of the essential nature of historical explanation—whether in the last analysis

25. D. J. Steinberg, D. K. Wyatt, J. R. W. Smail, A. Woodside, W. R. Roff, D. P. Chandler, *In Search of Southeast Asia* (New York, 1971)

26. W. F. Wertheim, "The Sociological Approach," *in* Soedjatmoko (ed.), *An Introduction to Indonesian Historiography* (Ithaca, 1965), p. 358.

27. *Ibid.*

it depends on a direct understanding of man's mental processes or upon general knowledge gained from observation of the regularities of man's behaviour, or both—remains unresolved. It was argued earlier that the philosophical debate about the nature of historical explanation and about whether or not history was a science had few practical implications and did not greatly affect the way in which historians actually pursued their enquiry. Equally it might be argued that the recent trends in historical practice have had few theoretical implications.

Second, the point of definition: In the end the common distinctions between history's territory and that of sociology, anthropology, or political science remain. The historian may find the conceptual schemes of the social scientists useful in helping to illuminate the past, and, indeed, he must be interested in man and society, not merely in particular men in a particular place at a particular time. He must be interested in the "morphology of human affairs," as Sir Lewis Namier called it.[28] But this interest must be anchored in events, not concepts. If his interest lies, for example, in the anatomy of revolution rather than in the French Revolution or the Russian Revolution or the Chinese Revolution, there will be a tendency to describe him not as a historian but as something else. Whatever the historian's concern with the "sort of thing" that occurred, he must have his special concern with what in fact occurred and with the fact that it happened in one way rather than another and at one time rather than another. His grasp of what happened may be aided by methods of conceptual analysis, but it cannot be replaced by them. For these reasons the alliance between history and its neighbours will continue, but perhaps from a base of more modest expectations.

A further dimension of the history–social science alliance concerns the role of value in historical studies. For some, no doubt the strengthening of history's claim to scientific status carried with it the possibility of a greater detachment matching the supposed objectivity of the natural sciences; but once again, fulfilment fell necessarily short of expectations— necessarily, since the social sciences are in this respect like history and cannot escape the influence of the interests and values of their practitioners. Together they are the "political sciences" as Stretton has called them,[29] though in so doing his purpose was not merely to draw attention to the mere presence of value and interest in even the most aseptic theoretical construct, or to the danger of bias in history, but rather to argue that value, so far from being undesirable, something that the analyst should feel

28. L. B. Namier, *Avenues of History* (London, 1952), p. 1.
29. Stretton, *op. cit.*

ashamed of and that he should try to rid himself of if possible, was in fact functionally necessary to his analysis. It helps to determine the end points of an enquiry, and it plays its part in deciding what elements will be taken as given and what ones will be isolated for investigation.

If one accepts the futility of attempting to pretend that history or social science can be value-free it is another matter to decide what prevailing interests may be discerned in the post–World War II expansion of Southeast Asian studies. B. R. O'G. Anderson has pointed to a shift from the historical—that is, noncomparative—method of George Kahin's history of the nationalist revolution in Indonesia to systems of comparative analysis of Southeast Asian affairs. The former "historical" approach was broadly "Western liberal" in its assumptions, sympathetic to Indonesian nationalism and looking to Indonesia's development within a democratic framework. The value content of comparative analysis, by contrast, has been such as to discredit nationalism and to give implicit support to American policies of social engineering in Southeast Asian countries, policies designed to secure economic development conceived in Western terms and to support nonrevolutionary elites.[30] Such a shift was a consequence of the emergence of a new academic establishment whose function, whether it was aware of it or not, was to support a new American role in the Far East and Southeast Asia.

Such a case can certainly be argued, and so far as its starting point is concerned, it is true that Kahin's *Nationalism and Revolution in Indonesia* (Ithaca, 1952) did wear its heart on its sleeve, as its author cheerfully admitted in the more recent paperback edition of the work.[31] Not only was there an overt sympathy for a particular element in the domestic politics of the Indonesian Republic during the revolution—the groups about Sjahrir, Hatta, and Natsir—but more fundamentally the work seemed to carry a hopeful expectation that competent nationalist leaders, working within a broadly democratic system, could lead Indonesia into the modern world with a minimum of disturbance. As a consequence of this approach, the early years of the Republic tended to be seen as disappointing the hopeful expectations of the revolution. Instead of democracy and development the story was one of inflation, corruption, disillusionment with parliamentary institutions, the gradual emergence of the malign figure of Sukarno, the growing power of the army, regional dissidence, and ultimately a move towards a new authoritarianism. Scholars, in considering these unpleasant realities, were apt to frame their

30. B. R. O'G. Anderson, "American Values and Research on Indonesia," paper presented to conference of The American Association of Asian Studies, March 1971.

31. Ithaca, 1970, Preface, pp. v–vi.

enquiries in terms of the implied question, "What went wrong?" and to give answers, still in the Kahin tradition, in terms of changing balances of domestic power and the emergence of a new constellation of forces inappropriate to the operation of parliamentary institutions.

To the critics of this view[32] the question "What went wrong?" was misconceived. Why should the fate of constitutional democracy be described in terms of "decline" or "breakdown" rather than in terms, say, of what Anderson called "the rise of Indonesian autonomism."[33] Terms such as "decline" were Eurocentric in their suggestion of a natural order of things upset by unfortunate circumstances. A structural approach, by contrast, it was argued, would underline the fact that parliamentary democracy was after all an artificial copying of Western institutions and suggest that its failure should not be regarded as unexpected or as a deviation from a norm. With its replacement by guided democracy, said Benda, "the Indonesian river is flowing more and more in an Indonesian bed."[34]

This is an overstatement. What constitutes an Indonesian river—what polity is likely to be most suited to the requirements of Indonesian society— must always be an open question. Parliamentary democracy, while it operated in Indonesia, did so in an Indonesian fashion, and to say that, necessarily and by its nature, it was unsuited to Indonesian circumstances would be to beg the question. Further, to be fair to Kahin, we should notice that his original analysis was certainly not the simple product of his system of values. At the time of his enquiry the divisions of Indonesian society which were later to be stressed by the structural analysts were obscured by the unifying effect of the nationalist struggle and also by the presence of a considerable degree of consensus about goals and how to achieve them amongst the very small elite. It was not at all unreasonable, on the evidence available at the time, to anticipate the establishment of a stable, democratic republic that would tackle the economic and social problems of independence vigorously. However, for the purposes of this discussion one may allow the main thrust of the argument that the sense of disappointment experienced by many scholarly observers of Indonesian developments from the early 1950's was all of a piece with a particular "liberal" framework of analysis. Similarly, it may well be that the orthodoxy of comparative studies and structural analysis, by setting up universal models of transitional societies, have consciously or unconsciously served

32. See, for example, H. J. Benda, "Democracy in Indonesia," *JAS*, 23 (May 1964):449–456, and "Decolonization in Indonesia: The Problem of Continuity and Change", *AHR*, 70, 4 (July 1965):1058–1073; and David Levine, "History and Social Structure in the Study of Contemporary Indonesia," *Indonesia*, no. 7 (1969):5–19.

33. "American Values and Research on Indonesia."

34. "Decolonization in Indonesia," p. 1073.

other values. Anderson argues that they mesh with a view of a particular road to modernization backed by American capital and technological aid.

The generality of this assertion, however, poses certain difficulties. It would certainly be legitimate to point to individual analyses and to notice that their value implications lean in such a direction. But whether *all* structural and comparative methods, *by their very nature*, are likely to reflect a *particular* set of values or a *particular* set of goals—social engineering, ordered economic development, or whatever—is much more dubious. Stretton, like Anderson, has been inclined to say that they are, that certain types of analysis naturally carry certain values.[35] How much support do the later products of the social science–history alliance in Southeast Asian studies really offer for such a conclusion?

If one had to sum up in a word or two the drift of recent trends of enquiry it might be said that their main feature has been a shift of interest from institutions and from the interplay of political forces to what are seen as more permanent things. To stay with the Indonesian example, the emphasis is placed on such things as Geertz's primordial loyalties, Soedjatmoko's cultural solidarity groups,[36] Feith's political cultures—in other words, on the things that do not change rather than on those that do. The emphasis on what are felt to be fairly intransigent cultural factors contributes to a sense of the immovability of tradition. Such analyses certainly play down such things as class divisions, and they help to support a view of Indonesian society as permanently divided by vertical rather than horizontal cleavages. In so doing they may minimize the possibilities of domestic change and may thus serve the interests of an existing elite. And this *may*, as Anderson suggests, fit naturally with the idea of ordered economic development, backed by Western aid and operating within an existing social and political order. So much may be admitted. Equally, however, such analyses may serve quite other purposes. They may support a lesser degree of involvement, a greater degree of detachment from the society under study, a greater respect for, and perhaps also humility in the face of, its distinctive patterns of culture. And at least one student has used the idea of structural analysis for a frankly radical purpose.[37] Though any individual analysis may carry its own values, the connection between *modes* of analysis and political purposes is not a tight connection.

Whether the connections are tight or loose their presence remains, of course, among the permanent problems of historians. They know that their

---

35. This, at least, seems to be his conclusion. See *The Political Sciences*, p. 235.

36. Soedjatmoko, "Indonesia: Problems and Opportunities," Dyason Lectures, *Australian Outlook*, 21 (December 1967):263–306.

37. Levine, *op. cit.*

work is bound to be interest-shaped and value-laden, and a good deal of ink has been spilt in worrying about the fact and in trying to devise ways of avoiding the imputation of systematic bias. Stretton's analysis, pointing out not only that value is inescapable but also that it has a necessary and technical function to perform, adds a new dimension to the discussion. Not only can the analyst never escape from his preferences: he ought not to, since value is necessary to good science. The next logical step might be to conclude that the old concern about the danger of implicit evaluations was a misplaced concern. But was it? Perhaps only in part.

First of all, does it follow from Stretton's argument that the historian's work is improved if he is aware of his values, or at least if he is aware that he has them? Stretton himself seems to suggest that since one cannot, and ought not to, escape valuing one should value consciously rather than unconsciously. Those who try to avoid valuing, he says, "discover less and also worse because they substitute bad judgment for good."[38] Anderson, too, suggests that new research formats may be "better" than their predecessors to the degree that their practitioners self-consciously accept them for what they are, the products of the values of their society.[39] These are doubtful propositions. Sometimes they may be true, and sometimes not. The quality of a man's work depends, surely, on the quality of his insights and of his observations and not necessarily on his own perception of his own values. The work of some historians and social scientists might well be completely inhibited if they were constantly stepping sideways, as it were, to observe themselves in action and to notice how their secret values shaped their questions and their observations. Others may do better by being self-conscious.

In either case, however, it must be emphasized that the enquiry is concerned, in quite an old-fashioned way, with the pursuit of truth. This point needs making. For some the inescapability of value has prompted the feeling that truth can never be caught, that conclusions are merely a matter of competing opinions, that old-fashioned notions of objectivity no longer have a place. In fact the argument does not lead to that conclusion. What we decide to study and what we notice when we study it, where we start our enquiry and where we terminate it, may all reveal preferences, choices, and interests. But this does not mean that to avoid bias is not important, that truth is no longer a relevant concept, or that objectivity

38. Stretton, p. 159.

39. "American Values and Research on Indonesia." Anderson and Stretton are not making quite the same point. Anderson is really making the best of a bad job. Values are inescapable, and we must simply accept that fact. Stretton, by contrast, welcomes them, holds that we could not manage without them. Both, however, appear to agree that self-consciousness about values is desirable.

is no longer a goal.[40] Scholarly enquiry takes place in the public view. Its findings must be defended in the light of evidence; the investigator may be made uncomfortable if critics are able successfully to identify the hidden purposes that his enquiry serves, but his conclusions are not thereby invalidated. The historian may have to accept, as cheerfully as he can, the fact that he cannot break out of the conditioning circle of his values, but this must not be allowed to deter him from his careful attention to the evidence and his pursuit of the truth. Part of the pursuit involves being wary lest his preferences blind his eyes to the facts or swing the enquiry in what could reasonably be called a wrong direction. To this extent it is still arguable that he should try to avoid the influence of his values.

Perhaps the elements of the problem may be clarified if distinctions are made between different kinds of value and between different effects of value. The first distinction can be made between embedded and unconscious values on the one hand and immediate and conscious preferences and purposes on the other. Both will combine to shape an enquiry. Neither should be allowed to cloud the enquirer's vision, though the influence of the former is more difficult to cope with than that of the latter. The second distinction is thus between the technical role of value, which properly aids and directs the enquiry, and the biasing or obscuring role, which improperly distorts or misdirects it. It is perhaps appropriate to reaffirm the importance of containing the latter in a volume designed to celebrate the work of a historian whose adherence to the strictest canons of scholarly integrity has been a model to his successors.

The problems of value are not new problems. They continue, as they have always done, to erode the security of the historian, and he has to live with them. His alliance with the social scientists has not liberated him from them any more than it has improved in other ways the scientific credentials of his own discipline. This is discouraging news only to those who expected more from the alliance than it was able to give.

40. Unless, of course, objectivity is defined to mean "a state completely free of the influence of value" or unless it carries the idea of Truth with a capital T, transcending the limited and partial criteria by which facts are selected—"absolute truth." But this is *not* the meaning of the term in ordinary usage. See, for example, W. H. Dray, *Philosophy of History* (Englewood Cliffs, N.J., 1964), p. 39.

The Limits of Nanyang Chinese Nationalism, 1912–1937

WANG GUNGWU

The Australian National University

The herculean efforts that went into Professor D. G. E. Hall's *History of South-East Asia* have been widely appreciated since the book first appeared in 1955. He was among the first to argue that the region was "an area worthy of consideration in its own right . . . to be seen from its own perspective," and he stimulated a whole new generation to see Southeast Asia quite differently than before. In this context, it is understandable that he paid little attention to the overseas Chinese communities in the region. The late Victor Purcell had produced a book on these communities only four years earlier, *The Chinese in Southeast Asia* (1951), and, from the point of view of Southeast Asian history, it would seem that the Chinese, whether within each territory or as interrelated communities in the "Nanyang," did not really belong. On the whole, many of them gave the impression of being transients who looked far more to China and did not care to identify themselves with the areas they lived in, and this was especially obvious in the way some Chinese seem to have responded to Chinese nationalism.

This was particularly true after the Chinese Revolution of 1911. The increase in the number of schools teaching in the Chinese National Language (Kuo Yü or Mandarin), the steady rise in remittances to China, and the reports of investments in new industries and other enterprises in China all contributed to a picture of these Nanyang Chinese becoming more and more nationalistic and increasingly committed to being the vanguard of Chinese power and influence over the region.[1] This was not merely a picture which hostile observers had of them. To some extent, many Nanyang Chinese have often seen themselves as loyal nationalists.

At the same time, there was also a conflicting picture. Many other Nanyang Chinese were unenthusiastic about China and apparently loyal to the various authorities under which they lived. They wanted to settle

---

1. Purcell 1951:127–131, 141–147, 453–467, 539–551; Purcell 1948:222–242; Ch'en 1939:173–197; Ide 1942:42–59; Narita 1942:460–474; Cheng 1943:47–129; Kikakuin 1940: 68–93.

down and make their homes in the region and resisted the pressure of those around them to behave like Chinese patriots. To the nationalists, these men were ignorant and selfish; they were short-sighted in their refusal to help China become rich and powerful and even more so in their lack of interest in vital political matters which must ultimately affect their own future overseas.[2]

Both views of the Chinese have been held by non-Chinese commentators and by the Chinese themselves. If the first view is more accurate, there would be good reasons why the Nanyang Chinese remain peripheral to Southeast Asian history. If the latter is more correct, then it may be argued that not enough has been done to integrate the Chinese into the main frame of the region's history. This essay surveys one aspect of this question. In trying to identify the limits of Nanyang Chinese nationalism during its most formative period, I hope to show how complex the problem of nationalism was for the Chinese and how difficult it is to measure the degree and the nature of that nationalism even when it existed.

Let me begin by noting that no nationalist leader arose independently from among the Nanyang Chinese before the visit of K'ang Yu-wei, Liang Ch'i-ch'ao, and Sun Yat-sen in 1900. Despite the generalization that the first prominent Chinese nationalists were mostly men from the Treaty Ports and the colony of Hong Kong and included men who had travelled and studied in the West or in the increasingly "Westernized" Japan, the Nanyang Chinese who lived under European rulers during the heyday of nineteenth-century European nationalism did not produce nationalists on their own. Distinguished men like Ku Hung-ming and Wu Lien-te of Penang, Lim Boon Keng (Lin Wen-ch'ing) of Singapore, and Li Teng-hui of Bogor in Java received considerable Western education, which prepared them for service in China, but they were not notable for their nationalism, nor were they the staunch supporters of the nationalist leaders who came from China during the last few years of the Ch'ing dynasty.[3] This suggests that early contact with Westerners and Western values was not sufficient to make them nationalists, and that other key factors were more important.

I do not mean that the Nanyang Chinese were not conscious of being Chinese, did not already have a strong sense of community, did not keep in touch with affairs at home, or did not know the importance of organization and how to organize effectively. On the contrary, their in-group loyalties and their speech-group identifications were, if anything, too pronounced, and their journeying to and from China whenever they could afford to do so was well known. Most of them probably felt that outside

2. This was a minority view. The fiercest criticisms came from Nanyang Chinese leaders themselves; for example, see Ch'en 1950:I, 31–42.

3. Liu 1967:269–272; Song 1923:234–238; and *Nanyang Hsueh-pao* notes on Lim and Li. Also Boorman 1967–1971:II, 250–252, 386–387; III, 440–442.

China they had common disabilities as Chinese because China had become poor and weak. Stories circulated that, whenever local governments became hostile towards their activities, it did not matter whether they were Cantonese or Hokkien, and, in extreme cases, it did not matter whether they were rich or poor, organized or not.[4]

Nor were the Nanyang Chinese totally illiterate, although the vast majority of the new immigrants during the latter half of the nineteenth century clearly had no education. In fact, among the settled Chinese population, a small educated elite was emerging in the major cities: for example, the English-educated in the Straits Settlements, the Dutch-educated in Batavia and Semarang, some of the Sino-Thai merchants and officials in Bangkok, and many of the Chinese mestizos in Manila.[5] Their education was largely the product of Western values and would have included some appreciation of the power of Western nationalism. But it was clear by 1911 that this education had mainly prepared the small Chinese elites to emulate and identify with the colonial and native elites wherever they were allowed to do so and that it tended to cut them off from the sense of "Chineseness" which their less-educated countrymen were to retain. Although some of the babas, peranakans, mestizos, and Sino-Thais found it possible to sympathize with Chinese nationalism, and even to recapture their "Chineseness" later on, they were never in a position to offer leadership in the new movement to identify with China's destiny.

Thus it fell to the reformers and revolutionaries *from* China to provide the stimulus to nationalism when they came to Southeast Asia as exiles and rebels in search of material support for their respective causes. Even then not many of the Nanyang Chinese openly supported these men. Most of them preferred to accept the status quo in China, partly because they had their homes in China to consider and partly because they were not convinced that anything they could do would make any difference to China. Others were close to the local colonial or native establishment and did not want to associate with men who uttered such dangerous bombastic talk.[6]

What distinguished the nationalist leaders from their Nanyang Chinese supporters, not to say from those who were cautious or hostile, was that these leaders from China were educated in Chinese and knew more about

4. The early nationalists realized that the Nanyang Chinese felt insecure and emphasized this in their propaganda successfully; see Feng 1945–1946:I, 170–174; II, 247–260; III, 205–215; IV, 145–181; V, 206–250; Wang 1959.

5. Song 1923:338–343; Skinner 1957:126–134, 143–154; Wickberg 1965:168–206. In Java, the peranakans had so many grievances against the Dutch colonial government that they emphasized their "Chineseness" for a brief period at the turn of the century and responded to Chinese nationalism, but this did not last long once the Dutch began to make concessions about Dutch education for Chinese after 1907; Williams 1960:27–41 and Liauw 1969:8–13.

6. Yen (1970:24–32, 1970:264) gives examples of this for Singapore and Malaya. For reasons mentioned in n. 5, the situation was somewhat different for a while in Java; Williams 1960:95–113.

the civilization they were proud of and that they had felt China's humiliations more deeply and directly and had studied Western learning specifically to find ways to restore China to greatness. They had concluded that the nationalism of the Western nation-states and, by this time, also of Japan was necessary to their task, but their perception of this need was rooted in their commitment to China's regeneration and their appreciation of the immediate dangers which China faced.

The quality of nationalism for the few Nanyang Chinese who were attracted to it at the beginning of the century seems to have been determined not so much by a passionate self-discovery because they were strangers being discriminated against in a foreign land or because they found new perspectives in the modern world away from home, but much more by the skilful persuasion of educated Chinese from China who were able to explain and confirm the sources of all their grievances. This produced, therefore, a taught nationalism that was made more relevant by being married to the apparent answer to all their problems: a strong China that would protect them. The Nanyang Chinese response to the nationalists, their sense of participation in the 1911 Revolution, and their remembrance of that response and that participation sustained many of them in their efforts to keep up with affairs in China for the next thirty years. But the question remains: How strong was this response?

The initial enthusiasm among most Nanyang Chinese for the Republic in 1911–1912 cannot be doubted. The kind of nationalism that expressed itself in terms of getting rid of the Manchus and establishing a government by the Chinese for the Chinese was genuine and widespread enough when its leaders finally succeeded after years of setbacks. The new leaders, furthermore, were southerners (many were natives of Kwangtung and Fukien personally known to the Nanyang Chinese), and they had promised to protect the Chinese from colonial governments and to welcome them to invest in China's rich and undeveloped mineral and industrial resources. By the time Sun Yat-sen passed through the region on his way to become the first provisional president of the Republic, the number of Nanyang Chinese who claimed that they had always supported his party had increased spectacularly and a great deal of money had been made available to the republican cause, including, for example, some $200,000 from the Hokkien community in Singapore to the new governor of Fukien to help pacify that province and another $50,000 from Tan Kah Kee (Ch'en Chiakeng) personally to Sun Yat-sen.[7] There can be little doubt that, at that moment, many Nanyang Chinese viewed their future with great expectations, and most observers were correct in describing them as being seized by nationalist fervour. Yet, thirty years later, Tan Kah Kee himself recalled:

7. Cheng 1964:62–63; Ch'en 1950:I, 3; Yen 1970:253–263, 320–329.

"At that time, our society was very immature and the overseas Chinese only believed fervently in devils and spirits. Their ideas of patriotism and public welfare were all very weak."[8]

Another period of enthusiasm that cannot be doubted followed the start of the Sino-Japanese War in July 1937. All writers attest to the zeal with which most Nanyang Chinese supported organizations like "national salvation movements" and to the large sums of money and large quantities of goods they collected and sent to the Chinese government. Particularly dramatic were the boycotts of Japanese goods throughout Southeast Asia which the colonial and native governments found very difficult to check. The Nanyang Chinese had had a great deal of experience at this; one could point to the efforts at boycotts in 1915, 1919, and 1923, and the more effective ones after the Tsinan Incident in 1928 and the Mukden Incident in 1931.[9] The picture, then, is of increasing solidarity among the Nanyang Chinese with their readiness and power to act as a united community.

Yet Tan Kah Kee, the man who emerged as the widely acknowledged leader of the Nanyang Chinese during the Sino-Japanese War, recalled that when Wang Cheng-t'ing (a former minister of foreign affairs visiting Nanyang Chinese communities just before the outbreak of the war) asked the Nanyang Chinese to organize themselves for greater unity, he had answered his visitor thus: "As for the word 'unity,' all the organisations of the overseas Chinese are mainly united in form only. Where substance is concerned, there is really very little worth talking about. . . . To talk emptily of unity when still like scattered sand, that is really to be regretted."[10]

Hundreds of young Nanyang Chinese, especially from British Malaya and French Indo-China, had directly helped Sun Yat-sen in his various attempts to organize uprisings in South China before 1911, and again, during the 1930's, thousands of Chinese from all over the region returned to China to study and eventually to fight for their country when war broke out. The two situations were obviously different—the first made them conscious of being members of a great nation awakening from a long slumber and the second alerted them to the possibility that their country might be bitten off in chunks by the Japanese. Yet Tan Kah Kee recalled that, for the first period, patriotism was weak and, for the second, unity was empty talk. Knowing how well he knew large sections of the Nanyang Chinese during the three decades, we cannot ignore his testimony and must wonder if the picture of a pervasive and growing Nanyang Chinese nationalism does not need qualification.

8. Ch'en 1950:I, 3.
9. Akashi 1968:73–86; Kee 1965:61–70. For the enthusiasm in 1937, see Akashi 1970: introduction and chap. 1.
10. Ch'en 1950:I, 33–34. "Scattered sand" refers to the well-known phrase used by Sun Yat-sen to describe the lack of political cohesion in traditional Chinese society.

The first series of qualifications relates to the complex divisions among the various Chinese communities in the different parts of Southeast Asia and to the changing political conditions in each of the countries. I have suggested elsewhere that our difficulty in having a clear picture of the political attitudes of the Nanyang Chinese is largely due to the fact that there was no single Nanyang Chinese community. In every country where they had settled, it is possible to find those who were intensely concerned with affairs in China, those whose primary interest was in preserving the strength of their communal organizations overseas, and those who were deeply involved in winning a political role for themselves in their country of adoption.[11] The first and third groups are relatively easy to identify for they were usually more outspoken and openly committed to their respective causes. The second group was inward-looking and built its strength upon watchful silence and the interlocking membership of its numerous organizations. It was also more flexible or opportunist and was prepared on occasion to throw its support to the first group where attitudes towards China were concerned and to the third group when relations with local authorities made such support necessary.

Where Chinese nationalism was concerned, it would be broadly true to say that the first group would be the most inclined to be nationalistic and the third group the least inclined. Their different attitudes were mainly determined by whether they were educated in local Chinese schools or in China or in native and colonial schools, although this was not always a reliable guide.

There were many prominent examples of the first group, and around these men were usually dozens, if not hundreds, of ardent supporters and assistants. The best-known were Siu Fat-sing (Hsiao Fu-ch'eng) in Thailand, Lim Nee Soon (Lin I-shun) and Tan Kah Kee in Singapore, Teng Tse-ju and Tan Sin-cheng (Ch'en Hsin-cheng) in Malaya, and Ty Han Kee (Cheng Han-ch'i) in the Philippines. Others who remained active in Chinese affairs throughout the interwar period include Lin Po-ch'i in Thailand; Teo Eng Hock (Chang Yung-fu), Tan Chor Nam (Ch'en Ch'u-nan), and Chuang Hsi-ch'uan in Singapore; Goh Say Eng (Wu Shih-jung), Cheng Lo-sheng, and Chuang Ming-li in Malaya; and Tan Pia Teng (Ch'en Ping-ting), Tjung See Gan (Chuang Hsi-yen), and Setoe Tjan (Ssu-t'u Tsan) in the Netherlands East Indies.[12] Some of them have left us

11. Wang 1970, 1972.

12. There were many more who clearly belonged to this group. They tend to be prominent in Chinese sources since they are actively concerned with China's affairs. This does not necessarily make them more important in Nanyang Chinese society, although Western and native sources do not give enough attention to other Chinese leaders for us to make reliable comparisons.

The names in the above two lists occur in a wide range of sources, the more notable being

information about their reasons for supporting Sun Yat-sen, the Kuomintang, or various political and philanthropic causes in China. At least three of them have published works reflecting their particular involvement in Chinese affairs.[13] What they say about nationalism, however, is not explicit. Their ties to China varied among respect for Sun Yat-sen and other national leaders, loyalty to a political party (mainly the Kuomintang), concern for the backwardness of their home towns or villages, distress at China's weakness and their own insecurity overseas, pride in being Chinese, or various combinations of all these. And these reasons led them to remit money regularly, contribute to specific funds, join political parties, visit China frequently, support local education and newspapers as well as finance schools in China, protest against local discriminations against the Chinese, organize anti-Japanese boycotts, and mobilize support for major policies of the Chinese government (especially in Nanking after 1928). As practical men, they were less concerned to reflect on the nature and quality of their nationalism and more interested in what a patriotic Chinese ought to do, but their commitment to serve China was usually unmistakable.

The third group also had its prominent men, but they tended to be successful individuals with influential friends rather than men who could depend on enthusiastic support from the Chinese community. The most successful examples are probably Lee Ah Yain (Li Hsia-yang) and Taw Sein-ko (Tu Sheng-kao) in Burma, Song Ong Siang (Sung Wang-hsiang) in Singapore, Tan Cheng-Lock (Ch'en Chen-lu) in Malaya, and Oei Tiong Ham (Huang Chung-han), Phoa Liong Gie (P'an Liang-i), Khouw Kim An, and Kan Hok Hoei in the East Indies.[14] There were many also in Thailand and the Philippines, but these, together with the Sino-Thai and Chinese mestizo, were often so rapidly assimilated into the native elite groups, once they sought to identify with them, that many cannot be described as Chinese. Whatever nationalism these latter felt may more appropriately be called Thai or Filipino nationalism.[15] For those in the British and Dutch territories, however, there was some ambiguity about identifying with the colonial elites or with the emerging indigenous nationalists. In Burma and Indonesia, local nationalism came earlier and this group of

Feng 1945–1946 and 1946; Chang 1933; Sun 1965; Ch'en 1950; Huang 1968 (especially vols. 45 and 48). Two recent studies have been very useful, Yong 1968:273–279 and Liauw 1969: *passim.* Boorman 1967–1971 contains biographies of Siu, Tan, and Teng (II, 90–92; I, 165–170, and III, 257–259, respectively).

13. Chang 1933, Teng 1948, and Ch'en 1950. Also see letters to comrades in Sun 1965:II and III; and Huang 1968–, vols. 45 and 48.

14. Purcell 1951:70; Song 1923:242–248; Yong 1968:262–271 groups Song Ong Siang with others I have placed in the second group (see n. 16); Liauw 1969:17–28, 61–68, 132–164; Soh 1960.

15. Skinner 1960; Wickberg 1965:237–237–246; Skinner 1957:143–154.

Chinese had a choice. But in Malaya and Singapore, this third group of
Chinese did not pay any attention to Malay nationalism until after World
War II, and the idea of Singapore nationalism based mainly on the political
consciousness of this group did not come about until after 1965. Neverthe-
less, it would be true to say that this group of Chinese throughout Southeast
Asia were aware of the appeals of Chinese nationalism for the Nanyang
Chinese. That they turned away from this emphasis on affiliations with
China must be seen as a deliberate political decision to affirm that they were
more at home where they were than in China.

The majority of the inward-looking, communally conscious Chinese in
between the first and third groups provide the greatest difficulty for those
who would like to describe their political interests and activities. Their
numerous organizations produced many community leaders at different
levels, but few of them communicated outside their communal limits unless
they had to. They had learnt that, for most of the things they wanted, they
could find enough China-oriented spokesmen or locally ambitious notables
to act for them. Thus they could concentrate on their social and economic
interests and appear to be politically noncommittal. In fact, their leaders
were probably politically more subtle and agile than the others, and thus
they were often seen as two-faced and untrustworthy, or at best ambiguous
and indecisive. It is therefore particularly difficult to place any of the well-
known leaders in this group, since some of them could claim that they were
either more China-oriented or locally oriented at some time or other in
their lives. But an attempt to identify them should be made. I suggest that
Dee C. Chuan (Li Ch'ing-ch'uan) and Albino Z. and Alfonso Z. SyCip
(Hsueh Ming-lao and Hsueh Fen-shih) in the Philippines; Hia Kuang Yam
(I Kuang-yen) in Thailand; Loke Yew (Lu Yu), Eu Tong Sen (Yü Tung-
hsuan), and Leong Sin Nam (Liang Hsin-nan) in Malaya; Khoo Seok Wan
(Ch'iu Shu-yuan) and Lim Boon Keng in Singapore; Liem Koen Hian
(Lin K'un-hsien), Kwee Hing Tjiat (Kuo Heng-chieh), and Thung Liang
Lee (T'ang Leang-li) in the East Indies; and possibly also Aw Boon Haw
(Hu Wen-hu) in Singapore and Burma may be considered to be members
of this group.[16] They were men who could not be called Chinese nationalists
but who were intensely involved in the welfare of the Chinese communities
in non-Chinese environments and were prepared to speak for these communities to colonial and native rulers and Chinese nationalists alike. Obviously Chinese nationalism affected these men in some way, if only to

16. *Hsin-Min* 1928; *Manila Chronicle*, Dec. 17, 1967; *Nanyang Hsueh-pao* note on Hia; Lee
1957; Yung 1967; Liauw 1972. For other examples, see *Nanyang Hsueh-pao* notes on Leow, Chin
and Tay; Li 1959:1–14. Boorman 1967–1971 has the biographies of Albino Z. Sycip and
Aw (II, 151–153, 177–180). T'ang Leang-li is well known as a publicist for Wang Ching-wei
in the 1930's but, as a peranakan, did not find it difficult to fit himself back into Indonesian
society after 1949.

heighten their awareness of themselves as Chinese, but they held back from the passion and enthusiasm which made non-Chinese frightened of what Chinese nationalists might be led to do. They seem to have reserved their judgment concerning the extravagant claims for China's regeneration and for China's capacity to protect them. They were proud to be Chinese and to receive the attention of the Chinese government, but they remained cautious about China's warm embrace in order not to be placed in a false position vis-à-vis the local authorities or committed irrevocably to any single political group which happened to have control of the Chinese government at the time. China's politics was obviously important and had to be watched, but these men were normally grateful that they could watch it from afar.

The above were not the only divisions in the Nanyang Chinese communities. Speech-group identifications, religious affiliations, educational backgrounds, wealth and status, and the fact of geographical separation by colonial boundaries, which were later confirmed as national boundaries, made it very difficult for all of them in the Nanyang to regard themselves as one people. Many had begun to realize that they were different from the Chinese in China in many ways; others had known that they were different from those Chinese who had grown up under a different set of colonial or native rulers; and still others remained always uneasy about crossing speech-group and religious boundaries, educational streams, and the barriers of wealth and poverty even among the Chinese within the same territory. All these differences continued to be real in most places right up to the outbreak of the Sino-Japanese War in 1937. Nationalism would have helped to break down some of these barriers, but obviously one could not live on the rhetoric of nationalism alone, and, except at moments of crisis, nationalism was not very meaningful to their lives.

What kept the Nanyang Chinese increasingly aware of nationalism were the activities of men who were really outside their communities. On the one hand were the expatriate Chinese who had been invited or sent to educate and exhort them; on the other were the native nationalists fighting against the colonial authorities.

Expatriate Chinese were those who came from China on specific missions and were recognizably different from Nanyang Chinese until they began to identify with the local problems of their overseas compatriots.[17] They were mainly those who followed a long and distinguished line of teachers,

17. It is difficult to determine why expatriates identified with the local Chinese. For example, Wu Pan-sheng (Go Puan Seng), the editor of *Hsin-Min Jih-pao* in Manila, married a local girl soon after arrival and stayed forty years (Go 1970:7–8). Other distinguished teachers and journalists like Hu Yü-chih and Wang Jen-shu (Pa-jen) exerted considerable influence and then returned to China. It remains important, however, to distinguish men like Wu who became *hua-ch'iao* from the latter two who never did.

journalists, and propagandists, who took jobs in the region but saw themselves mainly on a civilizing and nationalizing mission. Thousands came out or were sent out between 1912 and 1941. Some stayed briefly and made little impression. Others stayed for years at their newspapers or their schools, informing the old and preparing the young. Still others came with specific political and financial missions, some were exiles or rebels or agents of one political party or another, seeking refuge, assistance, moral support, money, and political followers; some came openly and boldly, while others came in disguise and under false names and false credentials. They followed a grand tradition, the tradition of K'ang Yu-wei, Liang Ch'i-ch'ao, Sun Yat-sen, T'ao Ch'eng-chang, Wang Ching-wei, Huang Hsing, and Hu Han-min from before the 1911 Revolution. But whether the new groups were rebels, exiles, or agents, each in its own way extended Nanyang Chinese interest and understanding of the problems of China and organized small groups of supporters for causes in China's national politics.[18]

Native nationalists impinged much less on the lives of the Nanyang Chinese except when they experienced a conflict of interest. This was particularly important in Thailand, where some prominent Sino-Thais identified with local nationalism and were more Thai than the Thai, and in Indonesia, where some peranakans were prepared to support Indonesian nationalism even when it was anti-Chinese.[19] The Nanyang Chinese were usually most aggrieved at this, but such acts did serve to remind them of the dangers of nationalism when it was turned against them. Whether or not it ever drove the Nanyang Chinese to espouse a fierce Chinese nationalism in defence and retaliation cannot be proved, but the rapid growth of native nationalism did help to polarize Sino-native relations, whether the Nanyang Chinese liked it or not. If this did not drive more Chinese to a stronger orientation towards China, it certainly made the large group of communal Chinese all the more defensive and the locally ambitious Chinese less certain if they could achieve their political ends without siding with local nationalists against other Chinese.

So far, I have discussed some of the attitudes various groups of Chinese had towards nationalism during the three decades after 1912. These attitudes explain some of the reasons why Tan Kah Kee found the Nanyang Chinese sense of patriotism weak in 1912 and their communities like "scattered sand" in the 1930's. It is further necessary to relate these attitudes to events in China during the three decades and how these events appeared to the Chinese overseas. The period was extremely eventful and the develop-

18. The list of names could be greatly extended. Other well-known names are Tai Chi-t'ao, Chü Cheng, Ch'en Chiung-ming, Li Lieh-chün, Teng K'eng, Hsü Ch'ung-chih, Ku Ying-fen, Sun K'o, Feng Tzu-yu, P'eng Tse-min, and Wang Cheng-t'ing. See Lo 1953–1968; Huang 1968–: vols. 45 and 48; Ch'en 1950:I, 20–47; Chang 1933; Lee 1957.

19. Skinner 1957:244–260; Liauw 1969:80–103.

ments in China most complex. It is doubtful that many Nanyang Chinese were able to follow these events in detail and to realize what was at stake outside of the two provinces, Kwangtung and Fukien, from which most of them had come and with which they retained some contact.[20] Only a brief outline of the major events which appeared to have elicited response from the Nanyang Chinese will be attempted here. It is recognized that newspapers, magazines, and books published in Chinese of this period are not a safe guide to Nanyang Chinese opinion since most of them were edited and written by expatriate Chinese, but to the extent that they provided the main reading matter for those Nanyang Chinese who kept up with affairs in China at all, these must have exerted some influence upon their attitudes. The materials should be used with caution and must be read together with Chinese writings in colonial and native languages, but we cannot afford to ignore them.

To begin with, the triumph of the Republic in 1912 was short-lived for those Nanyang Chinese who had acclaimed Sun Yat-sen. He had soon given way to Yuan Shih-k'ai, and the 1913 "second revolution" had failed miserably. By early 1914 it was clear that the Nanyang Chinese were almost back to pre-1911 conditions of being treated as potential financiers of rebels against the government in Peking. The main difference was that this time the enemy was not the Manchu dynasty but a Chinese Republic which was supposed to embody modern principles of government. Sun Yat-sen's reconstituted Chung-hua ko-ming tang (Chinese Revolutionary Party) now had to argue for a more subtle political cause: the cause of people's rights in a true republic as against selfish bureaucrats and warlords and, in 1915–1916, against Yuan Shih-k'ai's imperial ambitions.[21]

It was soon obvious that this was not a popular cause. The former revolutionary leaders were themselves split, and notable figures like Huang Hsing, Li Lieh-chün, and Ch'en Chiung-ming who went among the Chinese overseas were openly critical of Sun Yat-sen's attempt to write off the Kuomintang (Nationalist Party) and start a new, more tightly-knit party. Also, other leading figures known to the overseas Chinese like K'ang Yu-wei and Liang Ch'i-ch'ao were influential in Peking and seemed to stand on the side of the new political establishment. At the same time, the Nanyang Chinese could look to the republican regime and its consular representatives for help and protection. They probably did not expect very much, but it was much safer than supporting an underground rebel group

20. T'ang (1936:9) speaks of "the special relations existing between various centres in Fukien and Kwangtung and the great Chinese communities settled overseas, between whom a special kind of civilisation has developed." This is obviously too strong, but Ch'en 1950:I, 1–46, and the special pages of news on the two provinces in *Nanyang Siang-pao* until the 1930's confirm that South China remained of primary interest to the Nanyang Chinese before 1937.
21. Huang 1968–: vols. 45 and 48; Sun 1965:III.

and risking police attention for their families in China and local police attention for themselves.[22]

The main surviving Chinese sources which refer to Nanyang Chinese for the 1910's and the 1920's are sympathetic towards Sun Yat-sen and his eventually successful Nationalist Party (Kuomintang or Chung-kuo kuo-min tang). They tend to give the picture of widespread support for the only true nationalist movement in China and thus accentuate the nationalist activities of Nanyang Chinese. The surviving list of over ninety Chung-hua ko-ming tang branches and subbranches in Southeast Asia in 1914–1917, most of them with impressive lists of party officials, cannot be dismissed as misleading. The fact that the party succeeded in persuading Nanyang Chinese to subscribe over one and a half million dollars in bonds and send hundreds of young men to help the cause in Kwangtung as they had done in the years before 1911 testifies to Sun Yat-sen's credibility as a leader. What becomes clear from the published documents is that the subtle political and moral arguments against the Peking government were far less important than factors like personal loyalty to Sun Yat-sen, regional interest in Sun's activities in Kwangtung and Fukien, anger at the extortionate warlord governments in those two provinces, and the frustrations many Nanyang Chinese felt on returning to their homes in China and finding the economy and public security as bad as ever if not worse.[23]

But Sun Yat-sen was not getting very far himself even in his home province of Kwangtung. His essentially pre-1911 methods of securing financial support from the Nanyang Chinese were wearing thin as each year passed and he was still unable to gain a firm foothold in China. By the time he called for another change of name of his party to Chung-kuo kuo-min tang towards the end of 1919, there was indeed very little fresh excitement about his leadership among the Nanyang Chinese. Until he survived the rebellion of Ch'en Chiung-ming and reorganized the party once again with the support of Soviet advisers and members of the Chinese Communist Party in early 1924, there was little to stir most of the Nanyang Chinese about Chinese politics. Indeed, many of them were angered by the arrogance of the Japanese Twenty-One Demands and the loss of Chinese rights in Outer Mongolia, the abortive "Restoration" of 1917 and the obvious lack of leadership in the Peking government, China's defeat at Versailles in 1919, and further threats to Chinese interests after the Washington Conference, but they seem on the whole to have been unmoved except where Japan was involved.[24] Most of them were certainly unaware of the growing ferment in Central and North China among students and intellec-

22. Huang 1968–.
23. Huang 1968–: vols. 45 and 48; Sun 1965:III
24. Akashi 1968:77–86; Kee 1965:65ff.; Ts'ui 1965.

tuals after the May Fourth Movement until several years afterwards. They had become obviously dismayed by the weak government in Peking and disappointed by the ineffectualness of Sun Yat-sen in Canton, and all but a few seem to have eschewed any enthusiasm to take part in national politics. Instead, the majority of those who felt nationalistic about China concentrated on solidifying the sense of Chinese identity through education of their children.[25]

The first dozen years after the Republic was established did change the Nanyang Chinese, but more in their faith in themselves as members of a Chinese nation than in their faith in the government of China. They seem to have recognized that the vast majority of them were illiterate and that, among those who were literate, few were literate enough in Chinese to lead them to a more meaningful Chinese identity. The most urgent task, there-fore, was to expand Chinese education on the lines of the modern national schools being built in China. Money spent on political causes in China now that there was a government ruled by Chinese seemed less fruitful than money spent on teaching their children about China. Their own under-standing of nationalism had been learnt the hard way from exiles and rebels. Their children should be taught properly and be prepared not only to appreciate better a modern China but also to represent better the Chinese people abroad. They should be thoroughly freed from the shame of being a people despised by both Westerners and Japanese. A sound modern Chinese education would enhance the status abroad of generations to come. It would make them proud of China's glorious past and potential greatness, and it would stop their children from becoming babas and peranakans and put an end to the process of cultural and physical assimilation which the nationalist leaders had so fiercely denounced. And finally, in due course, it would make all Chinese abroad think less of themselves as Cantonese, Hok-kiens, Hakkas, Teochius, and Hailams and more as Chinese compatriots.

This, then, seems to have been the principal way a large number of Nanyang Chinese thought fit to respond to nationalism during the first republican decade. The power of youth after May Fourth, the Kuomintang-Communist alliance, the Northern Expedition after the death of Sun Yat-sen, and the apparent Kuomintang victory over warlords and Communists alike in the late 1920's and early 1930's opened up a new era for Nanyang Chinese nationalism. Many new factors contributed to the heightening of nationalist emotions. Developments in China were certainly crucial, but changing local conditions had also made the Nanyang Chinese more re-sponsive to events in China. Communications with China had improved considerably; the literacy rate was higher, and there was the promise of

25. Chang and others 1962:I, 273–289, 340–350; Li 1959; Hsü 1950:7–12, 19–58.

better schools, better teachers and students, more bookshops, and more books from China; there were better newspapers, and weekly and monthly magazines had begun to appear; the quality of writing, reading, and thinking had begun to rise. And as the power of nationalism began to be understood in China by more of the modern-educated, so also did the Nanyang Chinese feel its protective warmth. And as the Chinese began to turn against the Western and Japanese imperialists in such cities as Canton, Hong Kong, and Shanghai, what there was of Nanyang Chinese nationalism also began to have new dimensions. And when the Kuomintang and the Communists split up, and new exiles, rebels, and agents went again to Southeast Asia, there followed fresh debates on what was and what was not good for China.[26]

But just as important was the fact that counter-nationalist forces were also growing, in particular in Thailand, British Malaya, and the Dutch East Indies, where the Chinese were the most numerous. These took several forms, but the most important ones concerned the control of Chinese schools, the end of unlimited immigration in all territories, the banning of specifically Chinese political activities, and the extension of the use of deportation as a political weapon. In addition, there was the concurrent growth of indigenous nationalism, in some cases clearly aimed at curbing Chinese enthusiasm and aggressiveness. And not least were the opening of more colonial and native schools to the Chinese, some of which offered prospects of careers in the professions and even in officialdom.

These forces together proved to be strong enough to arrest the spread of the post-1925 tide of nationalism. Even the open support for Overseas Chinese nationalism by the Nationalist government in Nanking after 1928 was to no avail. Both colonial and native authorities had become alarmed at the likelihood of Chinese government intervention and sought determinedly to divide the Chinese communities within themselves and to check the hold that that government might come to have over all their Chinese subjects. They had no difficulty with expatriate Chinese, who could be stopped from coming or could be deported without fuss. As for the three main groups of the more settled Chinese, the first, the fully and openly China-oriented ones were still relatively few and, with care and watchfulness, they could be isolated. The third, the locally ambitious ones could be easily tempted with jobs, honours, and higher social status. There remained the second group, the large communally conscious group which needed delicate handling. They were potentially nationalistic as soon as all their

26. Mainly in the editorial and literary columns of *Nanyang Siang-pao* and *Sin Chew Jit Pao* in the 1930's. The turning point was probably the anti-British boycott after the May Thirtieth Incident (see *Straits Times* and *Nanyang Siang-pao* for June 1925), but the main discussion centred on Japanese imperialism.

children had been through modern Chinese schools. But if they were encouraged to go on organizing themselves in traditional community associations and were rewarded with tolerance and only the minimum curbs on their Chinese fervour, they were likely to be moderate and even grateful. Thus the various governments in Southeast Asia, each in its own way, restrained the China-orientated, won over some of the locally ambitious, and carefully cultivated the inward-looking tendencies of the majority until they were content to preserve their "Chineseness" without bouts of fervent nationalism.

I do not wish to suggest that the local governments were always successful. Their task in some countries was easier, especially where the Chinese were few or where upward social mobility followed quickly after assimilation, as in Burma, Cambodia, Vietnam, the Philippines, and Thailand. In British Malaya and the Dutch East Indies, the task was much more difficult. All the same, the fact that the Chinese were so divided made it possible for British and Dutch policies to have some effect in dampening the nationalism which had spread so freely among the younger generation of Chinese. They did this not a moment too soon, for, when the war with Japan finally came in 1937, the floodgates of nationalist emotion were truly opened. By that time, the machinery for channelling and moderating that nationalism had been tried and refined, and the Chinese in many areas could be safely permitted to vent their nationalism against an enemy who was external to Southeast Asia and who was also the chief rival and economic threat to the Western colonial powers themselves.

It required a traumatic conflict like the bitter defeats by the Japanese in 1937 to move the Nanyang Chinese to act as a single community, and the nationalism which the war engendered was indeed impressive. But we should perhaps note that it followed a new wave of nationalism in China itself which the threat of war had produced: the United Front, the end of civil war, the final unification of most of the people of China against a common enemy. With China at last apparently united, could the Nanyang Chinese appear to do less?

I suggested earlier that no nationalist leader arose independently from among the Nanyang Chinese and that, at the turn of the century, these Chinese had been taught the elements of nationalism. This nationalism was rudimentary, and although it reflected hopes in a strong China which would protect the Nanyang Chinese, it still fed itself upon hopes of eventual prosperity for their native provinces, Kwangtung and Fukien. It was not only a conditional nationalism but also a peripheral and dependent nationalism which did not have the capacity to generate itself. It depended on China to continue to take an interest in them and on expatriate Chinese to continue to prepare later generations to be nationalistic. Otherwise, the

Nanyang Chinese probably would not have overcome their distance from China and believe, as some did, that they were as Chinese as those at home and only different because they were temporarily abroad.

This became more obvious after 1920 as more Nanyang Chinese began to settle in Southeast Asia and immigration laws everywhere kept the numbers of newcomers and expatriates down. The question of how to teach their children to keep this nationalism alive among the new settlers became paramount. Local conditions were changing almost as fast as in China, and those who were themselves nationalistic feared that younger Nanyang Chinese who were born in the region and had not been back to China would be seduced by colonial and native rulers to forget their origins. Anti-Chinese extremists were appearing among the indigenous nationalists who could help to confirm the "Chineseness" of future generations, but local anti-Chinese sentiments were ultimately dangerous and had to be fought. But fighting this growing trend among the local nationalists created new dilemmas. In most cases, it meant choosing between local assimilation and remaining Chinese and eventually returning to China, between abandoning Chinese nationalism and sustaining that nationalism at the risk of being kicked out. At this point the choice again depended on what China wanted of them and what China could do for them. For those who had little faith, the answer was to be watchful and decide how to act only when they were sure. Hence both the nationalists and the advocates of assimilation among the Nanyang Chinese were always the articulate minority at opposite ends of the spectrum, while the majority who said little considered the relative strengths of China and the local governments while they carefully erected defences to ensure the survival of their communities.

That this kind of nationalism was calculated and controlled cannot be doubted. It stemmed from the fact that the nationalism was indirect and dependent on factors in China beyond the reach of Chinese overseas. The separation from China meant that the nationalism which was kept alive among younger generations of the Nanyang Chinese was more abstract and cerebral, taught, as it were, through textbooks in the modern Chinese schools and subtly worded articles in local Chinese newspapers and maga-zines but cut off from where the action was. It was a nationalism held in reserve while the settled Chinese learned to emulate their fathers in pro-fiting from the colonial framework and the laissez faire capitalism of the 1920's and 1930's. This in turn modified that nationalism even further as their careers and occupations in mainly modernized urban conditions led them to new divisions along educational and class lines. The divisions be-tween the rich and the poor, the Western-educated and the Chinese-educated, had become more meaningful, but they were not yet sufficiently strong to transcend other divisions by speech groups and orientations towards politics in China. The situation for the Nanyang Chinese in the early 1930's had become so complex that only something with great emotional force that transcended their local preoccupations could lift them from their multiple and divisive calculations. This the war in China succeeded in doing, but it made all the more manifest the dependence of Nanyang Chinese on China to make them nationalistic and keep that nationalism purposeful. Perhaps Tan Kah Kee was really perceptive when he complained of the lack of substance in Nanyang Chinese "unity" in the 1930's and added: "What I hope for is that our government can rule effectively and lead the people to unity. By providing an example for the overseas Chinese, surely the Chinese will respond. If our government is unable to lead the people to unity and the overseas Chinese are expected to achieve this [by themselves] first, then it is no different from climbing a tree to catch fish."[27] The observation does not explain the nature of the Nanyang Chinese nationalism, but it does clearly point to the limits of that nationalism. And when these limits are recognized as having been determined by Southeast Asian realities, it is less easy to dismiss the political activities of the Nanyang Chinese as peripheral to the history of Southeast Asia. Even in their political activities, the Chinese were directly under pressure from other political actors and factors in Southeast Asia and could not but influence the policies of colonial and native governments and the social and economic developments among the indigenous peoples of the region. To the extent that they did, such Chinese responses to nationalism, even to nationalism in China, need to be given their place in the course of more recent Southeast Asian history.

REFERENCES

Akashi Yoji. 1968. "The Nanyang Chinese Anti-Japanese Boycott Movements, 1908–1928: A Study of Nanyang Chinese Nationalism," *Nanyang Hsueh-pao*, 23, 1 and 2 (1968–1969):69–96.

——. 1970. *The Nanyang Chinese National Salvation Movement, 1937–1941.* Lawrence, Kans.

Boorman, Howard L. (ed.). 1967–1971. *Biographical Dictionary of Republican China.* 4 vols. New York.

Chang Yung-fu (Teo Eng Hock). 1933. *Hua-ch'iao yü ch'uang-li Min-kuo.* Shanghai.

Chang Ch'i-yun and others (eds.). 1962. *Chung-hua min-kuo k'ai-kuo wu-shih-nien shih-lun chi.* 2 vols. Taipei.

Ch'en Chia-keng (Tan Kah Kee). 1950. *Nan-ch'iao hui-i lu.* 2 vols. Foochow.

Ch'en Ta. 1939. *Nanyang hua-ch'iao yü Min-Yueh She-hui.* Changsha. English version: *Emigrant Communities in South China: A Study of Overseas Migration and Its Influence on Standards of Living and Social Change.* New York, 1940.

27. Ch'en 1950:I, 34.

Cheng Lin-k'uan. 1943. *Fukken Kakyō no sōkin*. Tokyo. The original Chinese version, completed in 1940, is not available.

Cheng, Shelley H. 1964. "The T'ung-meng hui and Its Financial Supporters, 1905–1912." *Majallah Pantai*, 2 (1964–1965):43–74.

Feng Tzu-yu. 1945–1946. *Ko-ming i-shih*. 5 vols. Shanghai. ——. 1946. *Hua-ch'iao K'ai-kuo Ko-ming shih*. Chungking.

Go Puan Seng (Wu Pan-sheng). 1970. *Refuge and Strength*. Englewood Cliffs, N.J.

Hsin-Min Jih-pao, Yuan-tan Chi-nien k'an. Manila, 1928

Hsü Su-wu. 1950. *Hsin-chia-po hua-ch'iao-yü ch'uan-mao*. Singapore.

Huang Chi-lu (ed.). 1968–. *Ko-ming wen-hsien*. Published by the Kuomintang Party Archives Committee, Taipei. Vols. 44–.

Ide Kiwata. 1942. *Kakyō*. Tokyo.

Kee Yeh Siew. 1965. "The Japanese in Malaya before 1942." *Nanyang Hsueh-pao*, 20, 1 and 2, (1965–1966):48–88.

Kikakuin. 1940. *Kakyō no kenkyu*. Tokyo.

Lee Ah Chai. 1957. "Policies and Politics in Chinese Schools in the Straits Settlements and the Federated Malay States, 1786–1941." M.A. thesis, University of Malaya, Singapore.

Li Ch'uan-shou. 1959. "Yin-tu-ni-hsi-ya hua-ch'iao Chiao-yü shih." *Nanyang Hsueh-pao*, 15, 1:1–14 and 2:19–44.

Liauw Kian-Djoe (Leo Suryadinata). 1969. "The Three Major Streams in Peranakan Chinese Politics in Java (1917–1942)." M.A. thesis, Monash University.

——. 1972. *Prominent Indonesian Chinese in the Twentieth Century: A preliminary survey*. Athens, Ohio.

Liu Ts'un-yan. 1967. "Ku Hung-ming and His Interpretation of Chinese Civilisation." In *Symposium on Historical, Archaeological and Linguistic Studies on Southern China, Southeast Asia and the Hong Kong Region*. Hong Kong. Pp. 269–281.

Lo Chia-lun (ed.). 1953–1968. *Ko-ming wen-hsien*. Published by the Kuomintang Party Archives Committee, Taipei. Vols. 1–43.

Manila Chronicle. "55 years of a Fruitful Career," special issue to Albino Z. Sycip, Dec. 17, 1967.

Nanyang Hsueh-pao, 1940–. Short notes in the following issues: 1, 2 (1940):130–131, on Leow Kiak Hoo (Liao Chieh-fu); 2, 1 (1941):113–114, on Chiu Mua Teng (Chou Man-t'ang); 2, 2 (1941):179–181, on Tay Seng Kwai (Cheng Ch'eng-k'uai); 2, 3 (1941):131–138, on Hia Kuang Yam (I Kuang-yen); 8, 2 (1952): 1–18, on Liu Shih-mu; 9, 2 (1953):38–39, on Li Teng-hui; 18, 1 and 2 (1962–1963), on Ch'en Chang-lo; 19, 1 and 2 (1964–1965):129–133, on Lim Boon Keng (Lin Wen-ch'ing); 22, 1 and 2 (1967–1969):2–18, on Lee Kong Chien (Li Kuang-ch'ien).

Narita Setsuo. 1942. *Kakyō shi*. Tokyo.

Purcell, Victor. 1948. *The Chinese in Malaya*. London. Reprinted 1967.

——. 1951. *The Chinese in Southeast Asia*. London. 2d ed. 1965.

Skinner, G. William. 1957. *Chinese Society in Thailand: An Analytical history*. Ithaca, N.Y.

——. 1960. "Change and Persistence in Chinese Culture Overseas: A Comparison of Thailand and Java." *Nanyang Hsueh-pao*, 16:86–100.

Soh Eng Lim. 1960. "Tan Cheng-lock: His Leadership of the Malayan Chinese."
  JSEAH, 1, 1:29–55.
Song Ong Siang. 1923. *One Hundred Years of History of the Chinese in Singapore*. London.
  Reprinted 1967.
Sun Yat-sen. 1965. *Kuo-fu ch'uan-chi*. 3 vols. (Hundredth anniversary ed.). Taipei.
T'ang Leang-li. 1936. *The New Social Order in China*. Shanghai.
Teng Tse-ju. 1948. *Chung-kuo Kuo-min-tang er-shih-nien Shin-chi*. Shanghai.
Ts'ui Kuei-ch'iang. 1965. "Hai-hsia chih-min ti hua-jen tui Wu-Ssu Yun-tung ti
  fan-hsiang." *Nanyang Hsueh-pao*, 20, 1 and 2 (1965–1966):13–18.
Wang Gungwu. 1959. "Sun Yat-sen and Singapore." *Nanyang Hsueh-pao*, 15, 2:
  55–68.
———. 1970. "Chinese Politics in Malaya." *China Quarterly*, 43 (July–Sept.):1–30.
———. 1972. "Political Chinese: An Aspect of Their Contribution to Modern
  Southeast Asian History." *In* B. Grossmann (ed.), *Southeast Asia in the Modern
  World*. Wiesbaden. Pp. 115–128.
Wickberg, Edgar. 1965. *The Chinese in Philippine Life, 1850–1898*. New Haven.
Williams, L. E. 1960. *Overseas Chinese Nationalism: The Genesis of the Pan-Chinese
  movement in Indonesia, 1900–1916*. Glencoe, Ill.
Yen Ching-hwang. 1970a. "The Chinese Revolutionary Movement in Malaya,
  1900–1911." Ph.D. thesis, Australian National University.
———. 1970b. "Ch'ing's Sale of Honours and the Chinese Leadership in Singapore
  and Malaya (1877–1912)." *JSEAS*, 1, 2 (Sept.):20–32.
Yong Ching Fatt. 1968. "A Preliminary Study of Chinese Leadership in Singapore,
  1900–1941." *JSEAH*, 9, 2 (Sept.):258–285.
Yung, Mabel Yuet-hing. 1967. "Contributions of the Chinese to Education in the
  Straits Settlements and the Federated Malay States (1900–1941)." M.A. thesis,
  University of Malaya.

Index

(Compiled with the assistance of William Koenig)

*Southeast Asian History
and Historiography*

Designed by R. E. Rosenbaum.
Composed by Syntax International Pte. Ltd.
in 10 point Monophoto Baskerville, 2 points leaded,
with display lines in Monophoto Baskerville.
Printed offset by Vail-Ballou Press, Inc.
on Warrens Number 66 Offset, 50 pound basis.
Bound by Vail-Ballou Press
in Columbia book cloth
and stamped in All Purpose foil.

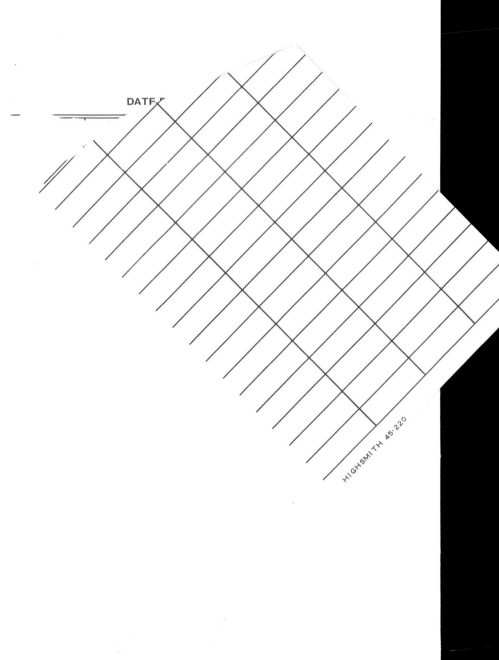

DATE

HIGHSMITH 45-220